Book of
British Villages

BOOK OF
BRITISH VILLAGES

A GUIDE TO 700 OF THE
MOST INTERESTING AND ATTRACTIVE
VILLAGES IN BRITAIN

Published by Drive Publications Limited
for the Automobile Association,
Fanum House, Basingstoke, Hants RG21 2EA

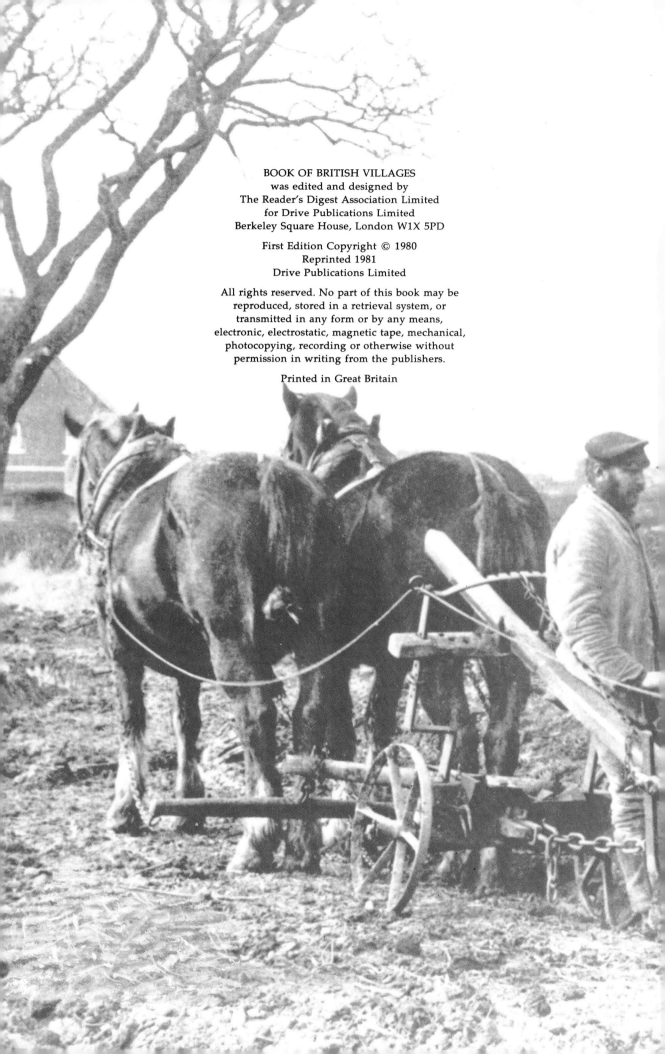

BOOK OF BRITISH VILLAGES
was edited and designed by
The Reader's Digest Association Limited
for Drive Publications Limited
Berkeley Square House, London W1X 5PD

First Edition Copyright © 1980
Reprinted 1981
Drive Publications Limited

Printed in Great Britain

CONTRIBUTORS

◆

The publishers would like to thank the
following people for major contributions to this book

ARTISTS

Peter Bailey Jill Coombes Richard Jacobs
Launcelot Jones Peter Jones Ivan Lapper
Robert Micklewright Peter Morter
George Tute Venner Artists

PHOTOGRAPHERS

Malcolm Aird Mike Burgess David Gallant
Neil Holmes Ian Howes Lucinda Lambton
Jane Lewis Sir Fitzroy Maclean
S. & O. Mathews Colin Molyneux
Patrick Thurston John Vigurs Trevor Wood
George Wright John Wyand

AUTHORS

Richard Adams John Arlott Anne Baker
Monica Belcher John Burke David Clarke
Robert Dougall Ross Finlay Bryn Frank
Dr Margaret Gelling David Green
Christopher Hall Terence Harris
Professor W. G. Hoskins John Hudson
Isobel Hunt J. Geraint Jenkins John Kitto
Philip Llewellin David MacFadyen
Sir Fitzroy Maclean Dr Venetia Newall
David Owen Rowland Parker John Physick
Miss Read Roger Redfern Richard Reid
Richard Shields Tony Venison
John Talbot White Ralph Whitlock
Gerald Wilkinson Ron Woodman
Alistair Wregg David Young

CONTENTS

SPECIAL FEATURES

ABBOTS BROMLEY
STAFFORDSHIRE

6 miles south of Uttoxeter (page 430 Bc)

A Butter Cross on the village green is a reminder of the days when Abbots Bromley was a market town. The six-sided timber building marks the spot where, as far back as the 14th century, local people did their trading in butter and other produce. There are several fine houses in the village, particularly in Bagot Street where the Bagot Almshouses date from 1705.

Abbots Bromley was in the Forest of Needwood in medieval times, and continues traditions associated with the forest. The Horn Dance is performed on the Monday after the first Sunday after September 4 and starts at 8 a.m. outside the vicarage. The horns are kept in the church throughout the rest of the year. The six sets of reindeer horns are of Saxon origin, but the dancers wear Tudor dress as they dance their way around an 8 mile circuit of local farms. The deer-men carry the horns on their shoulders and are accompanied by a Fool, a Hobby Horse, Maid Marian and a Bowman. The Horn Dance is probably an ancient version of a 'beating the bounds' ceremony.

Richard II hunted in the forest, and was often the guest of the Bagot family. As a reward for providing him with good hunting, Richard gave the Bagots a herd of goats whose descendants, known as Bagot goats, are in a special park at Blithfield Hall. The house was built by the Bagot family in Elizabethan times.

The Church of St Nicholas stands slightly downhill from the village, and although of medieval origin has a Queen Anne tower with a balustraded top. The ceremonial horns are kept at the east end of the north aisle.

Near the church is the school of St Mary and St Anne, a public school for girls. It was founded in 1874, and became part of the Woodard Foundation in 1921.

ABBEY RICHES *The great, grey, buttressed gable of this enormous 14th-century thatched barn looms over Abbotsbury. In medieval times it swallowed a tenth – or a tithe – of everything the villagers grew or raised in their farms and fields. The barn formed part of a rich Benedictine abbey, now a ruin, its size testifying to the power of the abbot, who levied tithes from a wide area around. Beyond is the 15th-century Church of St Nicholas, inside which is a marble monument to one of those powerful abbots.*

ABBOTSBURY
DORSET

8 miles north-west of Weymouth (page 421 Ca)

St Catherine's Chapel, set on the summit of a steep 250 ft hill, commands the large and spread-out village of Abbotsbury. The chapel – built in the 14th century with thick stone walls, sturdy buttresses and a heavy, barrel-vaulted roof – overlooks the barns, thatched cottages and orange-stone houses that make up the village. Some of the buildings' stones came from old monastery sites, and the area's meadows and gardens abound in mullioned windows, age-blackened timbers, ancient stone roof-tiles, and paving on raised footpaths – most of them half-buried in ivy.

The abbey which gave the village its name was founded in the middle of the 11th century. Today, with the exception of the half-ruined but imposing Abbey Barn, little remains of the abbey and its related buildings. The tithe barn was built in the 14th century, and measures 272 ft by 31 ft. It is one of the largest buildings of its kind in Britain and, together with an adjacent pond, marks the nucleus of the abbey site. Near by is the 15th-century Church of St Nicholas, which contains a marble monument of an abbot, dating from the early 13th century. To the west of the church are several large, post-Reformation houses – including Abbey House, Abbey Dairy House, the Old Manor House, and the Vicarage.

Abbotsbury lies in a sheltered, green valley about 1 mile from the coast. Just beyond the encircling hills is the northern end of Chesil Beach, a massive rampart of pebbles piled up over the centuries by strong tides and stretching 17 miles from Bridport to Portland. Behind the beach is a long, narrow and brackish lagoon called The Fleet, and for the past 600 years the western corner of the lagoon has housed a colony of swans, which feed on a rare grass in the area, *Zostera marina*.

Each May, hundreds of crammed-together nests, each occupied by a pair of swans, provide a fascinating sight. The Swannery is open to the public – as are the 18th-century gardens on the Beach Road west of the village. The gardens are so sheltered from the sea winds, and so frost-free, that subtropical plants grow there in the spring. Unusual shrubs flourish later in the year.

A mile-and-a-half to the north-west of the village is Abbotsbury Castle, an Iron Age earthwork set on a hill and covering some 10 acres.

ABERDARON
GWYNEDD

14 miles south-west of Pwllheli (page 428 Ab)

Steep lanes plunge down to this compact little village that faces south over a broad, sandy bay speckled with rocky islets. Aberdaron has a tranquil character, emphasised by the fact that the bank opens for just two hours each week.

New buildings stand on the landward slopes, but the heart of the village is a small square where the shops, two hotels and the post office – designed by Sir Clough Williams-Ellis, the architect of Portmeirion – are all within a few-dozen paces of each other. Y Gegin Fawr (The Big Kitchen) is a low, whitewashed building of stone, now used as a cafe, where medieval pilgrims rested before making the perilous crossing to the holy island of Bardsey. It is said to have been built about 1300, but is at least a century younger than Aberdaron's church, St Hywyn's.

West of Aberdaron is Mynydd Mawr, a 524 ft high hill on the tip of the Lleyn Peninsula. In fine weather it is a magnificent viewpoint, and is the best place from which to see Bardsey Island.

ABERDYFI
GWYNEDD

9 miles west of Machynlleth (page 428 Ba)

Bright terraces line the main street, looking out over the broad Dyfi Estuary to the rolling mountains of mid-Wales. Immediately behind the village, slopes rise so steeply that some houses are built into the cliffs. To the west, sand dunes and a golf course sweep down to a beach that runs along the coast for 4 miles. Sands and a sheltered anchorage for small boats combine to make Aberdyfi a delightful example of the trim, elegant little seaside resorts that developed on the coasts of Wales in Victorian and Edwardian times.

Ships were the main links with the outside world until 1808, when a road was built along the estuary. The road was rebuilt in 1827, but it was the arrival of the railway that enabled Aberdyfi to develop. It had been an isolated but prosperous little port for hundreds of years, shipping slate and wool to all parts of the world. Many fascinating reminders of that period are displayed in the Snowdonia National Park information centre by the pier.

ABEREDW
POWYS

3 miles south-east of Builth Wells (page 425 Db)

The tiny village, one of the most secluded in Wales, nestles in a deep, wooded valley with the impressive limestone crags of Aberedw Rocks rising to more than 1,000 ft above the south bank of the River Edw. Among the rocks is a small

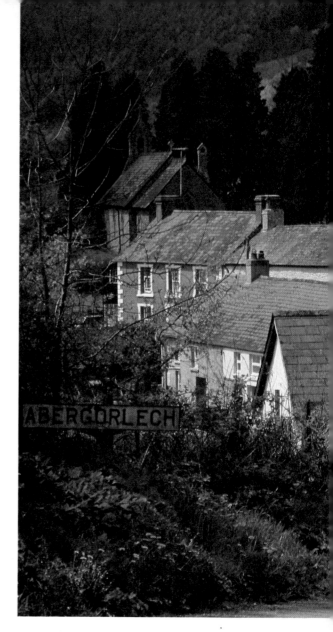

cave where Llywelyn ap Gruffydd, last of the original Princes of Wales, is said to have hidden shortly before being killed by English soldiers in 1282.

Legend maintains that when Llywelyn was in hiding at Aberedw he asked the local blacksmith to reverse the shoes of his horse so that the English could not follow his tracks in the snow. The smith is said to have passed the information on to the prince's enemies.

The remains of the mound on which Llywelyn's castle stood lie beside the road between Aberedw and the waters of the Wye.

The attractive heart of the village is a cluster of stone cottages that stand by the Seven Stars Inn. The neighbouring church, roofed with mossy slates, has a low but massive tower and dates from the 13th century. It is dedicated to Cewydd, a Celtic saint. A steep footpath from the highest point of the churchyard runs down to the rushing River Edw through lichen-covered trees, ferns and moss-covered boulders. The village post office, a few hundred yards up the valley, is one of the most picturesque in Wales. Clad with ivy and other creepers, it is reached by stone steps that pass under an arch of trimmed evergreens.

ABERFOYLE

CENTRAL

8 miles south-west of Callander (page 441 Ee)

At Aberfoyle the Scottish Lowlands end and the Highlands begin. The village has expanded since the Duke's Road was built for the Duke of Montrose in 1820 to give easier access to the Trossachs. This 5 mile wide strip of birch-covered mountains, rocky crags, streams and moorland was the setting for Sir Walter Scott's novel *Rob Roy* and his poem *Lady of the Lake*. The old village of Aberfoyle, mentioned by Scott, was south of the River Forth. Its church is now a ruin.

Modern Aberfoyle is north of the Forth, and some of its older houses were built for workers in the slate quarries on the Menteith Hill behind the village. The quarries were worked for almost 200 years before closing in the 1950s. In the main street, opposite the Bailie Nicol Jarvie Hotel, a small iron ploughshare hangs on a tree, recalling an incident in *Rob Roy* when Bailie Nicol Jarvie used a red-hot blade to set fire to a Highlander's kilt during an argument.

ABERGORLECH

DYFED

8 miles north-west of Llandeilo (page 425 Cb)

Forest-clad hills rise steeply to more than 1,000 ft above Abergorlech, which shelters in the narrow valley of the River Cothi.

The approach to the village along the road from Llansawel is particularly attractive as the road drops down to a bridge over the River Gorlech, from which Abergorlech takes its name. The combined post office and village store stands on one bank, looking across the clear stream to a picnic place, shaded by red oaks, that won a Prince of Wales award in 1975. It is also the starting point for a waymarked forest walk of just under 2 miles.

On the far side of the village an old three-arched bridge spans the Cothi, and is overlooked by a delightful terrace of cottages. Salmon and 'sewin' – the Welsh name for sea trout – can often be seen in the river below the bridge. Near by, the 19th-century church is tucked away on a slope behind the Black Lion Inn, and has a splendid collection of brass paraffin lamps. One wall of the village chapel is hung with slates to keep out the wet south-westerly winds that gust up the valley.

ABERSOCH
GWYNEDD

6 miles south-west of Pwllheli (page 428 Ab)

Immaculate houses look down on a small, tidal harbour where old stone cottages have been tastefully restored at the water's edge. There are three bustling boatyards, but in summer the sleekest yachts and cabin cruisers are to be seen offshore, moored in St Tudwal's Road. The headquarters of the South Caernarvonshire Yacht Club overlooks the anchorage from a rocky headland where tracks and footpaths offer views of Cardigan Bay and the peaks of North Wales.

A semi-circle of low hills and headlands make Abersoch a safe anchorage, and also contribute to a mild climate in which palm trees flourish on the southern slopes. From the centre of the village, where Victorian and Edwardian buildings cluster round the junction of three streets, a lane runs down to the sandy beach. More than 1 mile long, the beach is backed by dunes and a golf course, and looks out to the islands named after St Tudwal, a 6th-century missionary.

On the other side of the River Soch – shallow enough to be crossed on foot at low tide – another huge beach curves northwards towards Llanbedrog. At the mouth of the river, a narrow path cut into the cliff leads to a small jetty where fishermen gather at high water.

ABINGER
SURREY

5 miles south-west of Dorking (page 422 Db)

Stone Age men had a settlement at Abinger, justifying its claim to be one of the oldest villages in England. There are two parts to the village: Abinger Common, with the Church of St James and Manor House, and Abinger Hammer with its ponds and hammer-clock on the Guildford to Dorking road.

The Church of St James is of Norman origin, but was largely restored in 1950 after being almost destroyed by a flying bomb during the Second World War.

In the grounds of the Manor House, behind the church, are the remains of a Mesolithic dwelling excavated in the 1950s. It is considered to be one of the finest examples of a Middle Stone Age settlement in Europe. More than 1,000 flint tools were found on the site and are housed in a small museum. In the same manor grounds

is a motte, an earth mound, surrounded by a ditch, probably of the Norman period.

In a corner of the small green are the wooden stocks, and close by the churchyard wall, in a private garden, is a small stone pound.

Down in the valley is the hamlet of Abinger Hammer, where a fast-flowing stream powered an iron-forging hammer in the 16th century. This was one of the last places in Surrey where the industry survived.

A clock overhanging the main road dates from 1909. The hours are struck by the figure of a smith striking a bell with his hammer. The clockhouse stands on the site of an old forge.

ABOYNE
GRAMPIAN

11 miles east of Ballater (page 443 Gc)

Most of Aboyne dates from the 1880s, when a Manchester banker, Sir William Cunliffe Brookes, rebuilt the village. Before then it had been known as Charlestown of Aboyne, named after Charles Gordon, the 1st Earl of Aboyne, who began to build a village near his castle in 1670.

Sir William became landlord of Aboyne when his daughter married the head of the Gordon family. He rebuilt the mansion house, which stands in private grounds and incorporates part of a 17th-century tower-house – all that remains of Aboyne Castle. The village is still largely as Sir William built it, with stone villas and cottages, wide streets and patches of woodland.

The village green forms a natural arena for the Aboyne Highland Games, held every August or September. The games were founded in 1867 and include athletics and Highland dancing.

QUIET WATERS *The stream which once powered the iron-foundry hammers that gave Abinger Hammer its name still flows through the village – but now it feeds watercress beds.*

ACTON BURNELL

SALOP

7 miles south of Shrewsbury (page 429 Db)

Timber-framed, black-and-white cottages and buildings of grey-green stone stand side by side in Acton Burnell, which lies close to a ruined castle of red sandstone. Robert Burnell – Lord Chancellor of England and Bishop of Bath and Wells in the reign of Edward I – built the castle about 1284. It was originally regarded as a fortified manor house. It is open to the public and overlooks the grounds of Acton Burnell Hall, built early in the 19th century and now a college.

The Church of St Mary stands near by and, apart from its Victorian tower, it is almost entirely 13th century. It contains ornate memorials of the Burnell family – and of the Lees, who owned the village in the 17th century. The Lees were ancestors of the American statesman Richard Henry Lee, one of the signatories in 1776 of the Declaration of Independence, and of General Robert E. Lee, commander of the Southern forces in the American Civil War.

ADLESTROP

GLOUCESTERSHIRE

4 miles east of Stow-on-the-Wold (page 421 Dd)

Edward Thomas immortalised this village in his short poem *Adlestrop*, because his train stopped there briefly one summer afternoon.

> *The steam hiss'd. Some one clear'd his throat.*
> *No one left and no one came*
> *On the bare platform. What I saw*
> *Was Adlestrop – only the name.*

The station has gone, but the nameplate that caught Thomas's eye is now in the village bus shelter, with the poem inscribed on a plaque below.

ROMANTIC RUIN *The shell of Acton Burnell Castle stands beside the village church. In spite of being called a castle, the building is a fortified manor house – the oldest in England. It was designed to afford protection against raiders in troubled times rather than to withstand the rigours of war.*

◆

Had Thomas left his train, he would have found a village of golden-stone houses and cottages, a Georgian mansion, and a 13th to 14th-century church. The mansion, Adlestrop Park, is in Gothic style with grounds landscaped by Humphry Repton. Neither the house nor gardens are open to the public.

The Church of St Mary Magdalene contains monuments to the Leigh family, who have owned Adlestrop Park since 1553. Thomas Leigh was the rector at the beginning of the 19th century and his grand-daughter, the novelist Jane Austen, was a visitor to the rectory, now Adlestrop House. It dates from the 17th century, and stands among magnificent cedar trees. The schoolroom, school house and a cottage close by are 19th century.

CHASTLETON Thatched cottages of Cotswold stone stand in the shadow of Chastleton House, a great mansion which looms like a castle above the village, 3 miles north of Adlestrop. The house dates from 1603 and is in its original state, right down to the furniture. There is a secret room where one of the Royalist family hid from Parliamentary troops during the Civil War. In the garden of a nearby house are box bushes trimmed to animal shapes.

◆

MELLOW COTSWOLD STONE *The stone-tile roofed cottages of* ▷ *Adlestrop are typical of the sleepy villages that nestle among the Cotswold hills. The walls and roofs of the cottages are made from local limestone, which ranges in colour from honey-gold to brown. The free-draining soil provides ideal pastures for sheep, which have roamed the Cotswolds since Roman times. In Elizabethan days this was the centre of England's wool industry, and rich wool merchants built most of the beautiful churches and manor houses still to be seen.*

Adlestrop

AE

DUMFRIES AND GALLOWAY

9 miles north of Dumfries (page 441 Eb)

The village with the shortest name in Britain is also one of the country's youngest. It was built in 1947 by the Forestry Commission and is set in a conifer forest of more than 15,000 acres. Ae takes its name from the Water of Ae, which flows below the village on its way to join the River Annan.

There are about 50 houses in the village, a village store and post office, a school and a community hall. There is a picnic site by the river. From the site there are two walks through the forest. The road from Ae to Closeburn also has some ornamental trees by the roadside.

The Forest Office near the bridge at Ae supplies information about walking routes and the forest.

ALDBOROUGH

NORTH YORKSHIRE

7 miles north-east of Knaresborough (page 436 Bc)

More than 2,500 years of history lie behind Aldborough, for this village was the capital of the Brigantes, the largest Celtic tribe in Britain in pre-Roman days.

When the Romans came they paid the subjugated Celts the compliment of turning the settlement into an important camp for the famous Ninth Legion, and called it Isurium Brigantum. Isura was the Celtic name for the River Ure, which flows to the north of the village. The camp was a fort close to the important military base at York. There were hot baths and luxurious villas with expensive mosaic floors.

Fragments of the red-sandstone walls that enclosed the city can still be seen, and there are personal items such as brooches and ivory counters in the museum at the southern end of the village.

There are several Roman pavements still preserved, including one behind the former Aldeburgh Arms Inn, now a private house. The pavements can be seen during the opening times of the museum.

The beautiful Church of St Andrew is thought to stand on the site of a Roman temple dedicated to Mercury, whose statue now gazes down the full length of the 14th-century nave to where, in a curious medieval carving, Daniel languishes in the lions' den. Opposite the church is the Ship Inn, which was once the churchwarden's house and may be as old as the church.

Aldborough's cottages are mainly red brick clustered around the village green, called The Square, with its maypole where the maypole-dancing takes place during the second week of May.

On one side of the sloping green is a flight of

TIMBER AND THATCH IN ALDBURY *Many of the village's cottages and houses are timber-framed and date from the 16th and 17th centuries, when they would have been thatched. Most now have tiled roofs, but a few, like these, still have thatch and dormer windows typical of the county.*

steps to a platform from which the results of parliamentary elections were once announced. Aldborough was a 'rotten borough', which, without any reference to the village's actual population, returned two Members of Parliament until the Reform Bill of 1832. An inscription notes that the platform is what remains of 'The Old Court House of the Ancient Borough of Aldborough and Boroughbridge at which Members of Parliament were elected until 1832'. Close by is a pair of stocks, but these are modern replicas.

ALDBURY
HERTFORDSHIRE

3 miles north-west of Berkhamsted (page 426 Bb)

If the Saxons called a place old – and Aldbury means 'old fort' in Anglo-Saxon – then by now it must indeed be ancient. The heart of Aldbury is its triangular green and duck-pond.

The old elm that stood on the green, and still figures in local postcards, survives no longer – a victim of Dutch elm disease. The stocks and whipping post remain, however, worn by time into quaintness. When first erected during the last century they were probably not considered so picturesque. Near by, beyond the pond, stands the long, low, creeper-clad Greyhound pub, which makes an excellent starting or finishing point for a hike through the edge of the Chilterns.

The backdrop is the rising beechwoods of Ashridge Park, crowned at their summit by an urn on a Greek Doric column, a monument erected in 1832 to the canal-building 3rd Duke of Bridgewater. The foreground, about the green, is a charming collection of timber-framed, brick-and-tile cottages, mostly 16th and 17th century in origin. Among them is the tiny, tall-chimneyed village bakehouse.

The Church of St John the Baptist, with its flint-faced tower, stands a little way back from the green. The church, partly 13th century, incorporates the imposing Pendley Chapel, within which lie the late-medieval effigies of Sir Robert Whittingham and his lady. Sir Robert's feet, for some reason, rest upon a 'wild man'.

A short distance from the village is Stocks House, home of the formidable Mrs Humphry Ward, the Victorian novelist, who was a vociferous opponent of women's suffrage, yet was one of the first female magistrates. Her nephews, the Huxley brothers – Julian, the scientist, and Aldous, the novelist – often stayed with her in this handsomely remodelled 18th-century house.

ALDERBURY
WILTSHIRE

3 miles south-east of Salisbury (page 421 Db)

Successive landlords of the Green Dragon, an inn by the triangular village green, have been proud to point out that Charles Dickens used the inn as a model for the Blue Dragon in his novel *Martin*

NORMAN PRIORY *The stone pillar is a reminder that an Augustinian priory founded in the 12th century once stood at Ivychurch, Alderbury. Figures of a pope and a saint from the ruins have been built into the wall of the nearby farmhouse.*

Chuzzlewit, published in 1843. A few steps away, on the other side of the green, is The Forge, which is still in use. And, over the road from the other side of The Forge, a path across the meadow leads to the remains of Ivychurch, a 12th-century Augustinian priory, founded by King Stephen. Its prior and 12 monks ministered to the spiritual needs of royalty when they were in residence at Clarendon Palace. Stones from the ruins of Ivychurch were used to build the fountain and drinking-trough on the village green.

Another inn with a story is the Three Crowns, on the Southampton side of the hamlet of Whaddon. Its name is thought to recall the fact that in 1357 Edward III hunted in nearby Clarendon Forest with two captive guests, the King of France and the King of Scotland. Another theory is that the inn is named after the three kings of the Nativity.

St Mary's is a 19th-century church with a tall four-gabled tower and spire. Across the road is the driveway to Alderbury House, a late-18th-century residence, said to be built of materials from the bell-tower of Salisbury Cathedral after it had been pulled down in 1789.

St Marie's Grange, 1 mile to the north-west, is the home built in 1835 by the architect Augustus Welby Pugin for himself and his young bride. The house was much altered after Pugin returned to London to help with the design of the new Houses of Parliament. It was while staying at St Marie's Grange that Dickens wrote *Martin Chuzzlewit*.

ALDERMASTON

BERKSHIRE

8 miles east of Newbury (page 426 Ba)

It was in the 1950s that Aldermaston first came to national prominence as the starting point of a series of ban-the-bomb marches, by members of the Campaign for Nuclear Disarmament and their sympathisers. But the square buildings of the Defence Ministry's Atomic Weapons Research Establishment, surrounded by acres of grass and miles of fencing, lie some distance off and do not impinge on the village.

Red, rose, pink and umber are the colours of the straight, broad main street, with brick and timber its only building materials. At the high end, the view is closed by the towering, half-rounded lodges of Aldermaston Court, bearing massive wrought-iron gates almost as tall as themselves. The Eagle Gates, as they are called, date from William and Mary's day, and were originally made for Midgham Manor. They were later said to have been won in a game of cards by a member of the Congreve family, who owned the Court. They were erected on their present site after the Congreve family crest – a falcon – had been added. Facing the gates, at the bottom of the street, is the Hind's Head, a 17th-century coaching inn with a great black-and-gold clock and a gilt fox weather-vane. Between the lodges and the pub, the houses and cottages on each side of the street are a jumble of styles and periods, ranging mostly from 17th-century timbered to Victorian Gothic.

At first sight, the church, which lies round the bend of the road beyond the entrance to the Court, is a disappointment. Some previous lord of the manor thought fit to cover the walls with pebble-dash, and the years since have not been kind to the material. But the interior (the key is kept in the vicarage, next to the pub) is one of the most colourful and interesting in the shire. Medieval churches must have looked like this, ablaze with painted walls and stained glass. Some of the paintings and the stained glass, too, are indeed medieval; others are late 19th century, but all blend with one another, leaving the impression of a building that a lot of people have loved for a very long time. Among them, no doubt, were Sir George Forster, a Tudor soldier, and his wife, whose alabaster effigies lie in the entrance to the Lady Chapel. Part of Sir George's effigy was damaged in a roof fall, but his face remains unscathed, and his hind's-head crest lives on in the name of the inn.

Church Acre, a piece of land off Fisherman's Lane, was granted as compensation to the church after the Enclosures Act in the early 19th century. It covers not an acre, but 2 acres, 1 rod and 33 poles, and its rents are determined every three years, on December 13, at a candle auction. In this, a horseshoe nail is driven into a candle 1 in. below the wick, and bidding continues until the flame reaches the nail. The last bid to be received before the nail falls to the table captures Church Acre for the following three years. The vicar and the bidders drink rum punch and smoke church-warden pipes throughout the proceedings.

The Star Inn.

ALDWORTH

BERKSHIRE

3 miles west of Goring (page 426 Ba)

Split flint, red tile and brick are the major materials of this attractive, remote-feeling village that stands at the top of a steep road above Goring and the Thames. The materials have been married especially well in some of the older houses – in the large farm on the eastern edge of the village, for example, where the tiles slope down almost to the ground over the flint; in the converted barn overlooking the green; and in the partly 13th-century church. Timber-framed and thatched cottages add variety to the scene.

The long, low Bell Inn is a pleasant pub that overlooks the village well. The well-head is a massive structure of great beams supporting ponderous cogs and wheels, no doubt necessary in the days when the well was used, for the shaft drops a fearsome 372 ft. It is now sealed over.

From the churchyard, the land curves away to the west, creating an effect of great airiness and space, particularly at sunset. Laurence Binyon, author of the First World War poem which includes the line 'They shall grow not old, as we that are left grow old. . .', is buried there, and the village's own dead are remembered by a simple wooden cross brought back from France. Also in the churchyard is an object resembling a giant fossilised sponge, from which there bravely waves a single green branch. This is all that remains of a 1,000-year-old yew with a 30 ft

St Andrew's and the Clergy House on the Tye.

Home-grown beef in the square.

Figurehead outside the Star.

BEAUTY AND THE BEASTS IN ALFRISTON

Alfriston calls itself the capital of the Cuck-mere Valley. Around the square are inns, shops and houses with fine timber frames, brickwork, tile-hanging and weather-board-ing. The timbers of the Star Inn are orna-mented with carvings of beasts. One carving is thought to depict St Michael and the dragon. At one corner of the inn stands a large red lion, formerly the figurehead of a 17th-century Dutch ship. On the edge of the green, called the Tye, is the Clergy House, a 14th-century house, the first building bought by the National Trust, in 1896.

girth that was blown down on January 2, 1976.

Unless you are prepared for it, the interior of the church is startling, for at first glance it appears to be a mausoleum of giants. All round the walls, beneath fretted stone canopies, lie the larger-than-life effigies of Sir Philip de la Beche, Sheriff of Berkshire and Oxfordshire in 1313 and 1314, and eight of his relatives. Or rather, some of them lie; the remainder lean on one elbow, balance on a hip, and turn in a friendly manner towards one another. Though the effigies were knocked about during the Cromwellian period, they are still impressive – resplendent in sculpted armour and draperies.

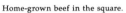

ALFRISTON
EAST SUSSEX

3 miles north-east of Seaford (page 423 Eb)

An old market cross, the only one to survive in East Sussex, still stands defiantly beside a chest-nut tree in the small square of the village, despite having been knocked down more than once by heavy lorries. It is a symbol of local pride, for Alfriston, after beginning as a Saxon settlement beside the River Cuckmere, became a market town before settling down as a village.

The narrow high street winds south from the square, revealing its architectural pleasures unex-pectedly. Many of the buildings are medieval in origin, notably the inns, the Star, the George and the Market Cross. An emblem of a bear and staff

on one of the timbers of the Star is thought to represent part of the arms of the Dudleys. It is said that the hostelry was built and maintained by the monks of Battle Abbey.

The village has long links with travellers, for it stands where an ancient ridgeway, used by pre-historic man, crossed the river. The long-distance walk of the South Downs Way now follows the route of the ridgeway. The South Downs Way enters Alfriston from the west by Star Street and follows River Lane to the riverside and the bridge. The river was a highway for smugglers, who came up from the sea, 3 miles away.

In the early 19th century, the Market Cross Inn – nicknamed Ye Olde Smugglers – was the base of the Alfriston gang, led by Stanton Collins, who used the quiet local paths for their illicit traffic and who once led an excise man to his death on nearby cliffs. Collins was eventually transported for sheep stealing.

The spaciousness and regularity of the 14th-century St Andrew's Church has earned it the title of 'Cathedral of the South Downs'. Its stone-work of small, square, knapped flints is unusual for Sussex churches, and its cruciform design is traditionally attributed to the sight of four oxen lying down in the shape of a cross when it was being built. The church's marriage register dates from 1504 and is probably the oldest in England.

To the west of High Street are the Twittens, narrow footpaths bounded by high flint walls. Scattered throughout the village, on the green, on the corners of lanes, even at kerb sides, are large smooth boulders which may long ago have marked the prehistoric cross-country ridgeway.

ALLENDALE TOWN
NORTHUMBERLAND

7 miles south of Haydon Bridge (page 438 Ac)

In the 19th century, Allendale was the centre of Northumbria's lead-mining area. The industry declined towards the end of the century when ore was imported from the Continent, and all that remains are the ruined furnaces and chimneys scattered throughout the dale.

The village stands high above the wooded gorge of the East Allen river, and claims to be at the exact geographical centre of Britain. Rows of rugged, golden stone buildings radiate from the broad, tree-lined Square towards desolate moorlands.

The austere Gothic-style Church of St Cuthbert, overlooking the river, dates from 1807 and is a stern reminder of the devoutness of the lead-mining community of the 19th century. But for many years the villagers have followed a New Year's Eve custom that dates from the Dark Ages. It is the Fire Ceremony, when men with blackened faces parade through the streets carrying tubs of blazing tar on their heads. They march to a bonfire in the market place, where the whole village turns out to celebrate the arrival of the New Year.

ALNMOUTH
NORTHUMBERLAND

5 miles south-east of Alnwick (page 438 Bd)

Firm, shimmering sands stretch as far as the eye can see at Alnmouth, where the River Aln meets the North Sea. A 56 mile stretch of this impressive coastline has been named as the Northumberland Heritage Coast by the Countryside Commission. The village was founded as a port between 1207 and 1208, and prospered as a shipbuilding centre and grain port until a great storm changed the course of the river in 1806. The harbour was abandoned, and Alnmouth became what it still is today – a quiet seaside place where brightly painted pleasure craft moor in the estuary during the summer.

Behind the broad beach lies an appealing jumble of houses, old inns and shops. Several houses are converted 18th-century granaries. Just south, facing the village but cut off by a loop in the river, is a grassy hill which is the site of a Norman church, St Waleric's, destroyed by the storm of 1806.

ALTARNUN
CORNWALL

7 miles west of Launceston (page 418 Cb)

Cottages of slate and granite line Altarnun's single winding street, and by the entrance to the churchyard a medieval packhorse bridge crosses the peat-stained stream known as Penpont Water.

The village lies just off the main road which descends the north-eastern flanks of Bodmin Moor, and is the centre of Cornwall's largest parish. Its old moorstone church, known as 'The Cathedral of the Moors' because of its size, is dedicated to St Nonna, mother of St David of Wales.

Just inside the churchyard is a stout Celtic cross, said to date from the 6th century. The 15th-century church contains 79 carved bench-ends depicting travelling musicians and entertainers, local characters of the time, and a flock of sheep.

The Methodist preacher John Wesley often visited Altarnun, staying at nearby Trewint in a house which is now a Methodist museum. Altarnun's Georgian Meeting House has a carved stone effigy of Wesley above the door, the work of the local sculptor Nevil Burnard, who was born in 1818.

Halfway across Bodmin Moor, about 4 miles south-west of Altarnun, is the hamlet of Bolventor and the slate-hung Jamaica Inn. The inn was built in the late 18th century and served as a resting place for travellers, but it became notorious as a meeting place for smugglers, whose activities Daphne du Maurier featured in her novel, *Jamaica Inn*. The view to the north from Bolventor takes in the 1,377 ft rocky tor of Brown Willy, Cornwall's highest point. Brown Willy is a corruption of the Cornish *Bron Ewhella*, which means 'highest hill'.

About 1 mile south-east of Bolventor lies Dozmary Pool, said to be where King Arthur's sword, Excalibur, was received by a hand rising from the water. According to legend, the pool is bottomless. In fact, it is only 9 in. deep.

Another legend tells of Jan Tregeagle, an unpopular local magistrate whose spirit was condemned to perform several impossible tasks, including emptying Dozmary Pool with a leaky limpet shell.

VILLAGE STREAM *Stone cottages face the ancient packhorse bridge which links the hillside village of Altarnun with its church, which stands on the other side of Penpont Water.*

ALVELEY

SALOP

6 miles south-east of Bridgnorth (page 429 Da)

One long street on the crest of a hill, lined by sturdy sandstone cottages, forms the central part of the village. In contrast to these are other buildings whose black-and-white fronts add a dash of traditional Shropshire 'magpie'. The dominant building is the elm-shaded Church of St Mary, which is also built of sandstone and is mottled with moss. It dates from the 12th century, but its exterior was heavily restored in 1878–9.

Inside the church, a brass commemorates John Grove, a native of Alveley who became a Freeman of the Grocers' Company in London. The memorial records how Grove, who died in 1616, left two annual gifts of £10 to the village. One was to employ a schoolmaster; the other was to help 'five poore aged . . . labouring men'.

There are several pleasant walks down to the River Severn, where steam-trains of the Severn Valley Railway run along the far bank.

ALVINGHAM

LINCOLNSHIRE

3 miles north-east of Louth (page 432 Be)

One thing in particular sets Alvingham apart from other villages: it has two churches in a single churchyard. One church, St Mary's, belongs to the neighbouring parish of North Cockerington. The other, Alvingham's parish church, St Adelwold's, lay abandoned for most of the 19th century, but was restored in 1933.

St Mary's Church was once the chapel of a Gilbertine priory, which was founded in Alvingham in the 12th century. The parishioners of North Cockerington were allowed to use it as their church when forced to abandon their first church as a ruin. It still retains some of its original Norman features, including the base of the font. There is part of a Saxon window in the chancel.

Across the yew-shaded churchyard stands the largely 14th-century Church of St Adelwold's, the only church in Britain dedicated to this Saxon saint. Adelwold became Bishop of Winchester in the late 10th century, and was a man renowned as a severe disciplinarian but an outstanding teacher.

Bordering the southern side of the churchyard is the old Louth Navigation Canal which links Louth, 3 miles south-west, to the sea. On the north side, Church Lane leads to a watermill near the two churches. A mill has stood on the site for at least 900 years. The present mill, housed in a three-storey building, has been partially restored and is open to visitors on certain days each week during spring and summer. There are two other craft workshops: the smithy in Yarburgh Road, which sells wrought-iron work; and a nearby pottery, housed in the old wheelwright's workshop.

Contrast in styles.

Bricks and stone.

Edge of paradise.

AMBERLEY
WEST SUSSEX

4 miles north of Arundel (page 422 Db)

'Dear Amberley', as it is affectionately christened by the official village history, is a lovely hodge-podge of styles, materials, periods and flower-draped walls set beneath a great wooded bluff of the South Downs more reminiscent of the Tyrol or the Highlands than of Sussex. Like Alfriston and Southease, it is a convenient halt for hikers along the prehistoric South Downs Way, a point that has been borne in mind by the landlord of the Black Horse pub, who has provided visitors to the bar with a small museum of Downland relics. Chief among these are a collection of sheep bells and hand-carved crooks amassed by 'Grassy' Olivers, a local shepherd; and a letter from Lord Selwyn-Lloyd, Speaker of the House of Commons from 1971 to 1976, proudly telling of his completion of the South Downs Way walk.

Across the end of a most attractive cul-de-sac, bordered by creeper-hung stone walls, is St Michael's Church, backed in turn by the broad-shouldered remains of Amberley Castle. The story of the church goes back to 681, when the land on which the village now stands was given to St Wilfrid by the Saxon King Cedwalla, whom he had converted to Christianity. Much of the building, however, dates from shortly after the Norman Conquest and is the work of Bishop Luffa, who also built Chichester Cathedral.

The interior of St Michael's is high, bare and silent, its roof supported on massive stone pillars. To the right of the lovely, worn chancel arch – part of Bishop Luffa's contribution – are fading purple wall-paintings of Christ in Majesty and the Resurrection, dating from the 12th century. Among the few but charming monuments are a brass of a knight wearing the armour and surcoat of the Agincourt period, and a poignant portrait plaque to a girl who died in 1919, aged 17 – 'A Dear Child', reads the inscription. In the tower is a peal of five bells, which were cast and hung in 1742. The peal is one of the lightest in Sussex.

Amberley Castle is also partly the work of Bishop Luffa, and of other medieval Bishops of Chichester, whose summer palace it was – something of an episcopal conceit, rather than a serious military fortification. Nevertheless, if you descend the slope behind the church and look up at the great cliff of masonry, with jackdaws swirling around its dizzy battlements, the castle is still extremely impressive. One end of the ruin, almost the oldest part, is the present Manor House. To see it, bright and living, among so much tumbled stone, is rather like travelling back down the centuries, to a time when the past was the present.

The high south face of the castle looks out over the wide-swinging Arun river and the Amberley Wildbrooks, an area that is sometimes marsh, sometimes stream and frequently flooded. The trains that run across the vast, flat plain look like toys, yet the embankments that carry them over the river and the treacherous ground were considered, when they were built in 1863, to be among the wonders of the Railway Age.

ARTISTS' PARADISE ON THE SOUTH DOWNS

No two houses are the same in Amberley, and each appears to have grown out of the edge of the road, gathering to itself the colours and materials – stone, brick, thatch, split flint, tile and timber – that happened to be available at the time of its creating. The streets of the village wind and twist to no particular plan, coaxing the visitor round each bend just to see what will happen next. It is all very peaceful, and past industry is acknowledged only in a nostalgic sort of way by adding the prefix 'Old' to the names of the buildings. There is a stone-tiled Old Brewhouse, a thatched Old Malthouse, a bow-windowed Old Bakery, the Old Bakehouse with curling brick steps and a black-and-white Old Stack Cottage. Artists come with brushes and palettes to capture the enchantment of this show village; fishermen come to display their patience on the banks of the Arun; while botanists and ornithologists come to study the plants and wildlife of the Downs and the Wildbrooks which between them enclose this idyllic corner of Sussex.

AMLWCH

GWYNEDD

15 miles north-west of Menai Bridge (page 428 Ac)

In 1768, what was then the world's richest source of copper was discovered on Parys Mountain, 2 miles inland from Amlwch. By 1801 the tiny hamlet had grown into a flourishing industrial centre, with some 5,000 people and a bustling port blasted from the cliffs. At their peak the Parys mines were producing 80,000 tons of ore a year. The falling price of copper and flooded workings combined to end the boom early in the 19th century.

Down by the harbour, now used by pleasure craft, are two dockside inns, the Liverpool Arms and the Adelphi Vaults. Old, ivy-grown buildings stand near the high-tide mark, overlooked by the stump of a windmill. Ships of up to 200 tons used to moor at the quays. The arrival of the oil industry, in 1973, led to the seaward end of the harbour being extended.

The heart of Amlwch is set back from the coast, with an elegant church, built in 1800 during the copper boom, at the head of the main street. It contrasts with the Roman Catholic church that stands beside the Bull Bay road, and is said to have been inspired by an upturned boat.

APPLECROSS

HIGHLAND

34 miles north-west of Kyle of Lochalsh (page 442 Cd)

Neither apples nor a cross have anything to do with the name of this village. It is a name derived from the Gaelic *Apor-crossan*, meaning 'the mouth of the Crossan river'. The village stands on a sandy bay, looking across to the island of Raasay and the mountains of Skye. All around are mountain peaks, some rising to almost 3,000 ft, and until the mid-1970s the only road to the village was over the narrow Pass of Cattle which snakes and hairpins between the mountains. A gentler route now follows the coast, starting from Shieldaig, 24 miles to the north.

The main street of Applecross is a neat line of cottages strung along the seashore among little groves of trees. In the village are four churches – the Church of Scotland, the Free Church, the Free Presbyterian Church, and the now unused Clachan Church, the previous Church of Scotland which stands on the site of an abbey founded in 673 by St Maelrubha, a Celtic monk.

APPLEDORE

KENT

5 miles south-east of Tenterden (page 423 Eb)

In the Middle Ages, Appledore – the name means 'apple tree' – was a centre for shipping. But that was before the marshes were reclaimed and the River Rother changed its course southwards after

fierce storms. Today, the sea is 7 miles away. The village has a violent history. The Danes pillaged it in the 9th century, and in 1380 it was sacked in a French raid, when the attackers burned the 13th-century church. Horne's Place, a medieval farmhouse with a 14th-century stone chapel, north of the village, was attacked by rebellious peasants under Wat Tyler in 1381. The owner, William Horne, was one of the commissioners appointed to put down the rebellion.

The village street, lined with houses of brick, tile and timber, broadens into an open space where a market used to be held, beside the church which was restored soon after its burning. The church has a battlemented tower and an ornately carved west door. A huge wooden screen, dating from the rebuilding, divides its interior. The church is also known for its timber roof and the quality of its eight bells.

The street crosses the Royal Military Canal, which passes through Appledore. The canal was built in 1804 as part of the coastal defences against the French. A stretch of it, 3½ miles long, is now in the possession of the National Trust, and trees have been planted along its route.

In the early 19th century Brookland, 5 miles south-east of Appledore, was a haunt for Romney Marsh smugglers. In the main street is Pear Tree House, the home of a doctor who was often led blindfold to treat their wounded. The church, where the smugglers used to hide, has a 60 ft

high, three-tiered wooden belfry, a 14th-century porch and, inside, a splendid Norman font of beaten lead.

Stone-in-Oxney, this 'island' village, 2 miles south-west of Appledore, stood on the Isle of Oxney before the marshes were drained. The Ferry Inn still displays a road-toll sign, and in the tower of the restored 15th-century church are a Roman Mithras-cult altar stone and the fossilised remains of an iguanodon dinosaur.

ARDELEY
HERTFORDSHIRE

5 miles east of Stevenage (page 426 Cb)

Perhaps the liveliest and most picturesque part of this small village is centred on its neat green, surrounded on three sides by fine black-and-white and thatched cottages overlooking a red-tiled well-head, and a village hall with a curiously arched doorway and wooden pillars.

The village is actually very old, and was known in early medieval times for its malt, a supply of which was sent regularly to the Dean and Chapter of St Paul's Cathedral.

These clergymen were so impressed, so it is said, that in 1240 they provided the funds to build the Church of St Lawrence that stands

opposite the green. Parts of this original structure were incorporated in the larger, present building, which dates mostly from a century later. To see the church, it is necessary to obtain a key from the vicarage next door.

The interior of the church is a delight, a record of the quiet continuity of village life over the centuries. The roof is supported by 12 carved wooden angels, all playing musical instruments and gazing down upon the many monuments and memorials. Especially touching is the monument to Mary Markham, a girl with a fine-boned, sensitive face who died in 1673 at the age of 24. The effigy of her dead infant son lies in front of her. The brass to the Shotbolt family, dressed in the rich robes of 1599, is also worth seeing.

On the road out of the village towards Walkern it is possible to catch a glimpse, over the treetops, of the turrets and battlements of Ardeley Bury.

A manor has stood on this site since the year 900, but its present resemblance to 'many tower'd Camelot' dates only from 1820. There is a lake in the grounds with a Tudor boathouse, but these are not open to the public.

MODERN MERRIE ENGLAND *The scene on the green at Ardeley, with its horseshoe of white-walled thatched buildings, is perfect Merrie England, yet it is actually all 20th century. The lord of the manor rebuilt most of the cottages and laid out the green in 1917. Eleven years later, the thatched hall was built to tone in with the surroundings.*

THE VILLAGE YEAR

A calendar of feasts and customs

The pattern of village life has always been closely linked to the perennial round of ploughing and sowing, new crops, first fruits and harvest. These weeks of hard work are punctuated by periods of relaxation, during which many of the traditional festivals, fairs and holidays are held.

January

New Year's Day and the Feast of the Circumcision, January 1 In some villages in Scotland and the North of England, New Year is ushered in by the First Foot, a dark-haired man who comes through the front door after midnight bringing symbols of plenty for the coming year: a coin, a piece of bread, or a lump of coal. At Allendale, in Northumberland, the First Foots set out after the New Year's Eve Fire Festival, when men parade with blazing tar barrels, which are thrown on to a great bonfire.

Plough Monday, first Monday after January 6 This day marks the beginning of the agricultural year. The Church Christianised the pagan custom of dragging a plough through the village and asking the gods to favour it. Today, the plough is blessed in Flamstead and other Hertfordshire villages, as well as in the dioceses of Chichester and Exeter.

At Goathland, in North Yorkshire, the Plough Stots still perform their traditional sword-dance on the Saturday following Plough Monday; 'stot' is an old North country term for bullock.

At Haxey, in Lincolnshire, Plough Monday is celebrated in the Haxey Hood Game, resembling a wild form of rugby and played using 13 hoods instead of a ball. Twelve are made of sacking rolled and stitched into a tight cylinder. The thirteenth is made of leather. Local legend dates the game from the 13th century, when the lady of the manor lost her red hood as she rode to church. Thirteen labourers retrieved it and, in gratitude, Lady de Mowbray bequeathed a piece of land known as the 'Hoodlands', so that the event could be re-enacted every year.

SWORD-DANCE *A web of swords is the climax to the dance performed by the Plough Stots – young men of the village – on the Saturday following Plough Monday at Goathland, North Yorkshire.*

FIERY FOOL *Smoking the Fool is part of the Haxey Hood Game celebrations. The Fool is one of 12 'Boggans' – people of the bogland – who lead the players to the field where men from five local hamlets compete.*

The Burning of the Clavie, January 11 Burghead, on the southern shores of the Moray Firth, celebrates Old New Year's Eve by burning the Clavie, a sawn-off tar barrel mounted on a long pole. The Clavie is filled with burning peat and tar and carried to the top of a nearby hill and smashed. Everyone scrambles for a burning fragment, which used to be treasured as a charm against evil spirits. The ceremony may relate to Norse fire-worship, when fires were lit in mid-winter as a plea for the return of the sun.

February

Blessing of the Nets, February 14 At Norham, Northumberland, the vicar blesses the nets at the beginning of the salmon fishing. The ceremony is held on Pedwell Beach, shortly before midnight. The first salmon caught is given to the officiating clergyman.

Shrove Tuesday Lent, the six-week Christian season of self-denial, begins on Ash Wednesday. During the Middle Ages, dairy products and eggs were forbidden foods in Lent, so on the eve of Lent, Shrove Tuesday, housewives used up their stocks to make pancakes. On the Tuesday morning the church bell rang, calling everyone to Confession – to be given absolution, or 'shriven' – hence, Shrove Tuesday.

At Olney, in Buckinghamshire, the Town Crier's bell announces the start of the annual Pancake Race. It is said to originate from 1445, when a housewife rushed in answer to the Shrove Tuesday bell carrying a frying pan and half-cooked pancake.

Shrove Tuesday games may be relics of pagan rites to encourage the fertility of the soil by driving out evil spirits, which explains the boisterous nature of many of the sports.

Silver-painted balls figure in the games still played in Cornwall – at St Ives, for example, and in Hurling the Silver Ball, at St Columb, which may involve 500 players. Goals are scored by dropping the ball into either of two stone troughs set 2 miles apart, or by carrying the ball over a parish boundary.

A football is part of a Shrovetide ceremony at Corfe Castle, Dorset. Each Shrove Tuesday the Company of Marblers and Stone-cutters of the Isle of Purbeck hold their annual meeting, when apprentice quarrymen, having reached the age of 21, are made freemen. It is then the practice for the freemen to kick a football around Corfe and over to Owre Quay, where the marble used to be shipped out.

March & April

Easter Sunday, March/April The conclusion of the Lenten fast is one of the main festivals of the Christian Church. Chocolate Easter Eggs are common throughout Britain, but in parts of the North villagers still decorate real eggs. These are known as Paste or Pace eggs, a corruption of the old English *pasch*, meaning 'Easter'.

In some Yorkshire villages, such as Midgley and Brighouse, a Pace-egg play is performed. Schoolboys, wearing simple costume, act a mummers' play in the market place or some other public place.

PRIZE EGG *In the North, Pace eggs are covered with petals and leaves and then boiled in onion skins to give a golden background. In some villages the best decorated eggs are awarded prizes.*

Bottle Kicking and Hare Pie Scrambling, Easter Monday This spring ritual takes place at Hallaton, Leicestershire. A hare pie is taken to Hare Pie Hill and scattered over the ground, symbolising the scattering of a sacrificial beast to promote fertility of the land. After this, the bottles – wooden barrels, two containing beer and the other one empty – are fought for by youths from Hallaton and the rival village of Medbourne. The teams try to carry the bottles over a brook into their own parish, and the members of the winning team share the contents of the full barrels.

May

RITUAL WEAR *Bonneted ladies carrying bundles of wood dance in Salisbury Cathedral each May 29. The dance is part of the Grovely Forest Rights ceremony, when the people of Wishford Magna renew their right to collect wood from the forest.*

May Day, first Monday in May The Celtic summer feast of Beltane, when bonfires were lit in honour of the sun, took place at the beginning of May. So, too, did the honouring of the Roman spring-goddess Flora, by decorating houses with fruit, flowers and trees. The maypole was originally a tree stripped of its foliage, and dancing round it symbolised the transition into summer.

Some villages still retain their maypoles. The one at Barwick-in-Elmet, Yorkshire, is, at 86 ft, the tallest in England.

Garland Day, May 13 Abbotsbury, Dorset, used to live by mackerel fishing, but today hardly anyone in the village makes a living from the sea. On May 13, two garlands, one of wild flowers, the other of garden blooms, are carried through the village by local children. The wild garland is sometimes thrown into the sea, as a reminder of the time when Abbotsbury depended on the ocean for its livelihood.

June & July

Well-dressing, Ascension Day, late May/early June Derbyshire observes its own attractive summer flower festivals in thanks for the blessing of pure fresh water from its wells and springs. Well-dressings are brightly coloured pictures of religious scenes. Natural objects such as moss and leaves, but chiefly flower petals, are pressed on to a prepared foundation of moist clay, spread over a wooden tray. Colourful well-dressings at Tissington, Barlow, Tideswell and many other villages can be admired at Ascensiontide and at varying times throughout the summer until September.

CHILDREN'S GALA *At Cockenzie, East Lothian, the Summer Queen is crowned in June after sailing with an escort of decorated boats from the old harbour to the new one at Port Seton. On the way a mock attack by pirates is repulsed.*

Tynwald Day, July 5 Every year an open-air meeting of the Isle of Man's 1,000-year-old parliament, the Tynwald, is held on Tynwald Hill, St John's, where the island's laws passed during the previous year are read out.

August

SAFELY GATHERED IN *Harvest Festival thanksgivings began in Victorian times, and at Swallowfields in Berkshire the harvest wagon was greeted by bands, banners and bell-ringers.*

Harvest Festival, August 1 Lammas, the festival of the first fruits, takes its name from Old English *hlâf-maesse*, meaning 'loaf mass'. The Harvest Festival, a thank-offering to God for the produce of the earth, is attributed to Robert Stephen Hawker, the Vicar of Morwenstow, Cornwall, who began it in his church in 1843.

Rush-bearing, August 5 The custom dates from the time when earthen floors were strewn with rushes once a year to keep them warm and dry. At Grasmere, Cumbria, on the Saturday nearest to August 5, St Oswald's Day, local schoolgirls dressed in green and white walk to church together with the vicar and congregation, carrying rushes.

Royal National Eisteddfod During the first week of August, Welsh poets, musicians and craftsmen gather at a site ceremoniously announced a year and a day before. The Eisteddfod is presided over by the Archdruid of the Gorsedd, or company, of Bards.

Burning the Bartle, Saturday after August 24 Opinions vary at West Witton, North Yorkshire, as to who Bartle was and why he should be burned, but the most popular theory is that he was a swine thief who lived in Wensleydale in medieval times. An effigy of 'Bartle' is paraded through the streets, a knife is plunged into his heart and he is set on fire.

September

Horn Dance, Monday following the first Sunday after September 4 The Abbots Bromley Horn Dancers' day starts at 8 a.m. and ends at dusk. Six men, carrying reindeer horns of unknown age, perform their ritual dance at the vicarage, the manor house and in the village. The dancers are accompanied by a Fool, a Hobby Horse, Maid Marian – the Man-Woman – and a Bowman. The origins of the dance are unknown, but it has remained unchanged for hundreds of years.

HORNED COMBAT *The high point of the Abbots Bromley Horn Dance is when the Deer Men lower the horns and act out a mock combat. The horns, three black and three white, are mounted on wooden replicas of reindeer heads.*

Crab-apple Fair, Saturday nearest to September 18 The highlight of this annual fair at Egremont in Cumbria is when apples are thrown to the crowd from a lorry as it drives down the main street. The fair dates from the 13th century, and Worcester apples are now distributed instead of crab apples.

Then follows traditional sports: street races, wrestling, cycling and terrier racing.

Michaelmas, September 29 The date coincides with the end of harvesting, and is a time of fairs and animal sales.

October & November

'PUNKY' LIGHT *Children parade in Hinton St George, Somerset, on the last Thursday in October carrying their 'punky' lanterns.*

Hallowe'en, October 31 This coincides with the ancient Celtic festival of Samain, when ghosts, witches and fairies walk abroad. On the last Thursday in October the villagers of Hinton St George in Somerset vie with each other to see who can make the best punky lantern – a hollowed-out mangel-wurzel with a lighted candle inside illuminating a carved face.

Caking Night, November 1, or following Monday The children of Dungworth, Yorkshire, used to go 'caking' before the Second World War. They wore masks and visited houses in the village, asking the householder to guess their identity. If he could not, he put money in a collecting box; if he could, he gave them a piece of treacle cake called 'parkin'. Grown-ups have moved in on the tradition, but they compete in a best-mask or fancy-dress competition.

Turning the Devil's Stone, November 5 A large stone on the village green at Shebbear, Devon, is said to have been dropped by the Devil on his way from Heaven to Hell. Unless the stone is turned over once a year an ill fate will befall the village, so on November 5 each year the bellringers of St Michael's Church ring a discordant peal, to challenge the Devil, and then make their way to the green where they turn the Devil's Stone.

Firing the Fenny Poppers, November 11 Since 1760 the 'fenny poppers', six small cannons, have been fired on St Martin's Day to celebrate the dedication of St Martin's Church at Fenny Stratford, Buckinghamshire. The 'poppers' are filled with gunpowder and are fired at midday, 2 p.m. and 4.10 p.m. on the Leon Recreation Ground.

BLAZING AWAY *Bonfires are lit at Ottery St Mary and at Hatherleigh on to which burning tar barrels are thrown.*

Tar-barrel rolling Playing with fire is a spectacular November pastime in Devon. The men of Ottery St Mary do it on the 5th, the men of Hatherleigh on the Wednesday following. The burning barrels are carried through the streets and eventually end up on a bonfire.

Ottery St Mary's festivities are probably similar in origin to Shrove Tuesday games. The Hatherleigh Fire Festival is a combination of Hallowe'en and Gunpowder Plot celebrations.

Laxton Jury Day, end of November Laxton, in Nottinghamshire, is the only village in England where the medieval system of farming survives. The villagers farm three fields which are shared among them each year by a jury. The jury is elected annually at the Court Leet which follows Jury Day.

December

St Nicholas Day, December 6 St Nicholas (Santa Claus) is the patron saint of children, and on his day, the choirboys of Par village, in Cornwall, appoint one of their number Boy Bishop. He is dressed in impressive robes and leads the others in the hymn singing.

Tom Bawcock's Eve, December 23 The fishermen of Mousehole, Cornwall, celebrate Tom Bawcock's deed on this day. The story goes that during a famine, a fisherman named Tom Bawcock put out to sea and brought back seven varieties of fish to feed the villagers.

Marshfield Mummers, December 24 At Marshfield, in Gloucestershire, the Christmas Mummers perform their ancient mumming-play – one of several performed in different parts of the country at this season. The players are heavily disguised by masks and strange tattered garments as they stylistically act out the simple plot of the triumph of good over evil, of resurrection over death. Once, probably in pagan times, the play symbolised the victory of the sun and spring over the death and darkness of winter.

PAGAN DRAMA *Mummers, at Marshfield, Gloucestershire, act out a simple play which symbolises the fight between good and evil, light and darkness and spring and summer.*

ARISAIG
HIGHLAND

7 miles south of Mallaig (page 442 Cc)

Some of the finest views in the West Highlands are from this village on the Morar coast. It lies at the head of Loch nan Ceall, a sea loch whose entrance is strewn with reefs and islets. Out to sea are three islands – the hump-backed Muck, the craggy Rum, and Eigg with its 1,289 ft pinnacle of rock.

Before the port of Mallaig was built 7 miles to the north in the 1890s, Arisaig's tiny harbour was busy with boats bringing produce from the Western Isles or taking livestock to the markets of southern Scotland. Now the harbour is busy again – there is a boatyard, yachts and pleasure craft call in the summer, and cruises are run to the islands. The Arisaig Hotel is a former stage-coach inn, and horses were stabled in the present lounge bar.

There are long stretches of sands along the coastline – silvery-white and accessible at Back of Keppoch bay, north of the village. About 2 miles south of Arisaig is Borrodale beach on Loch nan Uamh, where Bonnie Prince Charlie landed in 1745 and whence he fled in defeat 14 months later. This was Jacobite country, the land of the Macdonalds. In the local Roman Catholic church there is a memorial to Alexander Macdonald, the celebrated Gaelic soldier-poet who fought with Charles throughout his campaign.

ARLEY, Cheshire (page 429 Dc)
(see Great Budworth)

ARNESBY
LEICESTERSHIRE

8 miles south-east of Leicester (page 430 Cb)

In the graveyard behind the red-brick chapel in Arnesby, a child in the late 1760s learned to read by studying the gravestones. By the time he was nine he was writing hymns. The boy was Robert Hall, son of the Baptist minister, and destined himself to become an internationally celebrated Baptist preacher. He was born in 1764 and lived next door to the chapel at the Old Manse, now a centre for religious conferences. A narrow street

in the centre of the village is named after him.

Unlike most villages, the ground-plan of Arnesby is roughly square, with the main road forming a boundary on one side, and barns and haystacks pressing up against the backs of a varied selection of houses on two others. It is a quiet and self-contained place with one pub, the Old Cock Inn.

The Church of St Peter, with its square tower, dates back to Norman times, and the nearby village of Peatling Magna was the birthplace of Elizabeth Jervis, who grew up to become Dr Samuel Johnson's much loved wife, Tetty.

ASHBURY
OXFORDSHIRE
7 miles east of Swindon (page 426 Aa)

A chalk village, whose older houses are largely built of square-cut chalk blocks, Ashbury leans against the chalk ramparts of the Downs that lead up to the Berkshire Ridgeway. Fading to pearl-grey as it weathers, chalk is an attractive building material, especially when patchworked with red

brick and brown limestone and surmounted by thatch, as happens in many of the cottages. It is also remarkably enduring; the church and the Manor House, both mainly of chalk, have stood since the 13th and 15th centuries.

The Manor House, from the rear at least, is rather like a Rhine castle in miniature, rising sheer from the ravine of the infant River Ock, a tributary of the Thames. The front of the building is largely obscured by barns, but the little you can see, peeping between the struts, is delightful. So, too, is the church, with its steep steps running up between the manicured yews of the church-yard to the 15th-century porch.

The Rose and Crown is one of the few pubs within striking distance of the 85 mile long Ridgeway, and is consequently much patronised by walkers. The notion of tackling at least part of the track is made the more tempting by the chalk and thatch cottages, and the old tree-stumps, hollowed into flower beds, that frame the way up to Wayland's Smithy.

According to legend, if you leave your horse and a silver coin outside this prehistoric burial chamber, which lies just off the Ridgeway, you will, on your return, find the horse shod and the coin gone. If you should be so fortunate, the person responsible is Wayland, smith of the Nordic gods.

ASHBY ST LEDGERS
NORTHAMPTONSHIRE
4 miles north of Daventry (page 430 Cb)

Narrow, tree-lined roads and hills with winding paths shelter Ashby St Ledgers, a village rich in cottages of stone and thatch. The village takes its name from the medieval Church of St Leodegarius, which has a fine Jacobean three-tier pulpit. The Coach and Horses Inn was originally a 16th-century farmhouse to which a Victorian façade was added in 1892.

Near by is the medieval manor house of Ashby St Ledgers, where, according to local legend, the Gunpowder Plot was hatched in 1605 in a room above the timbered gatehouse. The mansion was owned by the Catesby family, and it was Robert Catesby who encouraged a small group of Roman Catholics to try to blow up Parliament and James I, and so strike a blow against Protestantism. But the plotters were informed on and the plot failed. Robert Catesby fled to Holbeache, in Stafford-shire, where, three days later, he refused to surrender and was killed. After this, the Catesby estates were sold and, over the centuries, they have passed from owner to owner. Today, the manor house is still privately owned.

PULPIT AND PLOT *Behind the Church of St Leodegarius, at Ashby, stands the timbered gatehouse to the medieval manor. It was in a room above the gate that, according to local legend, the Gunpowder Plot was planned in 1605. The Catesby family owned the manor, and Robert Catesby encouraged a group of Roman Catholics to attempt to blow up Parliament and the King. When the plot failed he fled, but was found and killed, refusing to surrender.*

ASHDON
ESSEX

4 miles north-east of Saffron Walden (page 432 Cb)

The lower stretch of the village lies in the vale of a stream called the Bourn, overlooked by the 17th-century Rose and Crown public house. One of the ground-floor rooms in the Rose and Crown still has its original wall decorations – painted panels with geometric patterns and texts in Gothic lettering.

The Church of All Saints crowns the hill above the village and dates from the 14th century, though the lower sections of the columns are thought to be Saxon. Next to the church is the early-16th-century timber-framed Guildhall, now a private house. Waltons, originally an Elizabethan house 1 mile north-east of Ashdon, was destroyed by fire in 1954, but was rebuilt by its present owner and given a Georgian front. He also restored the derelict 18th-century post-mill in a field opposite the house.

The Bartlow Hills, 3 miles north, are Romano-British burial mounds. There were eight at one time, four of which remain in good order. In the 1830s, these graves were opened up and yielded bronze, enamel and glassware which were obviously the possessions of men of high rank. The best examples were taken to Easton Lodge, near Great Dunmow, but were destroyed in a fire there in 1847.

ASHFORD-IN-THE-WATER
DERBYSHIRE

2 miles north-west of Bakewell (page 430 Bd)

Ever twisting, the River Wye meanders through Ashford, a limestone village with narrow streets and three ancient bridges. The 17th-century Sheepwash Bridge has a stone enclosure at one end in which sheep were penned before being washed in the clear water long ago.

Near the Sheepwash Bridge stands the parish church of the Holy Trinity, largely rebuilt in 1870. The lower part of the tower is 13th century. In the north aisle are four maidens' crants, garlands carried at the funeral of a young unmarried woman and hung in the church with a paper glove bearing her name and age. The crants probably date from the 18th century. Ashford holds a well-dressing ceremony on Trinity Sunday – the day of the church's patronal festival.

Behind the church are traces of a moat, all that remains of a fortified house which was the home of Edmund Plantagenet, brother of Edward II. The present Ashford Hall is a dignified Georgian building at the eastern end of the village, overlooking the Wye.

In the 18th century, Ashford was noted for its black marble, quarried locally and used mainly for church furnishings and for fireplace surrounds. In the church is a tablet to Henry Watson, who founded the industry, and also an example of the black marble – a table with an ornate inlaid top.

VILLAGE POND *The hub of Ashmore is the old pond. For centuries it was a watering place for cattle. Today, it is a home for ducks – and occasional geese and other waterfowl. The fine cedar beyond the pond stands in the garden of the Old Rectory, an 18th-century stone-built house.*

ASHMORE
DORSET

5 miles south-east of Shaftesbury (page 421 Cb)

Few chalk-country villages are set on hilltops – but Ashmore, situated more than 700 ft up on Cranborne Chase, is the highest village in Dorset. It consists largely of thatched cottages and a sprinkling of handsome 18th-century houses of grey-green stone and flint. Ashmore's many vantage points provide magnificent panoramic views. On a clear day the Isle of Wight is visible, some 40 miles away to the south-east.

The largest farm in Ashmore surrounds the Church of St Nicholas, with its modern stone brackets shaped as various animals. There are a

number of barrows, or ancient burial mounds, in and around the village.

On the Friday evening nearest to Midsummer's Eve a celebration known as Filly-Loo takes place, with singing and dancing round the village pond. Morris dancers from all parts of southern England join the villagers for the occasion. Ashmore has a fine cricket ground and, although the population is only 150, they claim to field one of the strongest village teams in England.

ASHURST
WEST SUSSEX

8 miles north-west of Shoreham-by-Sea (page 422 Db)

Cottages and farm buildings are scattered round the lanes which make up a rough square, and they display a wide variety of building materials and techniques. Some are half-timbered, some decorated with tile-hanging. Others are weatherboarded and some are even built of flint, though the Downs, where flints are found, are several miles away.

Ashurst looks as though it may not have changed much in basic layout since the Saxons established it in a clearing, or 'hurst', in the forest of the Sussex Weald. Its setting in the woods, away from the main roads, gives it a remote atmosphere. The lanes frequently broaden out into greens with buildings around their edges. A timber-framed inn, the Fountain, stands at one corner of the lanes, alongside barns and a 16th-century cottage which seems to lean on the tall brick chimneys that have been built against it. Some of the farmsteads are medieval, some even older. Eatons Farm, for instance, set round a small green on a trackway leading to a river crossing, is mentioned in the Domesday Book.

The flint used for some of the cottages was also brought in to build the 12th-century church. It stands in isolation from the main village, on a quiet lane with a large brick rectory and a cluster of cottages and farms. Inside the church, hanging on a wall, is a black 18th-century 'vamping horn', once used to accompany church singing.

ASHWELL
HERTFORDSHIRE

4 miles north-east of Baldock (page 426 Cb)

Ashwell, a long, large village set among huge fields and low hills, owes its existence and its name to the springs that bubble up in a dell surrounded by ash trees at the eastern end of the main street. The springs, crossed by stepping-stones, give birth to the River Rhee, which later becomes the Cam. Their waters are said to remain at exactly the same temperature throughout the year.

Probably the first inhabitants of the area were the Iron Age people who built a hill-fort, the Arbury Banks, to command the Icknield Way, an ancient road linking south-west England and the east coast. Traces of their hut circles within the fort can still be seen from the air.

Few villages present so complete and continuous a picture of human habitation and activity. Ashwell was an important town long before the Norman Conquest; and having lived, only just, through plague, tempest and fire, it looks what it is – an experienced, triumphant survivor. Five-hundred years of building styles jostle each other without apology, occasionally pushed aside by well-tended grass verges. Ashwell houses are for living in: medieval cottages with Elizabethan additions proved too small for Victorian families, whose improvements were in turn streamlined by the 20th century.

All the same, there is much that has escaped alteration. Bear House, on the corner of Bear Lane, is mostly medieval; so is the Chantry House, which in the 1540s was the home of 'John Smarte, clerk, a man of godlie conversation'. Several farms – Westbury, Dixies and Ducklake – date from the same period, as does the Rose and Crown pub, with its overhanging gables and its ghost that opens windows and thumps about in the cellar.

In Mill Street, in 1681, the Merchant Taylors' Company established a school, largely financed by a local benefactor. It is now the local library. The same mixture of conservation and economy is apparent in the old Maltings, superbly converted into a pair of modern houses, and the Old Mill, restored in the style of the miller's house. It retains an ancient, gigantic water-wheel turned by a stream. Its function is entirely decorative, since none of the mill machinery survives.

The lovely timber and whitewashed Guildhouse in the High Street had little to do with crafts; it was the home of the Guild of St John the Baptist, a religious body, and dates from about 1510. It is common knowledge, too, that the name of the Engine pub does not refer to the railway. Once it was called The Engine and Drum, because its landlord, in the 1850s, had a drum threshing machine for hire.

All Ashwell's links with the past, from prehistoric times onward, are summed up in the village museum, which is maintained entirely by local people and contained in the Town House. There is a sense of continuity, for in the 16th century this handsome building was probably used as the local tithe office.

But commanding past and present, from any viewpoint in the village, is the 176 ft tower of the church. Gauntly buttressed and crowned with a spike, it rears from the great 14th-century hull of the church itself. Its very size proclaims Ashwell's long-ago prosperity as a market town. Beneath the grass to the left of the path lie the victims of the Black Death that shattered the village in the mid-14th century.

The interior of the church, all clear light and whitewash, is remarkably puritanical in effect. There are few furnishings and fewer official monuments; unofficial ones, however, abound. One thing that Ashwell men have had in common down the centuries is a wish to immortalise themselves and their thoughts in stone, and consequently the church walls are covered with whirls, scrawls and scratches dating from the last century ('Wm. Law 1873') back to the days when the church was built.

ASKHAM
CUMBRIA

4 miles south of Penrith (page 435 Dd)

As attractive as its setting, on the Lake District National Park's eastern rim, Askham lies below rolling fells that sweep gently down towards the River Lowther. The far bank – almost vertical, and thickly wooded – is crowned by the towers and turrets of Lowther Castle, a romantic ruin. From the top of the village there are memorable views over the rooftops to the castle and the distant majesty of the highest Pennine peaks. Tracks and footpaths run westwards over the hills to Pooley Bridge and Ullswater.

Askham is built around two greens, separated by a central crossroads and a tight little knot of buildings which includes the 19th-century village school. The lower green, where geese waddle beneath scattered trees, is very broad and rises steeply on one side. Many of the cottages are of whitewashed stone, and date from the 17th century. One, near the Queen's Head, is an arts centre and base for walking tours. The upper green is less spacious, but has impressive views.

The Church of St Peter, standing just above the Lowther a short distance from the village, was built in 1832 on the site of an earlier building. Parish records list vicars since the 12th century. Inside is a chapel dedicated to the Sandford family of Askham Hall, who settled in the village in 1373. The hall, set back behind a wall at the foot of the village, dates from that period, but was substantially altered at the end of the 17th century. It is not open to the public.

HERTFORDSHIRE SPIKE *The glory of Ashwell's church is its magnificent tower, which dominates the landscape. It is crowned by an octagonal lantern and topped by a leaded spike, a typical feature of the churches in Hertfordshire. Inside, the church is probably unique in the amount of graffiti carved on its pillars and walls. On the south wall under the tower is a drawing of old St Paul's Cathedral, in London, and on a pillar a message, carved by a love-lorn mason, which declares in Latin 'Barbara is a vixen'.*

THE COTTAGE GARDEN

The old cottage garden rolls back the centuries. Its borders, packed with flower species hallowed by time, and with such scented shrubs as rosemary and lavender, flank a path leading to a bower draped with old-fashioned roses. Honeysuckle, and perhaps a close-pruned pear tree hug the cottage walls, and clematis clambers among the ancient plum and apple trees. Beyond the vegetable patch stand hives for bees, whose droning is the voice of summer.

White jasmine.

The attractive, well-stocked cottage garden owes much of its beginnings to the Dissolution of the Monasteries by Henry VIII in the 1530s. With the break-up of the monasteries, the villagers' supplies of medicinal herbs grown within the cloister came to an end.

Village gardens then became not only larders for peas and beans to grind into flour, and for other vegetables and fruit, but also medicine chests and spice boxes.

Hollyhock.

Many villagers exercised their right to graze cattle and pigs on common land. Each autumn, many of these were killed, because there was not enough feed to see them through the winter; and herbs were needed to flavour the none-too-sweet meat. Dried aromatic plants, such as lavender, were mingled with rushes to cover floors.

Everything in the garden was useful, as well as being lovely. Many of the plants associated with the

old ways of life remain favourites today. A lotion from columbine leaves was used as a cure for sore throats and liver complaints. Clipped topiary figures, usually in box or yew, kept evil spirits away, as well as providing handy surfaces for spreading laundry out to dry. Witches could not pass an elder bush, which also deterred flies, and house-leeks clustering on the roof warded off lightning. 'Nothing wasted' was the cottagers' motto.

LATE REFLECTIONS *By the mid-20th century, the more picturesque aspects of the traditional cottage garden were translated by the 'new' villagers – retired, commuting, weekending – into masterpieces like this one in Hampshire. Though vegetables have been banished from the front of the house, the old-fashioned flowers and shrubs, exquisitely tended, remain.*

Primrose.

A DISTANT SUMMER *The delightful and gently muted watercolours of Helen Allingham (1848–1926) did much to foster the Victorian town-dweller's idealised notion of cottage gardens. Minna, painted about 1886 in Mrs Allingham's own Surrey garden, shows superbly planned and planted borders beyond the finances of most cottagers of the period.*

◆━◆

Hazel bushes concealing the privy yielded pea-sticks, bean poles, twigs for besom brooms and thatching pegs, as well as 'lamb's tail' catkins for decoration and nuts.

Many an old apple or plum variety was first raised in a village garden, and every district clung affectionately to its own particular varieties of fruit and, to a lesser extent, vegetables and flowers. An old apple called the Norfolk Royal still grows around Norwich; and the original Bramley's Seedling apple tree still stands in a cottage garden in Nottinghamshire, where it was grown from seed in 1815.

Cottage gardens are generally thought of as being small. But, during the building boom of Elizabeth I's reign, a statute of 1589 proclaimed that no rural cottages were to be constructed or buildings converted for habitation unless each was provided with at least 4 acres of land. These plots were actually smallholdings, supporting livestock and growing corn, as well as vegetables and fruit.

◆━◆

STATELY PLOT *The Charsfield, Suffolk, cottage garden of Mr and Mrs Ernie Cole shows what can be done with limited growing space – provided every spare minute is devoted to it. Produce from the garden, which is open to the public, makes the Coles almost self-sufficient.*

Honeysuckle.

Everlasting sweet pea.

Canterbury bell.

Stock.

Golden rod.

Double paeony.

LIVING SCULPTURE TOPIARY

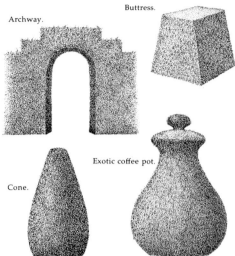

Archway.

Buttress.

Cone.

Exotic coffee pot.

The art of training and clipping trees and shrubs into fantastic shapes is thought to have been invented by a friend of Augustus Caesar. The art has always been popular in Britain, where suitable plants, such as box, yew and privet, flourish, and the alternative, ornamental stonework, is expensive. Its traditional setting was the formal gardens of great houses, but after the landscaping craze of the 18th century, it was generally relegated to smaller plots. Topiary requires infinite patience; shapes like those above may be decades in the making.

But the Enclosure Acts, especially those that took place between 1760 and 1860 as a result of the Agrarian Revolution of the period, caused many large cottage gardens to be reduced in size as landowners enclosed ever more strips of land.

William Cobbett, the author of *Rural Rides*, published in 1830, praised 'those neatly kept and productive little cottage gardens round the labourers' houses, which are seldom unornamented with ... flowers'. But just how long ago cottagers began to grow flowers solely for their beauty is difficult to determine. As long ago as the 9th century, Abbot Strabo extolled 'the appreciation of plant forms'. And roses, such as the White Rose of York, and Madonna lilies, were grown in medieval monastic gardens for church decoration. There is little doubt that these flowers found their way into cottage gardens. So, too, did variations discovered by villagers among wild flowers, such as double primroses, white 'bluebells', and Hen and Chick

BEAUTY WITH UTILITY *The traditional cottage garden was and is a combination of larder, herbarium and medicine chest. Beauty is incidental, yet the time-honoured mixings of flowering plants with vegetables and shrubs create a deep and subtle harmony of colours.*

daisies bearing flowerheads encircled by smaller daisy flowers.

As garden styles changed, and manor gardens were altered to conform to the latest fashions, outmoded and discarded varieties of flowers found their way to humbler plots. This was especially the case during the 18th century, when landscapers such as William Kent and Capability Brown swept away entire parterres, walled

gardens and avenues to permit parkland to lap the very walls of the houses. Plants changed hands by barter and gift, for few country folk spent meagre earnings on such luxuries.

In any case, the countryman's traditional conservatism and suspicion of everything new debarred plant novelties. This applied equally to new vegetables. Even potatoes, which saved families from starvation when corn harvests failed, remained superstitiously associated with the forbidden fruit of Eden. Until the turn of the 20th century, in many districts, custom dictated they must always be planted on Good Friday.

Unwittingly, cottage gardeners created plant museums. Their discovery during the latter years of the 19th century, by gardening writers and designers such as William Robinson and Gertrude Jekyll, has been compared to the discovery of medieval paintings by Burne-Jones and Rossetti.

Gardens entered into the horticultural equivalent of a Pre-Raphaelite period in which simple, hardy flowers inspired a return to Old English if not truly cottage-garden style. The most sophisticated examples included colour-planned borders, sunken rose gardens and naturalised 'wild' areas. Vegetables became segregated and hidden away.

The essential character of the country garden has been copied, with varying degrees of success, in urban housing estates and equally in grand 20th-century country gardens, such as Sissinghurst in Kent and Hidcote Manor in Gloucestershire.

Perhaps gardens surrounding council cottages most resemble old-style plots, with their higgledy-piggledy mixtures – sweet peas next to cabbages, roses beside currant bushes, and tomatoes ripening among the chrysanthemums.

Instead of a limited choice of plants available to cottagers, for whom flowers counted among family heirlooms, there is now a surfeit. Colours tend to be too startling; the mixtures too varied. Yet a visit to Anne Hathaway's Cottage at Shottery, near Stratford-upon-Avon, and to other village gardens up and down the country, confirms that the unique character of cottage gardens lives on in Britain today.

LOCAL COLOUR *The variety and individuality of old British gardens has always leaned on a seemingly casual use of local materials. Here, in Gloucestershire, bright flowers illuminate limestone slabs, recruited from the mason's yard to form a hedge.*

Columbine.

Madonna lily.

A COTTAGE GARDENER'S CALENDAR

Snowdrops decorate churches in February.

Primroses illuminate the winter-seared grass.

Daffodils – brave trumpets proclaiming spring.

Lily of the Valley – perhaps the first cottage flower.

Columbine – grown to stave off the plague.

Double paeony – a favourite since the 16th century.

Pansy – a relative newcomer to British gardens.

Madonna lily – a survivor from monastery gardens.

Moss roses – perfect companions for old cottages.

Honeysuckle – provided food for goats and hens.

Everlasting sweet pea – rare, but lingers on.

Stocks – for sweet-scented summer evenings.

Foxgloves – made mittens for fairies.

Canterbury bells ring all summer long.

Marigolds – a delicate flavouring for broths.

White jasmine's fragrance lasts until October.

Lavender sprigs – for protection against clothes moths.

Hollyhocks were an invaluable source for indigo dye.

Golden rod was thought to indicate buried treasure.

Christmas rose clumps may last for 100 years.

ASTBURY
CHESHIRE
1½ miles south-west of Congleton (page 429 Dc)

Two lines of cottages on either side of a little green are the heart of Astbury. At the top end of the green is the Church of St Mary, which is quite out of proportion to Astbury's size. When it was built, St Mary's was the parish church for Congleton, 1½ miles to the north-east.

It took almost 200 years to build, between the 13th and 15th centuries, and the changes in styles and fashions in church decoration during that time show that the upper part of the nave was added after an original, lower church had been built. The beautiful timber work inside has made the church famous, as has the unusual combination of one spire and two towers.

The original tower of the church is offset to one side. Although its foundations are Norman, it was finished in the 14th century. A link to the north aisle of the church was built when the second tower was put up a century later.

The gateway to the churchyard, with its short flight of steps, was added in the 17th century.

ASTON CANTLOW
WARWICKSHIRE
4 miles north-east of Alcester (page 430 Bb)

The Norman family of de Cantelupe acquired the manor at Aston in 1205, when it was known as Estone, and gave the village its name. They built a castle on the banks of the River Alne, but within two centuries it had fallen into ruin and today no trace of it can be seen.

The village is grouped around a small green and has some fine old buildings, including the 17th-century King's Head Inn and the black-and-white timbered Guild House. In the early 16th century the Guild House was the centre for Aston Cantlow's weekly market and annual fair. The building, restored by local funds, now serves as the village hall.

The Church of St John the Baptist dates mainly from the 13th century, and one of its early rectors, Thomas de Cantelupe, became Bishop of Hereford and Chancellor of England. He was made St Thomas de Cantelupe in 1320. The church is also said to be the place where William Shakespeare's parents were married in 1557.

ATCHAM
SALOP
4 miles south-east of Shrewsbury (page 429 Db)

On the main road into the village a tiny thatched cottage – like an outsized dolls' house – contrasts with the elegantly Classical lodge and gateway to Attingham Hall. Set in wooded parkland through which deer roam, the 18th-century mansion is now owned by the National Trust. Facing the lodge is a charming Georgian inn, the red-brick Mytton and Mermaid. A large metal sculpture of a mermaid is in the adjacent stable-yard; and the name 'Mytton' refers to 'Mad Jack' Mytton, an early-19th-century squire and MP, whose wild exploits and eccentric behaviour made him a local legend. On one occasion he alarmed his guests by entering a room astride a bear. The joke misfired when the bear bit him in the leg.

Atcham is set on a bend of the River Severn, which is crossed by two bridges. The older bridge has five arches, and was built in 1769–71 by a founder member of the Royal Academy, John Gwynne of Shrewsbury. The modern road bridge dates from 1929.

Behind the inn is the red-sandstone Church of St Eata, a 7th-century Celtic bishop. It is the only church in England dedicated to him, and he is commemorated by a fine stained-glass window.

AUCHMITHIE
TAYSIDE
3 miles north-east of Arbroath (page 443 Gb)

On the red-sandstone cliffs north of Arbroath stands the village of Auchmithie, one of the oldest fishing settlements on the Angus coast. The centre of the village is a double row of restored fishermen's cottages. A rough track leads down to the tiny harbour built among the rocks in the 1890s, but before the harbour was built the women of the village used to wade into the sea to launch the boats, and again to haul them in when they returned with their catches.

Herring was the main catch, and a fisherman's weekly wage included two bottles of whisky. In the 1820s several families moved to Arbroath to start the fishing industry there, but Auchmithie continued to run a small herring fleet until the 1920s.

Sir Walter Scott used Auchmithie as the model for his 'Musselcrag' in *The Antiquary*. The artist William Lamond spent 40 summers in the village, and painted scenes of Auchmithie and its fisherfolk.

AVEBURY
WILTSHIRE
6 miles west of Marlborough (page 421 Dc)

Entering Avebury from any direction is like stepping back into the past. Before the centre of the village is reached, the road passes through an immense circle of brooding stones which stand like petrified ghosts of an age about which little is known. The circle was raised about 2300 BC by Celtic farmer-shepherds, and was probably an

BROKEN CIRCLE *The southern inner circle of stones at Avebury lies close to the Red Lion public house, in the heart of the village. Some of the original stones were buried in medieval times, for superstitious reasons, others were used for building in the 18th century. Plinths mark where they stood.*

open temple where fertility rites were practised.

The heaviest stone in the outer ring weighs some 40 tons. Inside there are two incomplete circles. Concrete plinths mark the gaps where stones have gone – some to be built into cottage walls in the village. The stones, called sarsens, came from the nearby Marlborough Downs, and all are naturally shaped. It is believed that they may represent human figures; the tall, narrow stones males, and the rough diamond shapes females. Surrounding the circle is a bank and ditch enclosing 28 acres which is divided into four parts by roads entering the village.

The centre of Avebury is a cluster of thatched cottages and farms, and an Elizabethan manor. The Church of St James, just outside the earthwork, combines Saxon masonry with broken fragments of stone from the prehistoric circle.

The Alexander Keiller Museum is reached through the churchyard and is named after its founder, who opened it in 1938 to house the material from his excavations at Windmill Hill. Now it also includes objects from the West Kennet Long Barrow, Silbury Hill and Avebury.

A mile or so south of Avebury lies Silbury Hill, an enormous man-made mound standing 130 ft high. It dates from at least 2500 BC, and it has been estimated that it would have taken 700 men ten years to build. Internally, the hill is a six-stepped pyramid, based on a core of turf. The hill may have served as a burial mound, but excavations have revealed nothing and its purpose remains a mystery.

On the southern side of the River Kennet stretches West Kennet Long Barrow, a chambered tomb 330 ft long. The remains of about 46 people have been found in the stone-built burial chambers which date from about 3250 BC. Many of the New Stone Age People buried there had suffered from arthritis, and one corpse, that of an elderly man, had an arrowhead in his throat. Another site, at Windmill Hill, about 1 mile north-west of Avebury, has given its name to the earliest New Stone Age culture in Britain – the Windmill Hill People. Evidence for an early Neolithic settlement, built about 3700 BC, was found below and beside the banks of a later causewayed enclosure covering an area of 21 acres, which was constructed 450 years later – in 3250 BC. Excavations of the causewayed enclosure, consisting of three concentric rings of banks and ditches, revealed evidence of crop-growing and cattle-breeding.

AXMOUTH
DEVON

1 mile north-east of Seaton (page 419 Eb)

The lazy River Axe sets the mood for a quiet village that was once a bustling port but is now 1 mile from the sea. In the 12th and 13th centuries, sea currents piled a pebble ridge across the harbour mouth and the river silted up. Before the end of the Middle Ages, a huge cliff fall hastened the decline of the port. Approached from the coast, the road runs alongside the Axe and enters the village between the Harbour Inn

and the church. A stream, springing from a well that once provided the local water supply, runs beside the main street and is bridged in places by stone slabs.

The bridge across the estuary, linking Axmouth to Seaton, was built in 1877 to replace the ferry, and was one of the first bridges in Britain to be made of concrete.

Axmouth, where an Anglo-Saxon settlement was established in the 7th century, stands at the southern end of the Fosse Way, the great Roman road which bisected England from Lincoln to Devon. Now it has finally settled for the quiet life. Yachtsmen sail the broad river estuary, its mouth now too narrow for ships to enter, while ducks, gulls, herons and many other species of water birds find a haven in the mudflats and meadows on its banks.

Most of Axmouth's old houses, a mixture of colourwash and thatch, natural stone walls and tiled roofs, are grouped around the Church of St Michael with its handsome Norman doorway and medieval wall-paintings. The village lies at the

Fan-trained apricot trees.

Limestone gravestones.

WHERE APRICOTS GROW ON LIMESTONE WALLS

Fan-trained apricot trees, sprawling on ancient limestone cottage walls, add to the charm of the pre-Norman village of Aynho. According to tradition, feudal lords of the manor once claimed the apricots as rent from their tenants. Limestone dominates the village and the villagers as much today as it did in medieval times when it was used to build a now-vanished wall as a defence against attack. The apricots, comparatively rare trees in Britain, thrive in the limestone soil, modern houses, just like the old, are built of the local stone, and even the gravestones in the churchyard pay silent tribute to the material that gave enduring life to Aynho.

Limestone houses.

foot of Hawkesdown Hill, where there are Iron and Bronze Age relics as well as a fortified earthwork clearly built to guard the estuary. To the east, coastal paths through rocks and tangled vegetation offer dramatic sea views. The path towards Lyme Regis makes for rough walking as a result of a series of landslips over the years. The greatest fall was in 1839, when millions of tons of earth and rock crumbled and opened up a chasm nearly 1 mile long.

AYNHO
NORTHAMPTONSHIRE

6 miles south-east of Banbury (page 430 Ca)

Apricot trees growing against cottage walls are one of Aynho's attractions. They flourish on the village's south-westerly aspect and its limestone soil. The trees flower in April, and the fruits are harvested in September. In the past, the lords of the manor, members of the Cartwright family, are said to have claimed the apricot fruits as part of the cottage rents.

Aynho is set on a hill, and its steep, narrow lanes and alleyways conjure up the past with names such as Skittle Alley and Blacksmith's Hill. At the bottom of the hill, high pavements with steps lead down past stone and thatched cottages to the Banbury road. The Church of St Michael was rebuilt in the early 1720s, but retains its richly decorated 15th-century tower.

From 1615 to 1954, when the last squire, Richard Cartwright, and his son were killed in a motor accident, the Cartwrights lived in Aynho Park. The house was burned down during the Civil War, and was rebuilt or added to three times – the last being in the early 19th century, when a triumphal arch was erected. Today, the mansion has been converted into private flats, and the parkland, once the home of a herd of deer, is now farmland.

The park was landscaped by Lancelot 'Capability' Brown between 1761–3.

Tudor cottage in Ayot St Lawrence's main street.

AYOT ST LAWRENCE
HERTFORDSHIRE

2 miles west of Welwyn (page 426 Cb)

Though only a few miles from Stevenage, Welwyn and the suburbs of north London, Ayot St Lawrence can only be approached by way of country lanes so narrow in places that two cars cannot pass one another; even a moderate snowfall can cut the village's connection with the outside world.

Ayot St Lawrence's most famous inhabitant, George Bernard Shaw, moved into the New Rectory in 1906 because, it is said, of a gravestone epitaph in the churchyard. This recorded the death of a woman who lived to be 70 with the comment 'Her time was short'. Shaw thought that a place that considered a life of 70 years short was the right place for him. With characteristic lack of modesty he renamed the house Shaw's Corner. He gave it to the National Trust in 1944, but continued to live there until he died in 1950, aged 94. It is a large house, built at the turn of the century, with pretty gardens. Shaw's study, still containing his notebooks and other relics, affords a fascinating glimpse of the playwright's life.

The village street begins a few yards down the road from Shaw's Corner. Lying back from the street, in a romantically overgrown churchyard, is a splendid Gothic ruin of a church, with a toppling, bird-haunted tower and, inside, a tomb on which lie the effigies of a knight and his lady. The story goes that in the 18th century the villagers were poor. The church fell into decay and the owner of Ayot House, Lionel Lyde, used this as an excuse to ask the Bishop of Lincoln, whose diocese covered Ayot St Lawrence, to build a new church. Money collected for the renovation of the old church was put towards the new one.

The curious new church lies at the end of a muddy track across the fields. The great portico, with massive columns and wide-spreading colonnaded wings, was modelled on the Temple of Apollo at Delos. The interior incorporates other items of 18th-century architectural interest, but the doors are generally locked after 6 p.m.

The Old Rectory.

Shaw's Corner.

A PLAYWRIGHT'S CORNER OF ENGLAND

When George Bernard Shaw went to live at Ayot St Lawrence he became so fond of his home that he wrote a short verse about it. He ended by saying that although Ireland was his birthplace, 'This home shall be my final earthplace'. He was talking about his house, Shaw's Corner, whose verandah and trim lawn became familiar settings for newsreel and newspaper interviews. But Shaw also loved the village, and his last published work was a booklet of verses about Ayot St Lawrence. It was a guided tour of the village, starting naturally at Shaw's Corner. The old church, standing behind the war memorial, he referred to as 'Our Abbey Church, five centuries old', and the war memorial moved him to suggest that the loss of lives 'Has been our country's gain'. The Tudor cottage next to the Old Rectory, Shaw thought was a lesson in village architecture.

The old church of St Lawrence.

Opposite the old church is a Tudor black-and-white cottage, flanked at one end by the Brocket Arms, a splendid 400-year-old pub with stone-flagged floors, a vast inglenook fireplace and a garden full of oak tables and benches for summer evening meditation. At the other end of the cottage is the Old Rectory, an elegant, white 17th-century house, built in the days when rectors had large families and larger incomes. The Tudor Manor House and Ayot House add variation and charm to the scene.

AYSGARTH

NORTH YORKSHIRE

7 miles west of Leyburn (page 436 Ac)

Wensleydale is the broadest and most fertile of the Yorkshire valleys. It is watered by the River Ure, which rises quietly on the western slope of Lunds Fell, 15 miles west of Aysgarth. Near the village the river gathers pace and comes to spectacular life as its green, translucent waters spill over limestone terraces and become a torrent of seething foam.

There is a series of three separate steps in the falls, known as Aysgarth Force, within a distance of 1 mile. The best view of Upper Force is from the 16th-century bridge spanning the Ure. The Middle Force is reached by a footpath on the north bank of the river, and a little further downstream is Lower Force, the most spectacular of the three.

Aysgarth village, less than 1 mile from the falls, spreads along its main street, backed by banks of trees. It seems unaffected by the closeness of one of Yorkshire's finest beauty spots, and the provisions for visitors – car park, cafe and a museum – are in the valley bottom on either side of the bridge.

The museum, housed in an old mill, contains a collection of old carriages. Aysgarth's parish church of St Andrew stands near by, apart from the village, in a spacious churchyard above the falls. It was rebuilt after a fire in the mid-19th century, but still contains relics, originally removed from Jervaulx Abbey, which were rescued from the blaze.

BADBY
NORTHAMPTONSHIRE

2 miles south-west of Daventry (page 430 Cb)

Wooded countryside surrounds Badby, which clings to the side of Badby Downs. In springtime, the wood outside the village is a mass of bluebells. Winding lanes, lined with attractive ironstone cottages, lead down to the village green. In the centre of the green stands the Gothic-style village hall, which used to house the local school and is now a private residence.

Badby is bordered by Fawsley Park, with its Tudor Great Hall and ruined Dower House, formerly the homes of the Knightley family. The park also contains a fine avenue of cherry trees, lakes and several picnic spots.

The 14th-century parish church of St Mary lies on high ground above the main street. Its war-memorial window shows St George and St Michael – complete with swords and flaming wings – slaying two dragons. On the roadside south of the village is the derelict Lantern House, a tiny, two-storey, early-19th-century building in the shape of a lantern.

BAINBRIDGE
NORTH YORKSHIRE

4 miles east of Hawes (page 436 Ac)

In the Middle Ages the heavily wooded country to the south of the River Ure was known as the Forest and Manor of Bainbridge, and the village grew up around a spacious green which still has its stocks, grazing sheep and a profusion of daffodils in the spring.

The earliest inhabitants were foresters, who

founded a custom that is continued to this day. Each autumn and winter night, between the Feast of the Holy Rood (September 27) and Shrovetide in early spring, a villager takes a great bull horn off the wall of the Rose and Crown, steps outside and blows it, as his predecessors have done for 700 years. On a calm night, its bellow can be heard 3 miles away, indicating the road home to lost and long-dead foresters, through forests that were cut down centuries ago.

The whitewashed and pebble-dashed Rose and Crown, one of several stone houses scattered around the green, is of considerable age judging by the date of 1445 cut into its wall.

The Lords Trustees – the elected representatives of the village – meet at the inn to discuss and settle Bainbridge affairs. The village has owned itself since the days of Charles II, when the villagers purchased the manorial rights from the City of London.

From the old Bain Bridge there are fine views of the cascading River Bain, said to be the shortest river in England. It drains out of the Semer Water and runs a brief 2 miles before it joins the Ure. On its way through the village it supplies power to a saw-mill. The water-wheel of a second mill, which used to grind corn, is being restored.

Semer Water, 2 miles south of the village, is

CENTURIES-OLD CUSTOM *Dense forests, long since cleared, once engulfed Bainbridge, and a tradition started by the old foresters has survived over the centuries. Each autumn and winter evening a great bull horn is blown on the village green to guide home any forest worker who may have lost his way. On a still night it can be heard 3 miles away.*

claimed to be Yorkshire's largest natural expanse of water. In summer it is popular with boating enthusiasts and water-skiers, but in winter it is closed to encourage migratory birds. Each autumn the local vicar preaches from a boat to crowds gathered on the bank.

The Romans came to Bainbridge about AD 80, and stayed for 300 years in a series of forts they built on Brough Hill. The remains of one of them can be seen opposite the bridge. An old Roman road, now a grassy track, runs south-westwards from Bainbridge to join the Pennine Way.

BALEDGARNO
TAYSIDE

8 miles west of Dundee (page 443 Fb)

No signposts point the way to Baledgarno, set in the rich arable lands of the Carse of Gowrie. The secluded and immaculately kept village is on private property – that of the 12th Lord Kinnaird – and five terraces of red-sandstone cottages are set around the entrance of his lordship's home, Rossie Priory. The cottages overlook the green, which is split by a rushing burn crossed by an old stone footbridge. The village layout is completed by two blocks of two-storey houses.

Originally, Baledgarno was pronounced 'Ballerno', and today it is referred to as 'Balleggernie'. The village owes its unusual name to Edgar, King of Scotland from 1001 to 1005. *Bal* is the Gaelic for 'farm', or 'settlement', so the name means Edgar's farm. He had a fortress there, possibly at a place called Castlehill just outside the village. Baledgarno did not come into existence until the 1790s, when Lord Kinnaird built it to replace an earlier settlement near by, called Rossie.

BALLASALLA
ISLE OF MAN

2 miles north-east of Castletown (page 435 Bc)

The musical name of Ballasalla derives from the Manx Gaelic words meaning 'village of the willow river', and the old part of the village with its picturesque church, grey cottages and stone barns presents an attractive cluster lining the road down to the ford across the Silver Burn river.

About a quarter of a mile upstream is the Monks' Bridge. Its narrow, cobbled surface is suitable only for pedestrians or the long-vanished packhorses for which it was built in 1350.

A few hundred yards downstream are the ruins of Rushen Abbey. The abbey was founded in 1134 when Olaf I, the fifth in the line of Viking kings who ruled the island from the 11th to the 13th centuries, invited the abbot and monks of Furness Abbey to build another abbey on this spot. The monks improved agriculture and live-stock-breeding on the island, but their main achievement was the compilation of *The Chronicle of Man and the Isles,* the earliest written record of the history of the Isle of Man. It was completed in 1374, and is now in the British Library.

BALQUHIDDER
CENTRAL

10 miles north-west of Callander (page 441 Ee)

Rob Roy MacGregor died near Balquhidder – pronounced 'Balwhidder' – in 1734, and lies in the churchyard. The village stands at the eastern end of Loch Voil, rich in salmon and trout, where stone cottages cluster around a rock-strewn torrent. All around are the steep and thickly wooded Braes of Balquhidder.

The red-haired outlaw was baptised on March 7, 1671, and for most of his life was a brigand, cattle-thief and extortionist. During the Jacobite rebellion of 1715, Rob Roy alternately supported and plundered the Jacobite and Government forces. His activities made him a folklore hero, but his career ended unheroically when he was put in London's Newgate Prison for his part in a bankruptcy swindle. He was pardoned and released in 1727, and retired to Balquhidder. The site of his farmhouse, Inverlochlarig, can be seen near the head of Loch Doine, about 6 miles west.

Although the MacGregors ruled the district at that time, Balquhidder and its surroundings were originally the domain of the Maclarens; there is a monument in the churchyard commemorating stirring chapters in the clan's history. Their feud with the MacGregors continued after Rob Roy's death. His son Robin shot and killed a Maclaren during a land dispute. For this, Robin was hanged in Edinburgh in 1754 and was brought home and buried in the grave of his brother Coll, next to the graves of their parents. The MacGregor graves are covered by stone slabs bearing rough carvings of weapons and wild beasts.

The old kirk is now roofless and in ruins, but a mid-Victorian church is in regular use. It, too, commemorates the dead outlaw, and houses an autographed scroll and inscribed bronze plaque, presented in 1975 by members of the Clan Gregor Society of America.

BAMBURGH
NORTHUMBERLAND

5 miles east of Belford (page 439 Bd)

Pleasant greystone cottages, tea-rooms, craft shops and some fine inns surround the wide, wooded green called The Grove. But the whole scene is dominated by the massive walls, keep and towers of Bamburgh Castle.

The fortress stands on a rocky cliff, towering 150 ft above the sea, and spreads for a quarter of

WARRIORS' REST *In the churchyard of Balquhidder's old and new kirks, mirrored in the waters of Loch Voil, lie the remains of Rob Roy MacGregor and members of his turbulent family. Near by are monuments to the Clan Laurin, the Maclarens or Maclaurins; the spelling is argued at considerable length on one of the stones. Others recall clansmen who died in far-off Walthamstow and a fearful slaughter of Maclaurins in 1558 '... upon the midnight ... by a banditti of incendiarists from Glendochart ...'*

a mile along the clifftop. Its history is as violent as the waves that pound the shore below. The Anglo-Saxon chieftain Ida built a wooden fort on the rock in 547. The Vikings destroyed the castle in 993 and, two centuries later, Henry II rebuilt it, but his stronghold was ruined by Edward IV's cannons during the Wars of the Roses in the 15th century. It was the first English castle to succumb to gunfire. In 1893 the castle was bought by the 1st Lord Armstrong, who converted it to a private residence, so that most of the interior dates from the 19th century. The castle is open to the public daily throughout the summer, and the most impressive parts are the King's Hall, rich in carved teak, the armoury, and the keep which has a well 150 ft deep.

Bamburgh is not noted only for its castle, however, for it was from there that Grace Darling rowed out with her father on September 7, 1838, to rescue nine crew members of the steamship *Forfarshire*, which was wrecked upon a rock. A small museum opposite St Aidan's Church commemorates the heroic action, and contains the small fishing coble used in the rescue. Near by, a plaque records Grace Darling's birthplace, and her grave and a monument to her are in St Aidan's. She died aged only 26 in a cottage, now next to a souvenir shop, beside the castle end of The Grove.

BANWELL
AVON

5 miles east of Weston-super-Mare (page 421 Bc)

A privately owned Victorian extravaganza, Banwell Castle, complete with battlements, turrets and all the standard features of a medieval fortress, stands guard over the south-eastern approach to the village; but once past it, and over the brow of the hill, a more serene picture unfolds. Narrow winding streets lined with small cottages surround the church, the 'Cathedral of the Mendips', which dates from the 14th and 15th centuries. The tower stands over 100 ft high, and the splendid interior is glorified by a beautiful gilded chancel screen, a fine Tudor doorway and a strikingly painted roof.

Nearby Banwell Abbey used to be the country residence of the Bishops of Wells, but it has been extensively changed since Bishop Bekynton built it in the 15th century. Above the village, on private land, Banwell Hill is crowned by an Iron Age earthwork, constructed more than 2,000 years ago.

Banwell lies at the tip of one of the westernmost headlands which the Mendip Hills throw out towards the Bristol Channel, and the steep hills above the village afford magnificent views to the west and north. Beneath the hills, in the early 19th century, the pioneer archaeologist William Beard discovered Banwell Cave, containing vast quantities of ancient bones, among them those of cave bears, cave lions and wolves, creatures that roamed the area in prehistoric times. Beard used many of them to build a curious bone wall in the cave, but now the cave is no longer open to the public.

BARNACK
CAMBRIDGESHIRE

3 miles south-east of Stamford (page 432 Bd)

Everything in and around Barnack is stone-built: drystone walls; grey and buff-coloured farm buildings looking like miniature castles; an 18th-century windmill; two old inns; the church – and England's largest and grandest Elizabethan mansion, Burghley House, which stands in parkland 2 miles north-east of the village. South of the village are the grass-covered hummocks of the long-abandoned quarries from which much of this limestone came. Workings there ceased in the 16th century, and the area is now the Hills and Holes National Nature Reserve.

The tower windmill was preserved in 1961, when a new cap was fitted, and although not in working order, the machinery is intact. The windmill is open to the public at weekends. The Saxons built the Church of St John the Baptist. Its tower dates from the early 11th century, and within the north aisle is a fine 11th-century sculpture of Christ in Majesty. The spire dates from the 13th century, but the pinnacles and a rood screen bearing the de Barnack arms were added in the 20th century.

During the Middle Ages the quarries provided material for the cathedrals at Ely and Peterborough, and for Corpus Christi and other Cambridge colleges. In Bishop's Walk, in the village, the old rectory is now named Kingsley House after its association with the novelist Charles Kingsley, author of *The Water Babies*, who went there at the age of five with his clergyman father.

During his childhood, Kingsley is said to have witnessed the ghost of a former rector who, after cheating a widow of the parish, was doomed to haunt the house dressed in a flowered dressing-gown and a night-cap with a button on it. The room in which the ghost is supposed to appear is called Button Cap. Kingsley House is now divided into two private houses, but still retains the exterior that Kingsley knew.

Burghley House was built between 1546 and 1587 by the 1st Lord Burghley, who was Elizabeth I's Lord High Treasurer. The house is open to the public daily during the summer, except on most Mondays and Fridays, and its rooms contain beautiful painted ceilings, silver fireplaces and a fine collection of paintings, tapestries and furniture. The present owner is the 6th Marquis of Exeter, who won an Olympic Gold Medal in the 400 metres hurdles in 1928. The Burghley Three Day Equestrian Event takes place in the park each September.

BARNWELL
NORTHAMPTONSHIRE

2 miles south of Oundle (page 431 Db)

A stream, bordered by green verges, tall trees and dipping willows, divides Barnwell from end to end. Communication between the stone-built cottages, with their worn stone fronts and neatly thatched roofs, is provided by a variety of bridges, some stone and hump-backed, others

BARNWELL MOST ROYAL *The manor house is the home of Princess Alice, Duchess of Gloucester, and of the present Duke and Duchess, but the quiet stone village wears the honour easily, as befits a place whose castle has been owned by the mighty Montagu family since the 16th century. Barnwell is divided by a stream and rejoined by bridges; this one conveniently unites the shop and the Montagu Arms pub.*

wooden. The main bridge, which is reminiscent of a garden rockery, connects the Montagu Arms pub with the general store and its attendant cottages, making as lovely a calendar picture as anyone could wish for.

From there, the street climbs a hill towards the church, opposite which is a delightful little square of stone-tiled almshouses with their own chapel at the far end. These could be of any age, but, in fact, they were rebuilt in 1864 on the site of an earlier charitable institution founded in 1601 by Nicholas Latham, the village parson from 1569 to 1620. 'Cast thy bread upon the waters', runs the inscription on the arch over the entrance to the almshouses, an injunction which the Reverend Latham obviously took to heart, since his generosity provided not only the almshouses, but also Cambridge scholarships, a new pulpit for the church and many other good works.

Medieval castle

The path to the 13th-century St Andrew's Church runs through precise flower beds, yews and hollies; but before entering it is worth walking round the outside, past the carved, leaf-shrouded head of the Green Man – a pagan nature-spirit – at the rear of the building, from where the view conveys the entire flavour of the village. A wicket gate in the churchyard wall opens on to a neat path, which runs straight down the hill and over a bridge to the grey-white bulk of a medieval castle. It was built probably about 1266 by Berengar le Moyne, who ten years later ceded it to the Abbey of Ramsey. At the Dissolution of the Monasteries, it passed into the hands of the Montagu family, who built the big stone manor house next door, and lived in it until the end of the last century. Both castle and manor are now the property of the Duke of Gloucester. Though the best view of the two buildings is obtained from the top of the church hill, perhaps the most picturesque is that from by the castle bridge, an extraordinary, long-legged, crouch-backed structure of stone. Bridge, stream, castle and manor are framed by weeping willows and flowering shrubs.

It has been said that St Andrew's is the model parish church. If this means that it distils the essence of the village, then the description is apt, for all of Barnwell's story is there. The interior is rough stone with a heavy, wood-beamed ceiling, much altered over the years, notably by Sir Giles Gilbert Scott in the 1860s. There is a splendid three-part stone reredos, probably brought to the church when All Saints' Church, at the other end of the village, was partly demolished in the 1820s. Round the walls are monuments to Barnwellians down the centuries.

Montagu monuments

There is a monument to the late Duke of Gloucester, who worshipped in the church for 35 years, and on the opposite wall a portrait in bronze of his son, Prince William, killed in an air crash in 1972. A seat in the porch, presented by the prince's many admirers in and around the village, is also dedicated to his memory.

To visit the only remaining fragment of All Saints' Church, a good way along the stream from the village centre, it is necessary to obtain a key from The Limes next door. When the church was demolished it was decided to preserve the chancel, partly for its Montagu monuments and partly to avoid disturbing the remains of the many members of the family who lie in the vaults beneath. The result is a foreshortened building of considerable charm, almost as broad as it is long and with great high windows.

A plaque records the names of many, though by no means all, of the formidable Montagu family, which began in the 16th century with plain Sir Edward, and by the 19th century included the Duke of Buccleuch, the Earls of Hinchingbrooke and Sandwich, and the wife of an illegitimate son of the Emperor Napoleon.

But what first catches the eye is an obelisk covered with armorial bearings and containing in a niche the painted effigy of a small boy in red Jacobean dress. This is the curious, and to modern minds, somewhat eerie, monument to three-year-old Henry Montagu, who drowned in a pond in 1625. The symbolism of the child's sad end seems to have gripped the sculptor to an almost ghoulish degree; the effigy holds a scroll that reads, 'Lord, give me of ye Waters', while the whole obelisk stands upon a pair of large, inward-turning human feet dripping with watery mud and holding between them an upturned gilt cup inscribed with the words 'Pour on me the joys of thy salvation'. The plinth records the grief of the boy's father, and that he was Master of Requests to the Majesties of King James and King Charles.

BARR

STRATHCLYDE

6 miles south-east of Girvan (page 441 Db)

Steep, twisting but well-surfaced hill roads are the only way of reaching Barr – whose comparative inaccessibility once made it a stopping-off place for smugglers and their pony-trains. Goods to be sold in the towns and cities of the Lowlands were moved along secret routes in the surrounding Carrick Hills – which, today, have largely been taken over by the Forestry Commission. The older part of the village lies on a hillside north of the Water of Gregg. On the west side, the Gregg flows into the River Stinchar.

Barr – with its sturdy stone cottages and deserted smithy – lies in a corner of a sheltered valley, where the Stinchar cuts through the hills. Among the nearby beauty spots are Polmaddie Hill to the south-east and, to the east, Changue Forest, which was started in 1936. The forest is approached by a small lane which goes by white-washed cottages overlooking the rocky course of the Water of Gregg.

Several breeds of sheep are reared in the area, of which the Blackface sheep are the best known. Barr also used to stage the colourful Kirkdamdie Fair – where shepherds and farmers mingled – on a riverbank site 2 miles down the valley.

Shortly after the First World War a number of smallholders started a jam-making co-operative on a farm. However, the project failed. Today, the venture is recalled by a house in the village, known as 'The Jam Factory'.

BARSTON, West Midlands (page 430 Bb)
(see Berkswell)

BASING
HAMPSHIRE

2 miles east of Basingstoke (page 422 Cc)

Between Basing and Basingstoke there is a world of difference, and the boundary between the two worlds is the River Loddon. On the west bank the industrial sprawl of Basingstoke makes ever greater inroads into the countryside; 100 years ago it was a market town with a population of around 6,000; today it is a noisy, bustling urban complex with a population more than ten times as great. Across the river, by contrast, the village of Basing is a timeless haven of peace, protected by a conservation order as well as by its river frontier.

It is a red-brick village, dotted with little gardens and set in tree-studded pastureland. All the bricks and tiles were locally made, but the kilns have been closed since the war. In The Street, in the heart of the village, is the Norman Church of St Mary, and a few hundred yards further on – set back from the road – is a fine 15th and 16th-century tithe barn with a recently restored roof.

The living beauty of the village is equalled by the ruined splendour of Basing House. Once one of the most magnificent mansions in the country, it was built in the 16th century by William

◆

BATTLE LONG AGO *Cream and whitewashed walls contrast with red brick and tiles by Basing's churchyard gate. The village was the scene of bloody fighting when Cromwell attacked the Royalist garrison there in 1645. It is said that the guards were playing whist, and there is a Hampshire saying that 'clubs were trumps when Basing fell'.*

Paulet, an important national figure during the reigns of six Tudor monarchs, from Henry VII to Elizabeth I. He was created Marquis of Winchester by Edward VI who appointed him Lord Treasurer of England, which office he continued to hold under the Catholic Mary and her Protestant sister Elizabeth I. When asked how he managed to keep office under these three very different monarchs, he said: 'By being a willow, not an oak.' Unlike most great houses of the day, Basing House was not only a palatial home, but it was also heavily fortified. During the Civil War, Royalists held it against heavy odds from 1643 to 1645, when Cromwell himself, who had come over from Winchester, led the final assault. The battered palace was then looted, and fire completed its ruin.

The area defended during the siege was 20 acres, and 1½ miles in circumference. Completely intact is the 16th-century dovecot, with its interior of chalk bricks laid to make nesting places for 500 pigeons.

BASLOW
DERBYSHIRE

3 miles north-east of Bakewell (page 430 Bd)

An ancient packhorse bridge over the River Derwent leads to the greystone cottages and riverside parish church of Baslow. At the village end of the bridge is a stone-built toll-house, thought to be the smallest in England. St Anne's Church stands in a picturesque setting, its beauty enhanced by trees on all sides. The church is mostly 14th century with a 13th-century tower and spire. One of its clock's two dials has the words 'Victoria 1897' round the edge instead of figures. There are parts of a Saxon cross in the porch, and a dog-whip, once used to drive unruly

BY A BABBLING BROOK *On the path to Chatsworth Park a little bridge crosses the Bar Brook and leads to Goose Green, Baslow. The two thatched cottages are called, appropriately, Thatch and Thatch End.*

dogs from the church, is kept just inside the doorway.

Another part of the village, Goose Green, has thatched cottages and a trickling stream, Bar Brook, over which a bridge and a footpath lead to the Chatsworth estate. Chatsworth House, home of the Duke of Devonshire, is about 1½ miles south of Baslow, and footpaths across the park give views of the Derwent Valley.

A lane from the packhorse bridge leads to the attractive hamlet of Bubnell. A 17th-century hall there was the home of the Basset family. The hamlet overlooks Bramley Dale and Baslow Edge, a bluff, stone ridge across the river above Baslow.

BAYTON
HEREFORD AND WORCESTER

6 miles west of Bewdley (page 425 Ec)

Because of its isolation among rolling hills on the Shropshire border, Bayton has retained much of its traditional charm.

The narrow lanes present unexpectedly picturesque vistas as they meander through the village. Cosy half-timbered cottages and mellow brick look out over their creeper-clad garden walls, and the whole village has an air of serenity.

Not far from the Wheatsheaf pub, which has been an inn since 1825, stone steps lead to the door of the village store and the post office, an attractive red-brick building looking like a large dolls' house.

At the other end of the village the parish church of St Bartholomew stands on a bluff of high ground. Its early-19th-century tower rises above Norman stonework, and inside is a drum-shaped Norman font and a Jacobean pulpit. The church was extensively restored in 1905. Just below the church, to the north, is the rectory, a red-brick Georgian house approached by an avenue of elms. To the east of the church lies the early-19th-century village school, single-storeyed and now a private house.

From the high churchyard can be seen the parkland of the red-brick Georgian mansion of Shakenhurst, 1 mile or so to the west. This imposing house is approached by a long, narrow track which passes one of Bayton's many architectural gems, a small black-and-white lodge looking as though it had been lifted straight out of a picture-book.

BEDDGELERT
GWYNEDD

12 miles south-east of Caernarfon (page 428 Bc)

Surroundings of awe-inspiring beauty make Beddgelert one of the most memorable villages in Britain. Set at the meeting point of two clear, pebble-bedded rivers, it nestles in the heart of a majestic landscape with the Snowdon range rising steeply to the north, and Moel Hebog's craggy summit, 2,566 ft above sea-level, less than 2 miles away to the south-west. Trees, bracken and great banks of undergrowth give a rich assortment of colours and textures to the steep slopes. Footbridges over the River Glaslyn lead to a village green with seats at the waterside.

A footpath beside the river leads to what is said to be the grave of Gelert, a dog owned by the 13th-century Welsh prince, Llewelyn the Great. The prince is said to have left Gelert to guard his baby son, but returned to find the dog covered in blood and the boy missing. Convinced that Gelert had killed his heir, Llewelyn slew the dog. Too late, he realised that the blood came from a wolf that had attacked the child and had been killed by Gelert.

The tragic adaptation of an old fable was actually invented by a local innkeeper in the 18th century to boost trade. He and his friends were also responsible for the alleged grave. Their promotional prank prompted the lines:

> *Pass on,*
> *O tender-hearted,*
> *Dry your eyes;*
> *Not here a greyhound,*
> *But a landlord lies.*

BEETHAM
CUMBRIA

6 miles north of Carnforth (page 435 Cc)

An almost 19th-century atmosphere has returned to Beetham since the M6 motorway drew away the traffic which used to roar along its main street. It has the neat, carefully planned air of an 'estate' village, as it slopes gently up from the banks of the River Bela.

Ashton House, large and elegant, marks the western edge of the village and contrasts with the neat, greystone cottages and cobbled forecourts found elsewhere. The Wheatsheaf Hotel, its bays faced with mock-Tudor timbers, stands next to a combined post office and shop. The post office has a split-level door, studded with iron bolts, which is flanked by Gothic windows, while the first floor has a loading bay complete with a little drawbridge.

The church is much older. Coins dating from Edward the Confessor's reign were found at the base of a pillar during restoration work in the 19th century, although most of the present structure is 12th century. The north wall is unusual in having a stained-glass window in which St Oswald and St Alban flank Charles I, who is described as a martyr.

BELLINGHAM
NORTHUMBERLAND

14 miles north-west of Hexham (page 438 Ac)

The ancient capital of the North Tyne Valley is an idyllic retreat set below some of the most barren of the Northumbrian moors. The village has a wide main street, a market-place flanked by sturdy greystone buildings and a good selection of public houses. Most of the buildings date from the 19th century: the Town Hall with its clock-tower; a handsome Roman Catholic church; and a bridge crossing the River North Tyne.

The valley of Hareshaw Burn, which joins the river below the bridge, leads upstream through the village and a wooded dell to the waterfall of Hareshaw Linn which cascades some 30 ft into a rocky chasm.

Bellingham's parish church of St Cuthbert dates from the 12th century, and its stone roof was to guard against the firebrands of Border Reivers, the marauding bands of cattle thieves who raided along the English–Scottish Border in the 16th century. Below the churchyard is St Cuthbert's Well, said to have healing properties, and which provides the baptismal water.

BENINGTON
HERTFORDSHIRE

4 miles east of Stevenage (page 426 Cb)

There is no doubt that the centre of Benington justifies the village's long-standing reputation of being one of the prettiest in Hertfordshire. Its classic ingredients – church, folly, stately home, pub, cottages and green – can be seen in one sweeping glance from a vantage point by the duck-pond, provided that its quarrelling complement of Muscovy ducks can be avoided. From the Bell, a delightful pub with overhanging gables, black timbers and white pargeting, a row of attractive old cottages sweeps steeply down the side of the green. Most are also black-timbered and white-plastered. Others, in an unusual style, have maroon-painted timbers.

To the right of the pond is the gate to The Lordship, a large Georgian house attached to the remains of a Norman keep that was partly demolished in 1212. When the house was built, the keep was to some extent restored and improved upon. On the whole, the fairy-tale look is highly successful, especially in spring when the mound of the keep is carpeted with snowdrops. Both the gardens and the Folly', as its owner calls it, are open to the public at certain times of the year.

Past The Lordship's gates is the church, on its mound above the green. Inside are faded medieval wall-paintings of maroon flowers – perhaps the inspiration for the maroon-timbered cottages. There are two tombs, each bearing effigies of a knight and his lady. One is 14th century, the other 15th century. The earlier knight wears chain mail and his lady has long, flowing hair. The later knight has plate armour, and his wife wears a wimple.

SUN AND SPLENDOUR *Basking in the timeless splendour of summer sunshine, a pathway leads past half-timbered and whitewashed cottages to the tree-screened church of Benington. A goat grazes undisturbed in the silent stillness of the afternoon. The short Hertfordshire 'spike' of the church lifts a tentative finger to the milky sky . . . inside, the aisle is bathed in the aqueous light that filters through stained glass . . . straight from heaven.*

BERKSWELL
WEST MIDLANDS

6 miles west of Coventry (page 430 Bb)

Behind the red-brick Victorian almshouses facing on to the green is a square stone well that belonged to a long-forgotten lord of the manor, called Bercul; which is how the village got its name. Opposite the almshouses is the bow-fronted post office and shop, while near by, beneath the trees on the green, is the old whipping post and stocks, the latter pierced by five holes. It is said that the fifth hole was put there to accommodate a persistent local villain with

only one leg. The real explanation seems to be that there were originally six holes and the sixth one has simply rotted away.

Beside the well there is a handsome, stone-faced 17th-century house that was once the Rectory, and along the main street stands the 400-year-old partly timbered Bear Inn, whose leafy frontage is guarded by a Russian cannon captured during the Crimean War. On the southern boundary of the parish is a windmill of 1826 that now houses a small agricultural museum.

The Church of St John the Baptist is considered one of the finest Norman churches in the Midlands. Its pink stone is well set off by an unusual timbered porch of two storeys, of which the upper is the vestry. Its chief glory, perhaps, is the beautifully arched double crypt, dating from the 12th century.

BARSTON Thatched cottages have managed to hold their own with modern development and help to maintain the village character of Barston, which is 2½ miles to the west of Berkswell. The Georgian Barston Hall dominates the eastern approach to the village's leafy main street. Smart new houses with well-trimmed gardens fit in well with 16th and 17th-century dwellings, some timber-framed in black and white, others of red brick. St Swithin's Church near by was rebuilt after a fire in 1721 and restored in 1899. Its churchyard has a well-groomed air, with tailored hedges and lawns.

BERRIEW
POWYS

5 miles south-west of Welshpool (page 429 Cb)

Black-and-white timber-framed buildings, topiary and spacious gardens bright with flowers combine with a delightful riverside setting to make Berriew one of the most picturesque villages in Wales. Such eye-catching concentrations of 'magpie' architecture are rare in the Principality. So is the 'roses round the door' atmosphere that contributes so much to Berriew's character. No fewer than ten Best-Kept-Village awards, including the coveted national trophy, have been won by this borderland community since 1960. The village is set among low hills, patchworked with woodlands, which roll away to the north and south, hemming the River Rhiw into a narrow valley. The river tumbles down towards Berriew's ivy-clad bridge in a series of miniature rapids, and flows into the Severn 1 mile further on. Berriew's name is in fact derived from *Aber Rhiw* – Welsh for the 'Rhiw's mouth'.

The oldest part of the village, with many buildings dating from the 17th and 18th centuries, is clustered in a circle round the wall enclosing St Beuno's churchyard. Beuno, a 7th-century Celtic saint, spent much of his life in North Wales, and is said to have sought refuge in Berriew from Saxon invaders. Many miracles are ascribed to him, including having restored the life of his niece, St Winifred, after a frustrated lover had cut off her head.

The original church, which had a wooden belfry, was demolished in 1802. It may have been founded by the saint, and was described in local records, shortly before its demolition, as 'a very ancient structure, and so greatly decayed in every part that the inhabitants cannot report there to hear Divine Service without endangering their lives'. The second church was itself replaced by a third in the 1870s. Inside are fine marble effigies of Arthur Price, a 16th-century Sheriff of Montgomeryshire, and his wives Bridget and Jane.

Immediately beyond the churchyard's eastern boundary stands Old School House, built in 1819. Building costs amounted to £1,581, and the first headmaster was paid £40 a year to preside over the education of 50 boys. Its modern counterpart stands on the western edge of the village, overlooking the river.

Modern houses have been built on the outskirts, but the compact heart of Berriew has surrendered little of its character. Even the new squash court by the Talbot Hotel is painted black and white, and there is no shortage of genuine timber frames. Several of the cottages have tall clusters of chimneys and small, weather-boarded outbuildings. Attractive 'magpie' houses stand opposite the Lion Hotel.

BERRY POMEROY
DEVON

2 miles east of Totnes (page 419 Db)

A drive through thick woodlands brings the sudden and dramatic view of Berry Pomeroy Castle, a gaunt ruin on a craggy bluff about 1 mile from the village. A thousand years of history lie behind its grim and forbidding gatehouse, the entrance to a site often described as one of the most haunted in Britain. Only two families, the

Pomeroys and the Seymours, have owned it since the Norman Conquest, and their ghosts are said to prowl the walls, staircases and dungeons of the castle, which fell into ruins nearly three centuries ago. A gallery built on to the parapet of the gatehouse still has openings through which boiling oil and lead were poured on attackers.

The remains of a Tudor mansion, built by a Seymour in the early 17th century, stand in the courtyard. Solitary stacks of stone are all that remain of the Great Hall which, together with the rest of the site, is now in the charge of the Department of the Environment. One attraction in the grounds is a wishing tree, which has the reputation of granting a visitor's desires provided he walks round it three times backwards.

Although the castle ruins dominate the tiny village of slate-roofed houses, Berry Pomeroy also has a much-admired church of red Devon stone, built by the Pomeroy family 500 years ago on earlier Norman foundations. Its greatest treasure is a church screen, 42 ft long and gilded in parts with fine tracings of saints and apostles.

◆

GABLES AND GREENERY *It is high summer in the Coln Valley, and the steep gables and tall chimneys of Cotswold stone seem half submerged in the green depths of motionless foliage. Bibury dreams of days gone by, when busy weavers lived in the ancient terraced cottages of Arlington Row and machinery rumbled in the mill by the old bridge across the Coln that is now a museum.*

BETCHWORTH
SURREY

3 miles east of Dorking (page 422 Db)

The heart of this long, strung-out village is a cul-de-sac of 17th and 18th-century cottages leading to a long timber barn and the impressive medieval Church of St Michael. Inside is a chest believed to be pre-Norman and cut from a log that was an oak tree when Christ was alive.

Part of Betchworth straggles along a lane that by-passes the churchyard to the east, and leads to the bridge over the River Mole. The 16th-century Old Mill Cottage and the Dolphin Inn, built around 1700, line the lane. But the most imposing building – set in fine parkland – is Betchworth House. It is built in a variety of styles including Georgian and early-19th-century stucco.

Betchworth has a 19th-century watermill in Wonham Lane, which is in keeping with its quiet Victorian atmosphere. The village once had a much higher status with a 14th-century castle – the last remnants of which are mouldering under earth banks in the local golf course.

Only St Michael's reflects the village's ancient grandeur. In the tower is a piece of Saxon stonework as well as a Norman arch. Most periods of church architecture have left their mark, but the prevailing white sandstone – quarried locally – gives the building unity.

Within the church is displayed a map of the manor in 1634, showing – among enclosed fields – the surviving narrow strips of medieval farming.

BIBURY
GLOUCESTERSHIRE

7 miles north-east of Cirencester (page 421 Dd)

William Morris, the 19th-century artist and poet, thought Bibury the most beautiful village in England. Another Victorian, J. Arthur Gibbs, wrote of it eloquently in *A Cotswold Village*, published in 1898.

The slow-moving River Coln snakes between wooded banks, and is spanned by a road bridge dated 1770. On the bank of the mill stream, which flows into the river, stands a terrace of gabled and stone-tiled cottages called Arlington Row. The cottages were converted from a 14th-century sheephouse in the early 17th century to house weavers supplying cloth for the nearby Arlington Mill. This was built in the 17th century and was both a cloth and corn-mill. It is now a folk museum and contains a collection of furniture from the Cotswolds Arts and Crafts movement. Some of the mill's machinery can be seen in operation. Next door is a trout hatchery, open to the public every day during the summer.

The centre of Bibury is the square, overlooked by the Saxon Church of St Mary and dignified stone-built houses. St Mary's has many later additions, mostly Norman and medieval, but much of its Saxon work is still visible, particularly in the chancel.

BIDDENDEN
KENT

5 miles north-west of Tenterden (page 423 Eb)

The main street looks like the set of a period film, but it is quite genuine and is full of perfect examples of English architecture from late medieval times to the 17th century. Timber-framed houses line the broad road which runs from east to west, linking the churchyard with a small green at a road junction. Many of the buildings date from the 15th century. Bricks and tiles made from local clay were used in the 17th century to build and decorate some of the other houses.

Throughout the parish are ancient causeways paved with irregular slabs of local marble, and in some places the faint outline of the fossils of small snails can be seen in the stone. The cause-ways were laid as hard paths for heavily laden pack-animals bringing in wool from outlying hamlets and farms.

The houses on the south side of the main street have attics which give a clue to the source of Biddenden's medieval wealth and fame. These rooms housed cloth-workers. Biddenden was a centre of the cloth trade in medieval and Tudor times. North of the main street is the Old Cloth Hall, a half-timbered building where the finished cloth was assembled. Beneath a protective carpet on the floor of the medieval church are 16th and 17th-century brasses, commemorating some of the wealthy clothiers.

The village sign on the green depicts the Biddenden Maids, the Siamese twins Elizabeth and Mary Chulkhurst, who were born about 1135, joined at the hip and shoulder. They lived until the age of 34 when they died within a few hours of each other. They bequeathed 18 acres of

VILLAGE OF THE GOLDEN FLEECE

Cloth-workers once lived in the half-timbered houses on the south side of Biddenden's High Street. One of the residences has a faded, golden head above a pair of doors known as the Tate Door. Further along the street a stained-glass window in Ye Maydes Restaurant depicts the village's most famous sisters, the 12th-century Siamese twins Mary and Elizabeth Chulkhurst, who, surprisingly, survived for 34 years.

Stained-glass twins.

The golden head.

Ancient House, Biddenden High Street.

land, known as the Bread and Cheese Land, earnings from which provided bread and cheese for the poor of the parish. Their act of charity is now remembered on Easter Monday, when biscuits are made embossed with an image of the twins.

BIDDENHAM
BEDFORDSHIRE

 beautiful

---
2 miles west of Bedford (page 426 Cc)

This is a village where dogs take the air in baskets mounted on the handlebars of old-fashioned bicycles; a quiet place of wide streets, of green verges wider still, and of dark, dignified cedars. Prosperity has always been assured by the nearness of Bedford, a mere couple of miles away. Certainly, there is a fine collection of large 19th-century merchants' houses, mostly of stone, with carefully tended gardens surrounded by walls dripping with aubrieta and alpines.

The oldest houses are three fortress-like farms that, interspersed with the colour-washed thatched cottages and the suave big houses, look like warriors among courtiers. The farm by the church, especially, with its massive walls and sturdy timber gate, seems capable of withstanding a siege. However, in one small area at least, these tough buildings have yielded to the general prettiness. On the corner of Nodder's Way, a long, low, thickset barn has been converted into the Village Hall; this, and the magnificently thatched Three Tuns pub, across the road, comprise the social centre of Biddenham.

Between there and the church is a whole range of highly individualistic houses – the pink Parsonage Cottage, for example, with its jutting, thatched eaves, and the blue-and-white, lattice-windowed creation behind the bus shelter that looks just like a Wendy house grown up.

The church itself – St James's – dates from the 12th century. The interior is pale-washed, rounded, and dimly lit by the intricately patterned windows above the altar; the chancel arch and the tower both belong to the years of the church's beginnings. The little, plain Children's Chapel is 15th century, and is divided from the nave by a carved Jacobean screen; the blue-and-gold cloth behind its altar was used in Westminster Abbey during the Coronation of Queen Elizabeth II.

BIGNOR
WEST SUSSEX

---
5 miles south of Petworth (page 422 Cb)

Farms and cottages are spaced round a rough square of four lanes at the foot of the South Downs. Wide stretches of the Downs are seen from several vantage points between the buildings, and the straight route of a Roman road runs off to the south-west. The village is situated beside one of the largest excavated Roman villas in England.

Facing one lane is an often photographed 15th-century thatched cottage, known as the Old Shop. Its frame is of oak timbers, with the spaces between filled with brick, flint and plaster. Brick-lined steps lead up to its oak doors, which show off best in the glow of afternoon sunshine. Farm buildings cluster round the corners of the lanes, their owners taking advantage of the fertile local soil just as the occupants of the Roman villa once did.

Two massive yew trees stand near the part-Norman, part-13th-century church at the north-west corner of the lanes. A large slab of Sussex marble, perhaps the remains of an altar table, lies by the porch. The honey-coloured stones of the church walls, like those seen in some other local buildings, may have been pirated from the Roman villa.

In Roman times, the locality was probably an important agricultural centre. The villa was discovered in 1811, when a plough disturbed a mosaic of a dancing girl. Excavations indicate that the spot was inhabited from the 1st to the 4th centuries, spanning the bulk of the Roman occupation of England. The villa, built round a courtyard, contains mosaic floors depicting the seasons, the head of Medusa, Ganymede and other legendary figures. In one room there is a six-sided ornamental water-basin made of white stone. A lead pipe in its base probably supplied a fountain. The villa is open to the public from March to October.

BIRNAM
TAYSIDE

---
13 miles north-west of Perth (page 443 Fb)

When the 6th Duke of Atholl refused to let the railway cross his estates in 1856, the village of Birnam came into being in a beautiful wooded setting beside the River Tay. The railway arrived at Birnam in 1856, but it took seven more years of negotiation before the duke agreed to a route over his land which allowed the line to be continued to Inverness. During that time, villas and hotels were built, and Birnam grew up as a separate village across the river from the town of Dunkeld.

Many English families used to rent villas at Birnam for the summer and autumn, and among them were the Potters from London. Their daughter, Beatrix, wrote picture letters, later expanded into *Tale of Peter Rabbit* and *Tale of Mr Jeremy Fisher*, on two successive September days in 1893, at the house called Eastwood.

The steep slopes of Birnam Wood, nowadays mostly silver birch and scrub oak, lie above the railway line. They can be seen from Dunsinane Hill, 12 miles to the south-east, where Shakespeare's Macbeth saw acted out the fatal prophecy that he would fall when Birnam Wood came to Dunsinane.

What is claimed to be the last oak of the original Birnam Wood is now an ancient tree, its branches held up by wooden supports, at the side of the Terrace Walk beside the fast-flowing waters of the Tay.

A personal portrait of Broughton-in-Furness in Cumbria by

RICHARD ADAMS

Funny how Richard Adams's Watership Down rabbits seem so like people.
But it's no coincidence really. In his chosen village he has trapped, as if in amber,
not only the solid stone and indefinable atmosphere of the place but the subtle flavour and
succinct dialogue of its inhabitants. 'Reckon he's real 'andy fella,' says one,
admiringly. 'Happen he is,' comes the considered reply. Clearly, Richard Adams is as
much at home in Lakeland as on the Berkshire Downs of his masterpiece and
the quirkily named Lhergy-Doo, where he lives now on the Isle of Man.

66 I have known the southern Lake District for thirty years and for me Broughton-in-Furness is a kind of personal gateway to that wonderful country of hills, sheep, honest beer and honest people. We used to drive up from the south by night, approaching Broughton in the early morning through places the very sound of whose names evokes the Lakes – Backbarrow, Haverthwaite, Greenodd, Gawthwaite, Grizeback. Then, by Wreaks End (where the hillside is a mass of wild daffodils at Easter), you take a bend up the hill, go a mile over the top by Boothwaite Nook, and there below lies Broughton; all grey – greystone walls, grey-tiled roofs with grey smoke drifting from them. And so down, to leave the car in the little square and start the holiday with breakfast at the 'Manor'.

The square, with its trees and horses' drinking-trough, is very quiet; dry and dusty in summer, sheltered from the wind in winter; a clock on the wall at one side, and in the middle a beautiful stone obelisk put up for George III's jubilee in 1810.

The 'Manor' used to be one of the three best pubs I have ever known. Twenty-five years ago it was kept by Gerald Gray, and we first became friends on the winter day when I, a stranger wandering in for direc-

tions, found behind the bar a bloke who'd named his cat 'Strafford' because he was a black Tom. There was a blazing 18th-century 'basket' fireplace alongside the bar, and for the past two-hundred years people had cut or burned their names on the oak mantel and surround. The floor was banded slate, very smooth and cool, the marking of each flag like damascene, a symmetrical, watered pattern of creamy-light and smoky-dark greys and blacks, melting into one another like the surface of a pool after a stone has been dropped into it. On market days the farmers would come in before going home – Tysons and Lindsays and Birketts and Longmires and Boows and Dawsons – and their dogs would lie in heaps on the flags while they themselves supped Gerald's ale. Each farmer, as he left, would call his dog – Flash, Jed, Fly, Wag, Bob, Mad, Rip or whatever – which would disentangle itself and follow him out. One day a shepherd's wife, who had been shopping and was anxious to get off home, came in to get him out. 'Still bidin' here, Jack, art tha, wastin' thy time?' 'Nay,' said he, 'Ah'm noan wastin' mi time, lass. Ah've soopped as mooch as t' next chap.'

Mister Hutchinson, the butcher ('Morning, Mistroochinson!'), kept a splendid

shop, full not only of lamb and steak (not dear, either) but also of tripe and black puddings and, above all, of Cumberland sausage. Cumberland sausage is about half as thick as your wrist and extends in a single rope several feet long, so that Mistroochinson, having weighed you one end while the other trailed over the edge of the scale, would then cut it for you like a draper selling a length of tape. Some people used to have Mistroochinson's Cumberland sausage posted to them in the south.

Cattle auctions in the market – what a row! The farmers, canny and taciturn, all lining the indoor ring as the poor old cow was prodded round and round by a boy. 'Any more, any more, forty-six, forty-six, forty-six, forty-seven, forty-eight, forty-nine, forty-nine, are you all done at forty-nine BANG!' and out goes the cow with one metal gate clanging ech'oingly behind her, and in come five sheep through the other. I never knew why the auctioneer has to keep up his unceasing bellowing; but they wouldn't like it if he didn't.

There was never much traffic in Broughton. The children could safely wander off on their own, promising to meet you in half an hour. They were usually late (no wonder and no blame) and you would idle contentedly in the square, where the fuchsia dropped its glowing, cerise petals, the climbing *Nasturtium tropaeolum* glowed, a deep crimson splash, up the greystone walls here and there, and the sycamores' propellers spun down in the sunny autumn air. About you, seeming, like bird-song, to delight and reassure without needing to mean anything much, sounded the quiet voices of passers-by. 'Art tha cooming to Barra Soonday, then?' 'Nay, Ah cann't.' 'Is t'lyle fella coomin'?' 'Ay, happen.' 'Reckon he's real 'andy fella, is yon.' 'Happen he is.'

Broughton has always seemed to me exactly what a community ought to be. It recalls the Basque fisherman's prayer: 'O God, I know I'm not worthy to attain to your beautiful heaven. Please let me just stay here.' 99

Richard Adams

A beautiful stone obelisk put up for George III's jubilee in 1810.

The 'Manor' used to be one of the three best pubs I have ever known.

There was never much traffic in Broughton.

The square...is very quiet, with a clock on the wall at one side.

Broughton; all grey—greystone walls, grey-tiled roofs with grey smoke drifting...

BISHOP BURTON

HUMBERSIDE

3 miles west of Beverley (page 437 Cb)

Set among wide vistas of farmland and woods, the village straddles the road from York to Beverley. To the right – travelling towards Beverley – is a large, crescent-shaped pond full of chattering geese and backed by the war memorial, set high on a plinth and reflecting in the water. A road curves to the right around the pond, past a massive wood-and-iron pump, and runs up the little hill on which the church stands. About the hill, and around the large green at the other end of the pond, there are a number of pretty black-and-white cottages.

Opposite the pond, and on the other side of the Beverley road, is the red-tiled and white-washed Altisidora pub, named after the horse that won the St Leger in 1813. The horse was owned by Mr Watt, whose house and handsome park lie behind the pub; the house is now an agricultural college.

'Bishop' in the village's name comes from a

maner house belonging to the Archbishop of York that stood in a nearby field called Knight's Garth until the Reformation. But long before the archbishops appeared on the scene, St John of Beverley had consecrated the village's first church – in 708. The present church, on the same site, dates from the 13th century, but was rebuilt in the 19th century – a powerful building of square sandstone blocks. A monument in the church commemorates the instructors and pupils who were killed at the RAF flying school at Beverley between 1917 and 1918 The plaque was given by the women of the district.

PREACHER'S CORNER *A pair of black-shuttered cottages, set into an old stone wall, and the white rails around the pond make a perfect subject for reflection by the still water. In spring and early summer the pondside is flamboyant with marsh marigolds. Then, as they fade, the climbing roses round the cottage doors burst into bloom. This corner of Bishop Burton was the scene of the most memorable day in the village's 1,200 years of recorded history when, towards the end of the 18th century, John Wesley, the founder of Methodism, preached on the green beside the pond. He so impressed the villagers that they hold an open-air service on the green every third Sunday in July, to commemorate his visit. A bust of Wesley, carved from the wood of the elm tree under which he preached, is in the church.*

BISHOPS CANNINGS
WILTSHIRE

3 miles north-east of Devizes (page 421 Dc)

All Wiltshiremen are Moonrakers, and if anyone should be credited with earning them the nickname, it is the villagers of Bishops Cannings. Not those who live there today, of course, but the smugglers of the 16th to 18th centuries, who ran a profitable and illicit black market in Hollands gin and other forms of liquor, slaking the thirst of the Dutch and Flemish wool merchants who had made their headquarters in Swindon.

The story goes that one moonlit night, a patrol of Excisemen discovered two villagers from Bishops Cannings raking the surface of a local pond. When asked what they were doing, the men pointed to the reflection of the moon in the water, and said they were trying to fish out 'thik yaller cheese'. The Excisemen took them for idiots and rode off laughing. But the Moonrakers had the last laugh. In fact they were collecting kegs of liquor hidden in the pond.

Bishops Cannings is one of the oldest villages in Wiltshire, much older than the town of Devizes. Throughout the Middle Ages it belonged to the Bishops of Salisbury (hence the name), and the dean and canons of Salisbury Cathedral had a manor there; these high ecclesiastical connections are still reflected by the splendour of the church.

Built in the 12th century, and added to later, the church bears a certain similarity in design to Salisbury Cathedral, not least in its elegant tapering spire, perched on a two-storey tower. The entire building is larger and more imposing than you would expect in such a small parish, and both inside and out it is rich in carvings of birds, dragons, human faces, grotesques and animals. The organ, constructed in 1809, was given to the church by William Bayley, a local man who sailed round the world as Captain Cook's navigator.

The village is a dignified place of thatch, half-timbering, box hedges and neat farms, set among elms (though not as many as formerly, since Dutch elm disease took its toll) on the level plain of the Pewsey Vale. The great rounded mass of Roundway Down, where Royalists won a bloody victory over Cromwell's forces on July 13, 1643, stands about 1 mile to the west. Along a ridge just to the north extends a section of the Wansdyke, the impressive but still largely unexplained earthwork which stretches from the Berkshire boundary through Wiltshire to northern Somerset.

◆

VILLAGE OF WISE FOOLS *Now a quiet place of thatch and timber, Bishops Cannings was, during the 17th century, a hotbed of smugglers who camouflaged their activities by cultivating a reputation for feeble-mindedness. As well as the famous moonraker story, they solemnly told strangers that they spread manure about the church tower to make it grow, and that once the whole village marched 3 miles to Devizes to see an eclipse of the moon. But at the same period the village had a minister, Mr Ferraby, who was a fine musician, and it was said that the parish . . . 'could challenge all England for musique, football and bell-ringing'.*

BISLEY
GLOUCESTERSHIRE

4 miles east of Stroud (page 421 Cd)

Local people call the village 'Bisley-God-Help-Us', because of the winter winds which sweep across this remote, hilltop community. Its remoteness also contributed to its decline as a textile village at the time of the Industrial Revolution, and an old rhyme tells of 'Beggarly Bisley'. But neither local cynicism nor unkind verse can detract from Bisley's unarguable charm.

When entered from the south-west, the village appears as an amphitheatre of gabled, greystone houses climbing in terraces on either side of the main street. At the top of George Street the Bear Inn, once the court house, has detached 17th-century columns supporting the upper floor. Close by is the old lock-up, dated 1824.

Church Hill climbs steeply to All Saints, with its lych-gate at the entrance to the churchyard. A crumbling stone edifice in the churchyard is a 13th-century 'poor soul's light'. It was used to hold candles for Masses said for the souls in purgatory, and is believed to be the only outdoor example in England.

The Church of All Saints dates from the 13th century, and was restored during the 19th century. Its rector at that time was Thomas Keble, brother of John Keble, the poet and divine, after whom Keble College, Oxford was named. Thomas Keble was also responsible for the restoration of Bisley's seven wells, which now gush from spouts set in a gabled semi-circle just below the church. The wells are dressed on Ascension Day.

BLAIRLOGIE
CENTRAL

3 miles north-east of Stirling (page 441 Ed)

The village is one of several communities, known as the Hillfoots, strung along the steep, southerly slopes of the Ochil Hills. Blairlogie, with its pleasant jumble of cottages in varying styles, looks out from its sheltered site below the Ochil crags across rich farmland which, centuries ago, was covered by an inlet of the North Sea. In the background is the 1,373 ft high Dumyat, with views over the Hillfoots.

Blairlogie grew up in the shadow of Blairlogie Castle, a 16th-century stronghold of the Spittal family. Each spring and summer, invalids came to take advantage of the mild weather and to drink health-giving milk from the goats which grazed on the hillocks behind the village. For many years, Blairlogie was known as 'Goats' Milk Spa'. However, in 1820, tonic mineral water was found at nearby Bridge of Allan, which quickly established itself as a spa. From then on, Blairlogie's days as a health resort were numbered.

Today, the village is much as it was in the last century. A small car park on the east side is linked to a network of footpaths which connect Blairlogie with the other Hillfoot settlements, and with the old rights of way into the Ochils.

BLAKENEY
NORFOLK

5 miles north-west of Holt (page 432 Dd)

Beside the main coastal road between Sheringham and Wells-next-the-Sea stands Blakeney's Church of St Nicholas. Its tower, over 100 ft high, is a landmark for miles around, and at the eastern end of the church is a smaller tower built as a beacon to guide ships into Blakeney harbour.

High Street runs from the main road down to the Quay between cottages of brick and flint and a few houses of red brick. On the Quay is the Georgian Red House. The old Guildhall, in High Street, which is now a hotel, has a 14th-century undercroft. The waterfront was a commercial port until the beginning of this century. Now the estuary has silted up, and only small pleasure craft can sail up the narrow channel.

The broad Quay faces the wide, flat marshes stretching into the distance towards Blakeney Point. This long arm of sand and shingle has a nature reserve, owned by the National Trust, which can be visited by boat from Blakeney Quay, if the tide permits, or by a 5 mile walk from the neighbouring village of Cley.

BLANCHLAND
NORTHUMBERLAND

9 miles south of Hexham (page 438 Ac)

There is a barracks-square neatness about Blanchland. Its trim, grey and yellow stone cottages stand in disciplined lines around a large L-shaped village square. The dwellings date from the 18th century, when they were built to house miners from the nearby lead mines.

The origins of the village, however, go back to the 12th century when an abbey was founded there, and the square was formerly the abbey courtyard. The present church is all that remains of the abbey, but the 15th-century gatehouse forms an imposing entrance to the village. The Lord Crewe Arms was part of the abbey's 13th-century guest house, though most of the present inn is Georgian. In the 18th century it was, for a time, the home of General Tom Forster who led the unsuccessful Jacobite rising in 1715. After his capture at Preston, Forster escaped and hid in a priest hole behind a fireplace in the house. The site of the hiding place is still there and so, it is said, is the ghost of his sister, Dorothy. She appears to visitors, imploring them to take a message to her brother who fled to France.

MONASTIC VILLAGE Isolation has preserved the character of the model village of Blanchland, which was built in the 18th century on the site of a ruined abbey. It lies deep in the valley of the River Derwent, surrounded by bleak moorland. This seclusion, local legend says, caused the Scots to miss it on one of their raids across the border in 1327. In thanksgiving for deliverance, the monks rang a peal of bells. But their joy was short-lived, because the Scots heard the bells and returned to sack the abbey.

BLETCHINGLEY
SURREY

3 miles east of Redhill (page 423 Dc)

At the widest part of Bletchingley's one curving street stands the Whyte Harte, proudly bearing the date 1388 but a public house only since 1704, and the old market hall in the Middle Row that occupies part of the market place. Behind is Church Walk, the old High Street which has a fine, early-16th-century timber-framed house.

The big, sandstone Church of St Mary looks out over open country to the North Downs. Inside, a small window opens on to a hermit's cell – possibly that of Roger the Hermit, who was recorded as being in Bletchingley in the 13th century. Medieval gargoyles enliven the nave and the south aisle, and a 16th-century brass on the floor of the tower is dedicated to Thomas Warde, a tanner, and his wife.

The massive effigy of Sir Robert Clayton, money-lender, Lord Mayor of London and MP for the City of London, is one of the finest in the country. The iron railing around the monument is of local craftsmanship. Sir Robert, who died in 1707, owned the 'rotten borough' of Bletchingley.

To the west of the village, on the top of the hill by Castle Square, a lane leads past the site of the old pound to private parkland where the ramparts of a Norman castle are covered with woodland.

Among the many fine farmhouses in the parish is Place Farm, 1 mile to the north of the village. This was once the home of Anne of Cleves, who received the manor from Henry VIII on her divorce in 1540. The present house dates mostly from the 18th century.

Near by is Pendell Court, a fine brick house which was built in Jacobean style in 1624. Next door is Pendell House, built 12 years later, in the Classical style.

BLEWBURY
OXFORDSHIRE

3 miles south of Didcot (page 426 Ba)

The oldest part of Blewbury lies within a loop from the main road, London Street, that passes south of the village. It is a place of narrow lanes and pathways, and white-painted, timber-framed houses. A mansion house, Hall Barn, is said to have been one of Henry VIII's hunting lodges. Even older are the thatched 'wattle-and-daub' walls lining a long pathway; they are believed to be of Saxon origin.

The part-Norman church stands among trees in the centre of the loop, surrounded by a patchwork of streams and watercress beds.

◆

ANCIENT CHARM *The beauty of Bletchingley lies in its ancient houses. Timber-framed buildings vie for pride of place with brick and tile-hung houses where flights of stone steps lead up to wooden front doors. Traffic skirts the quiet High Street and a huge tree watches over the peaceful scene.*

Kenneth Grahame, author of *The Wind in the Willows*, published in 1908, came to live at Blewbury in 1910.

About 1 mile to the east is Blewburton Hill, topped by an Iron Age hill-fort. To the south are the Berkshire Downs and the Ridgeway.

BLISLAND
CORNWALL

4 miles north-east of Bodmin (page 418 Cb)

The village is perched on a hillside on the western edge of Bodmin Moor, where the barren, unfenced moorland gives way to deep valleys and woods. It lies in a parish of isolated farms and cottages, marshes and ancient hut-circles.

Around the green, a rare feature for a Cornish village, are granite cottages, mostly Georgian, a small post office and store and the Royal Oak Inn.

Blisland's chief glory is its church, dedicated to St Protus and St Hyacinth. The Norman and medieval building of slate and granite is pleasing on the outside, and breathtakingly beautiful within. Leaning granite columns support a white-painted wagon roof with carved ribs and bosses; a screen dating from 1894 is carved in medieval style and painted in turquoise and gold.

Near the hamlet of Pendrift, 1 mile north, is the massive Jubilee Rock, carved with a figure of Britannia, coats of arms and other symbols to mark the Golden Jubilee of George III in 1810.

BLYTH
NOTTINGHAMSHIRE

6 miles north-west of East Retford (page 430 Cd)

Elm trees shade the triangular green at Blyth, lending a pastoral charm to what was once a busy street on the old London to York highway, the Great North Road. The village lies within a loop of the River Ryton, crossed by an 18th-century bridge, and was a staging point in Georgian times. The Angel, built in the early 18th century, is the oldest of three coaching inns.

Facing the green are red-brick cottages with pantiled roofs, and a stone building with a 700-year-old doorway. The building is said to have been founded by the Hospitalers of St John of Jerusalem in the 12th century as a leper hospital.

North of the green stands the priory church of St Mary and St Martin, one of the oldest examples of Norman architecture in England. It formed part of a Benedictine monastery founded in 1088, and the north aisle, which was originally the nave, dates from that time. The 100 ft high tower was added in the 15th century. The eastern end of the church was demolished in the 1680s and the space became part of the gardens of Blyth Hall, which was demolished in 1972. Only the gateway remains, but next to it is a row of cottages built by William Mellish, a rich local merchant. They were once a single building, probably the rectory. Mellish also built the bridge over the Ryton, and the almshouses.

BOLTON-BY-BOWLAND
LANCASHIRE

6 miles north-east of Clitheroe (page 435 Db)

There are two village greens at Bolton. The smaller, below the church, has the stump of a 13th-century market cross and stocks posts at its centre. It is flanked by the Coach and Horses Inn, and by Rose Cottage – a substantial house built in 1835. Two rows of whitewashed cottages run down from the green. One cottage has outside steps leading straight to the upper floor, another has a mounting block for horse riders.

The other green is screened by trees, and lies above the 13th-century Church of St Peter and St Paul. The old church school of 1874 is at the top end of the green, and halfway down the side is the former Court House, with its weather-vane in the shape of a fox. The court used to decide rights of dwelling in the Forest of Bowland.

The church houses the tomb of a 15th-century landowner, Sir Ralph Pudsey, whose three wives and 25 children are also commemorated. Sir Ralph was hailed as a local hero when, in 1464, he hid the Lancastrian King Henry VI, who was fleeing from his Yorkist enemies.

SAWLEY Centuries ago Sawley was known as Salley, after the Cistercian abbey which stood there. The abbey ruins are near the village, which straggles along the bank of the River Ribble, 2 miles downstream from Bolton-by-Bowland.

BOLTON PERCY
NORTH YORKSHIRE

3 miles south-east of Tadcaster (page 436 Cb)

White limestone blended with red brick gives a pleasant dappled effect to the buildings of Bolton Percy. The mixture is seen also in the village inn, the Crown, and the white stone, now greying with age, was used in the walls bordering the road to the church and in the 15th-century church itself. In contrast, a half-timbered 15th-century gatehouse with delicately carved woodwork stands in isolation beyond the churchyard.

The Church of All Saints was built in the early 15th century. The medieval stained glass in the east window includes the coat of arms of Richard Scrope, Archbishop of York, who joined with the Percy family in a plot to overthrow Henry IV. He was executed for treason at York in 1405. In his *Henry IV*, Shakespeare calls the archbishop Richard Scroop. The Percy from whom the village takes its name was probably William de Percy, who held the manor in 1086.

◆

BORTH-Y-GEST *The sheltering crags of Moel-y-Gest, which form a backdrop to the picturesque harbour of Borth-y-Gest, bore silent witness to history in the 12th century. For it was from these quiet waters that Prince Madog, son of Owain Gwynedd, is said to have set sail to discover America more than 300 years before Christopher Columbus.*

BORTH
DYFED

5 miles north of Aberystwyth (page 425 Cc)

The village, which is little more than a stone's throw wide, stretches like a tightrope for almost 2 miles along a high, narrow bank of pale, sea-smoothed shingle. On one side there is a huge sandy beach, on the other the marshy wilderness of Cors Fochno, a raised bog of reeds and semi-liquid peat.

Victorian and Edwardian villas mingle with more modern buildings near the golf course; to the south, the single street runs between austere chapels and colourful little cottages whose back doors open on to the piled shingle. A short lane leads to the isolated village church on the edge of Cors Fochno.

Upper Borth clusters round a road junction, and spreads up a rocky headland towards the war memorial on Craig-yr-Wylfa. The memorial is a splendid viewpoint from which the mountains of North Wales and the great sweep of Cardigan Bay can be admired. At the foot of the headland, numerous rock pools contrast with the beach that spears northwards for 4 miles to the mouth of the Dyfi Estuary. In the distance, shingle gives way to rolling sand dunes which can be explored by a nature trail.

BORTH-Y-GEST
GWYNEDD

1 mile south of Porthmadog (page 428 Bb)

A pleasant wooded road, overlooked by the crags of Moel-y-Gest, leads from Porthmadog to this quiet little seaside village. Terraces of neat 19th-century houses huddle together in a shallow bowl that sweeps down to a sheltered bay where small boats moor. The shore is somewhat muddy, but there are pleasant sandy coves a short walk away over the western headland. Few seaside villages in Wales offer such splendid views. The huge open expanse of Traeth Bach – carved by the Glaslyn and Dwyryd rivers – contrasts with the wooded peninsula of Portmeirion and the rugged Rhinog Mountains that rise to more than 2,000 ft in the south-east. Harlech's crag-perched castle and the great road-bearing embankment across the upper Glaslyn Estuary are notable man-made landmarks.

Borth-y-Gest has retained its personality as a trim, Victorian village. It stands at the end of a cul-de-sac and remains peacefully aloof from through traffic. Mersey Street is particularly attractive. Running up from the bay, it passes between terraced cottages before petering into a footpath that leads over the headland to a golf course and the dune-backed sands of Black Rock.

BOSBURY
HEREFORD AND WORCESTER

4 miles north of Ledbury (page 425 Eb)

Before mechanisation, the hop-gardens surrounding Bosbury echoed every September to the accents of the South Wales valleys and industrial Midlands, as the pickers and their families moved in by the hundred to help with the harvest. Now machines strip the green vines, and the autumn invasion is just part of village history – a history stretching back to Saxon times and beyond.

The village, which probably derives its name from Bosa, a 9th-century local landlord, has seen invaders before – Saxons, Normans and marauding Celts. It is believed to have been a large town in pre-Saxon times, but it was destroyed by the Saxons and never regained its importance.

It is a traditional village, a pleasant mixture of half-timbered, stone and brick buildings. Dominating the whole village is the massive, detached stone tower of the 12th-century church. It is one of seven free-standing church towers in Herefordshire, and was built as a fortified refuge from the Welsh raiders who pillaged these border lands until the 15th century. Its six bells were installed in the 16th century.

In the churchyard stands a rare 14th-century preaching cross.

BOSCASTLE
CORNWALL

5 miles north of Camelford (page 418 Cb)

Many vessels have foundered near the entrance to Boscastle's harbour, the only shelter for miles along Cornwall's northern coastline. The narrow inlet snakes between high slate cliffs to a small stone jetty originally used for exporting slate and gràin, and sailing ships had to be towed to it by rowing-boats and ropes from the shore.

Beyond the quay the sea bursts through a hole in the cliffs, just before low tide. In rough weather this blowhole sends sea and spray booming across the harbour in spectacular fashion. But the village of Boscastle lies half a mile from the harbour in the Valency Valley, with narrow streets of slate cottages climbing the hillside. There is an inn, the Napoleon, at the top of the village, and the Wellington Hotel at the bottom of the hillside, as well as craft shops, a pottery and a Museum of Witchcraft.

Two miles east of the village is St Juliot, where the novelist Thomas Hardy, while a young architect, restored the church in 1872.

BOSHAM
WEST SUSSEX

4 miles west of Chichester (page 422 Cb)

Closely packed cottages line the quayside, with the church spire rising above them. Boats are tied up in almost every available spot. When the tide goes out, gulls, oystercatchers and wildfowl settle along the irregular shoreline.

Bosham is outstanding among the villages around the indented coast of Chichester Harbour. It occupies a small peninsula, jutting into one of the inlets of the sea. The road there is often flooded at high tide, and the houses all have high front doors approached by flights of steps to keep them beyond reach of the tide. A narrow High Street runs parallel to the quay, flanked by cottages, shops and inns of red brick, stone and flint, many decorated with hung tiles.

The tip of the peninsula is an open space known as Quay Meadow. The High Street and quayside run north-east from it. Beyond is the church, and then an avenue of evergreen oaks and holly trees leading to Bosham Lane which is lined with cottages, some thatched and dating from the 17th century.

The tower and chancel arch of the church are Saxon. It was in this church that Harold Godwin, later King Harold, prayed before sailing from the village in 1064 on his momentous journey to Normandy. He was captured by William, Duke of Normandy, whom he swore to assist in attaining the English crown. Harold's breach of his oath led to the Norman invasion of 1066. The church is depicted in the Bayeux Tapestry. Rough-hewn crosses in the stonework round the porch were cut by Richard I's Crusaders before departing for the Holy Land, intending to complete them on their return.

TIDAL CREEK *Bosham harbour is a safe haven for small boats, but the streets are sometimes flooded by high tides which even a king could not stop. Other places claim to be the site where Canute commanded the tide to roll back, but Bosham at least has evidence that the king may have visited the village. According to legend Canute's youngest daughter was buried there, and about 100 years ago a stone coffin of the Saxon period containing the skeleton of a young child was discovered in the church.*

BOSHERSTON
DYFED

4 miles south of Pembroke (page 424 Aa)

Large ponds noted for their lilies, and a spectacular stretch of coastline flank this tiny village. Most of the cottages and farms are finished in the whitewashed style that is typical of Pembrokeshire, but the slate-hung walls of Styles Farm near the church provide a picturesque contrast. Spruce blue-and-white coastguard houses stand by the St Govan's Inn. Ivy and

lichens abound, the latter paying tribute to the purity of the coastal air.

The church, built towards the end of the 13th century, stands beside a path that leads down to the pools where the lilies are at their best in June. The church's stained glass includes windows depicting St David and St Govan, who carries a model of his tiny chapel. The original chapel, thought to be built in the 6th century, huddles in a dramatic, wave-washed chasm just over 1 mile south of Bosherston.

BOTTESFORD
LEICESTERSHIRE

7 miles west of Grantham (page 430 Cc)

As it flows through Bottesford, the River Devon is little more than a swollen brook. Yet it manages to flood the road near the church. A narrow footbridge, built about 1600, crosses the river south of the churchyard.

There has been a settlement in the area at least since the Norman Conquest. A Norman baron, Robert de Roos, founded an encampment close to where Belvoir Castle now dominates the Vale of Belvoir. Bottesford had a market in medieval times, and Robert de Roos put up the market cross, the remains of which stand at the centre of the village to this day. Another relic of the past – the stocks and whipping post – stands beside the cross.

Bottesford's pride is the Church of St Mary which has a 113 ft spire, the tallest village spire in the country. The church has splendid monuments which were started between 1543 and 1684 for the first eight Earls of Rutland. One of the monuments depicts two Rutland children, who died in infancy of a 'loathsome disease' brought on by a coven of witches. When the witches were arrested, one of them called for a trial by ordeal. She asked to be given bread to eat, saying that if she choked on it and died it would be proof of guilt. She was given a slice of bread and duly choked to death. The rest of the witches were tried and hanged in Lincoln Gaol.

Discovering VILLAGE HISTORY

*A village is . . . a village is . . . a village, back through
layers of time; the same yet different, evolving
with centuries and generations. To peel away those layers
is to discover the stuff of history,
to take flight in a time machine of the mind.*

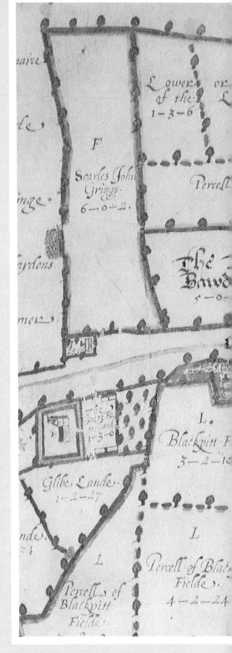

There is no such thing as an uninteresting village. In almost every village in Britain, men and women have lived, worked and died for 2,000 years or more. They lived through times of peace and war, famine and prosperity, cruelty and benevolence. Their experiences could not fail to become permanently imprinted on the place in which they lived.

Discovering a village's history is not always easy; often, much of it has been obscured by progress or eroded by time. Some villages are lucky enough to have attracted the attention of literary men in the past who recorded faithfully, but not always factually, rural life in their time. George Lipscombe, for instance, wrote an eight-part history of Buckinghamshire in the 1830s. But village historians often have to rely on legends and hearsay handed down from one generation to another – often inaccurate and coloured by romanticism and local pride.

The starting point for exploring village history can be something as simple as its name. Castle Acre sounds interesting; Chew Magna is intriguing; and how did Wendens Ambo get such a strange name? But it is not always the prettiest names that denote the prettiest vil-

lages. The name Bosham could hardly be plainer, but few villages are prettier, while rural-sounding Peckham Rye is now buried in London.

Local knowledge

There are three good sources of information in every village – the church, the pub and the village shop. Even in the smallest church you will probably find a booklet on sale giving the church's history and perhaps a short history of the parish.

Britain's parish churches are living monuments, as well as places of worship. In their size and style they reveal much about the village they serve, its past prosperity and the piety of the parishioners. The monuments and brasses may record the names of important local families going back 600 years or more; and in the churchyard the gravestones will tell you the names and ages of generations of humbler folk. If a churchyard is elevated several feet above its surroundings, that will often tell of many more generations, unknown and unrecorded, who are buried there.

The parish registers will contain the names of nearly all who were baptised, married and buried in the parish as far back

as the 16th century. But in most cases, except for those in current use and in the care of the rector or vicar, the registers will be at the County Record Office. They can be seen there on application or by appointment.

Most village folk take an intense pride in their community, and next to the vicar the most knowledgeable person is often the landlord of the pub. It is worth talking to the regulars, too, especially the older ones who can remember what life was like around the turn of the century. The village shop, which often includes the post office, usually has booklets on sale describing the parish history.

THE OLD AND NEW FACES OF AN ESSEX VILLAGE

More than three centuries separate two views of East Hanningfield, and together they show how little the village has changed over the years. The map, drawn in 1615 by a cartographer named John Walker, is remarkable for its accuracy when compared with the aerial photograph. The photograph shows that the main street, and the road leading to it from the west, are almost unaltered in shape and width since Walker's time, and that the green, called the Tye, is still the heart of the village. Even the shapes of the fields are much the same, and the only obvious differences after more than 300 years are the factory buildings on the edge of the village and a housing estate.

Learning about a village by talking to its inhabitants can be pleasant and rewarding, but anyone who wants to delve deeper must refer not only to parish registers but to other written records.

First there are the Manorial Records, which for six centuries or more chronicled the transactions of the manor-courts, dealing mainly with the transfer and tenancy of property. They also incorporate the deliberations of the court leet, or parish government. Those still existing – thousands have been lost or destroyed – are all in County Record Offices. From 1733 on they are in English and in book form. Those for the preceding 100 years or so are in a mixture of Latin and English, but before 1600 all are in Latin.

These early records are on rolls of parchment and difficult to read – but fascinating when you can. In some cases manor-court rolls of the 13th and 14th centuries can still be found, but they are likely to be in college libraries, the Public Record Office in Chancery Lane, London, or the British Museum. They are priceless treasures – the very stuff of medieval and Tudor life, recording even offences against local bye-laws.

Then there are the church-wardens' and overseers' accounts, dating mostly from the 17th century and continuing well into the 19th. All are now – or should be – in the County Records Office, and give a fascinating insight into every-day life in the village as seen by these officials as they went about their duties, dealing with paupers, vagrants, road-mending and more dramatic events like the raising of militia.

The church's diocesan and archidiaconal records should not be overlooked, dealing as they do with matters of general morality, nonconformism and payment of tithes. They are mostly in Latin, difficult to read, but well worth the effort, containing occasional verbatim reports in luridly lucid English – sometimes deliciously shocking. They are usually kept in diocesan archives; sometimes in university libraries.

Wills, maps and ancient records

But no single surviving document is likely to reveal more about an individual, his family, property and way of living, than that written just before he died: his will. Probate was in the hands of the church courts until the early 19th century, and since inventories of a person's possessions were part of the probate procedure, an inventory may often be found with the will. Careful study of it will give a fair picture not only of his house, but also the way it was furnished. Copies of wills can be found in Somerset House, diocesan archives, university libraries and occasionally County Record Offices.

Old maps give a splendid, but not always reliable, guide to the look of a village – frequently they are more decorative than factual. Most informative and detailed of all are the enclosure maps, which accompanied enclosure awards. These date from about 1770 to 1880 and show in remarkable detail every field, house and road. In particular they are an invaluable source of information on field names that have survived for centuries. They exist in great numbers and photo-copies can

ANCIENT RECORDS OF LIFE AND DEATH

Wills give a poignant insight into village history, often telling much about the testator's life style and his worldly goods. In the will of John Chapman, a baker of Ardeley in Hertfordshire, which he made in 1718, he was able only to give 'to my son William Chapman 1s (1 Shilling) and to my daughter Mary Canon 1s'.

Parish registers recorded baptisms, marriages and burials, but were not always well kept as the register for the Hertfordshire village of Great Amwell shows. The entries are very brief, not in chronological order and give only the names of the bride and groom and the date of their wedding.

John Chapman's will, dated 1718, disposes of his few possessions 'In the Name of God, Amen'.

Great Amwell's Parish Register goes back to the 17th century.

be obtained from County Record Offices.

Usually the earliest appearance of a village is in the Domesday Book, the national survey ordered by William the Conqueror in 1086 to discover the true wealth of the country. It records briefly how many serfs, villeins and cottagers there were; how many mills, how much meadow and woodland, and what it was all worth in taxes. It is often difficult to understand, but translations in printed form are available in public libraries and the County Record Office.

The same sort of information in greater detail is contained in the Hundred Rolls, the returns of governmental inquiries held under Edward I in 1274-9. They have been transcribed and printed in large volumes, also to be found in records offices and reference libraries. Often they give the name of everyone living in the village. But there is a snag: again you need Latin, as they are not translated.

MONUMENTS TO THE HIGH AND THE HUMBLE

In many parish churches, brasses set into the floor record the names, and often the effigies, of important local people of the past. A particularly good example is the brass dedicated to Sir Simon Felbrigg and his wife in St Margaret's Church, Felbrigg, in Norfolk. The brass dates from 1416, and the figures are 5 ft 4 in. long. The passing of lesser folk is usually recorded on tombstones in the churchyard, though these are often ornately inscribed and still clearly readable.

TRADEMARK *A sign bearing the motto of the Blacksmiths' Society decorates the wall of the blacksmith's shop in New Abbey, Dumfries and Galloway.*

Other books worth consulting are Lyson's *Magna Britannia* (1808, text in English) for manorial history, and Cobbett's *Rural Rides*, a penetrating survey of agricultural England from the saddle. Directories and gazetteers, too, give a potted history of villages and a list of their principal inhabitants: they were published at ten-year intervals from about 1800.

But by far the fullest records are those assembled in the *Victoria County Histories*, mostly written about 1900 and lately being updated and expanded to include village history. They are in the main excellent and make a first-rate starting point for inquiries, being available in all public libraries.

Finally, do not forget the county's archaeology officer. He – or she – can supply information on recent or current discoveries and investigations, and tell you where to find aerial photographs of the district. These can reveal fascinating aspects of features often quite invisible at ground level, such as ploughed-out barrows, deserted sites of medieval villages, and ancient forts.

And if, in the course of a stroll, you should happen on any interesting artefacts like coins, pottery fragments or even a stone axe, please do let the archaeological officer know!

Country yarns

Researchers delving into the past will inevitably come across the well-worn stories beloved of local guide-book writers and farmgate philosophers. Villagers are fiercely proud of their local history, and will boast of events which are, in fact, common to most villages. For example, the fact that the village was mentioned in the Domesday Book is hardly unique – so were most of them. Another popular story is that Cromwell's troops were billeted in the village, but as the Civil War touched most parts of the country this, too, is not unusual.

Cromwell's men are often unjustly blamed for the destruction of the local castle. Their artillery may have knocked it about a bit, but the chances are that local farmers did the rest by stripping it to build barns and walls.

There is a tendency also to exaggerate the age of buildings, such as the inn or manor house, which may be described as 14th century when they obviously date from the 16th century. And the old manorial system dies hard. The present owner of the manor house is often referred to as the Lord of the Manor, but there have been no manors or lords of manors since 1922.

Finally, there are the legends and myths which have grown from seeds sown in the distant past and have become embellished and distorted over the years. They are mostly untrue – but no village history is complete without them.

BOURTON ON THE WATER
GLOUCESTERSHIRE

15 miles east of Cheltenham (page 421 Dd)

The 'water' in the name is the River Windrush, flowing gently through the village beneath low stone bridges – two of them 18th century – and alongside a tree-shaded green. A riverside path leads to quiet corners where willows dip their tresses in the water, and beyond the green are secluded lanes with cottages and houses of golden Cotswold stone.

But the village can also be explored in miniature, by visiting the model built in the gardens of the Old New Inn. It was the work of the present landlord's father and a small team of craftsmen in the 1930s, and is a one-ninth scale replica of Bourton complete in almost every detail – including a model of the model itself.

Fascinating though this Bourton-in-miniature is, however, it is a place where nothing moves, which cannot be said of the village's other major attraction, Birdland. There, in the grounds of a Tudor manor, brightly plumaged parrots and macaws fly among the trees, and penguins swim in a glass-sided pool. There are flamingos and toucans in the aviary, and hummingbirds and sunbirds can be seen in the tropical houses.

In Sherborne Street, by the bridge, a corn-mill – now a motor museum – and its adjacent cottages date from the 18th century or earlier. The Old Manse, close by, was built in 1748 and is now a hotel. Across the bridge in the High Street stands the Church of St Lawrence, with a 14th-century chancel and Georgian tower.

BOWMORE
STRATHCLYDE

On east side of Loch Indaal, Islay (page 440 Bd)

Daniel Campbell, 'Lord of this island', constructed the unusual circular parish church of Kilarrow, which is the village's outstanding building. An inscribed panel on the church tower tells of Mr Campbell and his title, and records that he put up the church in 1769.

It is one of only two round churches in Scotland, and the roof has an extra-strong central pillar for support. According to local lore, the church was built in this shape so that the Devil could find no corner in which to hide.

Bowmore is the largest village on the Island of Islay, in the Inner Hebrides, and the unofficial capital. Whitewashed houses sweep up a hillside from the shore of Loch Indaal, and the streets are wide and well laid out.

Islay has many whisky distilleries, and the one at Bowmore, founded in 1779, is the second oldest on the island. For many years it was owned by the Mutter family, who ran their own steamer the SS *James Mutter* from the port – then the main one of the island. The Mutters emigrated to Canada at the end of the 19th century, but the distillery, which is open to visitors, continues to produce its single-malt whisky.

Many of Bowmore's old tiled and slated houses have been renovated or replaced by modern buildings. The village is one of Islay's chief holiday resorts, and there are two roads going south to the island's main harbour at Port Ellen – a low road near the shores of Laggan Bay, and a high road further inland.

BOXFORD
SUFFOLK

4 miles west of Hadleigh (page 432 Cb)

Entry to the former Anglo-Saxon settlement of 'the ford by the box trees' is downhill from any direction. All the roads twist sharply until they reach the huddle of houses and cottages in pale pink, off-white and light green. The pastel shades are occasionally broken up by red-brick Georgian façades, many of them added to old half-timbered buildings.

The Old School House, with its massive chimney, was a grammar school probably from Tudor times until the 18th century. The high latticed windows in some of the village's buildings show they were probably weavers' halls. Boxford played an important role in the woollen industry in the 16th century, rivalling that of the better-known Lavenham to the north-west.

Butcher's Lane, which runs off Broad Street, is lined by colour-washed timber-framed houses with overhanging upper floors and bowed ancient roofs. Some date back to the 15th century.

Inside the church, which dates from the 14th century, is a touching brass to David Byrde, son of the rector, who died in infancy in 1606. It shows him in his cot with his shoes below. Another memorial records the fate of Elizabeth Hyam, four times widowed, who after a fall 'was at last hastened to her end in her 113th year'.

BRADBOURNE
DERBYSHIRE

4 miles north-east of Ashbourne (page 430 Bd)

An 8th-century Saxon cross gives distinction to this remote village on a hill overlooking the narrow valley of Havenhill Dale Brook. The cross, depicting a scene from the Crucifixion, is one of the finest in Derbyshire. It stands in the churchyard of All Saints, whose square Norman tower, which dates from 1140, stands on a Saxon base.

All Saints contains many monuments to the local Buckston family. One commemorates Thomas Buckston, described as 'one of the oldest officers in H.M. Service' when he died in 1811. The south door of the church tower, with its moulded columns and wedge-shaped arch stones, is one of the best Norman doorways to survive in any part of the county.

Near the churchyard stands Bradbourne Hall, a greystone Elizabethan mansion, which was built on the site of a grange used by the monks of Dunstable Priory who once farmed the lime-

Bradford on Avon near Bath

stone hills of the district. During the Middle Ages, the lords of the manor were the Bradbourne family. Their seat, Lea Hall, still exists 1 mile to the south-west of the village.

The hamlet of Ballidon, with its partly Norman chapel in a field, lies to the north, as do ancient burial mounds on Minninglow Hill – which rises more than 1,000 ft above sea-level.

BRAEMAR
GRAMPIAN
17 miles west of Ballater (page 443 Fc)

At Braemar the Clunie Water, tumbling down from ski slopes of the Cairnwell Pass, flows into the River Dee. The village is flanked by the mountain scenery of the Grampians, with the Cairngorms lying to the north-west. In this rugged setting, Braemar stands 1,100 ft above sea-level, divided into two halves by Clunie Water.

It was there, in 1715, that the Earl of Mar raised the standard of James Stuart, the 'Old Pretender', at the start of the Jacobite rebellion against the English throne. The site of the standard-raising is now covered by the Invercauld Arms Hotel. Braemar Castle was built in 1628 by the 2nd Earl of Mar, and became the residence of the Farquharson family in the 19th century. It is an impressive, turreted building with a round central tower, a star-shaped outer wall and an underground prison. The castle is open to the public during the summer.

When Queen Victoria and Prince Albert bought Balmoral Castle, 6 miles away, it became fashionable to spend summer holidays on Royal Deeside, and many of Braemar's hotels and villas date from that period. Robert Louis Stevenson stayed in the village in 1881 – the cottage can still be seen – and wrote *Treasure Island* there.

The highlight of Braemar's year is the world-renowned Highland Gathering, held every September in the Princess Royal Park, which includes athletics, piping and caber-tossing.

Annual festivals of music and drama are held in the Invercauld Festival Theatre, which was once a church.

BRAMHAM
WEST YORKSHIRE
4 miles south of Wetherby (page 436 Bb)

Close your eyes and it is easy to imagine a stage-coach clattering into this village astride the Great North Road and pulling into The Square. There, passengers would alight for refreshment at the Red Lion or across the way, where a former inn still has a splendid bas-relief of a cart-horse on the wall, with the date 1700.

Old Bramham today has lost little of its charm, though it is cheek-by-jowl with more modern development, and is ideal for exploring on foot. Pleasant little lanes lead off narrow streets bordered by cottages of pale-yellow limestone.

Low Way leads from the central square to the

early-12th-century Norman Church of All Saints. In spring, the spacious churchyard is carpeted with daffodils. Among those who lie there are some of the men who fell at the Battle of Towton in 1461, during the Wars of the Roses. A number of Cavaliers and Roundheads were also buried there nearly two centuries later.

About 2 miles south-west of the village is Bramham Park, a Classical Queen Anne mansion set in 70 acres of gardens and containing fine furniture, pictures and porcelain. It was built between 1698 and 1711 by Robert Benson, 1st Lord Bingley, and is still occupied by his descendants. He is believed to have taken personal charge of the design of the house and garden. A fire severely damaged the house in 1828. Restoration work was carried out at the beginning of this century, and kept as closely as possible to the original design. The grounds are landscaped with pools, cascades and tall hedges in the style of Versailles, the great country palace created by Louis XIV of France in the 17th century. When Bramham Park was laid out, it took something like 30 gardeners to look after the grounds. House and gardens are open to the public in spring and summer.

BRAMPTON, Cambridgeshire (page 432 Bc)
(see Buckden)

BRAMSHAW
HAMPSHIRE
5 miles north of Lyndhurst (page 422 Bb)

Open moorland, with patches of beechwood and holly undergrowth, sprawls across the northern fringe of the New Forest, and Bramshaw lies scattered and hidden among the trees.

Most of the visible houses are at the extremes of the parish – Brook in the south, Nomansland in the north and Fritham in the east.

At Nomansland, so called, it is said, because it was originally built by squatters, red-brick houses sit back from the village green with its cricket pitch. Bramshaw Telegraph is a 419 ft hill about 3 miles west of the village. In the 19th century a semaphore signal stood on the hill, one of a chain of telegraph posts between Portsmouth and the Admiralty in London.

Bramshaw's church, St Peter's, stands on a small hill flanked with rhododendrons. Parts of the church, including the tower, are 13th century, but most of the brick, timber and stone building dates from 1829. There is a memorial to seven men of the parish who died in the *Titanic* disaster in 1912. They had set out as emigrants to seek a new way of life in America.

WANDERING WILDLIFE *The sprawling village of Bramshaw is* ▷ *largely a collection of farms and smallholdings, where pigs and donkeys graze by the roadside along with the inevitable New Forest ponies. The wiry, sure-footed ponies, which range in size from 12 to 13½ hands, are considered to be descendants of the jennets – small Spanish horses – which escaped and swam ashore from the wrecks of the Spanish Armada in the 16th century.*

BRAMSHOTT
HAMPSHIRE

1 mile north of Liphook (page 422 Cb)

Peace and quiet played little part in Bramshott's past. From Roman times until the 18th century the village was a centre for the mining and smelting of Wealden iron; and in the 16th and 17th centuries, when the industry was at its height, the woods were stripped by charcoal-makers, the land was pockmarked with excavations for ore, and even the streams were diverted to power the hammer-mills.

But times have changed. The village rests now, and only a few fragments remain to bear witness to its bustling past. A narrow overgrown lane winding out of the village and over the common leads to Waggoners Wells, three large ponds which were part of a system of waterfalls designed to operate the giant hammers. The wells, and 639 acres of surrounding commons and woodlands, now belong to the National Trust. The last mill in Bramshott was working until 1924, more than 300 years after it was built; but by then it had become a paper-mill, manufacturing the paper used to make postal orders.

The poet Tennyson knew Waggoners Wells, though in his day they were known as Wakener's Wells. He visited them one day in the summer of 1860, wrote a small poem about them, and so fell in love with the area that he had a house built on Black Down, over the border into Sussex.

The Church of St Mary dates partly from the 13th century, as does the manor house near by. The nave and aisles, and the broach spire, are Victorian. Ghostly carriages are said to rumble by night over the roads around the village, particularly along the lane to Waggoners Wells.

BRANSCOMBE, Devon (page 419 Eb)
(see Salcombe Regis)

BRAUGHING
HERTFORDSHIRE

7 miles west of Bishop's Stortford (page 426 Cb)

The village green at Braughing – pronounced 'Braffing' – is reached by a ford over the River Quin which has two hazards, ducks and a tendency to flood. Downstream, where the Quin joins the River Rib, part of the bank fell in a few years ago, to reveal the foundations of a Roman villa: a reminder of the days when, after St Albans, Braughing was one of the most important Roman centres in Hertfordshire.

Beyond the ford, the road opens on to the green, backed by pollarded trees and the late-Victorian shop. To the left, there is a charming grouping of houses about the church; first, the white pargeting of Causeway House, then, on a sharp half-twist on the road, an 1860 cottage of timber and herringbone brick. Round the bend, Church End contains several brightly washed cottages and one superb example of the pargeter's craft in dark blue and white.

VICTORIAN EXUBERANCE *Famed chiefly nowadays for its sausages, Braughing was for centuries an important road junction, reflected in the grandeur of its church and some of its houses. Here, a Victorian architect has summed up the ages in a joyous conglomeration of Tudor chimneys, herringbone brick and lattice.*

The sumptuous interior of the church belongs almost entirely to the early 15th century. At the altar end the blue and gold ceiling backs a magnificent pair of stiff-winged angels. Each beam end is supported by a knight, a lady, a monk, a demon or, in one instance, a frog-like creature in a waistcoat, all carved in oak. Beside the altar, one above the other, recline the effigies of two Jacobean brothers. Every detail of their armour is perfect, and both have similar, strong faces. Alongside them are an angel blowing bubbles, signifying the pointlessness of earthly vanity, and Father Time. Near by, the Freeman family – a name that still occurs in the district – is commemorated in a fine series of 18th-century portrait medallions. There are some interesting houses at the end of the village, including The Gables, with a gallows sign proclaiming that it was built 'Circa 1400'.

BRAUNSTON
LEICESTERSHIRE

2 miles south-west of Oakham (page 430 Cc)

Two superb cedars overhang the tiny village green, which has a flourishing lime tree planted in 1897 to mark Queen Victoria's Diamond Jubilee. Braunston's rural character is preserved by a stream, a continuation of the River Gwash, which runs through the village on its course towards the reservoir known as Rutland Water, the biggest man-made lake in Britain.

The village church, All Saints – with its considerable remains of medieval wall-paintings – dates in part from the 12th and 13th centuries. Outside is a grotesque stone carving which is probably an ancient fertility goddess.

LANGHAM Inside the church at Langham – 3½ miles by road from Braunston – is a memorial to the 1st Airborne Division which attended service there before being dropped at Arnhem in September 1944.

BREAMORE
HAMPSHIRE

3 miles north of Fordingbridge (page 422 Bb)

A Saxon church, a maze, a 16th-century manor open to the public and a countryside museum combine to make Breamore – or 'Bremmer' as it is pronounced locally – a splendid visitors' village. Most of the cottages, built of typical New Forest brick and tile and with neat garden hedges and paddocks, cling to lanes fringing the common, known as the Marsh, though it is not at all soggy. Local tradition has it that Henry II instigated the murder of Thomas Becket while riding across the Marsh, even though most historians assert that his fateful raging against 'that turbulent priest' took place in France.

On the higher ground behind the Marsh lie the farms of the Breamore Estate and the Elizabethan Breamore House, home of the Hulse family since 1748. It contains a fine collection of paintings and furniture, and an absorbing Countryside and Carriage Museum has been established in the grounds and in the old stables. The museum shows the historical development of agricultural tools and machinery, and features old steam-engines and reconstructed workshops, including a smithy. Both house and museum are open to the public in spring and summer.

On the other side of the manor's boundary wall is the ancient parish church, built about the year 1000. A Saxon inscription on one of the tower arches has been translated as 'Here the Covenant becomes manifest to thee'. The formation of some of the letters in the inscription helps to date the church to within the reigns of Ethelred and Canute – about 980.

The maze, or Miz-Maze as it is called, is cut into the turf of a small coppice about 1 mile away. It is believed to be Anglo-Saxon and forms an intricate pattern 87 ft in diameter. Such mazes were sometimes constructed near monastic houses as a penance for monks, who had to crawl round them on their hands and knees.

BREDON
HEREFORD AND WORCESTER

3 miles north-east of Tewkesbury (page 425 Eb)

High above the River Avon, a slender church spire rises from the meadows and acts as a landmark for Bredon. The main village street, with the church and its lych-gate in the background, is lined with charming thatched black-and-white cottages, with here and there buildings of Cotswold stone or mellow brick.

The church, dedicated to St Giles, has examples of the work of most periods from the Norman Conquest to the Reformation. Particularly notable are the Norman west front, north porch and nave, the Early English south chapel and the collection of 14th-century heraldic tiles in the chancel. These recall many important local families, including the Berkeleys, Despensers, Hastings and Mortimers. Among the wealth of monuments and memorials is a magnificent 17th-century canopied tomb, in marble and alabaster. It has splendid effigies of Sir Giles Reed, his wife Catherine, and their six sons and two daughters. The family were Bredon benefactors and founded the almshouses at the end of the main street.

Near the church are some exceptionally fine buildings: the Elizabethan rectory; the Old Mansion, an outstanding example of 17th-century red brick with mullioned windows and dormers; and the elegant 18th-century Manor House.

To the west of the Manor House is the 600-year-old Bredon Tithe Barn. It is 132 ft long – one of the largest stone barns in England. In one of its two porches is an upper room with a fireplace. The property is now owned by the National Trust and is open to the public.

Bredon has two inns, the 17th-century Royal Oak and the Fox and Hounds, a thatched, half-timbered building dating from the 16th century. The novelist John Moore, who died in 1967, was a frequent visitor to the Fox and Hounds.

BREEDON ON THE HILL

Breedon Church rules the Leicestershire landscape from its hill that has borne in turn stronghold, monastery and priory. The church's remarkable Saxon carvings are a legacy from the 8th century, and may well have been inspired by the illuminated manuscripts for which the monastery was famed.

The church on the hill.

Saxon carvings.

BREDWARDINE
HEREFORD AND WORCESTER

11 miles west of Hereford (page 425 Db)

In the west of Herefordshire, near the Welsh border, the peaceful village of Bredwardine sprawls down a hillside to the church beside the River Wye. Its name comes from Old English, and, appropriately, means 'place on the slope of a hill'. In this quiet, rural setting the Reverend Francis Kilvert wrote his mid-Victorian diary of parish life.

Kilvert, son of a Wiltshire clergyman, became Vicar of Bredwardine in 1877, but already knew and loved the area, having spent several years at nearby Clyro. He died of peritonitis at the age of 38, only a month after his marriage in 1879, and is buried in the churchyard. His marble cross bears the inscription 'He being dead · yet speaketh'.

The church itself, on a knoll overlooking orchards and cattle pastures, goes back to the 11th century. The south doorway and nave are original Norman, as is the huge font hewn from a single rock.

Most of the village homes cluster near the 17th-century Red Lion Hotel, a fine red-brick house. It is a good base for walkers exploring this serene border backwater, and for anglers congregating along the Wye near the village's distinctive six-arch river bridge.

BREEDON ON THE HILL
LEICESTERSHIRE

5 miles north-east of Ashby de la Zouch (page 430 Bc)

The great age of the village is apparent even in the tautology of its name. *Bre* means 'hill' in the Celtic tongue of the pre-Roman Britons, *dun* means the same thing in Anglo-Saxon; Hill hill-on-the-Hill, in fact.

The feature that attracted the attention of so many different peoples is a massive 180 ft high limestone bluff that has been topped in turn by an Iron Age fort, a 7th-century monastery sacked by the Danes 200 years later, a 12th-century priory and the present church. Within the ancient defences, known locally as The Bulwarks, a cemetery thought to be connected with the old Saxon monks has been discovered.

The church also contains one of the most remarkable examples of Saxon carving in northern Europe – a 60 ft fragmented frieze, probably of the late 8th century, depicting leaves and geometrical patterns, armed men on horseback, a demure Virgin and an enchanting angel. It is thought that the frieze was hidden and preserved by the Saxon monks after the destruction of their monastery, and was later discovered and set up in its present position by the Augustinians.

The village itself is gathered around one side of the hill, the other being occupied by an awesome limestone quarry. There are three pubs, two of which, the Holly Bush and the Lime Kiln, date from Tudor times.

BRENCHLEY
KENT

2 miles south of Paddock Wood (page 423 Eb)

Houses faced with white weather-boarding are spaced round an oak in the centre of a tiny green at Brenchley, which stands on a hill in the High Weald. A half-timbered house opposite the war memorial was once a workhouse and dates from the early 17th century. The Old Vicarage, a white weather-boarded cottage by the churchyard lych-gate, claims a date of 1320. A timber-framed butcher's shop stands on the east side of the green. The most impressive building is the heavily restored Old Palace, a timber-framed Tudor house now divided into cottages and shops. It was once the manorial home of the Roberts family, whose brasses can be seen in the church. Clipped yew trees, 350 years old, line the path to the sandstone church, which has some features of the 13th and 14th centuries, including a 14th-century west doorway.

Around the village are some fine old houses including Brenchley Manor, a 16th-century half-timbered structure about a quarter of a mile north. Another half-timbered mansion, Marle Place, just over 1 mile south, has a prominent cluster of chimneys. It was built in 1619, but has 19th-century tile hanging.

BRENT KNOLL
SOMERSET

2 miles north-east of Burnham-on-Sea (page 421 Bc)

Iron Age people who lived in the 4 acre fort on top of Brent Knoll enjoyed a sweeping view from its 449 ft eminence over what is now lowland Somerset and its enclosing hills.

The earthwork on the Knoll is thought to have been re-fortified during the Danish invasions of the 9th century. The *Anglo-Saxon Chronicle* records a battle in which men of Somerset and Dorset banded together to defeat the Danes in AD 845 – perhaps near Battleborough Farm under the southern flank of the Knoll, which is said to have been a farm since the 9th century.

Brent Knoll village, sometimes known as South Brent, has some fine old stone houses, set in orchards and well-maintained gardens. But the village's great pride is the Church of St Michael, with its Norman doorway, carved oak roof and three remarkable carved bench-ends. The story goes that some time in the Middle Ages the Abbot of Glastonbury tried to seize revenues from the parish priest, who succeeded in foiling him – and the bench-ends were carved to celebrate the village's victory.

The first shows a fox dressed in the abbot's robes rounding up a group of animals and a flock of geese; in the second, the victims are shown in revolt, stripping the abbot of his robes and putting him in the stocks; and, finally, he is hanged, with the geese pulling on the rope. To add to the insult, the abbot's monks are carved with pigs' heads.

BRETFORTON
HEREFORD AND WORCESTER

4 miles east of Evesham (page 425 Fb)

Hidden away in the Vale of Evesham lies the mellow village of Bretforton. Its documented history goes back more than 1,200 years to a Saxon deed of 714. The Saxons called it Brotfortun – 'the ford with planks' – possibly a reference to a footbridge alongside the ford. The village is set in a rich patchwork of fields and orchards, halfway between Evesham and the steep western edge of the Cotswold Hills. These hills supplied the honey-coloured stone for many of Bretforton's buildings. One of its showpieces is the Fleece, a quaint old inn tucked in a corner of The Cross at the heart of the village. The inn was originally a farmhouse, believed to date from the 14th century, and is one of the few inns owned by the National Trust. Creepers ramble over its oak-beamed walls, framing lead-lined window-panes under a roof of mossy Cotswold stone. Inside, on the stone floor, there are 'witch marks' designed to keep out evil spirits – a reminder of the inn's medieval past. Among its antiques, many worthy of a museum, is a 48-piece set of Stuart pewter.

The Fleece shares its corner of The Cross with

in the 1530s. Elizabeth I later gave the manor to her favourite courtier, the Earl of Leicester. The church, part of whose decoration seems to have been inspired by that of Wells Cathedral, has round medieval piers with capitals carved in fantastical designs, and monuments to the Ashwin family, whose links with the village and Manor House go back to Tudor times.

An avenue dark with yews links the churchyard to the Manor House, a handsome gabled mansion which dates from the 14th century but was rebuilt in the early 1600s. The old village stocks stand in the grounds. Bretforton Hall, on the opposite side of the road, stands out against the village's mainly traditional architecture. Built in 1830, it is an elegantly eccentric stone house with a balcony, arched windows, ornate ironwork and a battlemented tower. The hall's neighbours include a cottage with a dovecot built into its northern gable. The nearby Evesham road is flanked by several other cottages in which gold or pale-grey stonework blends with thatch and oak beams.

Facing the churchyard is the 130-year-old village school, crowned with a bell-cote. Beside it is a row of cottages with stone-mullioned windows, one with a front doorway little more than chin high. Bridge Street, at the western end of the churchyard, is another attractive blend of stone, brick and thatch leading to a stream which joins the River Avon near Evesham.

Bretforton's Main Street approaches the village square, known as The Cross, swinging right and left before opening out on to the square. Part of the area is now a car park, but the rest is still green, crossed by footpaths and roads. On one part of the green is a solitary tree ringed by an iron seat, from which the Fleece and the church can be admired at leisure. A cul-de-sac off Main Street leads to Bretforton House Farm, where brickwork combines with stone corners to create a façade at once Classical and sturdy.

VIRTUE TRIUMPHANT *One of the medieval capitals in the Church of St Leonard depicts a gleeful dragon devouring St Margaret. All but her feet and the hem of her dress have vanished into the maw of the creature, yet it seems unaware that she has already cut her way out with her Cross, and is emerging, triumphant and serene, from its side. Other piers in the church are decorated with lively representations of heads and trumpets.*

NATIONAL FLEECE *When Henry Byrd converted his ancestors' farmhouse into the Fleece Inn in 1848, he dispensed good ale and cider between 5.30 a.m. and 10.30 p.m. each day. His great-grand-daughter, Miss Taplin, maintained a similar service, though at more conventional hours, until she died, aged 83, in 1977. She left the inn, and its furniture, pewter and pottery, to the National Trust.*

Byrd's Cottage, another delightful old building with walls leaning at gravity-defying angles. A carved face guards one of its doors.

St Leonard's Church has stood at the northern end of The Cross for nearly 800 years. Like the rest of the village, it was the property of Evesham Abbey until Henry VIII dissolved the monasteries

BRIGHTLING
EAST SUSSEX

6 miles north-west of Battle (page 423 Eb)

The village is a small, quiet community of stone and brick cottages in the High Weald. Its landscape is dominated by the eccentric buildings and constructions of a local Member of Parliament known as Mad Jack Fuller, who died in 1834 and is buried beneath a pyramid which he had built in the churchyard in 1810. Legend asserts that Fuller sits inside the 60 ft pyramid, wearing a top hat and holding a bottle of claret.

The grounds of Brightling Park are adorned with a rotunda and a Classical temple which Fuller had built. He is also responsible for a 40 ft stone obelisk, now known as Brightling Needle, on the highest point of the district. In order to win a bet that the spire of the neighbouring Dallington Church could be seen from his home, he built a folly tower, sugar-loaf in shape like the church spire, within sight of his house. It still stands in a copse beside the road to the southeast.

BRILL
BUCKINGHAMSHIRE

6 miles north-west of Thame (page 426 Bb)

Behind an ancient windmill the village is grouped around a green and a square, where many of the dwellings have Georgian facades built on to older buildings.

The local clay used to build these cottages and houses also provided the material for pottery, and excavations have uncovered kilns dating back to about 1200. There are examples of Brill pottery in the Ashmolean Museum at Oxford and the County Museum at Aylesbury.

An Elizabethan manor house overlooks the square, and next to it are 17th-century stables with oval windows. Brill's three inns – the Red Lion, the Sun, and the Pheasant – all date from the 17th century or earlier. The writer Roald Dahl was a frequent visitor to the Pheasant, where he collected material for his short stories by listening to local yarns.

All roads into the village ascend steep hills, and one, Tram Hill, is a link with the days when a railway connected Brill with the heart of London. In 1872 the Duke of Buckingham had a tramway built which ran from the bottom of the hill to the main line at Quainton, 6 miles away. The line was taken over by the Metropolitan Railway in 1891, and until 1935 trains ran from Brill direct to London's Baker Street Station.

◆

HILLTOP LANDMARK *Brill stands 603 ft above sea-level, and its windmill looks across the flat countryside of Buckinghamshire and Oxfordshire beyond. The mill dates from 1689, and is one of the oldest post-mills in England. Its machinery is intact and can be seen on Sunday afternoons. Below the mill are grassy mounds thrown up when the ground was quarried for the clay from which the bricks of Brill were made.*

BROAD HAVEN
DYFED

6 miles west of Haverfordwest (page 424 Ab)

As its name suggests, this village, backed by low hills that are typical of inland Pembrokeshire, runs gently down to a wide, sandy shore. The firm, gentle slope of beach is set between spectacularly folded cliffs and looks out over the great semi-circle of St Brides Bay. Dramatic sunsets bring many summer days to a breathtaking close as sea and sky are fused into a glory of reds and golds.

Broad Haven's beach, which offers safe bathing, especially for children, has been attracting visitors since the 19th century, when the village became a small but fashionable resort for holiday-makers from Haverfordwest and Milford Haven. Many new houses have been built since the 1950s, but the Victorian atmosphere lingers in such places as Trafalgar Terrace and Webbs Hill, where a neat little chapel built in 1841 stands beside a sparkling stream.

The National Park Information Centre, which stands in a large car park set back from the shore, provides a wealth of information about this spectacular National Park coastline. The car park is also the starting point for guided walks that combine exercise with education. The village should not be confused with the National Park's other Broad Haven – a dune-backed bay on the south coast of Dyfed, near Bosherston.

LITTLE HAVEN Steep, twisting lanes snake down between high banks to Little Haven, and the clifftop road from neighbouring Broad Haven is particularly dramatic. A short walk leads to a rocky headland with superb views across St Brides Bay.

BROADHEMBURY
DEVON

5 miles north-west of Honiton (page 419 Ec)

On a summer evening, the sound of ancient church bells pealing out over the village seems to turn back the pages of history. Tucked away down leafy lanes only 5 miles from a busy holiday route, Broadhembury breathes an atmosphere of serenity and timelessness. Many of its buildings date from the 16th century; most are buff-washed, and all but a few nestle beneath a traditional covering of heavy thatch from which quaint little semi-dormer windows emerge. The builders mainly used flint and cob, a remarkably strong mixture of clay, straw and animal hair.

Hembury Fort, the finest prehistoric earthwork in Devon, crowns a steep wooded hill to the south-east. Excavations suggest that the fort was a Neolithic settlement of about 3000 BC, and was resettled and used by Iron Age dwellers until Roman times, almost 2,000 years later. Archaeologists have also uncovered traces of a huge western gateway and cobbled causeway.

The noble old Church of St Andrew, dedicated in 1259, stands at the top of the gently sloping main street and overlooks the village square. The elegant church tower, 100 ft high, is decorated with gargoyles and a golden weather-cock. The church, which has a finely carved stone porch, contains many memorials to members of the Drewe family, whose links with Broadhembury go back to the early 17th century. Among those buried in the church is Francis Drewe, who died in 1675 and is watched over by two winged cherubs, one clutching an hour-glass and the other a skull. Another of the memorials is to Augustus Montague Toplady, who wrote the hymn *Rock of Ages*. He was Vicar of Broadhembury from 1768 until he died ten years later at the age of 38.

The most memorable buildings in the village are scattered round an area where the main street divides, immediately below the churchyard. The earliest parts of Church Gate Cottage, with its leaded windows and slate roof, are believed to be as old, or even older, than the church itself.

A 15th-century inn, the Drewe Arms, occupies the south side of the square against a background of chestnut trees and larches. Opposite the inn are two gently curving terraces of thatched cottages. Just above the terraces, set back from the road in a garden where rhododendrons bloom in late spring and early summer, stands Broadhembury House, a mansion-in-miniature with a thatched roof, leaded windows and walls tangled with wisteria. Another fine private house, the Grange, stands just outside the village. It was completed in 1610 by Sir Thomas Drewe, son of the Sergeant-at-Law to Elizabeth I.

BROADWAY
HEREFORD AND WORCESTER

5 miles south-east of Evesham (page 425 Fb)

Not without reason has Broadway been called 'the show village of England'. The long, broad main street is lined with gracious houses and cottages, built of the honey-coloured Cotswold stone and in the style of the 16th and 17th-century builders who knew best how to use this

PRIDE OF THE COTSWOLDS *The cottages in Bankside, Broadway, are typical of England's most famous 'show village'. There, the art of the builders in Cotswold stone can be seen at its best, with walls, tiles and even the stone mullions of the windows seeming to glow with a golden radiance.*

attractive material. There is a pleasant lack of uniformity in the houses that front the green-verged roads. Steep gables thrust their shoulders above the roofline of dormer-windowed cottages, bay windows peer out from under stone tiling, and here and there thatch and half-timbering soften the bluffness of weathered stone.

In the centre of the village is a wide green, overlooked by the Broadway Hotel. The Lygon Arms Hotel, which dates back to the 16th century, still looks like the large private house it once was. Both Charles I and Oliver Cromwell stayed there at different times.

Near to the Lygon Arms is the factory of Gordon Russell Ltd, the furniture manufacturer who began by repairing the furniture for the hotel in 1904 and went on to build up a business in hand-made furniture.

Broadway's High Street climbs gently from the green for almost 1 mile. Then it steepens at Fish Hill, topped by the odd-looking Fish Inn. The building was originally a summer-house built on the estate of a local landowner in the 18th century, and has a sun-dial on its roof. The inn stands at 800 ft above sea-level, but further on along Buckle Street the ground rises to more than 1,000 ft and is crowned by one of the best-known landmarks in the Midlands – Broadway Tower. It was built in 1800 by the Earl of Coventry as a glorious folly, with no other purpose than that it could be seen from his family seat at Worcester, almost 20 miles away.

About 1 mile from Broadway Tower is the old Church of St Eadburgha, dating from the 12th century. It is one of two parish churches in Broadway. The other, St Michael's, was built in 1839 and is near the village green.

BROADWINDSOR
DORSET

3 miles west of Beaminster (page 421 Bb)

Some 40 cottages and houses, most of them dating from the 17th century, are the pride of Broadwindsor. They are listed as of historic interest by the Royal Commission on Historical Monuments, and perhaps the most notable of them stands in the centre of the village, at the crossroads near the church. It is a plain, tiled, cream-washed cottage in a terrace, and it bears a plaque stating that Charles II slept there on the night of September 23, 1651, when fleeing to France after his defeat by Cromwell's forces at the Battle of Worcester. The cottage, now a private house, was then part of the old Castle Inn. The king's stay is also commemorated by a plaque in the church.

Broadwindsor is large and compact, and is built up of terraces amid the west Dorset hills. Houses at one level look down on the chimneys of those below. The 19th-century brownstone Church of St John the Baptist stands on a plateau overlooking the village. It has a 15th-century tower, a seven-sided Jacobean pulpit, and an 18th-century picture, on boards, of Moses and Aaron.

A prehistoric ridgeway cuts across the parish, which contains two 19th-century turnpike tollhouses. Among visitors to Broadwindsor were the poet William Wordsworth and his sister Dorothy, who lived at Racedown House, on the western outskirts, from 1795 to 1797. They both wrote about the village, and Dorothy described it as: 'The place dearest to my recollection upon the whole surface of the Island.'

BROMPTON REGIS
SOMERSET

10 miles south of Minehead (page 420 Ab)

Ghida, mother of King Harold, is said to have refused to surrender Brompton Regis – then called *Brunan tun*, 'the enclosure by the Brendon Hills' – to William the Conqueror's forces after she escaped from the siege of Exeter in 1068. She was allowed to live on there in her manor, under a form of house arrest, until her death when she was buried in the Saxon church there. Both the manor and its little wooden church were razed after her death.

Then nothing much of interest to the outside world happened in this tiny, remote village for about 900 years – until the winter of 1978–9, when a new 161 ft high dam on the Haddeo river came into operation and water began to flow into the 4,500 million gallon Wimbleball Reservoir, 1½ miles to the east. The main purpose of the 370 acre man-made lake is to supply water to the Taunton, Yeovil and Bridgwater districts of Somerset, and the Exeter and Tiverton areas in Devon, but it has already been stocked with brown and rainbow trout, there is a sailing club established, and the reservoir now forms part of the Exmoor National Park.

The village, which has several cottages dating back to the 16th century, is penned in by steep hills. From the porch of St Mary's Church there is a splendid view of 1,163 ft Haddon Hill, 1½ miles to the south. The church was rebuilt in the 15th century, but the tower and some features are 200 years older. Inside, is this touching poem on a 17th-century brass memorial to a girl of 19:

Reader, Tis worth thy Paines to know
Who was interred here belowe.
Here Lyes good nature, Piettie, Witt,
Though small in volume yet most fairly writ.
She died young, and so oft times Tis seene
The fruit God loves He's pleased to pick it greene.

BROOKLAND, Kent (page 423 Eb)
(see Appledore)

BUCKDEN
CAMBRIDGESHIRE

4 miles south-west of Huntingdon (page 432 Bc)

Two coaching inns, the black-and-white 16th-century Lion and the red-brick 17th-century George, face each other across Buckden's wide High Street – a reminder that this quiet thoroughfare was once part of the main road from London to the north. Most of the houses are brick; many are of the Jacobean and Georgian periods, but the village is dominated by the 15th-century palace of the Bishops of Lincoln. Behind its red-brick walls stand a Tudor gatehouse and massive, turreted tower, all that remains of the original palace used by the bishops from the early Middle Ages until 1838.

Adjoining Buckden Palace is the contrasting greystone church where Laurence Sterne, author of *Tristram Shandy*, was ordained in 1736. In the churchyard are buried two uncles of the nine-day queen, Lady Jane Grey.

BRAMPTON, 2½ miles north-east of Buckden, has houses in an agreeable jumble of styles around its green. Samuel Pepys lived in a farmhouse there, revisited it often, and fled there from the plague in 1665.

BUCKLAND IN THE MOOR
DEVON

3 miles north-west of Ashburton (page 419 Db)

The moor is Dartmoor, and the tiny village clings to the steeply sloping banks of the River Dart in one of its most romantic reaches. A straggle of thatched, greystone cottages and a medieval church built of stone from the moor hide among groves of beeches in sheltered hollows. Grey lichen clings to the trees, and the rocks on the river bank are half buried in moss and ferns.

St Peter's is medieval, and typical of the moorland churches – ruggedly built and with a sturdy tower. Instead of numbers, the church clock has letters which read MY DEAR MOTHER. A local landowner, William Whitley, had them placed there in the late 1920s. Inside the church is a screen with medieval paintings on its panels.

A mile or so to the south-west is Holne, where two 15th-century bridges cross the Dart. The writer Charles Kingsley was born in the vicarage in 1819. Holne had a Ram Festival in pagan times, when a ram was ritually slaughtered on a granite stone and then roasted and eaten by the villagers. The feast, traditionally held in midsummer, is occasionally revived.

BUCKLERS HARD
HAMPSHIRE

2 miles south-east of Beaulieu (page 422 Bb)

Many of the mighty men-of-war used by Nelson in the Napoleonic Wars were built at Bucklers Hard in the 18th and early part of the 19th centuries, when it was the home of one of the country's busiest shipyards. A double row of brick cottages, once the homes of shipwrights, stand on either side of a broad roadway leading down to the quay on the Beaulieu River.

The great days of Bucklers Hard are recalled in its maritime museum, part of which was a former inn. John, Duke of Montagu, who owned Beaulieu Manor, planned to import sugar from the West Indies, and created the shipbuilding industry to construct the vessels he needed for the venture. Oak from the New Forest was plentiful and there was an ironworks at nearby Sowley Pond, where a powerful forge-hammer was operated by a water-wheel. The river anchorage had a hard bottom, an advantage that was incorporated in the name of the flourishing shipyard. But Montagu's venture failed when the French colonised the islands, and the shipyard lay idle until the 1740s, when warships were needed for the war with France.

Fifty-six ships for the Royal Navy were built there between 1745 and 1818, including the 64-gun *Agamemnon* and two other vessels in Nelson's victorious fleet at Trafalgar in 1805 – the battle that ended with the admiral's death. Parish records describe how as many as 4,000 spectators would assemble on launching days, when 'every vehicle and saddle horse within miles was in motion'. Stacks of oak timbers, piled for season-

ing in and around the town, were higher than the rooftops.

Decline set in with the end of the Napoleonic Wars. The shipyards closed and vacant houses crumbled into ruin. Still standing there is a fine old brick mansion which was the home of Henry Adams, the master builder of Bucklers Hard. The house is now the Master Builder's House Hotel. Next door to the hotel is an unusual chapel; it is a consecrated room in a cottage, and can hold no more than about 30 people.

Yachtsmen now moor on the river and pleasure boats ply from the quay.

BUCKNELL
SALOP

4 miles east of Knighton (page 429 Ca)

Steep, conifer-clad hills shelter the village, which is largely of 'rustic' architecture. A cottage near the church has a thatched roof, and there are substantial houses of pleasant, grey-green stone.

Bucknell is divided by a small, attractive river, the Redlake. It flows past the little Church of St Mary, which dates from Norman times. Inside, by the door, is a tub-shaped Norman font. On the west wall are 'benefaction boards', recording annual gifts of 'four grey cloth cloaks' to 'four poor old women' of the parish – and four smocks for their male counterparts.

From the church, a narrow lane follows the Redlake downstream. It passes farms, hay-filled barns, and black-and-white cottages. Near by is the station, built in 1860. With its freestone walls and Tudor-style chimneys it is a rich example of 19th-century railway Gothic.

A neighbouring hill, Coxall Knoll, is crowned with the remains of an Iron Age fort, one of several sites said to be where the heroic British chieftain Caractacus made his last stand against the Romans in the 1st century AD. The actual site has never been confirmed. Caractacus escaped after the battle, but he was finally betrayed by a supposed ally and taken to Rome. Although his life was spared by the Emperor Claudius, there is no record of him gaining his freedom.

Bucklers Hard's wide main street rolls down to the harbour.

A blossom-capped doorway in the village.

Figurehead in the museum.

Master Builder's drainpipe.

WHERE THE WOODEN WALLS OF ENGLAND WERE BUILT

The main street of Bucklers Hard was made wide enough to allow great oaks from the New Forest to be rolled right down it and into the harbour. Many thousands were – 2,000 alone for the building of the mighty 64-gun Agamemnon, *commanded by Nelson from 1793 to 1796. He called her his favourite ship and later she fought in his fleet at Trafalgar. There is a fine model of her in the local Maritime Museum. Between 1745 and 1822 this now-tiny hamlet launched 56 of England's 'wooden wall' warships and 15 merchantmen – most of them from the slipways of the shipbuilder Henry Adams and his sons Balthazar and Edward. Until his death, at the age of 91, Henry would spy on his workmen from a crow's-nest on his house. The house is now a hotel.*

BUNBURY
CHESHIRE

7 miles north-west of Nantwich (page 429 Dc)

Like many Cheshire villages, Bunbury is a cheerful mixture of styles and periods ranging from timber-framed Tudor cottages to Georgian brick with a sprinkling of black-and-white farmhouses. The streets are narrow and twisting and the village grew from three separate settlements. The original village developed around the church; there was further growth in Tudor times around the common; the final expansion took place at Bunbury Heath when the common land there was enclosed.

The church has been built or added to four times. The first occasion was in the 14th century when Sir Hugh Calveley established a college in the church. In the 16th century the top parts of the tower were added, together with the battlements and the Ridley family chapel. The church was restored in Victorian times and again after a German bomb destroyed the roof during the Second World War. Two important monuments survived both events; one to Sir Hugh Calveley, and the other to Sir George Beeston who was born in the last year of the 15th century and lived to see the beginning of the 17th. He fought in the army of Henry VIII in France and 60 years later, at the age of 89, commanded the *Dreadnought* in the battle against the Spanish Armada.

One mile north-east of the church, on the road to Alpraham, is Bunbury Locks, once an important stopping place on the Chester Canal, which was built in the 1770s to link Nantwich with Chester. There are two locks, and each – like all the others on the Chester–Nantwich stretch of what eventually became the Shropshire Union Canal – is twice the width of the narrow 7 ft locks common to most of the British canal system.

Beside the locks stands the canal warehouse, now a workshop, and near by is a long, low building in which canal cruisers are built. This was originally the stables where changes of barge horses were kept.

BURGHCLERE
HAMPSHIRE

4 miles south of Newbury (page 422 Bc)

Hazel, Fiver and the rest of the rabbits who made their home on Watership Down in Richard Adams's famous novel might well have looked down from their warren on to Burghclere: for the real Watership Down stands just south-east of the village, on the great scarp of the north Hampshire Downs. Close by is a very different yet equally evocative stronghold – Ladle Hill, a former Iron Age camp raised on a high point of the Downs.

Burghclere was once an important wool village, producing fleeces for the cloth and blanket mills of Highclere and Newbury. Later, lime became its source of income. Although the lime kilns are now disused, and have been for about the last 40

years, traces of them are still visible at Old Burghclere, ivy-hung and half buried in vegetation. The cottages where the kiln workers used to live still stand near by, and the fields around the village are pitted with shallow depressions – the marl pits from which chalk was dug to spread over the arable land.

Watercress beds are another of Burghclere's obsolete industries. Vestiges of the old beds still line some of the streams which flow down to the little River Enborne.

The artist Stanley Spencer spent six years painting the murals in the Sandham Memorial Chapel, now a National Trust property. The paintings depict scenes from his experiences as a Royal Army Medical Corps orderly, and also as an infantryman in Macedonia in the First World War. The subject matter is at once macabre and moving, illuminated by flashes of bitter humour – the reactions of an exceptionally gifted man to the cataclysm of war. Admission to the chapel is free, and the key can be obtained from the almshouses next door.

BURNHAM THORPE
NORFOLK

9 miles north-west of Fakenham (page 432 Cd)

The village inn at Burnham Thorpe is called the Lord Nelson. The village hall also bears the great admiral's name, while in the church, a cross in the chancel arch and a lectern are both made from timbers taken from HMS *Victory*. In this way Burnham Thorpe pays tribute to Horatio Nelson, who was born in the village in 1758.

A roadside plaque and a sign half a mile south of the village mark the site of the rectory where Nelson was born. His father, Edmund, was the rector of Burnham Thorpe until his death in 1802; in the following year, the admiral's birthplace was demolished and replaced by the present rectory. Horatio returned to live in the village with his wife from 1787 until 1793, when he was given command of HMS *Agamemnon*.

The village has a wide green overlooked by brick-and-flint Georgian buildings and the 13th-century Church of All Saints. The church was restored in Nelson's honour in the 19th century, and there is a marble bust of the hero above his father's tomb.

The naval theme is maintained in the east end of the church where the flags flown by the battle-cruiser HMS *Indomitable* at the Battle of Jutland are displayed at the chancel crossing. On the west wall is the crest of the Second World War battleship HMS *Nelson*, and her white ensigns are in the western arch of the tower. There is a fine 15th-century brass in the chancel floor to Sir William Calthorp, who lived at the Manor House.

At one time Burnham Thorpe was one of seven Burnham parishes, and the largest remaining one, Burnham Market, lies about 1 mile to the north-west. It has a large green enclosed by gracious 18th-century houses. Burnham Overy, to the north-west, has an early-18th-century watermill by the River Burn, and a church, St Clement's, with a Norman central tower.

BURNSALL
NORTH YORKSHIRE

10 miles north-west of Ilkley (page 436 Bc)

A massive five-arched bridge over the River Wharfe leads to Burnsall, where a broad village green with a maypole spreads out along the river bank, which is shaded by trees.

Burnsall's narrow main street winds up through the village from the river past an imposing Methodist church, built in 1901, to the Church of St Wilfrid. A lych-gate leads to the churchyard, and inside the church there are fragments of 10th-century 'hog-back' gravestones. The church itself was rebuilt in 1859, but still retains its 16th-century tower. Beside the church and set back from the road is Burnsall's most attractive building, the old grammar school, now a Church of England primary school. It dates from 1602, and looks like a manor house with its gabled porch and rows of mullioned windows. The school was founded by Sir William Craven, who was born in Burnsall parish around 1548 and became Lord Mayor of London in 1610.

Every August, crowds gather at Burnsall for a day of athletic events whose main attraction is the fell race from the village green to the top of Burnsall Fell and back.

BURPHAM
WEST SUSSEX

4 miles north of Littlehampton (page 422 Db)

A secluded collection of flint and brick cottages, some hidden behind hedges and flint walls, stands at the end of a 3 mile long lane which winds north from the Arundel to Worthing road. The lane climbs between the houses until it reaches an open space by a part-Norman church and an 18th-century inn. Tracks radiate northwards to the Downs and link the main village with outlying farm hamlets.

The 12th and 13th-century church, St Mary's, is built almost entirely of local flint, though Roman tiles appear here and there in its fabric and part of a Roman pavement was uncovered near the north transept. The impressive, spacious interior is white and airy, with elaborately carved pillars. By the churchyard is a timber-framed cottage. Beyond is a recreation ground, merging into a grassy plain, with a footpath leading by steep steps down to the river.

BURRINGTON
AVON

10 miles east of Weston-super-Mare (page 421 Cc)

More than 200 years ago, the Reverend Augustus Toplady took shelter from a storm beneath overhanging rocks in Burrington Combe. The experience inspired him to write the hymn *Rock of Ages*. Burrington Combe clefts deep into the Mendip Hills for a distance of 2 miles and is flanked by towering cliffs with caves that provided shelter for prehistoric man.

The village lies at the northern end of the combe and clusters around the late-15th-century Church of Holy Trinity, with its tower and spirelet. The gardens of the cottages are bright with flowers in spring and summer. The ramparts of an Iron Age fort stand on Dolebury Warren, 2 miles west of the village.

One of the largest lakes in the West Country, Blagdon Lake, is 2 miles to the east of Burrington. Many species of wildfowl can be seen there.

BURTON AGNES
HUMBERSIDE

5 miles south-west of Bridlington (page 437 Dc)

An Elizabethan beauty used to haunt Burton Agnes Hall, the manor that stands above this fascinating village. Her name was Anne Griffith, youngest daughter of the landowner who built the house. She was buried in the church near by, shortly after the house had been completed, despite her dying wish that her skull should be kept in the home she loved. In revenge, she haunted the graceful rooms and galleries until her skull was disinterred and put in an unrevealed place in the hall.

Anne's father, Sir Henry Griffith, a landlord powerful both in Yorkshire and his native Staffordshire, built Burton Agnes Hall between 1598 and 1610. The latter date is carved above the double doors of the splendid gatehouse. The hall is said to be one of the least-altered Elizabethan country houses. A vast Long Gallery occupies the whole of the top floor, and a fine collection of Impressionist paintings – including works by Gaugin, Cézanne, Corot and Matisse – can be seen there. The hall is open to the public, and its ghostly reputation is belied by the welcoming air imparted by its warm red brickwork and a bright interior lit by many elegant bow and bay windows. It is owned now by the Burton Agnes Preservation Trust Ltd, but Mr Marcus Wickham-Boynton, who built up the collection of paintings, still lives there. The gardens, with woodlands and herbaceous borders, are also open to the public.

The Norman manor that stood before the hall, stands there still between house and church, its substantial remains protected by 17th-century brickwork. It was built by Roger de Stuteville about 1170, with the living quarters in a great hall, reached by a spiral staircase from the sturdily pillared ground floor. Near by is an old donkey wheel.

Box pews fill the nave of the part-Norman Church of St Martin, which is entered through a tunnel of yews. Inside are several Griffith tombs, including that of Sir Henry and his two wives – decorated by three black coffins and carved skulls. Pantile-roofed cottages of cream-washed brick are scattered around the duck-pond below the church and hall, and there is an attractive little Methodist chapel, with Gothic windows, built in 1837.

COUNTRY STYLE *Picture-postcard thatched cottages line the labyrinthine lanes which add to the attractiveness of Burton Bradstock. One of the cottages is now the village post office and fits prettily beside its neighbours – which have ivy climbing up the walls, spreading across porches, and reaching to the small, upstairs windows. Many of the cottages date from the 17th century and have outwardly changed little since then.*

BURTON BRADSTOCK
DORSET

3 miles south-east of Bridport (page 421 Ba)

Each spring, migrating birds arrive in Burton Bradstock to take advantage of its situation in the warm and sheltered Bride Valley. Early spring flowers bloom throughout the area, which is filled with water-meadows; and the River Bride passes through a narrow gap in the hills on its way to the sea. The centre of the village is largely made up of stone or rubble-walled houses and cottages with thatched, stone, or slate-tiled roofs. They are mostly some 300 years old and are packed together in the narrow, curving streets, and in the lanes which lead to the north off the main road.

The 14th-century parish church of St Mary, which contains some handsome medieval panelling stands beside the village school in a quiet cul-de-sac in the heart of Burton. Not far away is the triangular village green, bordered by White House bearing the date 1635 and a Wesleyan chapel of 1825, now the village library. Two other houses, The Rookery and Ingram House, in Church Street, are also 17th century – although they have been greatly changed and renovated.

Several of the surrounding hills are topped by prehistoric hill-forts, and they have magnificent views across the English Channel. Below Burton Cliffs, which shelter the village from the sea, is a beach with a car park. Three miles north-east of Burton is the hamlet of Chilcombe, which has a tiny Norman church in the farmyard of the 16th-century manor.

BURWASH
EAST SUSSEX

6 miles east of Heathfield (page 423 Eb)

An almost unbroken line of brick-faced old shops and cottages forms the High Street of this outstandingly attractive village, which was once the home of Rudyard Kipling.

Burwash, spread along a ridge between the rivers Rother and Dudwell, was an important centre of the iron industry three centuries ago when the Weald was England's main source of iron ore. The village sign, which shows an iron-worker hammering a billet of iron, testifies to the ancient work of the Burwash forgemen who used to celebrate the feast of their patron, St Clement, on November 23, by hammering gunpowder on their anvils.

Inside St Bartholomew's Church, at the east end of the village, is a 14th-century iron tomb slab set into a wall at the end of the south aisle. It is claimed to be one of the oldest of its kind in the county. The church has a Norman west tower with twin bell openings.

Kipling wrote that he first saw the house where he was to live, Bateman's, a stone mansion with towering chimneys, when he ventured from the village down 'an enlarged rabbit hole of a lane'. The description still fits the steep valley lanes there.

The house, now in the possession of the National Trust, was originally built by an iron-master in 1634. Kipling bought the house in 1902 and it remained his home until his death in 1936. The works he wrote during this period include *Puck of Pooks Hill* and the poem *If*. His study remains just as it was when he was alive. Bateman's is reached down a narrow lane which turns south at the western end of the village. Upstream from the house is a watermill, cased in gleaming white weather-boarding, which has been restored to working order. Near by is the water-driven turbine which Kipling had installed in 1902 to light his mansion with electricity.

CAERWENT
GWENT

5 miles south-west of Chepstow (page 425 Da)

Vivid links with the past make Caerwent one of the most remarkable villages in Britain. Its war memorial, which stands on a Roman base opposite the church gates, marks what was once the bustling centre of Venta Silurum, one of the most important Roman towns in South Wales. The village is surrounded by walls built about 1,700 years ago to protect a prosperous Roman community whose town buildings included a forum, temple and public baths.

Caerwent House stands on the site of the forum, but the temple's foundations can be seen near by, and a row of Roman shops has been uncovered in Pound Lane. The most impressive sections of the town walls, more than twice the height of a man in some places, flank the Coach and Horses Inn, by the original east gate. Smaller relics of the Roman era are displayed in the 13th to 15th-century church, where splendidly grotesque gargoyles glower down from the tower. The 44 acre Roman town was founded in about AD 75, after the Romans had spent about 25 years pacifying the local Silures tribe, after whom they named Venta Silurum.

CALBOURNE
ISLE OF WIGHT

5 miles west of Newport (page 422 Ba)

Winkle Street, a terrace of 18th-century stone cottages, some roofed with thatch, others with lichen-stained tiles, is the unspoiled showplace of Calbourne. Unspoiled because the narrow street is a cul-de-sac, and visitors have to leave their cars and walk. The cottages, each fronted by a narrow bed of flowers, face the Caul Bourne where watercress waves temptingly in the crystal-clear current. At the entrance to Winkle Street, an elegant bridge, guarded by gates and a polygonal flint gatehouse, leads over the bourne – there dammed to make a lake – to Westover, a Georgian mansion standing in parkland. From Westover, the main road through the village runs steeply upwards past a sloping triangular green, at the point of which stands the church. The

ON GUARD *A many-sided flint-faced gatehouse stands at the entrance to the Georgian mansion of Westover. It also marks the start of Winkle Street, an unspoiled beauty spot which delights visitors to Calbourne. The dust and noise caused by motor-cars is unknown to the row of 200-year-old cottages which face the flower-bordered stream that gave its name to the village more than 1,000 years ago.*

building itself, venerable though it looks, dates only from the 13th century. 'Only', because it stands on land given to the Church by King Egbert in 826. Inside is a brass of 1383, showing a man in armour, commemorating William of Montacute, son of the Earl of Salisbury. William was hit in the eye by his father's lance while jousting, and died. The sorrowing earl is said to have put a similar brass in the church of every village where he held land. From the church gate, flanked by two old yews, there are views over the rooftops of the facing cottages to the Downs beyond.

CALDBECK
CUMBRIA

11 miles south-west of Carlisle (page 435 Cd)

An elaborate headstone carved with hunting horns stands near the door to Caldbeck's church, marking the grave of John Peel who died in 1854 after falling from his horse. A local man, born in 1776, he fathered 13 children after eloping to Gretna Green with Mary White. Peel loved hunting, often following the hounds on foot in traditional Lakeland style, and is immortalised in the song *D'ye ken John Peel*. The words were written by his friend, John Woodcock Graves, who worked in a mill making the grey cloth mentioned in one of the verses. A sandstone shelter opposite the churchyard gate is dedicated to Peel and Graves, but there is no mention of William Metcalfe, the Carlisle Cathedral organist who set the song to music.

Although Peel's grave is the main attraction, Caldbeck is a captivating little village in its own right, with fine views southwards to the Lake District's serried peaks. The attractive church, restored in 1932, dates from the 12th century. It is dedicated to St Kentigern, who is said to have preached at Caldbeck on his way from Scotland to Wales in AD 553. The churchyard is overlooked by a handsome 18th-century rectory with Gothic windows, and there are 18th-century cottages in the middle of the village, known as Midtown. A picturesque stone footbridge arches over the Caldbeck, behind the church, and leads to Friar Row, a group of stone cottages tiled with Cumberland slate and built about 1800.

COLD STREAM *An old brewery stands beside the Caldbeck – a tribute to the cold, clear water which gave the village its name. Caldbeck, which means 'cold stream' in Old Norse, grew up where two hill streams meet in a valley below the Cumbrian fells.*

CAPEL CURIG
GWYNEDD

5 miles west of Betws-y-coed (page 428 Bc)

This small village, spread out along the Holyhead road, is surrounded by some of the most majestic scenery in Britain. Woodlands soften the view down the road to the east, but elsewhere the eye is swept up to such peaks as Moel Siabod (2,860 ft) and Glyder Fach (3,262 ft). The craggy summit of Snowdon, at 3,560 ft the highest mountain in Wales or England, can be seen in the west. Until the Holyhead road was built by Thomas Telford, at the start of the 19th century, this was a remote wilderness rarely visited by outsiders. Today, Capel Curig is a centre for tourists in general and climbers in particular. The earliest of the village's hotels, now known as Plas-y-Brenin, is the National Centre for Mountain Activities, run by the Sports Council. Near by, where the crystal clear River Llugwy is crossed by a bridge, stands a small and ancient church built of massive, irregular boulders.

Shops selling local craftwork and mountaineering gear cluster round the main road junction in the village. Hotels and a school look out to Moel Siabod. An old stage-coach outside the Tyn-y-coed Hotel has been a colourful local landmark for many years. It has 'Falmouth to London' painted on its side, but there is some doubt about its authenticity. The Cwm Glas Crafnant National Nature Reserve, where alpine plants grow, is 2 miles north of Capel Curig.

◆

DOWN IN THE VALLEY *Boulder-strewn mountain slopes tower above Capel Curig, and in the distance the misty peaks of the Snowdon range form a jagged skyline. The local peaks were used by Sir John Hunt's team to prepare themselves for their ascent of Everest in 1953. They stayed at the Pen-y-gwryd mountain inn, on the twisting road that runs through the valley alongside the River Llugwy. Every five years they return on a nostalgic visit. Capel Curig also attracts anglers, who find good trout-fishing in the twin lakes of Mymbyr.*

CARDINGTON
BEDFORDSHIRE

3 miles south-east of Bedford (page 426 Cb)

Reminders of Cardington's most famous off-spring – the airship R101 and the great brewing family of Whitbread – are everywhere in the village. Samuel Whitbread's initials on plaques appear on many of the houses, like seals of approval, while over everything loom the vast, twin grey-green hangars, from one of which the R101 set forth on her maiden flight to India on October 4, 1930. She crashed early next morning on a hillside near Beauvais in France, with the loss of all but six of her 54 passengers and crew. Today, the shed that housed her is considered a place of ill-omen. Both hangars – the other one sheltered the R100, dismantled after nine successful flights – are now occupied by the Royal Aircraft Establishment, the government-run aircraft research body.

The houses of Cardington are set most attractively around an expansive green, and if there is a uniformity among them, this is due to the first Samuel Whitbread, founder of the family fortunes who was born in Cardington in 1720, and to his friend, the penal reformer John Howard. Between them, they built the bridge and many of the houses, while a later Samuel Whitbread carried out a good deal of restoration, including the rebuilding of the church, at the beginning of this century. Though somewhat severe in style, the dark stone and red-brick cottages running down to the King's Arms pub blend very pleasantly against the green. In the garden of the pub there is a model railway. John Howard's house, a three-bay early-18th-century building, stands north of the church in Church Lane. The almshouses he built stretch along the western side of the green and date from 1763 and 1764.

Probably the most elegant house is a large 18th-century building with intricately latticed windows, and a large bow window on the north side. This faces the church, a handsome structure with a stately tower. The interior is abbey-like, austere stone soaring up to the massive beams of the roof. Rebuilding, it seems, became necessary around 1900 because the foundations had been weakened by too many burials over the centuries. Apart from the monuments, not much of the original church is left.

The monuments, however, are superb and most thoughtfully reinstated within the new building. There are a number of 12th-century coffin lids set into a wall and several remarkable brasses, including one to Sir William Gascoigne, Comptroller of the Household of Cardinal Wolsey, in heraldic dress. But the monuments that immediately catch the eye are those to the Whitbread family – great allegorical 18th-century marbles in which Faith and so forth are depicted summoning Whitbreads to Heaven. Above their Greek drapes, their English faces look faintly incongruous. Near by is a memorial to John Howard, the reformer, who died of typhus while inspecting prisons in Russia.

On the opposite wall, the R101 tragedy is recalled by the airship's tattered ensign in a glass case, a plaque from the Royal Airship Works and a photograph of the dirigible at her moorings. There is a further monument to passengers and crew in the churchyard extension.

The font in the church is well worth seeing. Presented by Harriet Whitbread in 1783, it is an extremely rare example of Josiah Wedgwood's work in black basalt.

CARDINGTON
SALOP

11 miles south of Shrewsbury (page 429 Da)

Three hills provide shelter and seclusion for Cardington, which clusters around the trees, grass and gravestones of St James's churchyard. To the north stands The Barracks, a private house built of stone and timber, with tall, narrow brick chimneys. To the west is a neat row of cottages. Also in the area is the Royal Oak pub, a pleasing blend of whitewashed stone and timber-framed, black-and-white architecture. A short distance away is a fascinating group of ancient, weather-beaten barns.

The Norman church is notable for its long roof and formidable tower. By the altar is the ornate tomb of Judge William Leighton, Chief Justice of North Wales, who died in 1607. His effigy lies on its side, head on hand, while his wife and six children are depicted, kneeling, on the side of the tomb.

Judge Leighton built and lived in nearby Plaish Hall. It was the earliest brick-constructed house of its size in Shropshire, and is complete with minstrels' gallery, ornate chimneystacks, and vast fireplaces.

CAREW
DYFED

4 miles east of Pembroke (page 424 Bb)

Small but fascinating, the history-steeped village of Carew stands on the southern bank of a tranquil creek where seabirds wheel and swoop above a nodding carpet of slender reeds. A pink-washed inn and terraces of small, colourful cottages stand opposite the entrance to Carew Castle, an impressive ivy-clad ruin, whose once-palatial grandeur is reflected by the creek at high tide. The castle dates from the 13th century, but was 'modernised' by later owners who included Sir John Perrot, said to have been an illegitimate son of Henry VIII. Perrot built the state apartments with the huge, mullioned windows that overlook the creek. He was found guilty of treason against Elizabeth I, but died in the Tower of London in 1592 before being sentenced. A few hundred yards downstream is one of the few working tidal mills in Britain, restored in 1972 after many years of dereliction. The mill is reached by a footpath that leaves a pleasant, grassy picnic area across the creek from the castle.

Carew's other treasure is a magnificent Celtic cross that stands beside the road near the inn. Almost 14 ft high and carved with intricate geometrical patterns, it is believed to date from the 11th century and is one of the finest in Europe. It commemorates Maredudd ap Edwin, joint ruler of the old Welsh kingdom of Deheubarth, who died in 1035.

One of Carew's architectural curiosities is a squat, round, free-standing chimney in the Flemish style, used as the village bakehouse until the beginning of the 20th century.

CARLTON
NORTH YORKSHIRE

3 miles south-west of Stokesley (page 436 Cd)

In the tongue of the Norsemen, who left an indelible mark on the lore and language of the North-east, a *Karl* was a 'free man'. And Carlton, brooded over by the scarred face of the Cleveland Hills, grew up in Saxon times as a settlement of freed slaves. The scars, like the lines on a lived-in face, have a story to tell. Grey screes near the summit of Carlton Bank are the spoil of jet mines, and the crater and bare patches to their left are from the workings of alum pits. Jet, an intensely black fossilised wood, has been mined in the area since the Middle Ages. In the heyday of the trade, which declined in the 1860s, packhorses carried the jet to Whitby, where it was polished and used in jewellery. The horses also carried alum – a mineral used in medicine and for the fulling of cloth.

Alum Beck, running through the middle of the village with sloping orchards, gardens and grassy banks on either side, takes its name from the old alum works that were abandoned late in the 18th century. The beck is crossed by a pretty ford and a number of bridges, and in spring the cottages look out over a dancing sea of daffodils. Overhead, gliders often soar high above Busby Wood. They are launched from a gliding club at Carlton Bank, where new members are welcome. When the wind is in the right direction, hang-gliders launch themselves giddily into space from the precipitous bank.

The privately owned Manor House, near the lower end of the village on the west bank of the beck, is Carlton's most impressive building. It dates from the middle of the 18th century and is a small villa, elegantly proportioned in the Palladian style, with two wings flanking a central block. Villagers call it the New Hall, to distinguish it from the old manor house, on the same side of the beck, which is now a Boy Scout centre. It has been much rebuilt, and this can be seen in the different styles of stonework.

The Church of St Botolph was built at the end of the 19th century, in 14th-century style. According to legend, a church was founded on the site in 675 by the Saxon St Botolph. The present church was built with funds raised by Canon John Kyle, an old-style sporting parson or 'squarson' who boxed the village lads (and thrashed them soundly), rode to hounds, ran three farms and kept a pub, the Fox and Hounds, until his death in 1943. When asked to explain why he became a landlord, he told the Archbishop of York it was so that he could close the pub on Sundays, and suppress the profane language and singing that came through the bar windows. The Fox and Hounds is now a private house, next to the village school, leaving the Blackwell Ox as the village's only pub. In the days of the drovers, there were five.

Carlton has had its fair share of colourful vicars, for a previous incumbent, the Reverend George Sanger, stood trial for arson. The village church burned down in 1881, and it was darkly rumoured in the village that the culprit was the

vicar, whose mind became deranged because a local girl was about to bear him an illegitimate child. He was found not guilty, but the villagers shunned him and he left soon after. The tragedy inspired a novel, *Peccavi* ('I have sinned'), by E. W. Hornung.

The route of the Lyke Wake Walk runs over Carlton Bank, coinciding for a stretch with that of the 93 mile Cleveland Way. Lyke has the same origin as lych: both come from *lic*, Anglo-Saxon for 'corpse'. The Lyke Wake Walk, 40 miles across the moors from Ravenscar to Osmotherley, symbolises the last journey of the soul. It started in 1955, when a local farmer challenged anyone to complete the 40 miles within 24 hours. Walkers who complete the distance inside the time limit are eligible to join the Lyke Wake club, whose badge is a coffin.

CARRADALE
STRATHCLYDE

On the east coast of Kintyre (page 441 Cc)

The village is on the east coast of Kintyre and has a clear view across Kilbrannan Sound to the Island of Arran, 3½ miles away.

Although Carradale retains much of its old character, there are numerous small, new houses with views of the mountains of Arran. The buildings blend harmoniously with the stone cottages, hotels and boarding-houses. The village became a resort in the 19th century, and one of its attractions was the iron pier, erected in 1871. Near by are the ruins of Aird Castle. On Carradale Point, at the east end of Carradale Bay, is an Iron Age fort. Its walls have been vitrified – fused into a glass-like mass – by extreme heat.

NOVELIST'S CREATION *The early fortunes of Carradale were founded on its fishing fleet that sailed from the small tidal harbour of Waterfoot. But modern fishing boats outgrew this tiny haven, and local fishermen were forced to seek elsewhere for a living. It was to prevent this stagnation of a once-fine industry that the novelist Naomi Mitchison suggested, and was largely instrumental in building, this new harbour at the foot of the wooded Kintyre hills, capable of taking large, deep-sea boats.*

◆

But how and why the heat was generated is not known.

The grounds of Carradale House, home of Naomi Mitchison the novelist and children's writer, are open to the public and have a wide selection of rhododendrons and azaleas. Most of the hills behind Carradale have been planted by the Forestry Commission, and there are many fine and unspoiled forest walks. There is a forest information centre opposite the wall of Carradale House gardens, beside some timber-clad houses.

CARTMEL
CUMBRIA

13 miles south-west of Kendal (page 435 Cc)

Cut off from the bustle of 'mainland' England, Cartmel stands on a stubby peninsula which juts out into the huge tidal waste of Morecambe Bay. It is one of the gems of north-west England, richly endowed with a character that has taken more than 1,000 years to develop.

Cartmel's greatest treasure is the Priory Church of St Mary and St Michael, which has all the grandeur and atmosphere of a cathedral. It dates from the end of the 12th century when William Marshall, Baron of Cartmel and later the 2nd Earl

The Prior's Lodging.

The corner of Drury Lane through Bailey Gate.

CASTLE ACRE, A VILLAGE WITHIN A FORTRESS

The entrance to Castle Acre's village green must be one of the most imposing in all England. It is, or was, the bailey gate to the great fortress that William the Conqueror's son-in-law, William de Warenne, built to command the point where the Roman Peddars' Way crosses the River Nar. At the other end of the green are the splendidly craggy ruins of the Cluniac priory, also built by the de Warennes. The only roofed building among them is the Prior's Lodging, which continued to be inhabited after the Dissolution and is now a museum of relics from the site.

of Pembroke, founded an Augustinian priory in the village. This was dissolved by Henry VIII and most of the priory buildings were destroyed, but St Mary and St Michael was spared – after the roof had been stripped of its lead – to serve as the parish church. The door in the south-west corner of the priory is called Cromwell's door. Holes in it are said to be bullet holes made by indignant villagers firing at Cromwell's soldiers who had stabled their horses in the nave.

The church has a wealth of carved oak, an east window with 15th-century stained glass, and the 14th-century tomb of the 1st Lord Harrington and his wife.

Opposite the churchyard entrance is a building which dates from the start of the 18th century and has arched windows framed by weathered red sandstone. Westwards, down the street, stone shops and cottages, many painted white or pale grey over the roughcast finish, lead to a little bridge across the shallow River Eea.

At the centre of the village is a square with tiny, cobbled forecourts, an old market cross and, in one corner, a house whose upper floor, supported by pillars, projects over the pavement. The lofty gatehouse, now owned by the National Trust, is all that remains of the priory buildings. The rest were demolished and served as a convenient material for Cartmel's 16th-century builders. An archway under the 14th-century gatehouse leads into Cavendish Street, where another collection of attractive buildings includes a tiny, bow-windowed cottage. More cottages of

charm and character face the street that swings northwards from the square and runs out into open country past Cartmel Racecourse, where meetings are held on four days a year.

On the opposite side of the village, a milestone with old-fashioned 'human' fingers gives 'over the sands' distances to Lancaster and Ulverston. It is a reminder of the days when travellers risked crossing the tidal estuaries rather than make lengthy detours. The Priors of Cartmel provided official guides, but many travellers who failed to beat the tide are buried in the village churchyard.

CASTLE ACRE
NORFOLK

4 miles north of Swaffham (page 432 Cd)

Set between the ruins of castle and priory, and built largely of flint quarried from both, Castle Acre is a severely attractive village. In the Domesday Book, Castle Acre and the neighbouring villages of South and West Acre are referred to collectively as 'Acra', from the Saxon word *aecer* – 'a field'.

Castle Acre commands the point where the Roman or prehistoric Peddars' Way crosses the River Nar, and must have been of considerable importance from very early times. The present village owes its form to William de Warenne,

William the Conqueror's son-in-law, who reared up the great motte or mound that still looms over the village, and set on top of it his huge flint keep. Much of Castle Acre, at least as far as the church, is contained within the outer fortification of the bailey. The remains of the castle, a ruin since the de Warenne line petered out in the 14th century, are now in the guardianship of the Department of the Environment. The well-maintained gatehouse is at the top of Bailey Street, which runs down to the river.

Both the street and the green are a pleasant blend of brick and flint. Even the modern houses are built of the same materials, and rapidly weather into the general harmony. Many houses are of considerable age, but others belong to the mid-19th century, when, during the agricultural depression of the period, Castle Acre was declared an open village. This permitted the poor, the homeless and the unemployed to use it as a base for seeking work, and to build houses there.

The houses round Stocks Green, an attractive oblong of grass, trees and gravel, illustrate the long history of brick-and-flint building in the village. Some of the houses are completely new, the big Ostrich Inn with its beamed ceilings and huge fireplaces dates from the 18th century, and one house, on the opposite side of the green, pre-dates the Reformation. This has a large red-brick cross set in its front, indicating that the house was once a hostel for pilgrims. Before the Dissolution of the Monasteries in the 1530s, they used to visit the priory to inspect the arm of St Philip and other saintly fragments.

The Church of St James stands at the end of the green, a vast, airy building filled with golden light from the tinted windows. There are some panes of medieval stained glass in the south aisle, and a marvellous screen and pulpit bearing medieval painted panels of saints in deep reds, blues and gold. The font cover, too, is remarkable – a gilt, green and red spire towering some 20 ft to the golden dove at its peak.

The priory ruins lie behind the church, a range of jagged crags set among decorous paths and lawns. Like the castle, the priory was founded by the de Warennes. Shortly after the Conquest, they brought 25 Cluniac monks first to their lands near Lewes, and then to Castle Acre. The west front of the church is especially lovely, standing as it does against a soaring background of uplands and sky. The Prior's Lodging, the only part that is still roofed, was a farm building until recently, and now contains a small museum.

CASTLE BOLTON
NORTH YORKSHIRE

5 miles west of Leyburn (page 436 Bc)

A steep lane climbs from the broad, green floor of Wensleydale to Castle Bolton's single street, where stone cottages line a rough green. Ahead stands Bolton Castle, its massive walls and towers jutting four-square above the soft folds of the hills. To the north lies Redmire Moor, and to the south the River Ure and the 1,792 ft Pen Hill.

Richard Scrope, Lord Chancellor of England, built the castle as a fortified manor in the 14th century. Mary, Queen of Scots was imprisoned there for six unhappy months in 1568, and a local legend tells that while trying to escape she dropped her shawl. This is said to be the origin of the name of Leyburn Shawl, a limestone hill behind the nearby market town of Leyburn.

Bolton Castle is remarkably intact, and the dining-room is now a restaurant. Close by the castle walls is St Oswald's Church, also 14th century and built of pale local stone.

CASTLE COMBE
WILTSHIRE

5 miles north-west of Chippenham (page 421 Cc)

Chosen in 1962 as the prettiest village in England, Castle Combe survived a Hollywood invasion four years later. Although it lies about 17 miles from the nearest coast, the village was transformed to look like a seaport for the film version of *Dr Doolittle*. A harbour wall and jetty were built on the cheerful little Bybrook, which sparkles along beside a row of 17th-century cottages. But the upheaval soon receded, and Castle Combe reverted to the slumber it enjoys between regular influxes of tourists.

Once a centre for cloth-weaving, the village lies in a hollow and is approached through a deep valley, shaded by tall trees. The valley leads down from the road between Chipping Sodbury and Chippenham. Visitors are expected to leave their cars at the top and walk down to the village, where parking is restricted.

The houses and cottages, church and 15th-century market cross are all of mellow, honey-coloured Cotswold stone. The roofs are pitched steeply to allow rain and snow to drain off the porous stone tiles.

Stone steps lead up to the covered cross, where a wool market used to be held. Below it is a three-arched bridge of rough-hewn stone. The manor house, which largely dates from the early 19th century, is now a hotel and stands behind a screen of trees.

St Andrew's Church, with its tower built in 1434 'at the expense of the clothiers of the district', is rich with decoration in wood and stone. Although it was restored in 1851, the church still has a chancel wall from the 13th century. In the north aisle is the 13th-century tomb of Sir Walter de Dunstanville, who built the now-vanished castle which gave the village its name.

FILM-STAR VILLAGE The title 'Prettiest Village in England' ▷
together with a starring role in the film Dr Doolittle *bring thousands of visitors to Castle Combe each year. But, by providing parking at the edge of the village, the inhabitants have managed to retain the character of their community. Castle Combe's renown is due to a happy coincidence of superb local building stone and medieval wealth based on the wool trade. The tower of St Andrew's Church was paid for by 15th-century wool merchants, whose market was at the top of the street beyond the bridge.*

CASTLE COMBE

CASTLE HEDINGHAM
ESSEX

4 miles north-west of Halstead (page 432 Cb)

For more than 500 years the powerful de Vere family, Earls of Oxford, were lords of the manor at Castle Hedingham. Their 12th-century castle was built to dominate the Colne Valley, and its imposing stone keep – almost 100 ft high – still stands on a mound above the village where narrow streets and lanes are clustered around the ancient market square.

Falcon Square takes its name from the 15th to 16th-century half-timbered house, once the Falcon Inn, on its north side. The square is, in fact, a triangle, with its apex at the entrance to the churchyard.

King John granted Castle Hedingham a market charter in the 13th century. The market has long since ceased to be held, but there are reminders of the days when this was a prosperous little town; from the 15th-century Moot House in St James Street to the elegant Georgian houses of the wealthy wool merchants in King Street and Queen Street.

So much of the village's medieval and Tudor atmosphere remains, that it is easy to imagine how its inns and market place must have buzzed with the stories of the latest events at the castle: of the death of King Stephen's wife Matilda in 1151; of how King John wrested the fortress from the defiant Robert de Vere in 1215; and of the visit by Elizabeth I in 1561. This was the last royal visit to the castle, which was partly demolished in the 16th century by the 17th Earl of Oxford.

The queen probably entered the castle by the Tudor bridge which spans the now-dry moat. Above, tower the 100 ft high turrets, and on the first floor is the great hall spanned by a soaring arch. In the grounds of the keep is a Georgian house built in 1719 from the castle ruins by Robert Ashurst, who bought the castle from the widow of Henry, the 18th and last Earl of Oxford. The keep is open to the public on Tuesday, Thursday and Saturday afternoons from May to September.

Parts of the Church of St Nicholas are possibly as old as the castle, but much of it is Tudor and an inscription on the tower says that it was 'renovated in 1616'. In the churchyard is a carved Norman cross, which for many years was used to prop up the cellar of the Falcon Inn. It was rescued from this humble task in 1921, and now serves as a war memorial.

CASTLE RISING
NORFOLK

4 miles north-east of King's Lynn (page 432 Cd)

According to a centuries-old legend, the ghostly screams of an imprisoned queen echo through the keep of the now-ruined Norman castle from which the village takes the first part of its name.

In 1330 Edward III sent his mother, Queen Isabella, to Castle Rising after her part in the downfall and murder of her husband, Edward II. Despite the stories of her screams of loneliness and remorse, however, she lived a fairly comfortable life in the castle and was often visited by her son.

'Rising' probably comes from the Anglo-Saxon, meaning 'people of the brushwood', or Old German, meaning 'Risa's people'. The castle was built there in 1150 by William de Albini, who married the widow of Henry I and became Earl of Arundel. It passed to the Howard family in 1544. Henry Howard, Earl of Northampton, founded the attractive almshouses to the east of the church in 1614.

The single-storey, red-brick houses were rebuilt in 1807, but behind the leaded windows are rooms containing the original 17th-century furniture. The almshouses are occupied by elderly ladies who, on special occasions, wear red cloaks bearing the Howard badge and tall, pointed hats when they go to church.

Surrounding the castle is a ditch, which is crossed by a 13th-century bridge. The keep is one of the largest in England and stands 50 ft high. A stone staircase leads to the first floor and a splendid Norman arch which was the original entrance to the great hall.

St Lawrence's Church, though greatly restored, retains its Norman character, particularly at the west end which has a decorated doorway and windows. To the west of the church is the village green with a 15th-century cross.

Castle Rising was a port on the River Babingley until the 15th century, when ships became too large to navigate the river and the trade went to King's Lynn.

CAVENDISH
SUFFOLK

4 miles west of Long Melford (page 432 Cb)

Thatched cottages with pink-washed walls huddle beneath the tower of St Mary's Church on the edge of the village green. The cottages, whose origins go back 400 years, have been rebuilt twice since the Second World War because of dilapidation and fire, but none of their charm has been lost. They stand by a spot known as Hyde Park Corner, near the waters of the upper Stour.

The village name comes from *Cafa's Edisc*, an Anglo-Saxon settlement of 'Cafa's people' where *Edisc* meant an 'enclosure'. From there came the family of the Dukes of Devonshire and that of Thomas Cavendish of Trimley, a parish in the south-east of the county. He sailed around the world in the 1580s, and died at sea on his second attempt in 1592. Another Cavendish – Sir John – was Chief Justice of the King's Bench, and was with Richard II in 1381 when he confronted Wat Tyler, leader of the Peasants' Revolt, at Smithfield. Angered by the killing of their leader by Sir John's son, some of Tyler's followers pursued Sir John to Cavendish, where he hid his valuables in the church belfry before fleeing. He was later caught at Bury St Edmunds and beheaded.

Sir John left £40 in his will for a new chancel

PEACE AND QUIET *The clock of St Mary's Church, Cavendish, says it is noon, and the village reposes in the midday calm. The church tower can be seen from all over the village, and it is distinguished by its pointed bell-cote. Some immaculate cottages, their thatched roofs capped with ornamental ridges, stand between the church and the green. For those wishing to rest, a wooden bench has been thoughtfully placed in a sheltered corner.*

◆

in St Mary's Church. Its 14th-century tower dominates the village and contains a chimney in the ringing chamber, which was formerly a priest's room. At a fork in the road beyond the church stands Nether Hall, a fine early Tudor house. The present owner's family has farmed there since the 16th century. The timber-framed Old Rectory, near the pond, was built in the 16th century. It is now the home of the philanthropist Sue Ryder, founder of the Sue Ryder Foundation for the Sick and Disabled.

CAWDOR
HIGHLAND

5 miles south-west of Nairn (page 443 Ed)

Cawdor Castle is the seat of the Earls of Cawdor, and dates from the 14th and 17th centuries. The earliest part, the keep, has a grim history, for it was there, according to Shakespeare, that King Duncan was murdered by Macbeth. A drawbridge guards the entrance and there are impressive 17th-century additions to the castle.

The community stands among woodland on the edge of the Moray lowlands, and across a narrow ravine from Cawdor Castle. Most of the stone cottages and houses in Cawdor were built for the estate workers.

CEMAES BAY
GWYNEDD

10 miles north-east of Holyhead (page 428 Ac)

Seen from high ground to the east, the clustered cottages of Cemaes Bay contrast sharply with the great bulk of the nuclear power station on the coast of Wylfa Head, 1 mile north-west of the village. But the modern intruder cannot be seen from Cemaes Bay itself, where the main street funnels down to a bridge by the little harbour.

The sandy beach lies snugly between sheltering cliffs, and much of the coast immediately north of the village is owned by the National Trust. Llanbadrig Church, perched on the cliffs and reached by a lane from Cemaes Bay, is said to have been founded by St Patrick after he was saved from a shipwreck on the nearby Middle Mouse reef.

When the church was restored, in the 19th century, a donation came from the 3rd Lord Stanley, a local landowner. He had become a Moslem, and insisted on the interior being decorated in the Islamic style.

CENARTH
DYFED

6 miles south-east of Cardigan (page 424 Bb)

Cenarth's 18th-century bridge, its arches pierced by circular holes, sweeps gracefully over the most spectacular stretch of the River Teifi. After many miles of lazy meandering down a fertile valley, the river is suddenly squeezed into a wooded gorge where it foams and thunders towards the bridge in a series of low but dramatic waterfalls. A picturesque old mill, that once ground corn, nestles in the riverside trees adding an old-world touch to the scene.

There are newer buildings on the road out towards Cardigan, but the heart of Cenarth is close to the river. Many of the stone cottages are bright with colours, and the smithy – opposite the Three Horseshoes Inn – which has been restored to its original state, displays tools used by the blacksmith – including the tongs he used in his capacity as the village dentist.

The White Hart, overlooking the bridge, has a bar named after the coracles that may still be seen on this part of the Teifi. These curious craft, shaped like half of a giant walnut shell, are built to a design that was old when the Romans invaded Wales almost 2,000 years ago. A coracle holds one man, weighs 30–34 lb., and is propelled by a single paddle made of ash. Once used by local fishermen, they are now used only for sport.

CERES

FIFE

3 miles south-east of Cupar (page 441 Fe)

Today, a hump-backed 17th-century bridge spans the burn at Ceres. It is for pedestrians only and, according to local legend, an earlier bridge on the site was crossed by villagers on their way to join forces with Robert Bruce at Bannockburn, where the Scottish patriot defeated the English under Edward II in 1314. It is said that, on their return, the men of Ceres celebrated the victory on the village green, and the Bannockburn Games are held there annually in June. The highlight of the games is the Ceres Derby, a horse-race which takes place on the tiny racecourse.

In the late 18th and early 19th centuries, hand-loom weaving was a thriving industry. It declined when the powered looms of the town mills took away the trade, but several groups of old weavers' cottages remain. Weaving and many other aspects of rural life are the subjects of the Ceres Folk Museum.

A number of stone carvings by a local 18th-century stonemason, John Howie, can be seen around the village. One, on a wall, is the figure of a jovial-looking man holding a jug. He is said to be the last ecclesiastical Provost of Ceres, appointed in 1578.

CERNE ABBAS

DORSET

7 miles north of Dorchester (page 421 Cb)

Giant's Hill, with its 180 ft tall outline of a naked man cut in the chalky turf, overlooks the entrance to the village. The Cerne Giant, as the figure is called, holds a 120 ft knobbly club in one hand and has been there for more than 1,500 years. He is a pagan fertility figure, and is said to be an early British version of the hero-god Hercules,

whose cult may have been brought to Britain by the Romans.

As late as the early 19th century, local women believed that sleeping on the hill at night would cure infertility, and so ensure that the village population grew and flourished. Higher up the hill is a rectangular earthwork called the Trendle, which until 1635 was the scene of maypole dancing. At the present time, Morris dancers perform on the hill at 7 a.m. on May Day.

At the foot of Giant's Hill is the site of a 10th-century Benedictine abbey. It forms the heart of the village, with its thatched, orange-stone and colour-washed cottages lining Long Street. There are half-timbered Tudor houses in nearby Abbey Street. Facing down Abbey Street is Abbey Farm, an impressive gabled Tudor building in flint and stone. The largest and most intact feature of the abbey, the three-storey Abbot's Porch, stands in the courtyard. Originally, this was the porch to the abbot's hall, and two other structures still standing are the Guest House and a small barn.

The abbey church stood in what is now the village burial ground. St Mary's, in Abbey Street, has a 15th-century tower and a fine east window which probably came from Cerne Abbey. In the burial ground is a wishing-well named after St Augustine – the first Archbishop of Canterbury – who, in the 6th century, is said to have blessed it. Water from the well flows into a flower-fringed pool, the home of ducks, moorhens and wagtails, by the green just below Abbey Farm.

CHADDESLEY CORBETT

HEREFORD AND WORCESTER

4 miles south-east of Kidderminster (page 425 Ec)

The village street at Chaddesley Corbett is a rare example of the harmonious blending of several architectural styles. Mellow Georgian brickwork and colour-washed rendering share the scene with black-and-white timbered buildings, the most notable of which is the 17th-century Talbot Inn. Its long frontage, close to the churchyard, is one of the village's most memorable sites.

The Norman church has an 18th-century tower surmounted by a recessed spire. Its dedication to St Cassian is unique in the Midlands, and probably in England. The saint was an early-Christian schoolteacher who is said to have been stabbed to death by his pagan pupils. A few yards away, in the churchyard, is an old brick school building which bears a plaque recalling its extension in 1809. The village street is among the finest in the area and contains several intriguing houses, including the early-19th-century Charity House, which consists of three matching brick cottages.

A mile and a half to the east, in Chaddesley Wood, is a 250 acre national nature reserve established in 1973 to protect the area as a fine example of oak woodland.

A mile to the west lies the moated Harvington Hall, an Elizabethan red-brick building noted for its abundance of priests' hiding places built in the 16th and 17th centuries, when Roman Catholics were being persecuted. It also contains some fine Elizabethan wall-paintings.

CHARING
KENT

6 miles north-west of Ashford (page 423 Eb)

The main road from Maidstone to Ashford divides just before Charing, leaving the village in a quiet spot between the two roads. The buildings in the High Street are mostly white weatherboarded, brick and tile, with patches of timber work. The street was once a busy stopping place for travellers to Canterbury along the Pilgrims' Way.

In High Street stands the ancient Pierce House, with overhanging gables, close timbers and zig-zag patterns in its brickwork.

One of the Archbishop of Canterbury's palaces was built at Charing about 1300. Part of the structure remains and has been transformed into a farmhouse, behind the gatehouse. A flint wall encloses the extensive grounds, and one of its stones, at the corner of Pett Lane, is carved with grotesque faces.

The palace and the village church are found down a short lane off the main street. The church has a high, typically Kentish, tower, begun in the 15th century, while parts of the main structure date from two centuries earlier. On some pew ends in the church are carvings of Jack-in-the-Green, the spirit of nature's spring renewal. The faces vary; some are old and some young. But they all have leaves and tendrils curling fancifully from their mouths.

◆

SPIRITED CHARLESTOWN *Due to the 'spirited and meritorious exertions of Charles Rashleigh', the little Cornish village of West Polmear gained a new harbour and a new name at the dawn of the 19th century. China clay was its main export, but today it is famed for mackerel – and as a film location.*

CHARLESTOWN
CORNWALL

2 miles east of St Austell (page 418 Cb)

The picturesque quayside and waterfront at Charlestown will be familiar to television viewers and film-goers, for the television series *Poldark* and *The Voyage of Charles Darwin*, and the film *The Eagle has Landed* were all partly filmed there. Charlestown's popularity with film producers is a measure of the charm of its little harbour which has scarcely changed since it was built between 1793 and 1801. It was planned by the engineer John Smeaton – who also built the third Eddystone lighthouse – for Charles Rashleigh, a local industrialist, after whom the village is named. Its main street is lined with beech trees and Georgian cottages and leads down to the quay with its stores, offices and loading chutes.

To the east and west of the harbour are shingle beaches. The village also has a museum called the Shipwreck Centre.

CHASTLETON, Oxfordshire (page 426 Ab)
(see Adlestrop, Gloucestershire)

CHAWTON
HAMPSHIRE

1 mile south-west of Alton (page 422 Cb)

For most of the last eight years of her life the novelist Jane Austen lived at Chawton, working on such masterpieces as *Mansfield Park*, *Emma* and *Persuasion*. The house she moved into in 1809 is now a museum, and remains much as it was

when Jane lived there. The garden has been restored to its original condition, and just outside the garden wall, on the Winchester road, are two oak trees which she planted in 1809. Indoors, her possessions include a beautiful patchwork quilt which she made with her mother, as well as her desk, her bureau and her music books. The museum is open daily, except on Mondays and Tuesdays in winter. Jane left Chawton shortly before she died, and spent the last two months of her life at Winchester where she is buried in the cathedral.

One mile of open road separates Chawton from Alton. For the journey to Alton, Jane kept a donkey and cart – the cart is now preserved in the bakehouse.

The original connection between Chawton and the Austen family came through Jane's brother Edward, who was adopted by the family's second cousin, Thomas Knight, owner of the Chawton estate, and later assumed the surname Knight when his benefactor died. The manor house Edward inherited lies a little way from the village centre – a fine 16th and 17th-century house set in a park studded with trees.

The handsome church near by is comparatively modern. It was built in 1871 to replace an earlier church destroyed by fire. But the design, by the architect Sir Arthur Blomfield, is magnificent, and the church contains some fine locally made furnishings.

Like many other villages in downland vales, Chawton has crystal-clear springs which tend to overflow in winter and early spring, flooding the meadows and creating a haven for wildlife.

JANE'S SHRINE *While settling into her Chawton cottage, Jane Austen wrote – in doggerel contrasting oddly with her usual style – 'that when complete, it would all other houses beat'. But modest Jane could never have envisaged the thousands of pilgrims who annually pay homage there in her old home.*

CHELSWORTH
SUFFOLK

4 miles north-west of Hadleigh (page 432 Cb)

Anyone who visits Suffolk and does not take time to stroll through gladed Chelsworth has missed one of the most entrancing villages in England. There are no great castles or mansions; no place to spend the night. The joy comes in walking among the old houses – gabled, thatched, timbered, tiled and colour-washed – which face the River Brett. The river is overlooked by beech and chestnut trees, which also shade the 14th-century Church of All Saints. Access to the church is through the entrance drive to the 17th-century Grangè. The village is noted for its gardens, of which 15 or so are open to the public on the last Sunday in June.

Sir Francis Meynell, the book designer who founded the Nonesuch Press in 1923, made his home at Cobbold's Mill, now a picture gallery, to the west of the village, and Chelsworth was the village best loved by Julian Tennyson, author of *Suffolk Scene*. Tennyson, great-grandson of the poet, was killed in the Second World War. John Appleby, the American airman who wrote *Suffolk Summer*, was in no doubt about Chelsworth's charms. He called it the loveliest village in the region.

CHERITON FITZPAINE
DEVON

4 miles north-east of Crediton (page 419 Dc)

One of the longest thatched buildings in Devon, perhaps in the whole of Britain, stretches 145 ft along the boundary of Cheriton Fitzpaine's churchyard.

Originally it was the church house, but today it houses the village school. It is the most impressive of the many thatched buildings in the village, which nestles high in the hills above the River Creedy. Most of them are buff-washed and made of traditional Devon cob – a mixture including clay and straw – and they cluster on many levels around the heart of the village, the red-sandstone Church of St Matthew.

The church tower, with its battlements and pinnacles, dominates the village centre, and while in the eyes of some people its rough-cast rendering lacks charm, at least the craftsmanship is beyond doubt. The rendering was put on in 1706, and has survived the centuries unscathed.

Just opposite the church is a magnificent farmhouse, one of the best of its kind in Devon, with bold stone chimneys and a fine set of mounting steps outside the entrance. At one end of the village there is a row of stone-built almshouses, with a stack of chimneys like buttresses, which were endowed in 1594 to commemorate the defeat of the Spanish Armada in 1588.

The village gets its name from the Anglo-Saxon words *Cyric* and *tun*, meaning 'church farm'. Fitzpaine, the surname of the owners of the chief manor, was added in 1300.

SUFFOLK IDYLL *The lazy River Brett is hardly perturbed by the 18th-century hump bridges that lead to Chelsworth's pretty main street with its thatched cottages and handsome Rectory. Julian Tennyson, the Chelsworth author killed in the Second World War and whose monument is a window in the Church of St Edmund at Southwold, wrote: 'Suffolk is England, and England Suffolk'.*

CHEW MAGNA

AVON

6 miles south of Bristol (page 421 Cc)

John Leland, antiquary to Henry VIII, wrote of Chew Magna in 1545: 'It is a praty clothing towne, and hath a faire chirch.' 'Praty' it still is, and its 'faire chirch' still stands in this red-sandstone village close to the Mendip Hills.

In medieval times Chew Magna was a thriving centre of the wool trade, and on every hand there are reminders of that prosperous era.

Outside the churchyard's main gate is the 16th-century Church Ale House, which has a tiled roof. Feast days were often marked by a parish party – the church ale was so named because the ale consumed was frequently brewed by the church – and proceeds went to parish funds. Initially, the church itself was the scene of these festivities, but gradually other premises were bought for the purpose, which became known as the Church House, or – in this instance – the Church Ale House. It may have originally housed clerks who managed the village's manorial estates, but was later used as a refuge for the poor and was a school from 1842 until 1894. From the Church Ale House, also known as the Old School Room, the High Street climbs gently westwards and is flanked for part of its length by pavements several feet above road level. South Parade, the highest section, has white railings and includes a range of whitewashed stone buildings and a pink-painted bank. Opposite are two inns, the 18th-century Pelican and the 19th-century Bear and Swan. Between the two inns is the Old Bakehouse. It is now a shop, but a long-handled baker's shovel still hangs outside.

Until the mid-18th century a maypole stood outside the Pelican, and the street was the scene of village fairs. Further along High Street, stone cottages rub shoulders with big houses of charm and character. Acacia House, set back from the road, dates from the 18th century and has an elegant façade and an astonishing array of chimneys. The Beeches is another Georgian house, built in 1762 by Ephraim Chancellor, a schoolmaster, whose earlier home was the Dutch-gabled Portugal House on the corner of Battle Lane.

Harford Square, tucked away behind High Street, is overlooked by the impressive frontage of Harford House. It was built in the 19th century by James Harford, an ironmaster who was lord of the manor. There was once a blacksmith's forge in the square, though it had no connection with Harford whose ironworks were in South Wales.

Silver Street runs down from Harford Square towards the north side of the churchyard and passes Church House, which dates from the 16th century but has a classical porch of the Georgian period. The Queen's Arms pub forms an attractive cluster with whitewashed cottages by a stream at the foot of Silver Street. A private house next to St Andrew's Church is known as Chew Court, and hides behind a high, sandstone wall. The house was once part of the 'Palace of Chew', the property of the Bishop of Bath and Wells in the 14th century. Much of the palace was demolished by a 16th-century bishop.

Link with medieval times

St Andrew's stands in spacious grounds, and is Chew Magna's strongest link with medieval times. Parts of the church are Norman, including the south doorway which is sheltered by a 14th-century porch. On the exterior right-hand side of the porch, and on the nave wall, are scratch dials – a series of carved lines radiating from a central point. It is still uncertain how these dials worked, but they are thought to have indicated the time of Mass. Gargoyles glare down from the 100 ft high tower that was added some time between 1440 and 1550.

Inside the church a tablet commemorates Alexander Whyte, a naval surgeon aboard HMS *Bellerophon* at Nelson's victories at the Nile and Trafalgar. Ten years after Trafalgar, in 1815, Napoleon surrendered to the captain of the same ship following his defeat at Waterloo. Whyte died at Chew Magna in 1838.

A carved oak effigy of a knight in the south aisle is believed to be of Sir John de Hauteville. According to legend, Sir John was a man of great strength who threw the Hauteville Quoit, an ancient standing stone, from the top of Maes Knoll to its present resting place between Chew Magna and the road between Bristol and Shepton Mallet. The effigy came from the chapel at Norton Hawkfield, which was destroyed in the 16th century. It has a Victorian inscription.

STANTON DREW 'Where in the world is Stanton Drew? A mile from Pensford, another from Chew,' goes an old Somerset rhyme. The village is also at the heart of a complex of stone circles. Local legend says the circles were formed when wedding guests danced to the tune of the Devil's fiddle on the Sabbath and were turned to stone

Ornamental bridge in manor-house gardens.

One of two village pumps.

Monument to Sir John de Hauteville.

THE CHARM
OF CHEW MAGNA

The picturesque 19th-century bridge in the gardens of the manor house was part of the pleasure walks when the house was a family home. Old Chew Magna is also remembered in the 19th-century pump. The church has one of Britain's few wooden tomb effigies.

for their sin. In fact, they date from the New Stone Age, about 2500–1250 BC, and were probably used for sun worship or astronomy.

The River Chew flows past the village to the north and is crossed by a fine 15th-century stone bridge built by Thomas Beckington, Bishop of Bath. Near the bridge stands the 15th-century thatched Round House. It was taken over as a toll-house for a turnpike road in 1790.

CHIDDINGFOLD
SURREY

5 miles south of Milford (page 422 Cb)

All the ingredients of the perfect village are at Chiddingfold: a medieval inn, a splendid church, a line of period buildings grouped around a large triangular green, and a pond.

The village was first recorded in the 12th century, when the last remnants of the ancient forest were being colonised for farming.

In the 13th century, Chiddingfold was the main centre of the glass industry, stimulated by immigrant craftsmen. Some of the glass-makers'

names appear on a brass tablet below a small lancet window, made of original glass fragments, in the Church of St Mary. Names such as William le Franceis and John Alemayn show their countries of origin.

The industry lasted until the 17th century, and in its heyday supplied stained glass far and wide, even to St Stephen's, Westminster. The prosperity of the glass-making period is reflected in the fine buildings around the green, the outstanding one being the Crown Inn which claims to be the oldest recorded inn in the county, being mentioned in 1383.

Other buildings are brick-faced and tile-clad, like Chantry House at the top of the green. The 18th-century façades of Manor House and Glebe House add a touch of elegance to the scene.

The thorn tree by the edge of the green may be as old as the inn, having weathered six centuries. To the east of the green, in a side lane, is Pound Cottage, named after the stone enclosure of the village pound which stands in its garden.

The church, built of local stone, stands at the south corner of the green, approached by one of the best lych-gates in the county with the timber slab, where the coffin was rested, still in place.

CHIDDINGSTONE
KENT

4 miles east of Edenbridge (page 423 Db)

A row of 16th and 17th-century timber-framed houses, so unspoiled that they have been used as background for films of the Tudor age, line the north side of the village main street. The south side is taken up entirely by the churchyard, dotted with yew trees and dominated by a large sandstone church, rebuilt in the 17th century after a fire but retaining some medieval traces.

Chiddingstone, near the River Eden in the Kent Weald, is one of those rural spots which became wealthy through the old iron industry in the 16th and 17th centuries.

The houses opposite St Mary's Church, with their overhanging upper storeys, heavy beams and patches of tile-hanging, are owned by the National Trust. The most striking building is the timber-porched Long House, dating from about 1550. The 17th-century mock castle was originally High Street House, seat of the Streatfeild family, local ironmasters. In the early 19th century it was given a sandstone shell to give it the appearance of a castle, complete with turrets and towers. It is frequently open to the public and contains a museum showing collections made by the Streatfeilds, which include Japanese armour.

There are many caves in the parish, including one in High Fields which may have been a prehistoric dwelling. A large sandstone rock, about the size of a small haystack, stands in the park behind the school. It is called the Chiding Stone, and is said by some to have given the village its name. But the accepted origin of the name links it to a Saxon called Cidda. The stone is believed to have been the site of ancient religious rites.

CHILDSWICKHAM
HEREFORD AND WORCESTER

2 miles north-west of Broadway (page 425 Fb)

Farms and market gardens surround Childswickham, an off-the-beaten-track village in the Vale of Evesham.

Although many new houses have sprung up in recent years, much of the village's old-world character has been preserved. Weathered red-brick cottages and others in honey-coloured stone contrast with those of black-and-white half-timbering and thatch to give a delightful visual variety to the place.

The old village cross lies to the south of the village. It is said to have been erected by the de Beauchamp family in the 15th century. The original cross at its summit was destroyed by Puritans and later replaced by an urn from the churchyard which is now preserved as an ancient monument. Near by is the old Manor House. From there a peaceful lane leads to the Norman parish church of St Mary – with its oddly patterned font, and its slender 15th-century spire enhancing a charming village scene.

CHILHAM
KENT

6 miles south-west of Canterbury (page 423 Fc)

A square of half-timbered houses lies between the churchyard and the gates of Chilham Castle. The houses, shops and inns date from late medieval times, but were partly refaced with brick in the 18th century. From each corner of the square, narrow lanes lead down from the small plateau on which the village centre is built, and these reveal more cottages. The main street leads past shops and a Wealden hall house with curved timbers to the Woolpack Inn.

The castle consists of a Norman keep and a red-brick Jacobean mansion, constructed in 1616 for Sir Dudley Digges, a high official of James I. In the mansion is the Kent Battle of Britain Museum, which is open to the public. In the mansion's park is a collection of eagles and falcons, and the birds swoop above the heads of visitors on the command of a falconer.

In the north-east corner of the square is St Mary's Church, whose 15th-century tower has a chequerwork of flint and stone; and some tiles in its structure may be of Roman origin.

Chilham stands on the old Pilgrims' Way to the shrine of Thomas Becket at Canterbury, and the pilgrims are remembered today by a 'pilgrims' fayre' held on Spring Bank Holiday, when local people in period costume sell goods from stalls in the square.

WHERE PILGRIMS TROD *A mixture of timber, brick and tile houses line Chilham's main street, where pilgrims once walked on their way to Canterbury.*

TREES
and the village

Most of Britain was a vast forest until New Stone Age man began slowly clearing it with fire and axe. But for thousands of years the forest remained the source of the raw material with which man built and heated his home, devised tools and fashioned many other essentials. And so it remained – at least in rural Britain – up to the middle of the last century.

Britain's great forests were mainly of hazel, alder, birch, beech, willow and oak. Houses were built with great curved beams of oak, elm or black poplar forming their arch-shaped frames. Smaller beams and poles braced the structure, and the spaces in between were commonly filled with wattle and daub. The wattles were split from hazel or other common 'underwood', and hazel double-pegs held the thatch in place.

Most of the spoons, bowls and platters were of wood. Few medieval village homesteads possessed anything of metal except a knife or two and a billhook or sickle. In winter, leather shoes were given a wooden sole, or made entirely of wood. Both spinning-wheels – often made with a single piece of bent ash for the rim – and weaving frames of heavy timber were made in the village.

Every village had a flour-mill, worked by wind or water. The buildings were usually of wood as were all the working parts of the mill, except for the stones. Mill gear wheels had teeth of especially hard woods, such as hornbeam or elm.

Cattle and sheep were fenced, when necessary, in the open fields by movable hurdles, usually made locally. Indeed the everyday work of the village depended on numerous locally made articles. Baskets by the dozen and many cradles were made from the 'withies' of the village willow swamp or osier bed – cut at regular intervals and dried, stripped, soaked or split to obtain different degrees of colour and flexibility. Thin strips of willow, or oak, were woven into hats and panniers. Fishing tackle, net and traps also came from the osier bed.

Ale was brewed in at least one house in every village, and kept in barrels shaped from subtly curved staves of oak.

Apart from their practical uses, many trees were believed

HOW EACH TREE PLAYED ITS PART IN THE LIFE OF THE VILLAGE

OAK

The wooden walls of England, both afloat and ashore, were built of sturdy oak, great beams and bulwarks of it shrugging off the centuries like passing showers. Almost anything, from furniture to fences and barrels to baskets was made of oak. Its bark was used in huge quantities for tanning leather. And its acorns went to fatten pigs. Even the galls were used – to make ink.

ASH

Spears and spinning-wheels were of ash; as were carts and crooks for shepherds; tool handles, barrel-hoops and ladders. Its hardness and elasticity gave it many uses.

ELM

Massive curved beams of elm went into houses and barns. It made furniture for the living, coffins for the dead, and gave teeth to the mighty cog-wheels of mills.

BEECH

Close-grained beech was used to make dozens of turned wooden objects about the house in southern Britain – birch replaced it in the North and Midlands. Butter casks and of course furniture were also fashioned from beech.

BIRCH

The versatile birch had many roles, from fuelling fires with its logs to beating and sweeping with its twigs. Furniture, turnery, broom-heads, even buoys marking channels in rivers, were all birch.

WILLOW

The picturesque yokes used by milkmaids to carry their pails were carved from willow. It was light and its flexibility helped to stop milk spilling. It would bend into barrel hoops; and hard leather balls would bounce from bats made of it.

ALDER

Clogs and wooden soles for shoes were carved from light and waterproof alder – though poplar, wych elm, willow and beech were used in its absence. Turnery and mouldings followed, along with window frames.

HAZEL

Wattle-and-daub walls were built up with mud and woven hazel wands. Tough and flexible, hazel was also used as thatching spars, for hurdles, to pen animals, bean rods and pea sticks. It also provided nuts to eat.

OTHERS

Many other trees were woven into the fabric of village life: poplar, like oak and elm, was used for large building beams, and elder made small wooden spoons. Longbows were of yew and especially hard or close-grained timbers, like hornbeam, boxwood, spindlewood, holly and elder were used for items liable to heavy wear or requiring precise craftsmanship, such as shuttles, spindles, measures and components for wooden machinery.

to have magical powers. Sprigs of mountain ash and wych elm were used to ward off witches and to prevent milk souring and beasts bolting. Elder was sacred to a Norse goddess in eastern and north-western England, while hawthorn was held to be connected with underground springs in the Celtic west. Yews, associated with Druidism, frequently dictated the site of a Christian church because the early Christians often built them in places already held sacred.

Rope was made from the inner bark, or bast, of limes, elms and Scots pine, and from thin twigs of birch, heather and green hazel. Dyes made from trees range from the bright green of buckthorn and privet, through blues and violets from elder, yellows from broom, gorse and barberry, to a rich brown from boiled unripe walnut shells.

One of the major uses of wood in the self-sufficient village was for fuel. Besides the logs and roots that simmered with turves and dung on the cottage fire, rapid heat for bread-making came from fag-

POLLARDED *The life-span of these beeches has been increased by pollarding – lopping them about 6 ft up the trunk.*

gots – bundles of dry twigs about 4 ft long – which were fed into the oven, burned and then removed as ash before the dough went in.

At the time of the Norman Conquest, any village with woodland had one or more cop-

pices of about 80 acres. Coppicing provides a perpetual supply of small timber for village craftsmen. Coppice trees are periodically cut to a level just above the ground. Certain types of tree – particularly lime, hazel, wych elm, oak and willow – lend themselves to this treatment and produce straight shoots which can be cut or thinned at any time between two and 20 years. The art of coppicing was known to late Stone Age Britons who used the poles for causeways which, in wet ground, have survived to the present day. Hazel forms most English coppices, but there are also coppices of alder, oak, wych elm and willow.

As well as coppicing, other trees were pollarded, or lopped about 6 ft up the trunk so that the resulting growth was beyond the reach of grazing animals. Pollarding lengthens the life of trees, and the frequently made estimate '1,000 years old' could well be true of some sturdy old trunks.

The pattern of the early medieval village and its woods and trees continued with only minor modifications until the

CUTTING OSIERS *Fishing tackle, nets and traps were among the many items made from osier cuttings. Villagers are pictured hard at work harvesting, bundling and binding the 'withies' of their osier bed.*

A LIVING SHELTER *A dozen people can huddle together in the hollow trunk of this mighty yew at Much Marcle, Hereford and Worcester. Many churchyard yews were there before the church was built – the tree was venerated by pre-Christian cults.*

great land enclosures of the 18th and 19th centuries. But even today, many features of woodland economy can be seen by those who can spare the time and will spend the effort.

A number of Britain's ancient and historic trees have been preserved. One of the most famous is the Royal Oak at Boscobel, in Salop. It is said to have grown from an acorn of the tree that sheltered Charles II from Cromwell's troops after the Battle of Worcester in 1651.

Other venerable oaks include the Cowthorpe Oak in North Yorkshire, which was considered ancient in the 17th century. The painter J. M. W. Turner visited it in 1816, and the tree can be seen in his sketchbooks. Then there is the Major Oak of Sherwood Forest, the hollow trunk of which is said to have concealed Robin Hood from his enemies. Estimates of its age range from 500 years to an improbable 1,500 years, but its trunk is an undeniable 30 ft around.

But the oak is beaten easily for longevity by the yew: one at Fortingall, in Tayside, is thought to be 3,000 years old.

ROBIN'S HIDEOUT *The Major Oak of Sherwood Forest is said to have sheltered Robin Hood. Now props support it in its old age – estimated at up to 1,500 years.*

Its trunk was 56½ ft around back in 1796, but today it is only a shell. At Darley Dale, in Derbyshire, there is another yew about 1,000 years younger with a 32 ft girth, while a mighty yew at Goudhurst, Kent, has a bench seating 12 in its hollow trunk.

Fine beeches include those at Burnham Beeches, in Buckinghamshire, with their quaint distortions caused by lopping. At Peper Harrow, in Surrey, there is a black poplar 126 ft high, and at West Dean, West Sussex, a great wych elm 130 ft tall.

CHILLINGHAM
NORTHUMBERLAND

5 miles east of Wooler (page 438 Bd)

The handful of cottages that make up Chillingham were originally occupied by workers of the vast estate centred on Chillingham Castle. The village lies about a mile east of the River Till, and to the east the countryside rises more than 1,000 ft to the prehistoric remains of Ross Castle, a double-ramparted earthwork.

Chillingham has a living link with the past in its unique white cattle, which have roamed the estate for more than 700 years. These crescent-horned animals, which have reverted to a near-wild state, are believed to be the closest relatives of the oxen used by the ancient Britons. They are on view to the public from April 1 to October 31.

Chillingham Castle is the ancestral home of the Earl of Tankerville, and is not open to the public. It dates from the 14th century and consists of four towers linked by walls that enclose a large courtyard. The grounds and the present village were laid out by Sir Jeffry Wyatville in 1828. At the bottom of the village lies the part 12th-century Church of St Peter, and in the south chapel is the magnificent tomb of Sir Ralph Grey, who died in 1443.

BRABIN'S BOUNTY *In 1682 John Brabin the dyer, 'being infirme of body', left money to relieve the poor of his native Chipping. The lasting results of his generosity are the old village school and a fine row of stone-built almshouses.*

CHIPPING
LANCASHIRE

4 miles north of Longridge (page 435 Db)

In old English, the word *chipping* means 'market', and until local industry began to flourish in the 17th century the village of Chipping was simply that – the market which served this region of Lancashire. Later, like the stone-built Gloucestershire villages it so closely resembles, it became a thriving centre for the wool trade: many of its buildings date from the 17th century, when trade was at its most buoyant. Sheep grew fat on the Bowland fells, which rise steeply to the north of the village. And their fleeces were processed by local weavers, who sold the cloth to towns such as Preston and Blackburn. At the same period, flax-spinning was another source of local prosperity.

At the southern end of Windy Street, a carved stone on what was Chipping's first village school – now a youth club – commemorates the village's most notable benefactor, a dyer and dealer in cloth called John Brabin. He died in 1683, having drawn up a will a year earlier leaving money for the relief of the poor and for the building of a village school. His name, and the date 1684, also appear on the gable end of the neighbouring terrace of stone-built almshouses, which were paid for with his money. Another inscription, at 22 Talbot Street, marks the house where Brabin lived, now a post office and crafts centre.

Windy Street's cobbled pavements pass some of Chipping's most attractive houses. These include numbers 17 and 19, which stand at right-angles to the road overlooking tiny gardens. Like many other houses in the village, they have quaint, stone-mullioned windows. A delightful little courtyard, overlooked by a house with diamond-paned windows, is tucked away near the shop on the corner of Talbot Street and Windy Street.

Talbot Street itself runs down to a bridge over Chipping Brook: from the bridge there are pleasant views downstream, with an old mill in the foreground complete with undershot waterwheel, and the long wooded crest of Longridge Fell in the distance. Just below the mill, which has been converted into a restaurant, the brook is crossed by a wooden footbridge.

Prosperous community

Chipping's roots delve back far beyond the Norman Conquest. The first church was built in 597, and the area around the village was given full parish status around 1040, shortly before the start of Edward the Confessor's reign. In the early 14th century, when the area was laid waste by marauding Scots, the inhabitants were described as 'few, untractable and wild'; but Chipping recovered to become a prosperous community attracting trade from neighbouring villages, hamlets and farms. Until the middle of this century, its markets and fairs remained highlights of the local calendar.

One fair was always held on St Bartholomew's Day, August 24, in honour of the village church's patron saint. The church itself has a tower built about 1450, while the rest of it was rebuilt in 1506 and heavily restored in 1873, by which time the roof was badly dilapidated and even the lead in the windows had decayed. A brass plate near the altar commemorates Marie and Anne Parkinson, the wives of Robert Parkinson, who died in 1611 and 1623 respectively.

Since the 19th century, Chipping has also been noted for its chair-makers, and examples of their craft can be seen in the church sanctuary. The chairs are made to the traditional Lancashire spindle-back design. One of the windows at the east end of the church is a memorial to John Berry, a local chair-maker who died in 1966, and depicts the tools of his trade. A board listing the Ten Commandments commemorates another local chair-maker – Thomas Harold Berry, who died in 1942.

Chipping's longest-serving minister, John King, is buried in the chancel near his son Richard. He was vicar from 1622 to 1672, surviving all the upheavals of the Civil War which forced many of his contemporaries to abandon their livings. One of his successors, John Milner, was a close friend of John Wesley, and accompanied the founder of Methodism on preaching tours of northern England and Scotland. Wesley preached in Chipping church in 1752, but a year later, on a return visit, a small group of parishioners shouted him down, and he had to finish his sermon in the vicarage, after the service.

CHIRBURY
SALOP

3 miles north-east of Montgomery (page 429 Ca)

Houses of rustic brick and black-and-white cottages are speckled throughout the village, which rests on a gentle green slope near the Welsh border. The spacious Church of St Michael stands in the north corner of the village. Its nave was originally part of a 13th-century Augustinian priory. Near by is a timber-framed school of 1675, with a central gable and gabled porch. From the churchyard there is a fine view of Chirbury Hall, thought to be a 16th or 17th-century timber-framed house, with a stone façade added in 1736.

The Herbert Arms has a colourful heraldic sign paying tribute to Lord Herbert, the Shropshire-born writer and soldier who, in 1644, surrendered nearby Montgomery Castle to Cromwell's troops in the Civil War.

CILGERRAN
DYFED

2 miles south-east of Cardigan (page 424 Bb)

Even on a grey Welsh day when the rain looks like lasting for ever, visiting Cilgerran is like discovering treasure: the ruined castle never loses its beauty, and its setting is always romantic. The ragged towers and crumbling walls, perched above the River Teifi, have enthralled tourists since the end of the 18th century; and they have

inspired a host of painters, from week-end amateurs to great masters of landscape like J. M. W. Turner and Richard Wilson.

The castle and the deep wooded gorge cannot fail to impress. But genteel Victorian explorers who ventured into the village itself may not have been so enchanted by village life. _The History of Cilgerran_, published in 1867, mentioned that ... 'the cottages, or rather hovels, in which the farm labourers dwell are squalidly wretched and unfit for human habitation'. It also revealed that employers even then were suffering from inflation. 'The price of labour has more than doubled within the last 30 years,' it said. 'Male servants who can handle a plough cannot now be obtained under £9 a year, and female servants generally get from £4 to £6 a year.'

Today, the hovels have gone and buildings of pale-grey stone, many of them lime-washed in typical Welsh fashion, flank the broad main street that runs parallel with the top of the Teifi gorge. One of the most eye-catching buildings is the 14th-century Pendre Inn. It stands near the eastern end of the main street, in the shadow of a solitary tree which is encircled by a miniature stone wall. A huge lantern fashioned from a barrel hangs over the door.

Coracles on the Teifi

The church, dedicated to St Llawdog, stands close to the Plysgog stream, which tumbles down past a group of cottages until it flows into the Teifi. St Llawdog was a 6th-century Welsh hermit who died on the holy island of Bardsey. In the south wall there is a stone with an inscription that reads, in translation, 'Trenegussus, the son of Macutrenus, lies here'. The inscription is carved in Latin and Ogham, an ancient script evolved in Ireland more than 1,500 years ago. The memorial probably dates from Llawdog's time, but the church itself was entirely rebuilt in the middle of the 19th century, except for the tower which dates from the 13th century.

All nine windows of the church have stained glass. Those in the north wall illustrate biblical sayings. Those on the south side depict scenes from 20th-century life; one shows ploughing and harvesting, the window next to it shows men sailing coracles on the Teifi below the castle.

On the west wall, near the font, a white-marble tablet commemorates Griffith Griffith of Cilgerran, a surgeon in the Royal Navy who was lost in a gale off Ireland in 1822, together with the entire crew of HMS _Confiance_. The memorial lists all the ships in which he served, and mentions his participation in a raid on Algiers that resulted in 2,000 Christian slaves being set free.

Once, according to the 12th-century chronicler Giraldus Cambrensis, the Teifi was remarkable both for its salmon and for the fact that it was the only river in England or Wales where beavers lived. The beavers vanished long ago, but the salmon are still there; and local fishermen still net them from coracles, as they have done for centuries. Coracle races are held in Cilgerran during a week-long festival every August, and beached coracles – their design hardly changed in 2,000 years – can usually be seen on a former slate quay by the river below the castle. It is reached by a narrow lane that drops down from

CILGERRAN CASTLE *J. M. W. Turner's oil-painting shows the castle at dawn, with an early-morning mist rising from the Teifi and Plysgog rivers.*

the main street of the village near the post office.

The castle's early history is uncertain. Parts of it date from the 12th century, and it is known that in 1164 it was captured for the Welsh by the powerful Lord Rhys. Henry II eventually acknowledged Rhys as ruler of Deheubarth, an ancient kingdom embracing most of South Wales. Rhys is said to have strengthened the castle to such an extent that a powerful force of Normans and their Flemish allies was driven off with heavy losses. But the triumph was short-lived. Rhys's sons fought among themselves after their father's death, and in 1204 Cilgerran fell to William Marshall, Earl of Pembroke. The balance of fortune tipped again in 1215. Llewelyn the Great recovered the stronghold, only to lose it after eight years to Pembroke's son, another William Marshall. He set about rebuilding the castle, and most of the ruins seen today date from that period.

Welsh stronghold

In the 14th century, when south-west Wales seemed to be the likely target for a French invasion, Edward III ordered the castles at Cilgerran, Pembroke and Tenby to be repaired and strengthened. The invasion, when it came, was further east, but Cilgerran was later taken by the Welsh for the last time when Owain Glyndwr made a bid to regain independence for Wales in the first decade of the 15th century. The castle seems to have played no part in the Civil War, and gradually became the ruin it remains today. It is owned by the National Trust and is open to the public.

CILYCWM

DYFED

4 miles north of Llandovery (page 425 Cb)

Enchanting Cilycwm is surrounded by forests and craggy hills. It stands beside the River Gwenlas as it rushes down from its source on bleak Mynydd Mallaen to mingle with the waters of the Tywi. The single street, flanked by cobbled gutters and pavements, runs parallel to the river and is overlooked by white and colour-washed cottages of stone. The chapel, set back from the street, has abandoned its traditional grey in favour of brightly painted walls. It is a cheerful reminder that this remote village was one of the first cradles of Methodism in Wales.

Like just about every other building in Cilycwm, the Neuadd Arms is a minor masterpiece of elegant simplicity. Its white walls, edged with black cornerstones, spring from a tiny cobbled courtyard. The inn backs on to the churchyard, where ancient yews flourish above the river. The church itself is perfectly in keeping with the overall character of the village. It dates mainly from the 15th century, and its interior is notable for frescoes. Its memorials include one to a local naval officer who died commanding a combined Anglo-French squadron in the Crimean War.

Narrow lanes wriggle north from the village to Llyn Brianne, a large reservoir opened in 1973 to supply the Swansea area. It is set in rugged country where rare red kites still breed.

CLAVERING
ESSEX

7 miles north of Bishop's Stortford (page 432 Bb)

The parish of Clavering, some 14 miles in circumference, consists of seven 'greens' – Deers Green, Stickling Green, and so on – many of which are hamlets of considerable charm. But the main part of the village is gathered about the church, and it is this portion that owes its existence to what is now a hillocky, tussocky field surrounded by a still impressive moat and bordered by the mini-ravine of the River Stort. This is all that remains of the castle built in 1052 by Robert Fitz-wimarc, a French adventurer who was sufficiently adroit to hold high office under both Edward the Confessor and William the Conqueror. Edward himself is said to have visited the village in order to dedicate a chapel to St John the Evangelist. On that occasion, according to legend, he presented his ring to a beggar by the chapel door. The ring was returned to him many years later by a pilgrim from the Holy Land with the news that the beggar had been none other than St John, and that the king would shortly be joining him in Paradise.

Clavering's inhabitants have gently adapted their village to their changing needs over the centuries; this is apparent in the mingling of architectural styles that occurs in most of the older houses. The Old Post Office, for example, one of the colour-washed houses in Middle Street, shows much 19th and 20th-century work, yet the roof still contains the blackened timbers of the 15th-century smoke hole alongside the 16th-century chimney. The five cottages in the chestnut-shaded Church End were built as one house in the 15th century; between the 1750s and 1836 it was the local workhouse.

The Church of St Mary and St Clement is a long, slow record of Clavering life from about 1370 to the present day. It has an altar presented by members of the Australian Air Force, who served near by during the Second World War, a Crusader knight transferred from an earlier church on the same site, some superb stained glass and, on the chancel screen, delightful medieval portraits of saints. The screen was covered with pitch during the Civil War and has been recently restored. Among the many monuments are two from the 17th century that recall the wives of Haynes Barlee. The first had 13 children, six of whom died in infancy and are represented by six small carved skulls. The second 'had no issue, but a great fortune', which her husband gratefully recorded on her memorial.

CLAVERLEY
SALOP

5 miles east of Bridgnorth (page 429 Da)

Many of the village's charming black-and-white cottages have raised foundations to 'keep their feet dry' in the event of heavy rain. Their studded doors and diamond-leaded windows mingle with buildings made of weathered brick, red sandstone and ancient timber. Many houses are covered with creeping plants, which add to their attractiveness. One particular home, opposite the Plough Inn, has a beautiful sunken garden.

◆

SMALL IS BEAUTIFUL *The tiny thatched and weather-boarded cottage by the ford at Clavering is one of the smallest houses in Britain. It dates from the 17th century and measures only 8 ft wide by 10 ft deep, with two rooms one above the other. The River Stort rushes past its doorstep, and the cottage is thought to have been the ford-keeper's lodge.*

Claverley is set on a wooded slope and has many eye-catching features. They include an early-19th-century pump and stone trough outside the post office. All Saints' Church is the centre-piece of Claverley, and was built 28 years after the Norman Conquest on the site of a Saxon church, which in turn stood on pre-Christian foundations. The church contains a large and dramatic mural of armed knights fighting on horseback. Which battle they are fighting is not clear, but some of the knights are wearing French armour. The mural dates from the 12th century, and was discovered during restoration work on the church in 1902.

The gabled, 15th-century vicarage faces the churchyard – which has a hollow yew tree.

CLAVERTON, Avon (page 421 Cc)
(see Wellow)

THE CLAYDONS
BUCKINGHAMSHIRE

6 miles south of Buckingham (page 426 Bb)

There are four Claydons within 4 miles of each other: East Claydon, Middle Claydon, Botolph Claydon and Steeple Claydon. As its name implies, Middle Claydon lies roughly in the centre of the group and stands on the northern edge of the parkland surrounding Claydon House. The village is small and compact. The church, which dates from the 13th century, stands near a group of lakes in the park. Both church and house have many associations with the Verney family who owned the house which they presented to the National Trust in 1956. In the church is a memorial to Sir Edmund Verney, who was standard-bearer to Charles I. He died at the Battle of Edgehill in 1642. After the battle his severed hand was found, still clutching the Royal Standard.

Claydon House dates from the mid-1750s, but two-thirds of it was demolished late in the century and only the west wing remains. Florence Nightingale was a frequent visitor. Her sister married into the Verney family, and the house contains a museum devoted to the 'lady with the lamp'. Also of note for their plaster-work and woodcarvings are the state-rooms and the Chinese Room.

North-west of Claydon House is Steeple Claydon, dominated by the buttressed tower and spire of St Michael's Church. The main road through the village, Queen Catherine Road, is lined with thatched and timbered cottages and houses of chequered brickwork. One carries the date 1856 in dark bricks on a side wall.

The village inn, the Phoenix, is thatched and timber-framed and is painted black and white. There is a tiny triangular green at the top of Chaloners Hill, and about halfway down the hill the Chaloners Public Library is a red-brick building bearing the dates 1656–1902.

East Claydon and Botolph Claydon are close together – almost one village. Both have timber-framed thatched cottages, and Botolph Claydon's village shop is thatched.

CLEE ST MARGARET
SALOP

7 miles north-east of Ludlow (page 429 Da)

Narrow, twisting lanes lead to Clee St Margaret, which is sheltered by the steep western slope of Brown Clee Hill. The name 'Clee' derives from the Old English for clay, or clayey soil. The hill – 1,772 ft – is the highest in Shropshire, and is lined with farmhouses and stone cottages. In the village itself the two main buildings are Church House and the Norman Church of St Margaret.

The first is an ancient half-timbered building with a dovecot in the south gable-end. The second is enhanced by yews and has clear views of the surrounding beauty spots, such as Cove Dale and the wooded crest of Wenlock Edge.

Although the church was restored in Victorian times, it still has its original Norman doorway, only 6 ft high, and Norman herring-bone masonry in the outer walls at the east end.

Brown Clee Hill, which is criss-crossed by footpaths and bridleways, has two main peaks – Abdon Burf and Clee Burf – both of which show traces of Iron Age forts.

Also in the parish are the impressive earthworks of Nordy Bank, situated at about 1,000 ft, below Clee Burf. The Clee Brook, which runs through the village, coincides with the main road for 50 yds, providing motorists with an unexpectedly long ford.

CLEY NEXT THE SEA
NORFOLK

4 miles north-west of Holt (page 432 Dd)

The village has not been 'next the sea' since the 17th century, when land reclamation left it 1 mile inland. Traces of the old quay remain, dominated by an early-18th-century windmill which has been converted to a private house. It looks across a landscape of marshes, creeks, gullies and mud-flats – and beyond is Cley's beach, a deeply shelving expanse of shingle and the site of a coastguard look-out.

Behind the old quay the main street of Cley, pronounced 'Cly', winds between flint-built houses. One of the shops, called Whalebone of Cley, has some unusual flint panels outlined in animal bones.

The church stands on Newgate Green, a patch of high ground south of the village and near meadows that were once the harbour. St Margaret's Church reflects Cley's former prosperity; it was rebuilt on a large scale in the 14th century, though the transepts fell into disrepair in the 16th century and are now roofless.

The marshes between Cley and Salthouse, to the east, are bird reserves of the Norfolk Naturalists' Trust. They can be visited by applying to the warden, in Cley, or to the Trust's headquarters at 72 The Close, Norwich. Two miles south of Cley is the Glandford Shell Museum containing shells from all over the world and exquisite examples of craftsmanship in shell.

CLIFTON UPON TEME
HEREFORD AND WORCESTER

6 miles north-east of Bromyard (page 425 Ec)

How the River Teme got involved with Clifton is hard to see. The village stands on a hilltop nearly 650 ft high and 1 mile away from the nearest point of the river. A sprinkling of modern houses has appeared in the village in recent years, but the main street retains considerable old-world charm. Black-and-white cottages with dormer windows mingle with others of grey stone, timber and red brick. The occasional Georgian facade adds a touch of elegance, and the post office is a study of white rendering and black beams.

The 12th-century Lion Hotel, with its massive ivy-clad chimney, incorporates part of the original manor house, and next door is the 13th-century parish church of St Kenelm, named after the county's own boy saint, murdered at the age of seven in 819.

The door to the church has the largest drop handle in Hereford and Worcester (there is a smaller version on the door of the old brick forge opposite), and above the tower rises a spire clad in Canadian cedarwood shingles and topped by a golden cockerel weather-vane. In the church is the effigy of a cross-legged knight of the 13th century, his feet resting on his dog. He is Ralph de Wysham, a crusader who once lived in nearby Woodmanton Manor.

Clifton, much of which is a conservation area, is the meeting place for the hunt which bears its name, and a centre for the many ramblers who come to explore the unspoiled countryside.

CLOVELLY
DEVON

9 miles west of Bideford (page 419 Cc)

Plenty of stamina is needed for a visit to Clovelly, one of England's showplace villages, where a single cobbled street plunges in broad steps between gleaming cottages to the sea, half a mile below. Transport up or down the steep and narrow slope is on foot. Sledges are used to carry milk, groceries and bread. Vehicles are left behind in a car park above the village. Once described as 'a village like a waterfall', Clovelly is unspoiled simply because there is virtually no room for further improvement.

Flower-decked cottages, all different in both design and colouring, seem to tumble over one another on both sides of the street. At some of the steepest points, the door of one house looks out on the roof of its neighbour. Far below is a small, curving quay with an inn facing the sheltered harbour waters, busy with pleasure boats. People staying at the inn can avoid carrying their cases up and down the cobbled street by using special vehicles which use a private road.

The best way to approach Clovelly is by the Hobby Drive, a rough road that winds for 3 miles along wooded cliffs east of the village. For a small charge, cars can use the drive to reach Clovelly.

Credit for preserving the village and maintaining many of its cottages goes to the Hamlyn family, lords of the manor, who first occupied Clovelly Court in 1738. Both house and village

A VILLAGE LEFT
BEHIND BY THE TIDE

In the Middle Ages Cley next the Sea was a busy seaport at the mouth of the River Glaven. Its ships carried wool to the Low Countries and brought back Dutch tiles that still turn up in old Norfolk cottages. Land reclamation since the 17th century has left Cley high and dry – its beach is now a mile away – even though coastal trade in coal and grain persisted into the mid-1800s. The size of St Margaret's Church, with its splendid brasses and carvings, recalls the village's former wealth and importance, as does the great windmill which towers above the last vestiges of the old quay beside the broad expanse of the marshes.

Brass children.

Frozen music.

The windmill, Cley next the Sea.

are owned now by a Trust. Near this great mansion at the top of the cliff is the Church of All Saints, which has a Norman porch, a Jacobean pulpit and a monument to the 19th-century novelist Charles Kingsley, author of *Westward Ho!*, who lived in Clovelly as a child. His father was rector for four years. The church and the original Court were built nearly 600 years ago. But the mansion has twice been destroyed by fire and rebuilt – in the Georgian era, and in 1944 when it was a convalescent home for war wounded.

On Shrove Tuesday, the children of the village drag tin cans and old buckets up and down the cobbled street to scare off the Devil before Lent begins.

CLUN
SALOP

5 miles north of Knighton (page 429 Ca)

People have lived in Clun since prehistoric times, and it has had an eventful past. But the village today matches its description in the poet A. E. Housman's verse from *A Shropshire Lad*:

> Clunton and Clunbury,
> Clungunford and Clun
> Are the quietest places
> Under the sun.

Locals have been known to change the word 'quietest' to 'prettiest', 'drunkenest' or 'wickedest'.

Clun is one of those character-packed settlements that grew around the Norman fortresses built along the border of England and Wales. But Clun is much older than its castle. In the Town Hall's small museum are flint and stone tools and weapons found in the area, the partly cremated remains of a Bronze Age inhabitant, and the plans of several Iron Age forts near by.

The museum's Iron Age relics are reminders that the British King Caractacus is believed to have fought his last battle against the Romans near Chapel Lawn, 3 miles south-east. An oval earthwork there, with 25 ft high ramparts, encloses the 12 acre site of a camp, where he is thought to have been defeated in AD 50, before being taken prisoner.

The village had manorial status from Norman times until the late 19th century, and silver maces from 1580 and 1614 are preserved by the Town Trust. The small Town Hall in Market Square is an attractive building of 1780, with cream roughcast above lower walls of natural stone, and an iron-studded front door.

The main part of the village, on a slope above the River Clun, is laid out like a gridiron, with streets running north–south and east–west. Many of its most interesting houses date from the 17th century. Down a lane off High Street is the Hospital of the Holy and Undivided Trinity, founded in 1614 by Henry Howard, Earl of Northampton, for '12 poor men'.

The gauntly impressive castle ruins are set among grassy earthworks above the point where the River Unk flows into the River Clun. On summer evenings, games of bowls are played on the green beneath the castle walls. Then, the ruined keep, outlined against the western sky, makes a memorable picture. The castle was built around 1100 by Picot de Say, who was granted the lordship by one of the Conqueror's most powerful barons, Roger de Montgomery. The de Says' male line ended in the middle of the century, and Isabel de Say married William Fitzalan, Lord of Oswestry, 35 miles north, who added Clun to his possessions. He was a distant but direct ancestor of the present Duke of Norfolk, who is still Baron of Clun.

CLYNNOG FAWR
GWYNEDD

9 miles south-west of Caernarfon (page 428 Ac)

Set back from the shore, but linked to it by footpaths, Clynnog Fawr looks out over Caernarfon Bay to the beautiful west coast of Anglesey. Its main street, part of the road between Caernarfon and Pwllheli, is flanked by rows of attractive cottages, some whitewashed and others of natural stone. They face a church that is as elegant and impressive as a miniature cathedral, and seems far too grand for such a small, remote village.

It indicates Clynnog Fawr's former importance as a religious centre – founded by St Beuno at the start of the 7th century. The present church, light and spacious, dates from the start of the 16th century, but almost certainly stands on the site of Beuno's original monastic cell. It is one of the most interesting buildings in North Wales, complete with such curios as a pair of extendible tongs used to remove unruly dogs. From the south-western end of the church a stone passageway, once used as the village lock-up, leads to St Beuno's chapel, where his tomb stood until the end of the 18th century. The chapel was Clynnog Fawr's school from 1827 to 1847. Its teachers included Ebenezer Thomas – also known by his bardic name of Eben Fardd – one of the greatest Welsh poets of the 19th century. St Beuno's well, just outside the village, has for centuries been credited with curative powers.

QUIET CLUN *A crumbling castle looks down on Clun, one of several reminders of a violent history stretching over 1,600 years from the last battle of Caractacus to a Civil War skirmish in which the village church was attacked. But that was more than 300 years ago and, since then, Clun has been minding its own business to such good effect that it earned a poet's praise as one of the 'quietest places under the sun'.*

A print in St George's Church shows that the castle was in ruins by 1731, and it is said to be the 'Garde Douloureuse' in Sir Walter Scott's novel *The Betrothed*. Scott certainly visited Clun while gathering material for the book, staying at the Buffalo, an inn that stands in a corner of Market Square. Buffalo Lane and Bridge Street form two sides of a triangle running down to the river, and in Bridge Street is Ye Olde Shoppe, built in 1619 and restored in 1928. It is now a private house, and across the street from it is the old stone-and-timber smithy. A narrow, medieval bridge crosses the river at the bottom of Church Street, which is dominated by the massive, pyramid-roofed tower of St George's. The tower is Norman, but the roof is a 17th-century addition. It is believed to stand on Saxon foundations and to have been a place of refuge from marauders before the castle was built.

Parliamentary soldiers occupied the church during the Civil War, and it was partly burned in a Royalist attack. Charles II ordered funds to be collected for repairs, and an £8,000 restoration was made in 1877. The lych-gate entrance to the churchyard was built in 1723, and benefaction boards dating from 1725 to 1869 hang in the church porch. They list endowments to provide such benefits as bread, money and schooling for the village's 15 poorest children. Inside the church there is a wealth of Jacobean woodcarving, including a fine pulpit. Five old prints near the lady chapel show how the church looked before it was restored.

CLYRO
POWYS

1 mile north-west of Hay-on-Wye (page 425 Db)

Low, rolling hills to the north shelter Clyro, which looks out over the River Wye's broad valley to the dramatic crests of the Black Mountains behind Hay-on-Wye. The landscape and its people inspired the Reverend Francis Kilvert to write his vivid and still popular diaries while he was Clyro's curate, from 1865 until 1872. He is commemorated by a memorial in the village church, and by a plaque on the wall of his home, Ashbrook House, which stands by a stream opposite the Baskerville Arms.

Set back from the road that follows the Wye towards Hereford, Clyro has retained much of the peaceful atmosphere that enchanted and inspired its Victorian curate. White and colourwashed buildings of stone, together with a small pottery, cluster round a church that dates from the 13th century but was largely rebuilt shortly before Kilvert became curate. Two particularly attractive cottages, roofed with mossy and lichened slates, stand at the churchyard's eastern gate, looking up a long avenue of yew trees.

A mound marking the site of Clyro's Norman castle stands beside the road that leads to Hay-on-Wye, and the remains of a Roman fort have been uncovered in nearby fields. Like the castle, it was built to guard one of the main routes into south-west Wales.

Sir Reginald Braybrok (1405).

MEDIEVAL MEMORIALS

There are over 7,000 brasses still in Britain – more than remain in the rest of Europe – and the Church of St Mary Magdalene in Cobham, Kent, has the finest collection of them all. Brasses, while in no sense portraits, are a guide to the fashions in armour and dress of the period, as well as testaments to the art of the medieval engraver. Below are some of the brasses in St Mary's.

Sir John de Cobham (1365).

Sir John de Cobham (1354).

Sir Nicholas Hauberk (c. 1407).

Sir Thomas Brooke and his wife (1529).

COBHAM
KENT

4 miles south-east of Gravesend (page 423 Ec)

Cobham is to brass-rubbers what the National Gallery is to art lovers. There, on the wide chancel floor of the Church of St Mary Magdalene, is the finest collection of medieval brass memorials in England – a pavement of brasses set in stone slabs and spanning the years from 1320 until 1529. Most of them commemorate the members of the de Cobham and Brooke families, lords of the manor. Just south of the church is the College, founded by Sir John de Cobham in 1362 as a chantry for five priests. The college buildings were converted into almshouses in 1598, and still serve that purpose today.

The houses in the village street date in most cases from the 18th century, but among them are the 17th-century Forge Cottage, near the war memorial, and the half-timbered Leather Bottle Inn which Dickens – who knew the area well – used as a setting in *Pickwick Papers*. Owletts, a fine brick building of Charles II's reign, stands in comparative isolation at the west end of the street. It belongs to the National Trust and is open to the public on Wednesdays and Thursdays.

Cobham Hall stands in parkland at the other end of the village, and is reached by a drive that turns off the road to Shorne. The Hall is an imposing red-brick manor of the late-Elizabethan period, to which many additions and alterations have been made over the centuries, the most obvious being the broad, colonnaded front added in 1662. The park is the largest in the south-east, and was originally the hunting park of the Cobhams.

The grounds of Cobham Hall were laid out in the early 18th century by the landscape gardener Humphrey Repton. The Hall is now a girls' public school, but is open to visitors on certain days during the school holidays. Among the rooms worth seeing is the Gilt Hall, with a gilded plaster ceiling completed in 1672. In the Long Gallery is the state coach of the Earls of Darnley.

All round the church, and on the corners of the lanes in the vicinity, are sarsen stones – large smooth boulders of brown crystalline sandstone that were known as 'sour stones' or 'saracen stones'. They were probably used by prehistoric men to construct megalithic monuments.

COITY
MID-GLAMORGAN

2 miles north-east of Bridgend (page 425 Ca)

From the hills above Coity, part of the Vale of Glamorgan and the waters of the Bristol Channel can be seen. In clear weather, the heights of Exmoor are a notable landmark on the horizon. A chambered long-cairn tomb about 4,000 years old may be visited a few hundred yards from Byeastwood Farm.

The character of the village with its pale grey-stone houses has changed with the growth of new housing, but Coity remains dominated by its great ragged ruin of a castle. According to tradition, the stronghold was built by a de Turberville in the 12th century, during the Norman conquest of South Wales. De Turberville and his family held Coity until the 14th century.

Small stone effigies of de Turbervilles rest in the 14th-century church beside the castle, which is surrounded by a steep, grassy bank and a dry moat. The church tower features some splendidly grotesque gargoyles.

COLLINGHAM
NOTTINGHAMSHIRE

6 miles north-east of Newark-on-Trent (page 430 Cd)

Two settlements, North and South Collingham, link up to form this long village. South Collingham has gabled, red-brick houses, one of them thatched. Close to the green a high limestone wall, set with Gothic-style gateways, surrounds The Cottage. On the green is a hollow-trunked elm tree planted in 1746 to celebrate the defeat of Bonnie Prince Charlie at Culloden.

There are two parish churches: the part-Norman St John the Baptist at South Collingham, and the 13th-century All Saints at North Collingham. Both are built of limestone and stand among trees in quiet waysides. All Saints is on high ground above the River Fleet, a tributary of the Trent, and a stone beside the churchyard gate is inscribed with the flood level of 1795, about 5 ft above road level.

COLSTERWORTH
LINCOLNSHIRE

7 miles south of Grantham (page 432 Ad)

Limestone houses are strung out along a ridge in this large village, with the infant River Witham flowing below. The straightness of the narrow main street provides a clue to its Roman origins. The Roman road, Ermine Street, leaves the line of the main modern highway near Colsterworth and runs straight north to Lincoln.

Colsterworth is the birthplace of Isaac Newton. The great scientist was born in the little 17th-century Woolsthorpe Manor on Christmas Day 1642. The record of his baptism is in the church register: 'Isaac, son of Isaac and Hanna Newton, January 1, 1642–3.' In 1665–6 the plague caused Newton to flee from Cambridge and return to Woolsthorpe Manor for a stay of 20 months. The manor is now maintained by the National Trust and is open on Mondays, Wednesdays, Fridays and Saturdays from April to October – when the public can see the study in which Newton did much of his most important scientific work during his stay.

The Church of St John the Baptist, part of which dates back to the 12th century, contains a sun-dial cut by Newton at the age of nine. It is set into the wall behind the organ.

COLSTON BASSETT
NOTTINGHAMSHIRE

9 miles south-east of Nottingham (page 430 Cc)

At the western end of the Vale of Belvoir the River Smite flows through Colston Bassett, a village set among trees above which rises the slender spire of the parish church. St John's was built in 1892 by Robert Millington Knowles, the lord of the manor, in memory of his wife, Alice, and his son. He spared no expense in providing a lavishly designed building. Battlements and pinnacles adorn the tower, crowned by the spire, some 150 ft high, and in the nave are richly carved stone arcades and slender pillars decorated with angels. A life-sized angel sculptured in marble commemorates Alice Knowles in the chapel.

South of the church a medieval cross stands at the junction of the main street and Hall Lane, which crosses the Smite over a stone bridge and leads to Colston Hall. The house was built in 1704, and is set in parkland which rises gently to the north to the ruined Church of St Mary. This was Colston Bassett's original church, and dates from Norman times. When Robert Knowles decided to build a new church, St Mary's was in a state of decay and Knowles ensured its status as a ruin by removing the roof.

The Vale of Belvoir is noted for its Stilton cheese, which is made in Colston Bassett.

COLWALL
HEREFORD AND WORCESTER

4 miles north-east of Ledbury (page 425 Eb)

Colwall Stone, a large piece of limestone, stands in the centre of this big and sprawling village set on the wooded western slopes of the Malvern Hills. According to one legend a giant who lived in a cave beneath the nearby Herefordshire Beacon hurled the stone at his beautiful but faithless wife, killing her on the spot. Another version says that the stone was put there by the Devil, and that each midnight the stone turns around. No one, however, has seen this happen.

The 1,114 ft Herefordshire Beacon is reached from the top of the village, along the scenic Jubilee Drive. The Beacon is the site of an Iron Age fortress and is close to Wynds Point, the former home of the Swedish soprano Jenny Lind. The 'Swedish Nightingale' gave her final recital at nearby Malvern in 1883 and died at Wynds Point. William Langland, author of *The Vision concerning Piers the Plowman*, one of the earliest poems in the English language, is believed to have been born in the area around 1330 and to have found much of his inspiration in the surrounding hills. He is said to have lived near Langland, the long field next to the south-west boundary of the parish, now bisected by the railway.

In the 1860s a well-known local engineer, Stephen Ballard, drove a railway tunnel through the Malvern Hills and linked the village with

London. Colwall grew up around the station and today it is the only Herefordshire village at which trains still stop.

Just outside the present village is the Church of St James the Great. It was built in the 13th century as a chapel for the manor of Colwall. Close by is Park Farm, a mainly 16th-century timber-framed building with brick infill. It was formerly a palace of the Bishops of Hereford, who owned the manor.

Colwall is one of several Herefordshire villages near which the Holy Thorn grows – blossoming, it is said, at midnight on Twelfth Night. The story goes that it was grown from cuttings from the Glastonbury Thorn, itself supposed to have budded from the staff of Joseph of Arimathea.

COMBE MARTIN
DEVON

4 miles east of Ilfracombe (page 419 Dc)

One of the strangest inns in North Devon can be seen in the straggling main street of Combe Martin. The Pack o' Cards Inn was built in the late 17th century by a notorious gambler, Squire George Ley, with his winnings from a card game. It has four storeys, each smaller than the one below, and originally there were 13 doors, the number of playing cards in a suit, on each floor. At that time there were also 52 windows, one for each card in the pack.

The inn is the most distinctive building in a main street which winds for nearly 2 miles down a narrow valley to a bay with rock pools and jagged cliffs. Most of the older properties in the street are typical Devon cottages with slate roofs and walls painted in a range of colours. Nearer the sea there are rows of Victorian houses, many offering accommodation for visitors. A chimney on the hillside to the east of the village is the only remaining relic of the silver mines which made Combe Martin wealthy some 700 years ago, when men were brought from all over England to work in them.

On one side of the main street stands the Church of St Peter ad Vincula – St Peter in Chains – built at least 700 years ago and locally renowned for its 99 ft tower with battlements and tiers of gargoyles.

THE COMBERTONS
HEREFORD AND WORCESTER

3 miles south of Pershore (page 425 Eb)

When Bredon Hill is shrouded in cloud, the people of the Combertons are reminded of a traditional Vale of Evesham saying:

When Bredon's got on his hat,
Men of the Vale beware that.
When Bredon Hill doth clear appear,
The men of the vale have nought to fear.

Both Great and Little Comberton, about 1 mile apart, are among the most attractive of the Bredon villages. Great Comberton lies on the northern slopes, its narrow leafy lanes encircling the yellow-stone Norman Church of St Michael, with its unadorned, 16th-century benches and stalls with Jacobean panels. The neat churchyard shelters beneath the spreading branches of a giant yew tree.

In the summer this is a place of blossom, colourful gardens and a rare tranquillity. There is not even a post office; the villagers have to go to Little Comberton which, despite its name, is larger and busier than its neighbour but no less enchanting.

Little Comberton's church is dedicated to St Peter, and its 500-year-old tower looks down on a rustic scene of yet more timber-framed thatched cottages, mellow red brick and gardens walled with stone lining both sides of Manor Lane. The Manor House, close to the church, dates from the early 18th century and has a 17th-century dovecot in the grounds and a 16th-century timbered barn.

A circular stone-built dovecot in the gardens of Nash's Farm is one of the largest in England, and is thought to be medieval. The 17th-century, timber-framed farmhouse stands almost opposite Old House, which was part of Henry VIII's provision for Catherine Parr, his sixth wife. Catherine, who survived the king, remarried, only to die in childbirth in 1548.

Bredon Hill rises to 961 ft above the villages, and on its summit is a 39 ft high 'tower' known as Parsons' Folly. It was built in the 18th century by a Mr Parsons, with the purpose, it is said, of raising Bredon's summit to 1,000 ft.

COMPTON
SURREY

3 miles south-west of Guildford (page 422 Cb)

Small villages are strung like beads along the thread of the Pilgrims' Way in Surrey, and Compton is one of them. The way lies just to the north of the village, following a track along a low ridge of sandstone through heath and woodland.

The Church of St Nicholas, standing at the centre of the buildings straggling along the main street, is the most memorable in the county. The path from the gate leads through a tree-dappled yard past walls of flint and dark-brown sandstone towards the Saxon tower, capped by a small steeple. Inside, all seems whiteness; not just of whitewashed walls but of stubby Norman pillars and round arches carved from the hard chalk of the Hog's Back to the north. The tops of the columns are beautifully carved with decorative devices. They lead the eye step by step to the chancel – a double chancel, unique in England. The lower one is vaulted and held within the confines of Saxon walls.

At the centre of the lower chancel is the focus of the pilgrims' devotions, a small east window with Norman stained glass depicting the Virgin and Child. The effect is overwhelming, unchanged since the pilgrims passed on their way to Canterbury in the years following the murder of Thomas Becket in 1170. The wooden balustrade of the upper sanctuary is also Norman,

and one of the oldest pieces of church timber-work surviving.

The medieval perfection of the church must have been much admired by the Victorian artist G. F. Watts, who lived in the village and to whose memory a large gallery is devoted. Close by is the cemetery chapel designed by his wife. They are buried together beside the chapel.

The stonework in some of the cottages in the village shows the typical galleting of the area: small fragments of ironstone inserted into the mortar between the irregular building blocks to create a pattern of spots. Near the church, the White Hart cottage, once an inn, is a fine example of a timber-framed house, its upper storeys jutting out over the street.

CONISTON
CUMBRIA

6 miles south-west of Ambleside (page 435 Cc)

Old slate quarries and copper mines have not diminished the majesty of the Old Man of Coniston. Its summit, 2,627 ft above sea-level and almost 2,500 ft above Coniston Water, completely dominates this village where buildings of dark local stone mingle with others whose walls gleam with whitewash. One of the most handsome architectural features of Coniston is a white-washed, seven-doorway terrace, right beneath the Old Man and overlooking the Church Beck's boulder-strewn waters. The terrace, which is known as The Forge, is about 150 years old.

Near by, in the main street, a museum commemorates the life and work of John Ruskin, the Victorian writer, critic and social reformer, who had a profound influence upon the general artistic taste of his time. Ruskin lived at Brantwood, on the far side of Coniston Water, from 1871 until his death in 1900. Spurning the chance of a grave in Westminster Abbey, he chose to be buried at Coniston and lies beneath a splendidly carved cross in the north-east corner of the churchyard.

Coniston Water has been used for several water-speed record-breaking attempts, it being more placid than Windermere.

A slab of inscribed slate commemorates Donald Campbell, who died trying to break the world water-speed record in 1967. His jet-powered *Bluebird* went out of control at more than 300 mph. Campbell's body was never found.

Coniston is a fine centre for walkers. Paths lead to the summit of the Old Man, but less energetic explorers can stroll beside the lake or wander through the Grizedale Forest on its eastern shore.

REGAL LAKELAND *Crowned with rain clouds, the Old Man* ▷ *of Coniston (left) looks darkly down on the village from which it takes its name. Coniston, which means 'king's village' in Anglo-Saxon, also gave its name to one of the jewels of the Lake District, Coniston Water, which spreads out before it on the valley floor. It is not known which king chose the village for his own, but he found a setting between mountain and lake that is unrivalled, even among the beauties of Lakeland.*

CONISTON

CONSTANTINE
CORNWALL

5 miles south-west of Falmouth (page 418 Ba)

Granite for London's original Waterloo Bridge came from around Constantine, which is near one of Cornwall's main quarrying areas. Many buildings in the village, from the 15th-century church to the terraces of quarry-workers' cottages, are built of this hard-wearing local stone.

The village stands on rising ground above the thickly wooded valley leading to the quiet creeks of the Helford river. Its main street has several shops, a restaurant and the Queen's Arms Inn.

In a field just north of the village is Piskey Hall, an ancient underground passage with granite walls and known as a *Fogou*, the Cornish word for 'cave'. It was originally part of a prehistoric fortification. Entrance to the remains is through Bosahan Farm.

South-east of Constantine is Porth Navas, on a wooded creek of Helford river where the Duchy of Cornwall has its oyster beds.

CORFE CASTLE
DORSET

4 miles south-east of Wareham (page 421 Ca)

In Anglo-Saxon, *Corfe* means 'a cutting' or 'pass', an apt term for the deep gully that slices through the main ridge of the Purbeck Hills. Two roads from the west and three from the east converge on Corfe, but none by-passes it, stressing the strategic importance of the castle, towering high above the village on the top of its steep little hill.

The village has grown up around the hill, which has been fortified since at least Saxon times. The present castle dates from the late 15th century, but stands on the site of a much earlier fortress possibly built or enlarged by King Edgar in the 970s. His son, the young King Edward, afterwards canonised as St Edward the Martyr, was stabbed to death there in 978 – according to legend on the orders of his ambitious stepmother, Aelfthryth – or Elfrida.

The military role of Corfe Castle came to an abrupt end during the Civil War. For a time, it was the only Royalist stronghold between London and Exeter, but it fell at last when a member of the garrison turned traitor and admitted the Parliamentary besiegers who destroyed it with gunpowder. The ruin is now much as Cromwell's sappers left it in 1646.

Much of the attraction of Corfe lies in its uniformity. The entire village and the castle is made of grey Purbeck stone – not just the walls, but the roofing slates too. Much of the old village is built of stone taken from the ruined castle.

Many of the houses have neat little dormer windows and tall stone chimneys, and Corfe's older buildings include the fine old manor house. The Company of Marblers and Stone-Cutters of the Isle of Purbeck, an ancient organisation of craftsmen, has its headquarters at Corfe. It meets

BLOOD AND BETRAYAL *Lowering clouds pile up behind the brooding ruins of treachery-haunted Corfe Castle, perched strategically on a hill to dominate a gap in the Purbeck range. Edward the Martyr was murdered there in 978, and the Duke of Brittany was starved to death in its dungeons with other French captives by King John. It was blown up finally in 1646 after a traitor in the Royalist garrison allowed Cromwell's Roundheads inside.*

every Shrove Tuesday at the Fox Inn, when church bells are rung, a football is kicked around and newcomers are initiated by having to carry a loaf and a mug of beer, harassed by the members, without spilling any.

The Church of St Edward the Martyr was extensively restored in 1859, having fallen into ruin through centuries of neglect aggravating the battle scars received during the Civil War. According to a contemporary report, the Parliamentarians found that 'the most advantageous part of their batteries was the church, which they, without fear of profanation, used not only as their rampart but as their rendezvous. Of the surplesse they made two shirts for two soldiers, they broke down the organs and made the pipes serve for cases to hold their powder and shot, and, not being furnished with muskett-bullets, they cut off the lead of the church and rolled it up and shot it without even casting it in a mould'.

From the church, the two main streets, West Street and East Street, lead away from the castle and village centre, slightly diverging. Between them lies meadowland, carefully preserved and registered as Common Land.

CORRIE
STRATHCLYDE

4 miles north of Brodick (page 441 Dc)

Goat Fell, the highest mountain on the Island of Arran, looms 2,866 ft above the coastal village of Corrie. A picturesque row of whitewashed cottages at the foot of the fell faces eastwards across the Firth of Clyde – and it has long been a

magnet to artists and photographers. The rest of Corrie's houses stand close to the shore, with wooded slopes rising sharply behind. Red deer come down from the foothills in the winter to forage, causing the residents to erect high wooden fences to protect their gardens.

For generations, Corrie's economy was based on fishing and quarrying. From the late 18th century, limestone was taken from the hills, and in 1882 a harbour was built to ship out sandstone from the local quarries. However, the harbour was not deep enough to hold the 19th-century tourist steamers – and today it is sanded-up.

Corrie is a good base for climbers and walkers – and, to the north, a coastal path leads to the impressive Fallen Rocks. In the hills behind the village is the hamlet of High Corrie. It was the birthplace in 1813 of Daniel Macmillan, who left Arran to found the London publishing house which bears his name. His grandson, Harold Macmillan, was Prime Minister from 1957 to 1963.

CORRIS
GWYNEDD

4 miles north of Machynlleth (page 428 Bb)

Nestling below the main road that runs south to Machynlleth, the village of Corris is squeezed into a narrow valley flanked by precipitous slopes thick with trees, gorse and bracken. The swift waters of the River Dulas tumble through the valley. The industry that was Corris's lifeblood in the 19th century is commemorated by the name of the Slaters Arms, an inn on the narrow main street. Virtually every building in Corris is made of slate from roof to foundations, including the cheerfully mock-Tudor village institute. One little street, hemmed in by neat terraces, runs down to an old bridge where the Dulas is joined by a turbulent tributary.

For almost a century, Corris slate was taken down to Machynlleth by rail, following the opening of a horse-drawn tramway in 1859. Steam was introduced 19 years later, and the line remained open until 1948. Relics gathered together by the Corris Railway Society are now displayed in what used to be the stables and coach-house of the village station.

Upper Corris, 1 mile to the north-west, is overlooked by abandoned slate workings. A craftshop selling souvenirs made from slate provides a link with the old industry, as do the buildings and the slate slabs used for fencing.

COXWOLD
NORTH YORKSHIRE

8 miles south-east of Thirsk (page 436 Cc)

Oliver Cromwell is said to be buried at Newburgh Priory, south-east of the village. The story is that his body was taken there by his daughter, Mary, after the Restoration of Charles II in 1660, and buried in a brick vault which has never been

opened. Mary was the wife of Earl Fauconberg, and the Elizabethan priory was his family home. He is remembered in the name of the village pub, the Fauconberg Arms.

Coxwold has changed little since the almshouses down the hill from the Fauconberg Arms were built in 1662. The main street is steep, and pleasantly lined with grassy banks and cobbled verges. Stone houses climb the hill on either side of the street.

The 15th-century Church of St Michael, up the hill from the Fauconberg Arms, has been much altered since Laurence Sterne, author of *Tristram Shandy*, was Vicar of Coxwold. Sterne preached there from 1760 until his death eight years later. He gave the title of his book to his house, Shandy Hall, a tree-shaded brick building on the western edge of the village. Several of its rooms have been maintained in the style of Sterne's time. The house is open to the public on Wednesday afternoons during the summer.

Behind the church, Colville Hall is a good example of early-17th-century design, with gables, mullioned windows and a huge chimney at the back. Opposite the church is another 17th-century building, the Old Hall, which was once a grammar school but is now a private house.

The ruins of 12th-century Byland Abbey lie 1½ miles from Coxwold on the Ampleforth road.

CRAIGELLACHIE
GRAMPIAN

3 miles south of Rothes (page 443 Fd)

Two rivers, the Fiddich and the Spey, join near the stone-built village of Craigellachie – whose terraces face west over open ground and a wooded island to the great crag of Craigellachie Rock. It was there that the engineer Thomas Telford built his beautiful Craigellachie Bridge, a single arch of delicate ironwork with twin ornamental towers at each end. The bridge was opened in 1815, and is still intact. However, it has been replaced as the chief crossing over the Spey by a new bridge, a short way to the east.

Craigellachie is noted for its salmon fishing, magnificent mountain scenery and whisky. In 1890, Craigellachie copied many of its neighbours by opening its own distillery, the White Horse. Near by is the cooperage, where wooden casks to store the whisky are made.

Just over 2 miles to the north-east is the 1,546 ft high Ben Aigan, from which there are spectacular views of the Spey Valley.

CRAMOND
LOTHIAN

5 miles west of Edinburgh (page 441 Fd)

For at least 1,800 years Cramond has stood at the mouth of the River Almond, which forms Edinburgh's western border. But the village – with its trim, whitewashed houses and small yachting harbour – is quite distinct from the city. Some buildings, including the church, manse and old schoolhouse, lie within the rectangular outline of a Roman fort. The fort was built in AD 142 as a supply base for the Antonine Wall, the northern limit of the Roman Empire. The first church was built in the 6th century, on the foundations of the old Roman headquarters. The present parish church – renovated in 1656 and containing some of the earlier stonework – stands on the headquarters' site.

Cramond is divided into two contrasting parts. One is on rising ground east of the Almond, which flows into the Firth of Forth. The main building there is Cramond House, built in the 1680s for the local laird. The other section is the cluster of ironworkers' cottages by the water. Near by is the Cramond Inn. Robert Louis Stevenson used to visit Cramond, and portrayed the village in his adventure novel *St Ives*, published in 1897 three years after his death.

Over the years, as Edinburgh grew closer to Cramond, the houses fell into disrepair. In 1958, 26 of them, although outwardly attractive, were condemned. A private fund was started to save them, and the local council then launched a full-scale restoration and modernisation programme.

A sailing club now stands on the Almond beyond the restored houses, and a small ferry plies the narrow river mouth. It takes visitors to the Dalmeny Estate, where stands Dalmeny House, the home of the Earl of Rosebery, with its wooded grounds, farmlands and walks. Following the Almond Valley, a short walk leads to the site of Cockle Mill, and, beyond that, Fair-a-Far Mill, where iron-founding was carried on in the 18th and 19th centuries. One of the weirs which diverted water to power the original forge hammers is still there. The dock where iron ore from Sweden and Russia was unloaded forms an inlet on the riverbank.

From Cramond Island there are views of the Forth Railway Bridge, opened in 1890 by the future King Edward VII. Behind it is the new road bridge, which Queen Elizabeth II opened in September 1964.

CRANBORNE
DORSET

8 miles north-west of Ringwood (page 421 Db)

Red-brick and colour-washed cottages give Cranborne a bright and attractive appearance. The narrow streets and market place are flanked with handsome town houses – many of them Georgian and late Stuart – and there is a multitude of shining roof tiles from the kilns down the River Crane valley. The village is set on the edge of the rolling chalk uplands, Cranborne Chase, one of the great medieval forests. Several monarchs – including King John and James I – hunted there, and for centuries the woodland was governed by Cranborne Chase Court.

The outstanding building in Cranborne is the Church of St Mary, St Peter and St Bartholomew. The church was originally attached to a 10th-century Benedictine abbey, but the oldest part now remaining is the Norman doorway in the north porch, retained when the church was rebuilt in the 13th century. The church has a fine barrel roof, and its treasures include a finely carved medieval oak pulpit and fragments of 13th or 14th-century wall-paintings. In the south wall there is a late-Victorian window to John Tregonwell, who died in 1885. He was the son of Lewis Tregonwell, a local squire who was the founder of the seaside resort of Bournemouth, some 14 miles to the south. Lewis visited the area, mostly heathland beside the Channel, in 1810, and because the climate suited him well, he bought land and built there.

Near the church is the greystone Manor House, the former administrative centre of Cranborne Chase. It is mainly Jacobean, but its central block dates from the 13th century and was probably a hunting lodge built for King John. Its gardens feature Italian statuary and specialise in sweet geraniums, roses, herbs and silver foliage. They are open to the public on certain days from April to October. Another notable mansion is Cranborne Lodge, built of traditional red brick in the 1740s.

In the centre of the village is the gabled Fleur de Lys Hotel, where Rupert Brooke stayed and about which he wrote the lines:

We somewhere missed the faces bright.
The lips and eyes we longed to see;
And Love and Laughter and Delight.
These things are at the Fleur de Lys.

Half a mile south-east is Cranborne Castle, with a well-preserved medieval motte (mound) and crescent-shaped bailey (courtyard).

CRANTOCK
CORNWALL

2 miles south-west of Newquay (page 418 Bb)

A narrow tongue of water, the Gannel, separates Crantock from the bustle of Newquay. It is an ancient village, named after St Carantoc who founded an oratory there in the 5th century.

Thatched and colour-washed cottages cluster around a tiny square and a walled orchard. During the 1860s and 1870s the village's three inns closed down, probably because of the influence of the Temperance Guild. Only one of them, the thatched Old Albion Inn, was re-opened, and then not until 1946. It is said to have a secret chamber, once used by smugglers, under its stone floor.

The Church of St Carantoc dates from the 12th to 15th centuries, but was carefully restored in 1902. Its interior has white walls which contrast attractively with the brown roof and screen. The village stocks are behind the church. They used to be inside the tower, which was locked at night. In 1817, a smuggler confined in them managed to free himself and climb out using a bell rope.

According to a local legend, Crantock was part of a city known as Langorroc. The lawlessness of its inhabitants invoked the wrath of God, and the whole area was enveloped in sand. Vast numbers of bones and teeth have been found in the area of this 'Lost City'. However, during Saxon times many Christians were buried near St Carantoc's.

CRASTER
NORTHUMBERLAND

6 miles north-east of Alnwick (page 438 Bd)

The tiny harbour at Craster has changed little since it was built in 1906 by the Craster family, in memory of a soldier brother who was killed while fighting in the Tibetan campaign. During the summer, sturdy, square-sterned fishing cobles are moored at a jetty littered with nets, ropes and lobster pots. Craster's fishing fleet is small, and fishes mainly for salmon, lobster and crab. Herrings brought from the west Scottish coast are smoked over whitewood chippings and oak sawdust in a harbourside shed. They are claimed to be the best in the world.

Fishermen's cottages, some of which have been converted to weekend retreats, line the harbour. Opposite the kippering shed is the Jolly Fisherman Inn. Half a mile inland stands Craster Tower, the home of the Crasters since the mid-12th century. It has a tower, dating from about 1400, and a Georgian wing.

Behind the village is the Great Whin Sill, a rocky outcrop from where stone was quarried until about 1939. The Sill extends to Castle Point, to the north, where it rises 100 ft sheer out of the North Sea and is dominated by the ruins of Dunstanburgh Castle. A coastal path runs the 1¼ miles from Craster to the castle, which is open to the public. It was built in the early 14th century by the 2nd Earl of Lancaster, and was a Lancastrian stronghold for much of the Wars of the Roses, surrendering to the Yorkists in 1462. It was recovered a year later, then re-taken in 1464. The Egyncleuch Tower, sometimes called Queen Margaret's Tower after the wife of Henry VI, still stands, with John of Gaunt's gatehouse of 1380 and the Lilburn Tower built in 1325.

CRAYKE
NORTH YORKSHIRE

2 miles east of Easingwold (page 436 Cc)

One of the most romantic homes in Yorkshire, Crayke Castle was built in the 15th century on the site of a Norman castle. This battlemented house – which is not open to the public – is at the highest point of the hilltop village, which has fine views across the vale to York Minster. The 15th-century Church of St Cuthbert is a short way down the hill. It preserves part of an Anglo-Saxon cross and has some attractive Jacobean pews. The pulpit dates from 1637.

The village is mostly brick-built. But one or two houses are roughcast – including the Durham Ox public house – and another is half-timbered, which is unusual for this part of Yorkshire. Cobblestone paving in a small lane leading off the main street adds to Crayke's charm. The radical churchman Dean Inge, Dean of St Paul's Cathedral from 1911 to 1934, was born in Crayke Cottage and there is a plaque to him on the wall.

In medieval times, Crayke was hidden in the dense forest of Galtres.

HARRY KELLY'S COTTAGE *Low stone walls and a thatched roof held down by ropes are typical of the old cottages of Cregneish, a fishing and farming community on the wind-swept Meayll Peninsula. Harry Kelly, who died in 1938, was a fisherman and farmworker. His cottage, right, is now part of the Manx Open-air Folk Museum in the village.*

CREGNEISH
ISLE OF MAN

1 mile west of Port St Mary (page 434 Ac)

There has probably been less alteration to Cregneish in the last 200 years than to any other village on the Isle of Man. For this reason, part of it has been taken over by the Manx Museum as a folk museum.

Set in a dip on high ground in the extreme south-west of the island, it overlooks the Calf of Man, a mile-square islet and bird sanctuary, separated from Man by the treacherous waters of Calf Sound.

Many of the dwellings in Cregneish are traditional Manx cottages, their thatched roofs held in place by ropes and nets fastened to stone pegs at the top of the gables and under the eaves.

The folk museum centres on a typical fisherman-crofter's dwelling known as Harry Kelly's Cottage, which has the traditional Manx *chiollagh* – open hearth and chimney – and furnishings. Other buildings are a crofter's farmstead, a smithy and a weaver's workshop with a hand-loom on which demonstrations are given in the summer. There is also a small, thatched building fitted up as a joiner's workshop. It contains woodworking tools, including a treadle lathe.

In the field, adjoining the museum buildings, two or three of the strange-looking, Manx four-horned Loghtan sheep can often be seen grazing.

The intimate little church in the centre of the village was built in 1878.

About 1 mile to the north of the village stands the Meayll Circle, the burial ground of a Stone Age culture which flourished there between 4000 and 2000 BC.

The circle consists of six pairs of chambers, each with a flagged floor. When they were first investigated during the 1890s, the chambers held the fragmentary remains of 26 burial urns, but originally there must have been many more.

CRINAN
STRATHCLYDE

6 miles north-west of Lochgilphead (page 440 Cd)

Until the Crinan Canal was opened in 1801 there was little on this lochside spot apart from a 7th-century church. Now the small harbour forms the western basin of the Crinan Canal, which runs 9 miles eastwards to Ardrishaig on Loch Gilp and links the Sound of Jura with Loch Fyne.

The canal was built by the Scottish engineer John Rennie but was never a commercial success, despite Queen Victoria's patronage when she sailed along it in 1847.

Nowadays in the summer months, slim, elegant yachts and tough, stubby fishing boats crowd each other as they wait to pass through the lock gates. Each July, Crinan is the starting point for the final leg of the Tobermory Yacht Race.

CROPREDY, Oxfordshire (page 426 Ab)
(see Warmington, Warwickshire)

◆

SHORT CUT *Crinan harbour shelters at the foot of low, wooded cliffs beside an inlet on the Sound of Jura. Its locks give access to the Crinan Canal, which saves a 130 mile trip round the often storm-bound Mull of Kintyre – provided that the craft is no more than 88 ft long, the length of the locks.*

CROSTON
LANCASHIRE

6 miles west of Chorley (page 435 Cb)

Deep banks and high walls hold back the River Yarrow, which twists and turns through Croston. The village lies in a vale, and its Old English name means 'Town of the Cross'. This name may commemorate a 7th-century wayside cross used by the Celtic missionaries who brought Christianity to much of northern England. But there is no Celtic cross in existence: the present village cross was placed there in 1950.

In the centre of Croston stands the late-Gothic Church of St Michael. It is reached by a narrow lane flanked by terraced houses, and has a fine stained-glass window over the studded north door. On one side of the church is a small cloister, on the other, the school – founded in

1372 by John of Gaunt, Duke of Lancaster. The duke virtually ruled England in the last years of his father, Edward III, and in the first years of the reign of the boy king, Richard II.

The school was endowed by James Hiet, the vicar of Croston, in 1660. Two years later, however, his living was taken away from him because he refused, as a Puritan, to conform to the Act of Uniformity, whose demands included the use of the revised Anglican prayer book. He died in 1663 and was buried 'without ceremony or book', but is remembered by a stone plaque on the school wall.

The main road through Croston passes beside the strengthened Town Bridge which, with its hump-back arch, has carried local traffic since 1682. A short way from the village are the chapel and remains of Croston Hall. The Hall was the home of the de Trafford family from the Middle Ages until the early 1960s – when the last of the de Traffords died and it was demolished.

CROWLE
HEREFORD AND WORCESTER

5 miles east of Worcester (page 425 Ec)

A pleasant mixture of architectural styles borders Crowle's long main street: black-and-white half-timbering, the occasional thatched roof, Georgian and Victorian red brick and modern houses.

Just off the village street, at the end of a cul-de-sac, stands the mellow stone parish church of St John the Baptist, approached through yew trees in a neat churchyard. It was largely rebuilt between 1881 and 1885, but its history goes back to at least medieval times. Inside is a stone lectern incorporating the figure of a kneeling man, which is believed to have been made for Evesham Abbey in the 12th century.

Near the church is another reminder of Crowle's past, the stone remains of a medieval manor house, still clearly visible among the brickwork of Crowle Court Farm. Another farm, near the Victorian village school, has a stud with riding stables. The old Chequers Inn, a few hundred yards north of Crowle, has an attractive modernised façade of bow windows and gables.

CRUDEN BAY
GRAMPIAN

7 miles south of Peterhead (page 443 Hd)

Count Dracula came to his grisly form of life in the peaceful village of Cruden Bay – for it was there that Bram Stoker developed his story about the vampire nobleman of Transylvania.

In 1798 the Water of Cruden, which originally flowed to the sea through a little valley through the ridge to the north, was diverted into its present course. The safer anchorage which this alteration produced was the site chosen in 1870 by the Earl of Erroll to build a harbour, which attracted fishing boats and a busy coastal trade.

The settlement at this place had earlier been known as Ward of Cruden, but after the earl's efforts its name was changed to Port Erroll. Then, in 1899, the Great North of Scotland Railway Company built the lavish Cruden Bay Hotel. By 1924 this had become so important to the local economy that the name of the village was changed once again, this time to Cruden Bay.

After the Second World War the hotel was dismantled, but the fine golf course behind the sand dunes remained in use. Most of the old fishermen's cottages have been unobtrusively modernised, the harbour is busy with summer yachts, and the sands are superb.

On July 30, 1914, a Norwegian pilot, Tryggve Gran, made the first solo flight across the North Sea, taking off from the sands at Cruden Bay and landing 300 miles to the east at Stavanger. In 1971, at the age of 83, he returned to Cruden Bay to unveil a memorial in Main Street to his historic flight.

The substantial ruins of the 17th-century Slains Castle dominate the cliffs to the east of the village.

CUXHAM
OXFORDSHIRE

5 miles north-east of Wallingford (page 426 Ba)

A white-fenced stream runs down one side of the half-mile-long street in this peaceful village of brick, colour-washed and timber-framed cottages. Cuxham's little Church of the Holy Rood has an early Norman tower which rises little higher than the nave. It is entered through a typical round-arched doorway which stands in the deep shade of a yew tree. Inside, an old brass commemorates J. Gregory, who died in 1506, his two wives and six children. The Half Moon, Cuxham's ancient, thatched village pub, displays a copy of its original indenture (licence) dated 1647.

Maps of the district link Cuxham with the adjoining hamlet of Easington, at the end of a narrow dead-end lane leading from the well-preserved Cutt Mill. There are three other mills within 2 miles, all sited on the stream and all now private houses. The tiny community of Easington has not expanded much since the 10th century. The church, which dates largely from the 14th century, possesses a north doorway at least 200 years older; originally it belonged to an earlier church on the same site.

A dower house, manor house, informal Georgian rectory and the cottages make up the rest of this rural retreat on the edge of the strangely remote plain below the Chilterns.

CYNWYL ELFED
DYFED

5 miles north-west of Carmarthen (page 424 Bb)

Wooded hills enfold this pleasant little village in the rolling, thinly populated countryside north of Carmarthen. Its main street, overlooked by a neat little chapel built in 1792, slopes down towards the point where two rushing tributaries of the River Gwili meet near the village church. Tucked away behind the blue-washed Blue Bell Inn, the church dates from the 14th century and was restored in Victorian times. Its unusual east window symbolises the Crucifixion, with the head, heart, hands and feet of Christ incorporated in a cross but separated by abstract patterns.

The village's slate rooftops and colour-washed cottages contrast with the green countryside that is never far away. Trim little porches with panes of coloured glass are among the small architectural details that catch and delight the eye. Y Gangell, an old farmhouse just over 1 mile from Cynwyl Elfed, is now a museum commemorating the Reverend H. Elfed Lewis, who was born there in 1860. He became one of the best-known Welsh hymn writers, and lived to be 94.

South of the village, the road plunges into a deep, wooded gorge carved by the River Gwili as it races down to join the Tywi near Carmarthen. To the north, the road to Newcastle Emlyn climbs sharply to just over 1,000 ft and provides memorable views into the heart of mid-Wales.

DALBY
ISLE OF MAN

4 miles south of Peel (page 435 Bc)

At sunset on a clear day the Mountains of Mourne, some 40 miles away across the Irish Sea, can easily be seen from Dalby. The name of the village derives from the Norse *dal-byr*, 'the croft in the glen'.

St James's Chapel is described by the Poet Laureate, Sir John Betjeman, in his book *English Parish Churches*, as 'pinnacled without and unrestored within'. Its eccentricity lies in the fact that it was both a chapel and a school. It is built in two tiers on a hillside, and two sets of immense sliding doors separated the chapel from the old school rooms, and the school rooms from each other. The school, closed many years ago, is now the village hall.

At Niarbyl Bay, a small rocky cove where the rare red-legged chough breeds, there are traditional Manx thatched cottages just above the tideline. Cliffs form a notable panorama to the south.

◆

SAFE HARBOUR *Yachtsmen find safe moorings off the shingle shore of Dale, overlooking the great natural harbour of Milford Haven. In contrast, Atlantic rollers make surfing a popular sport on sandy Westdale Bay, half a mile west.*

DALE
DYFED

11 miles south-west of Haverfordwest (page 424 Ab)

Few villages in Wales stand closer to the setting sun than Dale, which overlooks the great natural harbour of Milford Haven and has become a sailing centre with safe moorings in Dale Roads. Most of the newer buildings are set well back from the shore, leaving it to a pair of terraces under a low headland, green with trees and overlooking a shingle beach crossed by a slipway. Giant oil-tankers can often be seen easing up and down Milford Haven, where a vast new port has developed since the late 1950s. Another feature of the seaward view is the drum-like Stack Rock Fort, built to defend the haven against the French in the mid-18th century. Dale Fort, from the same period, stands on a rocky headland near the village and is used as a centre for field studies. Mill Bay, between the fort and St Ann's Head, is where Henry Tudor landed in 1485 and marched to Bosworth Field.

A road that runs due west from Dale passes the village church and Dale Castle, and a footpath continues to Westdale Bay, a sandy beach used by surfers when the westerlies send great rollers crashing in from the Atlantic.

DALRY

DUMFRIES AND GALLOWAY

2 miles north of New Galloway (page 441 Eb)

An ancient block of stone in the rough shape of a chair stands at the top of the village on the eastern side. It is called St John's Chair, and a local legend says that John the Baptist rested on it during his supposed travels through Britain. St John was the patron saint of the Knights Hospitallers – the medieval religious order – who once owned the land on which Dalry lies. Because of this, the full name of the village is St John's Town of Dalry.

The village lies at the end of a chain of lochs in the Ken Valley. It stands on high ground, and its bright cottages, colourful gardens and riverside meadows justify its reputation as the handsomest village in the area. St John's Kirk of Dalry

– near which flows the Water of Ken – dates from 1831. It replaced a church of 1770 on the site, and the ruins of a 16th-century predecessor are alongside.

The churchyard contains a Covenanter's Stone. It marks the grave of two men who were 'murdered by Graham of Claverhouse, Anno, 1684, for their adherence to Scotland's Reformation and Covenants National and Solemn League'. It is a reminder that, in the 17th century, Dalry was the heart of Covenanting country, when Presbyterian churchmen were hounded by troops of the Episcopalian government of Charles II. An uprising in 1666 began in Dalry, and ended in torture and hanging for the Covenanters at Rullion Green in the Pentlands.

Three miles north-east of Dalry is Lochinvar, the small loch with the ruins of an island castle which is said to have been the home of Young Lochinvar, dashing hero of the romantic ballad by Sir Walter Scott.

DANBY

NORTH YORKSHIRE

12 miles west of Whitby (page 436 Cd)

From the wooded River Esk, Danby's main street makes its way towards the wild, heather-clad expanse of Danby Low Moor. Drystone walls, farm buildings and stone cottages, roofed with ruddy tiles, line the way and blend gently into the surrounding countryside. A delightful terrace of cottages, tucked snugly behind walled and hedged gardens, overlooks the road in from the east. ·The terrace commands memorable views southwards to Danby Rigg and Danby High Moor, which rises steeply to 1,400 ft. Down by the Esk, beyond a white-railed bridge over a tributary beck, lies Bridge Green. Sheep graze there, round a chapel erected in 1811 and restored in 1901.

Briar Hill, which runs east from the Duke of Wellington Inn, leads to Danby Lodge, once a shooting lodge and now an information and exhibition centre for the North York Moors National Park.

The railway through Eskdale – one of Britain's most scenically attractive rail routes – runs through the village. The arrival of the line encouraged Danby's development in the 19th century, and helps to explain why the present-day village is centred almost 2 miles north-east of its imposing parish church of St Hilda. The church, in Danby Dale beyond the adjoining village of Ainthorpe, dates from Saxon times. It is the burial place of Canon John Christopher Atkinson, the rector for 53 years until 1900, and was restored in memory of him in 1903. His *Forty Years in a Moorland Parish* retains its place in literature as an accurate account of North Yorkshire life in Victorian times. About 1 mile south-east of Danby the remains of Danby Castle, with its dungeons intact, are incorporated in a farmhouse. The castle, built in the 14th century, was the home of Catherine Parr before she became the sixth wife of Henry VIII.

DEBENHAM

SUFFOLK

11 miles north of Ipswich (page 432 Dc)

A wide main street of colour-washed and timbered houses slopes down gently from Debenham's 14th-century Church of Mary Magdalene, whose squat tower is believed to be pre-Norman. The road continues past a row of pollarded trees to a little street, aptly named Water Lane. Most of the time the lane is submerged under the waters of the Deben which trickles alongside the main street, under it and then out of the village.

A fire destroyed about 40 houses in 1744, but many of those that survived can be seen today. The old craft of rush weaving is still carried on in a building near the stream, and can be watched through the windows. All about the village are imposing old halls and farmhouses, several moated, such as Kenton and Aspall. Cider is made at Aspall, about 1 mile north of the village. Crow's Hall, named after the man who occupied it in the 15th century, is a sturdy red-brick mansion whose 9 ft deep moat is crossed by a four-arched brick bridge.

Six miles to the east of the village sits Saxtead Green's post windmill. A mill is thought to have stood there since the 13th century, and the present one, dating from the 18th century, is kept in working order. Perhaps the biggest curiosity in the area is the Groaning Stone, between the village and Brice's Farm. It is said to turn over and groan every midnight.

◆

GEORGIAN FACELIFT *This pretty pink-and-white confection, with its bowed Georgian window, is Debenham's ancient Guildhall which, despite appearances, has stood in the High Street since about 1500. The icing-sugar look was added in the 18th century. Nowadays, the building is divided in two – one half serves as the post office, the other as an antique shop.*

A personal portrait of New Alresford in Hampshire by

JOHN ARLOTT

The rich Hampshire voice of John Arlott is as English as cricket.
Of which he is the expert, the connoisseur, the arbiter of taste and style. He succeeded
the late, great Sir Neville Cardus as cricket correspondent of The Guardian,
broadcasts the season's great matches for the BBC and has written several
authoritative books on the game. So it is perhaps fitting that he
should live in a village that once boasted five cricket grounds – a village that
he fell in love with as a boy, and which he describes here with pride and affection.

❝ New Alresford is constantly mispronounced, T-shaped, honeycombed with cellars, packed with antique shops, riddled with woodworm, surrounded by watercress. The name – which means 'ford by the alders' – is pronounced 'Allsford'; and no one ever uses 'New', though they do call the adjoining village Old Alresford. Looking out of the bedroom window on this quiet spring Sunday morning, the thought came that it might have been the scene seventy years ago on the far side of two wars.

My first sight of Alresford was in 1921, when as a seven-year-old boy I cycled wheel-rim-deep through the dry grit of the Basingstoke Road into the summertime village that moved at walking pace. That memory suddenly came back, forty years later, when, with my wife, I drove into the village, saw that the first house on the edge was for sale, pulled into the yard, and bought it.

If it now seems simply a smart, residential area, one of its attractions is the unobtrusive evidence of its richly historic past – so appreciated by the newcomers that they have formed an Alresford Historical Society. It was a Saxon free borough and already a busy corn, woollen, farming and sheep-market town when William the Conqueror made his capital in neighbouring Winchester. In 1190, the Norman Bishop de Lucy, by virtue of his bishopric Lord of Alresford, embarked on an engineering operation of immense extent for his time. He had the marsh where the tiny Alre (a tributary of the Itchen), Sutton and Bighton streams met, turned into a vast 200 acre dam to make the river navigable from Alresford, out through Southampton Water, to all the world. He rebuilt the town based on a generous square and market house. The market house is now gone, but the Broad Street remains – one of the widest and most handsome in the county. The increase in the size of ships defeated his ambition for the river, but Alresford Pond – heavily silted but still covering some 60 acres – attracts water birds as rare as the osprey, and makes a spectacular mark on the landscape. Still, too, the pointed 14th-century arch of the

Great Weir links the two villages of New and Old Alresford.

Over the years between 1160 and 1736, seven fires destroyed much of Alresford's property, which explains why so venerable a place has such an 18th-century air. Only when you go to the backs of the deep-cellared houses do you find the brick-and-timber, or wattle-and-daub, behind the later façades, and the pin-pointing of the wood-worm which have invaded every beam in the place.

For a number of years in the 18th century, Alresford had five cricket grounds and was second only to Hambledon as a power in that game. Now it has not even a team – but Old Alresford has.

Its railway, the Mid-Hants, built in 1851, but axed in 1970, is kept puffing by enthusiasts for weekend trippers. The smell of its smoke, the nostalgic chug of its pistons and the sound of its whistle combine to carry me back more than a decade.

It was a rather sleepy village until the First World War, the greatest upheaval rural England has ever known, and the beginning of the end of the village life England had known for centuries. Some of the returning soldiers settled down in the village again – others did not. Certainly many of their sons escaped from what seemed to them village servitude. Tractors and milk-ing machines and silos replaced horses and men; and the motor bus and motor car brought Winchester to Alresford's door.

Some far-sighted farmers yoked the chalk streams of the Alre, Bighton, Sutton and Itchen again, in the classic combination – deep-sprung pure water, gravel seeding on chalk bedding – for growing watercress which, from the 1950s, became a major feature of the county's agriculture.

The original villagers drained away, drawn by the opportunities for employment, High Street shopping and entertainment in bigger towns. The shops which had met their needs were gradually taken over to form a nucleus of antique, book and art shops – eighteen of them – numerous enough to make the journey attractive to collectors from considerable distances.

Its water supply, crystal bright from a well in the deep chalk, was lost – grabbed by Southampton. Its tiny cinema, that changed programmes three times a week, became, simply enough, uneconomic. In common with other villages, Alresford began to change to a completely different kind of place – more comfortable and convenient than ever before. Meadows and poultry farms on the south side disappeared under a carpet of new housing. Yet the essential and original 'T' of Broad Street, crossed by East Street and West Street and watched by a vigilant Alresford Society, showed no adverse effect; rather the opposite.

Alresford is inhabited almost entirely by people who live there by choice, solely because they like the place. But that has not always been the case. When the Second World War came, the romantics saw it as the end of the old village life; but it was also the beginning of the new. Now, out in the garden, away from the traffic, the church bells – most faithfully rung – give it a timeless quality. **99**

Steam and the local cash crop.

The smell of smoke, the nostalgic chug of pistons...
combine to carry me back more than a decade.

*Alresford is inhabited...
by people who live there by choice, solely because
they like the place.*

*Laid out in the 13th century,
the Broad Street remains one of the widest
and most handsome in the county.*

*The 15th-century fulling mill on the River Walk
between New and Old Alresford.*

DEDDINGTON
OXFORDSHIRE

6 miles south of Banbury (page 426 Ab)

Deddington was a flourishing market town from the Middle Ages until the latter half of the 19th century. It still has a large market square, with a town hall of 1806, ironstone cottages and a gabled 17th-century inn, the Kings Arms.

In New Street, the main road through the village, there are a number of fine old buildings, including the Crown and Tuns Inn and Leadenporch House, which is a rare medieval hall with its original doorway. There are several good 17th-century houses and cottages on both sides of the street, including Grove Farm House, Plough Cottage and Trebolford.

The Church of St Peter and St Paul is basically 13th century, but its tower was built in the late 17th century to replace the original, which fell in 1634. It is crowned by eight pinnacles with gilded vanes, which give a flamboyant air to the building. North of the church is Castle House, formerly the rectory and dating from the 14th century, although most of the present building is 17th century.

Charles I stayed there on the night after the battle at Cropredy Bridge in 1644; and Piers Gaveston, Earl of Cornwall, a favourite of Edward II, is said to have been held there before his death in 1312 at the hands of nobles who detested him for his influence over the king.

Castle End, in Castle Street, is part 17th century and part Georgian, and is divided into two dwellings. Its gabled porch bears the date 1647. The castle was built by the Normans, and was in ruins by the 14th century. The castle mound, banks and a ditch are near the Oxford Road.

DEDHAM
ESSEX

6 miles north-east of Colchester (page 432 Db)

At Dedham, beside the River Stour, the painter John Constable's father had a watermill, now replaced by one of Victorian red brick. Constable's painting of the original mill is in London's Victoria and Albert Museum. Dedham Vale was 'Constable Country', and Dedham church tower featured in many of the painter's works.

The road into the village winds past houses of brick and plaster with luxuriant gardens, to a junction where the main street opens out and the

◆

MERCHANT'S LEGACY *Though belonging to an area where splendid churches are commonplace, Dedham's church is nevertheless outstanding for the richness of its carvings. Even the ceiling of the passage through the tower is beautifully worked with designs of the Tudor Rose and Portcullis, interspersed with the trademark of Thomas Webbe, the wool merchant whose money provided for the building of the church. In the late 1500s, Dedham was a famous centre of advanced Protestantism, and enthralled audiences packed the church for the Sunday and Tuesday lectures.*

battlemented church tower rises above shops, Georgian-fronted houses and old inns. The Sun has a coaching archway leading into its yard, where a Tudor stairway climbs to a rear wing. The Marlborough Head was the home and workshop of a clothier and then a dyer in medieval times, and became an inn only in 1702.

Diagonally opposite the Marlborough Head stands what was once the grammar school, attended by John Constable in the 1780s. It is now two private houses. Above one of the doors is a Latin inscription which records that 'Thomas Grimwood was master of the school in 1732'. Grimwood's son was Constable's Latin master. Sherman's Hall, opposite the church in the High Street, derives its name from the Sherman family, ancestors of the American Civil War general, who were wool merchants in the 15th century.

The 15th-century Church of St Mary the Virgin has heraldic symbols in the nave roof. Among other things, they depict the mark of Thomas Webbe, a wool merchant who financed the building of the church. A pew bears a medallion commemorating the first landing on the moon.

South of the village the road passes Castle House, the home of the painter Sir Alfred Munnings. Some of his paintings are on view in the house, and can be seen on Wednesday and Sunday afternoons from mid-May until October.

DEENE
NORTHAMPTONSHIRE

4 miles north-east of Corby (page 431 Cb)

Associations with the Battle of Balaclava are an intriguing feature of Deene, which lies in the shadow of Deene Park, once the home of James Brudenell, 7th Earl of Cardigan. It was Cardigan who, in 1854, led the disastrous charge of the Light Brigade. The earl – who gave his name to the warm garment worn today by both men and women – collected various military uniforms and mementoes. These are now on display to visitors in the house, which has been the home of the Brudenell family since 1514.

The park and the village are fringed by Willow Brook, which has been dammed to provide a series of artificial lakes. Many of Deene's tile-roofed cottages are built of stone from quarries at the nearby village of Weldon. Close by is the 13th-century Church of St Peter, which was restored in the late 1860s by Lord Cardigan's widow and dedicated to his memory.

DENT
CUMBRIA

4 miles south-east of Sedbergh (page 435 Dc)

Although in Cumbria, Dent lies within the Yorkshire Dales National Park. It stands slightly above the sparkling River Dee and is watched over by a cluster of steep, sheep-grazed hills – Barbon High Fell, Middleton Fell, Rise Hill and Whernside, at 2,414 ft the highest point in the park.

The narrow streets that twist and turn through the compact heart of Dent are surfaced with cobbles which, in the absence of pavements, spread right across from doorstep to doorstep. Sturdy cottages of grey stone sit snugly beneath thick-slabbed roofs built to defy the upland weather's most ferocious moods. Natural stone is dominant, but many cottages are colour-washed and have bright doors and window-frames. The Sun Inn is an attractive black-and-white building, and has an old mounting block outside as a reminder of the days when horsepower meant four legs and a saddle.

A huge piece of rough-hewn Shap granite stands in the centre of the village as a memorial to Adam Sedgwick. Born at Dent in 1785, he became a pioneer geologist and a Fellow of Trinity College, Cambridge, in whose chapel he is buried. Behind the monument, which also serves as a drinking trough, a path flanked by neat railings leads across the spacious churchyard to St Andrew's Church. It stands on 11th-century foundations, but was rebuilt in 1417 and has been restored three times since then. Its interior, light and airy, has several memorials to the Sedgwick family.

DENTON
LINCOLNSHIRE

4 miles south-west of Grantham (page 432 Ad)

Two 19th-century gatehouses of the former manor make an impressive entry to the village. They stand by the road close to a junction that leads to the village centre, where every building seems to be made of golden ironstone. They include the imposing double-fronted inn, the Welby Arms, and the church overlooking a lake.

The present manor house was extended in 1962, and is the home of the Welby family whose ancestors came to the village in the 16th century. Welbys also occupy Welby House, the former school built by William Welby in the 18th century. The Church of St Andrew is early 14th century, with a tall tower which rises in five stages. The lake in the grounds of the manor is fed by a spring called St Christopher's Well.

HARLAXTON A little more than 1 mile from Denton is Harlaxton, with its bizarre 19th-century manor – a monument to Victorian architectural exuberance. It is large and rambling, with turrets, cupolas, pinnacles and tall chimneystacks in styles ranging from Baroque to Gothic. The village, by comparison, is small and pretty with timber-framed cottages near the church and a 17th-century mansion, Nether House.

DIABAIG
HIGHLAND

On the north side of Loch Torridon (page 442 Ce)

The switchback road to Diabaig – pronounced 'Jer-vague' – passes through some of the most exhilarating scenery in Scotland. It skirts the foothills of Ben Alligin, a 3,232 ft peak of red sandstone topped with white quartzite, and descends through Bealach na Gaoithe (The Pass of the Wind). With a final swoop, the road plummets down into Diabaig, where cottages are dotted across the slopes of a rocky semi-circle.

The village is on Loch Diabaig, an inlet of Loch Torridon on the Wester Ross coast. There is a small pier used by local fishermen, but most of the villagers are crofters who graze sheep further along the coast at Craig.

WHERE HILLS ARE ENFOLDED BY A SILVER SEA *Loch Torridon, off which Diabaig lies, is usually described as the most beautiful sea-loch in the Highlands. But 'beautiful' is too gentle a term for this wild, brooding place, whose silences on calm evenings seem almost uncanny. Much of this quality resides in the hills leaning over the loch. They were old and worn when the Himalayas were young, but some of the atmosphere comes, too, from an awareness of more recent centuries. Wars, clearances and hardship have so depopulated the area that, standing at the end of the lonely mountain road from Inveralligin, the little fishing and crofting village of Diabaig (below), crouched by the shore, has something of the air of a last and gallant outpost in the wilderness.*

DINAS-MAWDDWY
GWYNEDD

8 miles east of Dolgellau (page 429 Bb)

Holiday traffic bypasses Dinas-Mawddwy, leaving the little village to live in peace in a landscape of outstanding beauty. Steep but smooth hills and mountains soar skywards on every side, with lower slopes that are thick with ferns and trees. The summit of Foel Benddin, just over 1,700 ft high, towers above the northern end of Dinas-Mawddwy's single street. It is part of the craggy-crested Arans that reach 2,970 ft before sweeping down to Bala Lake.

Immaculate buildings of rough stone line the street, contrasting with sternly elegant chapels built in the 1860s when Dinas-Mawddwy had a prosperous slate industry. Old workings, slowly vanishing beneath hardy conifers, overlook the main road below the village. One of the quarry buildings is now a woollen-mill, open to visitors.

Dinas-Mawddwy's street makes a sharp right turn by the Red Lion Hotel, and then becomes a narrow lane leading into the mountains. Cwm Cywarch, a beautiful cul-de-sac, ends beneath dramatic crags, but the road over Bwlch y groes (The Pass of the Cross) climbs steeply to 1,790 ft.

DIRLETON
LOTHIAN

2 miles west of North Berwick (page 441 Fd)

In the 12th century, the Anglo-Norman William de Vaux built a castle at Dirleton, probably of wood, on a stretch of rising ground some way back from the Lothian shore.

In the 13th century, a stone-built castle replaced de Vaux's stronghold, and over the next 400 years it was the centre of many sieges and intrigues. The last notable event was its capture by Cromwell's troops in 1650.

Soon after that, a new mansion house was built at Archerfield on the other side of the village, and the old castle fell into disuse. It is now in the care of the Secretary of State for Scotland, and has been preserved, complete with its prison, 'murder-hole' and more peaceful 17th-century bowling-green.

The village is pleasantly laid out at the foot of the castle hill. Cottages run round two sides of a green which leads to the attractive parish church. One feature of this church is a stained-glass window which features 90 birds and animals found on the Archerfield estate. At the east end of Dirleton, the old Ware Road leads to the Yellowcraig nature trail, and to the shore.

◆

PICTURESQUE RUINS *The imposing massive walls of ruined Dirleton Castle rise straight from sheer rock. The 13th-century castle was built to dominate what was once the main invasion route between England and Scotland, and the village which has grown up around it is considered to be one of the prettiest in Scotland. The ruins include a three-storey Renaissance portion, with three drum-towers and a dovecot.*

DODDINGTON
LINCOLNSHIRE

5 miles west of Lincoln (page 432 Ae)

The main attraction at Doddington is 17th-century Doddington Hall, but the village has its charm too. Groups of red-brick cottages, mostly 19th century, and farmland alternate along the main road. Doddington Hall stands close to the road behind a Tudor-style gatehouse and high brick walls.

The hall has been the home of the Jarvis family since the middle of the 19th century, and is open to the public from May to September. The rooms and furnishings are mostly 18th century, with outstanding tapestries and collections of china. From the outside the house is plain and symmetrical, with three jutting bays of red brick, each topped by a small dome. It is believed to have been designed by Robert Smithson in 1600, for Thomas Taylor, Recorder to the Bishop of Lincoln.

The Church of St Peter stands beside Doddington Hall. It was rebuilt in 1770 by Sir John Deleval, then owner of the hall, as a fitting burial place for his daughter who had died suddenly. Later, when Sir John's only son died, the church was painted black for the funeral, and traces of the black paint can still be seen.

DOLWYDDELAN
GWYNEDD

5 miles south-west of Betws-y-coed (page 428 Bc)

Halfway between Blaenau Ffestiniog and Betws-y-coed lies this ancient village set in a breathtaking landscape of forests, waterfalls, sparkling rivers and soaring mountain peaks. It once had flourishing slate quarries, but the old workings on the south side of the valley are returning to nature and in no way detract from Dolwyddelan's natural splendour.

The main street, dominated by a huge Victorian-style chapel, runs parallel to the River Lledr, with pine-covered slopes and the rocky Moel Siabod forming a magnificent background. The mountain is 2,861 ft high, and its precipitous crags shelter a lonely lake known as Llyn-y-Foel. Another broad street, flanked by sturdy buildings of local stone, runs down towards the river and passes one of the quaintest and most interesting old churches in North Wales. Dedicated to St Gwyddelan, a 7th-century Irish missionary, it is hemmed in by ancient yews and was built at the start of the 16th century. Its treasures include what is said to be the saint's bell, and there are brass memorials to the Wynne family who built the church.

Dolwyddelan Castle, west of the village, stands in ruins on a crag above the road. It dates from the 12th century and is believed to have been the birthplace of Llewelyn the Great, the warrior and statesman who ruled the whole of Wales before his death in 1240. Its restored tower is a landmark which can be seen from miles around.

DORCHESTER

OXFORDSHIRE

4 miles north-west of Wallingford (page 426 Ba)

Beside the River Thame and set among masses of willow trees is Dorchester Abbey, a reminder that this village was once a city. It stands on the site of a cathedral built by the Saxons in 634, as the headquarters of a diocese that extended as far north as Yorkshire. After the Conquest, the bishop moved to Lincoln, and in 1170 the Normans founded an Augustinian abbey on the cathedral site. This, with 13th and 14th-century additions, is the present abbey church of St Peter and St Paul.

In the 3rd century, Dorchester was a walled town on the road between the Roman cities of Silchester and Alchester. There is nothing to be seen of the Roman town now, except for a few fragments of the wall, but the winding High Street follows the line of the old road.

The village is on the west bank of the River Thame, about half a mile from where it joins the Thames. The 19th-century bridge crossing the Thame once had stone seats along its parapets,

◆

JESSE WINDOW *Part of the renowned 14th-century window in the sanctuary of Dorchester Abbey that represents Christ's descent from Jesse – King David's father. The vine tree springs from Jesse's loins to terminate with the figure of Jesus.*

but these were stopped up soon after the bridge was built and remain so to this day.

The abbey churchyard is entered by a massive oaken lych-gate erected in 1852 by William Butterfield, who was the architect for several college buildings at Oxford. A 14th-century gabled building in the churchyard was the village school in the 17th century. It now houses Dorchester's museum. Also among the graves and willows is an attractive thatched cottage.

Inside the church the long, Norman nave has a delicately traced 14th-century stained-glass window at the eastern end. The chancel north window, from the same period, is a Jesse window – one of the finest in the country. The figure of Jesse, ancestor of Christ, lies on the window-sill, and from his body springs a stone tree. His descendants are shown as fruit on the branches, some in stone and some in glass. At the top is the figure of Jesus.

Opposite the lych-gate is the George Hotel, a gabled building with overhanging upper storeys, which may have been part of the abbey buildings in the 15th century. The hotel is one of many charming old buildings in the High Street; the White Hart is a 17th-century coaching inn, and along the length of the cobble-paved street are brick-built and timber-framed houses and shops.

To the left and right of the High Street are lanes and streets full of character. Malthouse Lane has seven thatched cottages dating from the 17th century; Samian Way, near the bridge, has Georgian houses and cottages, including Molly Mop's Cottage, dated 1701, which has a thatched roof and walls of flint and red brick set in stripes and diamond shapes.

Between the southern end of the village, called Bridge End, and the River Thames runs a double row of ramparts and a ditch known as Dyke Hills. They enclose a site of more than 100 acres beside the Thames and probably date from the Iron Age.

DORSTONE

HEREFORD AND WORCESTER

6 miles east of Hay-on-Wye (page 425 Db)

Nestling under the Welsh hills at the head of the Golden Valley is a small package of history called Dorstone, which links the Stone Age with the present. Above the village, on Dorstone Hill, stands Arthur's Stone. A great slab set on upright stones, it was the entrance to a collective burial chamber around 3000 BC, and later a landmark for travellers.

In the village below, trim stone cottages stand around a small green, and spread out into a network of lanes. St Faith's Church, with its squat tower, can be reached across a small stream. It was rebuilt twice during the 19th century, but retains evidence of much earlier churches. It has a link with a murder which shocked England, for Richard de Brito, one of the four knights who killed Thomas Becket in 1170, founded a chapel there after serving 15 years' penance in the Holy Land. Inside the church is a superb late-19th-century pulpit in stone, which bears representations of the four Evangelists.

Even in the pub, the Pandy Inn, the past lingers on, in a history going back more than 500 years. Oliver Cromwell is listed among past guests. The cottages and houses near by span the years, sharing an atmosphere of pride and care rewarded by a plaque on the green which reads: 'Best-kept Village.'

The village's name has its roots in legend. One theory is that Arthur's Stone was used to worship the god Thor, hence Thor's Stone, corrupting to Dorstone. Another, more likely, theory is that it comes from the Anglo-Saxon and means the tun, or village, of Deorsige's people.

DOWNHAM
LANCASHIRE

3 miles north-east of Clitheroe (page 435 Db)

For centuries, most of Downham has been in the hands of a single family, the Asshetons. Thanks to them, the village has retained its unity of atmosphere and style over the centuries. The first Asshetons built Downham Hall in the 13th century, but it was not until the early 1800s that the family really made their mark. In 20 years of almost continuous building, two William Asshetons, father and son, gave Downham its vicarage and school. They added a Regency facade to the hall, and made improvements to the largely medieval Church of St Leonard with its short, thick tower and gargoyles which adjoins the hall.

An indication that nothing in Downham is allowed to be out of keeping is the public telephone box – which is painted grey to blend in with the stone houses around it.

The village sits on the slope of a limestone hill, beside the old Roman road linking the forts at York and nearby Ribchester. One of the legionaries died beside the road, and was buried near where he fell. His gravestone is said to protrude from the base of a wall surrounding Downham Hall, just to the left of the gates.

The church (with the stocks opposite), Downham Hall and the inn, the Assheton Arms, are around the village green at the top end of the village. Below them, stone cottages are grouped around another green and the stone bridge across the village stream. Near by is Old Well Hall, a Tudor house with mullioned windows and a square porch.

DOWNTON
WILTSHIRE

6 miles south of Salisbury (page 421 Db)

Two rows of houses, mostly brick and thatch, line a wide street with a broad strip of grass down its centre. This is The Borough, the medieval Downton built by the Bishop of Winchester about 1205.

The River Avon divides the village in two, and at its centre is a tannery, built in 1918 and still in use, with its frontage on the river bank. High

HAUNT OF WITCHES *Pendle Hill, 1,831 ft high and rising above the village of Downham in Lancashire, was associated with devil-worship during the 16th and 17th centuries. Ten witches who lived in the area were tried and hanged at Lancaster Castle in 1612. Forty years later, George Fox claimed to have had a vision on the summit – a vision that led him to found the Society of Friends, later known as the Quakers.*

Street is a continuation of The Borough on the eastern side of the river and has several 18th-century houses.

The Church of St Lawrence is large, with mixed architecture from 12th century to Victorian. It stands on the site of an earlier church, consecrated by St Birinus in 638. Inside are monuments by Peter Scheemaker, the 18th-century Dutch sculptor. South of the church is Moot House, an 18th-century building with a garden laid out on earthworks which are all that remain of a Norman castle. The small amphitheatre facing Moot House – which resembles a Saxon meeting place, or moot – is the result of 18th-century landscaping.

A Roman villa with seven rooms and a bath house was excavated near Moot House in 1955. It dates from about AD 300.

Nowadays, Downton is renowned as an angling centre for the Wiltshire Avon and its neighbouring chalk streams, the Wylye, Nadder and Ebble. Lord Radnor's estate, on the northern edge of the village, has a trout farm with more than 100 breeding pools. The long, low, 300-year-old Bull Hotel, on the Salisbury to Bournemouth road where it turns into The Borough, has attracted anglers since pre-war days. Its walls are hung with superb stuffed specimens of trout, pike and perch.

DREWSTEIGNTON
DEVON

3 miles north of Moretonhampstead (page 419 Db)

A modern castle and a Stone Age tomb are contrasting attractions near this granite and thatched village on a ridge above the Teign Gorge. Castle Drogo looms on a granite outcrop overlooking the river. It was designed by the architect Sir Edwin Lutyens for Mr Julius Drewe, a wealthy grocer, in 1910 and was completed 20 years later. The all-granite house has battlements and towers and stands in extensive grounds. The principal rooms in the building, now owned by the National Trust, are open to the public in summer. Two miles west of Drewsteignton stands a New Stone Age tomb, Spinsters' Rock, a 12 ft slab supported by three others more than 6 ft high. The monument is thought to be the tomb of a local chieftain, although folklore claims that three unmarried women assembled it before breakfast one morning to work up an appetite.

The heart of Drewsteignton is a square with a restaurant and inn, cottages and the granite-built church, Holy Trinity. The churchyard can be entered from the square through a lych-gate leaning casually against a tiny almshouse.

The 17th-century Fingle Bridge spans the Teign – a noted river for salmon and trout – at the foot of the gorge below the village.

DUNSFOLD
SURREY

4 miles south-west of Cranleigh (page 422 Db)

A broad ribbon of green stretches more than 1 mile along the centre of Dunsfold. The inns, chapel, shops and cottages cling to the perimeter of the green where it widens to a common at the southern end. Some houses on the east side are hidden behind hedgerows. The hedges carry a variety of species such as maple, hawthorn, blackthorn, yew, ash, oak and wild rose that suggests an age of seven centuries at least for this broad fold enclosed from the Wealden forest. Several trees, including some mighty oaks, stand on and around the green, which is also marked with marshy ponds and hollows.

Apart from the prominent inn, the Hawk and Harrier, most of the cottages are of brick overhung with tiles. The only obvious omission to complete the rural picture is the church, and that is to be found more than half a mile to the west, along a quiet road approached through tunnels of clipped yew. A legend explains this isolation. Every time the building was started in the village, the stone was spirited away to the present site and so, in the end, the church was built there.

St Mary and All Saints stands on a mound, which may have been artificially raised and which may have been a pagan burial mound. The Victorian poet-craftsman William Morris described this church as 'the most beautiful country church in all England'. It is a perfect example of 13th-century architecture. Even the oak pews,

showing the original tool marks, date from 1300. Each farm in the parish was responsible for supplying its own seat, and also for maintaining a section of the churchyard wall. The original altar stone, made of Sussex marble, lies in the churchyard under the shade of a massive yew tree.

A holy well, whose water is said to cure eye diseases, stands below the church by a stream.

The low-lying ground to the east of the village tempted the early canal-builders to make a connection between the River Arun, flowing south to the Sussex coast, and the River Wey, flowing north to the Thames. Stretches of this disused canal, built in 1816, are still to be seen. The canal was never a commercial success, and was used only briefly. It is said that the oak beams in some of the cottages were brought to the village by barge from the south coast, but most of the early timber construction must have come from the oaks of the local woodland, like the giant with a 20 ft girth standing by the Sun Inn.

DUNURE
STRATHCLYDE

5 miles north-west of Maybole (page 441 Dc)

The tiny harbour at Dunure is the only legacy of a former fishing industry, and an ambitious scheme devised early in the 19th century by the estate owner, Thomas Kennedy, to make the village a sea-port. He planned to bring in a railway from the Girvan Valley coalfields, but ran out of money soon after the harbour had been built. It has since silted up and is no longer suitable for commercial fishing.

Before Kennedy's scheme, Dunure was a quiet fishing village and a centre for the 'Arran water' trade – a local term for whisky smuggling.

On a headland to the south stands the remains of Dunure Castle, once the seat of the Kennedy family and the scene of a cruel torture. In 1570 the 4th Earl of Cassillis roasted the Abbot of Crossraguel over an open fire in the castle kitchens, to force him to hand over the rich abbey lands.

Two miles to the south of Dunure is Electric Brae – an optical illusion that makes the road seem to go uphill when, in fact, it is descending.

SMUGGLERS' COVE *This small and peaceful bay at Dunure in Strathclyde was once the place where 18th-century smugglers brought ashore 'Arran water' – their name for whisky.*

DUNWICH
SUFFOLK

4 miles south-west of Southwold (page 433 Dc)

Sea erosion has taken its toll on Dunwich, and what was once a great port is now a small village crouching behind a shingle bank and crumbling cliffs. An unclassified road, leading off the Blythburgh to Westleton road, passes through a dark forest to a shaded car park and picnic area. From there secluded paths wind into the village. The road passes the Victorian Church of St James and the ruined chapel of a 12th-century leper hospital. The village's one straggling street, containing a small museum and the Ship Inn, leads to the shore with its fishing boats, shore winches and a smoke-house near the water's edge.

Continual erosion has buried almost all of Dunwich's history under the sands. The Romans are thought to have had a fort there, which may lie 1 mile out beneath the sea, and the capital of the Saxon kingdom of East Anglia once stood there. In the 12th century, the men of Dunwich built 11 ships of war for the defence of the realm. King John granted the port its charter in 1199 for a fee of 200 marks and 15 falcons, and by the 13th century it was a station for more royal galleys than London. But from then on the sea began to take over, reaching the market place and refusing to stop. At least nine churches and hundreds of homes were engulfed in turn. The last to go was All Saints: its roof was dismantled in 1778, and part of the last buttress of the tower was removed from an unstable cliff in 1923. It can now be seen in St James's churchyard. But bones from its graveyard can sometimes be seen in the still-crumbling cliff face. There are also tales of old church bells tolling below the waves. The shell of the 13th-century Greyfriars' Monastery is today only 30 ft from the cliff edge, and it is estimated that the cliff is eroding at the rate of 2-3 in. a year. Some idea of Dunwich before the sea took its toll can be gained from a series of models in the village museum.

The road past the inner wall of the monastery goes on to Dunwich Heath, a windy expanse of heathland cared for by the National Trust. Beyond a row of coastguard cottages the land falls away below a parking space which offers a fine view of Minsmere bird reserve, and beyond that is Sizewell Gap which smugglers may have used to land their booty.

VICTIM OF THE SEA *A contemporary engraving showing the coastal town of Dunwich, in Suffolk, as it was in 1587. Most of what it shows now lies beneath the sea. In 1326 the first stage in a continuing saga of disaster occurred, when a storm swept away three of the town's nine churches and hundreds of houses. Successive centuries of erosion have buried old Dunwich beneath the North Sea. All that remains of Dunwich today is a small village.*

DURNESS
HIGHLAND

13½ miles north-west of Tongue (page 443 Dg)

Viking explorers gave the name Durness – Point of the Wild Beasts – to this spot on the wild north-west coast of Scotland. The village which now bears the name was created by smallholders evicted from inland valleys in the bitter days of the Highland clearances a century and a half ago. It is probably the remotest village on the mainland of Britain.

Like many crofting settlements in the Highlands, Durness is a scattered place, but unlike most others it has the advantage of being built on limestone, which breaks down into good soil for the crofters' fields. In summer the grasslands at Durness are knee-deep in wild flowers.

On the coast beside the main road to Tongue are the spectacular triple-chambered Caves of Smoo. To the west of the village, on the road to Balnakeil, is a craft hamlet where potters, jewellers, cabinet-makers and leatherworkers all ply their trades.

At Balnakeil stands the ruin of a church dating from 1619, containing the grave of Rob Donn, one of the most celebrated Gaelic poets. Near by is the old mansion of Balnakeil, once the Tigh Mor – Big House – of the chiefs of Clan Mackay, who controlled all this district before selling out in 1829.

Balnakeil Bay has a magnificent half-mile beach looking west across the Kyle of Durness to the forbidding country known as the Parph, which leads towards Cape Wrath. Just south of Durness, at Keoldale, is a passenger-ferry across the Kyle of Durness. It links up during the summer months with a minibus service to the lonely Cape Wrath lighthouse, built of granite in 1827 on a headland 400 ft above the sea. To the east of the lighthouse, some of the highest cliffs in Britain soar 800 ft above the wild Atlantic rollers which pound the shore below.

EAGLESHAM
STRATHCLYDE

4 miles south-west of East Kilbride (page 441 Ed)

In 1941 Eaglesham became the centre of national attention when the Nazi leader Rudolph Hess landed near by after his flight from Germany. It is the only claim to fame of the village, which is content to remain in quiet anonymity.

The 10th Earl of Eglington laid out the village in the 1790s on the edge of moorland 500 ft above sea-level. Inspired by an Italian village admired by the Earl, the street plan is in the form of a letter 'A' with the point at the top of a hill leading to the moors. Down the hill, between the two main streets, a small river runs to meet the White Cart Water. The ground beside the river is an elegant, tree-shaded green called the Orry.

At one time there were many hand-looms in the village, and in the 1830s, 400 weavers lived in the area. A cotton-mill stood on the Orry, and used water power to drive more than 15,000 spindles. The mill burned down in 1876, and the coming of power-looms in the industrial towns put many hand-weavers out of business.

Present-day Eaglesham is much as the 10th Earl designed it, including the parish church with its eagle as a weather-vane on its spire. In 1968 it became one of the first Scottish villages to be listed as a place of special architectural interest.

EARDISLAND
HEREFORD AND WORCESTER

5 miles west of Leominster (page 425 Dc)

All but a few buildings in this remarkable village are fine examples of the traditional black-and-white timber-and-plaster architecture of Herefordshire. Many date from the 17th century, but some are much older. Substantial parts of the Church of St Mary and the magnificent Staick House were standing when Edward III defeated the French at Crécy in 1346. The great hall at Burton Court, a mansion nearly 1 mile south of the village, also dates from the 14th century.

Eardisland grew round a castle built to guard a road between England and Wales, where it crossed the placid River Arrow. This was the road taken by Henry Tudor in 1485 as he marched to defeat Richard III at Bosworth Field, near Leicester, and become Henry VII, founder of the Tudor dynasty. The castle has long since vanished, but the great moated mound where the keep once stood can still be seen, now covered with trees

◆

GRACEFUL PRUDENCE *Eardisland began as a cluster of cottages huddling cautiously beneath the walls of a Norman castle for protection. Of the castle, only the mound remains, and in the more peaceful years since its disappearance, the village has gradually spread along the gentle River Arrow, each century adding its quota to the dignity of the scene.*

and bushes, placed between the church and river.

The road in from Leominster passes scattered black-and-white cottages and an old stone barn before reaching Staick House, just by the river. This is a superb timber-framed mansion, its beauty enhanced by topiary in the front garden, creeper-clad walls, leaded windows and a mossy roof. The oldest part is 14th century, and the most recent addition is the 17th-century dovecot-gabled east wing, which runs down to the road. Beyond the house oak beams, brick, roughcast and wisteria-webbed stonework mingle in a row of cottages on the river bank. These overlook the front gardens of an equally attractive row of houses and cottages on the other side of the Arrow, which date from the mid-16th century. The whole scene is best appreciated from the bridge across the river below Staick House, which also overlooks Millstream Cottage, formerly known as the Old School House. This was built in 1652 at a cost of £50, and remained a school until 1825. With another cottage it shares a tongue of land, between the river and a mill-race, that is almost an island. At the end facing the road is a whipping post.

On the other side of the mill-race is the 16th-century Court House, which in turn looks across the road to a tall brick-built dovecot with a fish-shaped weather-vane, built around 1700. It stands in the grounds of the Old Manor House, a 17th-century building which had its timbered façade extended in brick a century later. Opposite the Old Manor a lane leads south to St Mary's. Most of the church is early 13th century, but the tower was rebuilt in 1728 after the original one collapsed. The stained-glass window nearest to the 14th-century south porch was added in 1964. One of its scenes shows Christ as the Good Shepherd, with a typical Eardisland black-and-white house in the background.

The lane runs on past the yew-dotted churchyard and several cottages of great character before swinging right towards The Latchetts, a thatch-roofed black-and-white house with wisteria-clad walls. Ruscote, its 17th-century neighbour, is also thatched, with three good dormer windows. Swinging right again, the lane runs back towards the centre of the village, passing several more timber-framed buildings – including the post office – before reaching Knapp House, probably the second-oldest house in Eardisland. It dates from the 14th or early 15th centuries.

At the south end of the village, a lane runs past The Latchetts to Burton Court. The medieval great hall now forms part of a house which dates mostly from the late 18th century. But the handsome Tudor-style façade dates from 1912 – an early work of Sir Clough Williams-Ellis, the Welsh architect best known for his astonishing Italianate fantasy village of Portmeirion, at the north end of Cardigan Bay. Burton Court has an excellent collection of European and Oriental costumes and curios, and is open to the public on certain days during summer.

Not only the buildings enjoy a long life in Eardisland. In 1902 the vicar, checking the parish registers, found that 38 local people had lived beyond the age of 90 since 1778, and before that a certain 'Widdow Hill' was said to be 111 when she died in 1676.

EARDISLEY
HEREFORD AND WORCESTER
5 miles south of Kington (page 425 Db)

Black-and-white half-timbered cottages line the single street of Eardisley, whose name is recorded in the Domesday Book as *Herdeslege* – Herde's clearing in the wood. At that time the village stood at the centre of a vast forest, the last surviving tree of which stands on Hurstway Common, half a mile east of the village centre. Called the Great Oak, it has a girth of 30 ft.

Eardisley is in the Marcher country – the borderland between England and Wales – and the Normans built a castle there. It was plundered by the Welsh, restored, and finally destroyed in the Civil War. Still surviving, however, is the Norman font in the Church of St Mary Magdalene. Dated 1150, it is in perfect condition and its high-relief carvings show Christ despoiling Hell; battling knights; an angry lion and other figures.

Legends of phantom hounds are common along the border, and Eardisley – where the castle was once held by the Baskervilles – is no exception, for Parton, just south of the village, is said to be haunted by ghostly black dogs.

A more recent tradition, established in the 1970s by an Eardisley man who had emigrated to Canada, is the village's annual Stampede. On May Bank Holiday Monday, the whole atmosphere of the village changes for a day from medieval England to pure Calgary. Stetson-hatted local cowboys canter through the lanes to the old Tram Inn or the newer Mountie for nerve-steadiers before tackling bucking hill ponies.

EASDALE
STRATHCLYDE
11 miles south-west of Oban (page 440 Cc)

Slate has been quarried on Easdale Island since the 16th century at least, and today the village of Easdale still has signs of its former industry. It is split into two parts – Easdale on the island itself, and Ellanbeich on the neighbouring island of Seil, across the narrow Easdale Sound. A small ferry connects the two sections, and in Easdale proper there are remains of the old quarry workings and large piles of slate.

Today, Ellanbeich is a quiet, neatly laid-out community beneath the crags of Dun More. Seil is connected to the nearby mainland by the single-arched Clachan Bridge. It spans Seil Sound – a part of the Atlantic Ocean – and is known as 'the only bridge over the Atlantic'.

By the first half of the 19th century, Easdale was producing 5 million slates a year, and some 800 people lived in the divided village. Gradually, however, the quarries were excavated deeper and deeper beneath sea-level. Then, during a violent gale in November 1881, the sea crashed through a thin crust of rock on the Ellanbeich side. It swamped the workings, and cost 240 quarrymen their jobs.

EAST AND WEST QUANTOXHEAD

SOMERSET

3 miles east of Watchet (page 421 Bb)

A partly Jacobean manor resembling a medieval castle stands on a hillside overlooking the grassy coastal plain around East Quantoxhead. Court House, just behind the church, is the home of the Luttrells, a family which has links with the village going back more than 700 years. No part of the parish has ever been sold since it was granted by William the Conqueror to Ralph Paganel – a direct ancestor of the Luttrells through a Paganel daughter.

The village is reached by way of a winding high-banked lane leading north off the Minehead–Bridgwater road past squat, deeply thatched cottages. In the very centre is a duck-pond, raised slightly above road level and brimming with clear water.

A footpath from the car park leads to the Church of St Mary, some 13th-century features of which were retained when it was largely rebuilt in the 15th century. The porch has a 'coffin squint', an aperture through which the waiting priest could watch out for the approach of a funeral party. There is some fine medieval panelling inside, with carved bench-ends and several memorials to bygone Luttrells, one of whom was rector there for 71 years. More picturesque cottages and a footpath from the pond lead across a field to the rocky shore half a mile away.

West Quantoxhead, 1½ miles to the south-west, has some handsome houses and an imposing mansion, St Audries – now a girls' school – built in the Tudor style in the 19th century, at the same time as the pinkish-buff stone Church of St Etheldreda – also called St Audrey – which has an elegant tapering spirelet.

Both villages are at the northern end of the Quantock Hills, with woodland and moorland walks and magnificent views across the Bristol Channel to Wales.

EAST BERGHOLT

SUFFOLK

7 miles north-east of Colchester (page 432 Db)

It was at East Bergholt, above the winding River Stour, that the painter John Constable was born. There is a surprising number of large, elegant houses in this small community – Tudor halls, Georgian brick, Suffolk plaster with mossy red tiles and creeper-clad porches. Many of these were built by the wool merchants who made large fortunes in the Stour Valley between the 13th and 16th centuries. One of the finest views is from Stour Gardens, a graceful landscape of lawns with flower beds, grassy clumps and small ponds laid out below the home of the journalist and author Randolph Churchill, who died in 1968.

The house where Constable was born in 1776

THE ESSENCE OF CONSTABLE COUNTRY YESTERDAY AND TODAY

East Bergholt was the birthplace of the artist John Constable, who declared that he loved 'every stile and stump, and every lane in the village'. His feelings were not restricted to words, and time and again he painted the scenes of his youth and young manhood. In 1816, when he was 40, he was working on Flatford Mill, a building owned by his corn merchant father and in which he had worked for a year as a miller before leaving for London to study art. At the time of Flatford Mill, Constable had arranged to marry his fiancée of five years' standing, Maria Bicknell, that September. However, in order to complete his new painting, he postponed the ceremony – which greatly upset Maria, who accused him of putting his career before her happiness. Touched by her pleadings, he agreed to marry her in London in October, and assured her that she was not going 'to oppose the habits and industry of a student, but to solace them'. The painting – now in the Tate Gallery – was not completed until the beginning of 1817. In it, the mill and the lock are seen in the background between the trees on the left. And the photograph shows Flatford Mill in slightly different perspective, as it is today.

no longer exists, but its site is marked by a plaque on the fence of the house called 'Constables'. On the other side of the road, and a little higher up, is the tiny cottage which Constable once used as a studio. Today, it is a private house. Constable's father, a wealthy miller, operated the mill at Flatford, which still stands 1 mile south of the village. It is now a field-study centre and is not open to the public. Close by is Willy Lott's cottage, made famous by Constable in a painting that now hangs in Christchurch Mansion Museum, Ipswich. The Lott family owned several farms in and around Bergholt; a number of its members, including Willy, lie in the churchyard. Constable returned to East Bergholt many times, and much of his most famous work was done in an area about 10 miles round the village.

The Church of St Mary the Virgin has altered little since Constable's day. Its 15th-century builders ran out of money and left the tower unfinished. They hung the bells in a wooden bell-cage in the churchyard as a temporary measure. They are still there today and are rung by grasping the shoulder stocks.

Constable's parents are buried in the north-east corner of the churchyard, and Willy Lott's remains are close to the pathway on the south side of the church. Inside the church is a memorial to the artist's wife, Maria, and there is a stained-glass memorial window to Constable himself. There is also a monument to Edward

Lambe, who endowed the Lambe School for poor children in the village in 1594.

In the north aisle there is a tribute to John Mattinson, a schoolteacher who died in 1723. It bears the intriguing inscription: 'Eleven years the beloved Schoolteacher of this Town, then unfortunately shott.' But it does not say why he was shot, or by whom.

EAST CLANDON
SURREY

4 miles east of Guildford (page 422 Dc)

There are two Clandons, East and West, set amid the broad acres of farmland on the chalk plateau of the North Downs.

Hatchlands, to the east of the village, was the home of Admiral Boscawen who built it in 1756 with prize money gained from naval actions against the French. Much of the interior work was carried out by the Scottish architect Robert Adam. It was his first major commission, and the house is now owned by the National Trust.

The trim village lies at the crossroads to the west of the house and its parklands. It is one of the most pleasant architectural groups in the area, a tightly knit village of mostly brick-and-tile cottages and farm buildings set around the

churchyard, the inn, the Manor Farm and the Old Forge.

The centrepiece of the village is the small Church of St Thomas of Canterbury, in which the use of local flint is very evident. The stonework of the nave is essentially Norman. The chancel also dates from the 13th century and the north aisle and vestry from 1900.

In between West Clandon and Guildford is the square, red-brick Clandon Hall, which is open to the public. It was built in the early 1730s for Lord Onslow in an external mixture of Italian, French and English styles. Inside, its chief glory is a magnificent, two-storey marble hall. Recent restoration work has uncovered much of the original decoration and ornate plasterwork.

EAST COKER
SOMERSET

3 miles south of Yeovil (page 421 Cb)

None of the golden-stone houses and cottages of East Coker is more interesting than the long, low, thatched home of the village's most renowned son, the great navigator William Dampier. He explored the west coast of Australia, and was navigator of the ship that rescued Alexander Selkirk – the real-life Robinson Crusoe.

Dampier was renowned in the 17th century as a pirate. A journal he kept of his buccaneering days is in the British Museum, and he is still remembered for his book about natural phenomena, *Discourse of the Winds*. He was brought up in Hymerford House, which still stands by the mill-stream at the north end of the village.

He was baptised at the Norman font of the village Church of St Michael, which houses a brass memorial to him. Another memorial commemorates the poet T. S. Eliot, whose ashes are buried there. His ancestors emigrated from the village to America. In his poem, *East Coker – 1940*, Eliot wrote:

> 'In my beginning is my end. Now the light falls
> Across the open field, leaving the deep lane
> Shuttered with branches, dark in the afternoon,
> Where you lean against a bank while a van passes,
> And the deep lane insists on the direction
> Into the village . . .'

Coker Court, its hall built in the 15th century and the front and wings added 300 years later, shares a low hillside with the church. A path shaded by dark yews and giant cedars leads up to it, past a row of low, gabled almshouses founded around 1640 by the Helyar family, who lived in Coker Court for centuries. The local pub, cosy and whitewashed, is called the Helyar Arms.

EAST GARSTON
BERKSHIRE

5 miles north of Hungerford (page 426 Aa)

Seen from above, as you descend the slope of the Downs into the Lambourn Valley, East Garston is a pretty mingling of thatch and tiles. Some of the tiles are ancient and moss-grown and some bright and dashingly patterned, as on the roof of the modern Manor Farm, behind the church.

The overall impression is still attractively venerable. There are a large number of timber-framed, brick-infilled cottages whose walls, sloping inwards and outwards at all sorts of angles, seem to echo the bold curves of the Downs above. Most attractive is the row of whitewashed and black-timbered cottages on the road to the church. Each has its own individual bridge over the Lambourn, and each front door is crowned by a little thatch hat. The large, flint-built late-Norman church is approached through smooth, green paddocks. The east window, with its three huge lights, is considered remarkable, and there is a fine Jacobean pulpit.

EAST HENDRED
OXFORDSHIRE

4 miles east of Wantage (page 426 Aa)

The Eystons, descendants of St Thomas More, have been squires at East Hendred since the 15th century, and still farm their ancestral acres from the square-cut, medieval Hendred House. In the parish church of St Augustine of Canterbury are Eyston monuments going back to the 16th century; and on the war memorial is the name Thomas More Eyston, killed in 1940.

The village once held the unusual distinction of being the 'Best Kept' in both Berkshire and Oxfordshire, the latter title being due to the switch in county boundaries that took place in the early 1970s. It wears its honours gracefully, as befits a once-famous cloth and ecclesiastical centre. Traces of the prosperous past remain in the lovely timber and herringbone-brick building that contains a shop; in the well-preserved black-and-white cottages in Horn Lane; the thatch-topped walls in Cat Street, Orchard Lane and

along the Newbury Road; and in the handsome Plough and Wheatsheaf pubs. Present-day villagers have maintained old standards in modern houses, whose brick is already mellowing, and in the deep, curving thatch of the beautifully converted Barn End with its straw, rooftop cockerel.

The Carthusians built the unusual grey ashlar Champs Chapel with its adjoining black-and-white timbered priest's house during the 14th and 15th centuries. It is now the village museum and parish council meeting place. It is open to the public on summer Sunday afternoons.

An interesting feature of the church is the invisible clock, which you can hear thumping away as you enter. Constructed in 1525, it is one of the oldest timepieces in England. It chimes the hours and the quarters, and every three hours it plays a hymn. But it has no faces. There is also a lectern whose base represents a crusader's foot trampling three dragons – possibly 13th century.

◆

OXFORD DOUBLE FIRST *Due to the 1970s adjustment of county boundaries, East Hendred has been the Best-kept Village of both Berkshire and its present Oxfordshire. Among its other distinctions is a 13th-century chapel that has been a place of Catholic worship since the day it was built; and King's Manor in the village still retains a rare Crown Stewardship.*

EAST ILSLEY

BERKSHIRE

9 miles north of Newbury (page 426 Aa)

Only visitors to East Ilsley wear trousers and skirts and carry handbags; the natives wear jodhpurs and carry saddles. Mobile starting-gates and horse-boxes stand parked along the kerbs, and behind every large house, it seems, is a red-brick stableyard, gleaming with fresh black-and-white paint and polished steel. Long before you see the lean, handsome heads peering mildly over the half-doors of the loose boxes, you know that East Ilsley's business is training racehorses. But this was not always so. From the 13th century until almost within living memory this was a drovers' village, and had a sheep market whose importance was second only to that of London's Smithfield. The site of the old market is marked by a plaque in the High Street.

The village streets climb up the side of a hill whose summit is crowned by the church; beyond is the wide curve of the Berkshire Downs that from here seem to run for ever, criss-crossed by miles of paddock fencing delineating the training gallops.

Looking down from the church, the village is a pleasant jumble of white, pink and rose-red brick walls topped by mossy tiles, descending to the Crown and Horns, an 18th-century sprawl of a pub near a duck-pond that contains a large number of strident fowl. There are several imposing houses, among them the severely flat-fronted East Ilsley Hall, which is classic Georgian, and Kennet House, built at the end of the 17th century. The front door of Kennet House is hooded by a lovely white-plaster scallop shell, and attached · to the building,

of course, is a stable block. This one is surmounted by a clock-tower with a bent weather-vane – the latter being the only disorderly object in sight. Wheatsheaf House, further up the street, shows how imaginative modern buildings can enhance an old village. Two houses have been joined together at the first floor, creating a bridge-room and an arch that charmingly frames some older cottages beyond.

The first thing that greets you on entering the church is a notice asking you not to vex the goat, since it renders valuable service in keeping the churchyard tidy. The knoll on which the church stands is said to have been holy ground since long before Christianity.

According to legend, a sacred thorn tree that grew there was a focal point of Druidic rites. The present church, however, dates mostly from the early 13th century, as the massive Anglo-Norman pillars testify.

EASTLEACH

GLOUCESTERSHIRE

4 miles north of Lechlade (page 421 Dd)

Two hamlets, Eastleach Turville and Eastleach Martin, face each other across the River Leach and together make up the village of Eastleach. Turville rises in terraces up the steep western bank and is divided from its neighbour by a road,

◆

PRIMITIVE LINK *An ancient clapper bridge crosses the River Leach, which links the joint villages of Eastleach Turville and Eastleach Martin. The bridge, with its huge flat stones and steps leading down to the water, is known as Keble's Bridge after the local lords of the manor. The imposing house behind it was once a row of Cotswold cottages.*

the river and a meadow. A road bridge over the Leach links the two communities. Originally, the two villages were separate and were ruled over in Norman times by different noblemen.

The Keble family held the manor of Eastleach Turville for five generations from the 16th century. John Keble, the divine and poet in whose memory Keble College, Oxford was founded, was made the non-resident curate of Eastleach's two churches in 1815. Both churches are Norman; St Andrew's at Turville has a 14th-century saddle-back tower with a gabled roof, St Michael and St Martin's was founded by Richard Fitzpons, a Norman follower of William the Conqueror.

There are a number of old cottages in the village, some 19th-century almshouses and several picturesque farms and farm buildings of Cotswold stone.

EASTNOR
HEREFORD AND WORCESTER
1 mile east of Ledbury (page 425 Eb)

There are two castles at Eastnor – one an ancient ruin, the other modern, a creation of the prosperous early 1800s. The older of the two, Bronsil Castle, was built by Richard Beauchamp, son and heir to John Beauchamp of Powycke, Lord Treasurer to Henry VI, in the 15th century, but was based on an older structure. It was burned in the Civil War and the only remains – not open to the public – are the moat and part of a gatehouse tower.

Eastnor Castle is a Norman-style mansion with tall, turreted towers. It was built in the early 1800s for the 1st Earl Somers to the design of Sir Robert Smirke, who also designed the British Museum. The castle, with turrets at each corner and a central keep, overlooks a lake and parkland. It remains in the family who built it and who still run the estate. It is open to the public on certain days in summer.

The church, school and some pretty timber-framed cottages are near the castle gatehouse, around a green with a roofed drinking well given by the temperance campaigner Lady Henry Somerset in the 1890s. The village has no pub to this day.

EBRINGTON
GLOUCESTERSHIRE
2 miles east of Chipping Campden (page 421 Dd)

There are few more appealing sights than the combination of golden Cotswold stone and neatly trimmed thatch, and it is never more attractive than at Ebrington. The village descends in irregular steps on the northern fringe of the hills, to a valley of cherry orchards and vegetable gardens.

There was a manor at Ebrington as far back as the 13th century, though most of the present house dates from the 17th century. The Church of St Eadburgha has a Norman nave and a medieval tower. A monument in the church depicts Sir John Fortescue, who died around 1476, in his legal robes of Lord Chief Justice.

Three miles north of the village is Hidcote Manor, a late-17th-century house with a Georgian frontage. The manor is notable for its gardens, now owned by the National Trust. They were laid out by Major Lawrence Johnston over a period of 40 years during this century, and are claimed to be among the finest in England. Each section is devoted to a particular type of flower, and the gardens are divided by hedges of many varieties.

EDENSOR
DERBYSHIRE
2 miles north-east of Bakewell (page 430 Bd)

When the 6th Duke of Devonshire looked out from Chatsworth House he saw that the magnificent view across the park was blocked by a village – so he moved it. The village was Edensor, pronounced 'E'nsor', and it stood on a ridge east of the house. About 1839 the duke's gardener, Joseph Paxton, was given the task of shifting the village to a new site to the west of Chatsworth Park.

The houses were designed by John Robertson of Derby, and no two were alike. In a riot of architectural fancy he gave them Swiss-chalet roofs, Italian-style windows, Jacobean gables, Tudor chimneys and Georgian doorways. Paxton made sure the houses were placed well apart, surrounding a broad green planted with laburnum trees.

The Church of St Peter was rebuilt on its original site 25 years after the village had been moved. The architect was Sir George Gilbert Scott and he employed the Early English style, giving the church a great tower and soaring spire that dominated the village. The Lady Chapel has a fine monument to William Cavendish, 1st Duke of Devonshire, and his brother Henry. Other members of the family are buried in the churchyard, which also contains the body of Sir Joseph Paxton who was knighted after building London's Crystal Palace in 1851, and who died 14 years later.

Kathleen, sister of the late American president John F. Kennedy, who married the present duke's elder brother, the Marquis of Hartington, is buried in the churchyard. She died in a flying accident in France in 1948, four years after her husband had been killed in action. An inscribed stone commemorates President Kennedy's visit to his sister's grave.

A lane continuing from the village street climbs for 1 mile and gives increasingly better views back over Chatsworth Park and the Derwent Valley. High in the woods above the valley is the Hunting Tower, which was part of the original 16th-century Chatsworth House, built on a different site to the present house. Another remnant of that age is Queen Mary's Bower, near the Derwent and Chatsworth Bridge. It is probable that Mary, Queen of Scots spent some time in this stone turret while a periodic prisoner at Chatsworth in the 1570s.

Village BUILDINGS
and their links with the past

[A] Holy Trinity Church, Staunton Harold, Leicestershire. Built in the Perpendicular style between 1653–5 of local limestone.

[B] Village school, Peasmore, Berkshire. A mid-19th-century building of red brick and sandstone, with a clay tiled roof.

[C] Shandy Hall – vicarage in Coxwold, North Yorkshire. Built in the mid-18th century with red brick and clay roofing tiles.

[D] Almshouses, Moretonhampstead, Devon. Built in 1637 of local granite and thatched with heather from nearby Dartmoor.

Most of our villages owe their charm to chance – the picturesque result of centuries of unplanned and undisciplined growth. Clustering around the original nucleus of parish church and manor house, the village community grew. A cottage was built here, a corner shop there, culminating with the need for such communal buildings as a school, an inn and a village hall. As a village grew, so its character emerged. Though there might be a pleasing jumble of variety between individual buildings, the village as a whole would take on its own look. This might be the result of using local building materials – the warm stone of the Cotswolds, for instance, or the snug thatch of the West Country – or it might be a character that expressed the nature of the village economy, producing a farming village, a fishing village, a colliery village or a weaving village. The village shown below is a composite one, for no single example exists with such a diversity of building materials and style. But every single building does exist – they are chosen from villages throughout the country. The result illustrates the range and variety of our village buildings.

E *House at Culross, Dunfermline. Built in the 16th century it has stone walls faced with rough-cast (sand and cement mortar dashed with pebbles) and colourwashed.*

F *Fleece Inn, Bretforton, Hereford and Worcester. A 14th-century, timber-framed building with brick infilling, and clay-tiled roofing. It was originally built as a farmhouse and converted to an inn in 1854.*

G *The Ancient House, Clare, Suffolk. A 15th-century timber-framed house on a brick foundation. The plaster-faced walls were decoratively pargeted during the 17th century. The roof is clay tiled.*

H *Old Post Office, Lacock, Wiltshire. A pair of 18th-century houses in a formal Georgian style, with smooth-faced limestone walls and clay roofing tiles.*

I *Corner shop, Hawkshead, Cumbria. An 18th-century house, with an early-Victorian shop front, colour-washed stone walls and a slate roof.*

J *Castle Inn, Chiddingstone, Kent. Late 16th-century/ early-17th-century building, having tile-hung timber-framed walls on a stone foundation. The bay gable has decorated bargeboards.*

K *Cottage at Penarvon Cove, Cornwall. A mid-18th-century building with colour-washed cob walls and a slate roof. The windows are fanciful 19th-century Gothic.*

L *Terraced cottages in Bibury, Gloucestershire. Built in the early 17th century, of local stone with stone flag roofing, the cottages were the homes of local weavers and spinners.*

M *Lamb House, Rye, Sussex. An elegant brick-built house that was finished in 1723.*

N *Farmhouse, from Abernodwydd, Wales. A 16th-century timber-framed house, with a straw-thatched roof. It is now at the Welsh Folk Museum, St Fagans.*

O *Mill at Bourne, Gloucester. It was built in 1591, and has been a cloth and a flour mill. It is a mixture of local stone, timber-boarding and clay tiles.*

P *Cottage, Blaise Hamlet, Bristol. One of nine similar homes designed by John Nash and built for the retired servants of a local merchant between 1810–11. The walls are random rubble stonework, with a straw-thatched roof. This contrived rusticity was popular in the early 19th century.*

Q *Cottage at Selworthy, Somerset. One of many similar cottages built in 1820 for retired workers of the Acland family. The cob walls, with a thatched roof, include a large baking oven at the foot of the chimney.*

R *House at Rhydycarw, Trefeglwys, Wales, built in the 17th century. It has close-timbered walls, with wattle-and-daub infilling, and a roof of slate.*

S *Priest's House, Smallhythe, Kent, built around 1500. The wooden walls, with wattle-and-daub infill panels, incorporate some old ship's timbers. The roof is red clay tile.*

T *Village Hall, Buscot, Oxford. A late-19th-century building of limestone walls and slate roof.*

U *Manor House, Woolsthorpe, Lincolnshire. Built in 1620 with stone walls and slate roof.*

Building materials and styles

Dramatic changes in the looks and character of Britain's villages can often be seen in places only a few miles apart.

This is because communities tended to use the most convenient local materials to hand, and to build by methods proved and improved by generations of craftsmen.

Where there was stone, that was what they used – flints, rubble, or shaped stone. Clay served in several forms – baked into bricks, mixed with other materials, or bonded with something fibrous, such as horsehair. Then there was wood, used everywhere except on moorlands and mountains where it was scarce or non-existent.

As the materials affected the methods of construction, the buildings, whether cottage, shop, inn or school, developed a pleasant unity of form and look. It ran like a theme through the areas where the same materials were used, so that distinct regional styles evolved.

Some of these materials and the styles that developed from them are described and illustrated here.

MATERIALS USED FOR WALLS

COB

A mixture of clay, chalk, gravel and straw. Thick walls built in 12 in. layers, each one dried out before the next was laid. Final coating of lime or plaster. Mostly in Devon and Dorset.

RUBBLE STONE

Random rubble walls were built of smallish odd stones laid to fit roughly together, using plenty of mortar. Heaviest stones were laid lower down to add strength. Walls never more than 2 ft thick. Found in many moorland and mountain areas.

For squared rubble walls, stones were crudely shaped and laid in rough courses about 12 or 18 in. deep. Stronger than random rubble, because of better jointing, but took longer to build. Found in many places.

FLINT WITH BRICK OR STONE

Flint is plentiful in the south, south-east and East Anglia, so was used to build brick-and-flint walls. Flints were knapped and laid between corner pillars of brick with brick bands every 3 or 4 ft for added strength.

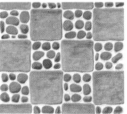

Flint was often combined with other materials to improve its strength and appearance. Square blocks of limestone were used with square panels of knapped flints to build chequerboard-pattern walls of flint and stone.

BRICK BONDS

English.

Flemish.

Header.

Stretcher.

Diaper.

Not only the looks but also the strength of a wall depend on how it is built – how its bricks are bonded to avoid a lot of vertical joints. English bond is strongest, Flemish more popular. Header bond is expensive; stretcher bond is common in cavity walls. Diaper has patterns of coloured brickwork.

WATTLE-AND-DAUB

An infilling used in timber-framed buildings. Hazel twigs were interwoven between structural timbers, daubed with clay and dung (reinforced with horsehair) and surfaced inside and out with a thin coat of plaster.

TIMBER CLADDING

Wooden boards were fixed horizontally to walls, and overlapped from top to bottom to form a stout weatherproof 'skin'. They were used mainly in Essex and the South-East.

WALL TILING

Elegant tile walls arrived towards the end of the 17th century. Plain or shaped clay tiles were nailed to wall battens, sometimes in pleasing patterns. Found most often in Kent, Sussex and Surrey.

REGIONAL DIFFERENCES IN TIMBER FRAMING

Northern England.

Eastern England.

Western England and Wales.

DECORATION

Brickwork *A practical and decorative way of filling spaces between wall timbers was with bricks – usually laid in herringbone pattern.*

Pargeting *Plaster was modelled while still wet into relief designs, and colour-washed. Used on timber-framed buildings in East Anglia during 16th and 17th centuries.*

Timber-framed buildings sprang up all over the Midlands, Wales and eastern England during the 15th to 18th centuries. For some reason still not understood – perhaps even a simple desire to be different – three quite distinct methods of construction evolved: Northern, Eastern and Western. All used the basic box frame, with the spaces between the timbers generally being filled by wattle-and-daub or brickwork. Where they diverged was in the way the timber framing was arranged. In Northern the verticals were set close together; the Eastern version had the timbers wider apart with more space between the horizontals; and Western style presented an almost square pattern. There were, of course, exceptions.

TRADITIONAL COVERINGS FOR ROOFS

PANTILES

These clay tiles had a wavy profile, so each overlapped its neighbours on either side to ensure a snug, weatherproof covering. Nailed to tiling battens. Widespread, except in the West.

PLAIN TILES

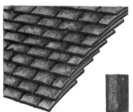

Plain clay tiles have been used since the 15th century – originally in places where slate or stone was not readily available. They are nailed to battens so that each row is overlapped by the row above.

STONE TILES AND FLAGS

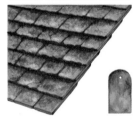

Thick, heavy slabs of sandstone covered roofs in the Pennines; thinner slabs of limestone were used in the Cotswolds and other parts of England and Wales. Both were fixed to stout battens with pegs or nails.

THATCH

Longstraw.

Norfolk reed.

Thatch was as practical as it was beautiful: warm in winter, cool in summer and adaptable to fit almost any shape of roof. Moreover the reeds and straw that made it were plentiful in rural England and Wales, where it was the traditional roof until the 18th–19th centuries. It was light, and the thatcher fixed it to the roof timbers with hazel pegs and metal hooks. Cob walls were often topped off with thatch. In moorland regions thatch was made of gorse or heather.

SLATES

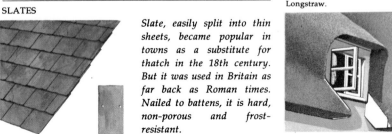

Slate, easily split into thin sheets, became popular in towns as a substitute for thatch in the 18th century. But it was used in Britain as far back as Roman times. Nailed to battens, it is hard, non-porous and frost-resistant.

EDINGTON
WILTSHIRE

4 miles east of Westbury (page 421 Cc)

Few people visiting Edington can fail to be amazed at the sight of its great church, matching many a cathedral in size and beauty. The Church of St Mary, St Katharine and All Saints stands below the village, aloof and impressive.

The building was started in 1351 by William of Edington, Bishop of Winchester and treasurer to Edward III. In 1358 his college of priests was transferred to the Bonshommes, hermits who followed the Benedictine Order. A local tradition says that it was the Black Prince, Edward III's son, who encouraged him to bring them to Edington from their only other English house, at Ashridge in Hertfordshire. The church was consecrated in 1361.

This noble building, with its battlemented tower and parapets, has a perfect background in the sombre lines of the Downs rising behind it. A medieval clock, apparently blacksmith-made and one of the oldest in England, is in the tower. A yew tree, said to be nearly as old as the church, flourishes in the churchyard. In 1450, the sanctity of the church failed to save the life of William Ayscough, Bishop of Salisbury, who had sought refuge there during Jack Cade's rebellion. Supporters of Cade, who was rebelling against the corruption of Henry VI's government and officials, dragged him out to the top of Golden Ham Hill, above the village, where they pelted him to death with flint stones.

Modern Edington, with a population of 700, is a village of farms and meadows, with some orchards and arable land extending over the flat landscape to the north. Its houses are scattered about the lower slopes of the Downs, and are approached by undulating lanes.

EDITH WESTON
LEICESTERSHIRE

5 miles south-east of Oakham (page 431 Cc)

The wide waters of Britain's biggest man-made lake lap quietly close to the slate-and-thatched-roofed houses at Edith Weston, and add to the village's pleasant air of seclusion. An ancient stone, possibly all that remains of a cross, marks the centre of the village, alongside a lofty lime tree. The road running in from the south is called King Edward's Way – a reminder that Edith Weston takes its name from Queen Edith, wife of Edward the Confessor, who inherited large tracts of land in the area when the king died in 1066. The Church of St Mary the Virgin dates from the 12th century, but the graceful tower was built 200 years later.

Rutland Water, the great reservoir alongside which the village now stands, was completed in 1975 and is almost as big as Windermere, with a 24 mile perimeter. A half-mile wide dam, 110 ft high, blocks off the River Gwash, and 3,500 acres of agricultural land – including seven farmhouses

and 16 cottages – have been submerged, along with the village of Lower Hambleton.

St Matthew's Church at Normanton, half a mile along the bank from Edith Weston, escaped a similar fate with the aid of £30,000 raised by voluntary subscription. The church, with its semi-circular portico and tower, was built in 1826-9 and designed by Thomas Cundy, then architect to the Grosvenor estate in Westminster. It stood alone in a meadow, but before the waters rose the ground around the church was raised and the crypt filled with limestone, rubble and a top-dressing of concrete up to the bottoms of the windows. Now the building stands above the surface of the lake, seeming almost to float, and is linked to the bank by a short causeway. Visitors can reach it from a car park, and view the interior through the windows.

There are sailing and trout fishing on the lake, and a bird sanctuary at its west end.

The 17th-century houses in the tranquil village of Wing, 3 miles south-west of Edith Weston, were built from stone quarried at nearby Barnack. A circular maze, 40 ft in diameter and cut from the turf of the village green, was probably made in medieval times to provide penance for wrongdoers who were taken to the centre and left to find their way out.

EDZELL
TAYSIDE

6 miles north of Brechin (page 443 Gc)

The road from the south runs straight as an arrow through the plantations of Edzell Wood, and enters the village through an arch erected in 1887 in memory of a local landowner, the 13th Earl of Dalhousie. Beyond the arch the village is spaciously laid out around a wide main street. At

LINDSAY'S RUIN *Edzell Castle was enhanced and ultimately destroyed by the addition of this Renaissance garden in 1604. The builder, Sir David Lindsay, squandered so much money on it that his family was left 'in extraordinary debt'. However, walls and flowers still blaze the Lindsay colours to the world.*

the northern end is a large tree-lined green known as Edzell Muir on which stands the parish church, built in 1818 with an iron belfry.

The modern village of Edzell was originally a hamlet called Slateford, and the earlier settlement was 1 mile to the west near Edzell Castle. The red-sandstone fortress was built in the 16th century by the Lindsays of Glenesk, and was once the most splendid in Angus. Mary, Queen of Scots stayed there in 1562, and so did Cromwell's men in 1651.

The castle was enlarged by Sir David Lindsay, who also added a walled garden in 1604. The carved wall-panels portray classical figures, and shrubs have been planted and trimmed to spell out a motto. The gardens are open on weekdays from Easter to the end of September.

EGTON BRIDGE
NORTH YORKSHIRE

7 miles south-west of Whitby (page 437 Cd)

Lush water-meadows and lofty trees at Egton Bridge, nestling in one of the loveliest parts of Esk Dale, provide a remarkable contrast to the high, rolling wilderness around the village. The scene seems to belong in the well-groomed grounds of a great country house. From the south, in a zigzag plunge from Egton High Moor, the road just past Key Green suddenly reveals delightful views of a rich, placid landscape. Pretty stone cottages overlook the river's northern bank, and a short footpath 200 yds beyond the post office leads to stepping-stones.

A railway bridge, which carries trains through Esk Dale, is flanked by St Hedda's Church – built in the 1860s and noted for its Stations of the Cross – 14 tableaux depicting the crucifixion of Christ – and The Postgate, an inn named after a local priest, Father Nicholas Postgate, who was one of England's last Roman Catholic martyrs. He was hung, drawn and quartered at York in 1679 after baptising a child into the Roman faith. The remoteness of Egton Bridge and other villages in the area allowed Catholicism to survive there throughout the Reformation and afterwards.

Near the inn stands a tiny railway station, dating from 1865, and up the hill from the church a rebuilt schoolhouse, now a private house, includes parts that have stood since 1685.

ELHAM
KENT

6 miles north-west of Folkestone (page 423 Fb)

An outstanding collection of old houses is found in this large village on the chalk downlands about 6 miles from the coast. A small square just north of the churchyard is joined by a narrow lane to a broad, curving High Street. The village houses range in style from the timber frames and overhanging upper storeys of medieval times to the elegant red brick of the 18th century. Many of the frontages are decorated with tile-hanging.

Elham lies in the Nailbourne Valley. The valley stream flows only occasionally, but when it does, there is likely to be flooding. Several cottages have wells: local mythology says that Christian missionaries and pagan gods competed to bring fertility to the valley during a drought.

The square was once a market place for which a royal charter was granted in 1251 by Prince Edward, later Edward I. Medieval timbers are hidden behind the tile-hung façade of the King's Arms Inn on its north side. In the Rose and Crown, which is part of a 16th-century coaching inn, is a courtroom dating from that period.

Abbot's Fireside, a house of 1614, stands in a prominent position in the High Street, its timbered upper storey resting on brackets carved into figures. It was Wellington's headquarters for a while during the Napoleonic Wars. In a lane called the Row, parallel with the High Street, is the Old Manor House, a timbered dwelling used by a 17th-century weaver, and a medieval hall house now converted into Well Cottage and Updown Cottage.

The church, dating from the 12th century with 13th to 19th-century alterations, is built of flint and ragstone. Inside are modern furnishings, fitted and carved in the early 20th century.

ELMLEY CASTLE
HEREFORD AND WORCESTER

4 miles south-west of Evesham (page 425 Eb)

There is no castle at Elmley today. The once-proud fortification, built in the 11th century and for many years the seat of the Beauchamp family, was a ruin by 1316. It was refortified in the 14th century, but fell into decay again in the 16th century.

The village, one of the most beautiful in England, has a wide main street, bordered by a tree-lined brook down one side, which presents a memorable picture of black-and-white cottages, thatched roofs, drystone walls and gardens.

At one end of the street stands a 15th-century stone cross, fairly well preserved. At the other end is the Square, containing the old village hall and a pretty Tudor inn. The inn sign shows on one side Elizabeth I, after whom it was named, and on the other a painting recalling her visit to the Savage family of Elmley Castle in 1575.

Near the Queen Elizabeth is the entrance to the churchyard, which contains two 17th-century stone sun-dials among the tombstones. The church, St Mary's, dating from the 11th century, is a treasure-house of village history.

SUMMERTIME BELOW BREDON *Nothing now remains of the* ▷ *Norman stronghold of Elmley Castle but its name and its stones, both taken over by the lovely timbered village that lies beneath Bredon Hill with its May trees and Iron Age fort, 50 of whose defenders were hacked to death in the 1st century AD by an enemy long forgotten. The bells of Elmley Castle church must have been among those that summoned the oblivious lovers who watched 'the coloured counties' from the hill in A. E. Housman's poem* Summertime on Bredon.

ELMLEY CASTLE

ELSDON
NORTHUMBERLAND

4 miles east of Otterburn (page 438 Ac)

During the Scottish Border Wars that flared throughout the Middle Ages, Elsdon was the capital of the Middle Marches. It lies amid the rugged moorland fells of south-east Redesdale, in the Northumberland National Park, and its heart is a spacious green where cattle were once herded in times of danger or severe weather. In a corner of the green is an old pinfold, or cattle pen, which is in good order. Between the nearby church and the school house, a stone slab is all that is left of a former bull-baiting ring.

The rest of Elsdon consists of a few 18th-century farmworkers' cottages, some modern houses, the Bird in Bush Inn, the church and the rectory. St Cuthbert's stands among trees at one corner of the green, and has a 17th-century bell-cote decorated with stone balls and a stubby spire. Most of the church is 14th century, and when it was restored in 1810 more than 100 skeletons were unearthed from beneath the north wall. They are believed to be some of the fallen at the Battle of Otterburn, fought 5 miles to the west of Elsdon in 1388 when the Scots had a resounding victory over the English.

Elsdon Tower, once the rectory, also dates from the 14th century and incorporates a pele tower – a small, fortified tower common in the Border country.

Elsdon Burn flows through a wooded ravine close to the village and is overlooked by two mounds. They were part of the fortifications of a Norman castle, built about 1080.

Elsdon is rich in folklore. In the church, three horse skulls found in the belfry in 1877 are said to protect the building from lightning and to improve its acoustics. The most grisly tradition is associated with a replica of an 18th-century gibbet which now stands 2½ miles south-east of the village, on the Newcastle road. The original gallows was called Winter's Gibbet, after a murderer who was hanged in Newcastle in 1791 and had his corpse displayed from the gibbet. There is a mythical belief that wood chippings cut from it will cure toothache if rubbed on the affected spot.

ELSTOW
BEDFORDSHIRE

2 miles south of Bedford (page 426 Cb)

Though now almost engulfed by Bedford, Elstow's claim to villagedom is still maintained by two fine rows of timber-framed, overhung, black-and-white cottages and the timber and herring-bone-brick Swan pub. Behind the pub lies the green, the Moot Hall and the church. All are splendid, and all are devoted to the recollection of Elstow's most famous son, John Bunyan, the site of whose cottage is marked by a notice peeping over the hedge on the right-hand side of the road from Bedford. His cottage birthplace,

Cottage gardens at Elterwater.

also long vanished, is indicated by a stone in the fields towards Harrowden.

It was while participating in dancing, wrestling and tip-cat on Sundays on the green that Bunyan heard a voice from above demanding: 'Wilt thou leave thy sins and go to Heaven, or have thy sins and go to Hell?' He chose the former course, and became a nonconformist preacher; this led to his imprisonment from 1660 to 1672 in Bedford Gaol, where he wrote *Pilgrim's Progress* during a later, six-month imprisonment. The Moot Hall, a 15th-century brick-and-timber market house, contains his few relics – including a door from his prison – and a museum of 17th-century life.

The church is a large fragment of a great Norman abbey, whose other remains lie beneath the fields beyond the churchyard. The picturesque ruins attached to the church are those of the mansion built by Thomas Hillersdon, using stone from the abbey, in the early 17th century.

By all accounts, until its nuns were pensioned off at the Dissolution, the abbey seems to have been fairly worldly – a place to which well-born ladies could retire from the world without too much hardship. Indeed, on several occasions, the Bishop of Lincoln was forced to upbraid both abbess and nuns for unseemliness in dress and behaviour.

The church they left – or the part that still remains – is glorious. Great high arches in the rough stone walls are echoed by tall clerestory windows above. The whole building is now warmly lit by 1880 stained glass illustrating Bunyan's *Holy War* and *Pilgrim's Progress*. Bunyan himself and his daughters were baptised at the font, and church furnishings from his day are incorporated in a chapel in the south aisle. The chapel was dedicated to Bunyan's memory by the Far East Prisoner of War Society.

IN THE VALLEY
OF THE BECK

*The sturdy stone cottages –
and colourful gardens – of
Elterwater shelter in the valley of Great Langdale Beck
beneath the exposed slopes of
Langdale Pikes. This is sheep
country, and at one time
wool was spun and woven by
the women who worked on
spinning galleries built out
from cottages at first-floor
level to catch the light.*

Spinning gallery.

ELTERWATER

CUMBRIA

3 miles west of Ambleside (page 435 Cd)

An open expanse of bracken-clad turf above the
village is a wonderful viewpoint, looking over
Elterwater's clustered rooftops to the craggy
Langdale Pikes which rise to almost 2,500 ft
beyond. The grandeur of the mountains is
emphasised by the fact that Elterwater is only
206 ft above sea-level.

Flanked by tree-clad slopes, the village is built
of attractive, grey-green stone and has as its focal
point a small green overlooked by a whitewashed
inn. Near by, a bridge spans Great Langdale Beck
as it splashes down over mossy boulders. Bridge
End, on the far bank, is an old cottage with a
periodic carpet of moss over its slate roof.

Elterwater was once a centre for charcoal burning. Charcoal made from juniper wood was particularly suitable for making gunpowder, which

became an important Lake District industry in
the 18th century. The gunpowder works at Elterwater did not close until the late 1920s. Today,
slate quarrying is a flourishing local industry and
much of the polished stone and slate goes over-
seas for the construction of important buildings.

Great Langdale Beck flows into Elter Water,
one of the area's smallest lakes, a few hundred
yards below the village. A lovely walk, much of
it through National Trust woodlands, leads
southwards for 1 mile or so to Skelwith Bridge,
where there is an impressive waterfall.

EPPERSTONE

NOTTINGHAMSHIRE

7 miles north-east of Nottingham (page 430 Cc)

A shallow stream called the Dover Beck runs
through the vale below Epperstone, and from its
northern bank the tree-lined village street climbs
up to the medieval church standing high above
the road.

The church, dedicated to the Holy Cross, dates
from the mid-13th century, but the Domesday
survey of 1086 records a church and refers to the
village as 'Epreston'. Opposite the church is
Epperstone Manor, with a red-brick dovecot of
1700 near the entrance gates. The manor was
formerly the seat of the Howe family, whose
best-known member was Admiral Howe
(1726–99), victor over the French fleet off Ushant
in 1794. It is now a police training school.

To the east of the village, about a mile downstream, is an old paper-mill – now a private
house – which made wads for the muzzle-loading
guns used in the Indian Mutiny and the Crimean
War.

ERBISTOCK
CLWYD

5 miles south of Wrexham (page 429 Cb)

The tiny heart of this scattered village is a beauty spot, secluded and tranquil on one of the loveliest stretches of the River Dee. The Boat, a 16th-century inn of mellow sandstone, looks out over the broad river to a steep, lofty bank thick with trees. Legions of flowers bloom outside the inn during spring and summer, while in autumn the river becomes a moving carpet of red, gold, brown and orange leaves. The inn originally catered for travellers who crossed the Dee by ferry. A bridge was later built downstream, but the little landing place has survived. The old windlass that hauled the boat from bank to bank still stands.

SLEEPY SECLUSION *The 16th-century Boat Inn, its sunlit sandstone wall clad in climbing roses, stands snugly amid the peaceful seclusion of Erbistock. This enchanting village is on one of the loveliest stretches of the River Dee and the Boat once welcomed travellers who crossed the water by ferry.*

The inn shares its idyllic setting with a prim Victorian church, also of sandstone, which stands just above the road and is sheltered by yews. Although it lacks the atmosphere that goes with great age, St Hilary's fits perfectly into its surroundings. The lane that meets the main road by the Cross Foxes Inn runs high above another memorable stretch of the Dee, where anglers fish for salmon. An old mill, restored and converted into a private house, completes the scene before the river flows away under a stone bridge.

ETAL, Northumberland (page 438 Ad)
(see Ford)

EUSTON
SUFFOLK

3 miles south-east of Thetford (page 432 Cc)

When Charles II visited Euston Hall it is said that he was much taken by the horse-racing in the park. He was also much taken, it seems, with his host Lord Arlington's five-year-old daughter,

Isabella, whom he considered a suitable wife for his illegitimate son by Barbara Castlemaine – the eight-year-old Henry Fitzroy. Henry later became Earl of Euston and Duke of Grafton.

Black-and-white cottages, some thatched, and flint-and-brick houses line Euston's main street. Euston Hall is still the seat of the Dukes of Grafton, and is open to the public on Thursday afternoons during the summer. It is approached on one side by a parapeted bridge crossing a stream which flows through the grounds to join the Little Ouse, but the visitors' entrance is through a gate on the main road. Back from the road is a red-brick mill disguised as a church, complete with battlemented tower. It is probably Georgian, as the grounds were laid out in the 18th century by William Kent, the architect of London's Horse Guards. Kent also designed an Italian temple above an underground ice-house in the grounds.

Euston Hall was originally built for Lord Arlington in 1666-70. It was enlarged and altered in 1750, but had to be largely rebuilt in 1902 after a disastrous fire. It was reduced to its present size in 1951. The main attractions in the house are the paintings by Stubbs, Van Dyck, Kneller and Lely.

CONTRASTING STYLES *A startling combination of black-and-white timbered cottages, flint-and-brick houses, thatch and tile adorns Euston's main street. Euston Hall, originally built in the 17th century, is the seat of the Dukes of Grafton. Within its grounds lie St Genevieve's Church – built by an unknown architect influenced by Wren – and a sleepy tributary of the Little Ouse.*

Euston's church, dedicated to St Genevieve, is in the grounds of the hall. Although there are traces of medieval work in the tower and walls, the church dates mostly from 1676. The architect is unknown, but he was obviously familiar with Wren's City of London churches. Inside the church are woodcarvings on the pulpit and screen, whose excellence supports the claim that they are the work of Grinling Gibbons.

EWELME
OXFORDSHIRE

3 miles south-west of Watlington (page 426 Ba)

Almshouses, a church and a school form the core of this village in the Chilterns. All date from the 15th century and were built by the Earl of Suffolk and his wife, Alice, who was the grand-daughter of the poet Geoffrey Chaucer.

Alice Chaucer lived in Ewelme at the time of her marriage to the Earl of Suffolk in 1430. He moved to the village, bringing with him the technique of building with brick which was fairly uncommon in Oxfordshire at that time. The village was built on three south-facing terraces of a fold in the hills: the church at the top, then the almshouses and, on the lower terrace, the school. All three buildings continue to function, and the school is probably the oldest in the country still in its original building.

The rest of the village consists of cottages from later periods, some thatched, a Georgian rectory near the church and the Manor House. Henry VIII and Elizabeth I used the manor as a country residence – Henry spent part of his honeymoon with Catherine Howard there in 1540 – and the present small house is Georgian.

The Church of St Mary contains the tomb of Alice, who was Duchess of Suffolk when she died in 1475. Her alabaster effigy lies beneath a richly carved canopy adorned with angels. There are angels, too, around the sides of the tomb chest, and beneath the tomb is a macabre effigy of a wizened corpse.

In the quiet churchyard is the grave of Jerome K. Jerome, the author best known for his *Three Men in a Boat*. Jerome lived in Ewelme for a short period in the 1880s, and his ashes were buried there in 1927.

Steps lead down from the church to the almshouses, which face inwards to a quadrangle. The steeply sloping tiled roofs were once thatched, and their overhanging eaves are supported on wooden pillars to form a cloister. In the middle of the quadrangle is a well with a cast-iron wheel for raising the water. The houses are occupied by 13 elderly people, as was specified in Henry VI's deed of foundation.

A spring wells up in the centre of the village, and watercress beds lie beside the stream running alongside the main street.

EWENNY
MID-GLAMORGAN

2 miles south of Bridgend (page 425 Ca)

The village slopes down to the River Ewenny, where a wooded lane leads to the impressive remains of Ewenny Priory, founded in 1141 by Maurice de Londres, Lord of Ogmore, as a cell of the Benedictine abbey at Gloucester.

Not much is left now of the original priory buildings, but the precinct wall that surrounded them has the massive grandeur of a medieval castle. Despite its appearance of impregnability, the wall was probably built more for prestige than defence, because there are no traces of fortifications on the eastern flank.

The parish church stands near by. It was built by the father of Maurice de Londres, and is one of the finest examples of Norman architecture in Wales. An interesting feature of the exterior is a Mass dial, marked to show the times of the four main hours of prayer in the Middle Ages. Inside, a gravestone inscribed in Norman-French commemorates the priory's founder. Although it is not far from the industrial bustle of Bridgend, this cluster of ancient buildings has retained an atmosphere of timeless tranquillity.

EYAM
DERBYSHIRE

5 miles north of Bakewell (page 430 Bd)

Plague Cottage, a 17th-century house near the green, recalls the dark past of this attractive moorland village.

Eyam – pronounced 'E'em' – stood remote and isolated in the 17th century, 800 ft up among the Derbyshire peaks. Yet it could not escape the plague that was raging in London. In 1665 a box of clothing was sent to Eyam's tailor, George Vicars. The clothing was contaminated with the plague germs, and Vicars became infected and died.

The plague spread rapidly, and many of the frightened villagers prepared to leave. But their rector, William Mompesson, persuaded them to

stay, and so stopped the disease spreading to other districts. The courage and self-sacrifice of Mompesson and his parishioners was paid for dearly – out of an estimated population of 350 some 250 died, including Mompesson's wife.

Plague Cottage was the home of George Vicars, and behind it is the Church of St Lawrence. In the church is a carved oak chair which belonged to Mompesson, and in the north aisle is the chest which is supposed to have contained the infected clothing sent from London.

Dotted around the village are the graves of whole families wiped out by the plague. Some have been turfed over, but Riley Graves to the west of the village can still be seen. In a limestone valley called The Delph is Cucklet Church, a natural cavern where Mompesson held his services after the village church had been closed to prevent the disease spreading. About three-quarters of a mile east of Eyam is Mompesson's Well, where supplies were left by neighbouring villagers; the money in payment was washed in vinegar and water which, it was believed, would destroy the infection.

But Eyam is not obsessed with its unhappy past, and has grown to be one of the largest and most pleasant of the Peak District villages. The Derbyshire custom of well-dressing is observed on the last Saturday in August, and there is a sheep-roast on the green on the first Saturday in September.

EYNSFORD
KENT

3 miles south-east of Swanley (page 423 Ec)

The ford, from which Eynsford takes its name, still crosses the River Darent, and a narrow, hump-backed bridge, believed to date from the 17th century, stands alongside.

Eynsford's moated castle, now in the care of the Department of the Environment, stands on the river bank. The circular outer wall, built of flint, dates from about 1100, but little remains of the early Norman castle except high, ruined walls and a deep well.

Close to the ford is a white-walled, timbered Tudor house, and on the other side is the Church of St Martin which is partly of 13th-century construction. A road near the ford forms a junction with Sparepenny Lane, reputedly a route once taken to avoid paying tolls on the turnpike. A toll cottage still stands at the junction.

The village was once well known for its paper-milling, founded by Huguenot immigrants in 1648, which produced high-quality hand-made paper until 1952.

The lane from the ford leads to the nearby Lullingstone Roman villa, one of the most important excavated sites of the Roman occupation of England. The Roman walls, mosaics and other finds are housed under a permanent shelter, and are open to the public.

Half a mile further along the road is Lullingstone Castle, a stately home with a Queen Anne front and a 16th-century gatehouse. Across the lawn is the Norman Church of St Botolph.

FARNBOROUGH

BERKSHIRE

4 miles south-east of Wantage (page 426 Aa)

Farnborough is a scattering of cottages, farms and a church lying 735 ft up in the Lambourn Downs. Small as it is, it is utterly lost in the gigantic, sunlit sweep of land and sky – mile upon mile of billowing, chalk-scarred plough and turf, criss-crossed by tracks that dip into hollows, reappear on the crests and, finally, like threads, disappear into the furthermost edge of the horizon. Some of these tracks, like Old Street and the Ridgeway, are of incredible age – much older than Stonehenge – and since they pass near by, may well be the reason for the village's existence. Farnborough, too, was a stopping place on the old packhorse trail between Hungerford and Oxford.

Though there is a lot of space between the groups of cottages, within the groups they huddle closely together – hardly surprising in this windy place. The two main groups are in pleasant contrast; one is an open-ended square of red brick, tile, thatch and latticed windows, while the other is a jumble of grey timber and white plaster.

The small Norman church, too, on the very edge of the tremendous view, seems to hunch its shoulders against the wind. The interior is airy and simple, with the exception of two surprising, skull-decked monuments on either side of the altar. Almost identical, they commemorate two men who died 20 years apart in the 17th century. Either they were friends, or the local sculptor's style had become stereotyped.

But the most unusual thing about Farnborough is the Rectory, which stands back from the road in a couple of acres or so of shorn hill-grass. Built in 1749, it looks exactly as though it had been extracted from a Dutch townscape of the previous century and miraculously deposited in the wild, wide Lambourn Downs.

FARNBOROUGH

WARWICKSHIRE

6 miles north of Banbury (page 430 Bb)

Stone cottages, a village store and the 17th-century Butcher's Arms Inn line Farnborough's winding main street. The parish church of St Botolph stands on high ground, which gives added height to the lofty spire built by Sir Gilbert Scott in 1875. The rest of the church is medieval, with some traces of Norman work.

At one end of the village street stands Farn-

OUTPOST OF THE COTSWOLDS

Farnborough Hall is largely the creation of the Holbech family, who added the property to their manor of Mollington, just over the Oxfordshire border, in 1684. According to a local tradition, the Farnborough terrace, still over three-quarters of a mile long, was intended to join with another terrace at Mollington so that the Holbech brothers, who lived in the two houses, could meet for a morning chat. But the Mollington house has long vanished. Like the Hall, Farnborough village is built of russet stone.

Warwickshire summer.

Farnborough village school.

Farnborough Hall, Warwickshire.

borough Hall, a 17th-century mansion built of russet ironstone with dressings of grey sandstone. The house is owned by the National Trust, and the principal rooms contain Italian paintings and sculptures. The house looks out across a picturesque lake to Edge Hill, scene, in 1642, of the first battle of the Civil War. The landscaped park has a terraced walk, a Classical temple, and an oval pavilion with an ornate plasterwork ceiling in the upper room. An obelisk of 1751 on the terrace marks the edge of the estate.

FECKENHAM
HEREFORD AND WORCESTER

6 miles north-west of Alcester (page 425 Fc)

Timber-framed cottages and elegant, red-brick Georgian houses face each other across Feckenham's quiet main street. The village is set around a small, tree-dotted green on which daffodils grow in the spring. A path from the green leads between the huge, weathered headstones in the graveyard and up to the Church of St John the Baptist. Parts of the church date from the mid-13th century and, inside, carved figures of angels playing musical instruments look down on the nave. On the west wall a benefaction board of 1665 records: 'King Charles the First of Blessed Memory Gave to ye ffree scoole of ffeckenham y yearly Sume of £6 thirteen shillings and ffoure Pence Payable out of ye fforest land.' The old school is now a private house, but a trust still distributes the money – on books and uniforms for the boys and girls of the village school.

Another tie with the past was the village's ancient Court Leet – a medieval form of local government – which sat until as recently as 1935. A red-brick manor house is on the Droitwich road, and there are several notable outlying farms – including the timber-framed and moated Shurnock Court Farm, built partly in the 16th century, to the east, and the early-16th-century Brick House Farm to the north.

FELMERSHAM
BEDFORDSHIRE

6 miles north-west of Bedford (page 426 Bc)

Admirers of medieval architecture will find one of the best examples in Bedfordshire at Felmersham. St Mary the Virgin was built in 1220–40, and has a beautifully arcaded west front and an abbey-like interior with splendid, deeply moulded arches. Two later additions – the perpendicular nave walls and the top part of the massive tower – make it even more impressive. Next to the church is a late-medieval tithe barn with tiled roof and buttresses; also near by is the stone schoolhouse of 1846, now a private residence. The gabled 17th-century Old Rectory was a farmhouse before it was enlarged in 1846.

The River Great Ouse sweeps round the hill on which Felmersham stands, and flows under the five arches of a stone bridge, built in 1818. At the

river's edge are two Victorian houses built in Jacobean style. Called East and West Grange, they were originally built as one, but earlier this century they were divided by the removal of a section from the middle.

Fresh bread and doughnuts are still baked in the brick ovens of the old bakehouse behind the village store. Further along the road is The Six Ringers, a 500-year-old inn of stone and thatch. Its recently restored copper and wrought-iron sign depicts six ringers sharing five bells. According to legend, the sixth bell was stolen from St Mary's by monks from the neighbouring village of Odell. They are said to have lost it in the Ouse when their boat capsized on the way home.

PAVENHAM Little more than a mile south of Felmersham, Pavenham's winding main street contains gabled farmsteads, thatched houses and cottages with tiny, square windows and low doorways. Mill Lane leads down to the banks of the River Great Ouse, and narrow grassy footpaths pass between the bowed backs of weavers' cottages, under stiles and into the neighbouring water-meadows. The Church of St Peter has a tall tower with a stone spire. There is a priest's room over the 13th-century doorway.

FINCHINGFIELD
ESSEX

8 miles north-west of Braintree (page 432 Cb)

PEACEFUL POND *All roads into Finchingfield converge on the white-railed village pond and the old brick bridge over the stream that feeds it. The jumble of old buildings beyond the bridge include the red-tiled and pargeted Fox Inn, which was a stage-coach stop in the late 18th century.*

Winding roads and lanes plunge down into Finchingfield through divided greens. Above the greens stand white-painted cottages and houses. Chief among them is the gabled and barge-boarded Finchingfield House, facing a row of Georgian houses and 16th-century cottages. The 17th-century house with a four-stack chimney beside the footbridge over the nearby pond – known as Bridge House – was once the village workhouse.

Crowning the curve of the hill is the Church of St John the Baptist with its Norman tower and Georgian-style bell-cote. The entrance to the churchyard is through the arch of the timbered 15th-century Guildhall, which contains four almshouses, a meeting room and a small museum of local bygones. Across the road is a house with plasterwork panels of animals, horseshoes, clover and other reliefs.

Just north of the village stands a windmill, dating from the 18th century, though a mill has stood on the site since 1100. A little further on is a six-sided thatched cottage called the Round House. It was built in the late 18th century by the local squire who lived at Spains Hall, 1 mile north-west of Finchingfield.

The hall dates from the 16th century and is built of red brick and stone, with curved gables, tall chimneys and mullioned windows. One of its 17th-century owners, William Kempe, remained silent for seven years as a penance for unjustly accusing his wife of infidelity. There are seven ponds in the grounds of Spains Hall, said to have been dug by Kempe to mark each year of his penance, which is recorded on a memorial shield in the church.

The hall was bought by the Ruggles-Brise family in 1760, and a plaque in the church commemorates Sir Evelyn John Ruggles-Brise who, in 1908, founded the Borstal training system. The present owner of Spains Hall, Colonel Sir John Ruggles-Brise, was Lord Lieutenant of Essex until 1978. The hall and gardens were opened to the public in the summer of 1979.

A STUART ECHO *By Finsthwaite's sturdy church there is a stone, erected about 100 years ago over a hitherto unmarked grave, to the memory of Clementina Sobieski Douglas. Legend variously says she was a Polish princess, or, more probably, the daughter of Bonnie Prince Charlie and his Glaswegian mistress, Clementina Walkinshaw. But how she came to lie there remains a mystery.*

FINDON
WEST SUSSEX

4 miles north of Worthing (page 422 Db)

Elegant 18th-century houses, mostly of flint and brick, and a 17th-century inn are grouped closely together round Findon's square. The village lies on the east side of the Findon Valley, where the land begins to climb towards the Downs. It is set apart from its church which stands on the opposite slope of the valley, about half a mile to the west, beside Findon Place, an 18th-century mansion in wooded parkland.

The driveway of Findon Place leads to the church, which is built of flint. Its original structure dates back to the 11th or 12th centuries. Both the nave and the aisle are roofed with a single span, producing a sensation of space. The church contains a rare 13th-century oak screen, and medieval oak pews showing the marks of the adze which fashioned them.

The Iron Age hill-fort of Cissbury Ring, with the remains of ancient flint mines, lies 1 mile to the east of the village. Riding stables are found on the tracks which lead from the village to the open Downs. In September a sheep fair of national importance is held at nearby Nepcote.

FINSTHWAITE
CUMBRIA

8 miles north-east of Ulverston (page 435 Cc)

One of the Lake District National Park's smallest villages nestles among low, wooded hills in a beautiful landscape near the southern end of Windermere. It is reached along narrow lanes, or by a walk of just under 2 miles which starts from Newby Bridge and skirts the grounds of Finsthwaite House. Another footpath runs on from the village into the heart of Grizedale Forest, where deer roam and buzzards wheel above the trees. Immediately north of the village, space is provided for motorists to park their cars and take a short, woodland walk to High Dam pool, in the lee of Finsthwaite Heights.

Finsthwaite itself is an attractive little cluster of typical Lakeland farms and cottages. Whitewashed walls contrast pleasantly with the bare, rough-hewn stones of their neighbours.

The buildings lie in a bowl which slopes gently down to the village church and the school, built in the 19th century and now used as a community centre.

The church, crowned by a squat steeple, has a timber-framed porch and, within, a fine coloured ceiling. The building dates from the 18th and 19th centuries and retains good features of both. On Finsthwaite Heights there is a tower commemorating the 'Officers, seamen and marines of the Royal Navy whose matchless conduct and irresistible valour defeated the fleets of France . . . and promoted and protected liberty and commerce, 1799'.

FINTRY
CENTRAL

5 miles north of Lennoxtown (page 441 Ed)

'Oot of the world and into Fintry' used to be the catchphrase for this strung-out village in the Endrick Valley, which still has an air of ancient remoteness.

Locked between the Fintry Hills and the Campsie Fells, its business is hill grazing and has been since the 13th century, apart from a brief incursion into cotton in the 1790s.

The Laird of Culcreuch at that time built a mill, the fine bridge that spans the ravine of the Endrick Water, and the group of workers' cottages that came to be known as Newton of Fintry. But transport difficulties eroded the enterprise, and in the 1840s the mill closed. Its ruins still stand close by Culcreuch Castle, ancient seat of the Galbraiths, and dating in part from the 15th and 16th centuries.

Fintry is actually four distinct hamlets. Near the bridge, under which the salmon and trout run to and from Loch Lomond, is the old settlement of Gonachan. Downstream lies Kirkton, beside the parish church built in 1823. Newton is now the long main street containing a tea shop, a crafts shop and the post office-cum-village store. Finally, there is the modern, and pleasant, Fintry Hills Estate.

From the Lennoxtown road, which crosses the Campsies, there are splendid views of the Clyde Valley, while 3 miles east of the village is the Loup of Fintry, a ribbon of white water plunging 90 ft from a rocky ledge.

FITTLEWORTH
WEST SUSSEX
3 miles south-east of Petworth (page 422 Db)

Groups of cottages are strung round the lanes and paths in the woodlands north of the River Rother, forming what is in effect the multiple village of Fittleworth. It is a quiet place that attracts artists and anglers.

One collection of dwellings makes up a rough triangle near the tile-hung façade of the Swan Inn which stands on Lower Street, just north of the River Rother. The cottages are of local stone with some brickwork, and the inn, which has a wood-panelled dining-room, is roofed with Horsham slate. An iron fire-back, dated 1622, is set in one of its open fireplaces. Many artists have stayed there, and its dining-room contains a collection of landscapes, including several by George Constable, brother of John.

Half a mile north, farm buildings, more cottages and a timber-framed house stand on a right-angled bend of the road, known as Hallelujah Corner. The Church of St Mary, close by, is set alone on top of a hill. It was extensively rebuilt in Victorian times, but has two medieval bells, the Sancta Toma Or, which dates from the 14th century, and the 15th-century Sancta Catarina.

Pleasant narrow lanes lead northwards up through wooded hills, passing old sandstone and ironstone quarries, near where charcoal-burners once worked among the oaks. In the heart of these woods is a cottage called Brinkwells where Sir Edward Elgar, the composer, is said to have lived for a while from 1917.

184

The VILLAGE CHURCH

From Anglo-Saxon times to the 20th century the church has been at the centre of village life: a meeting-place, a focus for hopes and fears and a symbol of village pride paid for and maintained by the parishioners themselves.

The church is often the oldest building in a village. It was built to last and was the one building on which generations of villagers lavished time and money.

During the Anglo-Saxon period, the church was built near the house of a local thegn or lord, who appointed the priest and gave him a glebe – a house and some land. Some of the early churches were built of wood, but were later rebuilt in stone.

The expense of the church and the priest were paid for by tithes, a system by which every parishioner was compelled to contribute one-tenth of his income in cash or kind, e.g., every tenth pig or sheep, every tenth bundle of corn, and so on.

As well as using the church for daily worship, parishioners used the nave as a communal 'village hall'. They gathered to watch Miracle or pastoral plays – Robin Hood was an established favourite – or participate in 'church ales'. These were revelries held on Holy Days (holidays), when no one worked and attendance at Mass was obligatory. A church ale seems to have been little more than communal drinking, followed by dancing, with the ale (often brewed on the premises or in a brew-house attached to the church) sold and drunk in the church or in the churchyard. The money raised was used to buy something special for the church, such as a bell.

Church ales were common throughout the 15th century, but the drinking often led to excesses and the events – discouraged by the more sensitive priests – gradually fell into decline and came to an end in the 17th century.

In medieval England, village life was hard, and the life of the workaday parish priest was little different from that of his parishioners. He lived in the same kind of house and tended his glebe land. He visited the sick and did as much as he could for the souls in his care – normally about 300 people. The priest was frequently poorly educated, but at least he could read and write. This, on top of his religious authority, made him the man to whom people turned for comfort and guid-

A CHURCH APART *Saxon lords often built churches as private chapels next to their homes, which usually stood some distance from the village. That is why, even today, many parish churches such as St Mary's at Breamore, Hampshire, stand apart from the communities which they serve.*

ance in all their problems.

During the later Middle Ages there was a surplus of parish priests and many clerics found employment as chantry priests. Families and religious guilds founded chantries – places where memorial prayers or obits were said for the souls of the dead. Most medieval wills made a bequest to pay for an obit for a number of years; some for perpetuity.

As most villagers were illiterate, church interiors were decorated with paintings, sculpture and stained-glass windows which told Bible stories.

When the medieval peasant stood for Mass, he was awed by the Doom, or Last Judgement, painting on the wall above the chancel arch. He was presented with two alternatives of life after death: eternity in Heaven with God, the saints and the angels; or everlasting torment in Hell.

He was also superstitious enough to believe the powers of witchcraft, and it became necessary in the 13th century for priests to lock all font covers in order to prevent Holy Water being stolen for Black Magic rites.

For the medieval law-breaker, the church was a place of sanctuary. A fugitive who entered the churchyard could stay in safety for 30–40 days and anyone who dared violate this sanctuary could be severely punished – even excommunicated. After this period of grace, the fugitive could elect to go for trial before the civil courts or plead guilty and flee the country – a form of self deportation.

During the mid-16th century, much of the decorative art in churches was destroyed as a result of the Reformation, when Henry VIII assumed Papal power and confiscated church wealth. Inventories of church possessions revealed a surprising amount of gold and silver plate and embroidered vestments, owned by small and otherwise poor parish churches.

In the following century, under the Commonwealth, the Puritans destroyed many statues, church decorations and stained-glass windows, and whitewashed over a great many wall-paintings. They introduced the dismal Sunday, when simple pleasures were frowned upon or forbidden, and the congregation were expected to listen to extremely long sermons.

During the 18th century, several great landowners rebuilt their churches in the Classical style, although the great majority of rural parish churches were gradually becoming more and more dilapidated. Family pride filled a few with marble memorials by the best sculptors, or memorial chapels, built near the manorial pew, with its velvet cushions and a fireplace to keep the squire comfortable during long winter services.

The squarson

For centuries it was the custom for younger sons of the landed classes to become clergymen – and often to take over the parish – or parishes – on the family estate. It was not uncommon for such parsons to inherit the estate on the death of an older brother and so come to combine the role of squire and parson – a squarson, as they came to be called. Most were conscientious, but in the 18th and 19th centuries some left their parishes in the care of underpaid curates, while they lived the lives of sporting squires, or absentee landlords.

In general, the 18th and 19th centuries saw the rise of the village parson in social status until eventually he became, like his medieval predecessor, the centre of village life. He set up schools, where on occasions he might teach, helped by his wife and daughters, with the parsonage gardens often the setting for bazaars, fêtes and Sunday School treats. By the end of the 19th century, the parsonage once again set the moral, educational and spiritual standards of village life.

The Victorian parson saw to it that his church was repaired, enlarged, re-paved and furnished with new pews, and

RECEIVING THE TITHE *An 18th-century print shows a boy bringing his parents' tithe of a pig and two geese to the parson. Every parishioner had to contribute a tithe or one-tenth of his income in cash or kind to the church.*

A CONSTANT REMINDER
OF HEAVEN AND HELL

The Last Judgement in a stained-glass window of the Church of St Mary at Fairford in Gloucestershire presented the medieval peasant with two alternatives of life after death. In the top half there is eternity in Heaven with God, surrounded by the saints and the angels. In the bottom half there is everlasting torment in Hell with the damned and with such creatures as the horned 'blue devil', depicted in gruesome and terrifying detail. It was the hope of Heaven and the fear of Hell that helped to drive the simple man to devote so much of what he could ill afford to the upkeep of the parish church.

heated – often with himself and the squire sharing the cost.

At times the restorations were over-enthusiastic and misguided, but had they not been done it is likely that many of our parish churches would not have survived.

One important office that has survived for over 800 years is that of the churchwarden, established in the middle of the 12th century. He took over from the parishioners the responsibility of maintaining the church fabric, and had the authority to haul people before the ecclesiastical courts, where moral and religious offences were judged.

Throughout the Middle Ages the churchwardens needed to be good businessmen, and after the Reformation they played an active role in local government. With churchwardenship carrying so many responsibilities, few people wanted the office. If they were elected by the parish

and declined, they could be heavily fined.

By the 17th century churchwardens, now assisted by sidesmen, were overseeing parish taxes (with the parish clerks), controlling the stocks and whipping post, and organising relief for the poor and for wayfarers. They were also keeping careful accounts of income from church properties and land, and many of these documents have survived to provide an invaluable insight into parish life.

The village church today

The churchwarden's office changed little throughout the next two centuries, particularly in village parishes where the effects of the Industrial Revolution were barely felt. The radical change came in 1921, when parish councils took over all parochial lay financial responsibilities, leaving the churchwarden as an honorary officer assisting the vicar.

The 20th century, particularly since the last war, has seen a marked change in the role of the church. With increased affluence and more mobility, fewer people are attending church and church-organised activities. Parishes are being forced to consider ways of using churches more economically – seven days a week instead of just on Sundays. Some churches are being divided up to provide the community with several different services, such as crèches, meeting-rooms and kitchens, with smaller areas retained for worship.

Even though the number of regular worshippers may have dwindled, the church is being brought back into the total life of the village in a way that has not been seen since the Middle Ages.

FLAMBOROUGH
HUMBERSIDE

4 miles north-east of Bridlington (page 437 Dc)

High on a chalk headland and exposed on three sides to the salt winds of the North Sea, Flamborough is rich in seafaring character. Its streets fan out towards the clifftops, and its sheltered North Landing harbours open-decked fishing boats, called 'cobles'. For at least 2,000 years the headland has also served as a fortress; while the villagers kept watch on the sea, massive raised earthworks protected them from inland attack. A 3 mile long barrier, known as Danes' Dyke, is clearly visible just west of the village. In spite of its name it dates from the 1st century at the latest – long before the Danes reached Britain.

St Oswald's Church, probably founded by Norman settlers at the start of the 12th century, was substantially rebuilt about 300 years later and remains the centre of the oldest part of Flamborough. It has a fine 16th-century rood screen and a bizarre memorial to Sir Marmaduke Constable which shows his heart laid bare. According to legend, his death in 1520 was due to eating a toad that in turn devoured his flesh.

Chantry Cottage, near the church in West Street, has the pale stone walls and crinkled red tiles that are typical of the older buildings. Some of the village stonework is so light-coloured that it seems to be coated with weathered whitewash, emphasising the dashes of colour that are provided by door and window-frame paintwork. In the straggling main street, overlooked by an inn called the Royal Dog and Duck and forming part of a traffic island, is another reminder of Flamborough's seafaring tradition. A memorial honours the crew of the coble *Two Brothers* who drowned with the men in another boat they were trying to rescue during a great gale in 1909.

FOCHABERS
GRAMPIAN

8 miles east of Elgin (page 443 Fe)

In 1776 the 4th Duke of Gordon decided to move the tumbledown village of Fochabers out of sight of his home, Gordon Castle, which had recently been rebuilt. The new village for farmworkers and fishermen was built on a grid pattern a short way to the south. Large-scale improvements were made by the Gordon family 100 years later, but many of the fine Georgian buildings were retained – including the late-18th-century parish church of Bellie, with its pillared portico, on the south side of the market square.

Fochabers (the stress is on the first syllable) lies on the edge of Speymouth Forest, to the east of the river. At the east end of the village is Milne's High School, opened in 1846 and built in Tudor Gothic style. It is named after Alexander Milne, who was employed at the castle – possibly as a footman – in the 18th century. He was dismissed by the autocratic duke when he refused to cut off his pigtail, which his employer felt did not fit

the castle's new image. Milne emigrated to America and made a fortune in New Orleans as a building merchant. He left $100,000 in his will to found the school which still flourishes.

The village is surrounded by miles of forest land with many fine walks, picnic spots, car parks and vantage points. Some extensive nurseries to the east of Fochabers have been owned by the same family since 1820. Visitors are welcome to see the large range of flowers, shrubs and trees. Half a mile west of the village, on the banks of the River Spey, is Baxter's food-processing plant, which grew from Mr and Mrs Baxter's village shop, opened in 1868. A replica of the shop is on the site and is open to the public from Monday to Friday, May to September.

FOLKINGHAM
LINCOLNSHIRE

8 miles south of Sleaford (page 432 Bd)

The broad main road climbs as it enters the village, and widens still further to form the Market Square, which is lined with brick and stone-built houses standing well back. At the summit a 17th-century coaching inn, the Greyhound, faces down the road, giving the centre of the village a most elegant and spacious air.

Folkingham, now merely a large village, was once an important place in the county. It was the seat of the Quarter Sessions Court, and its austere former House of Correction, or prison, stands to the east of the village. The building consists of the original 19th-century gateway and Governor's House, faced in cold-looking grey stone and with arched windows half blanked off and half grilled. It occupies the site of Folkingham Castle, built by Henry de Beaumont in Norman times and destroyed by Cromwell during the Civil War.

Justice was undoubtedly swift and severe in Folkingham at one time; the stocks and whipping post are preserved in the church.

FORD
NORTHUMBERLAND

7 miles north-west of Wooler (page 438 Ad)

A horse-riding accident led to the appearance of Ford as it is today. In 1859 the Marchioness of Waterford rebuilt the village as a memorial to her husband, who had died after falling from his horse. A tall column of polished Aberdeen granite carrying the figure of an angel also commemorates the Marquis of Waterford. It stands at one end of an avenue of elegant houses set well back from the road.

Ford's most interesting building is the old school, now called Lady Waterford Hall, which has a room decorated with water-colour frescoes by Lady Waterford. She was a painter in the Pre-Raphaelite style, and between 1861 and 1882 she painted biblical scenes on paper which were then transferred to the walls. Visitors can see them by applying to the caretaker next door.

Ford Castle was heavily restored between 1861 and 1865 by Lady Waterford. It is a fine example of a 13th-century square-built fortress with towers at each corner. Three of the original towers remain. James IV of Scotland spent the night there before his defeat and death at the hands of the English on Flodden Field in 1513.

Even older than the castle is the Church of St Michael, dating from the early 13th century and with its original bell-cote. Restoration in 1853 was by John Dobson, designer of Newcastle upon Tyne's streets and many of its buildings.

ETAL A street of thatched and pantiled cottages runs the length of the village, which lies 2 miles north-west of Ford. Their gardens make a colourful approach to the ruin of Etal Castle, built in the 14th century but destroyed by James IV of Scotland in 1496. Near the entrance tower are two cannons from the warship *Royal George*, which capsized at Spithead in 1782.

FORDWICH
KENT

2 miles north-east of Canterbury (page 423 Fc)

A small half-timbered town hall stands on an old quay in the centre of this village on the River Stour. Medieval ships, carrying wine, stone and other goods from the Continent, unloaded at the quayside when Fordwich was a thriving port for Canterbury. In the 1880s, Fordwich lost its mayor and corporation, but in a local government reorganisation of 1972 the parish, because of its long tradition, was again granted town status.

Fordwich's character, however, is still that of a village. Cottages, inns and a church are gathered near an 18th-century humped-back bridge of brick. Most of the buildings are brick faced and tile hung, and many are at least 200 years old.

The 16th-century town hall has an overhanging upper storey of timbers filled in with brick. The lower storey is of stone and flint rubble. There are stocks outside and the museum inside contains a ducking stool.

Across the small square, behind some cottages, stands the Church of St Mary the Virgin, with evidence of Saxon workmanship in its tower of flint and rubble. The church's main structure is 13th century, with an early-18th-century east window. Inside is the Fordwich Stone, said to be St Augustine's tomb, a single block of stone carved into the model of a cloistered building and thought to date from about 1100.

FORTINGALL
TAYSIDE

7 miles west of Aberfeldy (page 443 Eb)

Ditches surround a rectangular earthworks to the south-west of Fortingall, which is the legendary birthplace of Pontius Pilate. The story goes that his father was an ambassador sent by the Roman

Emperor Augustus to the Scottish King Mercellanus, and his mother was a MacLaren or a Menzies from Balquhidder, 20 miles to the southwest. The earthworks are known locally as the 'Praetorium', or governor's residence. Present-day archaeologists, however, state that the site is medieval, and that it housed no more than an ordinary fortress of the Middle Ages.

Fortingall lies in a narrow valley at the mouth of Glen Lyon, which stretches for 30 miles – the longest glen in Scotland. Its cottages, church and hotel were renovated in the late 1800s by Sir Donald Currie, a wealthy shipowner who lived at Glen Lyon House, in the west of Fortingall.

At the east end of the village, near the hotel, is the Cairn of the Dead. This was the burial ground of plague victims in the 7th and 14th centuries. A stone pillar is their memorial and near by is the churchyard, with the split and twisted remains of a giant yew believed to be some 3,000 years old. It is one of the oldest living things in Europe, and a stone wall protects it from village boys – who used to light fires in the fork in its trunk during May Day festivities. The River Lyon runs past the village, and the district is dominated by the Culdaremore Hills to the west, and the heavily wooded Drummond Hill to the south.

FOTHERINGHAY
NORTHAMPTONSHIRE

4 miles north-east of Oundle (page 431 Db)

Little is left of Fotheringhay Castle, renowned as the place of imprisonment and execution of Mary, Queen of Scots. It was built around 1100, rebuilt in the 14th century as a royal castle, and used regularly as such until its decay and demolition in the 17th century. Today, only the earthworks are left. Each summer, Scotch thistles grow to great heights on the site of the castle. According to legend, thistles were planted by Mary a short time before she was beheaded – shortly after 8 a.m. on February 8, 1587.

The magnificent tower of Fotheringhay's Church of St Mary and All Saints is an outstanding local landmark. Rising in stages, it is topped by a gilt falcon, badge of the House of York. The church itself, almost cathedral-like in its size and decorations, has numerous large windows which allow in floods of light.

In the main street, limestone cottages stand solid and four-square with heavy slate roofs. At the east end is a house with a 15th-century gateway and Gothic arch, believed to be part of a hostel built in the 15th century by Edward IV when he was resident at the castle.

FROM THE SHADOWS *The lantern tower of the Church of St* ▷ *Mary and All Saints at Fotheringhay shines through the deepening shadows of the great trees that frame it ... shadows matched in darkness by those less visible that haunt the village where the final tragedy of Mary, Queen of Scots was enacted in 1587. Only thistle-barbed grassy earthworks remain of the place of her execution, Fotheringhay Castle. An unseasonable sun illuminated the graceful tower just as brightly on the February morning when she died.*

FOTHERINGHAY

FOWNHOPE
HEREFORD AND WORCESTER

6 miles south-east of Hereford (page 425 Eb)

In the Domesday Book the village name is recorded as Hope – the Saxon word for a settlement under the side of a hill. 'Fown' was added later to make the distinction from Woolhope, possibly referring to a painted building. The village stands above the River Wye, beneath the tree-covered slopes of Cherry Hill and Capler Wood – both sites of pre-Roman camps. It has one of the largest churches in the county, early Norman with a 14th-century broach spire, clad with wooden shingles. Inside are a fine 12th-century Norman stone carving showing the Virgin holding the infant Jesus, and a 14th-century parish chest, 9 ft long, carved from a single log of oak. Outside the churchyard, reminders of the days of harsh justice, are the old village stocks and whipping post. Opposite the church is Manor Farm, a fine Elizabethan house.

Fownhope is famous locally for its annual Heart of Oak Club Walk, which takes place in the first week in June, when members carry flower-decorated sticks in procession to the 15th-century Green Man Inn. Originally called the Naked Boy, it is said that the Roundhead, Colonel John Birch stayed before taking Hereford from the Royalists in 1645. It became a coaching inn, and later was used as a court house. The cell and judge's room still exist.

The village's most famous son, born at Rudge End in 1795, was Thomas Winter, who became a professional prizefighter under the name Tom Spring. A bare-knuckle fighter, he was champion of All England in 1823–4. He had one fight of 77 rounds (a round lasted until someone was knocked down) which lasted 2 hours 29 minutes.

FOYERS
HIGHLAND

18 miles south-west of Inverness (page 443 Dd)

The two parts of Foyers lie on the wooded eastern shore of Loch Ness. Upper Foyers, high above the loch, is on the modern road which follows the line of General Wade's military route of the 1730s. Opposite the village shop is the start of a series of steep footpaths down the wooded ravine where the Falls of Foyers gushes out from the rocks and drops 90 ft in a spectacular white cataract. The lower part of the village lies where the river settles down again before flowing into Loch Ness.

Almost all the houses were built in the 1890s to accommodate the workers at Britain's first aluminium works. The factory was built in 1896, and used hydro-electric power generated by water diverted from the falls. Bauxite ore, the raw material for aluminium, was brought by ship from Ulster, through the Caledonian Canal and was landed at the village pier. The factory closed in 1967, but the buildings are still there and, near by, is a modern hydro-electric power station

which began supplying power to the National Grid in 1974. The waterfront road ends at a Loch Ness Monster investigation centre, which has a public information booth.

FRAMPTON ON SEVERN
GLOUCESTERSHIRE

7 miles west of Stroud (page 421 Cd)

Many villages have a green, but few can beat the one at Frampton for size and splendour. Three ponds and a cricket ground lie within its 22 acres, and it is surrounded by Georgian houses and half-timbered buildings. The Bell Inn is conveniently sited for cricketers and supporters, and there is a 15th-century barn near the church.

The outstanding house on the green is Frampton Court, screened by trees and built in the Palladian style in the 1730s for Richard Clutterbuck, a Bristol customs official. A canal in the grounds is overlooked by an orangery built in Gothic style, and peacocks strut on the lawns.

Frampton is said to be the birthplace of Jane Clifford, Henry II's mistress, 'Fair Rosamund', reputedly poisoned by Queen Eleanor in 1177. She is remembered in the village by the green, which is named Rosamund's Green.

The 14th-century Church of St Mary is reached by a footpath across a water-meadow, and beside it is the Sharpness Canal which links Gloucester with the River Severn. The sight of sea-going vessels passing within a few feet of the church tower is an occasional attraction.

FROXFIELD
WILTSHIRE

3 miles west of Hungerford (page 421 Dc)

On moonlit nights, the Hounds of Hell can be seen pursuing the ghost of Wild Darrell across the fields around Froxfield. That is the story villagers tell about the 16th-century owner of Littlecote House, who murdered a new-born baby by throwing it on to a blazing fire. Darrell escaped justice through the intervention of powerful friends, but later broke his neck when jumping over a stile.

The magnificent Tudor house, 2 miles north of the village, is open to the public at weekends and on Bank Holidays during the summer. Its Great Hall has a fine collection of Cromwellian arms and armour.

A magnificent Roman mosaic has recently been uncovered on the site of a Roman villa on the Littlecote estate.

Pleasant brick-and-flint cottages, some with thatch, make up most of the village, but its dominant group of buildings is the Somerset Hospital, or almshouses. On a high bank stands a quadrangle of 50 houses, built in 1694 by Sarah, Duchess Dowager of Somerset for 20 widows of clergymen and the widows of 30 laymen. An imposing archway, added in 1813, leads to the quadrangle with its small chapel surrounded by immaculate lawns and colourful flower borders.

In contrast the parish church of All Saints is small and plain, with a wooden bell-turret added during a 19th-century restoration.

FULBECK
LINCOLNSHIRE

9 miles north of Grantham (page 432 Ae)

Part of the village stands on rising ground over-looking the Brant Valley. To the west of the main Grantham to Lincoln road are narrow winding lanes bordered by old cottages nestling close together, and the Hare and Hounds Inn links the village and the main road. The inn sign depicts the master of the Per Ardua (RAF) Beagles in the hunt uniform, and was erected in 1961.

Fulbeck Hall dates from 1733 and stands at the end of an avenue of great lime trees. Its wrought-iron gates are believed to date from the early 18th century. The house and inn form a group

◆

NORMAN SAINT *Fulbourn's Gothic church is dedicated to St Vigor, a native of Artois, who is chiefly celebrated for demolishing a large and popular pagan idol in Normandy. Probably he would have been astonished to find himself commemorated in far-off Cambridgeshire. The church contains some splendid monuments, mostly to medieval prelates of St Vigor's, and of All Saints', a church that once shared the same holy ground but is now long vanished; however, there are also a couple of charming miniature brasses to ladies of the same period. From the village, a footpath leads to the Fleam Dyke, one of the earthwork defences that bestride the prehistoric Icknield Way. There, in 905, invading Danes massacred an English army, but the Dyke is now better known as the habitat of chalkland flowers and butterflies.*

with the 14th-century Church of St Nicholas, which has a tower with eight pinnacles. Inside are memorials to the Fane family, who have lived at Fulbeck Hall since it was built for Sir Francis Fane, who was a Fellow of the Royal Society. His son, another Francis, was knighted at the coronation of Charles II in 1661. He became known as a successful playwright – his *Love in the Dark or The Man in Business* was successfully performed at London's Theatre Royal in 1675.

FULBOURN
CAMBRIDGESHIRE

5 miles south-east of Cambridge (page 432 Cc)

Beetle-browed, reed-thatched houses line the streets of Fulbourn, which also has a trim line of single-storey almshouses, a timber-framed farm-house and a basically 13th to 14th-century church dedicated to St Vigor. The Normans brought the name of the saint to England – Vigor was the Bishop of Bayeux in the 6th century – and Fulbourn's church is one of only two in England dedicated to him. The other is at Stratton on the Fosse, Somerset. The church has several fine brasses, including one of the earliest known of an ecclesiastic in a cope. It is a life-size figure, in the chancel floor, of William de Fulburne, who was rector from 1377 to 1386 and was chaplain to Edward III.

To the east of the village is Fleam Dyke, a massive 7th-century earthwork built to defend East Anglia against the Mercians. South-west-wards are the Gog Magog Hills – about 250 ft above sea-level – which give fine views over the city of Cambridge.

GADDESBY

LEICESTERSHIRE

6 miles south-west of Melton Mowbray (page 430 Cc)

The village of Gaddesby was originally given by
Henry II to the Knights Templar. It passed to the
Knights Hospitallers in 1312 when the Templars
were suppressed by the pope. It eventually
became a parish in its own right in 1874.

The ivy-covered Cheney Arms is named after
Colonel Edward Hawkins Cheney of the Royal
Scots Greys, who fought at the Battle of Waterloo
in 1815. Four horses were killed under him
during the battle, and a fifth was wounded. An
almost life-size marble monument in the church
represents the colonel astride a fallen horse. The
colonel was more fortunate than his mounts, and
lived until 1848.

The Church of St Luke is one of the largest
and most beautiful in Leicestershire. Parts of it
date from the end of the 13th and the beginning
of the 14th centuries. The south aisle is the
showpiece of the church, with a richly carved
and battlemented parapet. On private land near
the church is the grave of the racehorse Bendigo,
winner of the first Eclipse Stakes in 1886.

Gaddesby Hall, which was built in 1744 and
enlarged in 1865, was partly demolished in 1950
and is now a private house.

GAINFORD

DURHAM

8 miles west of Darlington (page 438 Bb)

Georgian and Regency houses cluster pic-
turesquely around the sloping village green,
which in springtime is carpeted with daffodils.
Gainford dates from Saxon times and, despite
new housing developments, its narrow streets
and huddled homes smack firmly of the past. The
oldest and most interesting parts of the village –
which was made a Conservation Area in 1971 –
lie between the main road and the River Tees.

◆

HEART OF ENGLAND *Good pies and cheese, good hunting
and good farming have made Leicestershire a county of
unobtrusive prosperity – a quality typified in Gaddesby.*

Once the retreat of wealthy Darlington merchants, Gainford retains an atmosphere of comfort and solidarity. Past prosperity is seen in the impressive three-storey buildings in High Green. They include the former St Colette's School, built in the early 18th century, and the dignified Georgian House.

Architecturally, the glory of Gainford lies in High Row – a terrace of distinctive, 'character' houses complete with gaily painted flower-tubs and window-boxes. In summer, the area – with its rear courtyards and walled gardens – is a blaze of colour. Honeysuckle clings to the ancient stone walls; and the well-tended cottage gardens on the south side are a patchwork of fruit, flowers and vegetables. High Row curves from the mock-timbered Cross Keys Inn to the tall and sombre Gainford Hall, today a private farmhouse. The hall was built in the early 1600s and features gables, high chimneys, and mullioned and transomed windows. In the gardens is a round, stone dovecot of the same period.

Equally outstanding is the spacious, 13th-century parish church of St Mary. The church is splendidly situated on a corner of the green above the Tees, at a point where the river once marked the county boundary. The Tees changed course in 1771 during a raging flood, leaving part of Gainford in Yorkshire – although today the village is fairly and squarely in south Durham.

Anglers still fish for trout in the Tees, and a short way upriver is Gainford Spa where, in the 18th and early 19th centuries, people came to take the waters.

GARVALD
LOTHIAN

8 miles south-west of Dunbar (page 441 Gd)

Fear of Viking raiders probably led to the establishment of settlements such as Garvald, tucked away in remote folds of the Lammermuir Hills. Garvald, built round a church founded in the 12th century, is still one of the 'hidden villages' of the Lothians.

Its heart is a group of well-preserved red-stone cottages with red-tiled or grey slate roofs. The village is bounded on one side by the oddly named Papana Water, beyond which is a wooded ridge sweeping up to the Lammermuirs.

An oddity of Scottish transport history is that there was once a Gifford and Garvald Light Railway, opened in 1901 as a branch route connecting with the main line to Edinburgh. Despite its name, in all of its 47 years it never managed to close the 4 mile gap between Garvald and Gifford.

The present parish church is on the site of a Norman building. In the churchyard are preserved the 'jougs', an iron collar and chain which were the Scottish equivalent of an English village's pillory. The lane beyond the church leads over a bridge and, unexpectedly, into a property called Africa.

On the slopes of the Lammermuirs south-east of Garvald is the old mansion house of Nunraw. The original house was given to the nuns of Haddington in the 12th century by the Countess of Huntingdon, wife of Prince Henry. A tower was built to defend the nuns' lands, and this tower is incorporated in the present manor, which has been greatly extended. In 1946, the Cistercians acquired the house and lands and lived there while building their Abbey of Sancta Maria, half a mile to the south-west.

GEDDINGTON
NORTHAMPTONSHIRE

3 miles north-east of Kettering (page 431 Cb)

All three roads into Geddington meet at Eleanor's Cross, built by Edward I in memory of his beloved Queen Eleanor. The queen had died in 1290 at Harby in Nottinghamshire, and Edward was taking her to London to be buried. The mourning king erected a cross at each of the places where her coffin rested overnight – 12 in all. Today, only three remain; the one at Geddington is the best preserved. The 40 ft high cross – with its statues of Eleanor, niches, pinnacles, coats of arms and flowers – towers above stone cottages with steep, pitched roofs of thatch.

The scene is overlooked by the 14th-century Church of St Mary Magdalene – to which local schoolchildren annually bear garlands and ride hobby-horses in celebration of the village May Queen. The hexagonal base of the cross is used for the crowning ceremony, and during the procession the youngsters pass near the medieval stone bridge and ford over the River Ise.

The fields outside Geddington bear the remains of more than 70 miles of tree avenues. They were laid out in the 18th century by the 2nd Duke of Montagu, nicknamed John the Planter. He had originally planned to plant an avenue from his seat, Boughton House, to his London home. When his neighbour, the Duke of Bedford, refused to let the avenue cross his estates, he planted avenues of equivalent length on his own estates. Dutch elm disease has destroyed much of his work. But the old trees are gradually being replaced with limes and beeches by Boughton Estates, the present owners of the property.

GIFFORD
LOTHIAN

4 miles south of Haddington (page 441 Gd)

A Norman called de Gyffarde, who came to Britain with William the Conqueror, gave his name to Gifford, one of the most attractive Lothian villages. His descendants were granted land in the area by David I of Scotland in the 12th century.

The original village was built close to the castle of Yester. At the beginning of the 18th century, as the present Yester House was being built, the 2nd Marquis of Tweeddale had the cottages cleared so that his parkland could be extended. In its place, he laid out the present village.

The finest approach to the village is along the

tree-shaded road from the south-west, uphill from the bridge over Gifford Water, giving a view of the wide main street with the parish church at the end. To the left are the restored mercat cross and, behind it in a little square, the old village hall. Opposite, a road runs between a splendid avenue of limes which leads to Yester House. On the death of the 11th Marquis of Tweeddale in 1967, the mansion was bought by the composer Gian Carlo Menotti.

Yester parish church dates from 1708. The Reverend John Witherspoon, son of the minister there from 1720 to 1760, emigrated to America and became one of the signatories of the Declaration of Independence, and the founding president of Princeton University.

GIGGLESWICK
NORTH YORKSHIRE

14 miles north-west of Skipton (page 436 Ac)

Across the River Ribble from bustling Settle, Giggleswick is one of the most peaceful and enchanting of Pennine villages. Its quaint stone cottages, with mullioned windows under carved dripmoulds, date mainly from the 17th and early 18th centuries. Most of the masonry is pale, natural limestone, although some walls are colour-washed. Some notably beautiful cottages and houses are clustered near the western end of the churchyard and beside a small square at the Settle end of the village.

An ancient market cross stands outside the main gateway to St Alkelda's Church – named after an Anglo-Saxon Christian said to have been martyred by the Danes. The church contains an effigy of Sir Richard Tempest, buried with the head of his favourite horse when he died in 1488. Beyond the church, the main street opens out to cross a small, clear stream where ducks glide beneath a slate-slabbed footbridge.

Flowers and shrubs enhance the cottages leading towards the impressive stone façade of Giggleswick School, a public school founded in the 16th century. About a mile to the north-west, on Buckhaw Brow, is a well which ebbs and flows.

GLAISDALE
NORTH YORKSHIRE

9 miles south-west of Whitby (page 436 Cd)

At the foot of the steep road that leads up to the village of Glaisdale is one of Yorkshire's well-known landmarks. This is Beggar's Bridge, a packhorse bridge over the River Esk, built in 1619, which has remained unaltered ever since.

The bridge is said to have been built by Thomas Ferris, a poor local youth who used to wade or swim across the Esk to court the squire of Glaisdale's daughter. The squire did not approve of the impoverished suitor, so Ferris left the dale to make his fortune. He returned a wealthy man, married the girl, and built the bridge to symbolise their love and to enable later generations to

cross the river dry-shod. Today, modern bridges carry road and railway on either side of Ferris's bridge.

The main part of Glaisdale is strung out along a steep hillside, 500 ft above sea-level, and commands splendid views down into the deep, wooded heart of Esk Dale. In the distance, high moors roll away towards the sea near Whitby. Neat, traditional stone cottages line the road, giving way to more modern houses as it swings westwards for Lealholm and Danby. Terraces of typically Victorian cottages, built to house workers at the village's three blast furnaces, fringe the lower part of the road before it twists and turns through woodlands, crosses the Esk and scrambles up the 1-in-3 gradient of Limber Hill.

GLAMIS
TAYSIDE

10 miles north of Dundee (page 443 Fb)

Shakespeare's Macbeth was the Thane, or ruler, of Glamis, and supposedly lived in the original 11th-century castle, outside whose gates the village was built. The present-day castle – in Scottish Baronial style and with a rich collection of

tapestries, furniture, paintings and weapons – dates mainly from the late 17th century, when it was renovated by Patrick Lyon, 1st Earl of Strathmore. Glamis Castle has been owned by the Lyon family since 1372 – and the Queen Mother, daughter of the 14th earl, spent much of her childhood there. Her daughter, Princess Margaret, was born there. The castle is said to be haunted by the 'Glamis Monster', the ghost of an 18th-century earl, trapped in a secret chamber.

The castle is open to the public from May to September, and from the battlements visitors have fine views of the Vale of Strathmore, the eastern Grampians and the Sidlaw Hills. The grounds – laid out by the 18th-century landscape-gardener Capability Brown – boast a 21 ft high sun-dial with 84 dials.

The village of Glamis, which is pronounced 'Glahms', lies in a wooded setting off the main road. In 1956 the 16th Earl of Strathmore, then owner of the castle, gave a row of cottages in the Kirkwynd to the National Trust for Scotland. They have been turned into the Angus Folk Museum, which contains the furnishings, clothes and tools of generations of farmers, weavers and local tradesmen. Near by is the manse, which has an 8th-century Celtic cross in the grounds. The cross is associated with St Fergus, who founded the kirk.

CASTLE OF FEAR *Glamis Castle is perhaps the most haunted stately home in Britain. The 'Glamis Monster' shares quarters with a grey lady in the chapel, a madman on the roof, a Lady of Glamis who was burned at the stake for witchcraft, and the wicked Earl Beardie, who has spent the last 500 years playing dice with the Devil for his soul.*

A WAY OF LIFE RECALLED *Many aspects of village life in the 19th century are recalled by the exhibits in the Angus Folk Museum at Glamis, housed in a row of 17th-century cottages.*

GLENCOE

HIGHLAND

On southern shore of Loch Leven (page 443 Dc)

Two monuments bear witness to the Massacre of Glencoe, which took place on February 13, 1692. Then, some 130 Government troops under the orders of Archibald Campbell, 10th Earl of Argyll, slaughtered 38 Macdonalds living in the valley. The victims' crime was their tardiness in coming in to swear allegiance to William III. For this, the Campbell troops – who had been billeted peacefully among the Highlanders for almost two weeks – hacked men, women and children to death and burned their homes.

VALLEY OF DEATH *Sunshine streams down on the modern village of Glencoe, near the shore of Loch Leven. But on the night of February 13, 1692, it was snowing when soldiers billeted on the Macdonalds of Glencoe turned on their hosts and massacred them. The 160 or so surviving Macdonalds fled to the hills above the glen, where many of them died of hunger and exposure. The English historian, Macaulay, later called the glen 'the very Valley of the Shadow of Death'.*

The first monument to the dead stands on a hill at the northern end of Glencoe village. A memorial service is held there on February 13 every year. A second monument was erected on the island of Eilean Munde, in Loch Leven, near the entrance to the glen – where the murdered Macdonald chief, MacIan of Glencoe, is buried.

The village is set in the glen surrounded by peaks and ridges. The whitewashed houses run along both sides of a long straight street. Two rebuilt heather-thatched cottages in the street house a folk museum, where Macdonald and Jacobite relics are on display. Near by, in the Church of St Mary, is a memorial to the last Macdonald laird of Glencoe – whose death at the end of the 19th century ended five centuries of the clan's influence in the area.

The Macdonald estate was later bought by Lord Strathcona, a Highlander from Forres who emigrated to Canada, became co-founder of the Canadian Pacific Railway, and came home as a millionaire. He left two landmarks near the village which are there today; his mansion, built in the woods above the village and now a hospital, and the ornamental loch which he created from an old peat bog.

GLENELG
HIGHLAND

8 miles west of Shiel Bridge (page 443 Cd)

Only one road leads to the scattered village of
Glenelg, which looks across the Sound of Sleat to
the Isle of Skye. It was taken by Dr Johnson and
his biographer, James Boswell, on their tour of
the Highlands in 1773, when the doctor spent
the night sleeping on hay. Then, as now, Glenelg
lay to the south of Bernera Barracks, built after
the unsuccessful Jacobite rebellion of 1715.
Today, the barracks are gaunt, massive ruins
overlooking the end of the Sound, and in the
churchyard there is a worn memorial to one of
the garrison officers.

Glenelg – which reads the same way backwards
as forwards – once formed part of the extensive
estates of the Macleod chiefs from Skye. The
village suffered badly under later landlords. During the Highland Clearances of the 1830s and
1840s, scores of local people emigrated to Canada
– where some of them founded a new settlement
in Nova Scotia. To the north-west of the village

is a side road leading to the landing-stage of a
ferry to Skye.

South from Glenelg is the narrow Glen Beag. It
contains the preserved remains of two brochs,
defensive towers probably built by the Picts some
2,000 years ago. Further south are the forest
plantations high above the Sound of Sleat. There,
at the water's edge, is the burned-out house of
Sandaig, the 'Camusfearna' of Scottish author
Gavin Maxwell's best-selling book *Ring of Bright
Water*, about his life with two pet otters.

GLYN CEIRIOG
CLWYD

3 miles south of Llangollen (page 429 Cb)

Poets who were inspired by the beautiful wooded
valley in which the village stands are commemorated by stained-glass windows in the Ceiriog
Memorial Institute. They include Huw Morus,
born at nearby Pontymeibion in 1622, the 19th-
century bard the Reverend Robert Ellis, and his
near-contemporary, John Ceiriog Hughes.
Another window depicts William Morgan,
Bishop of St Asaph in 1601. Some of the institute's furniture was presented by the Welsh
colony in Patagonia in 1910–11.

Glyn Ceiriog is cradled by steep, wooded slopes
and runs down to a small stone bridge over the
River Ceiriog, from which it takes its name. Slate
was quarried and mined in the area until after
the First World War, but the old workings are
vanishing beneath shrubs and hardy conifers.
Beyond the institute, Church Hill clambers a
1-in-4 slope to St Bridget's Church, built in 1838.

On the opposite side of the village another
steep, narrow lane leads to a plateau, more than
1,400 ft above sea-level. On a clear day the views
include the Berwyn Mountains, at the head of
the valley, and the Pennines far away to the east.
The radio-telescope at Jodrell Bank is a notable
man-made landmark.

GNOSALL
STAFFORDSHIRE

6 miles west of Stafford (page 430 Ac)

Two pubs, the Navigation Inn and the Boat Inn,
stand on opposite banks of the Shropshire Union
Canal, an attractive waterfront area bright with
gaily coloured boats. This part of the village,
known as Gnosall Heath, dates largely from the
time the canal was opened in the early 19th
century. Buildings from that period include the
Coton Mill – originally a steam-powered flour
mill, but now a private house.

The heart of the village lies a quarter of a mile
east of the canal. The Church of St Lawrence –
largely 13th century with some fine Norman
details – has an impressive central tower, and
stands on a rise overlooking the Heath.

Near by is the former village lock-up, built in
1830, which was moved to its present position
from its original site in the village street.

SCENIC WALKS *Rugged walking country encircles Goathland, where sheep graze among the cottages of the scattered village greens. Near by are several waterfalls, with romantic names like Mallyan Spout, Nelly Ayre and Water Ark Foss.*

GOATHLAND
NORTH YORKSHIRE

7 miles south-west of Whitby (page 436 Cd)

Sheep graze on the coarse grasses where the moors come right among the greystone houses of this straggling village. A series of huge greens – more like heathland than conventional village greens – breaks the village up into pockets of houses, hotels, shops and tidy terraces of mixed styles of architecture. Goathland has had so much room to grow, that the economical use of space, so frequently associated with the English village, is completely lacking.

The whole area is fine walking country, and a network of footpaths fans out from the village on to the moors. There are several waterfalls, the nearest just beyond the village to the west. To the south-west is a stretch of Wade's Way, a preserved Roman road.

Goathland is one of a handful of English villages that celebrates Plough Monday. This takes place on the first Monday after January 6. For centuries the following week was looked upon as a farmworkers' holiday, and on Plough Monday the local farm boys, known as bullocks, jacks or stots, paraded a plough at their church to be blessed. Then they went from door to door, dancing and 'fooling', dragging the plough behind them. Nowadays the dancers, wearing rustic costume, go from door to door asking for money to finance their dancing at local festivals.

The Church of St Mary is pleasant and unassuming, and was built in the last decade of the 19th century.

GODSTONE
SURREY

5 miles east of Redhill (page 423 Dc)

Local historians suggest that Godstone grew during the Elizabethan period when it was a centre for the leather trade. Queen Elizabeth's name appears on a wall of the White Hart Inn in the High Street. It is one of three royal connections with this ancient hostelry, which claims a history going back to the time of Richard II and visits by Queen Victoria.

There are few other buildings in the village that can claim such age or such distinction, although there are several other old inns, some of Tudor origin, such as the Hare and Hounds. Tucked between the village green and the High Street is a pleasant jumble of buildings set in narrow alleyways which give a sense of intimacy.

Silence and solitude are easily found in Godstone by walking east from the White Hart, down Bay Path that leads to Bay Pond. The pond is now a nature reserve run by the Surrey Naturalists Trust. The word bay was used for the dam which was built to hold the water which powered the hammers of the medieval iron industry. The Godstone bay and pond may have later supplied power for the gunpowder industry, once widespread in Surrey.

Much of the wealth of the Evelyn family came from this industry, and their 17th-century black-and-white marble tomb can be found in the Church of St Nicholas. The church lies at the end of Bay Path, a good half a mile from the main

PAST REFLECTIONS *Some of the houses around the large tree-shaded green at Godstone date back to the 16th and 17th centuries, brick fronts and tile-hanging hiding many structures from earlier periods.*

village. The small church hamlet harbours the prominent but delightful almshouses of 1872, but the nearby cottages are much older. The 16th-century Old Pack House, a short walk down the lane south of the church, has fine timber-framing.

LIMPSFIELD The grave of the composer Frederick Delius is among the yews in the churchyard at Limpsfield, 3 miles east of Godstone in wooded countryside. Although he died in France, Delius wished to be buried in 'a quiet country churchyard in a south of England village'.

GOLSPIE
HIGHLAND

17 miles south-west of Helmsdale (page 443 Ef)

Although Golspie is mentioned in documents of the 13th century, the present village was created in the early 19th century. It is a neatly laid-out place, with sweeping pinewoods on the hills to the west and a fine coastline with golf links.

In wooded grounds north of the village stands Dunrobin Castle, the ancient seat of the Earls and Dukes of Sutherland. Part of it is thought to date from the 13th century although most of the modern building, built 1835–50 in turreted style above formal gardens, was the work of Sir Charles Barry, architect of the Houses of Parliament. It was restored after a fire in 1915.

When the Highland Railway extended northwards in the latter part of the 19th century, the 3rd Duke of Sutherland insisted on having a private station near the castle, his own carriage and, for a time, his own locomotive. The station is still there, but trains no longer stop.

The 1,293 ft summit of Ben Bhraggie, which overlooks the village, is crowned by a statue of the 1st Duke of Sutherland, who died in 1833. Although he was responsible for many improvements in the north of Scotland, he is remembered most for the callousness with which his agents evicted thousands of people from their holdings in the Sutherland glens to make way for sheep.

GOODRICH
HEREFORD AND WORCESTER

4 miles south-west of Ross-on-Wye (page 425 Eb)

The majestic ruins of a red-sandstone castle, deliberately mutilated by Cromwell's troops, stand on a green promontory above a bridge across the River Wye. The earliest part, the Norman keep, was built about 1160 by Godric Mappestone, to guard the ford against the Welsh. Godric's Castle became Goodrich Castle, and gave its name to the village which grew up beneath its walls.

The castle, now cared for as a national monument and open all year round, has romantic ghosts, too. In the Civil War it was the last castle in the county to hold out for Charles I against the Parliamentarians, eventually falling after a long siege to Colonel John Birch. His niece had eloped, taking refuge there, and was drowned in the Wye with her lover as they tried to escape. It is said that to this day their spirits haunt the castle towers.

The village lies in a hollow between castle and church. Its pale sandstone and greystone houses have a slightly Gothic flavour, seen in full-blooded form in the romantic-looking pinnacled inn, Ye Hostelrie Hotel, which dates from 1830.

WHEN WINTER COMES *A soft mantle of snow lies across the orchards and hop-fields of the Kentish Weald, and Goudhurst settles down to wait for the spring. Then the fields will come alive with colour, and the air will become fragrant with the smell of fruit blossom as the Garden of England awakes from its slumbers.*

GOUDHURST
KENT

4 miles north-west of Cranbrook (page 423 Eb)

Good manners, good taste and a rising curve of ancient, red-tiled prosperity from the village pond to the church at the top of the hill – that is Goudhurst. Even the Muscovy ducks, waddling beside the pond, share in the general affluence, for they know that should the weather turn inclement they can shelter in their neatly thatched mid-pond dwelling, thoughtfully provided with a ramp running up out of the water. Close by is a pretty tea shop, which a number of notices claim dates back to the 16th century. Intellectual refreshment, should it be required, may be obtained in the elegant village hall, with its lattice windows and little white tower, that lies behind the pond.

The beginning of the village street is most attractively framed by the Vine pub on one side and the village store on the other – both build-ings in gleaming-white timber cladding. Beyond, climbing up and reaching over one another, are the red-and-gold roofs of the steeply rising street – surely one of the finest massed tributes to the tiler's craft in the country. In many cases the tiles, carved or curved, extend down the walls. The lift of the street shows a whole range of tile marriages: tile with black-and-white timber fram-ing, tile with sandstone, tile with brick, but always, everywhere, tile lending its glow to the large and handsome houses. A slightly incon-gruous note is struck by the National Westmins-ter Bank beside the Vine, a tiny dolls' house of a building, about the size of a garden shed, in herringbone-patterned brick.

Many of the old houses have shops on their ground floors, making it unnecessary for the inhabitants of Goudhurst to travel far in search of supplies. They are also well supplied with pubs, for in addition to the Vine there are the Eight Bells and the Star and Eagle, standing next door to each other at the top of flights of steps at the high end of the street. The Star and Eagle, a late medieval, half-timbered building with leaded windows, is particularly fine.

The church door, framed by a neatly clipped yew arch, looks down the street, while the view from the back of the churchyard across the weald is glorious. It all looks too good to be true – as peaceful a picture of England as any tourist could wish to see. It has been like that for centuries –

GRAFTON UNDERWOOD
NORTHAMPTONSHIRE

4 miles east of Kettering (page 431 Cb)

One of Grafton Underwood's singular charms is a stream, running alongside its main street. Because of the stream, most of the ironstone cottages on the west side of the street are approached by their own stone bridge. The parish church of St James, surrounded by meadows and burly chestnut trees, has stood for more than 700 years and is noted for its Norman arcades.

As well as the greystone and thatched cottages of the village proper, there are three farms in the parish – which used to be the heart of Rockingham Forest. The whole area still has many trees and justifies the village's name. There is a pleasant woodland picnic spot, in Grafton Park Wood, where tables and chairs have been set out.

GRANGE-IN-BORROWDALE
CUMBRIA

4 miles south of Keswick (page 435 Cd)

At the point where Borrowdale opens out to meet the southern shore of Derwent Water, the village of Grange lies in a landscape of soaring splendour. Grange itself is barely 250 ft above sea-level, but scree-covered slopes patchworked with turf and bracken tower immediately behind the village. There are craggy peaks more than 2,000 ft high little more than 1 mile away.

The clear, pebble-bedded River Derwent is spanned by a graceful but narrow bridge which links Grange to the Keswick road.

Until the road was built, probably in the 18th century, the small, scattered villages of Borrowdale could be reached only on foot or horseback. The bridge is overlooked by a little Methodist chapel built from local green stone at the end of the 19th century. Beyond it, cottages and a farm are grouped round an open space which forms the centre of the village. It is a pleasant blend of natural stone and whitewash. Stone slabs set on end form a fence in front of the Chapel of the Holy Trinity, built in 1860 beside the road between Grange and Braithwaite.

with occasional interruptions. In 1747, the churchyard was the setting for a spirited battle between the notorious Hawkhurst Gang of smugglers and the Goudhurst Militia. While it was going on the villagers locked themselves in the church, emerging only when the militia gained the upper hand. The ringleaders of the gang were eventually hanged at Tyburn.

The interior of St Mary's Church, some of which dates from the early 13th century, is of massive, plain sandstone, making it look almost like a castle. It is all spaciousness and light, the latter quality being due to two German land mines that removed a considerable amount of gloomy Victorian stained glass during the Second World War.

Among the chief glories of the church – and there are many – are the painted wooden effigies of Sir Alexander Colepeper and his lady. Sir Alexander, resplendent in green-and-gold armour, had a foundry at Bedgebury, just south of the village, and there he cast many of the guns that smashed the Armada. The Colepepers were of considerable importance at this period. Catherine Howard, Henry VIII's fifth queen, was a member of the family, and so was her cousin, Thomas Colepeper, executed with her for treasonable adultery.

GRAFTON REGIS, Northamptonshire (page 431 Ca)
(see Stoke Bruerne)

GRANTCHESTER
CAMBRIDGESHIRE

2 miles south-west of Cambridge (page 432 Bc)

Can walk from Cambridge
Cream Tea @ the Orchard where Rupert Brook frequent

A homesick poet immortalised the church clock in this serene little village set among meadows beside the River Cam and loved by generations of Cambridge students and dons. Travelling in Germany shortly before the First World War, Rupert Brooke mused about 'the lovely hamlet Grantchester'. His poem, *The Old Vicarage, Grantchester*, asked wistfully:

 'Stands the Church clock at ten to three?
 And is there honey still for tea?'

Brooke lived at The Orchard between 1909 and 1910, then later at the Old Vicarage. There, in the garden, he wrote much of his verse. A mock-Gothic building halfway down the garden, known as Widnall's Folly, was created by Samuel Widnall, who bought the Old Vicarage in 1853 for his photographic and printing work.

The splendid chancel of the Church of St Andrew and St Mary places it high above the run of Cambridgeshire village churches.

TRUMPINGTON The sumptuous Church of St Mary and St Michael, Trumpington, 2 miles east of Grantchester, contains the finely preserved brass of Sir Roger de Trumpington, dated 1289 – the second-oldest brass in England. It shows Sir Roger, legs crossed, in armour and with a shield bearing his coat of arms.

GRASMERE
CUMBRIA

3 miles north-west of Ambleside (page 435 Cd)

William Wordsworth spent 14 of his most creative years in Grasmere – living at Dove Cottage, Allan Bank and The Rectory – and described it as 'the loveliest spot that man hath ever found'. Buildings of rough-hewn local stone nestle in a great natural amphitheatre, with the 2,003 ft high summit of Heron Pike dominating the view eastwards. Wooded lower slopes, many acres of which are protected by the National Trust, sweep down to Grasmere's little lake.

The village and its valley are seen at their best from the surrounding hills, but motorists can enjoy fine views from the Keswick road as it sweeps down from the north. On the left is the Swan Hotel in which Sir Walter Scott is said to have had breakfast when staying with the frugal Wordsworth. Swan Hill, opposite the hotel, runs gently down towards the centre of Grasmere after crossing the River Rothay. An old, creeper-covered house by the bridge is perhaps the most attractive building in the village. Shops and houses of grey-green and purple-tinged stone flank Broadgate, the main street, which has a pleasant little public green at its junction with College Street. Several hotels are clustered in the heart of Grasmere before the main road reaches St Oswald's Church, on the banks of the Rothay. The small building by the lych-gate was the village school from 1660 until 1854. Since then it has been notable for 'Sarah Nelson's Original Celebrated Grasmere Gingerbread', which is baked on the premises to a traditional village recipe. Wordsworth knew the church well and described it in his epic poem, *The Excursion*:

> 'Not raised in nice proportions was the pile,
> But large and massy; for duration built;
> With pillars crowded, and the roof upheld
> By naked rafters intricately crossed,
> Like leafless underboughs in some thick wood,
> All withered by the depth of shade above.'

The church, which dates from the 12th or 13th centuries, has outer walls faced with rough-cast.

Inside, a plaque commemorates Sir John Richardson, 'the constant companion of Sir John Franklin in Arctic exploration'. Richardson, who died in 1865, is buried near the lych-gate. Near the altar, an inscribed profile in white marble depicts Wordsworth between slender daffodils and bluebells.

Every year, on the Saturday nearest to August 5, St Oswald's Day, a colourful 'rush-bearing' procession wends its way through Grasmere to the church. The ancient ceremony, kept alive only in Grasmere and a few other North of England villages, dates from the time when church floors were of bare earth and had rushes scattered over them for warmth and cleanliness. Grasmere's church was paved with flagstones in the 19th century, but children still take symbolic gifts made of rushes and flowers to the church. The rush-bearers are given pieces of gingerbread stamped with St Oswald's name.

One of eight yews planted by Wordsworth in 1819 stands near his grave, in the south-east corner of the churchyard. The poet is buried with his wife, Mary, who died in 1859. In the same corner are the graves of Dorothy Wordsworth, William's devoted sister, and three of the poet's children, Dora, Catherine and Thomas – who died at The Rectory in 1812. Another stone commemorates William's younger brother, John Wordsworth, who died at sea off Portland in 1805 and is buried in Lyme Regis.

Homes of the Wordsworths
Beyond the church, Stock Lane skirts fields leading to Grasmere lake before reaching Town End – a delightful 'mini suburb' of stone, slate-roofed cottages with superb westward views. Dove Cottage, originally an inn called the Dove and Olive Bough, is in a small lane just off the road. William and Dorothy moved there in December 1799, paying an annual rent of £8. Three years later the poet married Mary Hutchinson, and three of their children – John, Dora and Thomas – were born at Dove Cottage during the following four years.

In 1808 the Wordsworths moved to Allan Bank, and the cottage became the home of their friend Thomas de Quincey, author of *The Confessions of an English Opium Eater*.

The Wordsworth Museum, 25 yds from Dove Cottage, contains many of Wordsworth's personal possessions. There is also a reconstruction of a typical farmhouse kitchen.

Allan Bank, where the Wordsworths lived until 1811, is private and not open to visitors. The poet and his family next spent two years in The Rectory, opposite St Oswald's Church, before moving to Rydal Mount – on the road between Grasmere and Ambleside – where Wordsworth lived until his death in 1850, a few days after his 80th birthday.

The village sports are held on a Thursday in late August, and regularly attract up to 12,000 spectators. The main events include traditional wrestling, races to the summit of Butter Crag and back, and hound-trailing in which dogs race over the surrounding hills following a scent laid earlier in the day.

GRASSINGTON, North Yorkshire (page 436 Bc)
(see Linton-in-Craven)

GREAT AMWELL
HERTFORDSHIRE

1 mile south-east of Ware (page 426 Cb)

The village centre in Great Amwell is like no other in Britain. With its shaven lawns and willows overhanging a pool of olive-green, slow-writhing waters, its gracious monuments and its islands inhabited by haughty swans, it looks like an exercise in 18th-century landscape gardening in miniature. Which is more or less what it is.

The prospect, which is seen best from the bridge leading to the church, was created in 1800 by the architect Robert Mylne as a memorial to Sir Hugh Myddleton, creator of the New River. Myddleton constructed the river in the early 17th century to feed water from the springs at Amwell and Chadwell to London, some 40 miles away. This enterprise gave London its first supply of clean drinking water, or, as one of the monuments puts it, brought 'health, pleasure and convenience to the metropolis of Great Britain'.

The pool lies in a hollow, with the church rising above it on one side and the main street curving upwards and round to join the Cambridge road on the other. The New River begins its journey to Clerkenwell on the left, as well-stocked with fish as it was in Izaak Walton's day, though perhaps it was not so expensive to take a rod to it then. All in all, with its air of discreet, if slightly antique, prosperity, it is one of the prettiest villages in the shire.

There are several large houses, all in different styles and generally connected with the Mylne family. The late-18th-century Amwell Grove, white fronted and pillared, was Robert Mylne's home, and W. C. Mylne built the Flint House in 1842–4. The garden contains a moss-covered pillar from the old Blackfriars Bridge, which Robert Mylne designed in 1768. In St John's Lane, near the pleasant four-square Victorian pub, there is an absurdly attractive 19th-century house, all pink wash, glowing brick and lofty chimneys.

A stepped path climbs up through the rhododendrons to the churchyard, which contains several large monuments, the most imposing of which, not entirely surprisingly, is the mausoleum of the Mylne family. The church itself is of great age, dating in part, possibly, from the 11th century. But the main impression is of Victorian and later prosperity.

GREAT AYTON
NORTH YORKSHIRE

5 miles south-west of Guisborough (page 436 Cd)

Reminders of Captain James Cook, whose voyages led to the colonisation of Australia and New Zealand, dominate this large village on the grassy banks of the River Leven. Cook's family moved from Marton, near Middlesbrough, in 1736 when he was eight, and he spent most of his childhood in Great Ayton. His school, now a museum, stands at the eastern end of the High Street, facing a waterfall. Members of the Cook family are buried in the 12th-century churchyard near Low Green, at the opposite end of the village.

The family cottage was dismantled and shipped to Australia in 1934, but a monument marks its site in Bridge Street.

The stone and mellow-brick buildings that surround High Green include the Royal Oak – an old coaching inn – which has a 1771 sun-dial set in the wall above its porch. An old pump and a stone trough recall the horse-and-cart days. Easby Moor, south-east of the village, is crowned by a 51 ft monument to Captain Cook.

◆

THE FAMOUS SWAN *A road sweeps past the greystone, slate-roofed houses of Grasmere to the broad, whitewashed front of the Swan Hotel. The 17th-century coaching inn was immortalised by Wordsworth in* The Waggoner, *in which he asked: 'Who does not know the famous Swan?'*

Gibraltar Mill.

A VILLAGE PRESERVES ITS PAST

The graceful white sails of Gibraltar Mill – a tower windmill built in 1661, added to 90 years later, and now part of a private house – dominate the skyline to the east of Great Bardfield. Their working days over, some of the millstones and the wooden gear-wheels have been made into steps leading up to the entrance to the mill, which is set on a gentle slope. Another local survivor from the past is the thatched Cottage Museum, tucked away in the High Street, which dates from the 16th century. It features displays of rural history and village crafts, and has a wide range of corn dollies, medieval symbols of the Harvest Spirit, now sold as decorations and good-luck charms.

Cottage Museum.

GREAT BARDFIELD
ESSEX

7 miles north-west of Braintree (page 432 Cb)

From the north the village is approached across a long, narrow stone causeway above shimmering water-meadows. From the south it begins with groups of low cottages whose upper windows peep out beneath eyebrows of thatch. But the centre of the village has majestic half-timbered buildings, Georgian houses and shops, and the 15th-century White Hart Inn, which is being restored as a private house.

High Street, where a fair used to be held, is wide and was probably once a green. Place House bears the date 1564 and the initials W.B.; it was the home of William Bendlowes, lawyer, MP and a governor of Lincoln's Inn.

Great Bardfield's church, St Mary the Virgin, is 14th century and has a fine stone screen across the chancel arch. The organ-case is said to be by Augustus Pugin, who designed the interior of the Houses of Parliament.

GREAT BEDWYN
WILTSHIRE

5 miles south-west of Hungerford (page 421 Dc)

In a hollow near Savernake Forest the large village of Great Bedwyn climbs gently up from the banks of the River Dunn and the Kennet and Avon Canal. Brook Street crosses the canal, river and railway, and near by is a square building which was once the village lock-up. At the top of Brook Street is the centre of the village, The Square, where a Victorian lamp standard stands on a traffic island.

In Farm Lane, running north from The Square, is Castle Cottage which has a cylindrical Norman chimney – thought to be all that remains of a small monastic building of the late 14th or early 15th centuries. The old Malt House, still with its kiln tower, has been converted into flats.

A walk southwards from The Square along Church Street takes in a stonemason's yard which has a collection of stonework of all types from the 18th century onwards. The Church of St Mary the Virgin dates from the 11th century and was enlarged in the 14th century. In the chancel is the tomb of Sir John Seymour, father of Jane who was Henry VIII's third wife and who died after giving birth to Henry's son, later Edward VI.

Above Great Bedwyn are the tall ramparts of Chisbury Camp, built by the Saxon leader Cissa to defend Wessex against the kingdom of Mercia. An indecisive battle between the two kingdoms was fought at Crofton, just south of the village, in 675.

At Crofton, by the canal, there is a pumping station with two beam engines, one dating from 1812. The station is owned by the Kennet and Avon Canal Trust, and the engines can be seen operating about seven times a year.

GREAT BUDWORTH
CHESHIRE
2 miles north of Northwich (page 429 Dc)

A parish that stretched 20 miles from Warrington in the north to Holmes Chapel in the south once centred on Great Budworth. It was the largest parish in Cheshire, embracing 35 townships. These are now all independent, but the prefix Great still dignifies the village name, and its imposing hilltop church is still there to bear witness to its former importance.

The village clusters round the hill, looking up at the red-sandstone mass of the church, which was built between the 14th and 16th centuries. Inside, changes in the style of the mouldings on the arches along the nave show that the church took many years to build.

On the southern side is the little private chapel of the Warburton family, lords of the manor, with its simple altar made of a single block of stone, its beautifully carved Tudor ceiling, and the heavy oak beam across the entrance arch now approaching its sixth century and in its third role. Originally, the beam was part of the nave roof when the church was built. Later, it was replaced and used as a roof timber in a nearby farm before being put up in its present position.

Another piece of massive timbering in the church is the medieval oak chest which has four locks, each capable of being opened only by a key kept by a church official. Three of the keys are kept by the churchwardens, and the fourth by the vicar.

The influence of a 19th-century squire, Rowland Egerton-Warburton, can be seen in the village. Outside the pub, the George and Dragon, on the corner facing the war memorial and lych-gate entrance to the churchyard, is a fence with carved mottoes such as: 'God speed the plough', 'Beware ye Beelzebub', and 'Rest all ye nigh aleyard and Kirkyard – do nought therein beset with sins'.

ARLEY Some 2 miles to the north of Great Budworth, among winding lanes, is the village of Arley. It belongs to Arley Hall, the Jacobean-style home of Lord Ashbrook. The hall is renowned for its gardens, which are open to the public.

GREAT COXWELL
OXFORDSHIRE
2 miles south-west of Faringdon (page 426 Aa)

Most visitors to Great Coxwell have come to see the barn – a vast, stone structure built in the 13th century by the Cistercian monks of Beaulieu and lovingly restored by the National Trust. Without particularly stretching his imagination, William Morris described it as being 'noble as a cathedral' – and certainly, in its cruciform shape and soaring interior, it is very cathedral-like. The wind soughs constantly among the great 50 ft high beams, and just to let your eye wander along the lines of ties, braces and struts is a lesson in medieval architecture. At the feet of the pillars, and dwarfed by them, are tractors, bailers, sacks of agrochemicals and other paraphernalia of the modern farmer; it is good to see that the barn is still doing its job after 700 years of continuous use.

Next to the barn, but separated from it by a large pond full of chortling geese, is the Court House, a mainly 17th-century farm with a mossy, stone-slate roof and lattice windows. In fact, most of the houses in the village are of limestone, including the modern ones, as though Great Coxwell were an outlier of the Cotswolds. It is a pleasant material and one that weathers quickly, so that within a very few years, ancient and modern look all of a piece.

The church lies at the far end of the village from the barn. The view from the knoll on which the church was built is tremendous; mile upon mile of farmland rising up to and bounded by the White Horse Hills and the broken, earthwork battlements of the Iron Age fort of Uffington.

The church, dedicated to St Giles, is ancient even by the standards of the neighbourhood. Much of it dates from about 1200 and, though it is small and not very grand, it has a pleasantly worn, loved look. The benches are scuffed Victorian, and lying on them are sets of kneelers embroidered by parishioners.

GREAT HAYWOOD, Staffordshire (page 430 Bc)
(see Milford)

GREAT HORWOOD
BUCKINGHAMSHIRE
5 miles south-east of Buckingham (page 426 Bb)

A disastrous fire destroyed the greater part of Great Horwood in 1781, and most of its houses and cottages date from after that time. But there are still some charming Jacobean cottages in the main street. Facing them, and occupying almost the entire length of the street, is St James's churchyard, entered by a lych-gate. The church dates from the 13th century and its handsome turreted tower dominates the village. One of its rectors was William Warham, who was appointed Archbishop of Canterbury in 1504 by Henry VII and officiated at the coronation of Henry VIII and Catherine of Aragon in 1509.

GREAT SALKELD
CUMBRIA
5 miles north-east of Penrith (page 435 Dd)

Red-sandstone buildings, typical of Cumbria's
Eden Valley, flank the road for almost half a mile
before forming a cluster around Great Salkeld's
ancient church. Monks are said to have rested
there with St Cuthbert's coffin after fleeing from
Viking raiders in the 9th century.

The church is dedicated to St Cuthbert and has
a sturdy, ivy-clad tower, built in the 14th century
to serve as a refuge when raiders swept over the
border from Scotland. The south doorway, sheltered by a porch, is a fine example of Norman
work with heavy, dog-tooth carving and
numerous heads. A sword and several pieces of
armour hang on the west wall. They were found
in 1644, after a Civil War skirmish.

Great Salkeld is a village where attractive
cottages and farmhouses blend with sandstone
barns. Several buildings have external staircases
of stone. The Highland Drove, a pleasantly
whitewashed, late 18th-century pub near the
church, recalls the days when Highland cattle-
men drove their herds south to English markets.

GREAT TEW
OXFORDSHIRE
5 miles east of Chipping Norton (page 426 Ab)

The 17th and 18th-century cottages of Great Tew,
cupped in a hollow of the Cotswold hills, make
up one of England's prettiest villages. Neat
greens and clusters of ornamental trees separate
these honey-coloured thatched and stone-roofed
dwellings, set amid encircling woods of dark
conifers. The immediate impression is of a harmonious wholeness rarely encountered, and
almost devoid of modern intrusions.

Even the solitary telephone kiosk is painted
grey so as not to disturb the felicitous blending
of evergreen and mellow stone. A row of
thatched cottages and the stone-roofed, 18th-cen-
tury Falkland Arms Inn face the tree-shaded
green, with its old stocks. Across the green are
the gabled Victorian school and teacher's house.
The 13th to 14th-century Church of St Michael
stands away from the village, on a hill and
approached through an avenue of laurels. Inside,
a charming monument to Mary Anne Boulton, by
Sir Francis Chantry, shows her reclining on a sort
of day bed, a book open on her lap. The Boulton

reedy north shore, where pebble-dashed cottages mingle with others of chunky, rough-hewn, pale-grey stone. A notably attractive outbuilding, complete with an outdoor staircase of stone, stands near the Derby Arms Inn. Great Urswick's other inn is named after General Burgoyne who surrendered his army to the Americans at Saratoga in 1777, during the War of Independence.

The lakeside lane runs eastwards to Birkrigg Common, where footpaths climb a low hill 446 ft above the nearby shore. There are splendid views over Morecambe Bay, which becomes a vast, gleaming desert of wet sand at low tide.

Great Urswick's church is set slightly back from the tarn, on a site where Christians have gathered for more than 1,000 years. Vertical grooves on the porch pillars are said to have been made by local men sharpening their arrows as they prepared for archery practice after the Sunday service. Inside, are fragments of a pre-Norman cross. They are carved with Scandinavian runic characters which say: 'Tunwinni set up this memorial to his son Torhtred. Pray for his soul. Lyl wrought this.'

GREAT WISHFORD
WILTSHIRE

5 miles north-west of Salisbury (page 421 Db)

Crossing the River Wylye on the way to Great Wishford, wild ducks, lapwings, moorhens, snipe and even a heron or two may be seen. Many of the village houses are made of Chilmark stone, quarried over the hill in the next valley. Some are interlaced with flint and others are thatched.

One of the first things that strikes the eye is the churchyard wall, with its stone inscriptions recording the price of bread in the village in times past. In 1800 it was 3s 4d a gallon, in 1801 it was 3s 10d, in 1904 only 10d and by 1920 it had risen again to 2s 8d. The sign is a reminder that bread was sold by volume, not weight. The church itself, St Giles, was rebuilt in 1863–4. It has two 14th-century effigies, possibly of Nicholas de Bonham and his wife, and floor brasses of some of the children of Thomas de Bonham, who died in 1473. A local tradition says that when Thomas returned from the wars after a seven-year absence, his wife was delivered of seven babies all at once. The old village fire-engine, bought in 1728 for £35, is kept in the church. Opposite the church are the stone-built Grobham Almshouses, founded in 1628, and Great Wishford School, made of chequered brickwork and founded in 1722 for the instruction of the children of the poor.

Oak Apple Day, May 29, is the ideal time to visit Great Wishford, for on that day the villagers reaffirm their ancient right of collecting firewood from Grovely Wood on the summit of the hill along the southern horizon. Before daybreak the young people of the village awake every household by banging tin pans and shouting 'Grovely, Grovely, Grovely and All Grovely'. Then, armed with billhooks, they trudge up the sunken lane to Grovely Wood. There they cut green branches for their houses, and a larger bough for the

THE PAST LIVES *A scarecrow stands guard over seedlings in a sunny corner of Great Tew. A few minor intrusions from the present – like TV aerials and the lamp over the cottage door – make little impression on a scene that has scarcely changed in the past 100 years or more.*

family bought the estate in 1815 and she died 14 years later. There is also a fine brass of the armoured Sir John Wilcotes and his wife Alice, dated 1410. In 1978 the Department of the Environment declared Great Tew to be 'of outstanding interest', and some painstaking restoration has been taking place; for the village has not escaped altogether the ravages of time, and some of its cottages are derelict.

GREAT URSWICK
CUMBRIA

3 miles east of Dalton-in-Furness (page 435 Cc)

Lost in a tangle of lanes, this quiet old village overlooks the placid waters of Urswick Tarn. The pool is less than 450 yds from end to end, but local legends say it is bottomless. The older part of Great Urswick is spread out along the tarn's

church tower. Later in the morning a party of villagers, led by the rector, go to Salisbury Cathedral, where four women, dressed in 19th-century costume and carrying nitches – bundles of sticks – dance on the cathedral green. Afterwards, the villagers go into the cathedral and the rector reads from the charter of 1603, confirming their rights in Grovely Wood.

Another vestige of bygone days is the Midsummer Tithes auction held just before sunset on the Monday of Rogation week, in late April or May, when the grazing rights on two small pastures from Rogationtide to August 12 are sold. The auction is conducted by the churchwarden, who walks up and down the church path collecting the bids. The moment the sun vanishes below the horizon he knocks down the bargain to the last bidder, using the church key as a hammer.

GRENDON

NORTHAMPTONSHIRE

5 miles south of Wellingborough (page 430 Cb)

Old stone cottages and houses line Grendon's long and twisting main street. The village is built on a slope, and the brown-and-grey tower of its 12th-century church is one of the best-known landmarks in the River Nene valley. It pokes up from between thatched and slated roofs, and overlooks an orderly patchwork of outlying fields.

The parish church of St Mary has been added to every century or so. The latest addition is a striking, black-and-white marble floor put in by a rector in 1914 in memory of his three children. The church also has a 17th-century clock mechanism, which is still in working order.

Grendon Hall is a Queen Anne mansion, once a home of the Compton family, earls and marquises of Northampton. The hall, now owned by the County Council, still has rooms with early-18th-century panelling. Two other notable houses in Grendon are the Grange, built in 1850, with a lantern cupola on its roof, and the gabled, 17th-century Manor Farm House.

GRETTON

NORTHAMPTONSHIRE

4 miles north of Corby (page 431 Cb)

Stocks and a whipping post stand on Gretton's placid green, as they have done for centuries. According to local lore, the stocks were last used in 1858 when a drunken churchgoer was put in them to sober up. A twisting maze of narrow streets jammed with ironstone cottages – one of which has an old sun-dial in its gable end – surrounds the green.

Gretton is built on a steep slope marking the edge of the Northamptonshire uplands. There are spectacular views across the Welland Valley and what used to be the tiny county of Rutland (today part of Leicestershire). The village came into prominence in the 19th century, when it was

the headquarters of the men who built the now disused Manton to Kettering railway. The workers also constructed the nearby Harringworth railway viaduct across the Welland Valley. It has 82 arches, is three-quarters of a mile long, and carries the railway 60 ft above the river.

The early-Norman Church of St James, with one of the highest towers in the county, is near the village centre. In the High Street are two imposing old buildings: the Georgian Gretton House – now a rehabilitation centre – and the 17th-century Manor Farm, which faces it.

GREYSTOKE

CUMBRIA

5 miles west of Penrith (page 435 Cd)

Hills sweep up to almost 1,200 ft above Greystoke, and on the edge of a vast, wooded park stands a castle. Seen from the road the castle is an impressive sight, but little of its medieval origins remain and the present battlemented, Elizabethan-style building was built in the 19th century by the Howard family. It is privately owned and not open to the public.

A stone gateway at the entrance to Greystoke Castle overlooks the village green. The Boot and Shoe Inn, on the opposite side, dates from the 19th century, and behind it are attractive 17th-century cottages with cobbled forecourts and dates carved above their doors. Most of the other buildings in the village are of the clean-cut stonework typical of the 19th century. Among them is the village school, built in 1838.

Greystoke's church, St Andrew's, was built in the 13th century, at about the same time as the original castle. Traces of that period survive,

VILLAGE OF THE PLAIN *The village of Grinshill huddles close to the southern foot of Grinshill Hill, a rocky sandstone outcrop which stands isolated above the vast sweep of the Severn Valley. Stone from the hill was used to build the village. It was also used by the Romans to build their town of Viroconium – now Wroxeter – which lies shrouded on the horizon, 10 miles south of the village.*

though the building was considerably altered in the 15th century. The east window has medieval stained glass showing incidents in the life of St Andrew.

To the east of the village are three farmhouses, built in the 18th century by the 11th Duke of Norfolk to 'enhance' the landscape. They are follies; Fort Putnam and Bunkers Hill are shaped like forts and Spire House resembles a church.

GRINGLEY ON THE HILL
NOTTINGHAMSHIRE

6 miles east of Bawtry (page 430 Cd)

Its position on a 200 ft high ridge gives Gringley outstanding views in three directions: northwards across peat land to the county border and Lincolnshire and Humberside; north-westwards towards the wooded hillocks of South Yorkshire; and south-east over the valley of the River Trent to the honey-coloured towers of Lincoln Cathedral, 20 miles away.

At one end of the ridge the land rises another 50 ft or so to form Beacon Hill, where there was a hill-fort in prehistoric times. Prince Rupert camped there in 1644 before capturing Newark for the Royalists during the Civil War.

The road climbs steeply to the village, passing fine red-brick houses and winding around the Early English Church of St Peter and St Paul.

Below the village, on the ridge's northern slope, the Chesterfield Canal follows the contours of the land on its way to join the River Trent. Once a busy waterway for barges laden with coal, bricks and timber, it is now maintained by a canal society and in the summer throngs with pleasure craft.

GRINSHILL
SALOP

7 miles north of Shrewsbury (page 429 Db)

Large, attractive houses line the narrow lane running through the heart of Grinshill. It is a small, well-cared-for village, lying beneath a steep and thickly wooded hill. The most imposing house is the Jacobean Stone Grange, which overlooks the cricket field. It was built in 1617 as a retreat for the teachers and pupils of nearby Shrewsbury School, who fled to it whenever plague struck the county town.

Several other fine old buildings stand at the opposite end of the village. They include the 17th-century Manor House; the red-brick Higher House, a century younger; and the black-and-white half-timbered Step House. The hub of the village, however, is the Elephant and Castle Hotel, a graceful example of early-Georgian architecture.

The red-sandstone Church of All Saints is tucked away up a lane leading from the village. It was built in 1839–40, and has a narrow west tower with a projecting parapet in the Italian manner. Higher up, the track leads to Grinshill Hill – a wooded, sandstone crag 630 ft above sea-level. There are superb views from the top of much of Shropshire, and the distant peaks of North Wales can also be seen.

211

GUITING POWER PRESERVED *A trust set up in the last decade ensures that many of the village's cottages and houses, clustered round and about the triangular green, remain in the hands of local people at modest rents. The move has greatly helped to preserve the rural aspect of this pretty village of Cotswold stone.*

GROOMBRIDGE
KENT

4 miles west of Tunbridge Wells (page 423 Eb)

A triangular village green is flanked on one side by a church beyond which lies parkland, where a 17th-century mansion stands among the trees and peacocks strut on the lawns. On the other two sides of the green are rows of cottages displaying brick, tile and weather-boarding. The Dower House, built about the same time as the mansion, is at the lower corner of the sloping green.

This old-world collection forms the Kent part of Groombridge, which spans the county border. On the opposite bank of Kent Water, a tributary of the River Medway, is the modern part of the village, in East Sussex.

The mansion, Groombridge Place, was built of brick some time between 1652 and 1674. It has hardly changed since then, set within its large medieval moat and surrounded by terraced gardens and formal avenues of trees. The church of 1625 was a private chapel of the estate.

GROSMONT
GWENT

10 miles north-east of Abergavenny (page 425 Db)

The little Town Hall is a quaint reminder that this small and sleepy place enjoyed the lofty status of a borough probably from Norman times until the 19th century. It stands in the middle of the village, among delightful buildings of mellow sandstone, and looks down a street undefiled by modern lamp posts. Instead, Grosmont is lit by old-style lanterns that hang from cottage walls and set the seal on a picture of infinitely memorable charm.

Grosmont Castle, immediately behind the village, stands above the River Monnow that marks the border with England. Surrounded by a deep,

dry moat and a cluster of oaks, the impressive ruins look out over rolling, wooded countryside of great beauty. The stronghold dates from the 12th century and, together with Skenfrith and White Castle, formed a defensive triangle in what was traditionally turbulent country. Henry III was forced to flee from Grosmont under cover of darkness when it was attacked by Llewelyn the Great's army in the 13th century.

The size of the 13th-century parish church is another reminder of the village's past importance. Its interior is particularly interesting, and includes the huge but crude effigy of an armoured knight.

GUITING POWER
GLOUCESTERSHIRE

6 miles west of Stow-on-the-Wold (page 421 Dd)

In the 1970s, a local landowner, Raymond Cochrane, set up a trust to ensure that his houses, about half of those in the village, would continue to be occupied by local people at uninflated rents. This action has helped to preserve the rural character of the village.

Houses and cottages of Cotswold stone cluster around a gently sloping triangular green. A cross on the green appears to be medieval, but is in fact a war memorial erected after the First World War. St Michael's Church, standing away from the green, has Norman origins but was heavily restored in 1903. In Well Lane, the old bakery dates partly from about 1600 and has a porch with a stone roof supported on columns.

The Cotswold Farm Park, about 2 miles north, has rare breeds of farm animals including Cotswold Lions – a heavily fleeced sheep.

Haddenham
BUCKINGHAMSHIRE

3 miles north-east of Thame (page 426 Bb)

White boundary walls capped with red pantiles give a Mediterranean air to Haddenham. They are made of wichert, a local material consisting of chalk marl mixed with straw. The old walls in the village have been matched in new buildings using modern materials in a similar style.

The village sprawls around its green and the 13th-century parish church. It is interlaced with streets, both broad and narrow, alleys and pathways which need to be explored to discover Haddenham's charm. Behind the wichert walls are thatched cottages and timber-framed houses. In High Street is the 17th-century Dove House,

◆

PAST PROSPERITY *A pond gently washes the churchyard wall at Haddenham, once the centre of a thriving local industry in raising ducks for the dinner table. The huge bell tower of St Mary's Church peers down on the thatched roof of Anchor Barn, a half-timbered 15th-century cottage.*

still with its dovecot, and Bone House, dated 1807 and decorated with the knuckle-bones of sheep on the outside walls.

A duck-pond laps against the churchyard wall, and it was there that local duck breeders founded a prosperous trade of raising birds for the table. There are ducks on the pond still, but the breeders have gone and the street where they lived, Duck Lane, is now Flint Street.

Hallaton
LEICESTERSHIRE

7 miles north-east of Market Harborough (page 430 Cb)

Every Easter Monday the villagers of Hallaton turn out in force to challenge neighbouring Medbourne in a boisterous 'bottle-kicking' contest, steeped in pagan ritual. First a huge hare pie is cut into portions and distributed by the rector. Some is left over to be scattered on Hare Pie Bank. Then the rival villagers tussle to carry

small casks of beer or 'bottles' over their opponent's boundary.

The winning scorer is chaired back to Hallaton's ancient conical buttercross to sample the beer, after which competitors and onlookers continue the celebrations at the village's three pubs – the Fox Inn, the Royal Oak and the Bewicke Arms. The contest almost certainly stems from fertility rituals and hare worship. But it has also been suggested that the custom survives from the sacrificial rites connected with the goddess Eostre, from whose name Easter is said to derive. A rector who tried to stop the custom in 1790 was met with the slogan, 'No pie, no parson'.

Mentioned in the Domesday Book as Alctone, the village lies in the rich grazing lands of the Welland Valley.

Castle Hill, just outside Hallaton on the Goadby road, was inhabited at least 1,000 years before the Normans came. Workmen building a railway across the Welland Valley in 1878 found pottery and fragments of clothing dating from before and during the Roman occupation. These are now in Leicester Museum.

St Michael's and All Angels' Church is a fine example of Norman and Early English architecture, dating from the 12th century. It has an imposing west tower and broach spire built in the 13th century, but the building as a whole has been extensively restored. Every three hours the clock peals a chime to which the villagers have fitted the words:

'Old Dunmore's dead, that good old man
Him we no more shall see
He made these chimes to play themselves
At twelve, nine, six and three.'

Hallaton Hall, an early-18th-century greystone house, is rich in associations with the hunting field, and many notable 19th-century sportsmen lived there. It is now occupied by the Torch Trust for the Blind and is known as Torch House. A museum of Hallaton antiquities, in Hog Lane, is open from May to October at weekends.

HALTON HOLEGATE

LINCOLNSHIRE

1 mile south-east of Spilsby (page 432 Be)

On the flat Lincolnshire Fenland any tall building becomes a landmark. And one of the most dramatic is the Boston Stump, the 272 ft high steeple of St Botolph's Church, Boston, which can be clearly seen at a distance of 15 miles from Halton Holegate, through clumps of small trees dotted around the neighbouring fields. Pastureland comes right up to the main street of the village, and the houses become more and more scattered until, finally, they give way to the Fens.

Halton Holegate has a landmark of its own – the handsome and spacious Church of St Andrew, standing on a little hill off the Spilsby road, visible from miles away.

Some of the woodwork in the church is 15th century, including several of the bench-ends which have carvings of angels, owls, monkeys and foxes running off with geese. The pinnacled tower was partly rebuilt in the last century.

Set among trees on the same side of the road as the church is the Old Hall, a largely 18th-century red-brick and slate-roofed building. Its somewhat faded elegance makes it one of the village's most imposing houses.

The low-beamed Bell Inn, believed to date from 1520, is locally renowned for its garden where giant sunflowers grow. In 1978, one reached the spectacular height of 23 ft 6 in. The Bell stands back from the road just west of St Andrew's Rectory, a mainly 19th-century building that was frequently visited by Alfred, Lord Tennyson.

One of the village's most notable sons was Thomas Grantham, a Baptist church leader born in 1634, who was persecuted and imprisoned in the struggle for nonconformist beliefs during the reign of Charles II.

HAMBLEDEN

BUCKINGHAMSHIRE

3 miles north-east of Henley-on-Thames (page 426 Ba)

A narrow stream runs through the brick and flint village of Hambleden, one of the most pleasant settlements in the Chilterns. At the centre of the village, where two roads meet, a pump stands beneath a chestnut tree. Until 1956 the pump was the village's main water supply. Close to the hump-backed bridge on the lane leading into the Hambleden Valley is a mid-19th-century smithy, its inside walls hung with tools of the blacksmith's trade, though decorative wrought-iron-work is now the main product from its glowing forge.

Hambleden's church, St Mary the Virgin, stands back from the square and is approached through a lych-gate. In the churchyard is a memorial to William Henry Smith, who built his family firm, W. H. Smith, into Britain's leading newsagent. Smith, who was given a posthumous peerage, lived at Greenlands, a Victorian manor house; his widow was made Viscountess Hambleden in 1891. Chief among the church's treasures are the Norman font and a wooden altar made from a 16th-century carved screen, said to be the head of a bed that belonged to Bishop Fox of Winchester, for the use of Cardinal Wolsey. The font was probably used to baptise Thomas of Cantelupe, who was born in Hambleden in 1218, became Bishop of Hereford in 1275, and was canonised in 1320. His shrine is in Hereford Cathedral. Also in the church is a 17th-century alabaster monument to the D'Oyley family.

A less-saintly son of Hambleden was the Earl of Cardigan, who led the disastrous charge of the Light Brigade in 1854.

SHOOTING YE LOCK *Though Hambleden's parish register records the death, in 1753, of a bargeman 'Kill'd by accident, shooting ye lock', the turbulent waters of Mill End weir on the River Thames, about a mile from the village, still attract canoeists. Not far from the mill, whose records go back to Domesday, is Yewden Manor, where the remains of a Roman villa, discovered in 1911, included the graves of 97 infants – 'unwanted', according to the parish guide.*

A personal portrait of Peasemore in Berkshire by

MISS READ

The delightful and popular books about village life and times by
'Miss Read' are the deceptively light-hearted works of an author with a deep
affection for, and profound knowledge of, the little worlds she has made her own – and ours.
Her enigmatic pseudonym preserves the anonymity of a charming schoolteacher who
lives with her husband in just such a village as those she has so fondly described over the past
20 years, from her original Village School *in 1955 to* Return to Thrush Green *in 1978.*
But the now-grown children of Peasemore, about whom she writes here, may well
recall the true identity of their acting/temporary headmistress when they read her words.
Please don't tell.

66 'The days that make us happy make us wise,' wrote John Masefield. And, of course, places can have the same effect. A favourite place must surely be one where we were happy and which has enriched our lives and supplied memories to warm us in years to come.

For me, just such a place is the village of Peasemore in Berkshire, whose charm lies in its modesty, its un-ostentatious variety of buildings and its position high on the noble downs. There was a settlement here in Saxon times, for the first church was dedicated to St Peada, son of the great King Penda of Mercia. The present medieval church has 18th-century additions paid for by 'William Coward, Gentleman', who, out of an annual income of £110, gave '*the Tower and great Bell of this church amounting to near 3 years' Revenue And by his Will left the Interest of Forty Pounds to the Poor of the parish forever such were the good effects of Virtue and Oeconomy Read, Grandeur, and Blush He dyd the 23rd Day of February Anno D 1739, aged 77'.*

But there are more personal reasons for

my affection for Peasemore. Here, early in the 1950s, I enjoyed the experience of teaching alone the sixteen pupils, aged five to eleven, who comprised the village school. My stay was for only a little over two months, until a perman-ent head teacher was appointed, but it was that golden time of the year, late August until the end of October.

I cycled the three miles each morning between hedges draped with spangled cobwebs and berried bryony. The last mile was uphill and almost always in the company of some of the children who came to meet me mainly, I think, for the pleasure of wheel-ing my bicycle. They were the friendliest, most unspoiled, children I ever taught and I grew very fond of my family. For that is what it was.

The oldest child was a girl of eleven, motherly and competent. One morning, when I was late, I entered the school full of anxiety. But I need not have worried – Irene was in full charge. The hymn books had been given out, the note struck on the yellow keys of the Victorian piano, and

sixteen voices were raised in approximate unison. The youngest was not quite five, and still missing his mother. Luckily, his sister of eight years old was there, and he sat in the same desk with her comforting arm around him when the charm of threading beads was overcome by homesickness.

As sole teacher, I was responsible for everything. When the school dinner arrived, we cleared the desks, pushed them together to form one great table, and I dished out. Afterwards, I patrolled the playground, relishing the exhilarating downland air and an occasional game of 'What's the Time, Mr Wolf?'

We often took a nature walk, enjoying the bounty of the hedges in early blackberries, sloes and nuts. The family feeling was intensified as we stopped to speak to mothers in the cottage gardens, or waved to distant tractors turning over chocolate-brown furrows and driven by 'my dad', or 'my Uncle Bob'.

One of our favourite walks took us by an ancient flint wall belonging to a fine old farmhouse approached by an avenue of lime trees. One of the flints had a deep recess in it. The children called it 'the lucky hole' and always tore ahead to see if there was anything in it. Usually there was – sometimes a wrapped fruit drop, or a few blackberries; sometimes a lucky halfpenny.

But whoever found the treasure must in all honour replace it with a gift of his own, even if it was only a pin plucked from the lapel of a jacket or a couple of the recently gathered hazel nuts.

The pond was another favourite place to visit. Moorhens strutted from the neighbouring bushes, and a bevy of Muscovy ducks, a study in black, white and red, waddled from the farmyard hard by to enjoy a refreshing splash. In our downland country, water is scarce. It made the pond doubly attractive to the children.

I think I learned more from my family than they did from me in the brief idyllic time we spent together. None of them much more than a mile from home, they carried the aura of a close-knit community as a shield against the unknown. They were unhurried, gentle and refreshingly grateful for all one did. They gladdened my heart.

It was obvious that the school would have to close one day, and a few years later the children were taken to the next village. I was not surprised to hear that they took some time to settle down in a 'big' school of about a hundred, despite an understanding headmaster and the fact that they were only three or four miles from home.

I visited the empty school one summer evening. There were cobwebs across the crack of the locked door. I found it poignantly forlorn. But there was a happy sequel, for the school was later converted into an attractive house so it is still lived in and loved.

Near my home are scores of beautiful villages, some in the willowy valleys of the rivers Kennet and Lambourn and the upper Thames, some impressive in glowing Cotswold stone. So why choose modest Peasemore as my favourite village?

The answer is simple.

I was happy there. **99**

Miss Read

Lych-gate to the church that 'William Coward, Gentleman' knew and loved.

Peasemore...whose charm lies in its modesty and its position high on the noble downs.

*I visited the empty school one summer evening.
I found it poignantly forlorn.*

*One of the flints had a deep recess...
The children called it 'the lucky hole'.*

*One of our walks took us by an
avenue of lime trees.*

HAMBLEDON
HAMPSHIRE

7 miles north-west of Havant (page 422 Cb)

An air of discreet Georgian prosperity pervades Hambledon, recalling the era when it was dubbed, erroneously, 'the birthplace of cricket'. Cricket was already long established by the 1760s when the Hambledon Club was formed by a group of wealthy landed gentry. The club's period of cricketing glory was brief, ending in the 1790s, but in 1777 Hambledon defeated an All-England side at Sevenoaks in Kent by an innings and 168 runs.

Memories of this golden age are preserved in the Bat and Ball Inn – 17th century but much altered – which stands opposite Broadhalfpenny Down, the original cricket ground. The Hambledon Club once used the inn as a clubhouse.

The village, contained by low, wooded hills, trails along the floor of a shallow valley.

East and West Street form a single thoroughfare running as a backbone through the village, flanked by neat, painted cottages of predominantly 18th-century brick. The George Hotel in East Street, a coaching inn in the 18th century, has stable yards scarcely altered since that time.

Bronze and Iron Age remains around the village, and traces of a Roman villa in the grounds of Bury Lodge, south of the village, indicate early beginnings, but the 13th century saw the first flowering of prosperity for Hambledon. In 1256, the Bishop of Winchester – to whom the village belonged – was given the right to hold a weekly market there. High Street, where the market was held, is the original heart of the village. It runs northwards from the point at which East and West Street meet to the 13th-century flint-and-rubble Church of St Peter and St Paul. Some stonework shows signs of the church's Saxon origins, and there is a 15th-century porch and an 18th-century west tower.

In 1612, a royal concession to hold two fairs a year gave a further boost to an already thriving community. At least 50 houses in Hambledon, though apparently Georgian, date from this period. A notable example is Tower House, in High Street, a timber-framed house disguised by an 18th-century 'face-lift' in brick. The village butcher is housed in a typical Tudor shop. Its shutters fold outwards, to form a counter protected by a small, tiled roof.

Manor Farm, in West Street, is a rare example of an early-13th-century manor house, shaped like a church with nave and chancel, in flint and stone. A large north wing dates from the 16th century, with a Victorian west front.

LIMESTONE COUNTRY *The abundance of good building stone in the Derbyshire countryside surrounding the village of Hartington is reflected in the medieval church, the cluster of 18th and 19th-century cottages at the foot of it, and low drystone walls marking the boundaries of fields. It was there, in the Dove Valley and the Beresford Dale, that Izaak Walton, author of* The Compleat Angler *(1635), fished with Charles Cotton – poet and landowner, who is commemorated by the Charles Cotton Hotel in Hartington.*

HANMER
CLWYD

5 miles west of Whitchurch (page 429 Cb)

In character, Hanmer seems more English than Welsh. It huddles at the end of a reedy mere sheltered by trees and, although in Clwyd, Hanmer is geographically part of the Shropshire 'Lake District' centred on Ellesmere. The lakes were formed about 10,000 years ago, when great glaciers melted at the end of the Ice Age. Attractive cottages look out on a scene so peaceful that lapping wavelets, stirred by the breeze, are often the loudest sound to be heard.

Village and mere gave their names to the Hanmer family, whose seat is at nearby Bettisfield. At the end of the 14th century, Margaret Hanmer married Owain Glyndwr – the last great champion of Welsh independence – in the village church. Approached up a long, gently sloping path, the sandstone building adds a noble touch to the scene. It was badly damaged by fire in 1889, but the tower and walls survived. A window depicting the four evangelists – Matthew, Mark, Luke and John – commemorates the consecration of the chancel, restored in 1936, and was presented by Sir Edward Hanmer. Six of his ancestors feature on a list of rectors and vicars that goes back to 1264.

Another stained-glass window, on the south side of the church, bears witness to the skill and dedication of two doctors, Hugh McColl and his brother Robert, who practised in the village in the early part of this century. A touching tribute, it was commissioned by 'their many grateful patients and friends' and symbolises the close-knit nature of this small, rural community.

HANSLOPE
BUCKINGHAMSHIRE

5 miles north-west of Newport Pagnell (page 426 Bb)

Standing a little apart from the village, St James's Church is a landmark for miles around. Its 186 ft steeple is supported by flying buttresses springing from tall pinnacles. Inside the church are long staves with claw-like heads, used for pulling thatch from burning houses before the days of fire brigades. The staves were too long to be kept anywhere but in the church tower.

The village centres around a small square, overlooked by a curving row of stone-built thatched cottages, appropriately named 'Horseshoe Cottages'. Several of the cottages in the village street have 17th-century date stones.

HARTINGTON
DERBYSHIRE

9 miles north of Ashbourne (page 430 Bd)

There was a market at Hartington in the 13th century, and the spacious market place with its pond forms the heart of the village. Around the market place are 18th and 19th-century limestone cottages, and on one side a market hall built in 1820. The Charles Cotton Hotel commemorates the 17th-century poet who lived at nearby Beresford Hall. He and Izaak Walton, author of *The Compleat Angler*, used to fish in the Dove Valley, and in Beresford Dale, about a mile to the south, is the fishing lodge built by Cotton in 1674. It is a stone, single-roomed building with a pyramid-

roof, and is now known as The Fishing Temple.

The church, St Giles, stands behind the square and is late 13th century. A stone coffin in the south transept has the carved head and shoulders of a 13th-century lady on its lid.

Hartington Hall, a gabled manor house of 1611, is on high ground at the eastern edge of the village. Bonnie Prince Charlie is said to have stayed there in 1745 while on his march towards London to seize the crown. It is now a Youth Hostel.

A cheese factory in Hartington is noted for its fine Stilton, and can be visited by arrangement.

HATHERSAGE
DERBYSHIRE

8 miles north of Bakewell (page 430 Bd)

There is a sturdiness about Hathersage that reflects the rugged grandeur of the scenery in which it is set. The village lies on a hillside above the Derwent Valley, and is sheltered by the long, low gritstone cliffs of Millstone Edge to the south-east and Stanage Edge to the north.

The Church of St Michael was built in 1381, enlarged in the 15th century and restored in 1851. It stands above the village, and its decorated spire is a distinctive landmark in the valley. A 14 ft long grave in the churchyard is said to be that of Little John – friend of the outlaw Robin Hood. The cottage where Little John is supposed to have died no longer exists, but across the road from the churchyard gate is the 15th-century Highbury Cottage, the oldest in the village. On the opposite hillside is a stone tower once used to house hunting dogs. Behind Highbury Cottage

are a ditch and mound that may be a Saxon earthworks or Norman motte-and-bailey.

The 18th-century vicarage was visited by the novelist Charlotte Brontë, and she based her 'Morton' in *Jane Eyre* on Hathersage. Her 'Moor House' in the novel is probably Moorseats Hall, which can be seen behind the vicarage.

The novelist probably took the name 'Eyre' from the Derbyshire family who have monuments in the church. Robert Eyre is said to have built houses for each of his seven sons during the 16th century. Five of these houses survive, including Hathersage Hall and North Lees Hall, which lies 1½ miles north of the village.

Dale Mill in Dale Road was built in the 1700s and was used for wire drawing – a process in needle making – once an important industry in the village.

HAWKSHEAD
CUMBRIA

4 miles south of Ambleside (page 435 Cc)

It is easy to understand how Hawkshead inspired the young William Wordsworth to write some of his earliest poems. The village is a place of great charm and character, and has a timeless atmosphere. It is set halfway between Windermere and Coniston Water, with the wooded hills of Grizedale Forest rolling southwards. Esthwaite Water

– on the southern edge of the village – is one of the region's smaller lakes.

Wordsworth was born in Cockermouth in 1770, but went to school in Hawkshead at the age of eight, following his mother's death. He spent much of his time there, lodging in the village, until going to Cambridge in 1787.

The rebuilt school still stands, and inside are the original desks, including one on which Wordsworth carved his name. Other features include chimneys like upturned tubs, and an old sun-dial set in the wall above the door.

The school was founded in 1585 by Edwin Sandys, a local man who became Archbishop of York. In the village church, set on a grassy hillock above the school, is the chapel he dedicated to his parents, William and Margaret. A church has stood on the site since 1150, but the present building dates mainly from the 16th century. Inside there are inscriptions on the wall dating from 1711.

The heart of Hawkshead is an enchanting little maze of narrow streets – snug squares, patches of cobbled pavement and low archways leading to secluded courtyards. Wordsworth lodged at Anne Tyson's Cottage, where Vicarage Lane meets Wordsworth Street. It is one of several cottages with flights of outdoor steps.

Several buildings in Hawkshead, together with land overlooking Esthwaite Water, were given to the National Trust by Beatrix Potter, the author of children's books, who lived 2 miles away in the village of Near Sawrey.

MAKING THE BEST OF IT *St James's Church at Hemingford Grey, set among a lovely tangle of waterways, meadows and old gardens, wears a curious stump on its tower. This is all that remains of a proud spire that was toppled into the river by a hurricane in 1741, when the parishioners, rather than rebuild, economically but inexplicably topped the stump with eight stone balls instead. The spire still lies on the river bed.*

HELPSTON
CAMBRIDGESHIRE

6 miles north-west of Peterborough (page 432 Bd)

At the crossroads on the village green stands a memorial to John Clare, the 'peasant poet' who was born in Helpston in 1793. The memorial, an obelisk ornately decorated in the Gothic style, stands at the top of Woodgate, the street where Clare was born. Beside his birthplace, is the Bluebell Inn, where he was once a servant.

Clare would have known the village cross, which dates from about 1300 and has a tall base with gables and battlements, and the attractive, greystone houses around the green. But the almshouses were built in the early 20th century.

The serene beauty of Helpston and the surrounding countryside inspired Clare who was, in his own words, 'A peasant in his daily cares, a poet in his joy'. Yet his life was one of turmoil and tragedy. He was at various times a ploughboy, herdsman, vagrant and failed farmer. He lived in constant poverty, and died in Northamp-

ton Lunatic Asylum where he had spent 23 years.

Clare's body lies in the churchyard of St Botolph, the village church by the green.

To the south-east of the village is Woodcroft Castle where Clare worked as a ploughboy. The castle, now a manor house, dates from 1312, and has 15th-century additions. During the Civil War the Royalist occupants of the castle were ruthlessly slaughtered by Cromwell's troops, and it is said that the sounds of battle and cries for mercy still resound through the castle.

HEMINGBROUGH
NORTH YORKSHIRE

4 miles east of Selby (page 436 Cb)

Yorkshire's industrial towns robbed Hemingbrough of its importance, and much of its population, during the early part of the 19th century. But the best of its past remains in the main street that runs southwards to the church.

Many of the houses date from the 18th century, and are built of dark-red bricks. A few have been painted in pastel colours. The architecture is simple though often elegant, particularly in the houses close to the church whose 189 ft steeple dominates the village. St Mary's Church was built in the 13th and 15th centuries of white stone quarried at Tadcaster. Its pencil-slim spire soars from a squat tower and is a landmark in the surrounding landscape of flat, open farmland.

The church is known for its bench-end carvings, showing figures of dragons, a monkey and a jester. A misericord – a hinged projection on the underside of a choir seat – dates from about 1200 and is possibly the oldest in England.

HEMINGFORD GREY
CAMBRIDGESHIRE

1 mile south-west of St Ives (page 432 Bc)

Graceful old houses stand by the edge of the Great Ouse and gaze down at the houseboats, skiffs and motor-cruisers which moor there. Set among the village's brick, timber and thatched cottages is a stout-walled and moated Norman manor house, said to be the oldest inhabited home in England. The original entrance to the house was on the first floor, but the external staircase leading to it has now gone. The house is privately owned.

Near by, on a willow-fringed bend of the river, is the 12th-century Church of St James. A short distance away is the 17th-century Hemingford Grey House, now a study and conference centre. In the gardens is one of Britain's biggest plane trees. It was planted in 1702, and has a girth of more than 20 ft.

A towpath leads to Huntingdon and Godmanchester water-meadows, and Hemingford Grey links with the village of Hemingford Abbots, where some attractive houses cluster around St Margaret's Church. St Margaret's was built about 1300, of brown cobbles.

HEPTONSTALL
WEST YORKSHIRE

1 mile north-west of Hebden Bridge (page 436 Ab)

Perched on a steep ridge, with open moorland behind and Hebden Bridge and the Rochdale Canal below, Heptonstall is a captivating old village best explored and enjoyed on foot. Towngate and Top o'th' Town, which together form the main street, are laced with blind corners and are no more than 9 ft wide in some parts. Packhorses clattered along them, after struggling up from the Calder Valley, before the Industrial Revolution cost Heptonstall its prominence as a centre of the handloom weaving trade.

A museum recalling the long history of the village is housed in a former grammar school in Churchyard Bottom. The school, which gave free education to 50 children at a time, was founded by a wealthy clergyman in 1642, rebuilt in the 1720s and continued until 1889. Some of the original school furniture is still there. One of Yorkshire's oldest Cloth Halls, now a private house, stands near by. It dates from the 16th century and is built of paler masonry than Heptonstall's usual dark stone.

Visitors can rest their feet in cobbled Weavers' Square, where seats overlook the yard of the two churches of St Thomas – one in ruins, but with some parts intact that go as far back as the 13th century; the other a prosperous-looking replacement built in the 1850s. The old church suffered heavy storm damage in 1847. A cockpit, which was still used for cock-fighting during the Napoleonic Wars, used to occupy the site of the vicarage.

Heptonstall's parish register records the names of Royalist troops who died in a Civil War skirmish in 1643. Oliver Cromwell's Roundheads occupied the village, and inflicted heavy casualties on the Royalist forces who battled up the hill from Hebden Bridge to try to dislodge them. The next Royalist assault, massively reinforced, found the Roundheads gone.

Steps lead down from Northgate to an unusual octagonal church, said to be the oldest Methodist church in the world still in regular use. Its foundation stone was laid by John Wesley, the founder of Methodism, in 1764.

HERTINGFORDBURY
HERTFORDSHIRE

1 mile west of Hertford (page 426 Cb)

The approach into Hertingfordbury from either direction is down a steep hill, with a sharp, left-hand bend at the bottom.

Until the main road from Hatfield to Hertford was diverted a few years ago, heavy lorries trundling through the village sometimes knocked chunks off corner buildings, but now the village has regained much of its former tranquillity.

It is a place of considerable charm, full of odd corners and unexpected things – a brick, mullioned window left unplastered in the middle of

a white wall; a tiny cottage with a delightfully pretentious Georgian door; a house called The Hill, which has an elegant chimney that runs down to a fireplace opening on to the street; and another very attractive house with a broad, arrow-shaped gable that leaves you puzzling over what the interior must be like.

The White Horse Inn dates from the 16th century, as does the pleasantly named Amores with its high, stone chimneys. There are also a number of fine rose-brick Georgian houses.

The church stands in a churchyard so steep that it would seem that some of the inhabitants must have been buried vertically; there is an odd monument by the door, shaped like a coffin standing upon lion's feet. The Church of St Mary itself, whose benefice is held by the Queen in her capacity as head of the Duchy of Lancaster, was massively restored towards the end of the last century, though not unattractively. The font, altar and communion rails, all of rose alabaster, reflect the high quality of 19th-century workmanship; so do the benches, carved by Joseph Mayer of Oberammergau in 1875. There is a whole chapel-full of monuments to the Cowpers, judges, statesmen and restorers of the church, and some fine early-17th-century effigies. The most charming of these is the little girl who kneels at the foot of the enshrouded Sir William and Lady Harrington; every detail of her sad face and Jacobean costume is perfectly clear. Near by is an elaborately dressed effigy of Lady Calvert, the mother of Lord Baltimore, the founder of the colony of Maryland in 1634.

Of slightly morbid interest are the 17th and 18th-century framed certificates of burial, declaring that the corpses concerned had been wrapped in woollen shrouds. For many years this was a legal requirement, as a means of encouraging the wool trade.

HIGH HAM
SOMERSET

4 miles west of Somerton (page 421 Bb)

Before the Somerset marshes were drained – between the 10th and 14th centuries – ships could sail as far inland as Glastonbury, and the hill on which High Ham stands was an island, looming large above the lagoons and swamplands of the region. It is still a notable landmark, rising some 280 ft above the surrounding flatlands and crowned by this delightful village, built with lavish use of the beautiful honey-coloured stone of the hill itself.

Although splendid vistas of the peat moors and distant hills can be enjoyed from the summit, the heart of the village is quiet and sheltered by tall trees, with ancient houses sitting around a small village green, on one side of which is the 14th to 15th-century Church of St Andrew. The church has an excellent carved roof, a magnificent 500-year-old rood screen and bench-ends decorated with poppy heads. But perhaps its most striking feature is an amusing row of gargoyles, including a trumpeter, a fiddler and a piper, a man throwing stones and a monkey nursing a baby.

From the other side of the green, a lane leads to Windmill Road and, half a mile to the south-east, a thatch-topped windmill kept in meticulous repair by the National Trust and open to the public on Sunday afternoons, or by appointment. The mill dates from about 1820 and is a tower-mill with a reed-thatched cap.

HINGHAM

NORFOLK

6 miles west of Wymondham (page 432 Dd)

Elegant Georgian houses and an impressive coaching inn, the White Hart, are grouped around Hingham's Market Place. In nearby Market Street are more Georgian houses, giving a dignified atmosphere to this 18th-century village – where each year fairs are still held in the street called The Fairland.

The village has strong ties with Hingham in Massachusetts, USA. In the early 17th century a rector, Robert Peck, rebelled against his superiors in the Church and emigrated to America to seek religious freedom. Some of his like-minded parishioners went with him, and together they founded Hingham, USA. A granite boulder in the Market Place was given by the citizens of America's Hingham, in exchange for an old mounting block which had stood outside a blacksmith's forge.

A local man who preceded Peck to America was Samuel Lincoln, whose direct descendant, Abraham Lincoln, became President of the USA. St Andrew's Church, where Samual Lincoln was baptised, has a bronze bust of the President – a gift of the Americans after the First World War.

HINTON ST GEORGE

SOMERSET

2 miles north-west of Crewkerne (page 421 Bb)

Rich golden stone from Ham Hill, 5 miles to the north-east, was used to build this village. Houses, cottages, barns and garden walls glow with it, and modern buildings blend pleasingly with the old, which date mainly from the 17th and 18th centuries. The broad High Street has a late-medieval cross with a carving said to be of St John the Baptist.

Several dozen of the houses and cottages are thatched, some with roofs renewed with reed, others with thatch bright green with moss. There are more fine houses in West Street, and from there a stone-paved footpath leads up to the mainly 15th-century Church of St George. Its battlemented and gargoyled tower has some scratch dials on its buttresses, which indicated the service times.

Hinton St George was the seat of the Poulett family, and the church has many Poulett memorials. It is said that Sir Amyas Poulett had the future Cardinal Wolsey put in the stocks for being drunk and disorderly when he was a young parish priest. The village inn is the Poulett Arms, and Hinton House, now converted into several private homes, was the family residence.

On the last Thursday evening of October the children of the village celebrate Punkie Night, when they parade with lanterns – punkies – made from mangel-wurzels. The custom dates from the Middle Ages, when the men went to a nearby fair and failed to return by evening, so their wives went out with punkies to look for them in the dark.

THE HERITAGE OF HINGHAM

The green by Hingham's Market Place is as smooth as a croquet lawn, and the elegant buildings around it form a pleasing picture with their trim red brick and white stucco fronts. Plants in tubs guard the lofty doorways. The unusual is the usual in Hingham, and one street has a traditional chemist's pestle-and-mortar sign on a decorative holder, while another has a house with a broad Dutch gable end.

Dutch gable.

Chemist's sign.

Georgian houses.

HOAR CROSS
STAFFORDSHIRE

7 miles west of Burton upon Trent (page 430 Bc)

Neither village green nor main street form the heart of Hoar Cross. Its houses and cottages are scattered along leafy lanes on the fringe of Needwood Forest, with an inn and a few houses at a crossroads, and Hoar Cross Hall and a huge church half a mile to the west.

The question most people ask at first sight of the church is – why? For this great and beautiful church serves, it seems, only a large house and a few cottages. In fact, when it was built in 1872 its builder was following the current fashion of commemorating a deceased relative with the best that could be obtained in church architecture.

The Church of the Holy Angels at Hoar Cross was built in memory of Hugo Meynell Ingram, of Hoar Cross Hall, by his young widow. She chose for her architect one of the finest church builders of the day, George Frederick Bodley. He used the 14th-century Gothic style, with a cruci-form plan – nave, tower, transepts and chancel.

The interior holds a wealth of decoration. The floor is paved with black-and-white marble. On the walls are 14 beautiful Stations of the Cross by two Antwerp woodcarvers, De Wint and Boeck. The vaulted chancel roof soars above the white-marble tomb of Hugo Meynell Ingram who lies buried near his wife, the Hon. Emily Charlotte.

Hoar Cross Hall was built for the Meynell Ingrams in 1862, in Jacobean style. The family moved out just after the Second World War, and now medieval banquets are staged there twice weekly in summer.

HODNET
SALOP

5 miles south-west of Market Drayton (page 429 Db)

Traditional Shropshire black-and-white buildings mark the core of Hodnet. Most of the half-timbered houses cluster around St Luke's churchyard. But, near by, an eye-catching Tudor house stands in picturesque isolation. There is also a modest 'folly' of Classical pillars.

From the ridge there is a clear view of Hodnet Hall and its wooded and pool-dotted grounds. The hall, which was built in Elizabethan style in 1870, stands on the site of a castle which belonged to one of Shropshire's most renowned families, the Vernons. Today, Hodnet Hall is the home of the Heber Percys – among whose ancestors was Bishop Reginald Heber, a 19th-century rector of the parish and the composer of several famous hymns, including *From Greenland's Icy Mountains*.

The most interesting structure in Hodnet is the 14th-century sandstone Church of St Luke. Its tower, octagonal from top to bottom, is the only one of its kind in the county. The church contains a chained Nuremberg Bible, printed in 1479. Also on display are a breastplate, helmet and sword which belonged to a Vernon.

THE EAGLE'S NEST *Lancashire hearts and Scottish blood were spent to raise the Eagle Tower of Hornby Castle, that soars so romantically above the placid River Wenning. Sir Edward Stanley built it after a grateful Henry VIII made him Lord Monteagle for leading Lancashire men-at-arms against the Scots at Flodden.*

HORNBY
LANCASHIRE

8 miles north-east of Lancaster (page 435 Dc)

Gargoyles on the battlements of Hornby Castle grimace down on the village, which is divided by the River Wenning. Below the castle, Hornby's main street leads down from the 19th-century Church of St Margaret to the three-arched stone bridge across the Wenning. The street is bordered by Georgian houses and cottages, and the Royal Oak Inn bears the names of its original owners, William and Emma Gelderd, with the date 1781.

On the other side of the bridge, the street broadens and runs between terraces of stone cottages and shops – some of which have bottle-glass windows. At the far end the street divides, one branch climbing past the old village school – now a car showroom – and the other running into the valley towards Lancaster. At the fork there is a Victorian drinking fountain, with a badge showing a cat with a rat in its jaws above a castle tower.

Hornby Castle, situated on a high hill, was built by the Normans, and the gargoyles were added by Sir Edward Stanley who commanded a contingent of Lancashire men-at-arms at the Battle of Flodden in 1513. Henry VIII created Stanley Lord Monteagle in gratitude for the part he played in the English victory over the Scots. In turn, the nobleman built the imposing Eagle Tower over the castle's central keep. He then erected the eight-sided tower at the west end of St Margaret's Church, with a Latin inscription which, translated, reads: 'Edward Stanley, Soldier, Lord Monteagle, caused me to be made.'

Later, the castle passed into the hands of the notorious forger and gambler Colonel Charteris. The colonel was cashiered from the Army for cheating at cards and, in 1713, he bought the castle with his ill-gotten winnings.

Hornby contains two churches. As well as St Margaret's, there is the small Roman Catholic Church of St Mary which was built around 1820 by its priest, the historian Dr John Lingard.

HORNING

NORFOLK

3 miles east of Hoveton (page 433 Dd)

The patchwork of lakes making up the Norfolk Broads is threaded together with streams, channels and rivers, and on one of these, the River Bure, stands the village of Horning. Unlike many of the villages that have sprung up with the popularity of the Broads, Horning is ancient. Earthworks have been found there and a ferry plied across the river for more than 1,000 years.

Horning Ferry no longer exists, but the Ferry Inn is still in business. Along the river, inlets lead to attractive houses with gardens and lawns sweeping down to the water's edge. This system of waterways, crossed here and there by rustic bridges, provides mooring places for many pleasure craft and gives Horning a slightly Venetian air. The village's main street runs parallel to the river, with occasional glimpses of it between trim, thatched cottages.

The flat landscape is relieved by the soaring towers of Horning's 13th to 14th-century Church of St Benedict, half a mile east of the village, and 14th-century St Helen's at Ranworth – 2 miles south as the crow flies but about 8 tortuous miles by road. St Helen's has a fine 15th-century painted screen and a rare Antiphoner, bequeathed in 1478: its 285 sheepskin pages, beautifully written and illuminated by monks, contain daily services in medieval Latin and 19 finely painted miniatures.

From the top of Ranworth Tower there are fine views across the Broads, bejewelled in summer by myriads of dancing sails.

About 3½ miles to the south-east is the ruined St Benet's Abbey, founded in the 11th century. Nobody seems to know when the last monks left – it was *not* dissolved by Henry VIII – but by 1702 only a few buildings remained.

The curious outline of the gatehouse is caused by the stump of a windmill built into the ruins about 200 years ago.

HORNINGHOLD

LEICESTERSHIRE

4 miles south-west of Uppingham (page 430 Cb)

At the beginning of this century Thomas Hardcastle, a farmer with large estates in the neighbourhood, decided to turn Horninghold into a 'garden village'. He erected stone, brick and half-timbered houses in a neat and symmetrical pattern and surrounded them with ornamental shrubs and a variety of trees. Overall, the village has an air of quiet and mellow prosperity.

Horninghold was originally a Norman settlement, but the only remaining building of that period is the Church of St Peter. It was skilfully restored in the Victorian era, and the north and south arcades date from the 13th century. Although the village has no public house, two cottages are on the site of the old Globe Inn. In keeping with the cosy atmosphere, the post office is situated in the front room of a private house.

There is a modest, triangular green on which stands the village sign made from oak and paid for with prize-money won when the village was judged the prettiest in Leicestershire in 1953. Between the green and the church is a restored, late-16th-century cottage which used to be the rectory.

Near by is the 16th-century Manor Farm – formerly the manor house – which was largely rebuilt by Thomas Hardcastle in 1909. He also converted an old farmhouse, Horninghold House, in mock-Tudor style, but kept the spacious, red-brick stables.

HORSMONDEN

KENT

4 miles south-east of Paddock Wood (page 423 Eb)

A neat, square green known as the Heath forms the centre of the village, set among pastures and orchards. The church is 1½ miles to the south. Plague in the Middle Ages may have made an earlier village around the church unacceptable, causing the survivors to move their homes to a 'healthier' site. Another theory is that a new village grew up around the forge of John Browne, gun-maker to Charles I, Cromwell and, it is said, to the Dutch navy when it was our enemy. The Gun Inn, beside the green, has above its entrance a copy of a gun made by John Browne and now kept at the Tower of London.

Sprivers, an 18th-century mansion, is set in a wooded park half a mile south-west and is now owned by the National Trust. Another mansion, Grovehurst, 1½ miles east, has a timber-framed structure dating from the 17th century.

The partly 14th-century church is of sandstone with a buttressed 15th-century tower. Among the memorials inside is an iron slab for John Browne's wife, dated 1644. A wall plaque records Simon Willard, who went to America and founded the city of Concord, New Hampshire.

Sheep sales are held every July on the village playing fields, and draw buyers from all over England. The sales are a living reminder of an older pastoral tradition before most of the local land went over to the growing of fruit and hops after the 16th century. Another reminder of an old industry is Furnace Pond, reached by a short track to the left about half a mile along Furnace Lane. It is a 'hammer' pond, so called because water power from it was used to drive hammers which beat iron into shape. Now this large pond is a haven for anglers and wildfowl.

◆

ON A SEA OF HOPS *Sail-like, the oast-house towers of Horsmonden seem almost to plough the rich soil of their Kentish hopfield like graceful yachts on a gently rolling sea. And sail-like, their wind vanes turn the angled cowls with the breeze to create a vacuum inside that draws up hot air to dry the hops on their slatted floors below. This is the Garden of England, and the village is surrounded by orchards and pastures, as well as hopfields – though it echoed once to the clangour of iron founders, who used the plentiful timber and water power of the region to make cannon.* ▷

HORSMONDEN

HORSTED KEYNES
WEST SUSSEX

4 miles north-east of Haywards Heath (page 423 Db)

The broad sweep of a well-tended green lies between the Crown Inn and an old forge in this village set in a clearing in the ancient woodland west of Ashdown Forest. The forge, like the inn, is still very much in business. On the green the village sign shows a knight and squire from the Bayeux Tapestry, recalling the Norman family of Cahagnes, some of whom fought at the Battle of Hastings, who later gave their name to the manor.

From the green the village stretches to the north, with timber-framed houses leading to the Norman Church of St Giles which stands on a ridge. Just north of the church, by a small school, stand two medieval buildings, Spring Cottage and Mote Croft, with some evidence of a moat around Mote Croft – surprising for such high ground. The outline of a circle with an earth-work, now hedged, appears to be a trace of a pre-Norman site, but the church itself is solidly Norman. Near the altar is the miniature effigy of a knight, estimated to date from the 13th century. A headless brass of a lady, with hands clasped in prayer, dates from the early 15th century.

Horsted Keynes station, about 1 mile to the north-west, is the northern terminus of the Blue-bell Railway, a privately owned line on which steam locomotives carry passengers.

Paths lead northwards through dense woods, passing ponds which once provided the water to power the hammers used by the local iron indus-try. Cinder and slag from the ironworkers' fur-naces may still be picked up on the pathways, and a nearby hill is called Cinder Hill.

HOVINGHAM
NORTH YORKSHIRE

8 miles west of Malton (page 436 Cc)

Fitting into its surroundings like a hand in a tailor-made glove, Hovingham is a fine example of an estate village planned with thought and impeccable taste. Its golden stone, ruddy-tiled cottages stand among flowers, creepers and trim little greens at the massive entrance to Hov-ingham Hall, the home of the Duchess of Kent's family. Her ancestor, Sir Thomas Worsley – George III's surveyor-general – designed the hall in the mid-1700s and much of the credit for the elegance of the village must go to him and his successors. The tunnel-arched hall gateway houses a riding-school stables.

Hovingham Hall overlooks a Victorian village school with an oriel window of startling size and appearance – almost like the stern of a man o' war of Nelson's time. Most of All Saints' Church, near by, was rebuilt in 1860, but its tower dates from the late Anglo-Saxon period – and a slab with eight sculptured figures, set into the con-struction, is thought to be an altar stone pre-served since about AD 800. A stream runs

through the northern end of Hovingham, with a ford beside the footbridge leading to cottages in Brookside. Near the ford is a garage with a weathercock that is linked to a compass – typical of Hovingham's attention to detail.

The Worsley Arms, a fine three-storey coaching inn built in the early 19th century, stands near the junction with a tree-lined country road to Coulton. Hovingham's other pub, the Malt Shovel, is further along the road to the north.

HOXNE
SUFFOLK

4 miles south-east of Diss (page 432 Dc)

Houses of timber, brick and plaster are dotted around the outskirts of Hoxne, whose attractive centre can be found down a shaded lane turning off from the main road. On the road towards Hoxne Cross the historic Goldbrook Bridge crosses a tributary of the River Dove.

A plaque on the bridge records that there the young King Edmund was captured by the Danes in 870 after his defeat in a battle near Thetford, some 20 miles away. Edmund's capture was due, it is said, to his betrayal by a bridal party who saw the glint of his golden spurs as he hid beneath the bridge. As he was dragged away by his captors he loudly cursed all future bridal couples who should cross the bridge. For cen-turies the curse was taken seriously, and even today it is considered unlucky for a bride to cross Goldbrook Bridge on her wedding day.

The Danes tried to force Edmund to renounce his Christian beliefs by tying him to a tree and shooting him with arrows. A stone cross stands on the site of an ancient oak tree which, when it collapsed in 1848, was found to contain an arrowhead.

Edmund was beheaded by the Danes, and for several years his body lay buried in the chapel of a nearby Benedictine priory. Nothing remains of the priory today, but the 16th-century Hoxne Abbey Farmhouse stands on the site.

Hoxne's church, St Peter and St Paul, dates from the 14th century. A screen bearing scenes of Edmund's martyrdom was made from the fallen oak tree.

HURSTBOURNE TARRANT
HAMPSHIRE

5 miles north of Andover (page 422 Bc)

One of the steepest and straightest hills in Eng-land is just to the south of Hurstbourne Tarrant. In less than 1 mile, Hurstbourne Hill rises to a height of 555 ft. Although it poses no major problem to modern motorists, it was a definite burden to the 19th-century stage-coaches. In those days the Oxford to Salisbury stage changed horses in the village before tackling the hill. Market wagons could not do this and a well-known farmer, Joseph Blount, kept a heavy horse which helped the wagons to the top.

Mr Blount lived at Rookery Farm House, at the foot of the hill, and the front-garden wall is known locally as 'The Wayfarers' Table'. This was because, in the 1820s and 1830s, Mr Blount left plates of bread and bacon on top of the wall for hungry travellers. William Cobbett – the journalist, politician and farmer – often visited him when gathering material for his *Rural Rides*. Cobbett's initials and the date 1825 are inscribed on a brick in the garden wall.

Hurstbourne Tarrant lies in a deep valley. Its only inn, the George and Dragon, was one of five which flourished in the stage-coach days.

The Norman Church of St Peter has two faded, medieval murals – the larger one showing three kings hunting in a forest and encountering three skeletons. The church's striking tower and spire date from restoration work in 1897.

Hurstbourne Tarrant has become a place of pilgrimage for artists and art-lovers. Bladon Gallery, formerly a Nonconformist chapel, stages some major art exhibitions during the year. It was opened 30 years ago by Augustus John, who helped found the gallery.

RURAL RIDE *The buildings of Hurstbourne Tarrant, one of the prettiest villages in Hampshire, are bunched about a little stream that oftens runs dry in summer, but flows a full spate of clear water after the spring rains. William Cobbett, the 19th-century reformer, loved the place, and in his* Rural Rides *describes it under its ancient name of 'Uphusband'.*

HUSTHWAITE
NORTH YORKSHIRE
7 miles south-east of Thirsk (page 436 Cc)

Unlike neighbouring villages beneath the lovely Hambleton Hills, where nearly every house is built of pale stone, Husthwaite is notable for its wealth of mellow, weathered brickwork. One quaint little Tudor cottage overlooking the village green is even more rare in North Yorkshire; it is half-timbered. The village's name reveals its antiquity; *Hús* is the Saxon word for 'house', and *Thwaite* is a Norse word meaning 'clearing'. The green is dominated by St Nicholas's Church, a medieval building with some Norman features including an early-12th-century doorway. Inside are pseudo-Norman nave windows inserted during a restoration in 1895. But it has genuine Norman windows, too; and high-backed pews with bobbinhead decoration.

Beacon Banks, just above the village, take their name from the fact that a beacon was set up there to warn of the approach of the Spanish Armada in 1588. The road up the banks gives a fine view of a White Horse, 314 ft long, in the hillside above Kilburn. It was cut not by prehistoric man but by the local schoolmaster in 1857. His pupils marked the outline, and the horse was dug by 30 local men.

Anybody who believes that the old craftsmen are a dying breed should take a look at a converted Victorian stables near the crest of Beacon Banks. They are the premises of Wilfrid Hutchinson, a woodcarver who learned his craft under Robert Thompson, the celebrated 'Mouse Man' of Kilburn. Just as Robert Thompson 'signed' his work with the carving of a mouse, so, too, his pupil, who fashions furniture out of local oak, has a trade mark – a squirrel.

HUTTON-LE-HOLE
NORTH YORKSHIRE
7 miles north-west of Pickering (page 436 Cc)

Westfield Wood provides a rich background for this charming village. Neat cottages and houses of pale stone, many roofed with weathered red tiles, are scattered along both sides of a grassy ravine carved by Hutton Beck as it rushes south from the moors. They rise to more than 1,000 ft between Hutton and Rosedale Abbey, 5 miles to the north. Little bridges and white wooden railings enhance the village's character.

'Hoton' was listed in the Domesday Book of 1086, but did not really develop until the 17th century, when it became a refuge for persecuted Quakers. Its oldest building, the Quaker Cottage of 1695, belonged to John Richardson, who emigrated to America and was associated with William Penn in founding Pennsylvania. One of the most attractive houses, built in 1782, stands at the northern end of the village, where the beck cascades down a series of rock shelves.

Ryedale Folk Museum, next door to the Crown Inn, recalls 400 years of village life.

ICKLETON

CAMBRIDGESHIRE

5 miles north-west of Saffron Walden (page 432 Bb)

There are traces of a fulling-mill at Ickleton, where cloth was thickened with 'fuller's earth'. It is one of two built in the village during the Middle Ages, when the wool trade flourished there. The surviving foundations of the mill are near Frogge Hall, a 16th-century house which gets its name from the fact that frogs once infested the damp streets of the village. The oldest house in Ickleton, The Hovells, once belonged to a Cistercian monastery, and Abbey Farm stands on the site of a late-12th-century Benedictine nunnery. A fishpond and fragments of the priory wall and an archway remain.

Much of the property in the parish was in monastic hands until the Dissolution of the Monasteries by Henry VIII, and several houses take their names from their old owners: Caldrees Manor, from Calder Abbey in Cumbria; Durhams, from the Canons of Dereham in Norfolk; and Mowbrays, from the Mowbray Dukes of Norfolk

who owned it before it passed to Clare College, Cambridge, in the 15th century. The poor of the parish were looked after by the Charity Commissioners at the Town Housen, a group of cottages which at one time incorporated a school. They date from the 17th century, except for one which was built about 1500.

The Romans had a military post at Great Chesterford, across the River Granta, and at Ickleton itself a Romano-British villa was excavated in 1842. The Roman Icknield Way passes close by, and it is probable that the road and the village take their names from the ancient British Iceni tribe, whose queen was Boudicca.

Evidence of the Roman occupation is present in Ickleton's parish church, which has Roman tiles in the stonework of its tower and Roman columns supporting Norman arches in the nave.

◆

A LADY'S GIFT *In the early 14th century, Elizabeth de Burgh, Lady of Clare, gave a farm at Ickleton as part of her endowment to University Hall, a failing Cambridge college. Soon afterwards the college became known as Clare Hall, in honour of its benefactor. A stone carved with the lady's coat of arms is set in the north wall of the farmhouse, Mowbrays, overlooking Ickleton churchyard.*

The church, dedicated to St Mary Magdalene, has an unusual feature in its clock bell, which is on the outside of the spire. Sadly, the interior of the church was recently gutted by fire.

Medieval stone carvings in the churchyard wall represent foxes, crocodiles and other beasts now unidentifiable through years of weathering. Animals are also a feature of the church pews – weird cockerels and a two-headed dragon.

A little more than 1 mile north of Ickleton is Duxford, with two spiky-towered churches. Duxford Chapel, below Whittlesford bridge, is a 14th-century chantry which became a travellers' hospice under the Order of St John. Near by is the RAF museum at Duxford Airfield, open at weekends, which has a large display of aircraft. Trapped there is the prototype Concorde, which flew in but can never fly out, because the runway was shortened to make way for a motorway immediately after its arrival.

ICKWELL GREEN
BEDFORDSHIRE
3 miles west of Biggleswade (page 426 Cb)

This is the kind of village that used to appear in magazine Christmas supplements under the title 'This England . . .' to remind expatriates of what they were missing. It possesses almost all the virtues: a vast, shaggy green; a velvety cricket pitch commanded by a symmetrical oak and a thatched yellow-washed pavilion; a maypole; vividly painted cottages and a smithy; and small girls riding docile ponies with all the hauteur of knights of old. The only things it does not possess are a church and a pub. For both these, villagers must travel half a mile or so to Northill, in whose parish Ickwell lies.

The cottages, all highly individualistic, are scattered round the edge of the green, creating considerable marches over muddy tracks between opposite dwellings. Most of the houses are old, and the few that are not blend very pleasantly into the scene, making up for their lack of years with perfect gardening. The buildings are dressed in a wide range of colours – primrose, ochre, dark honey, old-rose brick – and good reed thatching is everywhere. Perhaps the best examples of the craft are on Stable Cottage, with its startling off-centre thatched peak, and Corner Cottage on Warden Road which has a superb swept-round hood, like a medieval head-dress, over the window above the front door.

The smithy, a little shabby now and no longer plying its trade, stands near the maypole on the green. It is distinguished by a brick doorway in the shape of a horseshoe and was, in the 17th century, the workshop of Thomas Tompion, the father of English clock-making. His cottage near by is marked by a plaque presented by the Clockmakers Company.

May Day is taken seriously at Ickwell, as it has been since the days of the Tudors. Prettily dressed children dance about the stout, striped pole, linked to it by ribbons of red, white and blue. Side-shows and tea-tents thrive, antiques are sold in the smithy and the whole proceedings

are governed by the gracious presence of the May Queen from her lofty green bower on a flower-decked farm cart.

Behind the green, a pair of white gates and a cattle grid lead to Ickwell Bury. The park is pure 18th century and the house a very reasonable imitation of the same period. The original was burned down in the 1930s, and all that remains of it is the 300-year-old stable block and dovecot.

IDRIDGEHAY
DERBYSHIRE
3 miles south of Wirksworth (page 430 Bc)

Green hills and meadowland surround Idridgehay, where the Ecclesbourne Valley cleaves into the southern edge of the Peak District. The village is strung out along the main street, and its houses and cottages are mostly Victorian, as also is the Black Swan pub with its Gothic-style windows.

In contrast, the house called South Sitch is a well-preserved 17th-century dwelling with close-set timbers and a rare timber-framed chimney-stack. The oldest part of the roof is still thatched.

The Church of St James, at the northern end of the village, was built in 1854-5, and has a tower and tall spire. Close by is the small Victorian school. Victorian architecture at its best can be seen at Alton Manor, 1 mile north. It was built in 1846 and was one of the early designs of George Gilbert Scott, best known for London's St Pancras Station and the Albert Memorial. At Alton Manor, Scott employed an Elizabethan style with gables, balustrading and a tower, rather than the Gothic style featured in his later works.

IGHTHAM
KENT
4 miles east of Sevenoaks (page 423 Ec)

Half-timbered medieval houses are dotted among brick-and-tile cottages arranged around a small square and along a curving main street. The centre of the village is in a dip, with a stream known as Busty running through it.

Ightham – which traces its history back to the 1100s, when it was Ehteham, or Ehta's settlement – is set in an Area of Outstanding Natural Beauty, on the road between Maidstone and Sevenoaks. The 15th-century Town House, with close-studded timbers and massive gable-end chimneys, is prominent among the old buildings clustered round the square. Near by is the George and Dragon, built in Henry VIII's reign, and opposite is the 16th-century Skynner's House, timber-framed and with an overhanging upper storey. Near an old oast-house in Sevenoaks Road is The Old Forge, now converted into a timbered house, where the anvil is still displayed. Across the modern by-pass at the end of Sevenoaks Road is Oldbury Lane, a narrow and hedged byway leading to the Iron Age camp of Oldbury Hill – a diamond-shaped enclosure of 120 acres, now

under the care of the National Trust. In the grounds of the Old Rectory, in Rectory Lane, is one of the best herb nurseries in Kent – open on weekdays and Saturday mornings.

The church, on Fenpond Road, was largely reconstructed in the 14th and 15th centuries, and has several sculptures and brasses. One memorial records Dorothy Selby, who died in 1641 and was noted for her needlework, a copy of which can be seen in the church. A plaque remembers Benjamin Harrison, a local grocer who made a national reputation as an archaeologist in the 19th century. His investigations of local sites included the Iron Age camp at Oldbury Hill. In the graveyard lies the victim in a classic unsolved murder case. When Mrs Caroline Luard failed to return to her home at Ighton Knoll from a Sunday afternoon walk in August 1908, her husband, Major General Charles Luard, went to look for her. He found her in nearby Fish Pond Wood, dead from shotgun wounds. Hounded by gossip, though his innocence was well established, he threw himself under a train. He is buried beside his wife.

About 2½ miles south of Ightham, near the village of Ivy Hatch, is the beautifully preserved medieval manor house of Ightham Mote, whose walls rise sheer from the tranquil water of a moat. The house may have been named from its moat or from the ancient word 'mote', indicating a meeting place. In the reign of Elizabeth I the house was bought by Sir William Selby, and remained in the Selby family for 300 years. The house is privately owned, but is open to the public on Friday afternoons.

At the other end of the parish, near its northern boundary, is Ightham Court, a 16th-century brick mansion distinguished by a Classical front of ordered columns and a pediment.

ILMINGTON
WARWICKSHIRE

4 miles north-west of Shipston on Stour (page 430 Ba)

Just beyond the northern edge of the Cotswolds the land rises again to form Ilmington Down, 854 ft high and the highest point in Warwickshire. The village has all the Cotswold hallmarks – mellow stone-built cottages, lichen-covered stone roofs and mullioned windows.

The village has two greens: Lower Green overlooked by cottages, an inn and the village store; and Upper Green, below which are cottages and houses, the Norman church, St Mary's, and an orchard. Crab Mill, at the western end of Upper Green, dates from 1711, and the Manor House from the 16th century.

Just south of the village is the 17th and 18th-century Compton Scorpion Manor, home of Sir Adrian Beecham, son of the orchestral conductor Sir Thomas Beecham. Foxcote is an impressive early-Georgian house with nine bays.

In so English a village it is not surprising to find that some rural traditions are kept alive; sheep hurdles are still made there by a centuries-old method, and the Ilmington Morris Dancers perform regularly in the summer.

INGLEWHITE
LANCASHIRE

7 miles north of Preston (page 435 Db)

In the 19th century, sheep and cattle fairs drew crowds from miles around to Inglewhite, and the winding lanes into the village were crammed with farmers and their animals. The markets were held on the village green, where the small stone figure of a Green Man – a supernatural forest-being – stands on top of the market column.

Inglewhite spreads out across flat and fertile fields to the east of the Fylde Peninsula. Although it no longer has a market, there is evidence of the various trades which flourished there. In Button Street, animal bones were used for making buttons for the local clothing trade. Silk was woven in some of the stone cottages. Two private houses were once inns – the Black Bull and Queen's Head. They were formerly rivals to the Green Man, built in 1809 and now Inglewhite's only pub.

The village has a Congregational chapel dated 1826, with arched windows. At Whitechapel, just over 1 mile away, is the Church of St James. It was built in 1738, enlarged 80 years later, and restored in 1889.

INKBERROW
HEREFORD AND WORCESTER

5 miles west of Alcester (page 425 Fc)

The village green at Inkberrow is bordered by a picturesque assortment of houses, some of black-and-white half-timbering and others, in pleasant contrast, in mellow red brick.

From the west side of the green, the three-storey Bull's Head Hotel looks across to one of the county's best-known inns, the timber-framed Old Bull, the model for the village pub at Ambridge in the BBC's long-running *Archers* serial. But it has an earlier and more distinguished literary association: Shakespeare stayed there in 1582 on the way from Stratford to Worcester to collect his marriage certificate.

Near by is the Old Vicarage, a fine 18th-century brick building in the Tudor style and now divided into two dwellings.

Opposite, stands Inkberrow's parish church of St Peter, dating from the 12th century but considerably rebuilt over the years. Its battlemented walls and tower are a familiar landmark. In safe keeping inside are some rare maps that were left in the vicarage by Charles I when he stayed there on May 10, 1645, not long before Naseby – the last battle of the Civil War, where he was defeated by Cromwell's forces. There is also the canopied tomb of John Savage, a high sheriff, who died in 1631. His effigy in armour has the figures of his six children standing along the base of the tomb. Several families in the village can still trace their descent from him.

The name of the village store, Forge Shop, recalls the days of the village blacksmith. Opposite, the colourful sign of an antique dealer attracts the attention of Inkberrow's visitors.

Four miles east of Inkberrow is Ragley Hall, a 17th-century mansion with parkland laid out by Capability Brown. The great hall in the house is 70 ft long with a decorated plaster ceiling 40 ft high. Chippendale furniture, Minton and Meissen china and carvings by Grinling Gibbons are among the house's treasures.

IRNHAM
LINCOLNSHIRE

6 miles north-west of Bourne (page 432 Bd)

Four roads meet at Irnham, yet there is little through traffic to disturb the peace of this self-contained greystone village set among tall trees in a fold of hills.

The village inn, the Griffin, stands at the crossroads and is mostly Georgian. The north to south road through the village leads to Irnham Hall. The hall was built between 1510 and 1531, but a fire in 1887 destroyed much of the interior and there were some exterior alterations in the mid-18th century. It is occasionally open to the public and can best be seen from the churchyard of St Andrew's. The church, which dates from the 12th century, contains an early brass of Sir Andrew Luttrell, Lord of Irnham in 1390, and some stained glass, most of which is 19th century.

Two attractive 18th-century houses stand near the church – the Manor House and the even grander Newton House.

ISLEORNSAY
SKYE (HIGHLAND)

7 miles south-east of Broadford (page 442 Cd)

Despite its name, the village of Isleornsay is not on Ornsay Island itself. Instead, it stands on the south-east coast of the Isle of Skye and faces its namesake across the Sound of Sleat. The breakwater island of Isle Ornsay provides a sheltered anchorage which sailors have used for hundreds of years. In the 18th century up to 100 fishing boats would sometimes crowd into it at the same time.

Isleornsay – with its pier and crofthouses – grew up beside an inn, dating from 1888, on the main road between the villages of Armadale and Broadford. The inn is still there, known by the Gaelic name of Hotel Eilean Iarmain. Gaelic is being promoted locally, and the hotel staff can all speak it. The village was once a port of call for Glasgow steamers, and trippers made excursions to the nearby and spectacular Cuillin Hills, and explored the surrounding green countryside.

At low tide, the white lighthouse on the smaller and neighbouring island of Eilean Sionnach can be visited. In the background rise the remote mainland peaks of Knoydart, whose 3,000 ft summits dominate the beautiful waters of Loch Hourn, which forms an arm of the Atlantic Ocean.

KELD

NORTH YORKSHIRE

18 miles south-east of Appleby (page 436 Ad)

Business hours at Keld's bank agency – just 30 minutes a week – point to the sleepy seclusion of the most westerly of Swaledale's villages. Hidden away down a cul-de-sac off the switchback road from Richmond to Appleby, its tiny cluster of greystone buildings emphasises the vast grandeur of the surrounding Pennine fells, rising steeply to more than 2,000 ft.

Keld was originally a Viking settlement – its name comes from an old Norse word for a well or spring. The village today consists of a few cottages and farm buildings, a hall and a chapel, all round or near a rustic square flanked by the River Swale. There are fine views eastwards from the grounds of the chapel, which was rebuilt in 1860. A neighbouring building has an unusual doorway, completely framed by four blocks of

---

◆

PENNINE ODYSSEY *From the granite hamlet of Keld, a path – still known as Corpse Way – climbs 12 miles over lowering Kismore Hill to the graveyard at Grinton. Six-foot stone slabs along its course mark where bearers rested the coffins.*

stone which together form its pillars, lintel and step. A few hundred yards away, a Methodist chapel and a few other buildings stand beside the main road.

Keld and nearby Muker are well known to ramblers in the Yorkshire Dales National Park and hikers on the Pennine Way, which is only a few hundred yards away. It can be reached by a footpath which starts near the letter-box. Other tracks lead to the waterfalls of Kisdon Force and Catrake Force.

Half a mile north-west of Keld a moorland lane runs 4 miles to Tan Hill Inn, near a disused mine in the heather. At 1,732 ft it is England's highest and loneliest inn.

KELMSCOT

OXFORDSHIRE

2 miles east of Lechlade (page 426 Aa)

Farmhouses and farmworkers' cottages make up most of the village, which lies in remote meadowland close to the upper reaches of the River Thames. A lane from the river bank leads to the village and its manor house, the home for

25 years of the poet and artist William Morris.

Morris came to live in Kelmscot in 1871, and when he started his private printing works at Hammersmith in 1890 he called it Kelmscott Press. He wrote of the Elizabethan, greystone house:

'. . . Thames run chill
twixt mead and hill.
But kind and dear
is the old house here.'

The house was restored in 1968 as a Morris museum. It can be seen by arrangement with the owners, the Society of Antiquaries of London, Burlington House, Piccadilly. Some of Morris's furniture can be seen, and several rooms are decorated with wallpaper designed by him.

At the far end of the village is St George's Church, with a Norman nave and a 13th-century gabled bell-cote. In a corner of the churchyard is the lichen-covered tomb of the Morris family. The tent-shaped stone was designed by Morris's friend and partner, Philip Webb.

A group of cottages near the church was built in 1902 by Morris's widow, Jane, as a memorial to him. They were designed by Webb, and a sketch by him of Morris was used for a carved relief on the front of two more cottages built by the poet's daughter, May Morris, in 1915.

KENMORE
TAYSIDE

6 miles south-west of Aberfeldy (page 443 Eb)

Robert Burns visited Kenmore in 1789, and was sufficiently moved by it to pencil a few verses on the parlour wall of the hotel in the square. Preserved under glass to this day, the work opens with the lines:

'Admiring nature in her wildest grace,
These northern scenes with weary feet I trace.'

The mid-18th-century houses flanking the square were built by the 3rd Earl of Breadalbane, who lived in nearby Balloch Castle. This building, of which all that remains is its magnificent arched gateway, was pulled down in the 19th century. Its replacement, Taymouth Castle, has had a chequered career since the 3rd Marquis of Breadalbane died in 1922; first a luxury hotel, then a military hospital and a boarding school, its future is now uncertain.

At the beginning of the 16th century, Kenmore was no more than a ferryman's house beside the Tay, but in the 1570s market fairs were established and – with the help of the Breadalbanes – the place flourished. With the completion of the bridge over the Tay in 1774, which is still there, prosperity was assured.

Kenmore lies in a conservation area, and still looks much as it did in Victorian coaching prints. A steep road rises above the south shore of Loch Tay and crosses the watershed into Glen Quaich – a walk rewarded with fine views.

At Croftmoraig, some 2 miles to the east of the village, is one of the most imposing prehistoric monuments in Scotland. It consists of a double circle of standing stones set on a 190 ft diameter stone platform.

RUSTIC CHOICE *When the 2nd Marquis of Breadalbane redeveloped Kenmore in the mid-19th century he favoured a style best described as Victorian rustic, represented here by a house called The Fort, on the outskirts of the village.*

KERRY
POWYS

3 miles south-east of Newtown (page 429 Ca)

A sign on the whitewashed Kerry Lamb Inn reminds passers-by that a hardy breed of sheep takes its name from the village standing in the tree-clad hills that run from Newtown to the English border. The main street, mainly stone and old brick, has a pair of Gothic lodges that once commanded the entrance to Dolforgan Hall. These delightful follies, built about 1818, have slender, eave-high arches painted to look like chapel windows, but, in fact, are of solid brick.

The Herbert Arms looks across The Square to the church and the churchyard, renowned for its yews, limes and snowdrops. In 1176, the church saw an extraordinary battle of clerics, in which the Bishop of St Asaph and Giraldus Cambrensis of St David's claimed the church on behalf of their respective dioceses. Each excommunicated the other, but victory went eventually to Giraldus. A plaque in the church recounts the details of the dispute, and the fact that the church was finally transferred to St Asaph's in 1849.

KERSEY
SUFFOLK

2 miles north-west of Hadleigh (page 432 Cb)

Of all the times to visit Kersey, the late afternoon is best, for then the great Suffolk fields with their serpentine hedgerows are filled from horizon to horizon with the pink-gold and green light that has brought so many painters to East Anglia. Standing against the light, as you approach along the Lavenham to Hadleigh road, Kersey Church on its hilltop grows ever more massive. The village itself, however, is invisible until you come to a corner with an archaic wooden pump high on the right bank, turn, and then suddenly, there it is – all of Kersey, running steeply down

KERSEY – 500 YEARS OF CRAFTSMANSHIP
ALONG A VILLAGE STREET

Long before Shakespeare's day, the name of tough Kersey cloth was almost a byword for the sturdy yeomen and tradesmen who wore it. It brought prosperity to the village that made it and christened it – a prosperity that has lasted down the centuries and is typified by the pre-Reformation weavers' houses, whose bricks and timbers are as defiant of wind and weather as the cloth that was once woven in them. Between its two hills, one crowned by the church and the other by the remains of an Augustinian priory, Kersey lies like an enamelled jewel in the cup of a giant's hand. The multi-coloured houses run steeply downhill to the water-splash, and each bears some delightfully individual stamp. A massive Elizabethan door on tiny River House, for example, or a horse's tail on an eave which shows where the horse doctor lived.

Kersey shopfront.

The old village pump.

Medieval weavers' houses.

Springtime in Kersey.

The Street to a water-splash through a tributary of the Brett, and up again, just as steeply, to the summit of Church Hill.

Seen all of a piece like this, in a picture that fits snugly into the lens of any camera, Kersey is a peaceful, multi-coloured Toytown of a village, whose red-tiled roofs are subdued by just the right amount of weathering and lichen, and whose overhanging gables thrust forward in a quiet brilliance of red-and-yellow ochre, pink, white and café-au-lait. Only a closer look reveals how old it all is. The Corner House opposite the pump, for example, has among its ancient timbers those of a filled-in doorway that must date from the early 16th century at least, while a few yards down The Street is a group of weavers' cottages, so old that their hollowed steps and time-hardened timbers seem to grow out of the pavement. Their high lattice-paned dormer windows lean forward in faint surprise towards the White Horse Inn across the road, as near a pink-and-white birthday cake as a pub can be.

In all of The Street there is scarcely a house without character, from the timber-framed Bell pub to River House by the ford, whose inhabitants for almost 500 years have had the murmuring of the river along the walls as a background to their lives. The same walls, when the Virginia creeper dies back in winter, show a date-mark of 1490.

On the right of Church Hill, beyond the ford, are three adjoining houses – The Little Manor, Woodbine Cottage, and Aran Cottage – built before the Reformation and smothered at one end by a twisting creeper that looks nearly as old. Just downhill is the entrance to The Green, a lovely group of pastel-hued cottages.

The sheer size and magnificence of the Church of St Mary argues a prosperity and a population far greater than the village possesses now. It is a reminder of the centuries when half the men in England wore hard-wearing Kersey cloth, just as the women wore Lindsey Woolsey, made in the neighbouring village of Lindsey. Built largely in the 14th century, St Mary's is a most impressive building whose walls are decorated with a mingling of square-split flint and stone. The roof of the south porch consists of 16 intricately carved wooden panels, a masterpiece of 15th-century craftsmanship. The interior of the church suffered considerably during the Reformation, as a number of headless angels and battered carvings bear witness, though a surprising number of its earliest treasures remain. There is, for example, part of a 15th-century screen depicting kings and prophets making those curious double-jointed medieval gestures with their hands, and an engaging wooden lectern of similar date. Each generation has contributed something to the church, including our own which, in addition to preserving the bells and fabric, provided the beautifully embroidered hassocks decorated with ecclesiastical motifs.

Just before leaving the churchyard it is worth studying a sturdily independent East Anglian epitaph:

> 'Reader pass on nor waste thy time
> On bad biography or bitter rhyme
> For what I am this humble dust enclose,
> And what I was is no affair of yours.'

KETTLEWELL
NORTH YORKSHIRE

13 miles north of Skipton (page 436 Ac)

Held tightly in the grip of the Pennine crags, Kettlewell is a haven of rest for travellers between Wharfedale and Wensleydale, and for climbers and walkers exploring some of the finest parts of the Yorkshire Dales National Park. But for them, the village might have gone to sleep after its heyday in the 17th to 19th centuries as a market town and lead-mining centre. Its steep surroundings have prevented any sprawling growth, and its buildings still cluster by Cam Beck, near where it joins the River Wharfe.

At the western end of Kettlewell both the Bluebell Hotel, built in 1680, and the nearby Racehorses Hotel have cobbled forecourts and whitewashed walls, contrasting with the natural stone used elsewhere in the village. Across the beck, near the old stone bridge, stands a shop that used to house the blacksmith's forge and has a top-and-bottom divided door. Upstream a street leads up to Kettlewell's third inn, the King's Head, and its church, built in 1882–5. A carved font is preserved from the Norman church that was there before.

A charming whitewashed house, dating from 1681, stands beside the narrow 4-in-1 road that zigzags north from Kettlewell and into Coverdale, climbing to more than 1,600 ft before the plunge into Wensleydale. From the village, spectacular mountain scenery greets the eye at every turn. The crags of Knipe Scar dominate the western skyline, Top Mere looms to the north, and the 2,309 ft ridge of Great Whernside soars to the east. Kilnsey Crag, 3 miles south of Kettlewell beside the road to Skipton or Ilkley, is among the most dramatic rock formations in England.

KILBURN
NORTH YORKSHIRE

6 miles east of Thirsk (page 436 Cc)

One huge horse and thousands of tiny mice have brought lasting fame to this pretty little beckside village at the foot of the steep, wooded Hambleton Hills. Village schoolmaster John Hodgson and his pupils cut the outline of the Kilburn White Horse, 314 ft long and 228 ft high, into the turf of an almost sheer hill in 1857, then Hodgson and 30 local men dug out the turf. Two generations later, a local woodcarver's contributions to church architecture – and his whimsical humour – were starting to make the name of Kilburn known throughout Britain. Robert Thompson, born in 1876, took to adding astonishingly lifelike church mice to his carvings. They became the trademark of a thriving business, and can be seen in hundreds of churches, including Westminster Abbey, York Minster and Kilburn's own restored Norman Church of St Mary.

The 'Mouse Man' died in 1955, but his grandsons carry on the business from a workshop in

WHERE THE WATERS MEET *The white waters of the Falls of Dochart make a last surge before they pass beneath the bridge at Killin to join the River Lochay, which flows quietly into Loch Tay.*

front of the church. Near the Thompson workshop, footbridges cross the beck to flower-filled gardens. They front the snug, stone cottages with tiled roofs that are typical of North Yorkshire. A pub, the Forester's Arms, faces a small square. Kilburn Hall, further along the street, has a 17th-century façade. Kilburn school has a plaque commemorating Edward Harcourt, Archbishop of York, who supported it until his death in 1847.

KILCONQUHAR
FIFE

7 miles east of Leven (page 441 Fe)

Whenever it is cold enough for thick ice to form, curling becomes Kilconquhar's great outdoor sport. The village, on the shore of Kilconquhar Loch, has long associations with water and ice. According to one local belief, the present loch was originally marshland called Redmire. The villagers dug the peat and turf for fuel. Then, in the 1620s, the burn which was its outflow to the sea became blocked, and the loch was formed. However, another story says that there was a loch there some time before that – and that the laird of Kilconquhar was drowned in 1593 when the ice gave way beneath him during a skating party. The loch is also a noted haunt of waterfowl.

Kilconquhar – which is screened by trees and set back from the main roads – is pronounced 'Kinn-uh-er' locally. The name means 'church at the head of a lake', and there has been a church on this site since the 12th century. There are some carved gravestones in the churchyard of the present church of 1821, and nearby Kilconquhar Castle has a fine 16th-century tower. In the 1840s there was a tannery in the village, and some corn and flax-mills near by.

WHERE THE WATERS MEET *The white waters of the Falls of Dochart make a last surge before they pass beneath the bridge at Killin to join the River Lochay, which flows quietly into Loch Tay.*

KILLIN
CENTRAL

16 miles north of Callander (page 441 Ee)

The area around the River Lochay, which runs along the northern side of the village of Killin, is a sportsman's delight, attracting yachtsmen, fishermen and botanists in the summer, and skiers in the winter. Killin is hemmed in on three sides by towering mountains – including Ben Lawers, almost 4,000 ft. From the south-west approach, the first row of houses is lined beside the Falls of Dochart.

The burial island of the Clan MacNab is situated near the Dochart bridge and not far from Kinnell House, the family seat of the MacNabs. The house was sold in the 1820s by Archibald MacNab, the clan chief, who emigrated to Canada, and it was not until 1949 that the family was able to buy it back. A feature of the building is a splendid vine, one of the biggest in Europe.

The Lochay and Dochart rivers join outside the village and flow into Loch Tay – at the head of which are the ruins of Finlarig Castle, the former stronghold of the Campbell Earls of Breadalbane. The castle, which is now eerily buried among yew, bracken and ivy, is described in Sir Walter Scott's novel, *The Fair Maid of Perth.*

The 'punishment pit' beside the castle is a reminder of the days when the Campbells ruled supreme over Killin and the surrounding district. In the pit – according to local lore – rich law-breakers were beheaded. Poor offenders were hanged on a nearby tree.

How villages got their NAMES

*Heroes, saints and chieftains whose deeds
are no longer remembered, communities that carved
out settlements in long-vanished forests and
marshes – many fragments of the past
are recalled in the place-names of these islands.
But the meaning is not always the obvious
one. Changes in spelling over the centuries have
often obscured the original meaning, leaving a
fascinating detective puzzle for later generations.*

Few items in our national heritage are so adhesive – or so ancient – as our place-names. Some of these names, such as 'Allen', which occurs in Allendale and Alnmouth, belong to a language so old that we do not know what it was called, or who spoke it, a tongue that is simply referred to as 'Pre-Celtic'. Others reflect the tongues, beliefs and life-styles of later peoples – Celts, Gaels, Anglo-Saxons, Norwegians, Danes and the French.

Oddly enough, there are few place-name survivors that can be definitely ascribed to the four centuries of the Roman occupation. The reason seems to be that the Romans tended to Latinise already existing place-names, and that during their occupation the greater part of the population of what later became England, Wales and a large part of Scotland, spoke not Latin but Brythonic or British, a Celtic language that was later to divide into Cornish and Welsh. It was the Anglo-Saxon settlement that eventually gave rise to the English language.

All the same, traces of old British or Welsh still linger, rather confusingly, in the village and town names of both England and Scotland. Cawdor and Calder in Scotland came from the ancient British words *caled dwfr*, meaning 'hard stream'. Lanark comes from *llanerch*, the Welsh for 'glade', while the names of Fintry and Traquair in Scotland are both derived in part from the Welsh *tref*, meaning 'village'.

In England, ancient British village names refer to nearby hills or rivers. Dent, Kinver and Penn belong to the first group and Bovey, Chew and Coker to the second. Peover, meaning 'radiant', is another British river name, occurring in both Lower Peover and Strathpeffer. Occasionally, as one language yielded to the next over the centuries, some curious hybrids arose. *Bre*, for example, is British for 'hill', and *dun* signifies the same thing in Anglo-Saxon. Therefore, Breedon-on-the-Hill in Leicestershire means 'Hill hill on the hill'.

All village names contain clues to the history and development of the place, though not infrequently the words themselves have become so distorted that it takes an expert to unravel them.

For the most part, the names fall into clearly defined categories: topographical, describing the location of the village; habitation names, in which a word for, say, a farm or mill occurs; ecclesiastical names, involving a church, monastery or the name of a saint; and names that recall that of an early owner of the village or people who lived there.

Among the topographical settlement names, an important category refers to rivers. In Welsh, the prefix *Aber*, meaning 'river-mouth', is usually followed by the river name, as in Aberffraw. The Gaelic *Inver* is used in the same way, as in Invernaver. The suffix -mouth, as in Axmouth, is the English equivalent. Some English names describe a stream, such as Bradbourne (broad stream).

Since the first requirement of any settlement is a water supply, many names of villages not situated on rivers refer to a spring instead. This is the commonest meaning of -well in English names – Amwell, Burwell and Ickwell, for example – though in some areas the word becomes -wall, as in Colwall. *Tobar*, as in Tobermory (Mary's spring), and *ffynon* are used in a similar way in Gaelic and Welsh. The names of other villages originally sited by a pool or lake often have the Anglo-Saxon element *mere* in their names – Bulmer, Grasmere and Hanmer among them.

River crossings

Next to a water supply, a convenient river crossing ranked high among the needs of the early settlers in England; and many village names, such as Ampleforth, Boxford, Durnford and Winsford, recall the fords that gave the original settlements birth. 'Ey' in a village name is usually a reminder of the Anglo-Saxon farmers' fondness for the lush pastures obtained by draining swamp lands. They built their houses on 'Eys' – dry islands above the marshes – which in time grew into villages with names like Cuckney, Fotheringhay, Kersey and Thorney. *Inis* or *inch* in

Fingerpost in Wiltshire.

Welsh milestone.

Automobile Association plaque.

Village signboard.

Symbolic sign in Norfolk.

Stone sign in Yorkshire.

MARKING THE MILES TO THOSE STRANGE-SOUNDING PLACES

The variety and complexity of Britain's place-names can be seen nowhere better than on the nation's signposts. The Romans set up milestones, and a few survive – there is one at Stinsford, Dorset. They were introduced again in the 18th century, and in Victorian times some gave the distances in miles and furlongs – useful information in the days before the motor-car when every yard counted to the traveller on foot or on horseback. The 'fingerpost' type of signpost was introduced in the late 17th century. Since then they have been made in all shapes and sizes, and all kinds of materials – from wood to cast iron, from stone to enamel. Ornate signs often identify a village, and occasionally the yellow-and-black enamel plaques put up by the AA in the early days of motoring can be seen.

Gaelic, and *ynys* in Welsh have almost the same meaning – 'a meadow near water'.

Village names in hilly districts make their own comment upon the landscape. *Glen-* and *Strath-* in Gaelic refer to valleys, *Mon-* and *Tor-* to hills, and the prefix *Drum-* to ridges. Moelfre in Welsh means 'bare hill', and Trawsfynydd means 'across the mountain'.

The Anglo-Saxons had many words for hills. These include *beorg*, as in Farnborough and Inkberrow; *dūn*, as in Clandon; *hyll*, which occurs in Bucknell and Grinshill; and *hōh* – Silsoe, Totternhoe and Wadenhowe. Valley words include *cumb* (Branscombe, West Wycombe, Widecombe); *denu* (Buckden and Stagsden); *halh* (Etal, Gnosall); *hop* (Stanhope and Wallop). Such words are not synonymous; they are used for hills and valleys of particular shapes and sizes. Places by cliffs, hillsides, river banks or the seashore may have the Anglo-Saxon *ōra* in their names, as do Broadwindsor and Eastnor.

Forest clearings

Settlement names often contain some reference to woodland, of which the most common is the Old English *lēah*; -ley, -le, leigh or -ly in modern spellings. The usual meaning is 'clearing in a wood', and these names often occur in areas that were forested in the Middle Ages. Stoneleigh in Warwickshire, for example, is on the southern edge of a great cluster of names, mostly ending in -ley, recalling that the Forest of Arden once covered most of north Warwickshire, and its villages were all set in woodland clearings.

When a name ending in -ley occurs in isolation, however, without other -ley names in the neighbourhood, the meaning is more likely to be 'wood'. Elmley Castle is a good example, standing alone among the circle of -ton names that surround Bredon Hill. This 'elm wood' was probably a jealously preserved stand of timber in a countryside where wood was scarce. Names ending in the Old English *-field* refer to open land, to distinguish them from woodland.

CELTIC AND PICTISH NAMES *From about 600 BC until the Romans came in 55 BC, most place-names in England were Celtic. Pictish names, found in eastern Scotland, date from 200 to AD 800.*

□ Picts.
□ Celts.

The most widely used of the names that refer to a habitation are the English ones that end in -ton, from the Anglo-Saxon *tun*. Middleton and Newton, probably the commonest of all English place-names, belong to this large class. *Tūn* was not much used in place-names during the first two centuries of Anglo-Saxon England, though after that it became the standard term for any settlement in open country, and it was used throughout the Middle Ages.

Bosherston in Dyfed is an exceptionally late creation that incorporates the name of the family who owned the manor in the time of Elizabeth I. Most *tun* names, however, date from before the Norman Conquest, and when they incorporate personal names (such as *Alfrīc* of Alfriston and *Cēolmund* of Chelmondiston), they are generally commemorating Anglo-Saxon landowners.

Less frequent than *tūn*, but still very widely used, is the Anglo-Saxon word *hām*, meaning 'village or estate'. Most of the names ending in -ham contain the ancient word for village; but a few, such as Bosham, Cuxham, High Ham and Long Wittenham, are based on another Anglo-Saxon word, *hamm*, which means 'land in a river-bend, a promontory, or dry ground in a marsh'.

The Anglo-Saxon *burh* and *byrig*, modern -borough and -bury, mean 'defended place'. Sometimes it refers to prehis-

GAELIC NAMES *The Isle of Man was a stepping-stone for the Gaelic language. It reached there from Ireland in the 4th century and spread to Scotland 100 years later.*

toric hill-forts, as at Blewbury, in Oxfordshire, Broadhembury, Devon, and South Cadbury, Somerset. Alternatively, the 'defended place' could be an early Anglo-Saxon fortification, as at Bamburgh, the capital of the most northerly of the Anglo-Saxon kingdoms. In some cases the suffix refers to the residence of a thegn – an Anglo-Saxon rank roughly equivalent to 'squire'. Bibury, in Gloucestershire, is an excellent example of this last meaning. Bibury means 'defended house belonging to the lady called *Bēage*', and an 8th-century document still exists by which the estate was leased by the Bishop of Worcester to the thegn Leppa and his daughter Beage.

Roman towns

Another Anglo-Saxon word for a defended place is *ceaster*, as in Dorchester, Grantchester and Ribchester; but this word – derived from the Latin *castra*, a 'fort' – was used specifically to describe Roman walled towns.

There are many Anglo-Saxon words for a farm or village. These include *worth* and the related words *worthig* (Selworthy) and *worthign* (Bredwardine, Leintwardine). Old English *wīc* had a number of meanings. In some early names it means 'port' (Dunwich is the only instance in this book); but most often it means 'hamlet' or 'dairy farm', and these are probably appropriate for Fordwich, Great Urswick, Parwich and Walbers-

ANGLO-SAXON NAMES *The first English names appeared between the 5th and 7th centuries, with the arrival and settlement of the Angles and Saxons from Europe.*

SCANDINAVIAN NAMES *Danish and Norse invasions in the 9th and 10th centuries account for the many Scandinavian names found in northern and eastern England and the Midlands.*

wick. In the compound *wicham* the word kept its original connection with Latin *vicus*, and Wickhambreaux is one of a group of some 30 names which refer to small Roman towns still flourishing at the time of the first Anglo-Saxon settlements.

The Old English *stede*, 'place, site of a building', occurs in Horstead, a place where horses were kept; Minstead, a place where mint grew; Polstead, a place by a pool; and Worstead, the site of a wood, or enclosure. *Stoc*, which has a similar range of meanings, is found in Erbistock, Greystoke and Stoke.

Many places in the north and east of England, and in the Isle of Man and northern and western Scotland, are in the Norse language. The most frequent Norse suffix is *-by*, meaning 'a farm or village', as in Danby. Other Norse words include *bekkr*, a 'stream', as in Caldbeck; *melr*, a 'sandbank', found in Cartmel; and *thveit*, a 'woodland clearing', as in Finsthwaite.

The most usual word for a farm in Gaelic names is *baile*, which becomes Balla- in Manx names, Bal- in Scottish names, and Bally- in Ireland. Welsh and Cornish names beginning with Tre- have a similar meaning. In Scotland, Dun- refers to prehistoric or Dark Age forts, while Welsh names use Dinas- and Caer- for prehistoric and Roman forts respectively. The Welsh and Cornish *din*, 'fort', sometimes becomes Tin-, as in Tintern and Tintagel.

A distinctive group among the English village names consists of those which end in -ing or -ings, like Basing and Bishops Cannings. These have been transferred from groups of people to settlements within (or on the boundary of) the territory they occupied. The people of the Basing district were known as the *Basingas*, 'followers of a man named *Basa*'.

Some of these group names are formed not from a personal name but from a river name or a topographical term. Horning, in Norfolk, means 'people who live at the horn', referring to the triangle of land between the rivers Ant and Bure. Not all the names in -ing belong in this category of group names. Deeping means 'deep place', Guiting means 'gushing stream', and Clavering means 'place where clover grows'.

Saints' names

The building of a church in a village often caused the old name to be replaced by a new one which referred either to the church or to the saint to whom it was dedicated. Minster Lovell and the two examples of Whitchurch refer to church buildings. The Welsh *Llan-* means 'church', and is usually followed by the name of the saint. In Scotland and the Isle of Man the Norse word Kirk- and the Gaelic word Kil- were used in this way. In Cornwall many parishes are referred to simply by the saint's name: Constan-

tine, Crantock, Madron, Veryan and Zennor are all saints. Merthyr in Cornwall and Wales refers to a church which has a *martyrium*, the grave of a saint.

Most English place-names originally consisted of one word, or of a compound of two words. After the Norman Conquest, Norman bureaucrats wanted to distinguish between places with similar names.

Often the name of the owner of the manor was added, but sometimes that of a river or nearby feature was included instead. The many villages called Stoke, for example, may be distinguished by the owners' names, as in the case of Stokesay and Stoke Bruerne, and by reference to places near by, in those of Stoke-sub-Hamdon and Stoke-by-Nayland. When an estate name was used by several neighbouring villages, words indicating their relative positions, size or importance were added – Nether and Over Wallop, or Great and Little Tew.

Clerical Latin

Government clerks made their own Latin contributions to names like Wendens Ambo ('both Wendens') that coalesced places earlier called Great and Little Wenden. The many Magnas and Parvas, often preferred to Great and Little, are an indication of how officials loved to parade their learning.

Generally, the origins of British place-names are seldom obvious, and conclusions can rarely be reached on the basis of modern spellings. Askham, Atcham and Bosham, for instance, all end in -ham in their modern forms, but they evolved from very different beginnings. Askham means the 'place of ash trees', Atcham is 'the village of Eata's people', but Bosham derives from *hamm*, 'a promontory of land which belonged to Bosa'. A few names, such as Broadway, Claybrook and Westmill, mean what they say in modern English, but these are the exceptions. There are no short cuts to the understanding of village names.

KILPECK
HEREFORD AND WORCESTER

8 miles south-west of Hereford (page 425 Db)

At Kilpeck stands one of the most remarkable little churches in Britain – a strangely beautiful and almost perfect example of Norman architecture, with a superb array of rare carvings in red sandstone.

The name Kilpeck is a corruption of the Celtic *Kilpedic* (cell of St Pedic), and in the Domesday Book it was listed as 'Chipeete'. An early Celtic church there was replaced by an Anglo-Saxon one in the 6th or 7th centuries. The present church was built on the same site in 1135, beside a Norman castle of which only the motte and a few fragments of masonry remain. The fact that the church has survived the ravages of more than eight centuries, in such a fine state of preservation, says much for the skill of the craftsmen who built it and for the care taken by generations of patrons and villagers.

The south-doorway carvings include a Tree of Life, two soldiers with a slightly Egyptian appearance, a flying angel, birds and alarming-looking dragons. Right round the outside of the church is a frieze with more than 70 fascinating and fanciful carvings of heads – human, animal and monster – including a sheila-na-gig, or fertility figure.

Special features inside are the handsome chancel arch; a primitive holy-water stoup, probably Saxon; and a massive Norman font carved from a single block of stone.

KIMBOLTON
CAMBRIDGESHIRE

7 miles north-west of St Neots (page 432 Bc)

Catherine of Aragon, Henry VIII's first wife, was confined in a 13th-century fortified manor house in the village from 1534 – the year after her marriage was annulled – until her death two years later. The original building has completely vanished under 18th-century alterations, which include a north gateway and outer gatehouse by Robert Adam. There are also reconstructions, made in the early 1700s by Sir John Vanbrugh, of the Queen's room and adjacent boudoir – which have been refurnished since Catherine's time. He also added the main staircase. The building, Kimbolton Castle, is now a school, and the state rooms and extensive grounds are open to the public on Spring and Late Summer Bank Holidays and some Sunday afternoons in July and August.

Kimbolton is set among gently undulating fields stretching from Grafham Water. The River Kym winds along the north-eastern fringe of the village, passing the former Baptist chapel and the section called The Rookery. There is a wide, mostly Georgian, main street, with buildings with brindled roof tiles. At the far end, the street curves around the churchyard of St Andrew's, built in 1219 with later alterations.

KING'S SUTTON
NORTHAMPTONSHIRE

4 miles south-east of Banbury (page 430 Ba)

People for miles around can see the graceful spire of the Church of St Peter and St Paul, in the heart of this large, ironstone village. The late-14th-century spire is 198 ft high and is the finest of its kind in the county. It is the church's main attraction, and overshadows the churchyard and the village green with its stocks.

King's Sutton was a fashionable watering-place in the 17th and 18th centuries, when the sick and the crippled came for the mineral water. The spa was situated in nearby Astrop Park, where the water was drawn from St Rumbold's well. St Rumbold, the shortest-lived of all saints, was said to have been born in Walton Grounds, just south of the village, about the middle of the 7th century. His mother was married to a pagan prince of Northumbria, and was on a journey when she suddenly gave birth to a son. Her baby died three days later – but not before he had spoken aloud. He stated he was a Christian, declared his belief in the Trinity, and also gave a sermon.

Today, his legend is perpetuated in a replica of the well, standing at a roadside near the park, and in a stone font in the village church in which he was supposedly baptised. Blacklands, the site of an extensive Roman settlement, is also situated near King's Sutton – which was a royal estate in Saxon times.

KINNAIRD
TAYSIDE

10 miles west of Dundee (page 443 Fb)

Since it was restored in 1855, Kinnaird Castle has been a private home. The red-sandstone castle is said to have been built in the 12th century by Randolph Rufus, founder of the Kinnaird family. For the next 300 years it was added to and altered. Then, in 1618, the Kinnairds sold the estate and moved to nearby Moncur Castle. Today, Kinnaird Castle, with its old stone dovecot outside the walls, looks down the Braes of Carse to the secluded village of Kinnaird.

The village's sandstone cottages are attractively grouped on a hillside overlooking the Carse of Gowrie – a fertile strip of land between the hills and the Firth of Tay, which is famed for its strawberries. There are several fine views across the Tay to the Ochil Hills, and the best of these is from the early-19th-century church. The graveyard contains the tombs of the Threipland family, landlords of Kinnaird from the 1670s until 1917. There is also a small memorial to a father and son who, successively, were the parish ministers of Kinnaird for 87 years.

Three miles north-east of Kinnaird is Rossie Priory, home of the 12th Lord Kinnaird. Set around the entrance is the secluded and immaculately kept village of Baledgarno, which was built in the 1790s by the 7th Lord, to replace an earlier

Saying it with flowers   When Kinnaird was presented with the old schoolyard as a pleasure garden in 1975, it showed its appreciation by planting a fine display of roses.

settlement near by. The village consists of two blocks of two-storey houses, and five blocks of red-sandstone cottages overlooking the green. The green is split by a rushing burn, which is crossed by an old stone footbridge.

Baledgarno, which used to be pronounced 'Ballerno', and is now called 'Balleggernie', gets its name from Edgar, King of Scotland from 1097 to 1107, who had a fortress there – possibly at Castlehill, just outside the village.

KINVER
STAFFORDSHIRE

4 miles west of Stourbridge (page 430 Ab)

Wool, and much later, iron screws and nails, created Kinver. The village lies between the great sandstone bluff of Kinver Edge and the double waterways of the River Stour and the Staffordshire and Worcestershire Canal. Part of the bluff bears the dramatic name of Hanging Hill, which rather disappointingly turns out to be the place where wool was hung up to dry. Most of the red-brick cottages in the long, winding High Street were built to house the early-19th-century nail workers. At the top of the High Street is a fine, half-timbered building that was once the workhouse. A little further up the hill stands the former Grammar School, built in 1511, which was converted to a private house by a local architect and won a European design award in 1975. The village centre has several well-preserved Georgian houses, a restored business-house of the 15th century and a coaching inn, the White Harte. The streets are bright with gardens.

St Peter's Church, perched on a 298 ft spur above the village, dates mostly from the 14th century and incorporates the remains of an earlier, Norman church. On the north side of the chancel is a lovely 15th-century chapel, built by the Hamptons, lords of Stourton Castle; among the many monuments is an early-16th-century altar tomb commemorating Sir Edward Grey of nearby Enville, his two wives, three sons and ten daughters.

The road up to the church climbs past Holy Austin Rock. Over the centuries, the local homeless carved cave dwellings into the soft sandstone. The entrances were extended outwards and faced with masonry. In the face of Kinver Edge itself there is a further tunnelled 'rock cottage', known as Nanny's Rock or Meg-a-Fox Hole. Once, reputedly, a highwayman's hideout, it has a flue running up through the cliff, and was still inhabited until the late 19th century.

There are pleasant hill and riverside walks in the area, one of which leads to the half-timbered Whittington Manor Inn, about 1 mile south-east. Inside are the remains of a priest's hole and a secret Jesuit chapel.

KIPPFORD
DUMFRIES AND GALLOWAY

4 miles south of Dalbeattie (page 441 Eb)

Many of the villages on the Solway Firth have a secret history of smuggling. One of these, in beautiful surroundings near the mouth of the Urr Water, is Kippford, now a sailing resort.

Its houses are a mixture of whitewashed one-time fishermen's cottages and modern bungalows and villas, stretching along the shore of the estuary of the Urr. Low tide uncovers wide mudflats, and most of the local yachtsmen use boats designed to stand upright on twin keels or multi-hulls as the tide recedes.

At one time, Kippford's best-known industry was boat-building for the coastal trade, but that died out in the early 1900s. There was also a busy local quarry on the hillside at the north end of the village. The jetty at which its stone was loaded on to coasters is now a mooring place for the Solway Yacht Club.

Low tide at Kippford exposes a curving spit of shingle leading to Rough Island, a National Trust for Scotland bird sanctuary. The walk to the island should be attempted only on the ebb tide, because incoming Solway tides flow swiftly.

ROCKCLIFFE A pathway, called Jubilee Path, links Kippford with its neighbour, Rockcliffe, 1 mile south. From this high-level vantage point there is a splendid view of the bay. Unlike Kippford, Rockcliffe was never a smugglers' haunt, but a Victorian resort for sea-bathing.

KIRK MICHAEL
ISLE OF MAN

6 miles north-east of Peel (page 435 Bc)

Probably the nearest of the Manx villages to being typically English is Kirk Michael, in the north-west of the island. Its long main street is flanked on either side by colour-washed cottages and small shops. Halfway down the street lies the English-looking stone church and bell-tower. The entrance to the churchyard is through a wooden lych-gate.

TROPHIES OF WAR *Two cannons taken from a French man-of-war, the* Belle Isle, *bear silent witness to a battle fought during the Seven Years' War between Britain and France. The stone commemorates the victory of a British naval squadron over French privateers off the Manx coast on February 28, 1760, and stands on a mound raised by Bishop Hildesley and named Mount Aeolus.*

◆

Kirk Michael has often been called the Bishop's village because on its outskirts lies Bishopscourt, until recently the residence of the Bishop of Sodor and Man, one of the smallest bishoprics in the Church of England.

Bishopscourt was built sometime before the 13th century as a fortress. Courts were regularly held there to try offenders against Church laws, and so great was the power of the island's bishops that they not only had a particularly harsh dungeon on St Patrick's Isle, Peel, for their prisoners, but they also held, and still hold, a seat on the Legislative Council, the upper house of the Tynwald, the Manx Parliament.

Opposite Bishopscourt are the 13½ acres of Bishopscourt Glen, in which there is a mound topped by a commemorative stone and guarded by two cannons. A shelf of rock in the glen is thought to have been used by earlier bishops as a seat for rest and meditation.

A small turning to the east from the village leads to a craft pottery. A turning to the west leads to the vast expanse of shore where the marine biologist Edward Forbes, born at Douglas in 1815, began his studies.

In June each year, Kirk Michael echoes to the thunder of high-powered motor-cycles as competitors in the TT races roar through the village. The sharp, right-hand turn there provides an exacting test of judgment for the riders before they accelerate towards Ramsey.

KNOCKIN
SALOP

5 miles south-east of Oswestry (page 429 Cb)

Mellow buildings of brick and sandstone flank the broad street, which runs the length of the village. Knockin (pronounced 'Nukkin') was fortified by the Normans, and stones from the stronghold were used in the early 18th century to build two small bridges – and their adjoining sheep-dips – which span streams at the bottom of the street. As for the castle itself, little remains but a grassy mound near the church.

Architecturally, the crowning glory of Knockin is Top Farm, a black-and-white Elizabethan building with quaint windows and carved timbers. It also has a very pretty gable. Opposite the farm is the old pound, a simple enclosure of sandstone blocks where stray animals were once penned.

Along the village street is a fanciful little shelter, built in 1887 to commemorate Queen Victoria's Golden Jubilee. It bears a plaque with the words: 'Welcome work – Welcome rest.' The parish church of St Mary, which stands beside the castle mound, was originally built as the castle chapel. It was heavily restored in 1847, when a yellow-brick belfry was added, but a fine Norman doorway, now blocked, survives on the south side. On the other side of the village street stands the old smithy, which is now a taxidermist's.

Knockin is best approached from the east, where the main road sweeps through a fine avenue of trees before passing Knockin Hall, formerly a home of the Earls of Bradford. The Bradford estate still owns most of the village and surrounding land.

LACOCK

All the character and atmosphere of medieval England are packed into Lacock's streets. The village is entirely owned by the National Trust and is a happy jumble of styles – no building is later than the 18th century, and many date from two or three centuries earlier.

The buildings crowd together in cheerful disorder. Whitewashed half-timbered houses are wedged between greystone and red-brick cottages; steep-sided gables jut above moss-flecked, stone-tiled roofs; and upper storeys thrust boldly forward over the pavements. In High Street, Porch House has two gables and close-set uprights in its timber frame; the Red Lion Hotel dates from the 18th century and has a frontage of mellow brick. In East Street there is a 14th-century barn with curved timbers.

These are some of the gems of Lacock, but its two glories are St Cyriac's Church and Lacock Abbey. St Cyriac's is mainly 15th century, and has a lofty nave with a traceried window above the chancel arch. A fan-vaulted side chapel contains the intricately carved tomb and monument of Sir William Sharington, who died in 1553. Sir William acquired Lacock Abbey in 1540, when it was one of the last religious orders to be dissolved by Henry VIII. It had been founded as a nunnery in the 13th century by Ela, Countess of Salisbury, and when Sir William Sharington adapted it as his manor house he retained all the abbey's features – the sacristy, kitchen, cloisters and chapter house – and all are still there. The house was altered in Gothic style in 1753.

Visitors wandering among Lacock's ancient streets and buildings reach instinctively for their cameras at every turn, and it was at Lacock Abbey that William Henry Fox Talbot carried out his experiments in the 1830s which later formed the basis for modern photography. His first recognisable photograph, showing a detail of the abbey, can be seen in the house. There is a museum containing some of Fox Talbot's work and equipment in a 16th-century barn at the gates of the abbey.

At the Lackham College of Agriculture is a museum of agricultural tools, farm machinery and granaries. The museum is open on selected open days from April until October, or by appointment.

◆

LOVER'S LEAP *In the 16th century, Lacock Abbey became the home of the Talbot family. It is said that the heiress to the owner, William Sharington, fell in love with John Talbot, but Sharington disapproved and locked her in the octagonal tower at the south-east corner of the house. Talbot visited her secretly, and one day she leaped from the tower into her lover's arms. This dramatic demonstration of affection caused Sharington to relent, and he allowed the couple to marry.*

LAMINGTON

STRATHCLYDE

6 miles south-west of Biggar (page 441 Ec)

Alexander Baillie-Cochrane was 21 when he travelled up from London to inspect the estate he had inherited in Lamington. He was appalled by what he called the village's 'rotting peat-roofed hovels', and determined to build the place anew. It was then 1837, and gradually Cochrane had the old village demolished and a new one constructed a short way to the north-west. Lamington originally stood on the Dumfries to Edinburgh road, and Cochrane had this road diverted to serve his new village. He entered politics and was created Lord Lamington in 1880. He also built Lamington House, now in ruins.

The village – which faces the Tinto Hills to the north-west and Culter Fell to the east – has changed little since his days. A double line of charming, colourful cottages leads to the entrance to Lamington House grounds. The parish church, with a Norman archway, is set a little apart.

LANCHESTER

DURHAM

7 miles north-west of Durham (page 438 Bb)

All Saints Church, with its four-square battlemented tower, dominates this straggling village. Opposite the ancient church, the wide, flower-bedecked green is flanked by prosperous-looking stone houses and shops.

The village is named after the Roman fort of Longovicium, situated on a hill half a mile to the south-west. The fort – which covers about 6 acres – was built in AD 122 to guard part of Dere Street, the Roman road between Hadrian's Wall and York. It was kept in excellent repair until the 18th century, when the stone was plundered to construct buildings, and little remains.

Lanchester's outstanding building is the Church of All Saints. The Normans who built it used stone from the fort, and Roman pillars support the north-aisle arcade. A 5 ft high Roman altar – unearthed locally – stands in the wide south porch. In the south window there are three superb pieces of 13th-century stained glass.

LANGHAM, Leicestershire (page 430 Cc)
(see Braunston)

LARGO

FIFE

11 miles south-west of St Andrews (page 441 Fe)

Alexander Selkirk, the real-life Robinson Crusoe, was born in Lower Largo in 1676. A statue of him in Crusoe-style clothing is mounted in the wall of the house which now stands on the site of his birthplace near the former fishing harbour. Largo is situated on Largo Bay and consists of Lower

Largo, on the coast, once known as Sea-town of Largo, and Upper Largo, set a little inland. The coastal section is mostly a holiday resort, with long, sandy beaches. Its single main street is lined by rows of whitewashed fishermen's cottages with outside stairs, red-tiled roofs and crow-stepped gables.

In Upper Largo, the 16th-century parish church is unique in Scotland as its spire, dated 1623, is supported entirely by the arched roof of the chapel. Largo's second sea-going hero, Sir Andrew Wood, was buried there in 1515. He was in command of two of King James III of Scotland's ships, the *Flower* and the *Yellow Caravel*, in the Firth of Forth. In 1490 he won national acclaim by capturing five English pirate ships in the Forth. Near the church are the remains of his castle. Sir Andrew so disliked travelling by land that he had a canal constructed between the castle and the church. Each Sunday, in his retirement, he was rowed to church in a barge said to have been manned by English prisoners of war.

Alexander Selkirk, a cobbler's son, was in trouble with the law at the age of 19. He ran away to sea and later became Sailing Master of the barque *Cinque Ports*, which was privately financed to prey on Spanish treasure galleons in the Pacific. However, Selkirk constantly quarrelled with his captain and, in September, 1704, was put ashore at his own request on the uninhabited island of Más a Tierra, 400 miles off the coast of Chile. He was marooned there for four years before being rescued.

LASTINGHAM

NORTH YORKSHIRE

6 miles north-west of Pickering (page 436 Cc)

Stone houses, mostly detached, and the magnificent Church of St Mary set prominently on high ground in the centre of the village make up Lastingham. Halfway along the main street is a fountain with the simple inscription:

CEDD
ABBIE LASTINGA FUNDATOR
AD 654

The fountain, which was erected before 1100, recalls that St Cedd founded an abbey – originally called Laestingaeu – there in 654.

Although the original abbey is presumed to have been destroyed by Vikings, Abbot Stephen of Whitby was allowed by William the Conqueror to settle in Lastingham in the 11th century.

When Stephen began his new church he built a crypt over the burial place of St Cedd, and this 11th-century crypt has survived. Close to the church is the Blacksmith's Arms, at least 250 years old and built of local stone. Towards the end of the 18th century the landlord of this inn was also the curate of St Mary's – and father of 13 children. A local story tells how the Archbishop of York remonstrated with him regarding his non-clerical activities; the curate replied:

'Your Grace, my stipend is but £30 yearly and my children go hungry without the inn. Give me but £20 more and I will eschew the alehouse and my children bless you.'

LAUGHARNE

DYFED

9 miles south-west of Carmarthen (page 424 Bb)

Laugharne's name – pronounced 'Larn' – is inextricably linked with that of Dylan Thomas, the Swansea-born poet who lived there 'off and on, up and down, high and dry', from 1937 until his tragically early death in America 16 years later, aged 39.

The road from St Clears runs down to the village through a green and gentle landscape of low, rolling hills. From the brow above St Martin's Church, where the poet was brought home from New York for burial, there are memorable views over the broad waters of Carmarthen Bay to the distant hills of Gower. The oldest parts of the church date from the 13th century, but it was rebuilt about 1350 by Sir Guy de Brian, Edward III's standard bearer at Crécy, and restored in 1873. The interior is notable for its Victorian stained glass, and for walls crammed with commemorative tablets. Several recall members of the seafaring Laugharne family, including Vice-admiral John Laugharne who died in 1819. Dylan's grave is marked by a simple white cross made of wood in a new part of the graveyard.

Several elegant Georgian buildings – one of which, near the post office, was Dylan's parents' home – and numerous attractive cottages line the long, tree-flanked main street as it runs down to the 18th-century Town Hall with its white tower, belfry and weather-cock. The tower looks down Duncan Street, where cottages of mellow red stone complement the brighter colours of their neighbours. Brown's Hotel, a block away from the Town Hall, was a favourite haunt of the poet. His other 'locals' included the black-and-white Corporation Arms, at the foot of Gosport Street, and the pink-washed Cross House Inn. Gosport Street and Wogan Street, which starts near the gateway to Castle House, slope down to The Grist, a shop-flanked square on the site of a monastery. One side opens out on to the shore, where small boats moor beneath the lofty walls of the ruined Laugharne Castle. Henry II was entertained there on his way home from Ireland in 1172, and the castle is believed to have been destroyed by Llewelyn the Great's army in 1215. In the 16th century it was repaired and altered by Sir John Perrott – generally acknowledged as an illegitimate son of Henry VIII – and was later held by both Royalists and Roundheads during the Civil War.

POET'S EYRIE ABOVE
HIS 'MUSSEL POOLED SHORE'

Above the Boat House, Dylan Thomas's home in Laugharne, is this simple wooden hut, where many of his later works – including Under Milk Wood *– were written. The house is a museum now, and the hut is much as he left it to go on his last fateful American lecture tour in 1953. The far window overlooks the 'mussel pooled and heron priested shore' of his* Poem in October. *His chair, characteristically minus a couple of slats, stands by his red-painted work-table. The hut is reached from the shore, or by following Victoria Street, Cliff Road and Dylan's Walk from the centre of Laugharne.*

Laugharne Castle.

Dylan Thomas's workshop.

LAVENHAM
SUFFOLK

6 miles north-east of Sudbury (page 432 Cb)

Gatherings of Tudor houses, sagging gracefully with age, offer a charming example of a Suffolk wool town as it must have looked during the prosperous times of the Middle Ages. The rich merchants have gone, as has the wool trade, but they have left their legacy in the buildings, especially the Church of St Peter and St Paul standing almost cathedral-like on a hill above the village.

The community has been so scrupulous in maintaining Lavenham's character that telegraph poles were removed in 1967 and the lines hidden underground. The market place looks much as it must have done in medieval times, with its cross which was probably originally a preaching cross. It was erected in 1501, paid for by the will of a clothier. The Angel Inn has stood for about the same length of time. The market place was laid out in the 13th century, and Water Street was so named because a river ran alongside it. The origin of Shilling Street has nothing to do with money, but comes from Schyling, one of several Flemish weavers 'imported' to teach their English counterparts how best to make their cloth. For

some years after 1786, Shilling Street was lived in by Isaac Taylor, author and engraver, whose daughter Jane wrote the nursery rhyme *Twinkle, twinkle, little star.*

Many of the items the family used during their stay are on show in the Guildhall, one of the finest Tudor half-timbered buildings in the country. It is now a museum, with exhibits of local history and industries. A display of coopers' tools and techniques is mounted in what used to be the guild of weavers' wine cellars. Many of the weavers' cottages have craft symbols in their plasterwork, including one to St Blaise, the patron saint of clothworkers. The old Wool Hall is now a part of the Swan Hotel, where a preserved section of the bar wall is covered with the signatures of American airmen of the 487th Bomb Group, who were based at airfields near by during the Second World War.

It was these same airmen who presented an electric blower for the organ in the Church of St Peter and St Paul, greatest of all the 'wool churches' in East Anglia and owing its magnificence chiefly to the 13th Earl of Oxford and the family of Thomas Spryng, 'the Rich Clothier'. They and other wealthy merchants endowed the church in thanksgiving for the end of the Wars of the Roses in 1485. The church's 141 ft tower seems to stand as a tribute to the still enterprising village below.

by the station is the Mines Tavern, with a bar-counter resembling the side and end of a tramcar.

The recently revived Laxey Fair takes place in July and has stallholders in Manx Victorian costume. Like most fairs on the island it is a relic of earlier pagan rituals practised by the ancient Celts. The water of Chibbyr Niglus – a well – on the site of an early Keeill, or chapel, near Laxey harbour – was believed to have powers to heal eye troubles.

LAXTON
NOTTINGHAMSHIRE

10 miles north-west of Newark (page 430 Cd)

In Laxton there survives the last remnant of the system of agriculture which operated throughout England in medieval times. Why Laxton survived the land enclosures of the 18th century is not known, but today three great fields – West, Mill and South – are still worked in much the same way as they have been for centuries.

The Court of the Manor administers the work in these fields, acting for the lord of the manor – the Minister of Agriculture. The court appoints a foreman and jurors to share out strips of land, to see that the boundaries are being observed, and to see that the ditches are kept clear.

Laxton's medieval beginnings can also be seen in the village; there are two streets with farmhouses built end-on to the roadway on narrow strips of land. At the road junction east of the church is the old animal pound. The Church of St Michael stands on a rise, its tower topped by a Victorian pyramid roof. Much of the medieval church was restored in 1861.

LEALHOLM
NORTH YORKSHIRE

9 miles west of Whitby (page 436 Cd)

Stepping-stones across the meandering River Esk offer an adventurous approach to Lealholm from the south. Alternatively, there is a single-arch stone bridge, dating from the middle of the 18th century. A little green running steeply down to the riverside makes a delightful picnic place; the game of quoits is played there during the summer. The Board Inn, close to the bridge, takes its name from a board that used to hang outside, listing the prices of food and drink inside. A small Victorian railway station at the opposite end of the village is served by the picturesque, single-track Eskdale line through the North York Moors National Park.

Stone cottages, roofed with slates or tiles, hem the lane that leads up the dale towards Danby. One bears a carved inscription 'Loyal Order of Ancient Shepherds', with lodge insignia and the date 1873 in Roman numerals. The Wesleyan chapel, an elegant building set back from the road, was built in 1839. Its stonework was carved by the poet, preacher and mason John Castillo. He was a 'lantern saint', one of the early follow-

IN THE WAKE OF TOIL *Cabin cruisers and yachts lie in the now-quiet waters of Laxey Harbour, though a scant 70 years ago the scene was very different. Then, ore-ships loading lead for England from the mines behind the village jockeyed for position with the boats of the herring fleet. But the mines closed in 1929, and little remains of the fisheries but the fine fishermen's cottages backing the quay.*

LAXEY
ISLE OF MAN

6 miles north-east of Douglas (page 435 Bc)

Snaefell, the Isle of Man's highest mountain, rises to 2,036 ft in the northern part of the island, and from it springs the Laxey river which runs through a grassy glen to the village below.

Laxey is the site of the 'Lady Isabella', a water-wheel 72½ ft in diameter – the largest in the British Isles. It was built in 1854 to pump water out of the now defunct lead mines. It was named after the wife of the Lieutenant-Governor of the time. The wheel still turns, but now only for the benefit of tourists.

From the tree-lined electric railway station which connects Laxey with Douglas to the south and Ramsey to the north, visitors can travel on the only electric mountain line in the British Isles to within 30 ft of the summit of Snaefell. Close

ers of John Wesley who met at night and lit their way with lanterns made from cow horns. Castillo lived in Poets Cottage next to the paper-mill, now a house, where his father worked.

Marks on the chapel wall show the flood height in July 1840, and in July 1930 – 14 months before Lealholm's once-famous rock gardens were washed away, when the Esk burst its banks.

LEINTWARDINE
HEREFORD AND WORCESTER

7 miles west of Ludlow (page 425 Dc)

Black-and-white cottages, and houses and shops of weathered brick and stone line the streets of Leintwardine. The village, which stands on a hillside, is a network of narrow, criss-crossing lanes. On a grassy bank at the junction of High Street and Church Street is a wall with the filled-in doorway of the local lock-up.

Leintwardine – pronounced 'Lentwardyne' – comes from the Anglo-Saxon, and means 'homestead by the Leonte', possibly an old name for the River Clun. It is set on the north-western tip of the county, where the rivers Teme and Clun meet. The Roman Watling Street passed a few yards to the east, and one of the village's two main roads is named after it.

The village has had an unsettled history. The Romans built two settlements in the area – one around Watling Street and another where the village stands now. Later, the Saxons built on the remains of the Roman fortifications. The village was then raided by the Welsh and later still taken over by the Normans. After centuries of violence, Leintwardine found peace only after the Civil War.

The Church of St Mary Magdalene is evidence of the village's turbulent past, for its 14th-century tower is clearly defensive – 76 ft to the top of its battlements, with 6 ft thick walls. Among the church's monuments is one to General Sir Banastre Tarleton, a cavalry leader who fought so fiercely in the American War of Independence that he was known by the rebels as 'Bloody' Tarleton. The general later retired to Leintwardine, and died there in 1833.

LENHAM
KENT

9 miles east of Maidstone (page 423 Ec)

Shops, inns and houses, many displaying timber-work of the late Middle Ages, surround a square which marks the centre of the village just off the main London to Folkestone road. A row of lime trees stretches along the north side of the square, where the pavement is cobbled and includes some slabs of Bethersden marble, the blue and brown stone from nearby Bethersden, which contains the fossilised shells of a freshwater snail. On the square's south-west corner is a chemist's shop bearing the strange name Saxon Warriors, which commemorates a discovery there. A 20th-

century owner found a 15th-century hall-house within the structure of the building, and in its foundations were three skeletons with swords, daggers and spearheads. The skeletons were dated to the 6th century, and are thought to be the remains of Saxon warriors.

Lanes lead off from each corner of the square, and the one from the south-west expands to become the High Street with brick cottages on both sides. The street bends to reveal on its north side a half-timbered house called Honywood. The initials of the builder, Anthony Honywood, and the date 1621 are set in its front.

A lane of 18th-century red-brick cottages leads off from the north of the square, past the stone façade of the old village lock-up to where the North Downs can be seen in the distance.

The south side of the main square opens on to the smaller Church Square, where some of the stonework in the cottages contains the remains of arches of ecclesiastical buildings once attached to the church. The parish church itself has one of the best examples of a Kentish tower, built at the end of the 14th century.

LIMPSFIELD, Surrey (page 423 Dc)
(see Godstone)

LINDFIELD
WEST SUSSEX

1 mile north-east of Haywards Heath (page 423 Db)

The road from the north crosses the River Ouse, rises through farmland to curl round the churchyard on a hill, and then broadens suddenly into a village High Street lined with old buildings, many of them medieval. The street drops down to a pond and a large common.

The High Street alternates between the timber frames of medieval houses and the elegant brickwork of the 18th century. The church house was once a coaching inn and still keeps its name, the Tiger. It has a red-brick facade and timber-framed sides. The Old Place, set back in a garden behind wrought-iron gates, is outstanding among the many timber-framed dwellings in the village. Dominated by a massive roof of local Horsham slate, it is a group of buildings added gradually to an original 15th-century structure, and includes a timbered cottage which is said to have been a hunting lodge of Henry VII.

The 18th-century brick of Lindfield Place and Lindfield House reflects the prosperity of the village when it manufactured such things as paper, gloves and candles. The 18th-century cottages in the street have tile-hung façades. A cluster of shops and inns marks the lower end of the village, where the pavement is raised and lined with lime trees. The name of the village is believed to have derived from the lime, or linden, trees which were once common locally.

Victorian villas, the village hall and another inn stand round the pond, and lead to the green where cricket matches have been played for two centuries. One row of cottages, Pelham Place, was built by a Quaker, William Allen, in 1826, as an industrial school for distressed workers.

THE VILLAGE THAT THE PLAGUE BLESSED *An old packhorse bridge spans the stream at Linton-in-Craven, a Dales village whose principal benefactor was Richard Fountaine, a local boy who made good by burying plague victims in London – or in a more prosaic version of the story, made a fortune out of rebuilding the City after the Great Fire of 1666. He spent his money in founding the almshouses in the village, and his name is remembered, too, in that of the pub on the green.*

LINTON-IN-CRAVEN
NORTH YORKSHIRE

7 miles north of Skipton (page 436 Ac)

'Loveliest Village in the North' was the title awarded to Linton in a national newspaper contest in 1949. The competition is no longer held, but Linton's standards have never slipped. It is a bewitching little place of stone cottages, ivy-clad walls, immaculate gardens, moss, lichen and tall trees whose upper branches are thick with the nests of vociferous rooks. The green, at the centre of the village, is overlooked by an early-18th-century almshouse of surprising size. It was endowed in 1721 by Richard Fountaine.

The village green slopes eastward to the grassy banks of Linton Beck. Road, foot and packhorse bridges span the stream.

GRASSINGTON This is another handsome Dales village – 2 miles away to the north-east – and one whose fortunes were founded on lead. Remains of the old workings, which were closed in the 19th century, can be seen on the surrounding moors. In Garrs Lane there is a pair of cottages built from part of an old theatre in which the tragedian Edmund Kean made frequent appearances during the early 1800s.

LITTLE DALBY
LEICESTERSHIRE

4 miles south-east of Melton Mowbray (page 430 Cc)

Local tradition claims that this is the birthplace of the Stilton Cheese. It is said that the first Stilton Cheese was made about 1720 by Mrs Orton, housekeeper at Little Dalby Hall, from milk of cows which had been grazing in the meadows outside the village. An innkeeper from the Huntingdonshire village of Stilton began buying the cheese in large quantities to sell to his patrons – hence its name.

Little Dalby makes few concessions to progress. There are no street names and only one properly made-up road, winding through the village from Great Dalby to Melton.

The Church of St James stands on a hill outside the village, half concealed by trees, and was built in the 1850s. Near by, in a densely wooded park, is the manor house, Little Dalby Hall. It was a private theatre in the 18th and 19th centuries.

LITTLE HAVEN, Dyfed (page 424 Ab)
(see Broad Haven)

LITTLE WALSINGHAM
NORFOLK

5 miles south of Wells (page 432 Cd)

In its woodland setting, the village provides a splash of colour with red-brick and timber-framed houses, whitewashed fronts and red, pantiled roofs. The High Street broadens out into a square, called Common Place, in the middle of which is a 16th-century octagonal pump-house. An iron brazier, known as The Beacon, on the stone roof of the pump-house was once the only form of street lighting in the village. On the south side of the square is the flint-faced Shire Hall, and next to it a long building with an overhanging timber-framed upper floor.

Another square, the small and secluded Friday Market near the church, has the red-brick Georgian Elmham House, formerly a grammar school.

In 1061, Lady Richeldis, the lady of the manor, had a vision in which she was commanded to build a replica of Nazareth's Holy House, where the Archangel Gabriel appeared to Mary. The shrine was built near two wells, and it was added to by Augustinian and Franciscan monks in medieval times. It became a place of pilgrimage, and was visited by Henry VIII in 1538. Yet it was he who destroyed it when he ordered the Dissolution of the Monasteries in the late 1530s.

The grounds of the priory are approached by a 15th-century gateway in High Street. Beyond the gateway is the tall arch of the 14th-century east window of the church, rising from trim lawns beyond which are the gardens of a Georgian house and the two wells. Some sparse ruins of the convent remain, including part of the refectory and a chamber connected to the house.

LLANAELHAEARN

GWYNEDD

6 miles north of Pwllheli (page 428 Ab)

A new building in Llanaelhaearn houses a unique enterprise. It is called Antur Aelhaearn, a village co-operative formed by the people of this Welsh-speaking community in the mid-1970s to give new life to the village. For years the village's population had dwindled as traditional sources of employment – quarrying and agriculture – became mechanised and people drifted away to the towns. Antur Aelhaearn, which was inspired by the local doctor, has halted the drift, by providing alternative employment, including the manufacture and sale of traditional knitwear.

Llanaelhaearn is set in a pass between steep, crag-topped hills on the Lleyn Peninsula. It is overlooked by a tiny church dedicated to Aelhaearn, a 6th-century saint. Cottages cluster around the entrance to the churchyard with its avenue of yews and Celtic headstones. The dramatic stone ramparts of a great Iron Age hill-fort crown a rocky peak to the west.

LLANARMON DYFFRYN CEIRIOG

CLWYD

9 miles west of Oswestry (page 429 Cb)

The name of this isolated village commemorates a local saint, and means 'Garmon's Church in the Valley of the Ceiriog'. It is generally abbreviated to Llanarmon or Llanarmon DC. A grassy mound by the entrance to the churchyard is said to be

Garmon's burial place. The church itself was restored in 1846, and is approached through some ancient yews.

Llanarmon is set in ruggedly beautiful countryside and has become a popular centre for fishing, shooting and walking on the Berwyn Mountains that rise almost 3,000 ft to the west. One clearly defined track runs right over the mountains, crossing moors and streams before plunging into the upper valley of the River Dee. The landscape inspired the Welsh lyric poet John Ceiriog Hughes, born at a farm near Llanarmon in 1832.

The village spreads out from a junction of lanes where a brook runs down to join the River Ceiriog. Two hotels cater for visitors – the Hand, and the quaint, 16th-century West Arms with its ancient beams, log fires and polished brasswork.

LLANARMON-YN-IAL

CLWYD

4 miles east of Ruthin (page 429 Cc)

Small and isolated, Llanarmon-yn-Ial is tucked away in the valley of the River Alun. The green Clwydian hills form a natural barrier in the west, rising steeply to more than 1,500 ft. Buildings of pale limestone, some attractively whitewashed, cluster round a church which has two naves set side by side. It was partially rebuilt in 1736, and its memorials include a 14th-century effigy of the Welsh leader Llywelyn ap Gruffydd. A brass chandelier with a figure of the Virgin Mary is said to have been rescued from Valle Crucis Abbey, near Llangollen, when the monastery was destroyed by Henry VIII.

The heart of the little village is seen to good advantage from the large and slightly elevated churchyard. The combined post office and shop stand near to the whitewashed Raven Inn. The road that approaches Llanarmon-yn-Ial from the south curls round the churchyard, and then runs down to a bridge over the Alun. A notable feature of this wooded dell is a cave, hollowed out of a limestone cliff, where a Stone Age axe was found in 1869.

LLANDDEWI BREFI

DYFED

7 miles north-east of Lampeter (page 425 Cc)

A triangle of hills shelters this village, which is set back from the Teifi Valley. The main road through the valley is more than 1 mile away, on the far side of the river, and steers traffic well clear of Llanddewi Brefi's attractive little knot of narrow streets. Roses and hydrangeas bloom in the gardens of immaculate cottages with colour-washed walls. The whole place looks clean and cared for, and won Cardiganshire's best-kept-village award three times before the county became part of Dyfed, and once since. Warm and welcoming, Llanddewi Brefi provides a vivid contrast to the high, wild and windswept hills that sweep down to it from three sides.

Despite its isolation, the village has strong links with David, patron saint of Wales, whose name it commemorates – *Dewi* is Welsh for 'David'. The ancient but much-restored church overlooking the tiny square stands on a grassy mound said to have risen miraculously beneath St David's feet when he visited the village to address a turbulent meeting some time in the early 6th century. A striking modern statue of the saint stands inside the church, depicting him as a wayfarer with bare feet, a stout staff, and a white dove on his shoulder. The impressive old building dates from the 12th century, but is notable for carved stones from the Roman and Celtic periods.

LLANDINAM
POWYS

6 miles south-west of Newtown (page 429 Ca)

One of the great Victorian industrialists, David Davies, was born in Llandinam in 1818. His first business venture was the purchase of an oak tree for £5. Davies sawed it up and sold the planks for £80. Shortly before his death, in 1890, he transformed Barry, in South Wales, from a fishing village of 85 people to one of the world's great coal-exporting ports with a population of 13,000. He is commemorated by a statue on the main road through Llandinam. The village hall was

◆

AUTUMN LEAVES *The year is waning. Evergreen yews stand dark against the russet leaves of autumn that carpet the churchyard at Llandinam. Headstones lean sleepily forwards and a gentle mist rises among the surrounding meadows, lending an air of melancholy beauty to the little village that bred one of Wales's most renowned sons – the industrialist David Davies, who created the great port of Barry.*

built in the 1900s and given to Llandinam by his grand-children, one of whom became Lord Davies in 1932. The main village street runs roughly parallel to the Newtown to Llanidloes road, climbing past St Llonio's Church with its large, timber-capped tower. A cluster of timber-and-stone cottages stands at the top of the hill.

LLANFAIR CAEREINION, Powys (page 429 Cb)
(see Meifod)

LLANFAIR PG
GWYNEDD

2 miles west of Menai Bridge (page 428 Bc)

All but the first 20 letters of the tongue-twisting name that made this Anglesey village famous were added by a local man in the 19th century. But the name has stuck and become the longest in Britain. Llanfairpwllgwyngyllgogerychwyrn-drobwllllantysiliogogogoch means 'St Mary's church in a hollow by the white hazel close to the rapid whirlpool by the red cave of St Tysilio'. The earlier name is Llanfairpwllgwyngyll, but the long name is the one displayed on the small railway station, and souvenir tickets are sold in a shop near by.

The village itself has a few rows of attractive old cottages and is strung out along the Holyhead road built by the civil engineer Thomas Telford at the start of the 19th century. A whitewashed octagonal toll-house stands beside the road and remained in use until about 1890. Old toll charges are still displayed on a board.

The approach to the village from Menai Bridge is dominated by a lofty Classical pillar, topped with a statue of the 1st Marquis of Anglesey, who lost a leg at Waterloo.

LLANGATTOCK
POWYS

6 miles west of Abergavenny (page 425 Db)

The limestone crags of Mynydd Llangattock – notable for one of the longest cave systems in Britain – climb to 1,735 ft, immediately south of this attractive little village. Llangattock is almost an island, bounded by the River Usk and the Monmouthshire and Brecon Canal. Many of its cottages were built for quarrymen when local workings provided limestone for the great 19th-century ironworks at Nantyglo. Cottages with long windows were the homes of 18th and 19th-century weavers.

The narrow street running down to the church starts by a stream, where cottages huddle round a tiny, stone-paved square, then passes between neat terraces lined by cobbled pavements. The picturesque Old Six Bells is now a private house, but has retained the stone mounting block once used by horsemen. The church is dedicated to St Catwg, the grandson of Brychan, a semi-legendary figure of Irish descent who is said to have ruled this part of Wales in the 5th century. Inside the largely 16th-century church are the old village stocks and whipping post and, on the north wall, a memorial to 'Ann, wife of Richard Lewis. She died February 21, 1773, aged 72, being a Midwife, she was an Instrument in the hand of Providence to bring this world 716 children.' From the churchyard a short, pleasant walk over fields leads to Crickhowell's multi-arched bridge over the River Usk.

LLANGENNITH
WEST GLAMORGAN

14 miles west of Swansea (page 425 Ba)

Three hills – Rhossili Down, Hardings Down and Llanmadoc Hill – shelter Llangennith, spread out along lanes that run westwards to the sands of Rhossili Bay and north-west to Broughton Bay. It is an excellent centre for exploring one of the loveliest and most interesting parts of the Gower Peninsula. The oldest part of the village is centred on a sloping green where springs bubble up from the grass. Many of the buildings have a roughcast finish, to keep out winter storms, and their gleaming whitewash contrasts with the grey stones of St Cenydd's Church. One end of the church merges into the outbuildings of College Farm, which stands on the site of a monastery founded by the saint in the 6th century.

Cenydd is said to have been the son of Gildas, chronicler of the legendary King Arthur. He was born with a deformed leg and was cast adrift in a cradle, but seabirds towed it to safety and Cenydd was cared for by angels. Scenes from the saint's life are carved on the lych-gate leading to the church, where Cenydd is said to be buried. The settlement he founded at Llangennith was sacked by Vikings in 986.

From the village there are fine walks over Rhossili Down and west over the dunes to Burry Holms, an islet joined to the mainland for two hours on either side of low tide. It has the ruins of a 6th-century religious settlement founded by St Cenydd, and the wreck of an early steam-boat that went down in 1840 can sometimes be seen.

An unusual custom is followed at Llangennith, when shotguns are fired at a wedding – to scare off evil spirits from the newlyweds.

LLANGRANOG
DYFED

6 miles south-west of New Quay (page 424 Bc)

Colourful buildings line narrow streets descending a steep, wooded valley that suddenly opens out on to a sandy beach sheltered by cliffs. It is a stretch of coast which claimed many victims in the days of sail, and runs from New Quay Head to Cardigan Island.

The sea-front street climbs and twists past the remains of an old lime kiln. It was built in the 19th century, like many others on the south-west coast of Wales. Lime brought in by sea was burned in the kiln to make fertiliser for the acidic soil, and to provide one of the raw materials for making cement. Near the kiln is the 19th-century Welsh Independent chapel, where choir festivals are held in the summer.

From the clifftop beyond the kiln there are fine views up the rugged coast. On the opposite side of the bay, steep footpaths from Llangranog climb a hill crowned with the remains of an Iron Age hill-fort.

BENEATH CLIFF-TOP WALKS *The small sandy beach at Llangranog, Dyfed – with a scattering of sea-front houses and cottages – lies on one of the few bays on the stretch of coast between New Quay Head and Cardigan Island.*

LLANGURIG
POWYS

4 miles south-west of Llanidloes (page 429 Ba)

Although it consists of little more than a single street, Llangurig was a haven for travellers in the age of horse-drawn transport. It has two attractive inns – the pink-washed Blue Bell, and the Black Lion Hotel, re-built in 1888 and hung with mellow red tiles. The village setting is remote and beautiful, with high, wooded hills rising steeply from the valley's lush pastures.

The village church, dedicated to St Curig, looks over meadows to the River Wye and the hills beyond. It was founded by the 6th-century saint, but the oldest parts of the present building date from the 12th century. In the late 19th century the church was restored by Sir George Gilbert Scott, who also designed the Albert Memorial in London.

LLANGYNOG
POWYS

10 miles south-east of Bala (page 429 Cb)

Lead mining and slate quarrying were once Llangynog's basic industries. Now it is a holiday village within 4 miles of the Snowdonia National Park. Dominated by the great crag of Craig Rhiwarth, it nestles at the head of the River Tanat's lovely valley and makes a fine centre for exploring the Berwyn Mountains. Sturdy stone buildings, many of them whitewashed, are spread out between bridges over the Tanat and its first major tributary, the Eirth, which flows into Llangynog down a deep valley of outstanding beauty.

The village church, surrounded by a high wall of massive boulders, is dedicated to St Cynog. Another church, dedicated to St Melangell, stands 2 miles away at Pennant Melangell.

Lead was discovered in the hills above the village at the end of the 17th century, and within 50 years the mines were producing annual profits of £20,000. Old workings can be seen from a footpath that runs northwards into the Rhaeadr Valley, with its spectacular waterfall.

LLANRHAEADR-YM-MOCHNANT
CLWYD

12 miles west of Oswestry (page 429 Cb)

Llanrhaeadr-ym-Mochnant is a sturdy place, built mainly of stone, with two little squares and several small but attractive terraces of cottages. One square leads to the west gate of the parish churchyard, which slopes down to a river with a steep, wooded bank on the far side. William Morgan, later to become Bishop of St Asaph, was the village priest in the second half of the 16th century, and was the first man to translate the

Bible into Welsh – it was published in 1588. Near where the road swings past the former village school, built in 1855, there is an ancient monolith, taller than a man and carved with Roman numerals showing the distances to Shrewsbury and London.

Although it is tucked away off the main road through the beautiful Tanat Valley, Llanrhaeadr is known to thousands of visitors who pass through every year on their way to Pistyll Rhaeadr, at 240 ft the highest waterfall in Wales or England.

LLANSILIN
CLWYD

5 miles west of Oswestry (page 429 Cb)

Wooded crags forming a natural barrier between Wales and England look down on Llansilin across a green, secluded valley. Neat cottages, many whitewashed but bright with splashes of colour, line a narrow street that runs gently down past the old church to the greystone Wynnstay Arms. The Williams Wynn family, from whom the inn takes its name, have a home at Llangedwyn, in the nearby Tanat Valley. Their estates in this part of the country were once so vast that heads of the family were dubbed the 'Princes *in* Wales'.

George Borrow, the tireless 19th-century traveller and writer, visited Llansilin while gathering material for his much-quoted *Wild Wales*. He was seeking the grave of Huw Morys, the poet born near Glyn Ceiriog in 1622, who is buried by the south wall of the lovely old church. Its interior is notable for a fine barrel-vaulted ceiling.

The road down the valley from Llansilin passes a prominent grassy mound – all that remains of Sycharth, a home of Owain Glyndwr – the medieval Welsh patriot and hero.

LLANSTEPHAN
DYFED

7 miles south-west of Carmarthen (page 424 Bb)

Small but elegant Victorian and Georgian houses line the narrow main street, climbing towards a little square shared by two inns and the former village pound, now a shop. They are overlooked by the 12th-century church, with a lofty Norman tower. The interior contains numerous memorials from the 19th century, when the church was restored. The Ancient Society of College Youths visited Llanstephan to 'ring in' the new peal of bells on New Year's Eve in 1876. Local legend maintains that their attempt had to be postponed until New Year's Day after the local ale proved too strong for London heads.

The Green, which overlooks the shore, is a bright collection of white, blue, pink and green cottages overlooked by the romantic ruins of Llanstephan's castle, built by the Normans in the 12th century. Set high above the beach, on a wooded headland, it inspired innumerable romantic artists of the 19th century.

259

LLANUWCHLLYN
GWYNEDD

5 miles south-west of Bala (page 429 Bb)

Summer visitors have come to know Llanuwch-llyn as the Bala Lake Railway's southern terminus. Completed in 1976, the narrow-gauge line follows the old GWR track for 4½ miles to the little station on the edge of the village. Near by, an old stone bridge spans a beautiful dell where the River Twrch tumbles down in a series of miniature waterfalls.

Llanuwchllyn spreads along a lakeside road for almost 1 mile. On one side, fields as flat as a billiard-table border the shores of the lake. On the other, the craggy-peaked Aran Mountains rise steeply to almost 3,000 ft. Many of the buildings feature the irregular grey stonework so typical of North Wales. One of the most eye-catching is the former village school, now a neatly whitewashed home called The Old School House. A plaque records that it was built in 1841 to mark the 21st birthday of Sir Watkin Williams Wynn. He and his family owned huge estates in the Llanuwchllyn area until 1944, when much of the land was surrendered in lieu of death duties after the 7th Baronet died. At the southern end of the village, iron gates leading to a burial ground commemorate Sir Owen Morgan Edwards, born in 1858, who became one of the great 19th-century champions of Wales and the Welsh language. His work, and that of several other locally born patriots, helped make Llanuwchllyn one of the most staunchly Welsh villages anywhere in the Principality.

LLANYBLODWEL
SALOP

5 miles south-west of Oswestry (page 429 Cb)

One man, the Reverend John Parker, left his stamp on this village scattered along a secluded stretch of the River Tanat. Mr Parker was Llany-blodwel's vicar in the mid-19th century, and he rebuilt the Church of St Michael to his own design. To its original Norman character he added a curious, cigar-shaped tower which is connected to the body of the church by an arch. An inscription on the arch reads: 'From thunder and lightning, earthquake and flood, good Lord deliver us.'

Despite the Welshness of its name – which means 'village of flowers' – Llanyblodwel is firmly in England, with the twisting national boundary just over 1 mile away. In the village centre stands the Horseshoe, a 16th-century black-and-white inn, which until recently had been kept by the same family for more than 300 years. The old smithy is opposite, joined to a timbered barn. Near by is the former village school, now a private house, whose turrets and gables are also Mr Parker's eccentric work.

Llanyblodwel is fringed by steep, wooded hills, which overlook the 18th-century Blodwel Hall – now a flourishing farm.

LLANYBYTHER
DYFED

4 miles south-west of Lampeter (page 424 Cb)

One of the loveliest rivers in Wales, the Teifi, loops and swirls down to Llanybyther through a lush valley hemmed in by range upon range of wooded hills. People are heavily outnumbered by livestock in this remote rural area, but despite its isolation Llanybyther is known to thousands because of what is now the largest horse sale in West Wales. On the last Thursday of each month the village streets are thronged with buyers and sellers, all making their way to The Mart, where official bidding starts at 11 in the morning. Pit ponies used to account for most of the business, but the popularity of pony-trekking provided the sales with a prosperous future as horsepower gave way to underground machines. The market has a distinctly 19th-century atmosphere as bargains are sealed and celebrated.

Llanybyther has an air of quiet prosperity. Numerous inns share the streets with prim Victorian villas and older cottages of stone. A mill on the road that runs south-east over the hills to Llansawel is open to visitors, and serves as a reminder that the Teifi Valley once had a thriving woollen industry.

LLANYSTUMDWY
GWYNEDD

2 miles west of Criccieth (page 428 Ab)

David Lloyd George, one of the 20th century's most remarkable politicians and statesmen, spent his early years in Llanystumdwy and is buried beside the River Dwyfor that flows through the village. Born in Manchester in 1863, the future Chancellor of the Exchequer and First World War Prime Minister was one year old when, his father having died, he went with his mother and elder sister to live with his uncle, Richard Lloyd, the village shoemaker.

The stone cottage that was his home until 1890 is marked with a plaque and stands beside the main Criccieth to Pwllheli road, opposite the Feathers public house. Beside the cottage is the wooden building where his uncle worked and where local Liberals gathered to talk politics. It was there that David Lloyd George, as a boy, joined in the debates of his elders and got his first grounding in politics. Near by, a striking bronze bust of Lloyd George in his lion-maned old age stands outside a museum filled with mementoes of his often-stormy career that included 50 years in the House of Commons.

His grave, designed by the Portmeirion architect Sir Clough Williams-Ellis, is set on a wooded bank above the river. It consists of a great boulder inscribed simply with the initials DLG and the dates 1863–1945. A footpath from the grave runs down to the river, where trees overhang the clear water as it rushes between mossy boulders and flows under an ancient bridge where the young Lloyd George carved his initials.

LLAWHADEN

DYFED

8 miles east of Haverfordwest (page 424 Bb)

Dramatic views of Llawhaden's ruined castle suddenly appear as the village is approached on the roads from the east, south and north. The ancient stronghold, once a residence of the Bishops of St David's, crowns a precipitous wooded bluff that towers almost 200 ft above the clear waters of the Eastern Cleddau. Near the castle is the 14th-century Llawhaden House, which Oliver Cromwell claimed and gave to one of his generals – William Skyrme – after the Royalist owner had been killed. The Skyrme family occupied the house for over 200 years.

The Church of St Aidan stands at the foot of the cliff, almost 1 mile by road from the rest of the village, and its land is bordered by the river. It dates from the 11th century, and has 14th and 17th-century alterations. An attractive 17th-century watermill, now a fish farm, stands near by and is overlooked by a medieval bridge.

The village itself is a scattered community of cottages, houses and farms, spread out along a single street that slopes gradually down towards the castle. At the west end of the street is the ruined 13th-century hospice, known locally as Pilgrims' Rest. It was built by Bishop Beck for the use of travellers, and was used as a place of rest by pilgrims on their way from Bardsey Island to St David's Cathedral.

Llawhaden is more than 20 miles from St David's, and provided the bishops with a safe refuge in times of trouble. The castle ruins date from the 14th century.

LOCHINVER

HIGHLAND

5 miles west of Loch Assynt (page 443 Df)

Although three roads lead to Lochinver, the simplest approach is probably by sea. The village, a fishing community, stands at the head of Loch Inver, in one of the remotest corners of the north-west Highlands.

The easiest of the three land approaches is the rebuilt road from the east along the shore of Loch Assynt. The southern approach is over a narrow, twisting, single track through the Inverpolly National Nature Reserve, home of red and roe deer, wildcats and pine martens. From the north there is an old-style switchback road past even more remote settlements like Stoer, Clashnessie and Drumbeg.

Beside the harbour at Lochinver stands the Culag Hotel, until 1888 a summer home of the Dukes of Sutherland. Visitors to the village often come for the angling, which can be on sea lochs, on rivers, or on one of the dozens of freshwater lochs threaded through the mountains of Assynt.

The surrounding mountains are among the most spectacular in Britain. The side road to Baddidarach, on the other side of Lochinver, gives a striking view of the whitewashed village by the shore, a ridge rising behind it and, looming over everything, the sugar-loaf peak of Suilven in the heart of the deer forest beyond.

Mountains and water are inseparable in this landscape. Even the local school, along the Inverpolly road, is in a dramatic situation below a wooded hill, on a spit of land reaching out into Loch Culag.

BOYHOOD HOME OF THE WELSH WIZARD

David Lloyd George.

The ancient bridge that crosses the River Dwyfor at Llanystumdwy was a favourite haunt of the boy who was to become Britain's first Welsh Prime Minister. On this bridge the young David Lloyd George carved his initials, little knowing that he was carving into history. In the village of Llanystumdwy, whose name means 'church at the bend of the river', Lloyd George breathed in the fervour that was to gain him the nickname of the Welsh Wizard. His eloquence and skill in debates took him rapidly to success; Liberal MP for Caernarvon at the age of 27, Chancellor of the Exchequer at 45, and Prime Minister at 53. In 1939 he bought a farm at Llanystumdwy, and retired there in 1944. He died a year later. The charm of the village never left him, for there, on the banks of the Dwyfor, he chose to rest for ever.

Llanystumdwy.

The VILLAGE GREEN

Village greens are steeped in history, often more durable than the ancient buildings that surround them, having witnessed the work and play of generations of our ancestors. To know something of a village green's origins and purposes is to understand more about its role in village history.

From the spring crowning of a May Queen to the last flickerings of a November bonfire, the village green serves as a hub of local life and a centre for recreation.

Yet greens were not conceived simply for relaxation. Although their exact origins are obscure, most date from medieval times and had more workaday beginnings. Then, as centres of self-sufficient communities, their main purpose was probably to enclose the village livestock, which were impounded at night against predators both wild and human.

There was often a pond, with its attendant ducks and geese, for watering grazing animals and horses. A pound served the extra purpose of enclosing stray animals, as well as protecting cottagers' animals by night. Later, a pump provided for both humans and animals. Lock-ups, stocks and whipping posts became standard features for the correction of wrong-doers.

The use of greens for recreation and village events followed naturally enough. They were the very centre of the community. May Day, with its maypole, queen and garlands of spring flowers, has for long been one of the happiest festivals, with many villages making their special contribution to the great occasion.

At Ickwell Green, in Bedfordshire, there is a permanent maypole. There, the May Queen is accompanied by moggies (raggedly dressed women) carrying besoms – birch-twig brooms.

At Offham, in Kent, tilting at the quintain provides a climax to the day's revels. A revolving bar mounted on a pole supports a board on one arm and a

REMEMBRANCE *Many villages, like Finchingfield, Essex, commemorate their war dead with memorials on the green.*

HEART OF THE VILLAGE *The traditional role of the green as a centre of village social life is carried into the present by a friendly game of cricket at Guiting Power, Gloucestershire.*

bucket of water on the other. Young riders carrying home-made lances career over the green to tilt at the board.

A miss is greeted with howls of derision. A hit results in the arm swinging round and the rider becoming drenched.

Versions of this sport date back to Roman times. Although an original quintain pole still stands at Offham – perhaps the only surviving example – the one now used each May Day is a replica, erected alongside the original.

Because of their value to the community, with shared rights and responsibilities, many greens have remained virtually unchanged for hundreds of years. In the days when each

WATERING PLACE *The village pond today is often just a place where ducks dabble and small boys fish for tadpoles. But for centuries it was essential for the livestock which grazed the green, as these cattle still do at Nun Monkton.*

OPEN AND CLOSED GREENS

The lie of the land, the position of roads or of water dictated the shape of most village greens, as at Nun Monkton, North Yorkshire.

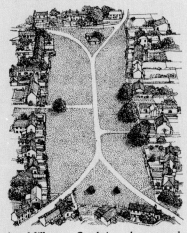

At Milburn, Cumbria, close-ranged houses surround a rectangular green, which could be sealed off in the event of attack.

village was a self-sufficient community, the only structures allowed on them were those with a communal purpose, including the church, market cross and smithy. In the 19th and 20th centuries these were often joined by the school, the village hall and war memorial.

Where other buildings, such as cottages, now stand, these may have been established by squatter's rights. Such rights, gained by more than 12 years of 'adverse possession', are likely to exist where a cottage without a garden stands within the old boundary of a green.

In 1965, when all common land had to be registered, there were more than 1,380 village greens in England and Wales. Their average size was 3 acres. Distribution in England varies greatly, from a single green in Cambridgeshire to as many as 116 in neighbouring Hertfordshire. The biggest concentration is in counties to the north-west of London.

Many Welsh counties, especially those in the mountainous areas of the north and west, are without greens. Scotland has its modest share, many of them in villages laid out by 18th-century landowners. For example, the Duke of Buccleuch included a green when planning the model village of Newcastleton, in Liddesdale, in 1793.

Local research shows that many more greens used to exist.

In Suffolk, for example, a number were enclosed and built over, in the interests of agricultural efficiency, between 1750 and 1850. Thus, the Great Green at Thrandeston, covering 50 acres, was enclosed in 1857, while that at Hinderclay vanished in 1819.

The old outlines of lost greens can often be traced in hedgerows and banks, and are especially clear in aerial photographs.

Shapes and functions

The distribution of greens in England has led historians to link them with the areas of Anglo-Saxon settlement that followed the decline in Roman power. Some may indeed be this old, or even older, but others have evolved since those days.

Archaeologists have shown that many of the older greens were tightly enclosed by buildings, opening out to the village's cultivated fields and common grazing by narrow lanes that could be closed by barriers or gates. This was the case at Milburn, in Cumbria, and these protected greens were common in the turbulent border counties of the north.

Throughout the land there is great variation in the shape and size of village greens, from the many of pocket-handkerchief size to a roadside common of 20 acres or more – as at Lindfield in West Sussex. Shape is equally unpredictable, suggesting that village greens originated at different times and for different purposes.

Triangular greens are perhaps the most familiar. They are found throughout Britain, and often became established where the junction of two or more roads formed a natural meeting place. Such greens were frequently the site of weekly markets and annual fairs.

Elsewhere, especially in Northumberland and Durham, there are many rectangular greens. Their regular geometry bears the hallmark of strict

CROSSROADS – WHERE MARKETS AND FAIRS WERE BORN

Many villages owe their origins to Anglo-Saxon settlements that grew up around the junction of intersecting roads – a natural meeting place for travellers and an ideal site for markets or fairs. Both events brought traders and entertainers in from the outside world, giving villagers a chance to meet new faces, enjoy a gossip and indulge in some horseplay.

SWINGS AND ROUNDABOUTS *The annual fair at Long Melford, Suffolk, in 1905.*

planning, perhaps due to the strong manorial authority of a Norman overlord.

Some greens occur in places where the expanding population of post-Norman Britain sought to establish new settlements in areas of woodland and scrub. The greens in such places may mark the original clearance in the wilderness, often indicated by place-name elements such as 'den' (woodland pasture for pigs), 'ley' or 'leigh' (a clearing in a wood), and 'field' (open land inside, or close to, woodland). The occurrence of the name 'green' in a place name, such as Wood Green, Turnham Green and Potters Green, usually indicates a very late period of settlement and many such places bear the look of a frontier settlement. Frequently they mark small hamlets in the parish at some distance from the central village. The name of the village often bears the name of a tradesman, landowner or a

MEDIEVAL SPORT *The price of accuracy without speed when tilting the quintain could mean receiving a clout on the back of the head.*

topographical feature, such as Heather Green and Rushey Green.

In recent years, archaeologists have shown that some village greens do not mark the original location of a village but sites which were colonised as their inhabitants migrated from an earlier site, which was often by a church. This explains why some country churches are found at a distance from the present village green.

There is not always an obvious reason for these movements. In some cases they were doubtless to do with security, or with the relative suitability of land for enclosing stock at different seasons of the year. In others, a community wished to distance themselves from a site stricken by plague or were removed against their will by a landlord wishing to extend or create a park.

Rights and privileges

The legal status of greens is complex but fascinating. Thus, some are common land, others are not. Yet every green is owned by somebody. Some, listed in early documents as 'manorial waste', were owned by the lord of the manor. Even so, other residents often had certain rights, those with frontages on the green having greater privileges than villagers living further away along the back lanes.

The complexity of such rights is demonstrated at Marsh Baldon, in Oxfordshire, where the custom was to enclose the green

TIME TO REPENT *A spell in the stocks was a commonplace punishment until Victorian times.*

ONE-MAN GAOL *The lock-up, basically a one-man cell for petty offenders, often survives on the village green.*

as a hay field from Lady Day (March 25) to Whitsun Eve. From Whitsun until the end of July it was thrown open to grazing horses. During the weeks after Lammas (August 1) it became common grazing land for cattle, while even later in

THE SOURCE OF LIFE *In the medieval village the well was often the community's only water supply.*

SPRING WELCOME *Dancing round the maypole on the green is an age-old custom – still practised in many villages – to usher into the community the fertilising powers of nature. The celebration shown was held at Kingskerswell, Devon, in the 1900s.*

the year it provided pasture for sheep.

Although such rights have been allowed to lapse in many parts of England, the owner of property adjoining a Scottish green may still be able to prove his feus, or rights, in a legal document.

The complex legal status of the village green is one of the reasons for its survival. Many have withstood the growth of even such major cities as London, which have swallowed up farmland and forests in their inexorable spread. They remain like green fossils amid the concrete and tarmac.

Richmond Green, in Surrey, was once the site of tourneys. Triangular Kew Green, with its 18th-century church and houses, was formerly the centre of the village. Even within inner London, ancient greens have survived in such urbanised surroundings as Stepney, Islington, Paddington and Camberwell.

The 'green' at Shepherd's Bush, now a fume-polluted traffic island, was called Gagglegoose Green in those distant days when it served as a meeting place for shepherds.

Even today, new greens are being created. To the south of the church at Charing, in Kent, a broad green space separates the old village High Street from modern buildings. In the same county, the post-war development of New Ash Green includes a grassed area, flanked by hall and inn, between its shopping centre and its bright new housing estates.

Village greens span the centuries. In their infinite variations they reflect the whole complex history of the peopling of our land, going back to the first settlements established by the Anglo-Saxon invaders who founded and named so many of our villages. When a village green is sited along the lines of a Roman road, as is the case in such villages as Ockley and Godstone – both in Surrey – it hints at an origin even further back in time.

Each green is unique, its very survival through centuries of change an incentive to delve into the history of the village that it serves.

LONG COMPTON
WARWICKSHIRE

4 miles north-west of Chipping Norton (page 430 Ba)

A saying in this village is that 'there are enough witches in Long Compton to draw a wagonload of hay up Long Compton Hill'. Local belief in witches existed at least until late in the 19th century, when a man accused of murdering a local woman claimed that she was a witch, and that there were 16 others in the district.

But there is no air of evil in Long Compton today – only stone and thatched cottages, antiques shops and the remains of a medieval cross adapted as a drinking fountain. The only magic potions mixed are those for a studio making stained glass.

The Church of St Peter and St Paul dates from the 13th century, and has an unusual lych-gate to the churchyard. The gateway is a two-storey thatched cottage with the ground-floor rooms removed. It now houses the village museum.

Just south of the village is a large stone, 8 ft tall and 4 ft wide, which stands apart from a Neolithic or Bronze Age circle known as the Rollright Stones. But local tradition gives a different version; it is said that the large stone was a king, and the smaller stones his courtiers, turned to stone by a witch to prevent him becoming King of all England. The stone is known as the King Stone, and the circle, the King's Men. A more distant group is called the Whispering Knights.

About half a mile west of the village is an old watermill, which stands on the site of a mill mentioned in the Domesday Book. Though the mill is no longer working, it still has its wheel, machinery and grinding stones.

LONG CRENDON
BUCKINGHAMSHIRE

2 miles north-west of Thame (page 426 Bb)

The road through Long Crendon weaves among thatched cottages, timber-framed houses and mellow stone walls. Needle-making was introduced into the village in 1558, where it flourished as a cottage industry until the 1830s, when factory-made needles took away the trade.

Long Crendon's prosperity in medieval times is reflected in its church, a stately, greystone building with a tall tower. It was begun in the 13th century, and was part of the endowment of the nearby Augustinian Notley Abbey. In the south transept there is an impressive alabaster monument to Sir John Dormer, a local landowner of the early 17th century.

Near the church stands a late-14th-century building with a timber-framed upper storey, most of which contains one long room. It was originally used as a staplehall, or wool store, but later it became a court house. Manorial courts were held there in the 15th century by the stewards of Catherine, wife of Henry V, who owned the manor. In 1900 the court house was one of the first buildings acquired by the National Trust.

Long Crendon Manor is the village's most imposing residence. It dates from the 15th century and has a courtyard reached through a stone gatehouse. The house itself is partly stone and partly timber-framed.

LONG MELFORD
SUFFOLK

3 miles north of Sudbury (page 432 Cb)

The main street through Long Melford stretches 3 miles along the route of a former Roman highway. At its north end the road crosses a stream by a bridge built in 1792 to replace the ford which gave Melford part of its name. The road splays out on to an attractive village green, then carries on past the long wall and turreted gatehouse of Melford Hall towards Bury St Edmunds. On the other side of the green an uneven row of cottages crawls upwards in leisurely fashion towards Elizabethan Trinity Hospital. Beyond them the Church of the Holy Trinity presents what is probably the best display of flushwork – ornate decoration in flint – in the county.

The village is rich in tradition. For example, there is the 16th-century haunted inn, The Bull, which has an old galleried courtyard. Some years ago, there were reports of objects being thrown about and furniture being rearranged during the night. From time to time there were also inexplicable chills near the dining-room door, where a murder was committed in 1648.

When the shrine and abbey of Bury St Edmunds grew in importance during the Middle Ages, Melford Manor was the country retreat and deer park of its abbots. Around the time of the Dissolution of the Monasteries, Henry VIII granted the manor to William Cordell, a rich lawyer who built both Melford Hall and the Hospital. Cordell went on to become Speaker of the House of Commons and Master of the Rolls. He entertained Elizabeth I at the hall in 1578, when she was welcomed by '200 young gentlemen in white velvet, 300 in black and 1,500 serving men'.

Since 1786 the house, whose 'pepperpot' towers stick up above the high wall, has been the home of the Parkers, a family of distinguished seafarers. Admiral Sir Hyde Parker sailed around the world with Lord Anson, and later commanded the North Sea fleet in 1781 in the indecisive Battle of the Dogger Bank against the Dutch. His son, another Sir Hyde, is remembered as the man to whom Nelson turned his blind eye when the order was given to break off the action at the Battle of Copenhagen in 1801.

The well-kept grounds of the hall contain a charming octagonal Tudor pavilion which overlooks the village green. A large monument to Cordell, in the 15th-century Holy Trinity Church, was designed by the royal mason, Cornelius Cure, who also designed the monument to Mary, Queen of Scots in Westminster Abbey. Among other local benefactors were the Clopton family of Kentwell Hall, just visible across the parkland

CENTURIES OF PROSPERITY
AT LONG MELFORD

A memorial inscription on Long Melford church reads, 'the work of well-disposed men'. It refers to the wool merchants who contributed to its building in the 1490s. The church is generally accounted the first thing that visitors to the village should see. Men of each age have added something to Long Melford – the Victorians included, who contributed elaborate shop fronts and ornate grave markers of cast iron.

The church from Long Melford green.

Victorian shop front.

Grave marker in the churchyard.

through a noble avenue of limes. The Clopton chantry in the church has a frieze of painted scrolls carrying a poem by the 15th-century poet monk John Lydgate, of Bury St Edmunds. On the east wall of the beautiful Lady Chapel there is a multiplication table marked out in the 18th century when the chapel served as a schoolroom. The tower was built in 1725, replacing one destroyed by lightning. In 1903 it was encased in flushwork.

LOWER PEOVER
CHESHIRE
5 miles east of Northwich (page 429 Dc)

Not one village, but two, Lower Peover – pronounced 'Peever' – consists of a group of cottages around a small green with a sign identifying it as the centre of the village, and another group of buildings up a cobbled lane almost half a mile away to the south. This group includes the church, the inn and two school buildings – the present village school and its predecessor, a mellow brick building, now a private house. This has a plaque in Latin recording that it was built for humble scholars and dedicated to God and the Church in 1710. It was restored in 1883. The bell which called the pupils to their lessons can still be seen on the roof.

The Church of St Oswald was built in 1269 of massive timber frames with a complex network of cross-braces. A stone tower was added some 300 years later. There is a wealth of carved wood inside: from pulpit to pews, screens to lectern,

and a large medieval chest made from a hollowed-out log of bog-oak with a massive lid. It is said that at one time local girls who wished to marry a farmer were supposed to lift the lid with one hand to show that they would make strong, hard-working wives.

Facing the church is Bell's of Peover Inn. Its name has nothing to do with the church bells, but recalls a former innkeeper called Bell.

LUND
HUMBERSIDE
7 miles north-west of Beverley (page 437 Cb)

The raucous cries of villagers betting on cock-fights once rang round the green at Lund, and lofty sycamores mark the place where the cockpit used to be.

Old brick buildings with tiled or slate roofs cluster round the little triangular green, which also has a medieval market cross, now headless, standing above steps hollowed by countless feet. Between the green and the church is the Wellington Inn. The pub has two signs – a hanging one shows the Iron Duke as a young man and the other, on a wall, portrays him in his later years. Manor House Farm, in Lockington Road near the inn, is a delightful 18th-century blend of brick and stonework. It can be admired from the road or the churchyard, which stands on high ground slightly above the centre of the village. The tower of All Saints' Church, with a trio of carved heads peering down from each belfry window, stands out in the low-lying landscape.

6kn Luss pre th fell climbing

LUSS
STRATHCLYDE

8 miles north-east of Helensburgh (page 441 Dd)

For more than 750 years the lochside village of Luss has been the home of the chiefs of the Colquhoun clan. In the middle of the 19th century the Colquhouns demolished the old thatched houses which made up the village, and replaced them with the attractive group of cottages standing today.

Luss Water flows by the village and into Loch Lomond. Between the river and the main road is a field in which the Luss Highland Games are held each summer. Near by is the parish church, built in 1875 by Sir James Colquhoun in memory of his father who was drowned in 1873 while returning from the island of Inchlonaig with venison for his tenants. Among the church relics are an ancient stone font and an expressive medieval effigy of the 6th-century St Kessog who brought Christianity to this part of Scotland.

LUSTLEIGH
DEVON

8 miles north-west of Newton Abbot (page 419 Db)

Huge granite boulders lie on the hillsides around this Dartmoor village, renowned for its ancient May Day Festival. The traditional ceremonies, including dancing round the maypole, are staged in what is known as the Town Orchard, now a permanent site for the festivities. Lustleigh, a village of deeply thatched granite cottages, lies in moorland dotted with fine old manor houses, many converted into farms. Higher Knowle, a house built during the First World War, opens its woodland gardens to the public during the summer. Another local beauty spot is Lustleigh Cleave, where the River Bovey flows through an avenue of trees.

The focal point of the village is the Church of St John, which dates in the main from the 13th century.

NORTH BOVEY A medieval stone cross stands on the edge of a green planted with sturdy oak trees in this lovingly preserved Dartmoor village 3 miles north-west of Lustleigh. Thatched granite cottages, many over 200 years old, and the 13th-century Ring of Bells Inn flank the green and form an attractive group by the 13th-century Church of St John.

LYBSTER
HIGHLAND

14 miles south-west of Wick (page 443 Ff)

It was the successful herring fishing which decided Captain Patrick Sinclair of Lybster to build a sturdy harbour at an inlet in the cliffs along the dangerous Caithness coast. In the 1830s the fishing industry boomed. The harbour was the base for more than 100 boats, and Lybster became the headquarters of one of the 26 fishery districts into which Scotland was divided, controlling the neighbouring harbours of Forse and Clyth and Latheronwheel.

Then the fishing declined and Lybster harbour is now used on a very much reduced scale, mostly by holiday sea-anglers. Some of the old fish-curing houses remain and are used as stores.

The main part of the village is above the harbour, and its wide main street still has some fine buildings, mostly of grey local stone. At the main crossroads stands the Portland Arms Hotel, once a staging-post on the old coaching route north from Inverness.

LYDFORD
DEVON

7 miles north of Tavistock (page 419 Db)

A winding street of granite houses leads to the ruins of Lydford Castle, a Norman keep that was once a byword for terror and injustice to the tin miners of Dartmoor. Its fearsome reputation, lasting down the centuries, now seems out of place in this pleasant, straggling village with its cascading river and woodland walks. Lydford was a prominent town in Saxon times, the site of a royal mint and a centre for the smelting of silver, lead and tin. Its castle, on a mound at the centre of the village, was for many years a prison for offenders against the savage Stannary laws which sent many illicit tin miners to their deaths. A local poet, William Browne, wrote in a 17th-century ballad:

> *'I oft have heard of Lydford Law*
> *How in the morn they hang and draw*
> *And sit in judgement after.'*

A ruined dungeon is still preserved in the square, two-storey keep. A side road just east of the castle leads to a field with a mound called Gallows Hill.

Close to the castle stands the 15th-century Church of St Petrock, which has an oak screen and bench-ends carved this century in the style of medieval craftsmen. A tombstone to a local watchmaker says he was 'wound up in hopes of being taken in hand by his maker and of being thoroughly cleaned, repaired and set going in the world to come'.

Around the corner from the church is Lydford Gorge, a thickly wooded ravine with a 100 ft waterfall carrying the swirling River Lyd down from Dartmoor.

◆

LUSTLEIGH *A village as indifferent to time's passing as the Dartmoor granite from which it is made. Church memorials recall 14th-century knights, Victorian parsons and a post-Roman Celtic gentleman with equal affection, while local records, without displaying any sense of awe, tell of an 18th-century curate who built a press to print his superbly unreadable, 32-volume work on the system of Divinity. Then, too, children used to crack nuts in a logan stone in nearby Lustleigh Cleave; the stone shifted and stabilised long ago, but it is still known as The Nutcrackers.*

MADLEY

HEREFORD AND WORCESTER

6 miles west of Hereford (page 425 Db)

One of the finest and most spacious village churches in England – dedicated to the Nativity of the Virgin – looks out over the brick-built houses of Madley. It was built of local sandstone in the 13th and 14th centuries, and has remained virtually unaltered since 1320.

The church houses several treasures, including one of the largest medieval fonts in Britain. Some of the beautiful stained glass in the east windows is 13th century, and today artists come to Madley to view the stained glass and sometimes to paint the village itself.

Madley's historical claims go back to the 5th century, when it was the birthplace of St Dyfrig, who is said to have crowned King Arthur. At the end of the Second World War, Rudolph Hess, the former deputy to Adolf Hitler, was flown from Madley RAF station – now closed – to be tried and sentenced at Nuremberg as a war criminal. More recently, the village has moved into the space age and is the home of one of Britain's newest Post Office earth satellite stations.

Madley lies between the River Wye and the Black Mountains. The cross in the village centre was rebuilt in 1975–6, and near by is the medieval, timber-framed Town House. Every year, at the beginning of July, a music festival is held in the church, at which leading orchestras and soloists perform.

MADRON

CORNWALL

2 miles north-west of Penzance (page 418 Aa)

Granite cottages, houses and the King William IV Inn are perched on the hill at Madron, whose Church of St Maddern was once the parish church of Penzance. From a lofty viewpoint above Mount's Bay the village looks across to the island of St Michael's Mount which seems to float upon the sea like a giant lily-pad.

Along a field path to the north-west of the village are Madron's wishing well and an ancient baptistry which still has its altar. About 3 miles from Madron, off the Morvah road, is the Mên-an-tol stone, which was once believed to have healing powers. The stone is an upright granite ring which formed the entrance to a prehistoric tomb.

Relics of prehistoric Britain abound in this part of Cornwall. A few miles north-west of the village is Lanyon Quoit, a giant 18 ft long stone supported on three upright stones. It was originally a covered burial chamber of the later Stone Age. The relics of an Iron Age village can be seen at Chysauster, 2 miles north-east of Madron. It is one of the earliest village layouts found in Britain and has a main street with four circular stone houses on each side.

In October 1805, the news of Nelson's victory at Trafalgar, and of his death, was brought to England by a Penzance fishing boat which had received the story from one of the returning warships. A thanksgiving service for the victory, and a memorial service for Nelson, were held in St Maddern, and a banner was made for the occasion. The banner is in a glass case near the north entrance to the church. A Trafalgar Service is held in the church each year on the Sunday nearest to October 21, and is attended by sailors and local dignitaries.

MAENTWROG

GWYNEDD

3 miles west of Ffestiniog (page 428 Bb)

A sympathetic Victorian planner combined with nature to make Maentwrog one of the most attractive little villages in North Wales. Although its roots delve back into the era of Celtic legends, most of the village was built by William Oakley, a 19th-century landowner whose family had extensive quarrying interests. Their home, Plas Tan-y-bwlch, is now a Snowdonia National Park centre, and stands in Victorian baronial splendour amid trees on the opposite side of the Vale of Ffestiniog.

Oakley created a village that could almost have been transplanted from an alpine valley. On one side of the single street, stone cottages linked by flights of steps cling to a slope so steep that the buildings appear to be standing on top of each other. They are framed by trees and a profusion of rhododendrons that tumble right down to the road by the Grapes Hotel.

A lych-gate, built to commemorate Queen Victoria's Diamond Jubilee in 1897, leads to a secluded churchyard dark with ancient yews. The church has a slate-clad spire and was rebuilt at the end of the 19th century, but a place of

◆

worship has almost certainly stood on the site since pre-Norman times. Like the village itself, the church commemorates St Twrog, who is said to have hurled a boulder into the valley to destroy a pagan altar. The rock on which the story is based still rests in the churchyard, and was probably deposited by a melting glacier at the end of the Ice Age.

MALHAM
NORTH YORKSHIRE

9 miles north-west of Skipton (page 436 Ac)

A bubbling beck divides the scattered stone houses of Malham, which stands amid some of the most rugged scenery in the Yorkshire Dales National Park. Malham beck emerges from the foot of Malham Cove, an awe-inspiring limestone cliff 280 ft high, a mile north of the village. It is shaped like a section of an immense amphitheatre, and has a resounding echo.

Low, cosy-looking limestone cottages, some of them gleaming with whitewash, share the village with two inns and a National Park information centre. A number of the houses are several hundred years old and although simple they are substantial. People walking the Pennine Way long-distance footpath are a familiar sight and the Buck Inn has a special bar for hikers. The Lister's Arms, across the brook, is an old coaching inn with the date 1723 above the doorway. It stands beside the steep narrow road that runs eastward to Gordale Scar, 1 mile away, where waterfalls plunge down a ravine 250 ft deep in places. A huge painting of this dramatic scene,

made by James Ward at the beginning of the 19th century, hangs in the Tate Gallery, London.

Sheep sales have been held in Malham every autumn for more than 200 years. Farmers pen their sheep on the green while the auctioneer conducts the sale.

One of Yorkshire's few natural lakes, the misty Malham Tarn, which belongs to the National Trust, lies high on the fells nearly 2 miles beyond Malham Cove. Malham Tarn House, now a field study centre, was once the home of the Liberal MP and philanthropist Walter Morrison, whose friends included Charles Darwin and Charles Kingsley, author of *The Water Babies*. It is said that some distinctive black marks on the cliffs of Malham Cove led Kingsley to imagine that a chimney sweep had fallen over the edge, and inspired him to write the famous children's story while staying at Malham Tarn House.

MALLWYD
GWYNEDD

10 miles north-east of Machynlleth (page 429 Bb)

Roads from Machynlleth, Dolgellau and Welshpool meet at Mallwyd, but this tiny village is set back from passing traffic and retains its atmosphere of charm and tranquillity. The Brigands Inn, on the outskirts of Mallwyd, recalls a notorious band of robbers who plagued this part of Wales in the 16th century, before they were trapped and executed in 1554.

Mallwyd looks out over the lush valley of the Dyfi to a landscape of high hills and pine forests. St Tydecho's Church stands at the foot of a steep hill, its slopes speckled with grazing sheep. In springtime, hundreds of daffodils bloom among the slate head-stones. The porch, built in 1641, is set with two huge fossilised bones unearthed near the Dyfi. They have been credited with prehistoric origins, but are probably the remains of a whale swept the 23 miles up the river from the sea by exceptional tides. The upper part of the little tower has boards inscribed in Latin.

MALPAS
CHESHIRE

5 miles north-west of Whitchurch (page 429 Cb)

In Norman French, Malpas means 'a difficult passage', and this referred to the route which ran down the hotly disputed border between Cheshire and Wales near which the village stands. The green mound behind the church, on the hill in the centre of the village, was the site of a small Norman castle, built to keep out the Welsh. The winding streets meet at the village cross, perched atop a flight of steps just below the red-sandstone church. All around are black-and-white cottages and Georgian houses.

In the late Middle Ages the landowners were the Breretons. Later, part of the village passed to the Cholmondeleys, who in the 18th century built the almshouses which have survived.

The village's most famous son was Bishop Reginald Heber, who wrote the hymns *Holy, Holy, Holy* and *From Greenland's Icy Mountains*. He was born in the rectory in 1783, and eventually became Bishop of Calcutta.

MANATON, Devon (page 419 Db)
(see Widecombe in the Moor)

MANORBIER
DYFED

4 miles south-west of Tenby (page 424 Ba)

Gerald de Barri, author of the most vivid account of life in medieval Wales, was born at Manorbier in 1146. He called himself Giraldus Cambrensis – Gerald the Welshman – and gathered material for his book, *The Itinerary through Wales*, while travelling with Archbishop Baldwin in 1188, seeking support for the Third Crusade. By coincidence, Manorbier's castle, which dates from the 12th century and was Gerald's birthplace, has often been likened to some of the great strong-

SEAT OF POWER *High above Manorbier Bay a Norman castle, built by the powerful de Barri family, dominates the green valley that leads down to the sea from the village.*

holds built by the Crusaders in the Holy Land.

Still inhabited, but open to the public during the summer, the castle stands between the village and the sandy, cliff-flanked shore of Manorbier Bay. There are splendid views along the majestic coast, and the remains of a prehistoric burial chamber – known locally as the King's Quoit – stand on the eastern headland. The parish church, which faces the castle across a narrow valley, dates from the 12th century. An effigy of a knight in chain mail lies to the left of the altar, and near the font is a brass memorial to the SS *Satrap*, lost with all hands off Manorbier in 1915.

MAYFIELD
EAST SUSSEX

8 miles south of Tunbridge Wells (page 423 Eb)

An exceptional variety of brick, stone and timbered buildings line Mayfield's High Street, which runs along a ridge of the High Weald. The views from the ridge sweep across the woods and farmland of the Sussex Weald.

A 15th-century sandstone gatehouse and a fine Tudor inn are the highlights of the main street. The gatehouse guards the remains of what used to be the palace of the Archbishops of Canterbury. A convent school has been built around them, but the medieval hall remains intact, its roof supported by giant stone arches.

Almost opposite the gatehouse stands a partially altered example of a 15th-century Wealden hall-house, known as Yeomans, its timbered wings filled in with a more recent central recess.

Featured on the village sign, and on the ornate sign outside the Middle House Inn, are scenes depicting the Devil. It was in Mayfield that St Dunstan, the Saxon Archbishop of Canterbury who founded the original palace, is reputed to have had several encounters with the Devil in various disguises. Legend says that the saint, a burly and skilled iron-worker, was in his forge one day when the Devil appeared as a beautiful girl, but St Dunstan spotted his cloven hoof. He seized the visitor by the nose with his red-hot tongs and the Devil reputedly jumped in the air, landing miles away.

Parts of St Dunstan's Church date back to the 13th century, but its porch was built 200 years later. It shows the Perpendicular style of architecture, with carvings, including a serpent, on the stone arches.

MEAVY
DEVON

6 miles south-east of Tavistock (page 419 Db)

Coming up from the Plymouth road, Dartmoor hereabouts is a three-tone watercolour of rock-strewn primeval wilderness, steep, dark-green patchwork fields, and a blinding-white moonscape of dizzyingly deep china-clay pits and towering spoil heaps. The steep, winding road to Meavy, wandered by sheep and cattle, climbs through and past all this, but its entry to the village, lying deep in a moorland bowl, is peaceful enough. At this point it splits. The right-hand fork goes over a hump-backed bridge; the left leads to a widening of the stream whose crystal-clear waters are forded by stepping-stones.

Beyond the stream, the branches of a fantastically gnarled oak frame the centre of the tiny village – the whitewashed pub, the Church of St Peter Meavy, the manor house that once belonged to the Drake family, and the shattered remains of an oak even more ancient than the one by the ford. Legend has it that this second tree, which may be older even than the Norman church, is the last 'dancing tree' in Devon – a focal point once of pagan rites, and round which the villagers whirled on May Day Eve and other festivals. On one occasion, it is said, nine men dined inside its hollow trunk; hard to believe now, as it leans exhaustedly on props to the churchyard wall. But all the same, its twisted branches are still in full leaf, suggesting that its centuries are not accomplished yet.

The interior of the church is simple, though it has a fine timbered roof with large, gilded bosses. Norman work is apparent in the chancel arch and in the crudely carved heads on a pillar. Other parts of the building, however, date from the late medieval period.

◆

VILLAGE IN A MOONSCAPE *Quiet, gentle Meavy is in odd contrast to the surrounding brooding miles of Dartmoor, dotted here and there with moon-like mountains of china clay and the remains of prehistoric settlements. But a touch of the wilder, older world perhaps, is embodied within the ancient oak propped upon the churchyard wall. It was once a centre of pagan rites. Or so it is said.*

MEIFOD
POWYS

6 miles north-west of Welshpool (page 429 Cb)

Wooded hills, known locally as 'allts', flank the lovely Vale of Meifod as it runs north-eastwards towards the Shropshire border. The steep slopes that rise behind this ancient village contrast vividly with the broad valley carved by the River Vyrnwy, one of the River Severn's main tributaries. The village is a neat collection of stone buildings, a few of which are whitewashed, speckling the green landscape. The King's Head Hotel, its walls clad with rambling ivy, looks across the main street to a large churchyard criss-crossed by a network of footpaths. The ancient church shelters a carved pre-Norman gravestone, and its windows are notable for 19th-century glass depicting coats of arms.

LLANFAIR CAEREINION This bright, busy village, some 6 miles south-west of Meifod, stands in lovely wooded countryside well known to the Romans who built a small fort near by on what is now called Gibbet Hill. The present village, of stone, brick and whitewash, runs down to the tree-lined banks of the swift River Banwy. The church was much restored in the 19th century, but incorporates many earlier fragments, including a 14th-century effigy of a knight.

On the outskirts of the village is the western terminal of the Welshpool and Llanfair Railway. Officially closed in 1956, it has been rescued and re-opened by steam enthusiasts.

A personal portrait of Strachur in Argyll by
SIR FITZROY MACLEAN

Brigadier Sir Fitzroy Maclean, Bart, CBE, Ll D, D Litt, distinguished soldier, diplomat, historian and traveller, may be found – when not still travelling – at Strachur House the home he found in Argyll, where his family has lived for centuries. He served Britain's embassies in Moscow and Rome, and parachuted into Yugoslavia in 1943 as Churchill's personal representative with the Partisans. He soldiered with the Camerons and the Special Air Service Regiment on operations behind enemy lines, was an MP from 1941 to 1974 and Under Secretary of State for War in the Churchill and Eden governments. He has chronicled his journeys to the Caucasus and Central Asia and written a history of Scotland.

❝ Since 1957, when we first came to live here, Strachur, in the county of Argyll, has for my wife and myself been the most important place in the world. Though Highlanders by birth, we had both spent much of our adult lives outside Scotland. Now, as a youngish married couple, we were bringing our children back to the land of our fathers.

We wanted to come to Argyll, where my family have had their roots for seven or eight-hundred years. We also wanted some land to farm. By a stroke of good luck Strachur House, which General John Campbell, laird of Strachur, built in the late 18th century, and a couple of thousand acres of hill, happened to become available at exactly the right moment – and at a price which, thanks to a literary windfall, I could almost afford.

At once it became clear that the decision we had taken had been the right one. Indeed, looking back twenty-two years later, the only possible one. After all those years on the move, we had at last come home. 'This,' in Alexander Gray's words, 'is

my country, the land that begat me. These windy spaces are surely my own.' What is more, the home we had found ourselves was the most beautiful that anyone could imagine. The house stands some way back from the shore, looking out across the sometimes sunny, sometimes storm-tossed waters of Loch Fyne to the hills beyond. The prevailing wind is the south-west, and when a storm is gathering you can see it coming up the loch long before it hits you. To justify the name Strachur Park, General Campbell planted the fields round the house with beech trees, now in full maturity. These gave the park a character rare in the Highlands where, as Dr Johnson remarked, fine forest trees are uncommon. A mile or two behind the house the great hill of Strachur Mhor rises steeply, its misty outline almost filling, as it did in the General's day, the middle bow window of the room in which I sit writing. But if John Campbell were to return to his library today, he would notice one significant difference. The two tall columns which he used to frame a fine equestrian portrait of

himself, now serve to set off the portrait of Prince Charles Edward Stuart, which the Prince sent to my family at a time when Campbell lairds could build themselves splendid houses, while families with known Jacobite sympathies were hunted and harassed and still deeply suspect.

The house and its policies (grounds) lie between what were once two or three separate hamlets. There is first of all the main village which clusters round the 18th-century church. Near the church is the Manse, built in 1780 and haunted by the dripping ghost of an imprudent traveller who, disregarding local advice, tried to cross Loch Fyne in a storm and was drowned.

On the south side of Strachur the name Glensluain, or Glen of the People, recalls a time when the narrow glen, with its two surviving cottages, was full of people. Here, as in many parts of the Highlands, people were replaced by sheep; but a few found employment as fishermen and made their homes in a row of neat cottages round Strachur Bay where the remains of an old pier recall the times when this was a little port.

A mile further north are the remains of a larger pier built about a century ago for the steamers that within living memory were an important means of transport. Long before the pier was built, Creggans (from the Gaelic *creagan*, meaning 'rock' or 'crag'), as this part of Strachur has always been known, was a regular landing place for boats, and it is here that Mary, Queen of Scots landed when she came to Strachur more than four-hundred years ago.

Across the road from the pier, looking over the loch, stands the Creggans Inn, of which my wife and I have been the proud proprietors for more than twenty years.

On the shore half a mile to the north is the site of MacPhunn's cairn. MacPhunn of Drip was a local laird who fell on hard times and took to stealing sheep. He was hanged at Inveraray on the other side of Loch Fyne and his widow, who was nursing a baby, was invited to collect his body. This she did by boat. Halfway across Loch Fyne she saw the body move, so mixing some of her own milk with a little whisky, she forced a few drops between MacPhunn's lips. He sat up, and a few minutes later the boat landed at the cairn which bears his name. Since the law did not allow him to be hanged a second time, he returned to Drip and lived happily there for many more years and is buried in Strachur churchyard.

It would be an exaggeration to say that life at Strachur continues exactly as it did in the days of General John Campbell or the lucky Laird of Drip, but much remains unchanged. Sheep still play an important part in the life of the community. Shinty, once a battle royal between villages, is still a far tougher game than hockey, its nearest Sassenach equivalent.

Forestry flourishes. Herring are still caught in Loch Fyne and converted locally into some of the finest kippers in the world. There are still salmon in the Cur, and the Kirk is as full as it was in General Campbell's time.

What is certain is that Strachur remains a place of great natural beauty, inhabited by people on the best of terms with each other. 99

Fitzroy Maclean.

Looking over the loch stands the Creggans Inn, of which my wife and I have been the proud proprietors for more than 20 years.

The house stands some way back from the shore, looking out across the waters of Loch Fyne.

The house is approached by an 18th-century bridge with an ice-house deep in its foundations.

A larger pier...built for the steamers that, within living memory, were an important means of transport.

The River Cur, full of salmon no one catches, makes its wild way to Loch Eck.

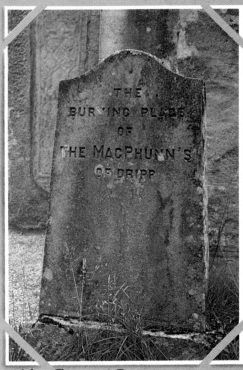

MacPhunn of Drip having survived his hanging by many years, lies now in Strachur churchyard.

MEIKLEOUR
TAYSIDE

4 miles south of Blairgowrie (page 443 Fb)

Just south-east of Meikleour is a long beech hedge bordering the home of the Marquis of Lansdowne. The hedge, which is almost 100 ft high, was planted in 1746. It is kept in perfect condition, and adds to the air of seclusion in this village set in the midst of rich farming and forestry country. The old-world atmosphere is maintained by the cottage-style hotel, which has an old notice saying it was a 'Posting and Hiring Establishment'.

Meikleour – pronounced 'Me-kloor', with the accent on the second syllable – has a market cross, dated 1698, in the village centre. Another relic of the days when Meikleour held three annual cattle fairs is the stone pillar – now half-hidden beside a roadside hedge – which supported the beam where goods were weighed. Also attached to the pillar were the jougs – an iron collar used to immobilise petty offenders in the same way as the pillory was used in England.

To the north-east of Meikleour is the Cleaven Dyke, dating from Roman times. It is thought to be associated with the legionary fortress of Inchtuthill, the remains of which lie 2 miles east.

BUSHY WONDER *The largest beech hedge in the British Isles is near Meikleour, Tayside. It stands almost 100 ft high, yet each tree is no more than 4 ft in girth. It is said that the men who planted the hedge, in 1746, left their work to fight at the Battle of Culloden, and never returned.*

MELBURY OSMOND
DORSET

5 miles south of Yeovil (page 421 Cb)

Thatched, stone cottages line the slope which leads down to Melbury Osmond's water-splash, a shallow, paved ford with a footbridge across it. The name Melbury is derived from the Old English word for 'multi-coloured hill'. The title is fully justified in the spring, summer and autumn – when the leaves on the enveloping wooded hills display their greenery, or turn to bronze and gold.

At the highest point in the village is the yew-surrounded Church of St Osmond, with the 17th-century former rectory near by. The nave, rebuilt in 1745, has a fine circular, stained-glass window – but little survives of its original furniture, except two coffin stools. The wall of the chancel bears a stone carving of a weird-looking animal believed to be a representation of Abraham's ram caught in the thicket.

Melbury Osmond is approached along a winding, sunken lane, its banks draped with hart's-tongue fern and – in spring and summer – spangled with flowers.

MELLS
SOMERSET

3 miles west of Frome (page 421 Cb)

The road into Mells winds past steep green banks and crumbling garden walls, radiant with flowers in the spring. It is a village of grey and yellow stone cottages, some thatched, set among greens and trees and forming an appealing group with the 15th-century church, Elizabethan manor and the 15th-century Talbot Inn.

A short cul-de-sac leading to St Andrew's Church is lined with cottages whose front doors open on to the road. The churchyard has two old yew trees, and among the graves is that of the Catholic theologian Monseigneur Ronald Knox, known for his translation of the Bible completed in 1955. He died at Mells in 1957.

The church has a 104 ft high tower, added in the 16th century, and a chapel dedicated to the Horner family who have lived at the manor since the 16th century. The centre of the chapel is dominated by an equestrian statue by Sir Alfred Munnings, in memory of Edward Horner who fell at Cambrai in 1917.

John Horner is said to be the 'Jack Horner' of the nursery rhyme. In the 16th century, when Henry VIII was dissolving the monasteries, the Abbot of Glastonbury is supposed to have sent the king the deeds of Mells Manor hidden in a pie, hoping that the gift would save Glastonbury Abbey from destruction. But the gift-bearer, Jack Horner, removed the deeds – 'the plum' – and kept them for himself. No evidence has been found to support this story, and the rhyme did not appear until 1725. The house was extensively restored in 1900, but retains its Elizabethan style of gabled roofs and mullioned windows.

THE BELLS OF MELLS *Every three hours, night and day, a chime of bells rings out from the slender windows in the church tower. There are four tunes, including Mells Tune which is of ancient but unknown date.*

MERIDEN
WEST MIDLANDS

6 miles west of Coventry (page 430 Bb)

A 500-year-old stone cross on the village green is said to mark the exact centre of England. Meriden also claims to be the home of English archery, still practised by the country's oldest archery society, the Woodmen of Arden. Their head-quarters are in the 18th-century Forest Hall stand by a field on the edge of the village, where the legendary outlaw Robin Hood is said to have competed in archery contests, and where archery is still carried on today.

A thatched cottage overlooks the wide green, and there are fine old buildings like the timber-framed Walsh Hall, of 15th-century origin, three-quarters of a mile north-east of the village. An 18th-century stone-built house, Meriden Hall, lies just off the main street. From the same period is the red-brick manor house, now a hotel and standing near the village pond, which has an attractive little gable-roofed waterfowl shelter in the centre. Two streams flow from the pond, one eventually joining the Humber and the other the Severn. The village also has an obelisk on the green erected in memory of cyclists who died in both World Wars. On a Sunday each May cyclists come from all over the country for a memorial service. Near by is a stone seat erected by the Cyclists Touring Club in memory of the cycling journalist W. M. Robinson – 'Wayfarer' – who died in 1956. Meriden was chosen as this cyclists' 'Mecca' because of its claim to be at the centre of England.

On a bluff overlooking the village, next to the half-timbered Moat House Farm of 1609, is the Church of St Lawrence, reputedly founded in the 11th century by Lady Godiva. About 1½ miles north-west is Packington Hall, ancestral home of the Earl of Aylesford, Lord Lieutenant of the county. Built in the late 17th century, it stands in extensive landscaped grounds, well known among fishermen for their well-stocked lakes. The estate church contains a small organ on which Handel is believed to have played.

MERTHYR MAWR
MID-GLAMORGAN

2 miles south-west of Bridgend (page 425 Ca)

Enchanting stone cottages, most of them thatched and whitewashed, nestle in peaceful woodlands patrolled by strutting pheasants. Even the public telephone box is buried in a stone wall to make it unobtrusive. Near the village green stands an elegant church, built in the middle of the 19th century but standing on ancient foundations. Merthyr Mawr is mentioned in a 9th-century manuscript, and the church has remains from the Celtic period. A medieval bridge over the clear waters of the Ogmore river has holes in the parapet through which sheep were dipped.

The lane that winds its way through the village continues to the ruins of Candleston Castle, a 15th-century fortified manor that was occupied until Victorian times. It stands in a romantic glade with a great wilderness of sand dunes, more than 200 ft high in places, rolling away towards Porthcawl. Blown inland by Atlantic gales, the sands cover what was once fertile farming land. Prehistoric remains, the oldest dating from the Bronze Age, have been found among the dunes.

MIDDLEHAM
NORTH YORKSHIRE
9 miles south of Richmond (page 436 Bc)

Strings of racehorses can often be seen cantering over the high, open countryside flanking the road that leads into Middleham from the south-west. This large, history-steeped community, once the 'capital of Wensleydale', is a centre of horse training, and there are several thoroughbred stables in the area.

Middleham resists definition: it is a village because it covers a single parish; but local people prefer to think of it as a town, and its parish council has the status of a town council.

At the top of the long, steep main street stand the massive ruins of Middleham Castle, once the home of Richard Neville, Earl of Warwick – Warwick the Kingmaker.

Lord Lytton, the Victorian novelist, wrote of Warwick and his stronghold: 'The mightiest peers, the most renowned knights, gathered to his hall. Middleham – not Windsor nor Sheen, nor Westminster, nor the Tower – seemed the court of England.'

When Warwick was slain at the Battle of Barnet in 1471, the castle was forfeited to the crown; and Edward IV, who had been held prisoner there during the Wars of the Roses, gave it to his brother, Richard of Gloucester, later Richard III. It was to become Richard's principal residence when he was Lieutenant of the north.

The massive Norman keep, begun about 1170, has walls 4 yds thick in places. It later became one of the ruins that Cromwell knocked about a bit in the Civil War.

Middleham has two crosses. The upper one, known as the swine cross, is thought to have been erected to commemorate Richard of Gloucester's grant of the right to hold a fair and market, twice yearly. A much-weathered animal figure on the cross may be the white boar that was his emblem.

A towered Victorian building near the cross was once the village school.

The Church of St Mary and St Alkelda was built mainly in the 14th and 15th centuries. Fragments of 14th-century glass in a west window depict the legend of Alkelda, said to have been a Saxon princess who was strangled by two Danish women for refusing to renounce her Christian faith.

Bones discovered during a restoration of the church in 1878 were pronounced to be the saint's, and were interred in the church. There is some doubt about the entire legend, though, for a spring rises near the church, and Alkelda could be a form of the Saxon *hal keld* – 'well in a valley'. There is also a legend that St Alkelda was beheaded by Muncius, a tyrant, because she refused his amorous advances.

About 4 miles from Middleham, on the road to Ripon, are the romantic ruins of Jervaulx Abbey. The Cistercian monks there were renowned for breeding horses and sheep. But possibly the greatest achievement for which they have been credited – apart from building the abbey – is the creation of Wensleydale cheese.

MIDDLETON
WARWICKSHIRE
4 miles south of Tamworth (page 430 Bb)

The countryside surrounding the ancient village of Middleton is an astonishing oasis in a desert of urban sprawl and industrial development. The village, which has a history going back beyond the Conqueror's Domesday Book, lies in an unspoiled landscape of leafy lanes and farmland between Birmingham to the south and west and Tamworth to the north.

The mainly 13th to 14th-century Church of St John the Baptist houses some fine memorials, one to the naturalist Sir Francis Willoughby, who died in 1675 and whose far-ranging studies of wildlife are still valued.

The Willoughby family entertained Elizabeth I and James I at Middleton Hall, a mile to the east, once a stately mansion but now a sadly neglected ruin, only the gaunt shell of which remains. The Marmion family, hereditary champions of the kings of England from the Conqueror's time, owned the place until the 15th century, when it passed to the Willoughbys. They kept it until the 19th century, after which it went through a succession of tenants and owners until it was abandoned finally in the 1960's. Now the house stands almost surrounded by gravel pits on land owned by a quarrying company, but plans have been laid to restore it as a conservation centre.

MIDDLETON IN TEESDALE
DURHAM
8 miles north-west of Barnard Castle (page 438 Ab)

Winding, drystone walls hem the roads leading into the village, which rises in terraces above the River Tees. Rugged sandstone houses and buildings and snug, whitewashed cottages reflect the non-conformist influence which once dominated Middleton.

Middleton House, former headquarters of the Quaker-owned London Lead Company, stands among tall trees overlooking the village. The company folded in 1905 and today the building is used as a shooting lodge. A further relic of the lead industry is the ornate, cast-iron Bainbridge Memorial Fountain, which commemorates the London Lead Company, erected in 1877 by one of its superintendents, Robert Bainbridge, with money presented to him on his retirement. It is painted blue and white and features the cherubic figure of a child.

The parish church of St Mary was completely rebuilt in the 1870s. Incorporated in the nave are several intriguingly decorated medieval tombstones discovered under the foundations of the former church. Just to the north of the church is a detached belfry. Built in 1557, it retains one of its three original bells, which is rung by using both hands and a foot.

Middleton is an ideal centre for exploring Teesdale. About 5 miles up river is the spectacular waterfall High Force.

MILBURN
CUMBRIA
6 miles north of Appleby (page 435 Dd)

Sandstone buildings, mottled with green and yellow lichen, form a defensive rectangle around Milburn's spacious central green. All face inwards, a reminder of the days when bands of bloodthirsty outlaws roamed the wild borderland between England and Scotland, killing, burning and rustling sheep and cattle. The narrow entrances at each corner were easily sealed against border raiders, leaving a few even-narrower 'through gangs' as the only means of communication with the outside world.

The shop and post office is housed in what was originally a stone barn. It looks out across the green to a lofty maypole, which stands on the base of a long-vanished preaching cross and is topped by a weathercock. The village school, at the top of the 400 yd long green, faces a small Wesleyan chapel at the opposite end. Both were built in the 1850s.

Milburn's setting does much to enhance its charm. The great wall of the Pennines rises steeply behind the village, reaching 2,930 ft at Cross Fell, only 4 miles away.

ROUND THE WORLD TO SHUGBOROUGH *The fortune amassed by Admiral George Anson, the Circumnavigator, after his four-year voyage round the world, helped to transform the family home into the magnificent creation it is today. The great white colonnaded mansion, set in exquisitely ornamented grounds within a bend of the little River Sow at Milford, is the home of Patrick Lichfield, the photographer earl. The county museum in the grounds houses a toy gallery which displays items covering the past 150 years.*

MILFORD
STAFFORDSHIRE
3 miles south-east of Stafford (page 430 Ac)

Some of the most delightful walks and drives in the county start at Milford, set in the beautiful valley of Staffordshire's modest little river, the Sow. The village is made up of attractive old cottages and newer, larger homes, many of them half-timbered with sweeping lawns and well-tended gardens. At Upper Home Farm, on the western edge of the village, two old cottages, a cart shed and a cow barn have been converted into new cottages, which won a Farm Building Award Scheme commendation in 1977. A stream in front of the buildings has been widened into a pool, which adds to the attractive scene. Opposite the Barley Mow Inn, the cottages and more elegant homes come to an end, and the road through the village opens on to the spacious Milford Common.

A short way through the common lie the entrances to Shugborough Park and Shugborough Hall, ancestral home of the Anson family, the Earls of Lichfield.

GREAT HAYWOOD Four waterways meet at this village, about 2 miles east of Milford: the Trent and Mersey Canal is joined by the Staffordshire and Worcestershire Canal and the River Sow flows into the Trent. Near the Clifford Arms a lane leads to Essex Bridge, believed to be the longest packhorse bridge in England. Its 14 arches span the Trent and Mersey Canal, the Sow and the Trent. It was built in the 16th century by the Earl of Essex.

MILTON ABBAS
DORSET

6 miles south-west of Blandford Forum (page 421 Cb)

In the 1770s, Joseph Damer, Earl of Dorchester, had the medieval abbey, from which the village takes its name, rebuilt into a magnificent new house. Proud of his house, he was displeased that its view of the wooded countryside was interrupted by the market town of Milton Abbas. He was so annoyed by this 'oversight' that he decided to have the town – which stood on his property – demolished. In the face of fierce local opposition, he razed the 'eyesore' of homes and commercial buildings. About 1 mile away, in a wooded valley, he erected a large 'model' village. And on part of the site of the old town he built an ornamental lake to enhance the beauty of the surroundings. Today, Milton Abbas is much as Lord Dorchester created it towards the end of the 18th century, and his house is now a public school.

Most of the thatched, cob cottages are washed in white or pale yellow. They are equally spaced and lie back from the road behind large unfenced front gardens, which together give the effect of a village green. The houses have flower borders in front, and long strips of kitchen garden behind. The rear gardens reach a steep escarpment which is crowned with trees. The main street cuts through the green, and in the centre of the village stand some 17th-century brick-and-flint almshouses, which Lord Dorchester had moved from their original site. At the lower end of the main street, in the old brewery buildings, is a museum devoted mainly to farming.

Opposite the almshouses is the 18th-century Church of St James. It was designed in late-Georgian Gothic style to fit in with the appearance of the new village.

The abbey church was restored in the 19th century by Sir Gilbert Scott, architect of London's Albert Memorial. Three-hundred yards to the east, a long flight of grass steps leads up to St Catherine's Chapel, dating from Norman times.

MINSTEAD
HAMPSHIRE

2 miles north-west of Lyndhurst (page 422 Bb)

An odd-looking church and an unusual inn sign catch the eye at Minstead, a village of thatched cottages, green lawns and holly hedges set in a maze of lanes in the New Forest.

What was once the village main street is now a cul-de-sac leading to All Saints' Church. A series of wooden galleries in the church are 'parlour pews', each the property of one of the big houses in the neighbourhood and possessing an outside entrance. Under a transept roof is the Gipsies' Gallery, which provided seats for the poor of the parish.

The Trusty Servant Inn at the village crossroads has a satirical sign. It depicts the ideal servant – a creature with a pig's head, standing for unfus-siness in diet, with its snout locked for secrecy. The ears are of an ass, for patience, and it has a stag's feet for swiftness. The left hand holds a brush, shovel and two-pronged fork. North-west of the inn are the 8 acres of Furzey Gardens which are open to the public.

The Rufus Stone, 1 mile north-west, marks the spot where William II, called 'Rufus' because of his red hair, was killed by an arrow while hunting in the forest. The king's death, on August 2, 1100, was said to be an accident, but the only witness was Walter Tirel with whom William had quarrelled the night before. Tirel, who immediately fled to France, was believed to have shot the arrow, but this he always denied.

MINSTER LOVELL
OXFORDSHIRE

3 miles west of Witney (page 426 Ab)

History and romance intermingle at Minster Lovell, for in addition to possessing famous legends, it also witnessed the tragic end of a great family and played a part in the closing chapter of the story of the Plantagenet Kings of England.

The older part of the village lies half-hidden just a few hundred yards north of the main Burford to Witney road, on a low mound bordered by the sinuous River Windrush. Wherever you go in this part of the village, from the narrow, multiple-arched bridge at its entrance, to the gaunt ruins of the 15th-century Minster Lovell Hall, at the east end, you are aware of the river, in which long green whips of waterweed coil incessantly in the slow-twisting current. Passing the bright gardens above the mill-race, it flows by the Old Swan Hotel which, despite its present elegant and chintzy metamorphosis, was built five centuries ago and once sheltered Welsh sheep-drovers on their way to the markets of eastern England. Much earlier it also entertained the retainers of Richard III, whose emblem, the Sun in Splendour, has been discovered in a bedroom behind the plasterwork. Leaving the creeper-clad stone pub, the Windrush then wanders off to the back of the cricket field, while the street rises, curves and dips to meet the river again behind the Hall.

Since the village is not quite of the Cotswolds, it lacks the uniformity of its tourist-packed neighbours to the west. Though many roofs are of stone, others are thatched. All the walls, however, are of grey-brown Burford stone, and it seems to make little difference whether they have stood for four centuries or were built in the last decade. A few years of weathering and allowing

UNCOMMON STREAM *The silky, sinuous Windrush, one of the loveliest of rivers, laces some of England's most famous villages – Burford, Bourton-on-the-Water and the rest – before joining the Thames on the old Berkshire border. Here, glass-clear and waving green banners of waterweed, it makes its grand entry to Minster Lovell, past Bridge Cottage, for centuries the property of Eton College, to the ancient bridge itself whose roadway is funnelled to permit the easier counting of Welsh sheep for toll charges.*

The Swan - Swinbrook - pub

the lichen to take hold, leaves them looking as if they had grown from the land itself. This effect is heightened by the wealth of creepers – roses, clematis and Virginia creeper – that cover the stone. Both houses and cottages display the versatility of local stone as a building material.

The rather grand Orchard House at the top of the street has massive pillars and a terrace of stone slabs, while a little further down the renovated front of the Old Post House glows red-gold from new-cut stone. From there it is possible to look back across most of the old village – thatch and stone breaking through the trees and lilacs, with vivid patches of roses and lupins – back to the other side of the river, where Bridge Cottage stands solitary.

Swallows curve through the tall windows of the ruined Minster Lovell Hall, and doves burble from the crag that was its watchtower. It stands among whispering willows by the riverside and is the subject of two village legends. The powerful Lovell family lived there from Norman times, and the hall was built around 1440 by William, Lord Lovell. But his grandson Francis, a Yorkist friend of Richard III, backed the wrong side in the Wars of the Roses and was declared a traitor by Henry VII, who confiscated his estates. During an unsuccessful rebellion in 1487, Francis was reported killed at the Battle of Stoke while fighting for Lambert Simnel, a pretender to the throne. But local legend has it that he survived, and went into hiding in a secret vault in the Hall known only to one servant. However, the servant died suddenly and Lovell, unable to get out, starved to death. In 1708, workmen altering the house found 'the entire skeleton of a man, as having been at a table ... with a book, paper, pen ... all much mouldered' in a hidden chamber.

During the 300 years following Francis Lovell's death the Hall passed from one owner to another until, finally, in 1747, it was dismantled by the Earl of Leicester and many of its stones sold locally for building materials. Even now the magnificence of the original house is still apparent, but the only complete secular building remaining is the great circular dovecot in the grounds of nearby Manor Farm, though the farm itself, and its barn, almost certainly incorporate the ruins of the chapel of St Cecilia, endowed by John Lovell in 1273.

The church, also built by William, Lord Lovell, stands just behind the Hall. It is dedicated to St Kenelm, the seven-year-old son of a King of Mercia who was murdered by his sister. The story goes that a dove immediately flew off to Rome to tell the Pope, who ordered an investigation. Meanwhile, the wicked sister was struck blind as she looked at her brother's body and the Bible she was reading was sprayed with blood. There is a painting of St Kenelm and his dove in the church.

There are also some interesting monuments, including one to a Royalist soldier of the Civil Wars who 'served not so much for the sake of pay as for the sake of Church and Prince', and a tomb, thought to be of William, Lord Lovell or his son, John, topped by a dignified, armoured effigy in alabaster.

The modern half of the village, correctly but

rarely called Charterville, is on the other side of the Burford road. There, in the 1840s, Feargus O'Connor, leader of the Chartists, built a number of houses, each standing in a few acres, and let them to working-class tenants. The scheme, however, quickly went bankrupt.

MONIAIVE
DUMFRIES AND GALLOWAY

16 miles north-west of Dumfries (page 441 Eb)

Three streams – Castlefairn Water and the Dalwhat and Craigdarroch Waters – meet near Moniaive and form the picturesque Cairn Water. The village, with its whitewashed houses and colourful gardens, was originally twin settlements facing each other across Dalwhat Water. In the Middle Ages the two communities – Minnyhive and Dunreggan – became one large estate. Minnyhive's original market cross of 1638 still stands in modern Moniaive.

The village is set in the uplands near the head of the Cairn Valley, and is surrounded by fine meadowlands and grazing hills. Three miles to the east of the village is Maxwelton House, birthplace of Annie Laurie – immortalised in the poem written by William Douglas, the man she jilted. In 1855 the poem was revised and set to music by Lady John Scott. Annie – a daughter of Sir Robert Laurie of Maxwelton – married Alexander Fergusson, owner of Craigdarroch, a mansion 2 miles west of Moniaive. The house was refurbished in 1729 by the Scottish master mason William Adam. Annie died there in 1764 and she lies in nearby Glencairn churchyard.

A memorial to the Reverend James Renwick – the last Covenanter martyr, who was hanged in 1688 – is on a hill to the west of the village, near the farm where he was born.

Montacute House.

MONTACUTE
SOMERSET

4 miles west of Yeovil (page 421 Bb)

A magnificent Elizabethan mansion, an ancient church, the remains of a medieval priory and narrow streets lined with buildings of golden Ham Hill stone, combine with more than 1,000 years of history to make Montacute a village of exceptional interest. Its roots go back to a 7th-century settlement; 200 years later it became known as Bishopston – now the name of the street that runs north from the church.

Immediately after the Battle of Hastings, Count Robert de Mortain, half-brother of the Conqueror, built Montacute Castle on top of St Michael's Hill, which dominates the village to the west. The name Montacute derives from the Latin *mons acutus*, meaning 'steep hill'. No trace of the castle remains, and the wooded slopes are now crowned by a folly tower built in 1760.

The stronghold was later given to a newly founded Cluniac priory, and many of the castle's stones seem to have been used when the priory was built. The priory's battlemented gatehouse survives, with adjoining buildings, and now forms part of Abbey Farm. Though not open to visitors, the gatehouse can be seen from the churchyard. The monks kept Montacute for more than 400 years, until Henry VIII closed it down and sold it in 1539.

Much of St Catherine's Church, standing where Middle Street turns north to become Bishopston, is Tudor, but the chancel arch and several other features date from the end of the 13th century. Inside are monuments to the Phelips family, who had links with the village from the mid-1400s. The beautiful Montacute House was built for Sir Edward Phelips by William Arnold, a Somerset mason whose other notable works

include Wadham College, Oxford. Sir Edward (who had been given the former priory estates by his father in 1588) was a successful lawyer, and built the house between about 1590 and 1601, when he became an MP. By 1604 he was Speaker of the House of Commons, and made the opening speech for the prosecution in the trial of Guy Fawkes in 1606. The house, like most of the village, is built of Ham Hill stone and is one of the finest Elizabethan mansions in Britain, with an immense gallery 189 ft long running the whole length of the second floor.

The grounds were laid out in the 19th century, but the Phelips' fortunes were fluctuating by that time and many of the family treasures were sold off. After being leased several times, the house was bought by a Mr Cook and presented to the National Trust in 1931. The most famous tenant was Lord Curzon, Viceroy of India and later Foreign Secretary, who lived there from 1915 to 1925.

The village itself is most attractive. Many of the buildings in Bishopston have stood since the 18th century, with stone-mullioned windows and mellow red-tiled roofs that contrast with that of Montacute's only thatched building, Monk's House (formerly The Gables), built in the 15th century. The Borough is a spacious square where the 18th-century Phelips Arms and the Old Bakery still stand. Near by are the wisteria-clad Montacute Cottage and The Chantry, adjoining buildings from the 16th century. The Chantry belongs to the National Trust, having once been a school and later the post office.

Many of the South Street cottages were weavers' homes when the glove trade flourished in the 18th century. The Baptist chapel in South Street, which dates from 1880, is one of the few recent buildings in the heart of the village. In Townsend is what used to be the Baptist manse, a 16th-century building that later became the Shoemakers' Arms and is now a private house.

ELIZABETHAN SPLENDOUR

Few visitors to majestic Montacute House spare more than a glance for St Michael's Hill, yet in the 11th century it was famed all over England due to the discovery of an apparently miracle-working Cross. When the relic was moved to Waltham, it was said to have cured King Harold's paralysis. So moved was he that 'Holy Cross!' was his army's war-cry at Hastings.

Abbey Farm.

Chantry window.

Folly on St Michael's Hill.

MONYMUSK

GRAMPIAN

7 miles south-west of Inverurie (page 443 Gd)

North-east Scotland's oldest Norman church still in use stands in the village of Monymusk. The building, on the east side of the square, was constructed around 1140 as a parish church, and continued in that role after the Reformation. Over the decades St Mary's, built of rich, red stone, was added to and improved. Then, in 1929, it was faithfully restored to its original state – when the Norman chancel arch and west doorway were uncovered. The Monymusk Reliquary of St Columba, that was carried before Bruce's army at Bannockburn, is now in the National Museum in Edinburgh.

Monymusk lies near the River Don, below Paradise Wood, and is surrounded by fertile farmland. It was established in 1713, when its site – then little more than a wilderness – was bought by the Grant family. In the 1750s the village was rebuilt by Sir Archibald Grant, and it was further remodelled by Sir Arthur Grant in the 1890s. The cottages were given an extra storey, and the thatched roofs were replaced by slates. The granite houses were left untouched, and a group of them surround a neat green.

A mile north-west, with the 1,470 ft Cairn Williams as a backdrop, Pitfichie Castle has been restored as a private residence. Three miles to the south-east stands Castle Fraser, built in the 15th century and expanded 200 years later. It is an impressive sight with its baronial hall, ornamental turrets and gargoyles.

MORWENSTOW

CORNWALL

6 miles north of Bude (page 418 Cc)

Atlantic gales constantly buffet Morwenstow, whose seven hamlets together constitute Cornwall's most northerly parish. The village is dotted with trees moulded into weird shapes by the wind, and above the trees rise the vicarage chimneystacks resembling miniature church towers. They were the whim of an eccentric 19th-century vicar, Robert Hawker.

Hawker is best known for his poems, especially his *Song of the Western Men* with its line 'And shall Trelawney die?', and for the Harvest Festival, a medieval custom which he revived and is now celebrated the world over. He spent much of his time in a hut made from driftwood, which he built on the cliff edge. The hut is now the property of the National Trust.

The church, St John the Baptist, is partly Norman, and has carved stone heads of men and beasts decorating the porch. A well in the vicarage orchard provides the water for baptisms.

Hawker's great concern was for the victims of shipwrecks, and more than 40 lie buried in the churchyard. The figurehead of the *Caledonia*, driven on to the rocks below the cliff in 1843, serves as a headstone for its captain and crew.

MOUSEHOLE

CORNWALL

2 miles south of Penzance (page 418 Aa)

Mousehole – pronounced 'Mouzel' – is a fishing community that has grown over the centuries into a fascinating maze of grey granite houses, tiny courtyards and semi-tropical gardens climbing a steep hill behind the harbour.

The Keigwin Arms, an old inn now a private residence, was the only building to survive when the village was burned by the Spanish in 1595. Another inn, the Ship, is the scene of Mousehole's Tom Bawcock's Eve celebrations on December 23, when fishermen gather to eat a fish pie called 'Stargazy Pie'. The pie is made with whole fish, their heads staring out through the crust. Tom Bawcock was a local fisherman who reputedly saved the village from starvation by sailing out in a storm and returning with a massive catch of seven different types of fish.

Mousehole was once the centre of Cornwall's pilchard-fishing industry and there are still a few fishing boats to be seen in the harbour.

On the hilltop above the village stands the parish church of St Paul, with a monument to Dolly Pentreath who died in 1777 and was said to be the last person to speak only Cornish.

South of the village is the Bird Hospital started in 1928 by two sisters, Dorothy and Phyllis Yglesias. Each year it tends to more than 1,000 sick wild birds brought in by the public.

MOUSEHOLE OF THE PHOENICIANS *The odd name of the village may be derived from an ancient Mediterranean word for watering place. Phoenician tin merchants anchored here 2,500 years ago.*

HENRY MOORE'S VILLAGE *Much Hadham's traditional pretti-ness makes an odd contrast to the powerfully simple works of the great sculptor who lives there, and who has donated a pair of heads to the church. The houses in the long main street record Hertfordshire prosperity down the centuries; despite appearances, the ones shown here both date from before 1600. But when one was given a Regency façade, the other sturdily maintained its late medieval timbering.*

MUCH HADHAM
HERTFORDSHIRE
4 miles west of Bishop's Stortford (page 426 Cb)

Standing in wide, wooded country, Much Had-ham is reputedly the most handsome village in Hertfordshire. Its chief glory is the main street, a charming mixture of Elizabethan cottages and rather grand gentlemen's residences of the 18th and early 19th centuries.

At the beginning of the street there is the 18th-century Lordship's stable block, crowned with a clock-tower like a decoration from an outsize wedding cake.

Down the street lies a fascinating range of architectural styles – Victorian almshouses, fine pargeting and black-and-white timber cladding.

Behind the main street is the original reason for Much Hadham's prosperity – the long, low, Bishop's Palace, the home of the Bishops of London for 800 years. It was also the birthplace of Edmund Tudor, the father of Henry VII.

The big, solid church is of flint, and a sign over the door announces 'This is the Gate to Heaven', while other unexpected pleasures include heads by Henry Moore, who lives in the village, ancient carving and ironwork, fine stained glass and a quilt embroidered by the village Women's Insti-tute for Queen Mary in 1935. It was later returned to them by Queen Elizabeth the Queen Mother after the death of George VI in 1952.

MUCH MARCLE
HEREFORD AND WORCESTER
7 miles north-east of Ross-on-Wye (page 425 Eb)

On February 17, 1575 Marcle Hill began to move – and kept on moving for three days. This strange movement of a mass of soil and rock, about 25 acres in extent, uprooted trees and hedges, killed cattle and sheep and even destroyed a small chapel in its path. The chapel bell was found during ploughing 265 years later. The cause of this convulsion, which moved the hill about 400 yds, remains unexplained.

The village played a large part in the develop-ment of cider making as a major local industry. As far back as the 1600s the local farmers had sold their surplus cider. One of the first men to start an actual factory for cider making in the 19th century was a Marcle farmer named Henry Weston, whose firm still operates at Bounds Farm.

The church is mainly 13th century and contains some of the finest carved effigies in the county. One, carved from a solid block of oak, dates from about 1350 and depicts a man – thought to be local landowner Walter de Helyon – lying cross-legged with hands clasped in prayer.

In the churchyard is an enormous yew tree, about 1,000 years old, whose huge trunk is split, and fitted with seats inside for seven or eight people.

Near the church are several old black-and-white farm cottages, and the village has two historic houses – Hellen's and Homme House. Hellen's, an ancient manorial house of brick and stone begun in 1292, is mainly 16th century. It has a dovecot built in 1641. The house is occasion-ally open to the public. Homme House, which is not, dates in part from the early 16th century. It was the seat of the Kyrle family and is still owned by their descendants.

NAPTON ON THE HILL
WARWICKSHIRE

7 miles west of Daventry (page 430 Bb)

The hill rises to almost 500 ft above Warwick-shire's flat countryside, and Napton has stood there since Saxon times. Thatched cottages, Georgian and Victorian houses and modern dwellings border the lanes around the village green, and towering above all, on the crown of the hill, is an early-19th-century tower-windmill. The old miller's cottage next door contains remnants of the original bread oven.

On the brow of the hill is the Church of St Lawrence, dating from the 12th century, which local legend says arrived there by mysterious means. It was originally planned to stand by the village green, but when the stones were placed ready for building they moved up the hill overnight. No one ever knew who moved them, but rather than tempt fate, the church was built in the new position.

The Oxford Canal winds its way around the hill, attracting boating enthusiasts, anglers and walkers who can enjoy the rural delights of its leafy towpath.

NAYLAND
SUFFOLK

7 miles north of Colchester (page 432 Cb)

The centre of Nayland is a jumble of colour-washed dwellings with overhanging timbers, patches of cobble, tiles turning sometimes to near orange, and a milestone obelisk which could be mistaken for a market cross. The village stands near the mouth of the River Stour, and can trace its history back to when it was the Domesday lordship of *Eilanda* – the Old English word for 'island'. This came about because the original manor stood on a moated field, now called Court Knoll, which was once so close to the river that its moat was always full.

High Street was once divided in two along its length by a row of cottages, but is now one street with detached gabled houses on one side and a

---

SILENT BY-PASS *Just beyond the second lock, the Oxford Canal turns sharp left to avoid Napton Hill, crowned by the tower of a derelict mill. The detour allowed Napton on the Hill to continue in a peaceful isolation that had already lasted for 1,000 years. Today, the canal – a mere 200 years old – shares the peace of the hillside village.*

continuous stretch of buildings on the other. The hub of the village is the 15th-century Alston Court, which has a big 17th-century door and mullioned windows.

The Guildhall, in the High Street, is a survivor of 16th-century prosperity from the wool trade. It is now a private house. The bridge over the Stour was originally made of wood and was maintained by a bequest from a wealthy clothier, John Abel, who died in 1523. His symbol – the letter A and a bell on the keystone – was preserved when the bridge was rebuilt in 1959.

In 1525, another Abel, William, presented a porch to the Church of St James, which dates from 1400. Its tower was damaged by an earthquake in the last century and it was replaced by the present spire in 1963. Inside, part of the Lady Altar covering was used at the coronation of Elizabeth II. On the altar is one of John Constable's three religious paintings, showing Christ blessing the bread and wine.

NETHER ALDERLEY
CHESHIRE

3 miles south of Wilmslow (page 429 Dc)

Hidden away on the western side of the road from Congleton to Manchester is the village of Nether Alderley. Almost the only landmark on the road is the huge 15th-century watermill, its vast sloping roof pierced by four dormer windows. The mill had two water-wheels, fed from Radnor Mere. The original entrance door is now blocked up, but one of the millstones can be seen below the new entrance. The mill is owned by the National Trust, and is open to visitors.

Almost opposite the mill a leafy lane, flanked by old brick cottages and shaded by great beech trees, leads past a handsome Georgian rectory to the 14th-century Church of St Mary. Nether Alderley belonged to the branch of the rich and powerful Stanley family, who lived at nearby Alderley Park. The church is full of their memorials and monuments, including a first-floor family pew with its own entrance from outside. The font, which dates from the 14th century, was buried in the churchyard to save it from destruction during Cromwell's Commonwealth – then forgotten. It was dug up in 1821, and 100 years later restored to use in the church. Among several old books in the church is a 'Vinegar' Bible of 1717, in which a misprint reads 'the parable of the vinegar' instead of vineyard.

At the entrance to the churchyard is an old stone school. A plaque records that 'Mr Hugh Shaw, Clerk, built this school, anno 1628'. But another wing was added by the Reverend Edward Stanley, brother of the 1st Lord Stanley of Alderley, in 1817.

A few hundred yards north of the mill a pleasant winding byway, called Artists Lane, leads from the main road to Alderley Edge, passing an inn and restaurant called the Wizard. The name recalls the legend of the magic cave of The Wizard of the Edge, where an army of knights waits ready to ride out on white horses if called upon to save the country.

NETHER WALLOP
HAMPSHIRE

7 miles south-west of Andover (page 422 Bb)

From the lovely old mill house standing sentinel at the southern edge of Nether Wallop, a winding lane opens up changing vistas of thatched cottages, cob walls of clay and straw, and colourful gardens. Willows are reflected in the bright waters of Wallop Brook. The through road stays on the north bank of the stream, but visitors can cross by a little bridge to examine the best of the cottages. Also south of the brook, on a low, tree-clad hill at the end of a cul-de-sac, is St Andrew's Church. It is of 11th-century origin, enlarged in the 12th to 15th centuries.

One of the finest features in the church is a 15th-century mural urging Sunday observance, entitled 'A Warning to Sabbath Breakers'. Christ is depicted bleeding from wounds inflicted by the tools and implements of people who work on Sundays. A whole range of medieval equipment is shown – but not of course the weapon for which Wallop became famous later throughout the cricketing world. Bats made by village craftsmen of the local willow were prized by top players, including W. G. Grace.

North-west from Nether Wallop are its companions, Middle Wallop on the busy Salisbury to Andover road, and Over Wallop. The name Wallop comes from the Anglo-Saxon, and means 'valley of the stream'. East from Nether Wallop a downland track leads 2 miles to the remains of an Iron Age fort on Danebury Hill. From there, another track leads to the River Test at Longstock, and on towards another fort at Woolbury Ring, 5 miles from Nether Wallop.

NETHY BRIDGE
HIGHLAND

5 miles south of Grantown-on-Spey (page 443 Fd)

Visitors go to Nethy Bridge from December until the end of April for the skiing. It is also a centre for fishing, walking and climbing – and its Victorian hotel has an attractive nine-hole golf course. The village straddles the River Nethy and spreads up the conifer-clad slopes above the water. There are several side roads containing old stone cottages.

In the 18th century, Nethy Bridge was the hub of a thriving timber trade, and saw-mills, brick kilns and a charcoal-fired ironworks were on a site in the north-east corner. The logs were bound into rafts, which were floated through the village on their way to the River Spey and on to the boatyards of Garmouth and Kingston on the coast.

The bridge over the Nethy was built about 1809 after the original one was washed away. The church is 1 mile to the north, next to the ruins of the Norman Castle Roy. Four miles south-west is Loch Garten with its renowned osprey eyrie, to which the birds return each April.

NEVERN
DYFED

7 miles south-west of Cardigan (page 424 Bb)

The historic roots of Nevern trail back more than 1,000 years, into the Celtic age of saints and legends. It is approached from the north by a winding road that twists and turns down a wooded dell, where ferns and mossy boulders lie beneath the trees. The village stands in a secluded valley washed by the River Nyfer as it flows towards the sea at Newport Bay. Clusters of buildings on both banks are linked by a narrow, medieval bridge with low parapets and stone steps that lead down to the clear water. Colour-washed cottages and a riverside inn stand beside a lane that climbs to join the Newport road.

On the other side of the bridge, attractive buildings of grey stone are set against a backcloth of low, wooded hills. The tower of the 15th-century church overlooks an avenue of ancient yews. The church is dedicated to St Brynach, a 6th-century missionary from Ireland, and a magnificent Celtic cross – richly carved and more than twice the height of a man – stands east of the porch.

NEW ABBEY
DUMFRIES AND GALLOWAY

6 miles south of Dumfries (page 441 Eb)

This Solway village grew up in the 13th century beside the Cistercian abbey that even now, in its ruined state, is one of the loveliest buildings in the Borders, and is known to all the world as Sweetheart Abbey. The building, and its name, are the legacies of the Lady Devorgilla who founded the abbey in memory of her husband John Balliol who died in 1273; some 20 years earlier the couple had endowed an even more famous establishment, Balliol College, Oxford. It is said that Devorgilla was so devoted to her husband's memory that she had his heart placed in an ivory casket and carried this 'sweet, silent companion' with her all her days until she was buried with it in the abbey in 1289. Within a century of her death, the story had gained sufficient currency for the building to become known as Abbey of Sweetheart, and so it has been called ever since.

Though the village is perhaps a little overawed by the abbey, it nevertheless contains some fine buildings including an 18th-century watermill, Abbey House – the former abbots' residence, a smithy bearing an 18th-century motto, 'By hammer and hand, All arts do stand': and some pretty, whitewashed cottages. One of these in the main street carries a crude stone carving of three figures in a boat. This is thought to celebrate the labours of three women who, when the abbey was being built, ferried the red sandstone for its facings over the Solway Firth.

NEW ALRESFORD, Hampshire (page 422 Cb)
(see p. 144)

NEW BUCKENHAM
NORFOLK

7 miles north of Diss (page 432 Dc)

The medieval pattern of streets set in rows and crossing almost at right-angles has been preserved in this village, though few of its buildings date from earlier than the 17th century. Georgian houses stand on the former market place, now a grass-covered green with a 17th-century market house built on nine wooden pillars. The one at the centre was the village whipping post.

The village became 'new' about 1150, when a Norman baron, William II de Albini, gave his castle at Old Buckenham to Augustinian canons and built a new one 1½ miles away. Its moated ramparts still stand, and in the centre are the remains of what is thought to be the first round keep in England. A barn near the keep was originally the castle chapel.

Until the 15th century, the castle chapel was New Buckenham's parish church. The present church, St Martin's, has roof timbers supported on stone effigies of the Twelve Apostles.

New Lanark

STRATHCLYDE

1 mile south of Lanark (page 441 Ec)

New Lanark was built as a model village in a thickly wooded gorge of the Clyde Valley by David Dale, a wealthy Glasgow merchant. In the 1780s he harnessed water power from the Falls of Clyde to run a cotton-mill, and the village was built to house the mill workers. The business was later run by his son-in-law, the social reformer Robert Owen, who introduced better sanitation and more humane working and living conditions.

Later, the mills were taken over by a new company, which operated them until 1968. By then, a local association had been formed to restore the buildings to their original outward form. Today, New Lanark is resuming its 'model village' image, and a school started by Robert Owen, rows of workers' houses and an old counting house are preserved in its centre. The counting house includes an exhibition area, and visitors are shown around the restored homes on certain days by their current occupants.

AGONY COLUMN *The central column supporting New Buckenham's market house once made a convenient whipping post for the punishment of village miscreants. On more pleasant occasions – market days – the upper storey provided shade for the stall-holders below who wished to keep their dairy products cool. The market house and its neighbouring row of attractive cottages stand on the market place, now a spacious, well-kept green planted with trees. It is planned to use the upper part of the market house as a museum.*

New Quay

DYFED

19 miles south-west of Aberystwyth (page 424 Bc)

Visitors throng the streets and beaches of New Quay in summer, but the village has managed to retain the enchanting atmosphere of a small, colourful fishing port. It is a miniature masterpiece of Georgian and Victorian good taste, with stacked terraces looking out over the tiny harbour and the splendid sweep of Cardigan Bay. Church Street is particularly attractive, wending its way to the shore between impeccable 18th and 19th-century houses. Elsewhere, palm trees pay graceful tribute to the mildness of the local climate.

The harbour is overlooked by a tall building with 19th-century port dues still displayed on one wall. Covering everything from cigars to barrel-organs, they are a quaint reminder that this was a flourishing port until road and rail transport killed the coastal trade.

NEW RADNOR
POWYS

6 miles north-west of Kington (page 425 Dc)

Almost 1,000 years of turbulent history lie behind New Radnor, which was 'new' at the time of Edward the Confessor. It was founded by Earl Harold Godwinsson in 1064, to replace Old Radnor as a stronghold commanding a valley leading from the English border into Wales. Two years later, in January 1066, the earl became King Harold, only to be killed at the Battle of Hastings less than 10 months later. New Radnor passed to Harold's conqueror, William, who gave the manor to one of his barons, Philip de Braose.

The Normans laid out New Radnor on a neat, gridiron pattern, with three main streets running from north-west to south-east, crossed at right-angles by five lanes. Walls entered by four gates protected the settlement, and an earthwork was built 1 mile higher up the valley to defend it against attack from the west. The Norman street pattern can be seen in map-like clarity from the steep, grassy mound which is all that remains of the Norman castle keep. Banks, ditches and hummocks mark the sites of the towers, moat and walls of the stronghold destroyed, rebuilt and destroyed again by the Welsh and the Normans during their 300 year tussle for this border town. New Radnor's last battle was fought in 1644, when it was held for Charles I but fell to Cromwell's men after a brief siege.

From the castle site can be seen the grassy banks which clearly define the western and southern sections of the old town wall. On a lower slope of the castle mound stands St Mary's Church, rebuilt in 1840-5 to replace an earlier church. The church overlooks a group of buildings that includes a black-and-white timbered cottage. A raised pavement passes a terrace of grey-green stone houses before the road turns sharp right into Broad Street.

This is the central thoroughfare of the village, where the Eagle Hotel stands on the site of the old prison, opposite the old town hall – reminders that New Radnor was a borough until 1886. Part of a lock-up can be seen behind the town-hall building, and the stocks stand on one side of the street near the hotel.

Near the bottom end of Broad Street, a row of whitewashed stone cottages line the road just before it curves to meet Water Street, another of the three main streets. At the junction stands the village's biggest single surprise – a memorial almost as large and as elaborate as Prince Albert's in London. Surrounded by gargoyles, arches, pillars and shields is the white-marble profile of Sir George Cornewall Lewis, New Radnor's MP from 1855 until his death in 1863. He was Chancellor of the Exchequer, Home Secretary and War Minister under Palmerston.

Water Street takes its name from a sparkling brook that flows its full length and is crossed by small bridges linking the houses to the street. At the top end of the street is Water Street Farm, which has timber-framed buildings.

The third of the three main streets, Rectory Lane, has an iron gate from where there is a good view of the old town walls. A whitewashed house near by was once New Radnor's Zion chapel, and next to it is a tiny graveyard – about 36 ft by 24 ft – with a single yew tree.

The scenery around New Radnor is spectacular, with the mountains of Great Rhos, Black Mixen and Bache Hill rising to more than 2,000 ft in the heart of Radnor Forest to the north-west.

SPACE SAVER *The massive chimney of this 17th-century house at New Radnor was built outside the main structure in order to make more room inside the house.*

NEWCASTLE EMLYN
DYFED

9 miles south-east of Cardigan (page 424 Bb)

The 'new' castle from which this large, bustling village takes its name was built in the 13th century to replace an even older fortress. The scanty but romantic ruins of its 15th-century successor – demolished by Cromwell after the Civil War – stand in a grassy hillock with the River Teifi forming a broad, natural moat on three sides. It is a delightful place for picnics and strolls in a peaceful atmosphere that belies the old stronghold's turbulent history. In 1288 alone, when the Welsh were still rebelling against the English, it is believed to have been attacked and changed hands three times.

The southern end of Newcastle Emlyn's lengthy main street is broad and flanked by several elegant buildings, notably a bank of brown-gold stone with little blue-painted balconies of wrought iron. To the north, where it funnels down into the oldest part of the village, the street is dominated by the old Town Hall, built around 1860 and complete with a clock-tower. The pavements at its feet are crowded every Friday when visitors flock in for the weekly market. The short hill that runs down to a bridge over the Teifi is flanked by colourful terraces, and is overlooked by the Emlyn Arms Hotel with its tiny, slate-paved verandah enclosed by iron railings. Slate from the now-abandoned quarries downstream at Cilgerran is also featured promi-nently in the mainly 19th-century parish church.

NEWCASTLETON
BORDERS

17 miles south of Hawick (page 441 Fb)

In 1793 the Duke of Buccleuch re-established the village of Castleton beside Liddel Water. The original village, called Copshaw Holme, is thought to have been destroyed in the 1650s by Cromwell's troops. The duke created Newcastle-ton as a village for general craftsmen, building cottages and leasing them to the villagers, as well as providing gardens and grazing ground. Although the new name was used from the time the village was built, it is still known locally as Copshaw Holme.

Newcastleton is set in the Border valley of Liddesdale, which features in Sir Walter Scott's historical novel *Guy Mannering*. Scott visited Lid-desdale many times collecting Border ballads.

The village has one main street with a large central square and a smaller one at each end.

In 1920 the Forestry Commission bought 3,500 acres of hilly land to the east of the village and covered it with spruce plantations. Newcastleton Forest is now part of the vast Border Forest Park, which extends into England. Every year, on the last weekend in June, musicians, singers and dancers congregate in the village for the annual folk festival, started in the early 1970s.

NEWPORT
DYFED

9 miles south-west of Cardigan (page 424 Bb)

Few seaside villages in Wales can equal New-port's bewitching blend of colour, character and history. In the Norman era it became the capital of the barony of Cemais, beneath whose castle it grew up. This stronghold – thought to have been sacked three times by the Welsh – is still there today, dominating the view up Market Street. Its tall gatehouse, that was partly demolished and converted into a house in 1859, contrasts pleas-antly with ivy-clad ruins near by. The broad streets that branch off at right-angles from the narrow main street running through the centre of the village are flanked by attractive buildings, dating mainly from the 18th and 19th centuries. Pinks, blues, greens, yellows and reds mingle with the pale grey of natural stone, and many of the houses are fronted by ornate iron railings

that add to the predominantly Georgian atmos-phere. A small public garden, neatly paved, stands at the top of Market Street and provides an ideal spot for surveying the scene.

Although now set back from the sea, this was a thriving port for many centuries. A lane runs down to the old harbour, overlooked by a former storehouse and ancient lime kilns. Many head-stones outside the restored 13th-century church bear the words 'mariner' or 'master mariner'. One inscription on a headstone near the church door commemorates 'John Morris, Master of the Schooner Jane of this Port . . . who with his crew perished in a Gale of wind at sea in a voyage from Galway to London in the month of August 1838. Aged 23 Years'. It is a poignant reminder that the age of sail was not all colour and romance.

NEWTON LINFORD, Leicestershire (page 431 Cc)
(see Woodhouse Eaves)

NEWTOWN
ISLE OF WIGHT

5 miles west of Newport (page 422 Ba)

A small red-brick building standing alone on a wide green verge is the first sign of a settlement on the road from the south into Newtown. The building is the Old Town Hall, erected in 1699 and now a museum in the care of the National Trust. It is the sole surviving evidence that the tiny village which lies beyond was once one of the boroughs on the island. That was more than 600 years ago when the name of the place was Francheville. It was a busy port, with a rich oyster fishery and a thriving salt-producing industry. Then, in 1377, during the 100 Years War, French raiders destroyed the town. Even-tually a few people returned and started to rebuild the 'New town' – the name which stuck. Although the town prospered – as the Town Hall indicates – it never regained its former import-ance. Even so, it continued to elect two Members of Parliament until the Reform Act of 1832, when there were just 68 inhabitants – and 39 voters – in the borough. Near the Town Hall is a house called Noah's Ark. This was the village inn until 1916 and was called the Francheville Arms.

Entering Newtown today, the road through the village makes several right-angled turns before running down to the marshes beside the New-town River. These turns are the remnants of the grid-iron street pattern of the medieval town, of which other traces remain only as leafy lanes or farm tracks. The first turn, just beyond the Town Hall, leads past stone-built cottages, whose charm has been acknowledged by the Post Office, who have painted the telephone kiosk grey, instead of pillar-box red. The tiny church was built in Victorian times to replace a predecessor which had decayed as the village declined. Where the road ends, a path leads down to the river, which is now a yacht haven. Where the path ends, a causeway continues out over the mud-flats beside a nature reserve where wildfowl and wading birds gather in huge numbers.

295

NORHAM
NORTHUMBERLAND

7 miles south-west of Berwick (page 438 Ad)

The historic village of Norham, pronounced 'Norrum', lies in rich meadowland in a loop of the River Tweed. There is a triangular green overlooked by stone buildings – some red-roofed and whitewashed – with the village cross, a 19th-century structure on a 13th-century base.

Norham looks across the Tweed to Scotland, and in medieval times was in the thick of many battles and skirmishes of the Border Wars. Its castle stands at the eastern end of the main street, on high ground. The massive rose-coloured walls and the great Norman keep make an impressive sight against a curtain of trees, and at the foot of the rocky bank the river is dwarfed to a silvery ribbon.

The Scottish poet and novelist Sir Walter Scott immortalised Norham Castle in his poem *Marmion*, calling it 'the most dangerous place in Britain'. It was built in 1157, and in 1291 was attacked several times by claimants to the Scottish throne. The 'red and honey-coloured walls' described by Scott are approached by Marmion's Gate, beyond which the imposing keep rises to 90 ft.

Up a lane from the north corner of the green is St Cuthbert's Church, with a long, flat-roofed nave and an oblong belfry tower at its western end. Parts of the church are Norman, but most date from 1846 to 1852. The elaborately carved 17th-century pulpit came from Durham Cathedral.

The Tweed is a salmon river, and the Blessing of the Nets ceremony heralds the start of the fishing season. Traditionally, the vicar is always offered the first fish caught.

QUEEN ELIZABETH'S OAK *Beneath this massive oak tree on Northiam's village green in East Sussex, Elizabeth I is said to have rested while on her way to Rye in 1573. According to tradition she changed her footwear there, leaving behind as a memento a pair of green silk damask shoes with 2½ in. high heels and sharp, pointed toes. The shoes are kept in the Jacobean mansion, Brickwall, which stands in parkland at the south end of the village. Brickwall was the home of the Frewen family for over 300 years.*

NORTHIAM
EAST SUSSEX

10 miles north of Hastings (page 423 Eb)

Cottages covered with white weather-boarding look out over a large village green where oaks and limes grow. One great oak dominates the scene, and it is beneath this tree that Elizabeth I is reputed to have rested on August 11, 1573. She was on her way to Rye when she stopped for breakfast at Northiam.

The white boarding, the general theme of the village centre, entirely covers the walls of a three-storey house by the green. To the north, several 17th-century houses and cottages front on to Main Street before the village straggles into bungalows.

A large yew tree rises from the churchyard, just above the village green. The church itself is Norman, and has a fine stone spire. It contains communion rails given by a local Puritan, Thankful Frewen, in 1638.

One of the houses by a recreation ground on the north side of the village was the site of a meeting on May 12, 1944, between the prime ministers of Britain, Canada, South Africa and what was then Southern Rhodesia. They met for talks before the D-Day landings and the Normandy Invasion.

Half a mile to the north-west is Great Dixter, one of the finest timber-framed buildings in Sussex. The house is believed to be basically 15th century, but was carefully rebuilt by Sir Edwin Lutyens in 1911. It is open to the public. Its garden is noted for its box and yew hedges.

NORTH BOVEY, Devon (page 419 Db)
(see Lustleigh)

NORTON ST PHILIP
SOMERSET

---

5 miles north of Frome (page 421 Cc)

Nine men of Norton St Philip were bound to stakes and burned alive after the Battle of Sedgmoor ended the Monmouth Rebellion in 1685. So says Geoffrey Coombs, the village contractor and undertaker, in whose family memories of the horror remain quite fresh. Geoffrey's ancestor Thomas Coombs was one of the men burned; and three other families in the village are descendants of three more. Eight of the men had languished almost 12 months in a dungeon before a judge – possibly the notorious Judge Jeffreys himself – arrived to exact terrible retribution from the pro-Monmouth villagers. Their gaol is now the Dungeon Bar of Norton's superb half-timbered George Inn, which has stood at the village crossroads for more than 500 years. The ninth man was an innocent bystander who held open the gate of the George when the men were led out – and was bundled away with the others to be burned in an orchard just east of the village on the Trowbridge road, says Mr Coombs.

There is no official record of these burnings, though mention has been made of 'hangings' in Norton. But Mr Coombs has examined the parish records and found that the church paid 12 shillings for 100 bundles of faggots for 'ye execution'. Other than that, the dark deed seems to have been kept dark.

It is all fairly recent history for the Coombs family, which has lived in the village since records began in 1220. At home Geoffrey has a cannon ball, picked up by one of his ancestors after a skirmish when Monmouth rebels barricaded the roads into Norton against the soldiers of James II. It has been used as a doorstop by the family ever since.

On show in the George is a section of oak beam replaced during renovations, in which is embedded a lead musket ball. It could be the assassin's bullet which local history says missed the Duke of Monmouth – illegitimate son of Charles II and pretender to the throne – when he stayed at the George on the night of June 26, 1685, just 10 days before Sedgmoor. Or it could have been fired during that skirmish near by, when fierce fighting took place in Chevers Lane – still called 'Bloody Lane' by villagers. An earlier visitor to the George was Samuel Pepys, who dined there with his wife while on his way to Bath in June 1668.

The pub, with its mullioned and bow windows, and its small courtyard and timbered balcony at the back, has hardly changed since Elizabeth I reigned. Cloth merchants met there in those days, when the village was a centre for the wool trade, had town status and was said to have 'the most noted cloth fair in the west'. Daniel Defoe called it Phillips' Norton in his list of Somerset's principal clothing towns.

The village is 1 mile west of the Bath to Warminster road, about halfway between the two towns. Its houses are grouped closely together in the friendly medieval manner. From about 1230 until the Dissolution of the Monasteries by Henry VIII it belonged to the great Carthusian priory of Hinton Charterhouse, 1½ miles north. The George, in its original simple stone form, may have served as a guest house for the monks: the upper part is believed to have been added as a wool store and extra accommodation. A pathway leads from the inn down a gently sloping field to the remarkable Church of St Philip.

The church's origins are also 13th century, but the present building was donated by a wealthy local merchant, Jeffrey Flower. He apparently took a hand in the design, and his fertile imagination produced a tower like no other in England, with oddly arched windows and elaborate niches. He died in 1644. Treasures inside include magnificent wrought-iron gates to the chancel and handsome screens of carved oak. St Philip's is said also to contain the grave of Siamese-twin sisters, the Fair Maids of Foscot. Pepys describes their tombstone, which he saw in 1668, as being carved with the figures of the girls, who had 'two bodies upward and one stomach'. They were born in Foxcote, a hamlet 3½ miles to the west. The carved faces from the tombstone are set into the wall inside the tower, but records of their birth are lost.

NUNNEY
SOMERSET

3 miles south-west of Frome (page 421 Cb)

A wooded fold among the valleys which ripple down from the eastern flank of the Mendip Hills is the setting for Nunney. It is a fairy-tale setting, with greystone, red-tiled houses grouped around a ruined medieval castle. A 10 ft deep moat and a stream surround the castle, forming an island which is maintained as a bird sanctuary.

The castle is reached by a footbridge, and although privately owned is open to the public. It was built in the 14th century by Sir John de la Mere, and is said to have been modelled on the Bastille in France. Three of the four sturdy towers are almost intact externally. During the Civil War the castle was a Royalist stronghold, but eventually fell to the cannons of Cromwell's artillery.

One of the 30 lb. iron cannonballs that demolished the castle walls is in All Saints Church, a 13th-century building greatly restored in 1874. In the south corner of the church there is a room containing a model of the castle as it appeared when built in the 1370s.

The early-18th-century Manor Farm near the castle is built of the same grey stone, as are the cottages bordering the stream. Some of the cottages bear dates of the 1600s and 1700s.

LOST VILLAGES

Thousands of villages have simply vanished from the map of Britain, wiped out by disasters, both natural and man-made – from plague to forcible clearances. But though the villagers have gone, the marks they left can still be seen.

Scattered about Britain, hidden among nettles, brambles and forests, are some 3,000 'lost' villages, each of which has contributed – in its own way – to the nation's history and heritage. Perhaps a cruel nobleman was waylaid and killed there; some treasure or contraband buried there; or maybe the overgrown ruins of a once proud and sturdy cottage housed a family whose loyalty to a long-ago and almost forgotten king was hailed at the time.

Some of the villages – with their particular histories, myths and legends – are completely lost from sight; while others can

still partly be seen on the surface.

A ruined church stands where a village once clustered around it; or else a faded pattern of green rectangular marks – made by the platforms on which village houses once stood – is an evocative reminder of the community which once lived and then died there. In rarer cases, a scattering of broken pottery on the ground can be the sign that a medieval village is completely buried below.

The 'green patterns' are among the best indications of a lost village. They can be located

A VILLAGE UNCOVERED BY THE SEA

One of the most remarkable archaeological sites in Britain was discovered when storm-driven seas cut into a mound beside the shore at Jarlshof, on the Shetland island of Mainland. In the windblown sand of the mound, archaeologists discovered remains of three village settlements. The earliest remains consist of four stone houses built about the 8th century BC. Near by are oval huts of the 5th and 4th centuries BC. At a higher level, an Iron Age broch tower and courtyard of about the 1st century AD protect a group of circular dwellings known as wheelhouses because of their shape. They are still partly roofed and are the most perfect examples to survive *in Britain. Later, the Vikings occupied the site, and the village they built was the last to be buried by the sand, some time after the 13th century. Below is an artist's impression of how the broch looked in the 2nd century AD.*

by aerial photography, and they can also be seen and identified by people – scholars or tourists – walking across ground which was trodden by earlier Britons.

There is no single reason why these once-thriving villages were deserted, or why they so often tragically disappeared.

Many of them were cleared in the 12th century as a deliberate policy of the monks who wished to establish monasteries on the sites. In seeking solitude the monks, particularly the Cistercians, removed all the inhabitants of an old village to a new site. This happened at Rufford in Nottinghamshire where two villages were destroyed about AD 1145 when

the monks established their community. Many such monastic depopulations may be found in eastern England.

However, one major factor in their demise was the Black Death, or bubonic plague, which came from the Continent and first ravaged England in the 14th century. From Weymouth, in 1348, the disease spread rapidly over the next two years, wiping out almost half the population and, in some cases, reducing villages to only a handful of able-bodied men. For the next 300 years or more there were hundreds of localised epidemics – which again took their toll of village life – and several national outbreaks. The disease culminated with the Great Plague of London in 1665 – although a few years later it flared up again on a small scale, when even more villages suffered.

However, it is too easy to blame the plague, ghastly though it was, for the loss of so

EVIDENCE FROM THE AIR *A lonely church in an empty field is all that remains of the village of Low Ham in the midst of the Somerset Levels. This aerial view shows distinct traces of where houses once stood. Excavations revealed a 3rd-century Roman villa, no trace of which remained on the surface.*

SAXON VILLAGE *At West Stow, in Suffolk, Saxon houses have been reconstructed on the site of a village which was abandoned around AD 650. In the reconstruction, two houses of oak and thatch flank a communal hall.*

many villages. In fact, only a few were wiped out completely and most of the inhabitants who had fled into the surrounding countryside returned to their old dwellings and farms.

Slowly, many villages came alive again, although it is likely that some villagers chose new sites for their homes and did not go back to infected buildings.

Excavations, where they have been made, show a slight shift of site, and indicate that life went on as before. This was certainly so at Coombe – and possibly at Steeple Barton – in Oxfordshire. But some villages – such as Tilgarsley, in Oxfordshire, Ambion in Leicestershire and Middle Carlton in Lincolnshire – were completely wiped out and never resettled.

As far as England was concerned, the plague did not wipe out a great number of villages at one lethal blow. But, returning every few decades, it gradually reduced the rural population. In Scotland there were other reasons for the disappearance of villages – notably the Highland Clearances of the 18th and 19th centuries, when the clan leaders and landlords turned many crofters out of

their homes to make way for the more profitable rearing of sheep. In Wales – as in other parts of Britain – villages were sometimes abandoned, or parts of them lost or destroyed, by a natural shift in the course of a river. Some Welsh quarrying and mining villages, together with those of south-west England, died 'natural deaths' when the minerals ran out in the 19th and early 20th centuries.

So, for a variety of reasons, many villages never recovered their former size, and landlords found there was a permanent reduction in the labour supply – certainly not enough men

remained to support an arable economy. Moreover, the price of wool and meat was rising in 15th-century England, and it paid a landlord to turn over the old arable of the open fields to large pastures – where one shepherd or cowherd could produce as much as a score of farm labourers.

Inevitably, the depopulated villages decayed under the new system of farming. But there were also many instances where the lord of the manor evicted the few remaining inhabitants against their will to turn the land into sheep and cattle pastures. The government became alarmed at these evictions – not

SHEEP BEFORE MEN *In the 100 years up to 1860 Highland landlords cleared whole villages to make way for sheep – often putting their tenants straight on to emigrant ships bound for the colonies.*

so much out of compassion for the victims, as for the fact that a large and fit peasantry was necessary to maintain the army during the continual wars with France. The so-called Domesday of Inclosures (1517) shows that most of the damage had been done before the reign of Henry VII began in 1485. However, the evictions and evacuations continued, and the records say repeatedly of Midland villages – where the problem was the greatest – that the villagers had 'departed in tears', or that 'they are idle or have perished'.

In a record of 1270, the village of Knaptoft in Leicestershire had some 32 farmers tilling the soil. By 1525, another record shows huge pastures of 600 acres, and only five families of labourers working for the squire in the sheep pastures.

The distribution of lost villages is by far the densest in the Midlands and the eastern side of England – the lowlands. This is largely because the heavy clays produced better pastures, and partly because it was a countryside of powerful landlords who could do as they pleased to their estates – often to the cost of the villagers living on them. In villages with numerous small free-holders, however, it was almost impossible to make such sweeping changes.

In Northumberland alone there are more than 100 known sites of lost villages. Other counties with more than 100 such sites are Lincolnshire, Norfolk, Oxfordshire, Warwickshire, Hereford and Worcester, Wiltshire, North Yorkshire and Humberside. There are fewer sites in the upland regions of the north and west, probably because these regions had fewer villages to begin with.

Some counties show no recorded sites, but this is often because – as in Lancashire – the necessary local research has not been done; or – as in the Midlands – because former villages have been built over.

Some villages survive as single farmsteads. For example, Crowndale Farm, near Tavistock in Devon, had been a hamlet with seven farmsteads in 1336. Sixty years later it had

FOR KING AND COUNTRY *The scattered village of Tyneham in Dorset was surrendered to the Army in 1943 as a war-time artillery range. On the church door a notice reads: ' . . . We have given up our homes where we have lived for generations to help with the war and to keep men free. We shall return one day . . .' But the villagers never returned. The ruined, deserted village still belongs to the army.*

been reduced to a single holding. Aunby, in Lincolnshire, was abandoned in the 15th century and is now simply a farm beside a stream.

Recently, archaeologists have concentrated on East Anglia and the nearby counties for their excavations. There, the shell of a remote church – perhaps in the middle of a field, perhaps near some tangled undergrowth – can suggest that an Anglo-Saxon village is literally underfoot. Excavations around the impressive and isolated church at Maxey, in Northamptonshire, have revealed a buried village within a few yards of it – although the present village is half a mile away. Similar diggings at Longham, in Norfolk, have uncovered totally buried villages near the now isolated church – and the site has also yielded pottery dating from Saxon times.

However, figuratively speaking, this is just scratching the surface as far as lost villages are concerned. Many more are still waiting to be discovered. And, in some cases, the signs of their presence are there for all to see.

But some sites are discovered purely by chance, as there are no surface indications such as a church to suggest that a village once existed there.

Such a site is West Stow in Suffolk where at least 60 hut sites have been unearthed. West Stow was inhabited as early as AD 400 and abandoned after 250 years of occupation. The most likely reason for its abandonment is that the settlers found a better site about 1 mile upstream, where the present medieval village now stands.

The occupation of the village ended abruptly, but peacefully, and archaeologists believe that there are many such peaceful evacuations still to be discovered.

It could be that the next historic and hidden village to be uncovered will be the result of someone wandering through a quiet country field. Someone who is knowledgeable, alert, and who is keen to restore to us something of our past.

OARE
SOMERSET

6 miles east of Lynton (page 420 Ab)

It was in the little Church of St Mary, at Oare, that Carver Doone shot Lorna in R. D. Blackmore's famous novel *Lorna Doone*. The village lies deep in an Exmoor valley less than 2 miles from the sea, yet bears little relation to the coast which can be reached only by winding lanes. The scenery in this remote corner of Exmoor is superb. Oare Water tumbles riotously through the narrow valley, a green ribbon amid towering round-shouldered hills that in autumn are carpeted with glowing heather.

Those wishing to envisage the dramatic scene when Lorna was shot at her wedding should remember that the church, though small, was even smaller in the 17th century, the period in which the novel is set. No more than a dozen people could have got inside, and Carver would have been only a yard or two from the bride when he shot her at the altar. The west tower was rebuilt and the chancel enlarged in the mid-19th century, and the box pews put in a little earlier. Doone country and the Badgworthy Water – where the novel's hero, John Ridd, stumbled into his adventures – lie approximately 2 miles to the south-west.

There is a local rhyme which says:

Culbone, Oare and Stoke Pero
Are three such places as you seldom hear o'.

Stoke Pero and Culbone are equally remote hamlets, respectively 5 miles south-east and 2½ miles east of Oare, a village of which few would have heard had not Blackmore immortalised it. There was a John Ridd serving as churchwarden at Oare as recently as 1925.

ODSTOCK
WILTSHIRE

3 miles south of Salisbury (page 421 Db)

In the south-east corner of Odstock's churchyard is the grave of a legendary local figure, Joshua Scamp, a gipsy who was wrongfully hanged for horse-stealing in 1801. Scamp became a martyr among his people, and each year they assembled around his grave on the anniversary of his death, after first drinking lengthily to his memory in the nearby Yew Tree Inn.

One year, the rector and his churchwardens decided to stop the riotous celebrations by locking the church door and uprooting a briar rose which the gipsies had planted by Scamp's grave. The thwarted gipsies put a curse on anyone who should in future lock the church door, and after sudden death befell two who defied the curse the rector threw the church key into the River Ebble, where it is said still to lie.

Another briar rose has been planted by Scamp's grave, marked by a headstone now splitting with age, and the Yew Tree Inn still flourishes in this tiny village of stone and flint cottages. St Mary's Church – largely rebuilt in the 1870s in flint and stone – sits alone at one end of the village street. At the other end of the village is The Parsonage, a 17th-century house that was once an inn where Oliver Cromwell is said to have stayed.

OFFHAM
KENT

7 miles west of Maidstone (page 423 Ec)

An irregularly shaped green marks the centre of the village, which stands among orchards and woodland above the Medway Valley. Cottages, Georgian houses and an inn cluster round the green. Along one side of the green stand two early 18th-century brick houses – the Manor House, its front ivy-covered, and the nearby Quintain House. Local stone and timber are found among the brick and tile of the cottages, some of which date back 300 years and more.

On the green is a tall white pole with a revolving bar across the top. This is Offham's quintain, or tilting pole, said to be the only one in England. Tilting at the quintain was once a favourite sport on English village greens, and survived until recently at Offham.

Offham's Norman church is half a mile away from the main village, along a lane to Addington. Norman stonework and windows can still be identified, and the outline of a Norman chancel arch remains above the 13th-century arch.

Beside the church is a farmstead which was originally the Manor House, built in the reign of James I. An ancient barn there has been recently re-thatched.

Offham began as a Saxon settlement, and its modern name is based on the old name 'Offa'. The village is first mentioned in AD 832, when King Ethelwulf granted 'Ofnehamne' to the Church of Canterbury.

OLD BOLINGBROKE

LINCOLNSHIRE

3 miles west of Spilsby (page 432 Be)

The remains of a castle in which an English king was born adds atmosphere to this sleepy village on the southernmost edge of the Lincolnshire Wolds. Only a few fragments remain of the castle, built some 900 years ago and occupied in the 14th century by the mighty landowner John of Gaunt, Duke of Lancaster. One of his friends and followers, Geoffrey Chaucer, is said to have frequently visited the castle. It was there that Gaunt's son – who was to become Henry IV – was born.

Henry's coat of arms is prominently displayed in the centre of the village, in a bed of red Lancastrian roses. Old Bolingbroke was a prosperous market town in the Middle Ages; now it is a rambling little community of narrow lanes overlooked by low, tree-clad hills.

The castle fell into ruin after being captured in the Civil War by Cromwell and his troops, who, despite being outnumbered, defeated Royalist forces in 1643 at the Battle of Winceby near by – when Cromwell's horse was killed beneath him.

For centuries, only tumbled, grassy mounds showed where the castle once stood, but recent excavations have uncovered substantial remains of the gatehouse, towers and curtain wall.

A turning past the village inn, the Black Horse, leads to the castle site. To the north, the parish church of St Peter and St Paul stands among yew trees facing a group of large houses on the other side of the road. The church is a mixture of 14th-century architecture – perhaps commissioned by John of Gaunt – and 19th-century restoration. The old work includes richly moulded windows, and a nave arcade reaching to the modern barrel roof. At the entrance to the church are two worn heads believed to represent John's parents, Edward III and Queen Philippa.

The church is flanked by 18th and 19th-century buildings, including Bolingbroke House, with its turret-style chimneys.

OLD BRAMPTON

DERBYSHIRE

4 miles west of Chesterfield (page 430 Bd)

Buildings of local ironstone set in a pastoral landscape make Old Brampton one of the most attractive villages in the county. This impression is enhanced by the medieval tower and spire of the Church of St Peter and St Paul.

The clock on the south side of the tower must be unique – it has 63 minutes marked upon it. Many years ago, a craftsman employed to repaint the clock face took refreshment at the inn at midday. He returned some time later with his concentration severely affected, so that there are seven divisions between I and II, four between IV and V, six between VII and VIII, and six between X and XI.

Opposite the church is The Hall, a handsome whitewashed building dating from the 16th or 17th centuries with a 19th-century porch. It has mullioned windows, two gables and a stone-tiled roof.

The narrow North Lane is an old bridle road leading to Linacre Wood, where there are three reservoirs which supply water to Chesterfield. Linacre House, now demolished, was probably the birthplace of Thomas Linacre who founded the College of Physicians in 1518. He is commemorated by choir stalls in the parish church.

TIME AND OLD BRAMPTON

For quite a while now there has been something worth recording about time in Old Brampton. Take the church clock, which – due to a mistake by a tipsy workman – has 63 minutes painted on it. Take the village itself ... a mellow place in which ancient houses and their gardens are a timeless mixture of past and present.

OLD DEER

GRAMPIAN

10 miles west of Peterhead (page 443 Gd)

Religious conflict beset the villagers of Old Deer in the early 18th century, when the Episcopalian congregation threw out the Presbyterian minister who had been assigned to them. The incident has gone down in local church history as the 'Rabbling of Deer', referring to the 'rabble' who acted in such an extreme way. Today, however, both denominations are happily established. The parish church of 1788 stands at the end of the main street, and opposite it is the Episcopal church, St Drostan's, built in 1851.

Old Deer is set in the centre of the wooded valley of South Ugie Water, near the ruins of a Cistercian abbey founded in 1218. The remains are open to the public from April to September. Near by, a monastery was founded in the 6th century by St Drostan – although the exact location is no longer known. The 9th-century Latin manuscript, the *Book of Deer*, belonged to the monks at one time, and in its margins are notes about the history of the monastery. The 11th to 12th-century notes are the earliest known examples of written Scots Gaelic. Today the manuscript is in Cambridge University library.

The Russells of Aden – pronounced 'Ah-den' – were the lairds of Old Deer from 1758 to 1937. The heart of their estate – now owned by the district council – was turned into a country park in 1975.

OLD WARDEN

BEDFORDSHIRE

4 miles west of Biggleswade (page 426 Cb)

Warden means 'watch-hill'; the prefix 'old' was added about 1500, but before then Warden pears, grown by local monks, and the Warden pies made from them, were famed throughout England. Most of Warden Abbey disappeared beneath the turf long ago, but the watch-hill remains, commanding endless miles across the Bedfordshire flatlands.

Mostly, the village is the creation of two families, the Ongleys and the Shuttleworths, who, during the 19th century and after, lavished money and imagination in pursuit of their ideas. These varied considerably – cottages and houses with and without rustic-beamed verandahs, reed thatch and timber framing, a pump in a roofed black-and-white shelter, a large red-brick post office, and a shop with bow windows and a clock-tower. It is all very attractive, and if there is a feeling of wonder as to why anyone should put a curly yellow chimney 4 ft across on top of a tiny cottage, or erect a huge gallows over a well, it is just part of the fun.

Both families have now departed, though the Hall, built for the Shuttleworths in 1872, still stands on a hilltop in a magnificent park.

Both hall and park are best seen from the opposite hilltop, on which the church stands.

This is a warm, friendly building of patchy brown stone, but however welcoming its exterior it cannot adequately prepare you for the surprise of the inside. There, from floor to ceiling, the whole place is a mass of dark, polished, carved oak. There is scarcely an inch of pew, pulpit, gallery or door that does not bear some biblical or saintly scene. The whole thing was set up by Lord Ongley, who brought most of the carvings back with him from his travels in France, Belgium and Italy in 1841. Some of the carvings are reputed to have come from Anne of Cleves's private chapel in Bruges; certainly, the initials 'AC' appear in several places in the church. The building's most treasured possession, however, is a medieval window depicting a Cistercian abbot, which came from the old Abbey of Warden.

TAKING TO THE AIR
IN A BEDFORDSHIRE VILLAGE

In 1930 Richard Shuttleworth bought his first aeroplane, a de Havilland Gypsy Moth; four years later he added a 1909 Bleriot and a 1910 Deperdussin to his collection. But Shuttleworth did not live to see his hobby develop into one of the world's most famous aircraft museums. When war came he left his ancestral home, Old Warden Hall, and joined the RAF. He died in a flying accident in 1940, and in 1944 his mother founded the Shuttleworth Trust in his memory. Since then the Trust has grown to include many rare planes, such as a 1918 Bristol Fighter, with the oldest Rolls-Royce engine still flying. The aircraft are housed on a tiny airfield in the park next to the mansion, and on the last Sunday of each month during the summer many of them take to the air.

Old Warden Hall, now a college of agriculture and forestry.

OLDHAMSTOCKS
LOTHIAN

6 miles south-east of Dunbar (page 441 Gd)

Remotely tucked away on the eastern edge of the Lammermuir Hills, Oldhamstocks overlooks the steep-sided valley of the Dunglass Burn. Henry Percy, Earl of Northumberland, came this way during his campaign into Scotland in 1532, reporting to Henry VIII that he had obeyed the royal command to 'destroy, waste and burn corn and towns to their most annoyances'.

Another visitor was Oliver Cromwell, who spent a night at the Oldhamstocks Inn before defeating the Scots at the Battle of Dunbar in 1650. The inn no longer exists.

Although Oldhamstocks was granted the right to hold regular fairs in 1672, and was noted a century and a half ago as a place to buy well-built carts, the population has dwindled with the mechanisation of agriculture.

It is now a well-preserved village of neat cottages with tiled roofs. At the west end of the single street stands the parish church, remodelled in 1701 from a much older building. In the graveyard is the watch house, set up in 1824 to guard newly buried bodies from the attentions of the 'resurrection men' – body-snatchers whose grisly trade supplied corpses to the anatomy schools of Edinburgh.

The little village green remains untouched, with its 18th-century water pump and the mercat cross as a reminder of the long-ago days of the bustling Oldhamstocks fairs.

Rooftop oddity.

The Avro Tutor, in service until 1946.

Bristol Fighter – First World War veteran.

OLNEY
BUCKINGHAMSHIRE

5 miles north of Newport Pagnell (page 427 Bc)

Pancakes, hymns, the poet William Cowper and lace have spread the fame of this large parish far beyond Buckinghamshire. Its long, broad High Street runs from the market, with stone houses rising straight out of the pavement, giving it a Georgian air – although many of the buildings date from the early 17th century, and one or two from the early 20th century. One is a curious, stepped-gable structure bearing the legend 'Bucks Lace Industry', surmounted by a stone relief of a bonneted old lady busying herself with bobbins. It is a factory, built in 1928, to try to revive the lace-making for which Olney was once renowned, but now makes lampshades.

Stone and mossy-tiled roofs give the High Street uniformity, but each house has its own individual characteristics. There are superb Georgian doorways such as the one fronting the Four Pillars Restaurant. The house at number 25 has a plaque that reads, 'This house was built by the Feoffees for the town of Olney, 1694' – the Feoffees are a local charity that still exists. The Georgian Olney House has two bronze nymphs clasping electric lamps which illuminate its entrance.

Market Place, with its triangular green and war memorial, is rich in antiques shops, coffee houses and, around the corner, a wine bar with 18th-century bow windows. At the bottom of Market Place is Orchard Side, a large, flat-fronted Georgian house in patterned brick. There, between 1767 and 1786, William Cowper wrote some of his most famous works, including *The Task, John Gilpin* and the *Olney Hymns*. He composed the Hymns in partnership with his friend John Newton, a slave trader turned parson.

The house is now a museum containing relics of both men, including a portrait of Cowper conversing with the three hares that for some time shared his home.

The huge 14th-century church, with a 185 ft high spire that can be seen for miles around, lies beyond Market Place. It contains Newton's pulpit and some fine stained glass, including a window depicting Cowper and his pet hares.

Every Shrove Tuesday, a pancake race is run between the Market Place and the church, in the course of which the competitors must each toss and catch a pancake three times. The prize is a prayer book and a kiss from the sexton.

OMBERSLEY
HEREFORD AND WORCESTER

4 miles west of Droitwich (page 425 Ec)

Even in a county celebrated for its black-and-white, timber-framed dwellings, the architecture of Ombersley is outstanding. The village street is bordered by a whole medley of buildings in this style, their gables, chimneys, differing roof-lines, and seemingly haphazard frontages together form a scene typical of old Worcestershire.

Particularly notable is the King's Arms pub, partly 15th century and with a 17th-century plaster ceiling. The early-17th-century Dower House, in its leafy setting, is another fine timber-framed dwelling. Near by are two medieval cottages – Cresswells, with a fine twisted chimney, and the Thatched Cottage.

In recent years, Ombersley's character has been saved by the construction of a by-pass. More than 20 of the village buildings have been listed as being of historic or architectural interest.

The parish church of St Andrew, which still has its original box pews, was consecrated in 1829 and serves both the village and the estate of Ombersley Court, built in the early 18th century as the family home of Samuel, Lord Sandys. The mansion, with its impressive pillared portico, stands in landscaped grounds on the edge of the village and is still the residence of the Sandys.

On a grass verge at the centre of the village is a rare 'plague stone' recalling that the Black Death, which reached England in 1348, swept through this part of the county. The trough-like stone, originally placed outside the village, was as close as traders from outside would come. The villagers left money in the stone, often covered with vinegar to disinfect it, and traders left their goods near by.

ORFORD
SUFFOLK

9 miles east of Woodbridge (page 433 Dc)

Daniel Defoe, writing in 1722, said of Orford that is was 'now decayed. The sea daily throws up more land so it is a sea port no longer'. The result, however, has not affected the beauty of the once-thriving port. It is now a quiet village of brick-and-timber buildings, which looks particularly attractive from the roof of its castle, built for Henry II between 1165 and 1167. Orford comes to life in summer, when pleasure craft come up the River Ore from the North Sea to tie up along the breezy quay.

From the quay, the road passes a car park where once the sea lapped. Across the way stands the Jolly Sailor, an inn with numerous secret cupboards hinting at past links with smuggling.

The road continues past a stretch of green, and a line of demure little brick cottages. Further on are sturdier terraces, and an elegant Georgian corner. Near by is the Church of St Bartholomew, parts of which date from 1166.

Market Hill twists up to a square from which every prospect pleases. There is a house in Pump Street with a dominating black gable end with a porthole-style window. On the other side of the square is the Orford Oysterage, with a sign depicting a merman. Ralph of Coggeshall, writing in the 12th century, recorded that Orford fishermen caught a man-like creature in their nets. He was wild, naked and covered in hair. The fishermen handed him over to the governor of the newly built castle. The merman ate anything, raw or cooked, but either he could not or would not talk, even when hung up by his feet

Village pump.

Chinese muff dogs.

ORFORD –
THE VILLAGE THE SEA FORGOT

Cottages as neat and trim as old men-o'-war stand in Orford's Pump Street, reflecting the sturdy character of a village that sent ships and men to fight in Henry V's wars and to challenge the might of the Armada. Orford seamen are found the world over, and one of them, about 100 years ago, brought back three tiny muff dogs from China. Their stuffed remains still astonish visitors to the Jolly Sailor pub. Though the village's associations with the sea are as strong as ever, its port has been diminished by the encroachment of Orford Ness – a great gravel bank that grows by some 15 yds a year.

and tortured. He managed to escape back to the sea, 'and was never afterwards seen'.

When Henry II had his castle built it was revolutionary in design. It is thought to have been the first in England to abandon the traditional square or oblong shape. Instead, it had an irregular, many-sided construction whose confusion of faces was intended to baffle attackers. The ramparts have been reduced to lurching waves of grassy ditch and hummock. But the keep has been perfectly restored and, from its roof, the view over land and sea takes in Havergate Island, a bird sanctuary where avocets now breed after being absent from Britain for 150 years.

OSMOTHERLEY
NORTH YORKSHIRE

6 miles north-east of Northallerton (page 436 Dc)

The 40 mile Lyke Wake Walk starts in Osmotherley and crosses the North York Moors to the coast at Ravenscar – a challenge to the endurance and tenacity of experienced walkers. Those who complete the arduous route within 24 hours can join the Lyke Wake Club, founded in 1955 by a

local farmer, Bill Cowley, who devised the walk.

The 100 mile long Cleveland Way, one of the national long-distance footpaths, also goes through the village, entering by way of a narrow passageway off which there is a Methodist chapel built in 1754. John Wesley, the founder of Methodism, preached there, and also from the cross in the village centre.

Osmotherley lies on a long hill on the far western edge of the North York Moors National Park, and is close to the Hambleton Hills and Cleveland Hills. Its steep main streets – known as North, South and West End – have cobbled pavements and grassy verges lined with trees and flowers. Most of the houses are stone-built and have tiled roofs.

In South End is the village hall, once the old school, built in 1836. One of the houses, number 27, used to be a cobbler's and clogger's, and has the sign of a clog on the upper wall.

In North End there is the old pinfold, or pound, in which stray animals were impounded until their owners paid a fine.

The parish church of St Peter has a Norman doorway, and was extensively renovated and added to in Victorian times.

About 1 mile to the north of Osmotherley is the Lady Chapel of Mount Grace Priory.

ARCHITECTURAL POT-POURRI *One of a long terrace of 18th-century cottages in Overton, Clwyd, all of which possess an odd mixture of both round and pointed brickwork arches. Towards the end of the 18th century a craze for a return to medievalism sometimes led to architects using a curious blending of styles – the round arch having its roots in Classical architecture; the pointed arch in Gothic.*

OVERTON
CLWYD

6 miles south-east of Wrexham (page 429 Cb)

The Hundred of Maelor, of which Overton is the traditional 'capital', is a strip of Wales that juts out between Salop and Cheshire. Until the old Welsh counties were reorganised in 1974, it was a detached part of Flintshire. The yews surrounding the handsome sandstone church in the centre of Overton feature among the 'Seven Wonders of Wales', listed in a traditional Welsh folk rhyme. A particularly ancient yew by the churchyard gate is now supported by baulks of timber.

Overton has several times won awards for the county's best-kept village. The broad High Street sweeps past a pleasant blend of 18th-century buildings with bricks and sandstone enlivened by a magpie dash of black and white. There is a particularly pleasing terrace of cottages near the playing field, where the Wrexham road swings to the left. At the other end of the street, the quaintly titled 'Cocoa and Reading Rooms' are now a bank, library and social club. Most of the traffic between Wrexham and Whitchurch passes well to the north of Overton, but the village bustles into life when point-to-point races are held in neighbouring Bangor-on-Dee.

OXTON
NOTTINGHAMSHIRE

8 miles north-east of Nottingham (page 430 Cd)

Handsome red-brick houses and a Norman church give Oxton a dignified air. It once stood inside the borders of the Royal Forest of Sherwood, when that great woodland spread further than it does today. A stream flows from Oxton Dumble, a tiny wooded hollow to the north-east, and runs past the churchyard, before joining the Dover Beck about half a mile to the south.

The Church of St Peter and St Paul stands near the centre of the village, its entrance overshadowed by a giant yew tree said to be 600 years old.

The Sherbrooke family have been lords of the manor since the early 17th century. Two flags in the church commemorate two members of the family. They are the Battle Ensigns flown by Captain Henry Sherbrooke on his ship, HMS *Tarantula*, during the First World War, and that of his son, Rear Admiral Robert Rupert Sherbrooke, who was awarded the VC in 1942. A note of his citation hangs in the church.

A mile to the north of the village are well-preserved earthworks called Oldox Camp.

OXWICH
WEST GLAMORGAN

11 miles west of Swansea (page 424 Ca)

The village trickles down a narrow, leafy lane to a long sandy beach on the Gower Peninsula. Some of its quaint stone cottages are roofed with thatch, and one, near the post office, bears a slate plaque commemorating the fact that John Wesley, the founder of Methodism, stayed there five times between 1764 and 1771. Another cottage has roses rambling round the door to complete a scene of picture-postcard perfection. Although the village has grown considerably in recent years, its charming old buildings have not been overwhelmed by newcomers. The 12th-century church is dedicated to Illtyd, a Celtic saint, and stands on a rocky ledge in isolation above the sea. The steep, wooded slopes of the headland, which rise immediately behind the church, make a fine setting for the old building. Inside are an ancient font – said to have been brought to the church by its patron saint – and a 14th-century altar-tomb, with effigies of the de la Mare family.

On a hill above the village are the ruins of Oxwich Castle, built as a fortified manor house in 1541 by Sir Rice Mancel.

The village is sheltered from Atlantic winds by Oxwich Point, a long limestone headland with steep flanks covered by ivy-clad trees. In sharp contrast, the land to the east is a reedy wilderness, dappled with pools and known as Oxwich Marsh. The whole area – which is more than 500 acres – is the home of rare birds and plants, and comprises a National Nature Reserve. A Nature Conservancy information centre is open during the holiday months.

Parracombe
DEVON
4 miles south-west of Lynton (page 419 Dc)

Cottages cling to the sides of the valley leading down to this stone village on the western edge of Exmoor. Other colour-washed cottages butt against the narrow road as it reaches the bottom of the hill, where the village inn stands next to the lively little River Heddon – hardly more than a stream in summer, but a torrent in winter.

Parracombe's proudest treasure lies outside the village – the medieval Church of St Petrock. A national protest movement saved St Petrock's from demolition in 1878, when a new church was built in the centre of the village. The interior of the old church has plain white walls, tiers of box pews and a 13th-century chancel.

According to legend, Parracombe was the first place in Devon to have a Christian church, which St Petrock himself built over 1,400 years ago. No trace of it remains, but Parracombe's other link with the past is the prehistoric hill-fort of Holwell Castle just above the village.

RESCUED BY RUSKIN *Among the dwellings that cling to the hillside in Parracombe, Devon, is the village's proudest treasure – the medieval Church of St Petrock, saved from demolition in 1878 by a protest movement, led by John Ruskin, the celebrated art critic. Unlike many country churches, St Petrock's interior escaped the hands of Victorian restorers and has retained its age-old simplicity.*

Parson Drove
CAMBRIDGESHIRE
6 miles west of Wisbech (page 432 Bd)

For centuries, Parson Drove was a centre for the production of woad, the dye with which ancient Britons smeared their bodies. It is fermented from the woad plant, whose bright yellow flowers and blue-green leaves produce the pigment which was also used for dyeing cloth. The industry was killed by the introduction of synthetic indigo in the 1890s, and England's last mobile woad-mill operated in the village until 1914. The woad-making process can be studied in collections of old photographs in Wisbech Museum, 6 miles from the village.

When Samuel Pepys and two relatives stayed at the Swan Inn at Parson Drove, in 1663, someone stole his uncle's horse. The enraged diarist wrote of the village as 'a heathen place', an unkind description of this pleasant community in the Fens. The village lies on a long street, behind both sides of which fields and dykes stretch into the distance. There are churches at either end of the street. St John the Baptist has a 15th-century tower and arcades of seven bays, but may have lost its chancel in a flood in 1613. It is now maintained by the Redundant Churches Fund. Since the mid-1970s most of its functions have been taken over by the Victorian Emmanuel Church, which stands next to the Methodist church.

PARWICH
DERBYSHIRE

5 miles north of Ashbourne (page 430 Bd)

Neat limestone houses and trim-gardened cottages stand beside a pleasant green at Parwich, set remotely among high hills. It is thought that the name Parwich – pronounced 'Parich' – comes from 'dairy on the River Pever', which was probably the original name for the stream running through the village.

Overlooking the humbler dwellings is the imposing Parwich Hall, dating from the middle of the 18th century. It overlooks terraced gardens, which are occasionally open to the public.

The parish church of St Peter, in the centre of the village, was rebuilt in 1873 and incorporates the original Norman doorway and chancel arch. A Norman carving above the doorway depicts the Lamb of God carrying a cross, a stag trampling on two serpents, a bird, a pig and a lion.

PAVENHAM, Bedfordshire (page 426 Bc)
(see Felmersham)

PATRIXBOURNE
KENT

3 miles south-east of Canterbury (page 423 Fc)

A group of 19th-century cottages, built for the tenants of a now-vanished estate, forms the heart of this small village. The seat of the estate, a mansion called Bifrons, has been demolished and its parkland turned over to farming. The cottages standing by the east boundary of the old park were erected by the manorial family of the time, the Conynghams, who had them designed in Tudor style. They have projecting gables, with ornately carved timbers supported by the figures of elephants, lions and other heraldic devices. The timber still looks fresh and bold.

The small church, dedicated to St Mary, is late Norman, and is built of flint and Caen stone imported from Normandy. It has a circular 'wheel window' on its east end and some exquisite carvings around its south door. Much of its stained glass is Swiss, and dates from the 16th and 17th centuries.

The first part of the village's name is taken from a Norman manorial lord, William Patricius. A manorial court was held in the village until the early 20th century.

Beside Patrixbourne runs the Nail Bourne stream, leading down from the east Kent chalk plateau towards the River Stour. It is sometimes dry for several years, and then rises suddenly to cause local flooding. The flowing of the stream is traditionally regarded locally as an omen of disaster, though there is a perfectly adequate scientific explanation: a bedrock of chalk soaks up rainwater like a sponge until it is saturated, at which point the stream begins to flow.

PEASEMORE, Berkshire (page 426 Aa)
(see page 216)

PEBWORTH
HEREFORD AND WORCESTER

6 miles north-east of Evesham (page 425 Fb)

Time has hardly touched Pebworth's Friday Street, and if Shakespeare strolled down it today, as he used to when he lived at nearby Stratford-upon-Avon, he would have little difficulty recognising it. The half-timbered cottages standing there now are the same ones he knew, many of them still trimly thatched and set in colourful country gardens. And if anyone asked him he might be able to explain how the village got its nickname – Piping Pebworth. Is it true, as people say, that after getting drunk at Bidford-on-Avon, just over the border into Warwickshire, he slept the night under a crab-apple tree; and next morning, waking up with a hangover and vowing never to drink in Bidford again, he composed the uncharacteristic jingle which keeps the nickname alive, as well as those of several other nearby villages?

> *Piping Pebworth, Dancing Marston, Haunted Hillborough, Hungry Grafton, Dodging Exhall, Papist Wixford, Beggarly Broom and Drunken Bidford.*

The village owes its proper name to an early Saxon landowner called Pybba. It is built in a figure-of-eight on a hill, and the mixture of red brick and Cotswold stone shows how close it lies to Warwickshire and Gloucestershire. The Church of St Peter, with its 15th-century battlemented tower, crowns the hill; halfway down, bordering one of the lanes, is the stone-built village store and post office; still further down, near the Mason's Arms, is Friday Street. Round about, among their more modest neighbours, are the large country houses which lend character to the village – mellow brick farm buildings which serve as a reminder of Pebworth's traditional association with the land.

PEMBRIDGE
HEREFORD AND WORCESTER

6 miles east of Kington (page 425 Dc)

Half-timbered cottages and inns, jumbled round a medieval market place make Pembridge an oasis of old English grace.

The open market hall, with its stone-tiled roof supported by eight oak pillars, dates from the early 1500s and once had a second storey. It shares the triangular market place with the rambling New Inn – also known locally as 'the inn without a name'. Founded in 1311, it was enlarged with matching gabled wings in the 17th century. Two ghosts are said to haunt the inn: one of a girl who appears only to women, the other of a red-coated soldier armed with a sword. Another old inn, the Greyhound, is a short walk east past the post office. It has stood, its overhanging upper storey supported by carved timber brackets, since early in the 16th century.

Old stone steps lead from the market place up to a knoll and the Church of St Mary. It is thought to have been built between 1320 and 1360, replacing an even earlier Norman church. Its most remarkable feature is the detached, pagoda-like bell-house. Mighty timbers, bracing one another in criss-cross fashion inside stone walls, relate to a Scandinavian building method adopted in East Anglia but surprising on the Welsh Marches. The walls are slitted with embrasures through which bowmen could fire, indicating that the belfry also served as a stronghold during border skirmishes. In the church itself, the west door is bullet-scarred from a Civil War attack.

Opposite Ye Olde Steppes, where Bridge Street starts north towards the River Arrow, are Duppa's Almshouses. Four remain from the six built in the 1660s. Another row of six almshouses, Trafford's, is at the eastern end of the village and dates from 1686. Glan Arrow Cottages, near the river, were built in the 1500s, and the row of three houses now known as Bridge House, beside the riverbank footpath, has a 14th-century hall.

WHERE THE MOUNTAINS BEGIN *Close to the Welsh border the village of Pembridge huddles below its church, and from its trim churchyard the view is much the same as it was in medieval times. Then, anxious villagers scanned the Welsh Marches for signs of border raiders. Now it is a view that attracts artists to this peaceful and unspoiled corner of England, and visitors from across the border shop in the black-and-white gabled grocer's shop or drink in the red-roofed Red Lion.*

PEN-CLAWDD
WEST GLAMORGAN

7 miles west of Swansea (page 424 Ca)

Broad, flat marshes on the Loughor Estuary provide Pen-clawdd with its basic livelihood – cockles. The cockle-women jog out over the marshes at low tide, riding on flat, horse-drawn carts. Forks, sieves and other implements are as traditional as the transport, although some carts have given way to modern transport. The daily harvest, unwillingly shared with wheeling hosts of seabirds, is taken to Swansea for sale. Traditional dishes include cockles fried in oatmeal with cloves and bacon or ham.

Pen-clawdd's neatly terraced cottages line one side of the village's lengthy main street, Beach Road, looking out over a wilderness of tidal creeks, marshland and salty turf grazed by sheep and sturdy Gower ponies. The view, bright with boats in summer, is more like East Anglia than South Wales.

Spreading inland, Pen-clawdd climbs steep slopes, clad with gorse and bracken, that rise to 340 ft in less than half a mile. Short walks lead to Pen-y-gaer, the site of an Iron Age fort with splendid views over the estuary and seawards past Whitford Point to Carmarthen Bay.

The village is dominated by two huge chapels, one built in 1911 and the other in 1912.

PENMACHNO
GWYNEDD

4 miles south of Betws-y-coed (page 429 Bc)

An old bridge over the River Machno links the two parts of the village, swinging the narrow road right and left before it climbs on to a lonely, lake-dappled expanse of windswept moorland, where it climbs to nearly 1,600 ft.

In the centre of the village, a large chapel, built in 1867, contrasts with the stone cottages built for quarrymen before slate ceased to be profitable. The church, on the opposite side of the street, is notable for having the oldest Christian gravestones in Wales. They date from the late 5th or early 6th centuries. A window commemorates William Morgan, Bishop of St Asaph, the scholar who first translated the Bible into Welsh in 1588. Morgan's birthplace, Ty Mawr, stands to the north-west of Penmachno. It is owned by the National Trust, and is reached by a scenic road through the Gwydyr Forest.

PENN
BUCKINGHAMSHIRE

3 miles north-west of Beaconsfield (page 426 Ba)

High on a ridge of the Chilterns stands the village from which a celebrated Buckinghamshire family took its name. It was the home of the ancestors, and some of the descendants, of William Penn, the Quaker who in 1682 founded Pennsylvania in America.

The village green is a broad triangle with a pond at one corner. Around the green stand 17th-century cottages; near Holy Trinity Church is the gabled and creeper-clad Crown Inn. The church has a 14th-century tower from which, the villagers claim, can be seen 12 counties. There are memorials in the south aisle to the Penn family; their portraits are engraved in brass plates set in the floor. A Norman font, a 12th-century stone coffin and a magnificent 14th century nave roof are among the church treasures. But pride of place goes to a medieval painting of The Last Judgment, which hangs over the chancel arch.

PENNAN
GRAMPIAN

10 miles east of Banff (page 443 Ge)

Fishing has long been the business of Pennan, and a few fishing boats still operate from the tiny harbour which is set below cliffs overlooking the Moray Firth.

The village, which fronts the harbour, is approached by a steep hairpin bend in the red-sandstone cliffs between Pennan Head and Troup Head. It is one of the few safe landing places for boats for miles along the rocky, north-facing coast. Even so, smugglers operating in the 18th and 19th centuries preferred to risk their boats to

store cargoes in the deep caves cut into the cliffs. One such place is Quinan Cave, to the east around Pennan Head, which has a socket in the roof from which the smugglers hung their lanterns.

Pennan harbour was originally built in the middle of the 18th century, but within 40 years the sea had caused heavy damage. Its replacement lasted little longer, and was superseded by the present harbour, built between 1810 and 1910.

PENSHURST
KENT

5 miles west of Tonbridge (page 423 Eb)

Approached from the east, the view of Penshurst is idyllic. It lies in fertile farmland near the junction of the rivers Eden and Medway. From Rogues Hill, down which the road descends to the village, the pinnacles of the church tower rise above a cluster of cottage rooftops. Lower down the hill, the towers and battlements of Penshurst Place, a 14th-century manor house with an Elizabethan front, come into view. As Rogues Hill slopes down, it passes a charming group of almshouses. At the other end of the village, a garage now occupies a forge, which was built in 1911 with an enormous horseshoe-shaped door and ornate symbols of hammer and spikes on its gable.

In Leicester Square – the original Leicester Square, named after a favourite of Elizabeth I – two half-timbered cottages are bridged by a cottage which is raised on posts, forming a sort

VICTORIAN MEDIEVALISM *The entrance to Penshurst's parish churchyard is through an open-ended square, flanked by 19th-century half-timbered cottages – an unashamed evocation of the past.*

of archway entrance into the churchyard. Near by is the post office, built by the architect George Devey in 1850. The church is of sandstone, with parts dating to the 13th century and extensive 19th-century reconstruction. It contains some impressive memorials to the Sidney family, who have owned Penshurst Place since Edward VI gave it to Sir William Sidney in the 16th century.

A footpath leads through the churchyard past Penshurst Place and its park. Within stone walls and towers that were enlarged in the 15th century and reconstructed in the 19th century stands the well-preserved great hall which was built by Sir John de Pulteney, a rich merchant who was Lord Mayor of London four times between 1331 and 1337.

Sir Philip Sidney, soldier, courtier, statesman and poet, was born at Penshurst in 1554. He won imperishable fame 32 years later at the Battle of Zutphen in Holland when, mortally wounded, he refused a drink of water and passed his flask instead to a wounded soldier, with the words: 'Thy necessity is yet greater than mine.' The present owner is his descendant, Viscount De L'Isle, VC.

The state rooms and picture gallery contain china, silver and portraits, and there is also a toy museum. The house and its formal gardens, which were laid out in the 1850s, are open to the public daily from April until October.

PIDDINGHOE
EAST SUSSEX
1 mile north-west of Newhaven (page 423 Db)

A flint-walled, winding street connects the buildings of this small village on the west bank of the River Ouse near Newhaven. Along the twisting route of the street, among more modern dwellings, are many old buildings including what used to be the forge and a former malthouse. The Royal Oak Inn has some anglers' bric-à-brac.

Two small greens, with flint cottages grouped around them, lie on either side of St John's Church, which is also built of flint and has one of the only three Norman round towers in Sussex. The tower, dating from the 12th century, is topped by a shingled spire with a golden fish-shaped weather-vane. Kipling called this a 'begilded dolphin', but local anglers regard it as a sea-trout.

The quayside, below the church, was used for unloading cargo until well into the 20th century, but it is now used by pleasure craft.

TELSCOMBE The attraction of Telscombe, 2 miles west of Piddinghoe, lies more in its secluded atmosphere than in any particular building. High flint walls surround most of the houses. The village, which has barely 40 inhabitants, is to a large extent in the possession of the National Trust. Trust properties include the Manor House with its sheltered gardens and a neo-Saxon tower. The church, built of local flint and Caen stone from Normandy, is a simple part-Norman structure.

PITCAIRNGREEN
TAYSIDE
4 miles north-west of Perth (page 443 Fb)

Trees shade the semi-circular green in the heart of the village, surrounded by houses, cottages and the inn. A garden nursery is beside the green, and near by are raspberry fields and rolling arable land. Beyond these stretch the wooded estates of Redgorton parish.

Pitcairngreen is set near the River Almond, which, in the 18th century, was harnessed to power textile mills. A local nobleman, Lord Lynedoch, created the village to house the mill workers, setting it on the slopes above the fertile Almond Valley.

The mills were abandoned by the end of the 19th century and the valley was later taken over by naval depots and workshops. However, Pitcairngreen is well away from recent industrial developments, and lies in a fold of rich farming country. To the north-east is a prehistoric burial cairn – some 100 ft in diameter and 13 ft high – made of boulders taken from the River Almond.

PLESHEY
ESSEX
6 miles north-west of Chelmsford (page 432 Cb)

The sight of the great mound on which Pleshey Castle once stood takes the breath away. It is first glimpsed between the pink-washed walls and thatched roofs of a row of cottages. Then, at the end of the row, suddenly there it is: the astonishing upsurge of turf, 60 ft high and 900 ft around, on which Geoffrey de Mandeville built a castle a few years after the Norman Conquest.

He may well have reshaped a prehistoric tumulus to his purpose, adding a moat, now inhabited by ducks and moorhens, and an inner bailey that stood on another 2 acre enclosure to the south. At any rate, the castle he built was so important that it remained the home of successive Lords High Constable of England for more than 200 years. It later passed into the possession of Thomas, Duke of Gloucester – Richard II's uncle – who, in fulfilment of a vow, built a College of Canons at Pleshey. The faint outline of the building can still be seen, at the end of dry summers, near the church.

In 1397, Richard, suspecting treachery, had Thomas kidnapped and murdered. The widowed duchess, according to Shakespeare, was left to mourn among 'empty lodgings and unfurnished walls, unpeopled offices, untrodden stones'. Now, even these have gone. The only building that remains above ground is the magnificent 15th-century bridge of red brick that connects the mound with the inner bailey. It survives through the rather touching generosity of Queen Elizabeth's Commissioners, who in 1558 discovered that the villagers of Pleshey were keeping rabbits in the castle ruins. Since the bridge was the only means of access to the animals, it was decided not to pull it down.

313

PLOCKTON
HIGHLAND

5 miles north-east of Kyle of Lochalsh (page 443 Cd)

Several landlords have been responsible for the layout and appearance of the fishing and crofting village of Plockton. Hugh Innes, who made his fortune as a sugar planter in the West Indies, bought the tiny village in 1801, evicted most of the tenants, reducing many to a state of abject poverty, and rented out the hill grazings for sheep farming. He planned a settlement of 280 houses, but only the lower part of the village, by a small inlet of Loch Carron, was built. Today, a tree-lined croft road marks the site of what were to have been Allan Street, Graham Street and Glasgow Street.

Innes died in 1831, and Plockton was inherited by his grand-niece, the wife of a wealthy Englishman called Isaac Lillingston. The Lillingstons helped the local men to build boats for inshore herring fishing, and trading sloops to sail down the west coast to Greenock and Glasgow.

A government-financed Relief Committee rebuilt the harbour wall, fenced the arable land above Plockton, and repaired the stone houses. When Lillingston died in 1850 the area was bought by the wealthy merchant Sir Alexander Matheson, who built Duncraig Castle on a rocky ledge above the south shore of Loch Carron. The castle is now a school.

After the First World War another rich merchant, Sir Daniel Hamilton, bought Plockton and the western part of Lochalsh. He repaired many of the houses and opened up pathways through the glorious hill and forest country from Loch Carron south to Loch Alsh. In 1946, Sir Daniel gave Plockton and much of the surrounding district to the National Trust for Scotland.

◆

OASIS IN THE NORTH *Lush, green Plockton lies among a wild array of islands, headlands, crags and mountains, yet is so blessed by its sheltered position – and a wandering arm of the Gulf Stream – that palm trees grow in its gardens. All these features and an abundance of wildlife, make the place especially attractive to painters, a number of whom live in the cottages strung round the fine natural harbour. This was once a haven for Baltic schooners and for the hardy Hebridean fishermen who thought nothing of rowing 70 miles across the Minch to Stornoway. But nowadays its waters seldom contain anything other than yachts. These reflect Plockton's chief occupation as a quietly prosperous summer resort – a far cry from its destitute years following the 19th-century Clearances.*

The VILLAGE AT WORK

Four-hundred miles, and totally different life styles, separate the Scottish fishing village of Whitehills from the Oxfordshire community of Ardington. One confronts the Moray Firth, the other lies within the seductive orbit of London. Yet they share the common quality of remaining thriving, independent communities, each with its separate identity, in an age when many villages are in decline.

WHITEHILLS

In Whitehills, 40 miles north-west of Aberdeen, the saying has for long been that 'when the fishing is good, everything is good'. It is still true, though only about 115 of the village's 1,200 inhabitants now earn their living on the grey waters of the North Sea.

The once-numerous fleets along the coast have nearly all vanished, their work now concentrated on a handful of bigger ports. But the Whitehills men continue to put to sea in anything short of a hurricane. The *Unison, Co-Worker, Felicity, Halcyon, Beryl* and the rest land as much as £30,000 worth of white fish – cod, haddock, plaice and related species – in a good week. Womenfolk gut and fillet the fish in harbour-side sheds. Other Whitehills men transport the fish to market.

Whitehills, alone among its neighbours, has survived as a fishing community by making change its ally.

A critical point in its fortunes came with the switch from line fishing to seine (net) fishing in the 1920s. Until then, a four-man boat trailed as many as 2,000 hooks, each hook baited with mussels collected laboriously by women and children of the village.

Seine fishing resulted in bigger catches than line fishing for less labour. But neighbouring villages, which did not make the change, no longer have a fishing fleet.

Wisely, the Whitehills men refused to be lured by the big money in herring in the 1960s, preferring to stick to white fish and their traditional hunting grounds in the Moray Firth. When herring became overfished, the Whitehills boats still prospered.

'There has always been fresh fish for sale on the quay at Whitehills,' says Bill Lovie, a member of one of the village's principal fishing clans.

But maintaining that tradition is no longer easy. A boat costs around £200,000, compared with £25,000 only a few years ago. Capital investment of this order means that more and more of the boats are owned not by partnerships of independent local fishermen, but by one or other of the two big firms that buy the catches.

Because modern fishing techniques need fewer men, the village has had to diversify in order to survive. Some people have jobs in Banff, 3 miles away, and nearly 100 work at the local mental hospital.

Some cottages have been sold or let to people from as far away as Edinburgh – 150 miles south – who want weekend homes. Beyond the headland east of the village is a site occupied by nearly 100 caravans – a source of local contention.

The village has lost some services, too. It still has eight small shops but the chemist, the two tailors, the shoemaker, the blacksmith, four of the five bakers and two of the three butchers have gone. Dr Beeching closed the railway station, but the village still has a good bus service.

Air of prosperity

In spite of all, the air of prosperity is unmistakable. In an exceptionally good year a fishing-boat crew member can earn as much as £10,000, though the average is lower. Most households run a car, so that only the old and the young depend entirely on public transport.

But success breeds its own problems. The village minister notes that the community's tradition of co-operation has been at least partly eroded by increased competition and overconfidence. The change is especially evident in the men's attitude to the dangers of the sea, and there is a feeling that the sea's toll today is higher than it need be when every Whitehills boat carries radar, sonar and wireless.

Death is always a fact of life in a fishing village, just as in a mining community. Down by the lower harbour is a plaque: 'Erected 1858 after the great loss of life on this coast.'

Though most of the fishermen have difficulty in recalling the year in which particular comrades were lost, they can remember the date and the day of the week with the precision

Whitehills, on Scotland's Moray Firth coast, is at once a modern and yet a traditional village. Because its fishermen have taken advantage of the most up-to-date fishing techniques, the community has succeeded in surviving changes that have killed its neighbours.

For the young, a landing of crab has a perennial fascination.

Supporting the fishermen who risk the dangers of the sea are those, including the women of the village, who clean, prepare and pack the fish. Other Whitehills men then drive the lorries which take the catch to market.

of personal grief, even when the tragedy is 40 years old.

But now needless risks are taken. As Bill Lovie puts it: 'Nowadays the boats carry only one man on watch. There always used to be two – watch-ing the sky . . . If the barometer fell they wouldn't go. But today they go anyway. Gale force, and still they go . . .'

Bill Lovie's wife is glad her three sons are not at sea, but she knows there is little she could have done to stop them if they had felt the urge. 'Many of the youngsters seem born to it, especially if their fathers were fishermen before them.'

One such father is Simpson Brown. He gave up the sea

when his son James was lost overboard from the boat *Diligence* in the autumn of 1968. James's one ambition when he left school was to follow his father to the fishing grounds. He started as boat's cook but begged for a chance, soon granted, to serve on deck. As the vessel was heading for port 'a lump of sea' struck it by surprise and 18-year-old James was carried away.

ARDINGTON

There is no place for such perils in the folk memories of Ardington, and its satellite hamlets of East and West Lockinge, 3 miles east of Wantage in what is now part of Oxfordshire.

Though much older in origin, Ardington is essentially the creation of Lord Wantage, a mid-19th-century banker-turned-country-gentleman. Its cottages – wonders of convenience in their day – were mostly built by him. They have since been modernised by the Lockinge Estate which he founded, and which maintains his tradition of paternal benevolence to employees, tenants and their families and pensioners.

Gerald Skidmore, now retired, used to be in charge of the estate's shire horses. There were still 12 of them as late as the 1940s. In 1895 the estate (apart from outlying tenant farms) consisted of some 1,300 acres. Today, it is down to what used to be the home farm.

The village population has declined in parallel. The 1871 census showed 851 people in Ardington and the Lockinges. In 1971 there were 469. But the estate is still the predominant social and economic influence in the village, even though only a score or so of households are directly dependent on it for their daily bread.

In the 1930s the estate automatically offered a job to every boy leaving school. Not any more. Now some work at the Atomic Energy Authority establishment in Harwell, others at the Didcot power station. Shops and offices in Wantage employ others.

But rather than see the old community dissipated, the estate has an active policy of creating new jobs in the village. A flavour chemist has his factory in the building which Lord Wantage put up to house a pioneer co-operative store. A plastics firm occupies the former blacksmith's and farrier's

No longer a village of shire horses and quiet lanes, Ardington has nevertheless been kept alive as a busy working community – rather than a dormitory – despite its proximity to London. The initiative of the local estate owner has ensured that when traditional jobs ran down, new trades were attracted.

Modern machines have given rise to a new type of farmer who has to be a technician as well as a man of the soil.

No longer does the farmer work from dawn to dusk. During harvest-time at least, he often works round the clock, using the combine harvester's powerful headlights to keep ahead of any change in the weather.

sheds. There is a pottery in the dairy, and two craftsmen make and repair rush-bottomed chairs in what was the grain-dressing shed. In the former watermill, another craftsman now makes oak and mahogany furniture to order.

Other buildings, which date from nearly a century ago when the estate was virtually self-sufficient, house an upholsterer, a vehicle paint and spray shop and a small firm which repairs vintage cars.

These enterprises have brought new life to the village. The buildings made available by the estate have been an obvious attraction, while the Council for Small Industries in Rural Areas has helped with technical and financial aid. The

craftsmen work and often live in the place, and so form part of its community. In this way, Ardington has escaped the fate of many similar villages near to large towns which have simply become dormitory settlements for commuters.

The newcomers' biggest impact has been on the village primary school. Five years ago it was down to 20 pupils and the Oxfordshire authority was threatening to close it. That spotlighted the way in which the village was becoming imbalanced, with too many old people and no new generation coming along. This was when the estate's present owner, Christopher Loyd, and his manager, John Haig, decided that something had to be done to

keep the community alive and so launched the present small-scale industrial revolution to provide new jobs for the people of the village.

Already the newcomers' children have pushed the school roll up to 26, and it seems a safe bet that the sound of children at play will remain part of the village's life for a good many years to come.

In their quiet way, under the downs that loom to the south of the village, the folk of Ardington are adapting and surviving as successfully as their more rugged counterparts in Whitehills.

PLUCKLEY
KENT

6 miles west of Ashford (page 423 Eb)

Narrow, round-arched windows, framed by white-painted brick, are found on nearly every building in Pluckley. These are the 'lucky' Dering windows, so called because, according to legend, a Royalist member of the local Dering family escaped through such a window from Parliamentarians during the Civil War. In many cases, the brick façades, constructed on the orders of Sir Edward Cholmeley Dering at the end of the 19th century, enclose older, timber-framed houses.

Brick cottages, with shops, a school and an inn, form a small square in front of the church in the village centre on the edge of a ridge near Ashford. The church, begun in the 13th century, is built of ragstone with a timber roof. It contains a 16th-century timber screen. Hop gardens stand close by the churchyard.

The Derings left more behind them than the marked style of the windows, for Pluckley has the reputation of being one of the most haunted villages in England, and the ghosts include members of the Dering family. The Red Lady Dering still looks for a lost child in the churchyard. The White Lady Dering haunts the burned-out ruin of Surrenden-Dering manor. Other ghosts include a pipe-smoking gipsy who burned herself to death, and a brick-worker who fell into a pit.

POLPERRO
CORNWALL

3 miles south-west of Looe (page 418 Cb)

The road into Polperro winds through a grassy valley which gradually deepens to become an almost sheer ravine. Small white and cream houses cling to its sides. Others line the River Pol which runs through the village. And around the wide harbour, cottages line the water's edge.

Polperro has a few plain though elegant Georgian houses, but many of its cottages are oddly shaped, as if designed to fit into the confined space. The House on Props is supported on wooden stilts and overhangs the brook. Among the cottages run streets and alleys too narrow for cars in places, and during the summer months motor traffic is banned from the village.

The oldest house in the village dates from the 16th century and stands by a Saxon bridge over the Pol. In the 19th century it was the home of Jonathan Couch, the village doctor, naturalist and author of a *History of Polperro*. His grandson was Sir Arthur Quiller-Couch, the novelist and poet who wrote under the pseudonym 'Q'. John Wesley, the Methodist preacher, went to Polperro twice while on preaching tours, and in 1760 stayed at the Old Market House on Big Green.

Like most Cornish villages Polperro has a history of smuggling, and there is a Museum of Smuggling in Talland Street, but its legal trade has always been fishing. In the 1850s, two-thirds of the villagers were engaged in fishing, and pilchards were the staple catch. The harbour is still busy, but in the summer most of the boats carry holidaymakers in search of mackerel. At low tide the harbour makes a fine amphitheatre for Polperro Fishermen's Choir, which regularly sings on the quayside in summer.

A MARTYR TO QUAINTNESS *The best time to see Polperro is in winter, for then the crowds that boil and seethe in its steep summer streets have departed, permitting the bones of the tough old fishing village to show through. But neither the motorists nor the artists who 'discover' the place can be entirely blamed, since the charm of its piled-up old cottages is undeniable. Each has its own character, like the Shell House, in the Warren, once the home of a fisherman who enclosed the whole of its front with seashells.*

POLSTEAD
SUFFOLK

4 miles south-west of Hadleigh (page 432 Cb)

Murder most foul made Polstead headline news more than 150 years ago, and it has remained famous as the scene of a crime that shocked and horrified the nation – the Red Barn Murder. It was there that 26-year-old Maria Marten, whose thatched cottage still stands in Marten's Lane, to the south-east of the village, was shot and stabbed to death by William Corder and her body buried in the Red Barn.

It was thought that Maria had eloped with Corder, by whom she had had an illegitimate child that died when it was two months old – some said by poison. But her stepmother dreamed three times that she had been murdered and buried in the barn. At her insistence, her husband went to the barn and dug at the spot indicated in the dreams and found his daughter's body.

A search was then made for Corder and he was found living in Middlesex, married to a woman who had met him through a matrimonial advertisement. He was convicted of murder and hanged at Bury St Edmunds in August 1828, and an account of the trial, wrapped in Corder's own skin, is preserved, together with his skull, in Bury's Moyses Hall Museum in the Butter Market.

Apart from Maria's cottage, only one other relic of the crime remains in Polstead, the farm where Corder lived in the centre of the village, which is now called Corder's Farm. The Red Barn burned down mysteriously shortly after the murder, and Maria's tombstone in the churchyard was so chipped away by souvenir hunters that the exact location is not known. A sign marks the approximate spot.

Every road into Polstead winds among cherry orchards thick with blossom in May, and the 'Polstead Black' cherry is claimed to be unsurpassed. Clusters of thatched and colour-washed cottages border the lanes, and huddle closer together around the green at the top of Polstead Hill. At the bottom of the hill is Polstead Pond, a broad stretch of water fringed with overhanging trees, and on a rise opposite the Georgian Polstead Hall stands the Church of St Mary. It dates from the 12th century and has brick-built arches and windows. The bricks are thought to be English and the oldest-surviving examples of their kind.

In the grounds of Polstead Hall, beside the churchyard, a small oak tree grows alongside the remains of the Gospel Oak, an ancient tree which was believed to be more than 1,300 years old when it collapsed in 1953. The spot may have been sacred in pagan times.

PORLOCK
SOMERSET

5 miles west of Minehead (page 420 Ab)

A series of hairpin bends and a 1-in-4 gradient make Porlock Hill a spectacular road down into Porlock village. Small, whitewashed houses with tall chimneys crowd in on the narrow, twisting main street, their gardens glowing with fuchsias, roses and creepers. Perhaps even more attractive are neighbouring West Porlock and Porlock Weir, 1 mile and 1½ miles down the road leading north-westwards out of the village. Both hamlets lie under the shoulder of a huge wooded hill which skirts the coast for several miles.

Porlock merits an unhurried visit, being surrounded by romantic countryside and other more remote hamlets, with many pathways to delight the explorer on foot. One fascinating walk is along a path going west from Porlock Weir. The path leads for some 2 miles along a ledge, through dense woods at the edge of the sea, to the 35 ft long Church of St Culbone – claimed to be the smallest medieval church in England – which has stood since Norman times. Porlock's own parish church of St Dubricius dates mainly from the 13th century, although it does have a fragment of a Saxon cross fixed to the west wall of the nave. In the 14th-century arcade is the alabaster effigy of a knight who fought alongside Henry V in France in 1417 – John Harington. He lies beside his wife on a superb table tomb, his hands clasped in prayer over his badge, and his head supported by angels.

HIGH AND DRY *The tiny harbour of Porlock Weir, with its snug, whitewashed cottages, lies below the hillside village of Porlock. At low tide, the boats in the haven are left stranded.*

At the east of the village is the 15th-century Dovery Court, now a museum and information centre. A mile along a minor road to the north-east is Bossington, another attractive village of thatched cottages.

PORT ISAAC
CORNWALL

5 miles north of Wadebridge (page 418 Cb)

White-painted and slate-hung cottages stand in tiers above the harbour of Port Isaac, and are interlaced with narrow passages called 'drangs', one of which is known as 'Squeeze-Belly Alley'.

A stream runs down through the village to the harbour where fishing boats unload their catches of lobsters and crabs. Long, stone-built fish cellars stand by the harbour, and close to it is the old Golden Lion Inn.

There is magnificent cliff scenery, with two picturesque havens just along the coast – Port Gaverne to the east, and Port Quin to the west. Port Gaverne has a small, shingle beach. In the 19th century, slate from the Delabole Quarry was loaded there by men and women who passed it hand to hand across the beach to the sailing ships. The quarry, 500 ft deep and 1½ miles round, is the deepest in England.

Port Quin was a 'dead' village for many years, due, it is said, to its only fishing vessel, manned by the entire male population, being lost at sea towards the end of the last century.

PORT-EYNON
WEST GLAMORGAN

13 miles west of Swansea (page 424 Ba)

Along the Gower Peninsula the road from Swansea comes to a sudden end in the dunes backing Port-Eynon's sandy beach. The road runs steeply down to the shore through a snug little village of whitewashed houses. To the west, spectacular limestone cliffs tower 200 ft above the sea, and there is a magnificent walk to the Worms Head peninsula and Rhossili.

Port-Eynon nurses tragic memories of the sea's fickle temper. In a corner of the churchyard, where old headstones mark the graves of many mariners, is a striking white statue of a lifeboat-man, erected as a memorial to three members of the local lifeboat crew who lost their lives in 1916 while trying to reach a ship in distress. The village no longer has a lifeboat, and the old lifeboat house at the west end of the bay is now a Youth Hostel. In front of the hostel are the old oyster pools, all that remains of a once-thriving oyster-dredging industry.

Many stories and theories surround Culver Hole, a short walk from the village round the headland. This great cleft in the cliffs has been sealed with a wall of rough masonry, pierced with openings 7 ft high by 3 ft wide. It may have been a smugglers' lookout post, or possibly a columbarium where pigeons were bred for food.

PORTMAHOMACK
HIGHLAND

At south-east end of Dornoch Firth (page 443 Ee)

In 1800 the only buildings at Portmahomack, on the coast of Easter Ross, were Tarbat parish church, three houses and two granaries.

The present village looks out over the Dornoch Firth to the mountains of Sutherland. It grew up as a fishing centre after the original harbour was improved to Thomas Telford's plans in the first half of the 19th century. Although the harbour is now visited mainly by holiday sailors and sea-anglers, the curving line of cottages beside the shore is still a typical fishing-village layout.

The parish church, on a hill at the south end of the village, is no longer used for regular worship. Below the church, just above the beach, is the Free Church, a striking building in 19th-century style.

The peninsula on which Portmahomack stands is well-farmed land. At the northern tip is the slim tower of Tarbat Ness lighthouse, built in 1830, altered in 1892 and one of the highest in Britain.

PORTMEIRION
GWYNEDD

2 miles south-east of Porthmadog (page 428 Bb)

A grandmother strolling through Portmeirion one blossom-scented summer evening was inspired to remark: 'My goodness, if I had ever honeymooned here I would have wanted at least two husbands!' Of all the visitors who have marvelled at this dream village – including members of the royal family – she remained a favourite of the man whose dream it was: the architect Sir Clough Williams-Ellis. For he, too, was inspired by love – his love for the sunny Mediterranean fishing village of Portofino, which he discovered while exploring Italy as a young man. Its 'gay rococo architecture backed by hanging woodlands' captivated him totally, and he returned home determined to create something equally enchanting in Britain.

The result is Portmeirion, an extraordinary masterpiece-cum-folly, a tasteful extravaganza of romantic buildings, exotic plants and warm Mediterranean colours set against the brooding grandeur of Snowdonia.

He spent several years combing more than two-dozen possible sites scattered between the Hebrides and Scillies, and had almost abandoned hope when, in 1925, an uncle asked him to find a tenant or buyer for a craggy, thickly wooded little peninsula in the sandy estuary between Porthmadog and Harlech. It was only 4 miles from Plas Brondanw, where his family had lived since the 16th century, but had been leased for years to an eccentric old lady who allowed the grounds to become so overgrown that, when she died, a path had to be hacked through the jungle so that the hearse could reach the house. 'Directly I got inside the perimeter wall I knew my search

was over,' Sir Clough recalled some time later.

He wanted to prove that a beautiful natural site could be developed without being spoiled and that architectural good manners could also mean good business. Portmeirion was a commercial venture and day-visitors are still charged an entry fee. In the past, notable visitors have included Edward VIII, when he was Prince of Wales, H. G. Wells, David Lloyd George, Bertrand Russell, King Zog of Albania, George Bernard Shaw, John Steinbeck, Thor Heyerdahl – and Frank Lloyd Wright, founding father of modern architecture, who 'took it all without a blink'. Noël Coward wrote his comedy *Blithe Spirit* there.

Above the main hotel, facing south for shelter and sunshine, is the great natural amphitheatre where Sir Clough created his colourful, richly detailed masterpiece from the tangled thickets.

A visitor entering the village through a tunnel at the southern end of Bridge House is stunned by a vision so unexpected and magical that it is tempting to reach out and touch the nearest pastel-shaded wall. The tall, elegant campanile, bells tinkling in the breeze, soars above the cobbled Battery Square with its shrubs, bow windows, shutters, weather-boarding, balconies and murals. The terrace of the green-domed Pantheon looks out over rooftops of mellow, red tiles that blend easily into a vista of paths, lawns, shrubs, flower beds and fish-filled pools.

Many buildings are pure Sir Clough. Others, like the 17th-century Town Hall, whose ceiling depicts the life and labours of Hercules, were rescued from demolition elsewhere, taken to Portmeirion stone by stone and carefully restored to their former glory. Sir Clough spent more than half a century collecting them for his 'Home for Fallen Buildings', as he dubbed the village.

Portmeirion's peninsula is surrounded by uncrowded beaches. Inland, miles of tranquil footpaths and bridleways explore the estate between banks of rhododendrons, mimosa, camellia, eucalyptus and palm trees.

Portmeirion was seen by millions of viewers as the setting for *The Prisoner* television serial. Any fears Sir Clough may have had for the future of his life's work were removed in 1971, when the buildings were designated as being of historical and architectural interest. He was knighted the following year – 'in time for it to look nice on my headstone,' he quipped. He lived until 1978, dying after 94 richly filled years.

LITTLE ITALY BY THE SEA *The Gloriette, an ornate and pastel-* ▷ *hued folly built out of architectural oddments, is typical of the wedding-cake buildings of Portmeirion – the Italianate village which Sir Clough Williams-Ellis created in North Wales. He concentrated the cottages, shops, reconstructions and monuments in and around the terraced gardens which cover the valley above Traeth Bach. Bubbling over with Welsh whimsy, he gave his creations names which fitted their fantastic appearance or function – from the Triumphal Arch, to the Dome, to the Cloth Hall, to the Ship Shop. He also acquired numerous 'eye-traps', including a colonnade from Bristol, a brewery clock and an abandoned ballroom. Timbers from HMS* Arethusa – *a 19th-century man-of-war broken up in 1933 – he incorporated into the hotel smoking-room. So Sir Clough staged what he rightly called 'a lighthearted "live" exhibition of architecture, décor and landscaping'.*

Portmeirion

PORTPATRICK
DUMFRIES AND GALLOWAY

6 miles south-west of Stranraer (page 441 Cb)

In the heart of Portpatrick are the preserved ruins of the 17th-century parish church in which runaway marriages were performed at a fee of £10 for the officiating minister. Many of the eloping couples came from Ireland, 22 miles away across the sea. Records state that '198 gentlemen, 15 officers of the army or navy, and 13 noblemen' were married there in the 50 years before 1826. It was then that the Church authorities put an end to the system which made Portpatrick Galloway's Gretna Green.

Portpatrick was the terminus of the main ferry route between Scotland and Northern Ireland. Its harbour was extended in 1820-1, when the Admiralty set up two workshops in the village. However, the harbour was severely damaged by south-westerly gales, and the steamer service was later transferred to Stranraer. The North and South Piers were pounded by the sea, and are now little more than lines of rubble.

In 1898, long after the last steamer had sailed to the Irish port of Donaghadee, the local estate passed to the Orr-Ewing family. They rebuilt many of the stone houses and cottages, and helped to turn Portpatrick into a holiday centre.

On the seafront, North and South Crescents mark the line of the tramway from Dashers Den quarry which provided most of the harbour stonework. Downhill are the surviving walls of one of the Admiralty workshops.

The ruins of the 16th-century Dunskey Castle are on a headland half a mile south.

PORTREE
SKYE, HIGHLAND

35 miles north-west of Kyleakin Ferry (page 442 Bd)

Bonnie Prince Charlie said goodbye to his rescuer, Flora Macdonald, in an inn on the site of Portree's Royal Hotel. After his defeat at the Battle of Culloden in 1746, Flora brought the prince over to Skye disguised as her maid. At the time, the village was no more than a handful of cottages. It did not grow any larger until 1819, when Thomas Telford built a harbour and a row of cottages. They are still there, along with Portree's oldest building, Meall House. It used to be the local gaol, and today is the tourist office.

Portree, with its bright, whitewashed houses rising from Portree Bay, is the capital of the Isle of Skye. It was on its site that, in 1542, King James V of Scotland came to demand homage from the island chiefs. Later, when the village was built, it took its name from the Gaelic *Port righ*, meaning 'King's Port'. The harbour looks out to the smaller island of Raasay, dominated by the flat-topped Dun Caan, almost 1,500 ft high. Dr Johnson and his biographer James Boswell visited Raasay in 1773, and Boswell recalls in his journal of *A Tour to the Hebrides*, that he and his companions danced a reel on the mountain top.

POWERSTOCK
DORSET

4 miles north-east of Bridport (page 421 Ca)

Flights of terraces make up the village, with the almost square, greystone Church of St Mary standing on the topmost layer. Around the church, at different levels, are stone cottages and large houses – some of them with thatched roofs. Glebe House, a few hundred yards to the north of the church, has the ruins of a 17th-century tithe barn in its grounds.

Powerstock is overshadowed by the 827 ft high Eggardon Hill, with its remains of a complex Iron Age fort. On another hilltop, to the south-east of the village, is the earthwork of Powerstock Castle. The castle was built in Norman times and was later converted into a hunting lodge for King John, who hunted in Powerstock Forest.

St Mary's is a Norman structure which was largely rebuilt in the 1850s. It has a row of gargoyles – probably Norman – and on the inside of the south porch are some fine 15th-century carvings of figures in relief, including a Virgin and Child, and a king with a staff and book. Just outside the door are the remains of a 13th-century dole table, from which loaves of bread were given to the poor.

Powerstock pastoral.

Virgin, Child and angels in the church.

WORKS, FAITH AND CHARITY
AT POWERSTOCK

Powerstock lies under the wing of Eggardon Hill, whose summit is a 20 acre sanctuary defended by mighty ramparts almost as formidable as when they were carved out of the chalk 2,000 years ago and more. The village itself is more subtly protected by a maze of deep lanes which, once negotiated, reveal a gracious collection of orchards, gardens and cottages set at all angles on a series of knolls. The chancel arch in Powerstock Church is one of the finest pieces of Norman workmanship in Dorset. A dole of bread was once given to the poor over a stone slab in the churchyard, but the gift is now one of coal.

Bread table in the churchyard.

PRESTBURY

CHESHIRE

2 miles north-west of Macclesfield (page 429 Dc)

There must be more good restaurants and antique shops in the main street of Prestbury than in any other village street in Britain. The road, which sweeps down to a bridge over the River Bollin, is flanked on its upper stretch by bow-fronted shops with an air of quiet prosperity. Their white-washed fronts contrast with the mellow red brickwork of the Georgian houses near the bridge and the beautiful little two-storeyed timber-framed house opposite the churchyard entrance. This marvellous example of Cheshire 'magpie' architecture was originally the priest's house, though it is now used as a bank.

The village does not figure in the Domesday Book, though pieces of a Saxon cross were found in the churchyard together with the doorway of a Norman chapel. Certainly the fabric and furnishings of the church contain work dating from Victorian times back to the 13th century.

PUSEY

OXFORDSHIRE

5 miles east of Faringdon (page 426 Aa)

The village takes its name from the Pusey family, who were given the estate by King Canute in the 11th century. The church and a mansion, both in the elegant Classical style that reached its peak in the Georgian period, were built for J. A. Pusey in the 1740s. A 'no through road' leads to the village, where attractive estate cottages stand among beech and horse-chestnut trees.

All Saints' Church is approached by a courtyard and entered by a porched doorway. Inside there are marble statues and Venetian screens. A monu-

RAINBOW'S END *A rainbow arches to earth beside the flint and pebble-dash Norman church at Pyecombe. The church's 13th-century tower, topped with a pyramid-shaped roof known as a Sussex cap, looks across windswept downland which has changed little during the 800 years of the village's existence. Today, life in Pyecombe is a tranquil affair, and has been so since Cromwell's troops invaded the village and violated the church.*

◆

ment to J. A. Pusey shows that he died in 1753, a few years after the church had been completed.

A path of red gravel leads to the park and Pusey House. The house is a private residence, but the gardens are open to the public during the summer, except on Mondays and Fridays. In the gardens are ornamental trees, classical sculptures, a lake with black swans and a Chinese bridge.

PYECOMBE

WEST SUSSEX

6 miles north of Brighton (page 423 Db)

Flint cottages and farm buildings occupy an exposed spot on the South Downs by the side of the road from Brighton to Hurstpierpoint. Some distance away is the village church which is small and built of flint and pebbledash. It dates from the 12th century. Tracks lead off to the remains of ancient burial grounds, Iron Age forts and Celtic field systems on the open South Downs. National Trust woods, known as New-timber, lie half a mile to the west.

Pyecombe was once a shepherds' village, and was well known as a centre from which shepherds' crooks were supplied. The top of the churchyard gate is in the shape of a crook, which is also used for the village sign.

The original village was close to the church, but the roadside hamlet which now contains the older dwellings was settled after a plague in 1603 had made the first site uninhabitable for a time.

QUAINTON
BUCKINGHAMSHIRE

6 miles north-west of Aylesbury (page 426 Bb)

At the top of Quainton's sloping, triangular green are the pedestal and broken shaft of a 15th-century cross. Behind the cross is an 18th-century chequered-brick farmhouse and the tower of a brick-built windmill constructed between 1830 and 1832. The Quainton Windmill Society is restoring the mill, which is open to the public on Sunday mornings.

Cottages line two sides of the green, and the area was the birthplace of George Lipscomb, who wrote an eight-part history of Buckinghamshire in the early 19th century. At its apex, the green meets the lower road which runs past the Sportsman Inn, where the thatched eaves are little more than head-high; past the village school, built in 1910, with its roof-top bell; and past the road leading to Quainton railway station – where, on summer weekends, the steam trains of the Quainton Railway Society run along the remaining two-thirds of a mile of track.

SHADOWS OVER THE CENTURIES *The red-brick almshouses at Quainton, with their dormers and Dutch gables, have sheltered the needy for almost 300 years. Today, they are the homes of pensioners and they still cast their shadows over the street leading to the 14th-century Church of St Mary.*

QUENIBOROUGH
LEICESTERSHIRE

6 miles north-east of Leicester (page 430 Cc)

Contrasting cottages of thatched roofs, white and colour-washed walls and red brick are presided over by the needle spire of St Mary's Church in this village in Quorn fox-hunting country. The 162 ft high spire is a landmark across the surrounding countryside, and stands vigil above the superb tower of pink granite. The oldest part of the church is the chancel in which one Norman window – no more than 6 in. wide on the outside – is preserved.

Approaching the village from the west, Coppice Lane on the left leads to Queniborough Old Hall with its memories of the Civil War. From there Prince Rupert, the Royalist general and nephew of Charles I, demanded over £2,000 from the mayor of Leicester to pay the king's forces who were camped around Queniborough. The mayor, however, pleaded poverty and sent only £500. A copy of Rupert's letter is housed at the Old Hall today.

Along the village's broad Main Street cottages stand back behind neat grass borders. A thatched cruck cottage about halfway along was built on the site of a carpenter's shop. Coffins were once made there and wheeled down a little cobbled path which is still preserved in the garden.

RADWAY
WARWICKSHIRE

7 miles north-west of Banbury (page 430 Ba)

Edge Hill, which rises above Radway, was the scene in 1642 of the first major battle of the Civil War. Some villagers say that the sounds of the battle can still be heard on occasions, and that a phantom soldier rides along the lanes looking for his hand, lost in the fighting.

Today the hill and the village below are peaceful, with only a castle-like tower as a reminder of the battle. It is said to stand on the spot where Charles I placed his standard, and was built in 1749 by a local architect, Sanderson Miller. It is now the Castle Inn. Radway's village green, with a pond, is surrounded by thatched cottages of yellow stone, and its Victorian church near the green is built of Hornton stone.

Sanderson Miller lived at Radway Grange, which he developed from an Elizabethan house. A later owner was Field-Marshal Earl Haig, British Commander-in-Chief during the First World War. His name appears on the church lych-gate.

◆

WENSLEYDALE WAYSIDE *Life is lived at an easy pace in Redmire, one of the most peaceful and least known of the Dale's captivating villages. Until the mid-19th century, lead and coal, torn from the moors, provided much of the village's livelihood. But each miner also kept a cow or two and subscribed to a Cow Club that paid the wages of the village herdsman, or By-law Man.*

REDMIRE
NORTH YORKSHIRE

10 miles south-west of Richmond (page 436 Bc)

The last passenger train from Redmire left with a clanking and a hiss of steam in 1954, allowing this attractive village to return to a tranquillity almost undisturbed by the 20th century. It lies at the east end of Wensleydale, down a quiet lane between Wensley and Castle Bolton. Sheltered to the north by limestone hills, it looks south across the wooded valley of the River Ure to the great plateau of Penhill, 3 miles away. Cottages of pale stone are scattered around a large green crossed by footpaths and narrow unfenced roads leading in and out of the village.

In one corner of the green a gnarled and ancient oak has grown out horizontally over a garden wall, and is propped up in its old age by wooden posts. Near by, a stepped base, said to be that of a medieval cross, now supports an inscribed pillar put up to celebrate Queen Victoria's jubilee in 1887. It was topped off with a lamp 90 years later to mark Elizabeth II's jubilee. On the opposite side of the green is one of the village's two inns, the King's Arms. Close by is the post office which was built as a drill hall for the Dales Volunteers about the time of the Napoleonic Wars. The other inn, the Bolton Arms,

stands near the former smithy beside the road to Castle Bolton. A little further along the road is the pinfold where stray animals were penned until claimed by their owners.

The parish church of St Mary is half a mile away to the south-east, in even more rural isolation. It has a finely carved Norman south doorway and a simple Norman font. Beyond the church wooded tracks and footpaths lead to Wensley, 3 miles further on in the same direction.

REEPHAM
NORFOLK

6 miles south-west of Aylsham (page 432 Dd)

An air of 18th-century prosperity lingers in Reepham, then an important market town, in the centre of a barley-growing and brewing region. The old market place has mellow, red-brick houses balanced by the pink colour-washed façade of the King's Arms.

One of the largest houses, Brewery House, is known locally as the Dial House because of its sun-dial above the wide portico. Behind the market place there is a narrow street, Back Street, where a large timber-framed house with an overhanging upper storey stands among tiny cottages with front doors that open directly on to the street.

The east of the market place is dominated by the tall tower of St Michael's Church, which strangely is not the parish church of Reepham but of neighbouring Whitwell. At one time three churches stood in the churchyard; Reepham's Church of St Mary is joined by its choir vestry to St Michael's, and the third church belonged to Hackford, but has been a ruin since 1543. Only a fragment of the tower wall remains.

About 1½ miles south of the village is the Norfolk Wild Life Park, which contains one of the largest collections of European mammals, including lynx, brown bears and wild boar. The aviaries hold a great variety of birds of prey.

REPTON
DERBYSHIRE

5 miles north-east of Burton upon Trent (page 430 Bc)

A 212 ft tall spire soars above Repton's parish church, a fitting crown for a village that was once the capital of a Saxon kingdom. In the 7th century it was the seat of King Penda, who introduced Christianity to the people of Mercia. A church was built and an abbey founded, but both were destroyed by the Danes in 875. The church, which is dedicated to the Saxon St Wystan, was rebuilt in the 10th century. Its chancel, part of the north transept and the crypt are among the best surviving examples of Saxon architecture in England. The aisles were rebuilt in the 13th century and the tower and spire were completed in 1340.

A priory was founded close to the church in 1172, and after it was dissolved in 1538 the

ruined building was used as part of Repton School, founded in 1557 and now one of Britain's best-known public schools. It can be seen through the Priory Gateway, and although most of the buildings are 19th century there are fragments from earlier periods, including the 15th-century Prior Overton's tower which is now part of the headmaster's house.

The broad, main street runs southwards from the church and school to the market cross, a column mounted on a base of octagonal steps and topped by a stone ball. Attractive town houses line the road, some timber-framed, others in Georgian red brick. Easton House, just off the High Street, was built in 1907 for a housemaster by Sir Edwin Lutyens, who designed the fountains in London's Trafalgar Square.

REVESBY
LINCOLNSHIRE

6 miles south-east of Horncastle (page 432 Be)

In summer, fallow deer can be seen grazing in the parkland close to this estate village on the southern edge of the Lincolnshire Wolds. The deer park in the grounds of Revesby Abbey seems appropriate for a place that was the home of Sir Joseph Banks, one of England's greatest naturalists. Banks accompanied Captain James Cook on his voyage round the world between 1768 and 1771. Sir Joseph's house stood about half a mile south of the present great house, known as the Abbey. On the main east-west road near the village, impressive iron gates open on to a long drive leading to the creepered walls of the house, built in the middle of the last century.

Surrounded by woodlands, Revesby consists of a dozen late 19th and early 20th-century cottages, almshouses and a church around a spacious green. The long, low almshouses, now empty, date from 1862. The Church of St Lawrence could almost be 14th or 15th century, but its small, fussy spire gives it away.

The church was, in fact, built in 1891 by the Stanhope family. Its east window is in memory of Edward Stanhope, Secretary of State for War, who died in 1893. In the aisle is a marble bust of Joseph Banks, a lawyer, who had built an earlier church in the same place. St Lawrence's has a set of tiles from a Cistercian abbey which used to stand on a site about half a mile south of the church.

Revesby reservoir, 1 mile along the Horncastle road from the village, is a magnet for fishermen and waterfowl. Another attraction is the summer fair, held in the park each year on the first Thursday in August.

RHOSSILI
WEST GLAMORGAN

15 miles west of Swansea (page 424 Ba)

Colour-washed cottages perch on cliffs 200 ft above a sandy beach that runs northwards for 3 miles to the little island of Burry Holms. Immediately behind the beach, whale-backed Rhossili Down rises steeply to 632 ft and is the highest point on the Gower Peninsula. In clear weather, views from the summit include Hartland Point, 40 miles away in Devon, and St Govan's Head, 30 miles away on the Pembrokeshire coast.

The oldest part of Rhossili huddles round the churchyard, where the headstones are thick with moss and pale lichen. Inside the church, which has a 12th-century doorway, is a memorial to Petty Officer Edgar Evans. A local man, he was one of the small party chosen by Captain Robert Scott for his final dash to the South Pole in 1911–12. Evans died on the return journey, along with Scott and the rest of the party.

A footpath past the clifftop Worms Head Cottage Hotel leads past the coastguard station to the Worms Head, a remarkable rock formation forming Gower's most westerly point, which is now a bird sanctuary. It can be reached on foot at low tide, and safe crossing times are displayed by the coastguard. Walkers may see hang-gliders swooping over the bay from their take-off point on Rhossili Down.

RIBCHESTER
LANCASHIRE
5 miles north of Blackburn (page 435 Db)

Beneath the streets of Ribchester is the site of a 5½ acre Roman fort, built around AD 80 to garrison some 500 cavalrymen. It was near there that, in the 18th century, a schoolboy found a magnificent Roman ceremonial helmet. The helmet is now in the British Museum, but there is a replica of it in the small museum just outside St Wilfrid's churchyard. The churchyard is situated

◆

CROMWELL'S NARROW ESCAPE *The magnificent castle at Ripley might well have seen the fate of England change course, for it was there that Oliver Cromwell sought rest after the Battle of Marston Moor. Lady Ingilby, wife of the Royalist owner, sheltered him for a night, but with a brace of pistols at the ready, prepared to shoot if he did not behave.*

directly over a corner of the fort's treasury building, and has a sun-dial with the inscription: 'I am a Shadow. So art Thou. I mark Time. Dost Thou?'

The village is encircled by green hills and lies in a curve of the River Ribble. It is a pleasant jumble of multi-coloured stone cottages in long, twisting terraces, and has two pubs, the White Bull, dated 1707, and the Black Bull. The White Bull has a porch canopy supported by four columns said to be from the Roman ruins.

Many stones from the fort went into the building of the 13th-century church. Inside is a Jacobean pulpit and a faded mural to St Christopher, the patron saint of travellers. The saint was often invoked by those about to cross the swift-flowing Ribble – a dangerous undertaking in the past and which, in the 13th century, resulted in the drowning of Ribchester's first recorded rector, Drogo. The river now has a bridge, which was built in 1774.

RIPLEY
NORTH YORKSHIRE
4 miles north of Harrogate (page 436 Bc)

There is a faintly continental air about Ripley, due to the whim of a lord of the manor, Sir William Amcotts Ingilby, who remodelled it in 1827 on the lines of a typical French village of Alsace Lorraine. But even though one building bears the inscription 'Hotel de Ville', the true Yorkshire character prevails in the greystone

houses, the cobbled square, the market cross and the village stocks.

The majority of the houses are terraced and set back from the single main street behind a tree-lined grass verge. At one corner of the square a life-size stone boar symbolises an association of nearly 700 years between Ripley and the Ingilby family, for the estate was granted to Thomas Ingilby who saved Edward III when he was attacked by a wild boar in Knaresborough Forest.

The Ingilbys still live in Ripley, in the magnificent part-16th-century castle west of the square. It is open to the public on Sundays and Bank Holidays from Good Friday to the end of September, and Tuesdays to Sundays during July and August. Among its attractions are lavishly decorated and furnished rooms and a secret hiding place. The grounds overlook lakes and the Thornton Valley, and the gardens were laid out by Capability Brown.

The 14th-century parish church of All Saints contains many monuments to the Ingilbys, and the church wall bears grim reminders of Cromwell's visit to the village. The stonework still carries the marks of bullet holes made when Roundhead troopers executed several Ripley men who had been captured at Marston Moor.

RIVINGTON
LANCASHIRE

3 miles south-east of Chorley (page 435 Db)

A long causeway spanning a vast, man-made lake approaches Rivington from the west, and an early glimpse of this captivating village is the stubby spire and weather-cock of its part-Elizabethan church poking above the trees of a wooded knoll. Half of old Rivington lies beneath the 2 mile long reservoir – formed in the 1850s to provide water for Liverpool.

OLD SCHOOL TIES *Generations of Rivington children have passed through this school, founded in 1656. Some rode in, tethering their horses to the stone post in the playground.*

Opposite, and slightly downhill from the church, is the village primary school, built in 1656 as a grammar school then rebuilt in 1714.

At the centre of the village is a triangular green, from which it is possible to peer over the vicarage wall and see the remains of a set of stocks. Overlooking the green is a graceful little Unitarian chapel, built in 1703.

Not far from the green is a handsome, white Georgian building, Fisher House, once the home of John Fisher who was Vicar of Rivington for half a century from 1763.

Rivington Hall, at the end of a long avenue of beech trees, is a handsome Georgian mansion built in 1780 by Robert Andrews. A hall has stood on the site since Saxon days. In 1900, the house was sold to the Lancashire soap-maker and multi-millionaire industrialist William Lever, later Lord Leverhulme, who restored and rebuilt the two vast barns that are among the glories of Rivington. These barns – one next to the hall, one at the other end of the beech avenue – also date back to Saxon days. They needed to be large because every winter they became Noah's arks, sheltering the farm animals and holding fodder to last until the thaws of spring. Both barns are of cruck construction, with massive paired oaks supporting the roof and walls. Lever, who turned most of the hall grounds over to the public as Lever Park, built a replica of long-vanished Liverpool Castle on a bluff towering over the lower end of the lake. He also built a tower on the 1,191 ft summit of Rivington Pike. Another tower there, square-shaped and partly obscured by trees, was built by the Andrews family in 1733. The hall is now owned by the North West Water Authority, and permits to fish for trout can be bought there. The barns are used as tea-rooms for visitors.

ROCKBOURNE
HAMPSHIRE

3 miles north-west of Fordingbridge (page 422 Bb)

In many villages the more attractive houses must be diligently sought out: not so in Rockbourne. Its single long street, which runs beside a winding chalk stream, is made up almost entirely of 16th to 18th-century houses, and some splendid cottages. There is no uniformity: clay-and-straw cob walls and thatch roofs stand happily next to brick and tile, timber and stone. Large gardens and a multitude of trees help in the harmonious blending of styles. Small bridges link the houses beside the stream to the village street. The stream is a winterbourne – it flows only in winter or other periods of high rainfall and is usually dry in summer.

At the north end there is a cluster of medieval farm buildings, including a great barn. They lie alongside a chalky track leading up to the downs. Across the gravelled courtyard in front of the manor house a long flight of steps flanked by an immense yew hedge leads up to St Andrew's Church, perched on a grassy hillside from which there is a fine view of the village.

The church has architectural features of almost

WINTERBOURNE SUMMER *Waterweeds ravel gently in the bottle-green depths of the lazy stream that divides a remote Hampshire village. It is summer, and the stream could well have been dry for it is a winterbourne, often flowing only in winter. But a good rainfall has kept it sparkling bright, to add a final touch to the setting of this perfect thatched house in Rockbourne – village of delightful houses. And its rose-red walls glow as the sun appears, and rain clouds roll away.*

every period from the 13th century to the present day, as well as a Norman arch. It houses imposing memorials to the Coote family, notably one to Lieutenant-General Sir Eyre Coote, who distinguished himself as one of Clive of India's officers at the Battle of Plassey in Bengal in 1757 and died in 1783. Behind the large churchyard is an unspoiled area of open country where nature lovers can observe the plants, birds and animals of the chalk downlands.

Half a mile south-east of the village are the excavated remains of a vast Roman villa. It has two wings, each with a bathing suite, and 73 rooms have been uncovered – some with mosaic floors. Coins found indicate that it was occupied from the 2nd century until the Romans left in the 5th century.

ROCKINGHAM
NORTHAMPTONSHIRE

3 miles north-west of Corby (page 430 Cb)

According to the Domesday Book, Rockingham was wasteland when William the Conqueror ordered a castle to be 'made' there. Today, as in Norman times, the castle stands sentinel-like on the tree-clad slopes of Rockingham Hill – with the thatched and slated cottages of Rockingham's wide main street spread out below.

The castle was the country retreat and hunting base of medieval monarchs. In 1530, Henry VIII gave it to Edward Watson, whose descendants still live there. Among its famous guests was Charles Dickens – who wrote much of *Bleak House* while staying there in the 1850s. The castle is open from Easter until the end of September.

Monuments to members of the family are in the mainly 17th-century Church of St Leonard, which stands below the castle's north courtyard. From the courtyard are fine views of the Welland Valley, the River Welland, and the Eyebrook Reservoir, a trout-fisherman's paradise.

ROSTHERNE
CHESHIRE

3 miles north of Knutsford (page 429 Dc)

In this beautifully kept estate village, all of the cottages lining the road to the church have carved slate nameplates and are named after shrubs and trees – Apple, Pear, Willow, Lilac, and so on.

A group of 12 houses form a square at one end of the village. They were built for estate workers in 1909 by Lady Margaret Egerton of Tatton, and bear the Egerton crest and the initials E of T. Lady Margaret also provided a bath-house and laundry with irons and free soap – remarkable innovations for their day. The lych-gate at the western side of the churchyard has an ingenious closing mechanism operated by a heavy wooden weight and a pulley system. The steeply sloping churchyard is dominated by the Gothic-style memorial to Joseph Simpson Esqre, presumably one of the successful Manchester merchants who moved out to this part of Cheshire to escape the expanding city during the last century. The Earl of Egerton restored St Mary's Church in 1888, on the 700th anniversary of its foundation.

On the north side of the church is a magnificent view over the waters of Rostherne Mere, the largest and deepest in Cheshire – some 100 acres in area and 100 ft deep. It is now a bird sanctuary, which harbours a variety of waterfowl. A local legend says that when the bells were being hung in St Mary's the largest rolled down into the mere, and that on Easter morning a mermaid raises and tolls the bell.

ROTHLEY
LEICESTERSHIRE

5 miles north of Leicester (page 430 Cc)

One of Rothley's two greens – Town Green – incorporates some of the finest timber-framed houses in the county. One or two are cruck-built, in which curved tree trunks are joined to form the framework of the house. Slightly more 'modern' are the Tudor box-frame houses.

Town Green lies on the edge of Rothley Park, site of Rothley Temple which was built in the 13th century by the Knights Templars. The temple was later incorporated into an Elizabethan house which was added to over the succeeding centuries and finally converted in 1960 to the Rothley Court Hotel. From about 1550 until the middle of the 19th century it was the seat of the Babington family. William Wilberforce, a family friend, drafted his bill for the abolition of slavery at the house while on a visit in 1791. A small monument records the occasion. In 1800, the historian Thomas Babington Macaulay – later Lord Macaulay of Rothley – was born there, and the hotel maintains the room as it was on the day he was born.

The original Templar chapel is still used for occasional services. The parish church of St Mary the Virgin has a carved Norman font and some fine memorials. In the churchyard is the shaft of a Saxon cross of the 8th or 9th century.

Rothley Station, which was built for the Great Central Railway in the 1890s, is being restored to its original condition, complete with enamelled and nostalgic advertisements. Its lamps are lit by gas, and the waiting-room has a portrait of Queen Victoria. It serves as the southern terminal for a 5 mile route which runs across the picturesque Swithland Reservoir to Loughborough. A steam-train service operates each weekend.

RUTHWELL
DUMFRIES AND GALLOWAY

6 miles west of Annan (page 441 Fb)

Scotland's finest Dark Age monument is in the parish church of Ruthwell, set deep in the farming country between Dumfries and Annan. The Ruthwell Cross was sculpted by unknown artists in the 7th or 8th centuries. Two of its four faces are carved with scenes from the Life of Christ, and the other two show scroll work and parts of a runic version of the ancient poem, *The Dream of the Rood*, by Caedmon of Whitby, the first Old English Christian poet.

The 18 ft high preaching cross was broken up in the 18th century and thrown into the churchyard; and it was not until 1823 that the parish minister, Dr Henry Duncan, realised the significance of the fragments and painstakingly pieced them together. He re-erected the monument in the manse garden, and today the Ruthwell Cross has pride of place in the church.

During his final illness the poet Robert Burns was sent to Brow Well, 1 mile east of the village, in the hope that its waters would help him. He stayed a fortnight, until July 18, 1796, then returned to his home in Dumfries, where he died three days later. Every year, on the anniversary of his death, a commemorative ceremony is held at the well.

RUYTON-XI-TOWNS
SALOP

9 miles north-west of Shrewsbury (page 429 Cb)

Next to the black-and-white Smithy House at the west end of the village is a monument commemorating the time in 1308 when Ruyton joined with ten other communities to form a small, rural borough.

Ruyton straggles along a main street more than 1 mile long, which runs atop a steep sandstone bluff above the River Perry. The Norman Church of St John the Baptist stands on the summit of the bluff, against a background of low, wooded hills. In the churchyard are the scanty remains of a castle, built in 1301 by Edward, Earl of Arundel, the creator of the borough.

Near by, the road passes a small, man-made cave which was cut into the sheer sandstone cliff as a memorial to the local men killed in two World Wars. Their names are recorded inside.

St Abbs
BORDERS

10 miles north-west of Berwick (page 441 Gd)

In 1832 a harbour was built at the fishing station of Northfield. The harbour is one of the few safe havens on a dangerous, rocky shore which includes the highest cliffs on the east coast of Britain. The village itself is built on a ridge above the harbour, rows of sturdy cottages over which spume is hurled by easterly gales.

A few years after the harbour was built, its name was changed to Coldingham Shore. Later still, it came to be known as St Abbs, after St Ebba, a 7th-century princess of Northumbria, who founded a nunnery near by.

North of the village is the imposing landscape of St Abb's Head, the site of St Ebba's foundation. The headland is capped by a lighthouse, erected in 1862. It is already so high above the sea that there is no need for a tower, and the keepers actually walk downstairs to the light.

On a farm on St Abb's Head is a 240 acre wildlife reserve, cared for by the Scottish Wildlife Trust. It can be reached by a footpath that starts just outside the village.

◆

STIPPY-STAPPY *This is a stepped row of tin-miners' cottages in St Agnes from which the men set off to work their shifts in West Kitty, Wheal Kitty, Blue Hills and the rest. When the last mines closed, in 1917, many of the miners went abroad; it is said that wherever in the world you find a hole in the ground, there you will find a St Agnes man.*

St Agnes
CORNWALL

6 miles north of Redruth (page 418 Bb)

In the 18th and 19th centuries, St Agnes was the bustling centre of a flourishing tin-mining area. It lies on a hillside, and the surrounding landscape is dotted with old mine workings, their tall chimneys and roofless engine-houses standing like the gaunt remains of deserted castles. The engine-houses drove the machinery and pumped water from the mine shafts, but before steam-engines were invented the miners burrowed into the cliffs and hills in search of tin and copper. Some of these old workings can still be seen along the coast.

Since mining ceased, early this century, the village has become a quiet, unspoiled community among some of Cornwall's finest scenery. Slate and granite cottages line the main street, some dating from the early 18th century. Old miners' cottages stand in a stepped terrace known as 'Stippy-Stappy'. Below the village lies Trevaunance Cove, which has had three harbours since 1632. All were destroyed by the sea, the last during a storm in 1916.

From St Agnes a coastal footpath leads to St Agnes Head, with a view that takes in a 30 mile sweep of the Atlantic coast from St Ives to Trevose Head, 9 miles from Newquay. At Trevellas, off the road to Perranporth, is the pretty thatched Harmony Cot where John Opie, the celebrated portrait painter, was born in 1761.

ST ASAPH

CLWYD

5 miles south of Rhyl (page 429 Cc)

Britain's smallest cathedral, smaller than many parish churches, gives St Asaph the unusual distinction – shared with St David's – of being at once a cathedral city and a village. The cathedral is impressive, despite its modest proportions, and stands on a short, steep hill overlooking lush meadows beside the River Elwy. It was completed in 1482, after two earlier cathedrals had been destroyed during the Anglo-Welsh struggles. Later, it suffered the indignity of being used as a stable by Cromwell's cavalry in the Civil War. Treasures displayed inside the cathedral include a first edition of the Bible in Welsh, published in 1588. It was translated by William Morgan, Bishop of St Asaph from 1601 until 1604. Other rare books include a 14th-century Latin hymnal and a 1549 prayer book that belonged to Roger Ascham, Elizabeth I's tutor, which has notes in his handwriting.

St Asaph stands at the mouth of the lovely Vale of Clwyd, but is set back from the main road to the North Wales coast and has a quiet, dignified atmosphere. Several old buildings line the High Street as it climbs towards the cathedral. The 14th-century parish church stands near the bridge over the Elwy, and its neighbour, the Kinmel Arms, is a former coaching inn that dates from the 17th century. There is a pleasant area of public meadow beside the river.

ST BRIAVELS

GLOUCESTERSHIRE

5 miles west of Lydney (page 421 Cd)

A castle that never saw a battle dominates St Briavels, standing high on a spectacular bluff above the Wye Valley. The castle dates from the 13th century, and during the reign of King John was used as a hunting lodge. It is now used as a Youth Hostel. The keep fell down in the 18th century, but the twin-towered gate-house survives.

The Church of St Mary is Norman and later, and outside the church the St Briavels Bread and Cheese ceremony is held every Whit Sunday. After Evensong, a local forester stands on a wall and throws pieces of bread and cheese to the churchgoers below. The custom is said to be 700 years old, and the villagers who catch the food retain the right to collect wood and graze animals in nearby Hudnalls Wood.

TINTERN On the west bank of the River Wye, 3 miles south-west of St Briavels, where the Wye sweeps through a magnificent wooded gorge, lies Tintern. The village extends for 1 mile from a small church at its northern end to the majestic ruins of Tintern Abbey, which was founded in 1131. The ruins – mainly 15th century – convey a striking impression of its former glory.

ST DAVID'S

DYFED

14 miles north-west of Haverfordwest (page 424 Ab)

The most westerly village in Wales also ranks as Britain's smallest city, thanks to its magnificent medieval cathedral, the shrine of the patron saint of Wales. Its heart, Cross Square, is named after a 14th-century preaching cross that stands on a stepped base by the neat little memorial garden. The square is enclosed on three sides by an attractive assortment of buildings that includes an eye-catching whitewashed cottage – now part of a restaurant – and Court House.

Most cathedrals dominate their surroundings, but St David's nestles in a leafy valley, and only the upper part of its lofty central tower is visible from Cross Square. It was almost certainly built on the site of a monastery founded by St David in the 6th century. The greater part of the present cathedral dates from the end of the 12th century, and is built of rich mauve stone hewn from the cliffs of nearby Caerbwdi Bay. The central tower was rebuilt after it collapsed in 1220. Inside, the cathedral has a fine, decorated roof of the 16th century and a richly carved 14th-century choir screen. Reached by a long flight of steps that runs down from The Pebbles, the cathedral shares its tranquil valley with the extensive and deeply romantic ruins of the medieval Bishop's Palace.

St Dogmaels
DYFED

1 mile west of Cardigan (page 424 Bb)

Tier upon tier of elegant Victorian cottages and small villas climbing up from the Teifi Estuary form the village of St Dogmaels. At night, the lights of the upper village seem to be magically suspended between earth and stars. St Dogmaels became a popular retreat for retired sea captains in the 19th century and has the atmosphere of a trim, nautical watering place despite being set slightly back from the estuary. Private craft moor offshore, and the river is noted for its salmon and 'sewin', as sea trout are called in Wales. To the north, where the Teifi meets the open sea, is the beach of Poppit Sands and the start of the Pembrokeshire Coast National Park.

From the top of the village there are peaceful views over hedges and fields to the clustered heart of St Dogmaels, with its ruined abbey and 19th-century church. The abbey was founded early in the 12th century and its remains, although scanty, give the village a romantic finishing touch. The church has a remarkable early-Christian monument, whose inscriptions enabled the previously baffling Ogham alphabet to be translated in 1848. Ogham was the script used by the ancient British and Irish scholars. Its mysteries were solved because the stone was inscribed in both Ogham and Latin.

A NATION ENCAPSULATED Every aspect of Welsh rural life, from cottage to castle, farm to workroom, has been gathered by the Folk Museum at St Fagans. However, the old village itself, thatched, whitewashed and peaceful is also immensely attractive, with little to show of the Civil War battle that caused the River Ely to run crimson with blood.

St Fagans
SOUTH GLAMORGAN

4 miles west of Cardiff (page 425 Da)

The Welsh Folk Museum draws thousands of visitors to St Fagans Castle every year, but the picturesque village on the outskirts of Cardiff is a tourist attraction in its own right. Castle Hill plunges steeply down to the Ely river, and is overlooked by thatched and whitewashed cottages with diamond-paned windows. They nestle behind neatly trimmed hedges and are watched over by the gables and chimneys of the castle, which shares its hilltop with St Mary's Church and the late-Victorian Plymouth Arms.

The 16th-century castle, built on the site of an earlier stronghold, was owned by the Earls of Plymouth from 1730 until 1946. Together with 100 acres of land, it was then handed over as a gift when plans for the folk museum were finalised. One of the finest collections of its kind in the world, the museum features every aspect of Welsh life, from domestic utensils to complete buildings rescued from dereliction elsewhere.

Village Crafts

Britain's craftsmen of the past knew nothing of mass-production and standardisation. The things they created were made to suit local needs and conditions, and they used readily available materials. In time, the products of factories and mills began to reach even the remotest parts of the country, and the old skills became neglected and forgotten. But country craftsmen, like old soldiers, never die, and a renewed desire for hand-made quality has ensured that it will be a long time before they finally fade away.

THE THATCHER

Thatching was once a basic skill of any competent farmworker, but today it has become a specialised craft.

Styles of thatching vary from the sharply angled and heavily ridged roofs of Norfolk, where reed is the prince of materials, to the softer, curving contours of West Country homes, where straw is the usual choice.

Straw tends to be laid in one of two ways. In Essex, Kent and parts of Sussex, wheat straw is laid with the stems aligned but with their heads and butt-ends arranged in random order: no attempt is made to lay them in the same direction. The stems are then combed with a long-straw rake to give the roof its characteristically smooth, flowing

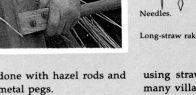

Norfolk-reed legget.

Combed-reed legget.

Shears.

Needles.

Long-straw rake.

Eaves' knife.

appearance. Another easy-to-recognise feature is the criss-cross pattern of stitches along the ridge, done with hazel rods and metal pegs.

Combed wheat reed, the alternative method of using straw, is found on many village buildings in Dorset, and in Devon where it is known as Dorset or Devon reed. The straw is laid butt-end downwards and has a crisp, cropped appearance.

Norfolk reed looks similar to combed wheat reed, but the eaves and gables are not cut to shape; instead they are beaten into position with a legget to form a tapered profile.

Like all other craftsmen, the thatcher has specialist tools, which vary from district to district according to the material used on the roof.

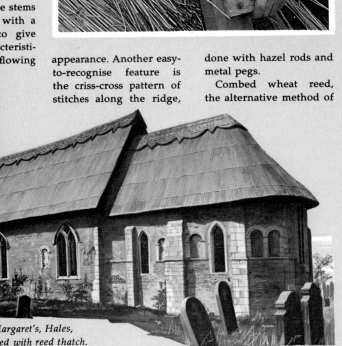

The Church of St Margaret's, Hales, Norfolk, partly roofed with reed thatch.

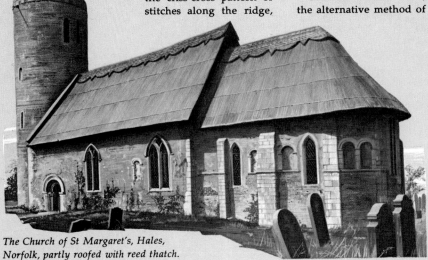

THE CARPENTER

The range of work handled by the traditional village carpenter was as varied as the types of wood and tools he used. Often he did the work of the village builder, roofer and jack-of-all-trades, as well as being called upon to make or repair agricultural implements such as ploughs or harrows, wheel-barrows and tool handles. He was also the man who made five or six-barred field gates – in collaboration with the blacksmith.

And, finally, there was the occasional need for the made-to-measure coffin – a characteristic of the village rather than the town, where ready-made coffins were available.

In some villages the plentiful supply of timber led to the growth of specialist crafts, as at West Wycombe, where the beechwood of the Chilterns provided material for a chair-making industry that gave birth to the celebrated stick-back or Windsor chair.

The carpenter's tools were his most treasured possession, guarded jealously and often handed down from father to son.

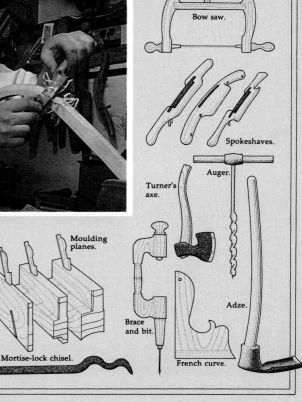

Bow saw.

Spokeshaves.

Auger.

Turner's axe.

Moulding planes.

Brace and bit.

Adze.

Mortise-lock chisel.

French curve.

THE BLACKSMITH AND FARRIER

When horses worked on the land the glowing forge and ring of hammer on anvil were common in every village. Horses are shod by a farrier, and a blacksmith works with wrought, or 'black', iron. But the village blacksmith was master of both trades. He shod horses, repaired ploughs and made farm implements.

Many forges remain in active use, whether for farriery, as repair shops for agricultural equipment, or as workshops in which wrought-iron articles are made.

With the forge and the anvil as his first essentials, the smith has a great many tools that are primarily used for bending metal. Chief among these is the swage block – a heavy square or rectangular block of cast iron with a number of different holes and V-shaped grooves in it. He also has several mandrels – cast-iron cones – used for making hoops and rings, and fullers and flatters – die shapes that fit into the anvil.

A farrier's stand – known as a 'lazy blacksmith' – is used to place a horse's forefoot on while trimming the hoof.

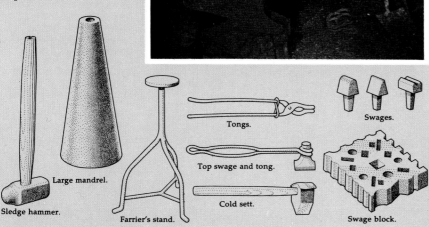

Large mandrel.

Sledge hammer.

Tongs.

Swages.

Top swage and tong.

Farrier's stand.

Cold sett.

Swage block.

THE MILLER AND THE BAKER

In former times, almost every parish had its corn-mill, whether driven by wind or water.

Watermills were driven by a wheel powered either by water passing under it – the undershot wheel – or by water channelled to the top and controlled by a sluice – the overshot wheel.

From the 12th century onwards, windmills appeared, introduced by Crusaders returning from the Holy Land.

Windmills were commonest in the flat landscape of East Anglia, where the slow-moving streams provided insufficient power to drive a wheel. There were two main types of windmill: the post mill and the tower mill. Post mills were built on a central post, and the miller had to turn the whole building to keep the sails facing into the wind. Tower mills had a revolving cap which carried the sails.

Until the end of feudalism – towards the close of the 15th century – most village mills were owned by the lord of the manor, to whom everyone paid a toll for grinding their corn. After this, mills were bought or rented privately, and millers ground villagers' corn in return for one-sixteenth of the flour. It was not until 1796 that a law was introduced making it compulsory to pay a miller with money.

The miller's work was physically demanding – he was forever humping heavy sacks of grain, and making running repairs to the mill's mechanism. Windmills depended upon the vagaries of the wind. This could mean working through the night, if that was when the wind decided to blow.

Bread was the staple food of the villager, and whereas many cottagers baked their own loaves there was usually a bakery in the village. The oven was brick-built and had a heavy iron door closing its mouth. Faggots of wood were used to heat the oven, and when they burned themselves out the embers were removed with a long-handled rake. A piece of sacking soaked in water was then placed in the oven on the end of a pole and was wiped around the oven floor to clear it of all cinders. The oven was then ready for baking a batch of loaves.

The loaves were placed in the oven on a long-handled wooden spade, called a peel, and were removed in the same way. Few village bakeries have survived into the age of factory bread, but the mouth-watering smell of newly baked bread pinpoints their location.

VILLAGE BAKERY *A typical 19th-century bakehouse – now in the National Museum of Wales – with three bread ovens. Each oven could bake about 100 loaves at a time.*

THE DRY-STONE WALLER

The craft of dry-stone walling dates from the 18th century, when the vast open fields of the Saxons were divided to suit the new, four-year crop rotation system. To enclose the fields the farmers turned to local materials, and in areas such as the Yorkshire dales, the Devonshire and Cornish moors and the Cotswolds that meant using stone.

Dry-stone walls have no mortar in their construction, and the art of the waller lies in his ability to select and grade each stone so that it fits exactly into a particular gap. A good stone waller seldom cut his stones to size – they are usually too hard to cut cleanly, except in the Cotswolds where a heavy, double-edged hammer is used.

A well-made wall is laid with the stones sloping away from the centre, so that they are self-draining in wet weather. Large tie-stones are inserted at regular intervals, and at right-angles to the length of the wall, to form a bond and increase its strength. The top is finished with large flat stones laid on edge.

Dry-stone walling is almost a lost art, and there are few men who can do more than repair existing walls. Fortunately their predecessors built well, and the dry-stone wall, climbing almost vertically up the sides of many a valley, will be a pleasant feature of the landscape for many years to come.

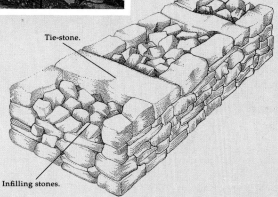

Tie-stone.

Infilling stones.

THE WEAVER

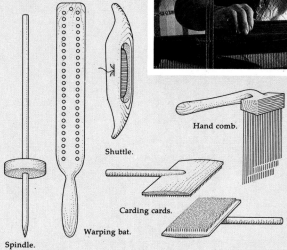

The cloth worker was as essential to village life as the blacksmith or wheelwright. Until the introduction of cotton in the 18th century, wool was the staple material for cloth, and cloth making was a major cottage industry in the West Country, Yorkshire and Lancashire. Most of the work was done in villagers' homes until the end of the 18th century, when water power was harnessed for mills.

In the early days of the craft, children were often used as carders, to straighten the wool fibres with the heads of teasels or combs. Spinners – usually women – twisted the fibres, either by hand or on a spinning-wheel, into yarn which was then twirled on to a spindle.

Weaving was generally done by men, working two to a loom. Cloth was made with two sets of yarn – the warp and the weft – woven at right-angles to each other. A shuttle used to 'throw' the warp through the weft from one side of the loom to the other. The warping bat was used in setting the pattern of the weave.

Where water power was available, the finished cloth was shrunk and thickened, in a process called fulling, under hammers driven by a waterwheel.

Weaving, spinning and dyeing are thriving crafts which are still carried out in many villages.

Hand comb.

Shuttle.

Carding cards.

Warping bat.

Spindle.

THE WHEELWRIGHT

The wheelwright was perhaps the most versatile of all country craftsmen, needing the skills of a woodsman, a blacksmith, a carpenter and a joiner. He built the whole cart, or wagon, not just the wheels. As well as having a sound knowledge of the stresses and strains in timber, he had to take into account local needs and conditions.

Wagons in different parts of the country had to carry different types of loads, and to cope with the local terrain. In the Cotswolds the wagons were lightly built, to lessen the strain for the horse on the many sharp inclines; and each wagon had a deeply waisted frame so that the front wheels could turn sufficiently to negotiate the twisting lanes. The wagon body had almost horizontal fore and tail ladders to hold corn sheaves.

Wagons in the Vale of Berkeley in Gloucestershire were built with four double-tyred wheels so that they would not sink into the clay-bound land. But the area's straight and level roads permitted high laden weights and a limited turning lock. Hay was the usual load, so

almost vertical fore and tail ladders were fitted.

To construct the wheels that carried such enormous loads, including the weight of the wagon itself, the wheelwright used special tools.

A boxing engine was used to bore a hole through the hardwood hub, into which a hardened metal casing was fitted to take the wear of the wheel on its axle. A spoke dog gave the wheelwright a means of levering pairs of spokes together when fitting the

felloe – or rim pieces – and a samson for cramping them together.

The traveller was used to measure the circumference of a wheel.

Now that the tractor has taken over from the horse, the wheelwrights have all but disappeared, but 50 or so are still engaged in the trade.

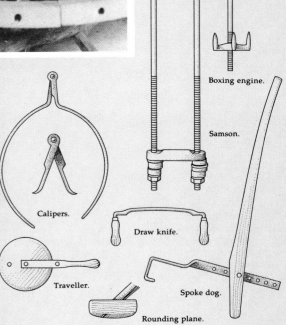

Boxing engine.

Samson.

Calipers.

Draw knife.

Traveller.

Rounding plane.

Spoke dog.

STAFFORD WAGON *The design of carts and wagons varied from region to region, according to the terrain and the loads they were intended to carry. The Staffordshire wagon (left) was particularly robust – its wheel rims could be up to 8 in. wide – and when fully loaded, needed as many as six horses to pull it.*

DISCOVERING VILLAGE BYGONES

The products of village craftsmen of the past can often be bought at junk shops, jumble sales and at country markets. They make interesting souvenirs of a bygone age, and their authenticity can be checked at rural museums.

TRIVETS
Simple, three-legged stands were used to support kettles and pans by the hearth.

LOVE SPOONS
The custom whereby a young man carved a wooden spoon as a love token has continued in Wales for centuries.

PIG FEEDER
A litter of piglets could feed from this many-spouted pottery feeding bottle.

BUTTER STAMP
The decorative designs on carved butter stamps often served as trade-marks of dairy farmers.

CAST-IRON POT
Iron cooking pots were hung from a bar over an open hearth from the early 18th century.

WINDSOR CHAIR
The seat was carved from a single piece of elm on all Windsor chairs. Bentwood backs were introduced in the mid-18th century.

BOTTLES
Old glass and stoneware bottles survive in many shapes and colours. The design often indicated the contents.

HORN BEAKER
Horners in the 19th century made beakers from cow horn. The horner's skill was in making a leak-proof base.

BRANDING IRON
Blacksmiths made branding irons with a distinctive mark for each local farmer.

CAST-IRON FRYING-PAN
With cast-iron pots, the long-handled pan was used for cooking on open fires in the 19th century.

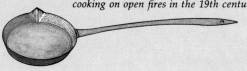

SHEPHERD'S CROOK
Crooks were often made by woodland workers. A ram's horn was sometimes used for the crook end.

SHEEP SHEARS
In the 19th century an expert could hand-shear a sheep in less than five minutes with these simple clippers.

MILKING STOOL
Low, three-legged stools, made by the village carpenter, took the back-ache out of milking.

FLAT IRON
The domestic smoothing iron used in the 19th century was heated on the kitchen fire.

KNITWEAR
Hand-knitting is one of the oldest cottage crafts. Many areas had their own patterns for particular garments, such as fishermen's jerseys.

SPINNING-WHEEL
From the Middle Ages until the 18th century, all yarn was spun on a wheel turned by working a treadle. Spinning-wheels are still made for craft hobbyists.

BIRD-SCARER
The rattle, beloved of football fans, was originally used to scare birds away from growing crops.

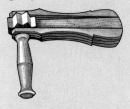

CLAY PIPE
The earliest clay pipes date from the 16th century. Complete pipes are rare.

SAMPLER
Most samplers date from the 18th and 19th centuries. This one was worked by the novelist Anne Brontë.

345

THE FLEMISH CONNECTION *The extraordinary towering chimney of this cottage in St Florence is 17th century, but its origins go back to the 12th century, when Henry II encouraged people from Flanders to cross the Channel and colonise the south Pembrokeshire area. They brought with them their wool industry, tall chimneys and wide fireplaces. St Florence became a centre of the industry, now long vanished.*

tially blocked when the railway was built in the 19th century. Until then, St Florence stood at the head of a tidal creek and could be reached by small boats at high water. The little river now flows to the sea through a marshy valley.

The parish church has a tall, plain tower, and its earliest parts date from the 12th century.

ST HILARY
SOUTH GLAMORGAN

2 miles south-east of Cowbridge (page 425 Da)

There is an air of quiet prosperity about St Hilary. Immaculate buildings of pale limestone can be admired from a tangle of little roads and footpaths that spreads out from the church. Many of the oldest cottages and houses, notably Village Farm, have been tastefully modernised without any loss of character, dignity or charm. Attractive modern homes flank a leafy cul-de-sac beyond the Bush Inn, with its thatched roof. The atmosphere is more English than Welsh, a reminder that this part of Wales lost its independence many years before the mountainous north.

St Hilary's Church dates from Norman times, but it was restored by Sir Gilbert Scott in 1862 as a memorial to the Reverend John Traherne, who had died two years earlier. Traherne was St Hilary's vicar, a landowner and a prominent local historian. The church memorials include an effigy of Sir Thomas Basset of Beaupre (pronounced 'Bewper') Castle, who died in 1423. The castle, a splendid mostly 16th-century mansion, is undergoing some restoration. It is reached by footpaths to the south of the village. One porch bears, in Welsh, the motto 'Better death than dishonour', which was later adopted by the Welch Regiment.

ST FLORENCE
DYFED

3 miles west of Tenby (page 424 Bb)

Such names as Flemish Close and Flemish Court are clues to the totally unexpected origins of this little village, set in a tangle of narrow lanes 3 miles west of the popular holiday resort of Tenby. They provide links with the people from Flanders whom the Norman kings encouraged to settle in West Wales during the 12th century. A quaint old cottage near the church has two enormous Flemish-style chimneys of grey stone.

The entire village has a timeless atmosphere that swiftly transports visitors back to an infinitely less hectic age. It has won several awards for its abundance of flowers and general neatness. High Street climbs a gentle hill, passing houses and colourful cottages on its way to the church. Several buildings have stone-framed doorways with pointed arches that enhance their already considerable character. Most of the newer homes have been colour-washed to blend with their neighbours. The village must have been even more attractive before the Ritec stream was par-

ST JOHN'S
ISLE OF MAN

3 miles south-east of Peel (page 435 Bc)

The historical heart of the Isle of Man is the village of St John's. An open-air meeting of the Tynwald – the island's parliament, introduced by the Vikings 1,000 years ago – is held in the village every year, on July 5.

The term Tynwald derives from the Norse words *Thing*, meaning 'assembly', and *Vollr*, meaning 'meeting place'.

On Tynwald Day, the Lieutenant-Governor, members of the Tynwald and other civic officials walk in procession from St John's Chapel over a rush-strewn path to take up their appointed positions on the four-tiered Tynwald Hill. Then all the laws enacted in the previous year are read out in both Manx and English, and an opportunity is given for anyone who wishes to present a petition of protest to do so. Several petitions have been presented in recent years.

For the tourist, Tynwald Day is the most colourful day in the island's calendar, since on that day there is also a fair and folk festival

with displays of Manx dancing and music.

St John's Chapel, at which a service of thanksgiving is held before the Tynwald ceremony, is worth a visit. Its primary function was originally that of a court house, and this can be seen clearly in the arrangement of the pews.

Although the village is small, its distinction in having the Tynwald field at its centre is because it sits at the junction of the main north-south road and the main east-west road. Its houses are colour-washed or rendered, with slate roofs, and it has three pubs. Perhaps the best known of these is the Ballacraine Hotel. It was through this hotel's door and into its bar that the comedian George Formby accidentally rode in a scene in his 1930s film about the Manx Tourist Trophy motorcycle race, *No Limit*.

St Keverne
CORNWALL

9 miles south-east of Helston (page 418 Ba)

More than 400 shipwreck victims are buried in St Keverne's churchyard, a grim reminder that the treacherous Manacle Rocks are just 1 mile offshore. The village, which stands on the high, flat plateau of the Lizard, has houses and cottages built of cob and local stone grouped around a large square. Towering above the village is the octagonal spire of St Keverne's Church, which dates from the 15th century. The spire was rebuilt in 1770, replacing the original one which was struck by lightning.

In 1497 the village blacksmith, Michael Joseph, joined with Thomas Flammock of Bodmin to lead a 15,000-strong rebellious army to London. They were protesting against heavy taxes imposed by Henry VII, but their venture ended at Blackheath where they were defeated by 25,000 men of the king's army. Joseph and Flammock were captured and executed.

St Mawgan
CORNWALL

4 miles north-east of Newquay (page 418 Bb)

Snugly pocketed in a deep and wooded valley, St Mawgan is protected from the Atlantic gales that sweep in from the western coast.

In the village there are stone cottages, a stream crossed by a ford and stone bridges, the Falcon Inn and a largely 13th-century church, St Mawgan's. There are many monuments in the church to the Arundell family whose manor house, Lanherne, stands in the village. It has an Elizabethan front, but the rear dates from the 17th and 18th centuries. Since 1794 it has been a convent for Carmelite nuns, and cannot be visited; but its chapel is open at all times.

In St Mawgan's churchyard is a simple wooden tablet, shaped like the stern of a boat, in memory of nine men and a boy who froze to death in a lifeboat after their ship foundered in 1846. This is a grim reminder that the sea is not far away, about 2 miles down the valley where it opens out to form the rocky cove called Mawgan Porth.

A LAND OF SAINTS

A spate of saints descended on the West Country after the Romans departed in the 5th century. They came from Brittany, Wales and Ireland, leaving in their wake hundreds of Celtic crosses marking holy sites and graves. This form of cross was elaborated upon over the centuries: all those shown here are in St Mawgan's churchyard – note particularly the beautifully carved lantern cross on the right, contrasting with the simple stone on the left.

Simple Celtic headstone.

Three variations on the theme.

The elaborate lantern cross.

SALCOMBE REGIS
DEVON

2 miles north-east of Sidmouth (page 419 Eb)

In the 9th century Alfred the Great owned Salcombe, a connection which earned it the title 'regis' (of the king). Alfred's grandson, Athelstan, gave the village to the monks of Exeter, but the royal appendage remained. Salcombe Regis stands in a valley which runs sharply down to the South Devon coast. At the upper end of the valley is a thorn bush which is said to have grown there since Saxon times, marking the boundary between the cultivated fields of the village and the common land on the hill. Local superstition holds that the well-being of the village depends upon the existence of the thorn, so that when one tree dies another is planted.

Houses perch along the sides of the valley as it descends to a shingle beach, but to reach it visitors have to walk down a path followed by 131 steps down the cliff face. Parking is available near the Church of St Mary and St Peter. In the churchyard lie the graves of two distinguished scientists – Sir Ambrose Fleming, who invented the wireless valve in 1904, and the astronomer Sir Norman Lockyer, who made pioneering discoveries about sun spots in 1886, and whose observatory still stands at the top of the hill.

BRANSCOMBE A steep hill, 2½ miles east of Salcombe Regis, runs down into Branscombe past the shimmering seascape of the English Channel. In the village centre a road leads up past an ancient smithy to St Winifred's Church with its late-Norman tower. The smithy has been working since the 15th century and must be one of the oldest in the country. From the square another road climbs up past the 14th-century Great Seaside Farm, looking across the valley to the sea at Branscombe Mouth.

SAMPFORD COURTENAY
DEVON

5 miles north-east of Okehampton (page 419 Dc)

A church tower with four pinnacles adorned by golden lichen dominates Sampford Courtenay, which has a special niche in Devon's history. White or colour-washed cottages under rounded thatch stand among trees and gardens on both sides of the village street, approached by a sharp turn at the 17th-century New Inn. At its top end the narrow, climbing street opens into a square overhung by the 15th-century granite tower of the hillside Church of St Andrew. Today, the square is a scene of peace and tranquillity, but in 1549 it erupted into violent rebellion.

The uprising was against a decree of Edward VI introducing a Prayer Book in English to replace Latin in churches throughout the country. Other parishes joined what became known as the 'Prayer Book Rebellion', and the peasants formed an army led by priests. The rebels besieged Exeter for five weeks, but were eventually driven back to Sampford Courtenay and defeated with fearful casualties.

The ringleaders were hanged in London. No reminders of the conflict exist in or around the village, or in the church where the uprising began. The interior of St Andrew's is light and spacious, with chairs instead of fixed pews. Probably the oldest single object in the church is the marble font, which is believed to date from about 1100 and clearly came from an older building.

Five granite crosses stand at various points

---◆---

BATTLES LONG AGO *Sampford Courtenay has changed little since Whit Monday, 1549, when the villagers, having murdered a Protestant zealot for attempting to force the Anglican Prayer Book upon them, raised the West Country and besieged Exeter. Retribution followed swiftly; the dismembered corpses of the ringleaders were nailed to London Bridge. The village remains, a gentle introduction to wild Dartmoor.*

around Sampford Courtenay, which is set among

around Sampford Courtenay, which is set among gentle hills and valleys, winding lanes and high hedgerows. Historians say they were put there as boundary marks by a medieval lord of the manor, but village tradition is that they were put there 'to keep out the Devil'.

OLD FRIENDS *The Church of St Nicholas and the Manor House form a honey-coloured cluster of Tudor buildings. Framed by the tree and the porch, the Manor Chapel contains memorials to the families who have dominated the life of Sandford Orcas for 400 years.*

SANDFORD ORCAS
DORSET

3 miles north of Sherborne (page 421 Cb)

Following a winding lane up a combe northwards from Sherborne, a striking view towards the Somerset plain opens up at the top and, on descending a steep hill, you come suddenly on the beginning of a straggling village which follows a stream down the valley. This contains a number of cottages and houses built of golden Ham Hill stone, some with stone mullioned windows and leaded lights.

Near a road junction at the lower end of the village several streams converge to flow eventually into the River Parrett.

On a rise beyond the centre of the village, the church and Manor House form a fine pair of early-Tudor buildings. The Church of St Nicholas has a Norman font and a 15th-century tower, and its small chapel contains a number of monuments. Among them is one dated 1607 to William Knoyle, whose family once owned the village.

The small, 16th-century Manor House is complete with arched gatehouse, stable court and walled garden. It was formerly the home of Edward Knoyle, who inherited Sandford in the early 1530s. There may well have been an earlier manor house on the same site – the property of the Orcas family – who, in the 12th century, gave the village the second half of its name.

SAPPERTON
GLOUCESTERSHIRE

5 miles west of Cirencester (page 421 Cd)

Many of Sapperton's modern buildings are indistinguishable from the 17th-century ones, thanks to the architects and craftsmen Ernest and Sidney Barnsley and Ernest Gimson. With their followers they became known as the Sapperton Group, and worked closely with William Morris.

The architects could have chosen no better setting for their work. The village stands at the head of a wooded valley of the River Frome, close to Cirencester Park, seat of Earl Bathurst. The centre of the group's activities was Daneway House, a 14th-century manor.

The Sapperton architects all built homes for themselves in the village. Ernest Barnsley built Upper Dorvel House in 1901; his brother built Beechanger in the same year; and Gimson built The Leasowes.

Memorial plaques to the three men are in the churchyard of St Kenelm's, a 14th-century church largely rebuilt during the reign of Queen Anne. Also buried there is Rebekah Mason, first wife of the 18th-century English astronomer Charles Mason, co-originator of the Mason-Dixon Line, which divided Pennsylvania from Maryland and was the northern boundary of the southern 'slave' states.

Sapperton is also known for the Sapperton Tunnel of 1789, which carried the Thames and Severn Canal for more than 2 miles beneath the

Bathurst estate. It fell into disuse in 1911, but its Classical eastern entrance, near Coates, has been restored. The 18th-century Daneway Inn, at the Sapperton end of the tunnel, was the haunt of bargees and the professional 'leggers' – men who propelled the narrow boats through the tunnel by lying on their backs and pushing with their legs against the tunnel wall. There is another canal pub, the Tunnel House, at Coates.

SAWLEY, Lancashire (page 435 Db)
(see Bolton by Bowland)

SAWREY
CUMBRIA

2 miles south-east of Hawkshead (page 435 Cc)

Far Sawrey and Near Sawrey, flanked by Windermere and Esthwaite Water, lie in a rolling, wooded landscape. Both villages are tiny, but Near Sawrey is famous as the home of the children's writer Beatrix Potter. She bought the 17th-century Hill Top Farm with royalties from *Peter Rabbit*, and there created such characters as Jemima Puddle-Duck and Pigling Bland. When she died, in 1943, the house and its contents were left to the National Trust. The house is as she left it, and a visit is like stepping back into the pages of a childhood story. Many of its contents appeared in picture form in Beatrix Potter's books, which she illustrated herself. The farmhouse backs on to the Tower Bank Arms, which is also owned by the National Trust. It overlooks a village of mainly whitewashed cottages surrounded by fields where sheep graze.

Far Sawrey, on a lane which ends at the Windermere ferry, stands among trees. A narrow lane runs southwards to the Victorian village church, set by a grassy hillock with pleasant views over Windermere to the hills above Kendal. Town End, opposite the churchyard entrance, is an attractive old pair of cottages whose whitewash gleams in the rich green landscape. The lane continues to Newby Bridge, rising and falling through woods where occasional breaks provide delightful views of Windermere.

SEDLESCOMBE
EAST SUSSEX

3 miles north-east of Battle (page 423 Eb)

The village slopes gently for nearly a mile down a Wealden hillside. Houses cluster round the church among dense hedges at the top, but the main settlement, known as Sedlescombe Street, lies at the lower end. There, a pump and pillared pump-house, dated 1900, stand on a long triangular green. On either side of the green are brick and tile-hung cottages, shops and inns. One thatched cottage, the last of its kind in the village, bears the date 1506. Just past the top of the green is a large timber-framed house with mullioned windows. Known as Manor Cottages it is thought to date in part from the 15th century.

The road is a main route to Hastings, and the village has always catered for travellers to the coast. Its inns and eating-places include a restaurant in a converted tanning-shed.

Although restored in 1866, the church retains its 15th-century tower and old roof timbers.

Oaklands, an estate to the south-east of the village once occupied by local gentry, now houses the Pestalozzi Children's Village. It was opened in 1959 by the Pestalozzi Trust which carries on the work of the Swiss educational reformer who died in 1827. The school is for deprived children of all Third World countries. Further south, just off the road to Hastings, at Norton's Farm, is a small museum of rural life.

SELBORNE
HAMPSHIRE

4 miles south of Alton (page 422 Cb)

Steep slopes deep-shaded by beech trees rise high above the mellow stone cottages of Selborne, birthplace and home of the Reverend Gilbert White, the 18th-century pioneer of English natural history. The Zig-Zag Path leads to the summit of Selborne Hanger, where White recorded many wildlife observations for his classic book *The Natural History and Antiquities of Selborne*, published in 1789. At the top is a monolith known as the Wishing Stone. The footpath and the Hanger are owned by the National Trust and are open to the public. White's house, The Wakes, which dates back to 1500, is now a museum and memorial library devoted to the naturalist; to Captain Lawrence Oates, who accompanied Scott to the South Pole in 1911–12 and died with him on the return journey; and to Oates's uncle, the explorer Frank Oates, who died on an expedition in Africa. White is buried in St Mary's churchyard, and is commemorated by a stained-glass window depicting St Francis.

The church is Norman, but much of it was rebuilt in the mid-19th century. Viewed from the village green – called The Plestor – it is half hidden by a huge old yew tree. In another part of the village, Gracious Street is flanked by pleasant houses. It leads to Wheelwright's, with its ancient smithy, and to Fisher's Buildings, the old workhouse.

At Lime End Yard, in The Street, is the workshop of one of Britain's leading restorers of horse-drawn vehicles. The yard is often gay with colourful gipsy caravans, in which he specialises. He can sometimes be watched at work at weekends.

About 1½ miles east of Selborne is the site of an Augustinian priory, founded in 1232 by the Bishop of Winchester. After a chequered existence it was finally suppressed by order of the Pope in 1486.

Finds made during recent excavations on the site include glass fragments identified as medieval alembics, or distilling apparatus. The original fragments are in the Science Museum, London, but replicas are on display along with other relics of the priory at The Wakes.

SELBORNE OBSERVED –
AN 18TH-CENTURY NATURALIST AND HIS VILLAGE

One critic said of Gilbert White's Selborne: *'Open the book where you will, it takes you out of doors' – about as close as anyone will get to pinning down the elusive charm of this minor classic that has delighted thousands of people with little previous knowledge of English natural history or antiquities. White was a brilliant observer, and the hills, gardens and woods he described have changed little since his day. Selborne is a modest and lovely place; and he wrote of it with modesty and love.*

Garden at The Wakes.

Detail from the memorial window.

One of White's letters.

White's favourite yew.

The village from Selborne Hanger.

351

SELWORTHY
SOMERSET

3 miles west of Minehead (page 420 Ab)

Thatched cottages are grouped around a pasture at Selworthy, reached by a lane where oak, ash and holly branches intermingle overhead.

The village is sheltered from the fierce sea winds by 1,013 ft Selworthy Beacon, rising above it to the north. To the south, across a green valley, lies Exmoor and its highest peak, 1,705 ft Dunkery Beacon – the best view of which can be seen from the steps of the largely 14th-century Church of All Saints. The church is perfectly proportioned, rich in stone carving and tracery, and has three magnificent wagon roofs, all lavishly decorated. There is a 14th-century tithe barn in the grounds of the former rectory.

Selworthy parish incorporates a number of outlying hamlets. Within easy walking distance are Lynch, 1¼ miles to the north-west, and Bossington, half a mile further on. Lynch has a 16th-century chapel of ease, built for the convenience of worshippers living some distance from their parish church, and at Bossington a stream gurgles into the sea over a pebble beach. Allerford, half a mile south-east of Lynch, has a two-arched packhorse bridge. At Tivington, under a wooded hill 1½ miles south-east of Selworthy, there is another, and lovely, chapel of ease. Dating from the 14th century, and thatched, it has a cottage attached at one end. All these hamlets have thatched cottages with cob walls of clay and straw mixture washed in pastel shades.

SHEEPWASH
DEVON

9 miles east of Holsworthy (page 419 Cc)

Hedge-lined lanes, in parts too narrow for cars to pass each other, lead through rich farmlands to this quiet village perched on a hill. The streets of Sheepwash radiate out from the village pump and war memorial, which stand in a gravel-covered square set among pink-washed cottages with thatched roofs. Fishermen come from many parts of the country to stay at the Half Moon Inn, which stands in the square and offers prospects of salmon in the nearby River Torridge.

Sheepwash has been a working rural community for 800 years, and there are farm buildings in natural stone right in the centre of the village. The 19th-century Church of St Lawrence, just off the square, has many slate tombstones in its graveyard. Great care has been taken to preserve the tombstones, many of which date from the last century and have gilded letters cut deeply into the slate.

Sheepwash was an important North Devon market town until it was devastated by fire in 1742. The site was afterwards deserted for more than ten years. The Church of St Lawrence is the third to be built on the site. The 'South Commons' are a medieval system of field 'strips', whose outlines can still be seen in the turf.

SHERIFF HUTTON
NORTH YORKSHIRE

9 miles north of York (page 436 Cc)

High grassy banks flank Sheriff Hutton's long main street as it climbs gently from a medieval church and past the village green. Little flights of steps lead to the brick and stone cottages perched above. York Minster's majestic towers can be seen 9 miles to the south, but the village skyline is dominated by the gaunt, jagged ruins of Sheriff Hutton Castle. However, of the earlier fortification, built by Bertram de Bulmer, Sheriff of York in about 1140 and from whose office the name of the village is derived, nothing remains, but it is associated in local memory with the earthworks to the south of the church.

The present castle was built by the Nevilles in the early 1380s, and a century later became one of the favourite residences of Richard III. The Duke of Richmond and Somerset, illegitimate son of Henry VIII, later lived there in royal style, but by the mid-17th century it had fallen into disrepair and had become little more than a quarry for local builders. Many of the older houses in

the village are built of the castle's stones; all the same, what survives is still vastly impressive. The remains are open to the public, and are reached by a private lane off the main street above the whitewashed Castle Inn.

The Church of St Helen and Holy Cross dates in part from Norman times, but major additions were made in the 14th and 15th centuries. Prince Edward, Richard III's only son who died a year before his father's defeat by Henry VII at Bosworth Field, is said to have been buried there in 1484. An alabaster effigy of a boy is believed to commemorate him. There is also an earlier monument to a 14th-century knight.

SHIELDAIG

HIGHLAND

On eastern shore of Loch Shieldaig (page 443 Ce)

In 1800, when the Napoleonic Wars were at their height and voluntary naval recruitment had reached an all-time low, someone at the Admiralty had a brilliant idea. Why not grow their own sailors? The seamanship of Highland fishermen was legendary – a superb quality that could be called upon by the nation in time of war. And so Shieldaig was born, as a kind of nursery for the Royal Navy. The new village was given grants for boat-building; guaranteed prices for fish; exemption from the salt tax; and a generous amount of land for each tenant. But, as the threat of war receded, the government's interest waned, and the village gradually went into a decline, from which it has now recovered.

Shieldaig is situated on the east side of Loch Shieldaig, an inlet of Loch Torridon. The village has a line of neat, whitewashed cottages overlooked by Ben Shieldaig and craggy ramparts of naked rock. Pine-clad Shieldaig Island, a National Trust for Scotland reserve, is just offshore. Inland, the road to Torridon, 7½ miles away, starts on the hillside behind the village and leads to some glorious and rugged countryside.

◆

BY ORDER OF THE LORDS COMMISSIONERS *The village of Shieldaig was born about 1800 out of an Admiralty scheme to encourage the growth of fishing communities – and hence of recruitable seamen – in the Highlands. However, Loch Shieldaig's fisheries potential had been exploited as long ago as the days of the Vikings, who called the place Sild-vik, 'Herring Bay'. The present name is a Gaelic adaptation of the Norse.*

SHIRLEY
DERBYSHIRE

4 miles south-east of Ashbourne (page 430 Bc)

Brick and stone cottages cluster about the junction of many lanes at Shirley, forming a pleasant patchwork among trim hedgerows and well-kept gardens. The village's name comes from the Old English term for 'a bright clearing'. The lords of the manor, who took their name from the village, later became the Earls Ferrers.

The Church of St Michael stands at the centre and highest point of the village. The chancel and south aisle date from the 14th century, but the rest of the church, including the tower, was rebuilt in the 19th century. A yew tree in the churchyard has a trunk 17 ft in circumference.

The white-painted Old Vicarage, on a hill towards Ashbourne, was the birthplace of the novelist brothers John Cowper Powys, in 1872, and Theodore Francis Powys, in 1875. Here, too, lived Countess Ferrers, widow of the 12th Earl, until her death in 1969. She and her husband are buried in Shirley churchyard. The Hall Farm, north-east of the church, was the home of the Shirleys, but has been much altered since medieval times, though traces of its moat remain.

SHORWELL
ISLE OF WIGHT

5 miles south-west of Newport (page 422 Ba)

Three manor houses – none open to the public – give an unusual air of distinction to Shorwell, which lies cupped in a wooded valley below the bare Downs. Not that Shorwell is a large place: it possesses only one apiece of those other essentials of village life – an inn, a shop and a church, St Peter's. The church is a hoarder's delight of many different treasures, including a 15th-century wall-painting, monuments, brasses, and a 500-year-old pulpit. There are also several rare books, including a Bible of 1541 and a Breeches Bible of 1579 – so called because it says Adam and Eve sewed fig-leaves together and made breeches, whereas the Authorised Version says they made aprons.

From the centre of the village, St Peter's looks towards Northcourt Manor, which was built by Sir John Leigh in 1615. In its grounds rises the Shor Well, which is the source of a stream that flows behind the cottages of the main street and through the garden of the Crown Inn. A little further on it passes the Elizabethan Wolverton Manor, second of Shorwell's three. The third manor, Westcourt, was started in the reign of Henry VIII and finished in the time of James I. It stands on the slope of the Downs, west of the Crown Inn. Near Westcourt's gates is the old village pound. About 1 mile south-west of the village, but still in the parish, is Yafford Mill, whose wheel is turned by the waters of the Shor Well stream. The mill, which was used until 1970, has been restored to full working order. It stands in what is now a farm park.

SHOTLEY BRIDGE
DURHAM

2 miles north-west of Consett (page 438 Bc)

Plain stone buildings skirting the main street seem to reflect the strict moral outlook and industriousness of the German sword-makers who settled in Shotley Bridge at the end of the 17th century. The craftsmen's work made the village famous, and their long and flexible blades rivalled those made in Toledo.

Shotley Bridge is idyllically situated in the tree-filled Derwent Valley, on the Durham-Northumberland border. In the centre of the village, a single-arched bridge spans the water linking the two counties. The upper reaches of the river have been dammed to form the Derwent Reservoir – a beautifully sited spot, where fishing, sailing and bird-watching are popular.

It was the river that attracted the Protestant sword-makers, who had fled from religious persecution in Germany. The soft water was particularly suited to early methods of steel-making, and some large stones in the Derwent have sharpening grooves left by the blades. The Mohls, Oleys and other families kept the industry going until the late 19th century.

The sword-makers mostly lived in small terraced houses – now demolished – with German inscriptions on the outside walls. But, in 1787, the Oleys built their own house – Cutler's Hall – at Benfieldside, high above the village.

The site of the former Shotley Bridge Railway Station is now a picnic spot. From there, a path along the old railway line runs 6½ miles to Rowland's Gill.

SILSOE
BEDFORDSHIRE

9 miles south of Bedford (page 426 Cb)

Pavement-hugging brick cottages with little gabled windows set in their tiled roofs line Silsoe's picturesque High Street. At its head is the George Hotel, a coaching inn in Georgian times, when the village was a staging-post between Bedford and Luton. Behind the High Street the village spreads westward along narrow, tree-shaded lanes, with houses ranging from 16th-century timber and thatch to Georgian. A lock-up with an arched doorway stands in the garden of a house in Church Road.

The ironstone Church of St James – rebuilt in 1830 – is in the village centre at the entrance to Wrest Park. The manor of Wrest was held by the Earls de Grey family from the late 13th century until the early 1900s. The present house, built in French Renaissance style in 1834, is not open to the public, but the landscaped gardens are open on summer weekends. They were designed in the early 1700s by Henry Grey, Duke of Kent, and later adapted by Capability Brown.

SIMONBURN, Northumberland (page 438 Ac)
(see Wark)

SINGLETON
WEST SUSSEX

5 miles north of Chichester (page 422 Cb)

A compact collection of 17th and 18th-century houses, set in a fold of the South Downs, forms the core of the village, which lies in the valley of the River Lavant where the main road from Chichester turns northwards towards Midhurst. The houses are almost entirely of flint and brick. Occasionally, there are glimpses of older timber work. Inns dating from the 18th century, the Fox and Hounds and the Horse and Groom, recall an era when Singleton was the home of the celebrated Charlton Hunt.

The church, which stands to the south of the village, shows evidence of Saxon work in its walls and tower. The pews are Tudor, and the oak roof beams date to the 14th century. Medieval graffiti – symbols such as pilgrims' crosses – are scratched into the stonework around the porch.

The Weald and Downland Open Air Museum is just outside Singleton, set in parkland. It consists of old buildings brought from other parts of the area and reconstructed.

A mile to the north, along the road to Midhurst, stands an 18th-century house called the Drovers, said to have been the headquarters of smugglers who used secret passages there.

SKENFRITH
GWENT

6 miles north-west of Monmouth (page 425 Db)

A soft landscape of streams and wooded hills surrounds Skenfrith, which grew up around one of three Norman castles on the border between Gwent and Herefordshire. It has a great deal of character, like many other places poised between Wales and England, and a delightfully peaceful atmosphere that belies its military origins. Buildings of warm sandstone overlook a lush expanse of greensward that surrounds the ruined 13th-century castle, with its circular towers and central keep. The stronghold's eastern walls were protected by the Monnow, a river noted for its trout, which flows past an old mill and skirts the whitewashed Bell Inn.

Skenfrith's church may be a few decades older than the castle, and has a sturdy tower that was probably used as a refuge in times of trouble. It is capped with an unusual dovecot of open woodwork that rises in two stages and is roofed with slate. In the north aisle is the tomb of John Morgan and his wife, Ann. Morgan, who died at Skenfrith in 1557, was the steward of the Duchy of Lancaster, the local MP, and the last governor of the three castles. The tomb's effigies are notable for the detail of their Tudor costumes.

WHERE BORDER FEUDS
WERE FOUGHT

The peaceful little village of Skenfrith in Gwent grew up in the shadow of one of three Norman castles – the others are at Grosmont and White Castle – which together formed a defensive triangle on the turbulent Anglo-Welsh border. On the southern wall of Skenfrith's ruined castle there is a watermill, founded in the 14th century.

The old watermill.

The village at peace.

MOORLAND VILLAGE *A stone bridge spans the River Hodder and leads to the greystone village of Slaidburn, set in the heart of Lancashire's moorland region known as Bowland.*

SLAIDBURN

LANCASHIRE

7 miles north of Clitheroe (page 435 Dc)

Cobbled pavements flank Slaidburn's narrow main street, which climbs from a stone bridge over the River Hodder. Slaidburn lies in a fold in the moors, where the Croasdale Brook joins the River Hodder below the Forest of Bowland.

Many of the village's houses and cottages are built of grey stone, and two of the main buildings bear inscriptions which proclaim their age. An elegant two-storey building in Church Street, which was once the grammar school, has a carved plaque over the door saying that it was 'erected and endowed by John Brennand, late of Panehill in this Parish, Gentleman, who died on the 15th day of May in the year of Our LORD 1717'. It is now the local primary school. At the lower end of the village, overlooking the green and the river, is a large stone barn bearing the words: 'Erected AD 1852 for the use of the industrious poor of the Township of Slaidburn, for ever.'

At the centre of the village, where Church Street and Chapel Street meet, stands an inn called the Hark to Bounty. The sign shows a clergyman listening to a dog baying at the full moon. Local legend says that Bounty was the name of a foxhound belonging to a 19th-century squarson named Wigglesworth, who was both squire and rector of the parish. Whenever he took a drink at the inn, Wigglesworth would leave the hound outside and, when it barked, would say to his companions, 'Hark to Bounty'.

THE SLAUGHTERS

GLOUCESTERSHIRE

10 miles west of Chipping Norton (page 421 Dd)

Beautiful villages of great character and charm are plentiful in the Cotswolds, but few can equal the mellow, picture-postcard attractions of Lower and Upper Slaughter. A mile apart, with the River Eye running through them, the 'twins' are memorable clusters of rich, honey-coloured stone buildings which blend perfectly into the roll-ing landscape of the Gloucestershire countryside.

Many of the buildings date from the 16th and 17th centuries. Lower Slaughter has several relatively new houses, some of which have windows with stone mullions and small, rectangular panes edged with lead. No houses have been built in Upper Slaughter since 1904, although some cottages in Baghot's Square, by the churchyard, were remodelled by Sir Edwin Lutyens in 1906.

Lower Slaughter's tree-shaded main street runs beside the river. The southern side is notable for Manor Farm, with its creeper-clad walls and mossy roof. The farm, enlarged in 1688, stands almost opposite what is now the Manor Hotel. Originally known as the Manor House, it was built in the mid-17th century for Sir Richard Whitmore, Sheriff of Gloucestershire and MP for Bridgnorth. Its 16th-century dovecot is one of the largest in Gloucestershire.

Members of the Whitmore family, including several distinguished soldiers, are commemorated by brass tablets in St Mary's Church. It was rebuilt by Charles Shapland Whitmore in 1866-7, but stands on medieval foundations.

From the church, a short and enchanting riverside walk leads to The Square, where picturesque cottages bunch round an old water trough whose spout is shaped like a lion's head. Flanked by cottages on one side and low, stone footbridges on the other, the path continues to the early-19th-century corn-mill – which worked into the 1960s and retains its water-wheel. It now incorporates the village shop, bakery and post office, and has practically the only brickwork to be seen in Lower Slaughter.

Mill Cottage, Malthouse Cottage, Ivy Cottage and their neighbours make Malthouse Lane a stroller's delight as it doubles back to The Square. As the administrative centre of a 'hundred' – an ancient form of local government – Lower Slaughter was the seat of a court which sat every three weeks from the Middle Ages until the 17th century. The village prison was in use until 1630, a century after the local scaffold had claimed its last victim. It is commemorated by the name of Gallow's Piece, a field south-west of the village.

Some of Lower Slaughter's most attractive buildings line the river's southern bank. Dene House, its ground-floor windows peeping out from 'frames' of trimmed box, stands next to the trim Victorian school which is now a private house. Their near-neighbour, Washbourne's Place, takes its name from a 15th-century owner and overlooks the village's main bridge.

Upper Slaughter stands on a gentle, grassy hill above Slaughter Brook and was once dominated by a Norman castle. The remains of a motte and bailey have survived behind the early-18th-century Home Farm, and stand in the centre of the village. Pottery from the 11th to 13th centuries has been found on the castle mound.

COTSWOLD TWINS *Upper Slaughter, a confection of honey-coloured stone and lush gardens, is rivalled for beauty by its 'twin', Lower Slaughter, to which it is linked by the limpid waters of the River Eye. The grim-sounding name which the villages share has nothing to do with death and destruction – it comes from the Anglo-Saxon word* slohtre, *which means nothing more gruesome than 'muddy place'.*

The path leading to the main entrance of St Peter's Church goes past the cottages of Rose Row with their long front gardens. The church dates from Norman times, but was substantially restored in 1877. Among those commemorated in the church are 16th and 17th-century members of the Slaughter family, and Francis Edward Witts, Upper Slaughter's rector from 1808 until 1854, has a canopied tomb in the north-east corner of the church. His *Diary of a Cotswold Parson* was published in 1978. The Witts's home, set in attractive grounds, is now the Lords of the Manor Hotel. Near by is the Manor House which was built by the Slaughters in the 16th century and is open to visitors on Friday afternoons from May to September.

The village school, east of the churchyard and reached from it by a narrow footpath, dates from 1846 and is on the site of its 18th-century predecessor. Immediately beyond it, a lane sweeps down a broad, open field, dotted with trees, to a pleasant stretch of river crossed by two foot-bridges and a ford. The approach to the ford is overlooked by one of the village's many picturesque cottages, while larger buildings on the far bank include a barn with a dovecot built into one wall. The Way's End, a handsome old house a short distance upstream, was the rectory from 1914 until 1955. Opposite the ford is a tiny Methodist chapel, dated 1865 but unused since before the Second World War.

A peaceful lane follows the river downstream, passing several pretty cottages and a fine old stone barn with a massive oak lintel. The Dingle, set on gently rising ground above the road bridge over Slaughter Brook, was built in 1905 as the manor's dower house. Many of the other buildings date from the 17th and 18th centuries and feature stone 'dripmoulds' above their windows. Most of the cottages were topped with thatch until, at the end of the 18th century, it gave way to chunky stone tiles.

SLEDMERE
HUMBERSIDE

7 miles north-west of Great Driffield (page 437 Cc)

Immaculate Sledmere and the Yorkshire Wolds for miles around are a tribute to generations of foresight by the Sykes family. Outside the parkland estate of Sledmere House, the village of pleasant red or cream-washed brick and the bountiful farmland beyond are rich in reminders of the dedicated tradition upheld by the family, who in Tudor times were merchants in Leeds. Richard Sykes started building Sledmere House in 1751, where a medieval manor once stood, its people in terror of marauding wolf packs from the surrounding wilderness. His work was carried on in the 1780s by his nephew Sir Christopher Sykes, whose addition of great wings gave the building its air of grandeur. Sir Christopher's major endeavour, though, was the development of agriculture on the Wolds. A Classical temple by the main gates to the house commemorates his achievement in building, planting and enclosing 'a bleak and barren tract of country'.

A 120 ft Gothic tower, which stands 2½ miles south-east at Garton Hill, commemorates Sir Tatton Sykes, who won fame as a bare-knuckle fighter. He died in 1863.

The great house was heavily damaged by fire in 1911, but lavishly renovated. Its magnificent Turkish Room was inspired by the private apartments of the sultans in Istanbul. The village was also rebuilt, on the north-east edge of the park, at about the same time. The new buildings, however, were designed to remain faithful to the appearance of their forerunners.

On the opposite side of the road from the church stands perhaps the most remarkable village war memorial in Britain. It is a 60 ft high copy of the ornate medieval Eleanor Cross at Northampton, set with brasses which depict the Sledmere men who died in 1914–18. Near by is another monument just as unusual. Its carved scenes tell the story of the Waggoners Reserve, a 1,000-strong corps of farm-workers assembled in 1912 by Lt. Col. Sir Mark Sykes each of whom was paid £1 a year. When war came in France, they provided horse-drawn transport for supplies to the front lines.

Sledmere's pub, The Triton, was an 18th-century coaching inn. A sign still proclaims that the landlord is 'licensed to let post horses'.

SLINDON
WEST SUSSEX

4 miles west of Arundel (page 422 Cb)

Narrow, hedged lanes form a rough square around which are grouped cottages of flint, their dates ranging from 1693 to 1922. Despite the time-span, the use of flintwork and traditional styles gives the place a sense of architectural unity. The village is surrounded by 3,500 acres of farmland and woodland owned by the National Trust, where the beech trees are among the finest in England.

Slindon occupies a shelf on the southern slopes of the South Downs, from where the view sweeps right across the coastal plain to the Channel. The village was founded by the West Saxons, and its name means 'sloping hill'. The village became a residence of the Archbishops of Canterbury, and traces of their palace are found in Slindon House, rebuilt around 1560 and much altered in the 1920s. It is now a private school. Archbishop Stephen Langton died there in 1228. He acted as a mediator during the negotiations which led to King John's acceptance of Magna Carta.

A thatched post office and the Newburgh Arms Inn stand at one corner of the lanes. In another is a pond, where walkways lead off into the beechwoods. On the other side of the village is the flint church, dating from the 11th century. The church contains the wooden effigy of a reclining Tudor knight, 5 ft long and dressed in armour. It is the only wooden effigy of its period in Sussex.

Nore Folly, a flint arch on a hill 1 mile north-west of the village, was built in the early 19th century for the Newburgh family, who used it as an outdoor dining place.

SMARDEN
KENT
7 miles south-west of Charing (page 423 Eb)

Houses with black-and-white timberwork and white weather-boards have been preserved in this village on the level clay plain of the Kentish Weald. Many of them have tall, elegant wooden gables. Smarden was once a market town, licensed by Edward III in 1332. In the 15th century, 66 men from Smarden – weavers, fullers, tailors and drapers – took part in the rebellion of small property holders led by Jack Cade, protesting against high taxes and prices. Later, when Elizabeth I visited the place, Smarden was noted for its cloth trade. She confirmed its right to a five-day fair with a charter.

The village's prosperity is recalled by the timber-framed houses in the main street called simply, The Street. Notable among them are Chessenden, a Wealden hall-house, and Dragon House, which is decorated by a frieze of dragons. Near by stands the village pump.

A group of medieval houses lies just to the west of the churchyard, on the road to Headcorn; first, Matthew Hartnup's house with his name carved on the main beam of the upper storey. Alongside stands one of the best surviving cloth halls in the county, with the hoist used for lifting bales of cloth still hanging from its gable end.

The pathway in front of the Cloth Hall and the entry to the churchyard are paved with a local limestone containing fossilised snails. St Michael's Church, which dates from the 14th century, is known as the 'Barn of Kent' because of its 36 ft wide roof-span over an aisleless nave.

◆

UNSELFCONSCIOUS CHARM *Tiled roofs and weather-boarded walls are characteristic of centuries-old cottages in Smarden, Kent – a peaceful little village that belies its bustling past as an Elizabethan market town and centre of the cloth trade.*

SOMERSBY
LINCOLNSHIRE
6 miles east of Horncastle (page 432 Be)

Little has changed in Somersby since Alfred Tennyson, who was to become Lord Tennyson and Poet Laureate of England, spent his boyhood there, roaming a countryside which he lovingly recalled as being rich 'with plaited alleys of the trailing rose'. The church where his father preached, and the former rectory where the poet was born in 1809 are much as they were last century. Barely a dozen houses, mostly hidden away among woods and along narrow winding lanes, make up the rest of the little community.

Alfred was one of 12 children brought up by the Reverend George Tennyson at the rectory, now Somersby House. The rambling, cream-washed building is set back behind hedges of holly and yew opposite the Church of St Margaret, but it is not open to the public.

A bust of Tennyson has a proud place in the church, where his father was buried in 1831, and a glass case contains some of the poet's relics.

Opposite the church is a battlemented house said to have been built in the 18th century by Sir John Vanbrugh, designer of Blenheim Palace.

STAGSDEN
BEDFORDSHIRE
4 miles west of Bedford (page 426 Bb)

An assortment of thatched, stone cottages lines Stagsden's main street. One has thatch sweeping down to head height. Two others – the White Horse and Dog and Duck – were once public houses. And Fir Tree Cottage was the village school. Lanes lead from the village to Hanger and Astey woods with their streams and bridges.

Stagsden is a thriving agricultural community with many outlying farmsteads. It lies on a low ridge flanked by gentle hills and green meadowland. The greystone vicarage was built in 1844, and next to it is the 13th and 14th-century Church of St Leonard. The interior was renovated by local craftsmen in 1976-7. The Tudor screen has been re-touched, broken Tudor roses replaced, and the organ has been restored. This was built in 1802, and was originally a barrel-organ, later converted to a manual organ.

Church Lane leads to Stagsden Bird Gardens. There, in 8 acres of woodland, some 150 species of British and foreign birds are kept.

◆

THE SMITHY AT STAGSDEN *Like many smiths who ply their ▷ trade a long way from racing or livery stables, John Lowe has abandoned shoeing as a means of making a living. Now his skills are applied instead to swift, long-lasting repairs on modern farm machinery – to combine-harvesters when the crop is threatened by thunderclouds, to ploughshare points broken on flint, or, as here, to hammering new harrow rings out of mild steel rod. Though working horses have largely vanished from the countryside, the blacksmith remains, an integral part of the community.*

STAGSDEN

BESIDE THE CRUEL SEA *A bluff headland wraps a protecting arm around Staithes, on the North Yorkshire coast, where gulls forage among pools left by the retreating tide. There could be no more tranquil scene – in summer. But Staithes also has to face the gales of winter, so the sea-front houses shelter behind massive stone walls.*

STAITHES

NORTH YORKSHIRE

9 miles north-west of Whitby (page 436 Cd)

Crouched between the twin headlands of Cowbar Nab and Penny Nab, and with a maze of cobbled streets running steeply up from the harbour, the village at first sight resembles the fishing hamlets of North Devon and Cornwall. But it lacks the cream teas, the balmy breezes of the south-west and the general air of colourful prosperity. Staithes – pronounced 'Steers' in the local dialect – is, and always has been, a tough, working village looking outwards to the sea and inland to the alum, potash and ironstone mines for its livelihood. Beyond unfailing courtesy and easy, ready conversation, it can afford few concessions to the tourist. And if old ladies taking the air on Seaton Garth by the harbour wall still wear the white, starched cotton bonnets of their ancestors, they do so without any sense of quaintness.

About the beginning of this century there were more than 100 fishing cobles in Staithes. Now there are no more than a dozen of these gaily painted craft riding to buoys in the outer harbour, or tied up along the Staithes Beck whose deep gorge divides the village in two. All the same, fishing still flourishes. Piles of D-framed, netted lobster-pots lie beside the lifeboat station; and, everywhere, men in seaboots and oilskins tinker with outboard motors or carry fishing tackle up through the streets. The adventure and tragedy of the sea runs through the village's story. Beowulf, the 6th-century Viking hero, may have been buried at the top of nearby Boulby Cliff, the highest coastal point in the north-east. James Cook began his career as a navigator when, in 1741, he quit his job as an apprentice grocer in a local shop and signed on as cabin boy in a Whitby ship. The original shop was destroyed in a storm, but its successor, behind the harbour, still bears a plaque recalling Cook's association with the place.

The American privateer John Paul Jones raided the village for supplies in 1779 and, later, a large number of Staithes men, caught by the press gang, fought and died at Trafalgar, or spent years in Napoleon's prisons.

Many of the waterfront buildings, including the attractive Cod and Lobster pub, have been knocked down by the sea several times over the last century or so and have been doggedly rebuilt. At least they served to protect the web of alleys that run between High Street and Church Street – alleys that bear extraordinary names such as Gunn Gutter, Slip Top, Stone Garth and Dog Loup. Dog Loup is reputed to be the narrowest street in the North of England and, since it cannot be more than about 18 in. wide, it probably is.

High Street and Church Street run uphill roughly parallel to one another, forming, in effect, the right and left boundaries of the village. Church Street takes its name from the 19th-century Church of St Peter the Fisherman, one of five places of worship in Staithes. The others are a Catholic church and three non-conformist chapels. St Peter's apart, the street contains a pleasant jumble of architecture – Georgian houses and rockery-girt cottages approached by steep flights of steps. Each building has its stamp of

362

individuality, like the black-tarred cottage which has a brightly painted figurehead of a Viking guarding its door.

The High Street also contains a number of fine stone buildings and one or two antiques shops, including The Smugglers, which has reproductions of superb Frank Sutcliffe photographs of Staithes taken at the beginning of the century. From these it can be seen how markedly the fishing fleet has declined. The difference is all the more pointed if you walk through the lane behind the shop to the edge of the cliff overlooking the beck and the harbour – a favourite view of Sutcliffe's. But though most of the boats have gone, the old houses still cling to Beckside.

STANHOPE
DURHAM

6 miles west of Wolsingham (page 438 Ab)

High fells and sprawling moorland embrace Stanhope, the 'Capital of Upper Weardale', a village built of the local limestone. The village radiates from the trim, 15th-century Market Place with its simple stone cross. In the south-west corner is Stanhope Castle, a pseudo-medieval fortress with battlements and towers, which was built in 1798 on the site of an old manor house. It is now a school. The North Wall of the adjacent Castle Park is noted for its unusual stone patterns – which are formed like a fish, a bull, and other creatures.

On the north side of the Market Place stands the 12th-century St Thomas's Church, with its stumpy tower. By the churchyard entrance is a 5 ft high petrified tree stump, believed to be some 250 million years old, which was unearthed in a local quarry in 1959. To the left of the church porch is a collection of 13th-century coffins in dark limestone quarried in the neighbouring village of Frosterley.

Near by, at the head of Church Lane, is Stone House, the former 17th-century rectory which was rebuilt in its original style in 1821. The sober, 19th-century Methodist chapel was attended by many of the miners and quarrymen who once dug coal, lead, iron, silver and limestone in the area. A terrace of miners' cottages has been restored in Chapel Street.

Stanhope Hall, an impressive, fortified manor house, is a mixture of medieval, Elizabethan and Jacobean architecture. The hall is not open to the public, but there are fine views of it from the west end of the village. Beyond the hall, in Stanhope Dene, are the remains of lead and iron mines. From there, Stanhope Beck leads upstream to Heathery Burn Cave, in which – between 1843 and 1872 – a number of Bronze Age artefacts were discovered.

The River Wear flows near by, and a short distance downstream is the privately occupied Unthank Hall, an Elizabethan farmhouse. Unthank means 'without permission' in Anglo-Saxon, and usually refers to a place first settled by squatters. Further downstream is the disused Unthank Mill, standing beside Stanhope Showground.

STANTON
GLOUCESTERSHIRE

3 miles south-west of Broadway (page 421 Dd)

The long main street climbs the gentle Cotswold foothills to end at the Mount Inn. On either side of the street the houses are of golden stone with steeply pitched gables, and were built around 1600. Yet their appearance today is much as it was when they were built, thanks to the efforts of the architect Sir Philip Stott who owned the estate from 1906 to 1937.

Sir Philip's former home, Stanton Court, is a fine Jacobean house with beautiful grounds. The gardens are sometimes open to the public on Sundays during the summer. The original manor house, Warren Farm House, is partly 16th century. Also of medieval origin is the village cross, another fine example of Stott's restoration work.

Furnishings by the architect Sir Ninian Comper can be seen in St Michael's and All Angels Church. His rood screen of 1923, organ loft of 1918 and a number of windows blend well with the church's Norman architecture. The east window, which was destroyed by prisoners shut in the church during the Civil War, was also restored by Comper. Some medieval pews survive, and deep grooves in their ends are said to have been made by the leashes of dogs brought inside by shepherds.

STANTON DREW, Avon (page 421 Cc)
(see Chew Magna)

STAUNTON-IN-THE-VALE
NOTTINGHAMSHIRE

6 miles south of Newark-on-Trent (page 430 Cc)

When Sir Walter Scott stayed at Staunton Hall he found the village typical of English pastoral beauty, and the hall became 'Willingham' in his *Heart of Midlothian* published in 1818. In more than a century and a half, little has changed. The houses still huddle together around the church and the hall which, standing close together, form the heart of Staunton-in-the-Vale.

The vale is the fertile Vale of Belvoir, watered by the River Devon flowing northwards to the Trent. The river winds past sloping lawns that run down from Staunton Hall, home of the Staunton family for more than 400 years. In 1794 the upper floor was heightened and bay windows were added. The Stauntons supported Charles I when he raised his standard at Nottingham in 1642, and their home was attacked by Cromwell's forces. Bullet holes can still be seen in one of the doors.

The Church of St Mary was extensively restored in 1853, but the tower, arcades and aisle windows date from the late 14th century. Inside are many memorials to the Stauntons, for they were associated with the village in medieval times. They commanded Belvoir Castle, 6 miles to the south, under the Normans, and its main tower is named Staunton Tower.

STENTON
LOTHIAN

5 miles south-west of Dunbar (page 441 Gd)

In a district which prides itself on its architectural heritage, few groups of buildings are in such perfect harmony as the red-tiled cottages and 16th-century church tower, now a dovecot, which surround the little green at Stenton.

On the green stands the old 'tron', or weighing-beam, once used in the busy days of the Stenton fairs to measure bales of wool. The heyday of the old fairs was also a time of witchcraft. On March 1, 1659, Bessie Knox and four of her friends, known together as the Stenton Witches, were strangled and their bodies afterwards burned.

The old church tower stands within the grounds of the present church, which was completely rebuilt in 1829. Beyond it at the east end of the village, beside the road to Pitcox and Dunbar, is the ancient Rood Well. This is covered by a tiny circular building with a conical roof topped by a stone ornament, which local tradition claims is meant to represent a cardinal's hat.

STINSFORD
DORSET

1 mile east of Dorchester (page 421 Ca)

Thomas Hardy's heart is buried in the village churchyard, and Stinsford is known to be the 'Mellstock' of many of his poems and novels – including *Under the Greenwood Tree*. Hardy, who died in 1928 and whose ashes are in Westminster Abbey, was born in nearby Higher Bockhampton in 1840, and his detached home is at the end of a row of cottages in a leafy lane not far from Yellowham Wood. 'Hardy's Cottage' belongs to the National Trust, and is open in the summer.

Stinsford is set in the wooded valley of the River Frome, which is a favourite place for trout-fishers. The main house in the village is the red-brick and gabled Stinsford House, a few yards from the 13th-century Church of St Michael.

In 1972 the remains of another great man of letters, C. Day-Lewis, the Poet Laureate, were buried in the churchyard, close to the resting-place of Hardy's heart. At Stinsford Cross, on the south side of the A35, is what is thought to be a Roman milestone.

STEYNING
WEST SUSSEX

5 miles north-west of Shoreham-by-Sea (page 422 Db)

A Saxon thatched cottage fronts on to a small green at one end of Church Street. It is surrounded by 17th-century cottages and is not far from a Norman church. Beyond the churchyard, partly hidden in its extensive grounds, stands an 18th-century brick vicarage. This jumble of building styles is typical of Church Lane itself, a street that shows off every type of local building material and several centuries of styles as it runs from the church to the village High Street. Flint, timber, brick, tile, thatch, Horsham slate and stone are found in its buildings. Cottages of the 15th, 16th and 17th centuries line the street. An old grammar school, bearing the date 1614 but with some 19th-century additions, is now used as a school library. At the end of the street, near its junction with the High Street, is a 17th-century house, which has a central recess with overhanging wings.

Shops and inns line the High Street, which rises to the Old Market House with a tile-hung front and a projecting clock-turret. Timber-framed structures survive behind many of the brick fronts of these buildings.

A stone which may have given the village its ancient name stands in the porch of the Church of St Andrew. The strangely carved slab has crude geometric designs and was discovered in an Anglo-Saxon burial ground at the east end of the present churchyard. The church itself has a decorated lofty interior and was built of stone imported from Normandy.

Half a mile to the east of the village, along the main road to Shoreham, is Bramber Castle, a ruin now in the possession of the National Trust.

STOKE BRUERNE
NORTHAMPTONSHIRE

4 miles east of Towcester (page 430 Ca)

Although comparatively few narrow-boats now pass along it, the Grand Union Canal plays a prominent part in the daily life of Stoke Bruerne. It winds through the hillside village, under the double-arched Canal Bridge, and on to Blisworth Tunnel. The tunnel extends for nearly 2 miles, and is the longest of its kind still in regular use in England.

Relics of canal life are housed in the nearby Waterways Museum – a converted 19th-century grain warehouse, which was opened in 1963. As well as a wealth of technical information and exhibits, it contains a life-sized model of the interior of a narrow-boat. Short trips are run along the canal in the summer, and there is a pretty walk along the canal towpath.

The heart of the village is the green, surrounded by limestone cottages and overlooked by the Norman Church of St Mary. The marble war memorial in the churchyard is unusual in that it bears a woman's name. Sister Elsie Bull, the daughter of a coachman at nearby Stoke Park, was a nurse in the First World War. She survived a typhus plague in Serbia; and finally died in 1918.

All that remains of Stoke Park - the first English house to be designed in the Classical Italian style - are two pavilions which were linked by the now demolished central block. The house was designed in the 1630s by the architect Inigo Jones. The design had been brought from Italy by Sir Francis Crane, the royal tapestry-maker. Sir Francis lived in Stoke Park, and in 1635 - the year before he died - he entertained Charles I at his showplace home.

GRAFTON REGIS Henry VIII courted Anne Boleyn, his second wife, at the Manor House at Grafton, 2 miles south-east of Stoke Bruerne. It became a royal possession in 1527, and in 1541, Henry added Regis to Grafton's name. In 1675 Charles II selected the manor for the title of the dukedom he conferred on Henry Fitzroy, his son by the Duchess of Cleveland.

STOKE-BY-NAYLAND
SUFFOLK

5 miles south-west of Hadleigh (page 432 Cb)

A stiff climb to St Mary's Church, rising out of the Stour Valley, is rewarded by a fine view of 'Constable Country'. Stoke is regarded as the heart of the area which the painter John Constable used in his Suffolk landscapes, and the largely 15th-century church itself features in several of his paintings. Its tower of flint and mellow, peach-coloured brick rises 120 ft, looking down on a neat rectangle of village streets and providing a landmark for miles around.

Perched on a hillside to the south of the church runs a row of timbered almshouses, looking as they probably did centuries ago. A stroll from the church to School Street leads to the fine 16th-century Guildhall and the Maltings, dating mostly from the same period. Now converted into four cottages, part of the Maltings was once a medieval hall-house.

Near the lych-gate in School Street is the building housing the well, down which a servant of Lord Windsor's fell to his death in 1603, and a tiny brick structure with a grating high up in one wall. This was once the village lock-up.

But the village possesses more momentous links with the past than these. Brasses and memorials inside St Mary's include a 16th-century brass of Lady Howard, an ancestor of two of Henry VIII's ill-fated wives, Catherine Howard and Anne Boleyn, who were both beheaded; and a 6 ft brass monument of a knight in full armour – Sir William Tendring, who fought at the Battle of Agincourt and who died six years later in 1421.

The 16th-century Thorington Hall, whose tall Tudor chimneys rise south-east of the village, is a fine example of a yeoman's house, virtually unchanged by the centuries.

A PAINTER'S INSPIRATION

Unsullied views for miles around drew the landscape painter, John Constable, like a magnet to Stoke-by-Nayland. Here he found peace and gathered inspiration for many of the masterpieces which will keep this picturesque corner of England alive for ever. Much of the village remains unchanged since his brush captured it on canvas. The 15th-century church, which he loved so much, contains memorials to the village's famous sons and daughters. Above soars its tower which looks down on the timber-framed Guildhall, below.

Detail of Sir William Tendring's brass.

Mourners from a floor brass.

STOKE SUB HAMDON
SOMERSET

5 miles west of Yeovil (page 421 Bb)

Meadowland divides Stoke Sub Hamdon into two parts – West Stoke, where most of the people live, and East Stoke, where the Church of St Mary stands. To the south is Ham Hill, sometimes called Hamdon Hill, now a country park. It is covered by a network of earthen ramparts, ridges and terraces created largely by a succession of peoples who fortified it in prehistoric times. But part of its outline is a legacy of centuries of quarrying for its honey-coloured stone.

This stone was used to build all the houses on the north side of the main street. Many of them, even the smaller cottages, have mullioned windows and well-proportioned gables and date back to the 17th century. On a road leading north from West Stoke stands The Priory, a complex of buildings begun in the 14th century to house priests from a long-vanished chantry. The Priory is now preserved by the National Trust, and its hall is open free to the public.

The church itself has a Norman nave and chancel arch, with a 15th-century panelled timber roof, carved bench-ends of the same period, and an iron-framed hour-glass by the Jacobean pulpit. Traces of 15th-century mural paintings, representing four angels, remain on the upper walls of the nave, and in the massive transept walls are squints – holes cut to allow a view of the altar.

STONE IN OXNEY, Kent (page 423 Eb)
(see Appledore)

STONELEIGH
WARWICKSHIRE

3 miles east of Kenilworth (page 430 Bb)

The tiny River Sowe flows through Stoneleigh on its way to join the Avon, and the early-19th-century Sowe Bridge forms an elegant approach from the east to this attractive village. There are many timber-framed houses and cottages with brick infilling, a black-and-white gabled farmhouse, and a smithy.

STOURTON'S SIMPLICITY AND GRANDEUR

For more than 200 years the Hoare family of City bankers dominated Stourton. The marble tomb of Sir Richard Colt Hoare stands under a Gothic stone canopy on a slope in St Peter's churchyard. It was placed there by Sir Richard in 1819 – 19 years before his death. The medieval church and the neighbouring cottages are linked by lawns to the Hoares' home, Stourhead. The house stands in one of the finest gardens in England, landscaped round an artificial lake overlooked by a pantheon.

Stourhead Gardens.

St Peter's churchyard.

The red-sandstone Church of St Mary is Norman, and contains a magnificent chancel arch and monuments to the Leigh family. Alice Leigh was a co-founder of the red-sandstone Old Almshouses in the village in 1594. In 1596, she married Sir Robert Dudley. She was made Duchess of Dudley by Charles I in 1645.

Stoneleigh Abbey, the ancestral home of the Leigh family, is a magnificent blend of the remains of the old abbey with a Georgian mansion. Part of the house and grounds are open on Sundays and Bank Holidays in the summer.

STOURTON
WILTSHIRE

3 miles north-west of Mere (page 421 Cb)

Unfenced lawns in front of neat stone houses border the road at Stourton, an estate village laid out in a deep, wooded valley leading down to a lake. Cars are normally left in a large car park on the plateau above the valley, the walk down through the trees being only a few hundred yards. Though always lovely, Stourton is especially so in the early spring when the daffodils are in bloom, and a few weeks later when the rhododendrons and azaleas glow with colour.

The great house of Stourhead was completed in 1724. The library and picture gallery were added later. An artificial lake was created by damming the headwaters of the River Stour. In 1946 the owners of the house, the Hoare family, presented it to the National Trust. Stourhead is perhaps one of the finest examples of 18th-century landscape gardening in England. The house has an outstanding collection of works of art and furniture by Chippendale the Younger.

STRATHPEFFER
HIGHLAND

4 miles west of Dingwall (page 443 De)

At the western end of Strathpeffer stands a youth hostel which was originally the home of Dr Thomas Morrison, whose enterprise created this Highland health resort. Dr Morrison visited the village at the beginning of the 19th century, and found that the waters – four sulphur springs and one chalybeate spring – relieved his ailments. He set up home there, and in 1819 he persuaded the local landowner to build a wooden pump-room over one of the springs – the Strong Well. The first hotel was opened in the 1830s, but Strathpeffer did not fully flourish until 1862, when a railway station was opened near by.

By then a new and larger stone-built pump-room had been erected, and in the 1870s it was extended to become the Baths Establishment – the site of which is now an extension of the village square, with some of the original stonework contained in the road surface. The proprietors built a pavilion facing it, and the shops in the square were painted white and green – the colours of the pump-room and pavilion.

STRETTON-ON-DUNSMORE
WARWICKSHIRE

6 miles west of Rugby (page 430 Bb)

In the heart of the village – which stands on Dunsmore Heath and straddles the Roman Foss Way – is a triangular green divided by a stream and crossed by low brick bridges. Around it are timber-framed and red-brick dwellings and farm buildings. A post office, some shops and two inns complete the rural scene, which is dominated by the lofty Victorian tower of All Saints' Church.

Each year on St Martin's Day, November 11, people from Stretton and other villages gather in a local field at sunrise to celebrate a custom that dates from Saxon times. An agent of the lord of the manor, the Duke of Buccleuch, collects 'Wroth Silver' – a payment which preserves the ancient right of villagers to drive cattle across the duke's land.

The amounts paid range from ½p to 21½p and total 47p. After the ceremony the villagers have breakfast at the duke's expense in the nearby Dun Cow Inn.

STRONTIAN
HIGHLAND

20 miles south-west of Fort William (page 443 Cc)

Strontium, the element discovered in 1786, got its name from the lochside village of Strontian, where it was found in the local lead mines. Strontium was isolated in 1808 by Sir Humphry Davy, the scientist and inventor of the miners' safety lamp. The remains of the mines, last worked in 1904, are to the north of the village.

Strontian was rebuilt in the late 1960s by the Department of Agriculture and Fisheries for Scotland. The Department divided the larger farms into smallholdings for crofters, and erected modern buildings in Strontian's magnificent setting of water and mountains.

The village is situated near the head of Loch Sunart, at the mouth of a wooded glen. The River Strontian runs through the village into the loch, and from the glen visitors can climb to the 2,775 ft high peak of Ben Resipol, with its breathtaking views over Loch Shiel and the Morven district.

STUDHAM
BEDFORDSHIRE

6 miles south-west of Luton (page 426 Cb)

High on the ridge of Dunstable Downs the hills dip into a shallow bowl of common land, giving shelter to this tiny village which began as a sprinkling of Saxon homesteads. Studham has grown haphazardly over the centuries, with clumps of cottages and houses scattered at random and linked by alleys and footpaths in an appealing informality. The common fronts the village in a broad expanse of coarse grass criss-crossed by roads. From across the common the lattice-windowed, whitewashed Red Lion pub stands out among its neighbouring cottages, with the grey tower of St Mary's Church rising behind.

Most of the church dates from the 13th century, with 15th-century additions by Sir Reginald Bray who built St George's Chapel, Windsor and Henry VII's Chapel in Westminster Abbey. The Norman font is surrounded by medieval tiles and the red-and-grey marble pulpit is Victorian. An unusual entry on the First World War roll of honour records that Olive May Hart died from shock due to Zeppelin raids, aged 22.

SUDBURY
DERBYSHIRE

5 miles east of Uttoxeter (page 430 Bc)

Rows of red-brick cottages, gabled houses and a dignified 17th-century coaching inn toe the curving line of Sudbury's main street. In the 17th century the mail and stage-coaches clattered through the village, and in the 20th century lorries and cars pounded the narrow roadway until a by-pass brought peace at last to Sudbury.

The coaching inn, the Vernon Arms, has a central arch beneath one of its three gables, and beyond are the stables used for the post-horses. Opposite the inn, the base of a high brick wall is where the stable boys sat waiting for the stage to arrive. The inn takes its name from its builder, George Vernon, who was also responsible for Sudbury's most distinguished building – Sudbury Hall.

The hall is in late-Jacobean style with two projecting bays and a heavily canopied porch. The red-brick façade is diamond-patterned in darker brick, and the windows are mullioned. Since 1967 the hall has been owned by the National Trust, and is open to the public from Wednesdays to Sundays throughout the summer. Chief among its attractions are the magnificent plaster ceilings and the fine woodcarvings by Edward Pierce and Grinling Gibbons.

All Saints' Church stands surrounded by a grove of yew trees next to the grounds of Sudbury Hall. The church, dating from the 12th century, was heavily restored in the 19th century.

SULGRAVE
NORTHAMPTONSHIRE

6 miles north of Brackley (page 430 Ca)

Visitors from all over America come to Sulgrave to pay homage at Sulgrave Manor, the ancestral home of their first President, George Washington. He was a descendant of Lawrence Washington, a wool merchant, who built the house in the late 1550s. Today, the two-storey greystone house is a Washington Museum. Among its many mementoes of George Washington and his wife are a chair from his Mount Vernon home; a wooden snuffbox bearing his features; and a piece of Martha Washington's wedding gown.

The much-altered and restored medieval Church of St James contains a brass monument to Lawrence Washington and his wife, Anne, and has a 17th-century pew used by the Washington family.

The road into Sulgrave is lined by grassy banks, and the cottages and houses have been there for centuries. One bears the date 1636 on its porch.

SUTTON
BEDFORDSHIRE

3 miles north-east of Biggleswade (page 426 Cb)

John of Gaunt, Duke of Lancaster, son of Edward III, and virtual ruler of England in the last years of his father's reign, held the manor of Sutton in the 14th century. His connection with the village lives on in the name of the pink-washed village pub and the John o' Gaunt Golf Club in Sutton Park. A moat near the clubhouse is said to be the site of his manor house.

A tributary of the River Ivel flows through the village, which is strung out along a leafy lane that dips through a ford beside a 14th-century packhorse bridge. On the banks of the stream a white, 16th-century farmhouse and cottages of multi-coloured brick and timber make a colourful group. Sutton Park, now the clubhouse of the John o' Gaunt Golf Club, was the home of the Burgoyne family.

There are monuments to the Burgoynes in Sutton's medieval Church of All Saints. The tomb of Sir John Burgoyne is dated 1604, and the monument to Sir Roger, who died in 1679, is by Grinling Gibbons.

The Old Rectory, next to the church, has grown with the centuries. It began as a wattle-and-daub priest's house in the 14th century, was extended in Tudor times and again in 1705, and was embellished by the Victorians.

SUTTON CHENEY
LEICESTERSHIRE

2 miles south of Market Bosworth (page 430 Bc)

According to tradition, Richard III took communion at the Church of St James in Sutton Cheney on the morning of August 22, 1485, just before he went to battle on Bosworth Field, 1 mile away. He was killed, Henry Tudor became Henry VII and the Wars of the Roses came to an end. Each year the Richard III Society hold a service in the parish church of St James on the Sunday nearest the anniversary of the battle.

Among monuments inside the church is a recumbent effigy of Sir William Roberts, who built the Carlton stone almshouses east of the church in the early 17th century. The almshouses have been renovated as a single residence.

A permanent exhibition at Ambion Hill on Bosworth Field, where visitors can follow the Battle of Bosworth, is open seven days a week from Easter until the end of October.

TWYCROSS Some of the oldest and finest stained glass in Europe can be seen in the Church of St James at Twycross, 6 miles north-west of Sutton Cheney. The glass, which dates from the mid-12th century, was smuggled to England in the wake of the French Revolution in 1789. William IV gave it to Earl Howe, of nearby Gopsall Hall, and it was later donated to the church.

SUTTON COURTENAY
OXFORDSHIRE

3 miles north-west of Didcot (page 426 Aa)

A long row of picturesque cottages and fine old houses climbs from the River Thames to Sutton Courtenay's large green, shaded by huge lime trees and overlooked by a Norman church, some medieval houses and a 17th-century manor.

The Abbey, on the south side of the green, stands in its own grounds and around a courtyard. It never was an abbey, but was built as a rectory in the 14th century. Older still is Norman Hall, a 12th-century manor house of plain stone opposite the church. Sutton Courtenay Manor is to the west of the green, dating partly from about 1670, but with a 13th-century hall.

Sutton Courtenay is a place to explore, both for its architectural treasures and for its pleasant walks beside the Thames. The Church of All Saints has a late-Norman tower, and the churchyard contains the grave of the Earl of Oxford and Asquith, Prime Minister from 1908 to 1916. George Orwell, author of *Animal Farm* and *Nineteen Eighty-Four*, is also buried there.

Lord Asquith lived at The Wharf, built from three cottages in 1912 and backing on to the millstream at the end of Church Street.

A footpath from the northern end of the main street follows the bank of Sutton Pools, a bend in the Thames where willows hang low over the river and the water rushes over two weirs. Across the meadows on the northern bank is Culham Cut, a waterway which bypasses the loop of the river.

SWAFFHAM PRIOR
CAMBRIDGESHIRE

5 miles west of Newmarket (page 432 Cc)

Two churches in the same churchyard stand above Swaffham Prior's curved main street, which is lined by a mixture of demure cottages and Georgian houses with shady gardens. The first church, St Mary's, was built in the 12th century. It has a fine 13th-century tower on to which a fibre-glass spire was recently added. The second church, St Cyriac's, dates from the 13th century and was built for a separate parish. The two parishes amalgamated in 1667, and both churches continued to function until St Mary's spire was struck by lightning in 1767 and the church was closed down for a time. However, it is St Mary's which is in business today, while St Cyriac's is used as a social centre.

Swaffham Prior gets its name from the Anglo-Saxon word 'Swaffham', meaning a 'homestead of the Swabians', an ancient tribe – and the Prior refers to the fact that it once belonged to the Prior of Ely. The village stands on one of the few hills in Cambridgeshire.

SWAFFHAM BULBECK This village, 1½ miles south-west, is named after a Norman family who founded a nunnery there. The yellow and red-brick Abbey House was built on the site in the 18th century, and the ground floor contains a small part of the nunnery crypt. In the 17th century, Swaffham Bulbeck was an inland port from which cereals were exported to the Continent. Although the waterway and quay are no longer used by commercial traffic, the port area – Commercial End, off the main road – retains much of its original character. The Dutch-style Merchant's House, the granary and the malt house are still standing, and the old stevedores' cottages are now private homes.

Just down the road from the playing-field is the 13th-century Church of St Mary, among whose treasures is a beautiful 500-year-old Italian chest – which is, in fact, a portable altar. The pew-ends are capped with the battered remains of fabulous beasts carved in the 15th century.

REACH Much of the limestone used in Swaffhams' churches comes from quarries near the neighbouring village of Reach. It claims to be the oldest settlement in the district on the basis of Stone Age flints found in the surrounding peat. The 7 mile earthwork of Devil's Ditch starts at Reach. Excavations carried out in 1924 showed that it was built in the 8th century as an East Anglian defence against Mercia, to the west.

SWANBOURNE
BUCKINGHAMSHIRE

2 miles east of Winslow (page 426 Bb)

Much of the village consists of brick and half-timbered cottages and farmhouses lining the main street, Winslow Road. The stone-built Church of St Swithin is in the centre of the village. Inside is a brass tablet in memory of Sir Thomas Fremantle, who fought alongside Nelson at Santa Cruz and Trafalgar. Admiral Fremantle's descendants still live at Old House, a basically 16th-century timber-framed house near the church.

To the north of the church is a large Victorian vicarage – now a private residence – and, opposite, a thatched, timbered house with herring-bone brickwork. Next to it is the 16th-century Manor House with mullioned windows.

By a road junction at the western end of Winslow Road is an antique shop, and from there a small lane called Smithfield Close leads to several groups of white-painted, 16th-century cottages with thatched roofs and low eaves. One group, called Barrack Row, is said to have housed a garrison of Royalist troops in 1643.

PARSON'S COMFORT *The great tithe barn at Sydling St Nicholas is built like a fortress, with massive flint walls and timbers almost as permanent. One of these bears the initials of Ursula Walsingham, the widow of Elizabeth I's Principal Secretary. The roof is of corrugated iron, but then the cost of thatching the nine-and-a-half bays would be horrendous.*

SYDLING ST NICHOLAS
DORSET

7 miles north-west of Dorchester (page 421 Ca)

Every road to the valley of the Sydling Water is lovely, but perhaps the finest way is over the hills from Piddletrenthide and Cerne Abbas, catching a glimpse of the Cerne Giant on the way. The valley is a green bowl carved out of the soaring, furze-patched Dorset hills. Long before the Romans came, and for several centuries after their departure, the steep slopes above the Sydling were dotted with farmsteads. But now all that remains of them are marks and lines that show and fade with the seasons, visited only by cattle and sheep.

Sydling St Nicholas, at the valley's heart, is of a respectable age even by Wessex standards. Probably it evolved as ploughs became strong enough to cope with the heavier valley soils, and there it has remained.

The principal building material is yellow stone, either by itself, or divided by double courses of split flint which is sometimes encased in frames of pink brick. Most of the cottages are capped by wheat reed thatch, a delightful material that lies close and sleek like an animal's fur, pale gold when newly put on and darkening to caramel as it weathers. In the High Street is the smithy, dated 1800, which has been run by the same family for three generations.

At the top end of the village is a neat, white swing-gate that looks as though it might lead into someone's garden, but is in fact the entrance to the churchyard. The Church of St Nicholas has yellow stone walls, topped by gargoyles to carry the rainwater off the roof. One of these had a minor role in the film version of Thomas Hardy's *Far from the Madding Crowd*, in which it was seen gushing water on to the grave of Fanny Robin. The village also appears as 'Sidlinch' in Hardy's story *The Grave by the Handpost*.

The interior of the church, much of which dates from 1430, was considerably damaged during the Cromwellian period, so that only fragments of its once glorious stained glass still remain. However, not even an Ironside trooper could make much impression on the massive font, which may well be carved from a Roman capital. More surprisingly, the chalice, the 400-year-old 'Sydling Cup', has also survived.

There are a number of charming 18th-century monuments to the Smith family, lords of the manor for many years.

Over the wall from the churchyard there is an enchanting glimpse of the gardens of Sydling Court, with ancient, moulded yew hedges running up the hillside and tall trees full of cawing rooks. The Court passed into the possession of Winchester College at the Reformation. Among its many tenants since then were the Elizabethan soldier-poet Sir Philip Sidney and his mother-in-law, Lady Walsingham. She was the second wife of Queen Elizabeth's Principal Secretary, Sir Francis Walsingham, the founder of her Secret Service.

Near the entrance of the lane leading to the church is the stump of the old market cross, and behind it are the handsome mullioned windows of the mainly Tudor vicarage. The yews in the garden are thought to be nearly 1,000 years old.

TALLEY
DYFED

6 miles north of Llandeilo (page 425 Cb)

Encouraged by its quiet solitude, Norbertine monks founded an abbey at Talley in the 12th century. Its ruins still stand just north of the village, beside a small lake of great beauty in a spot sheltered from the west by the steep, wooded slopes of Mynydd Cynros, which rises to just over 1,000 ft.

A handsome Georgian farmhouse stands among trees in one corner of the village, but Talley's heart is an attractive ribbon of cottages whose view towards the rolling eastern hills is dominated by the abbey's scanty but impressive ruins. Wars, weather and local builders who used it as a convenient source of ready-dressed stone all combined to destroy what had been the only foundation of White Canons in Wales. The lofty remains of the central tower, with its high, pointed arches, give the village of Talley a romantic atmosphere.

An attractive 18th-century church stands beside the ruins, its graveyard running down towards the lake with its background of trees. Another lake lies a few hundred yards to the north, immediately beyond the trees, and can be seen from a narrow lane. Talley's whitewashed inn and post office stand beside the road to Llandeilo, about 500 yds from the rest of the village.

TARBERT
WESTERN ISLES

At head of E. L. Tarbert, Isle of Lewis (page 442 Bf)

One of Scotland's most westerly villages is perched on an isthmus between North and South Harris. Its white cottages dotted across grey mountain slopes give it a Scandinavian appearance when seen from the ferry crossing the Minch from Skye. The impression is heightened by the names of some of the peaks that rise above Tarbert: Straiaval, Gillaval, Uisgnaval, Oreval, Cleiseval and Clisham. Most of the villagers speak Gaelic as their first language. They have typical Harris-men names such as Macleod and Maclennan, Maclean and MacDonald.

To the west of the village is a fertile coastal strip backing on to the Atlantic. To the east, are dark fjords which extend deep into the interior of North Harris. As well as fishing, holiday-makers can observe otters, red deer, golden eagles and wild swans in the area. There is fine walking country all around, ranging from beaches, to tracks over the surrounding hills.

◆

END OF THE LAKES *This is the translation of Tal-y-Llychau, Talley's ancient name, and an accurate description of the site that attracted the White Canons in the 12th century. Their abbey has long been a ruin, despite an annual award of £6 made by Henry VII to the abbot. Henry may have stayed in King's Court in the village on his way to Bosworth.*

TARBERT

STRATHCLYDE

On east coast of north Kintyre (page 441 Cd)

Neat fishermen's cottages, holiday homes, craft shops, small hotels and pubs ring the tiny, landlocked bay where East Loch Tarbert ends. Sheltered however the wind lies, it is a near-perfect haven for small boats. More houses spread up the northern and western hillsides, but the finest views of the village and loch are from the ruins of Tarbert Castle, on a hillock immediately behind the village on the south side of the bay. Castle Street leads up from the harbour near colourful Fish Quay.

Today, only two storeys of the castle's 15th-century keep remain standing. The decline of the fortress followed the coming of stable government to Argyll and the Hebrides. For centuries before, Tarbert was a focus of struggle between warring Scots factions, and between them and Viking invaders. Whoever held the castle could command the low, mile-wide isthmus between Knapdale and Kintyre. This strip was not simply the only land route, but also a portage where goods could be shifted between the eastern and western lochs. Boats, too, could be dragged overland, short-cutting the voyage from the Clyde to the Western Isles.

When Magnus Barefoot, King of Norway, launched an invasion in 1098, the Scots king, Edgar, desired peace with the English. To keep the Norsemen at bay, he agreed that they could take any island around which they could travel. Magnus, who also wanted the fertile Kintyre peninsula, sat at the tiller of his longboat as it was dragged across the Tarbert isthmus – the name Tarbert is derived from the Gaelic for 'a portage' – and claimed the 'island' as his own. Robert Bruce also dragged ships over the route in 1315, in order to attack Castle Sween. He occupied Tarbert Castle, and in 1326 enlarged it and strengthened its fortifications.

TATTERSHALL

LINCOLNSHIRE

8 miles south of Horncastle (page 432 Be)

Cromwells have been linked with Tattershall since the 14th century, and the heritage is still vividly alive in the splendours of an ancient castle, church and market cross. The magnificently restored keep of Tattershall Castle and the Church of Holy Trinity are both monuments to their builder – Ralph Cromwell, Lord High Treasurer of England under Henry VI.

◆

GLASGOW MAGISTRATES' HAVEN *Big, plump Loch Fyne herring, known locally as 'Glasgow Magistrates', are equally delicious fresh-cooked or kippered. Though not so plentiful as they used to be, they are still landed here at Tarbert beneath the ivy-draped ruins of the castle that King Robert Bruce restored as part of his attempt to control the fertile Kintyre peninsula.*

The market cross on the village green serves as a reminder of the medieval times when Tattershall was a flourishing market town. Houses and shops now surround the small village green and its trees in the heart of this little community beside the River Bain where it forms part of the Horncastle Canal. Some of the buildings in and around the village, and a number of exceptionally tall trees, prevent the castle from being a major landmark. But although the 110 ft high keep does not dwarf its surroundings, its battlements provide stunning views of the surrounding flatlands.

Walls 22 ft thick form the base of the four-storey building, which is spacious enough for a large hall on each floor. It was restored by Lord Curzon, Marquess of Kedleston, former Viceroy of India, between 1911 and 1914 and subsequently handed over to the National Trust in 1925, which opens it to the public most days of the year. The moated keep is all that is left of the castle which Ralph Cromwell built.

Ralph Cromwell died in 1456, only a year after the castle was completed. He was buried no more than 400 yds away, in the greystone church that he also built – although, in fact, Holy Trinity was not finished until the 1480s. A gatehouse, now a museum and National Trust shop, stands between the castle and the church.

Plainly furnished and almost without orna-

ment, the church is 186 ft long and has more than 60 windows through which light streams unimpeded. Most of its original stained glass has been broken, or taken to other churches. In the north transept, among several fine brasses, a sadly mutilated one commemorates Ralph, 3rd Lord Cromwell, who gave such lustre to Tattershall.

The Dogdyke Steam Pumping Station at Bridge Farm preserves a beam-engine of 1855, once used for land drainage. About 1 mile from the village, on the Sleaford road, is an old railway warehouse, home of the Lincolnshire Aviation Society's museum, which is open most weekends. The museum's collection includes six complete aircraft, many models and other relics.

TAYNUILT
STRATHCLYDE

9 miles east of Oban (page 441 De)

Cannon balls, thought to have been used at the Battle of Trafalgar, were made at Taynuilt, and the local furnacemen erected the first public memorial to Lord Nelson after his victory at Trafalgar, in October 1805. Before Nelson's body was back in England, the workmen hauled a 4 ton prehistoric standing stone up a nearby hillside. They placed the stone near the local church, with the inscription: To the memory of Lord Nelson, this stone was erected by the Lorn Foundry Furnace Workers, 1805.'

Most of Taynuilt dates from the mid-18th century, when a charcoal-fired ironworks – the Lorn Furnace, Bonawe – was established on the south shore of neighbouring Loch Etive. Its raw material was iron ore shipped from Ulverstone, in the Lake District, to a harbour on the loch. The return cargo was pig iron from the furnace. Although the ironworks stopped production in 1874, the buildings have been carefully restored as a monument of the Industrial Revolution. The lintel of the forehearth of the furnace bears the date 1753.

Taynuilt is situated where the Pass of Brander meets Loch Etive, and is surrounded by magnificent mountains – the tallest of which is the 3,689 ft Ben Cruachan. The village attracts many anglers and walkers, and nature-lovers can visit Glen Nant to the south – with its acres of birch, hazel, holly, guelder rose, oak and ash. The glen is administered by the Forestry Commission and Nature Conservancy. In 1977, and again in 1978, Taynuilt won an award for the Best-Kept-Village in Argyll and Bute.

TEALBY

LINCOLNSHIRE

3 miles east of Market Rasen (page 432 Be)

Landing lights burn on not-too-distant plateaux, and black aircraft with their wheels down wobble overhead like flying dinosaurs. This is RAF country, and has been ever since the Second World War when the roar of Lancasters, Halifaxes, Wellingtons and Stirlings was the most familiar sound in the Lincolnshire landscape.

Tealby, however, set on and among the ups and downs of a hillside crowned by its church, remains aloof from most of this and concentrates on good gardening instead. Airfields apart, most of the village looks upwards and outwards to the wide, airy rim of the Wolds. From the church, the main street runs steeply down to a water-splash through the River Rase, past the Gothic school with its metal spire, the Memorial Hall, defended by a cannon and containing plaques recording Tealby's many wins in the Lincolnshire Best-Kept-Village competition, a lane called The Smooting and a good many attractive cottages of varying dates. Most of the older buildings are of reddish-brown ironstone with mossy-tiled roofs, and almost all have stone-embanked gardens, richly planted and expertly maintained. The one belonging to Garden Cottage is particularly well planned, with a little river running beneath its walls, while nearby Watermill House – formerly a corn-mill – has a small but forceful waterfall crashing past a side window.

Beyond the water-splash – known as the Beck – the river flows through some cottage gardens within the precincts of Bayons Park, where once stood a manor that was one of the most remarkable buildings in the shire. It was built in the 1830s by Alfred, Lord Tennyson's uncle, Charles Tennyson, MP, who, piqued at not being offered a peerage, capitalised on his Norman lineage by calling himself Tennyson-d'Eyncourt, and building a mock-Norman castle at Bayons complete with keep, drawbridge and barbican. It was occupied by the Army during the Second World War, and later fell into disrepair. It was dynamited by the Royal Engineers in 1964, and all that remains is a rocky, ivy-covered mound.

Climbing back from the river towards the church, it is worth having a look at the King's Head, a handsome stone pub with yellow shutters and a very fine Norfolk-reed thatch. The three-layer, patterned crown and the thatched cap over the door make one of the finest examples of the craft for miles around.

All Saints' Church, stoutly built in ironstone and dating in part from the mid-12th century, overlooks the entire village. The interior is rough-hewn, with a low tower arch, seemingly of greater strength than the present building requires and possibly late Norman. There are some fragments of 14th-century glass, and monuments to the Tennyson-d'Eyncourts and a number of their servants. The family must have been excellent employers, since the memorials include mention of 30 and even 50 years' service at Bayons Manor.

On the south-western outskirts of the village is the picturesque hamlet of Tealby Thorpe. Thorpe Mill – built in the late 18th century and now a private residence – is open on a few Saturday and Sunday afternoons in the summer, when the mill can be seen working.

UNRUFFLED STREAM *Lily-pads pave the sunlight-dappled waters of the River Rase in a peaceful corner of Tealby.*

TEFFONT

WILTSHIRE

10 miles west of Salisbury (page 421 Cb)

There are two Teffonts – Teffont Magna and Teffont Evias, so named after Ewyas in Herefordshire whose barons once owned the manor house. The two lie close together in the lovely Nadder Valley, and a tumbling stream – the Teff – gushes from the ground just north of Teffont Magna and flows through both villages. The name Teffont comes from the Anglo-Saxon words *teo*, boundary and *funta*, stream.

Teffont Magna is a charming village with thatched cottages clustering round the medieval Church of St Edward, where the 13th-century bell is kept on the window-sill. The stream is crossed by numerous miniature stone bridges. Fitz House, a gabled building of the 17th century, was once the collecting house for locally grown wool and its fine barn still stands.

At Teffont Evias some of the houses are more imposing; cream-coloured Chilmark stone has been used imaginatively to build a series of mansions within spacious, stone-walled grounds. A fine example is the beautifully proportioned Howards House which is now a private hotel. The nearby Chilmark quarry, now disused, provided stone for Salisbury Cathedral and for many

CHURCH AND MANOR *The slim grey spire of St Michael and All Angels soars 125 ft, yet seems almost dwarfed behind a great sprawling cedar. Alongside, the battlemented tower and tall chimneys of the manor house stand sharp against the dark, wooded hillside beyond. Together they make a gentle introduction to the Nadder Valley village of Teffont Evias.*

◆

of the old buildings in the Teffont neighbourhood.

Towards the end of the village the woods close in, almost overshadowing the early-19th-century parish church of St Michael and All Angels with its graceful and richly ornamented spire, 125 ft high. The adjoining turreted manor is a most imposing early-17th-century building, now converted into flats, which has its own private chapel in the church. Church and manor house together make a striking picture. A huge box hedge overhanging the stream marks the garden boundary.

TELSCOMBE, East Sussex (page 423 Db)
(see Piddinghoe)

TERLING
ESSEX

6 miles north-east of Chelmsford (page 432 Cb)

There is a certain magnificence about the trees, a neat uniformity of fencing and a four-square, discreet opulence about the pub, that tells any experienced wanderer in southern England that he is approaching a village whose chief means of

livelihood is the working of a great estate. This is certainly the case at Terling, where the pub is called the Rayleigh Arms. Further clues are provided by milk-floats bearing the legend 'Lord Rayleigh's Dairies: A Family Business', and a number of signs indicating the whereabouts of various departments of Lord Rayleigh's Farms. These are the outer glimpses of one of the finest dairy-farms in the country. Some 2,400 cattle graze in fields that are almost manicured in their perfection of fences and ditches. The originator of all this grandeur was the Hon. E. G. Strutt (1854–1930), a younger son of the 2nd Lord Rayleigh. He was made a Companion of Honour for his services to agriculture during the First World War: now he and his wife are remembered by a pair of bells in Terling's church.

Though the village is of much greater age than the farm, it would almost appear that the two were made for one another. The broad green with its clipped turf is bounded by old cottages, decently and quietly clad in primrose, ochre or white. Next to the church, which has a handsome red-brick tower of the 18th century, is a small Tudor manor house with high octagonal chimneys.

From the green, the road bends around into a neat pastel-coloured grouping of cottages and shops, beside which stand the discreet pillars marking the entrance of the drive to Terling Place, home of the present Lord Rayleigh. Further along, the road passes a low E-shape of red-brick estate buildings, obviously modern, yet all of a piece with this sensible, attractive and businesslike village.

375

THAXTED

ESSEX

7 miles south-east of Saffron Walden (page 432 Cb)

At the heart of Thaxted stands the Guildhall, an ancient building of dark-silver oak framing with plaster infill. It was built about 1400 by the Cutlers' Guild as a meeting place for men of the craft, and to declare the prosperity of the Thaxted cutlery trade. It is best seen looking up the hill from the bottom of Town Street. From there, it seems protected rather than dwarfed by the slender 181 ft blade of the church spire. The Guildhall is at the junction of four streets. The houses of Town Street belong to all kinds of periods. Few are distinguished in themselves yet, taken together, the jumble of eaves, overhangs and colour-washed walls is extraordinarily pleasant. At the top of the hill, opposite the church, is an imposing building, Clarence House, built of elegant red brick in 1715. Below the Guildhall, in Town Street, is the Recorder's House, which probably dates from the 16th century. There, in the days of Thaxted's wealth, the Recorder, or magistrate, lived. It is now a restaurant.

The cutlers' industry declined in the 16th century, possibly in part because of a shortage of trees on which they depended for fuel.

In Town Street a plaque is displayed on the house where Gustav Holst lived between 1917 and 1925. He worked on several famous compositions there, including the setting of the favourite school hymn, *I vow to thee my country.*

To the right of the Guildhall runs the appropriately cobbled Stony Lane, lined on one side by fine, overhanging medieval houses. One of them bears the legend 'Dick Turpin's Cottage', denoting where the highwayman may, or may not, have lived at some time in his career. No one seems to know for certain.

At the top of the lane is the south entrance of one of the most glorious of all Essex churches. Like the Guildhall, much of its soaring mass advertises the wealth of the medieval tradesmen who dedicated their church to Our Lady, St Lawrence, patron saint of cutlers, and to St John the Baptist. The interior, some of which dates from the 14th century, is all clear light and airy spaciousness, perhaps even a little bleak, an effect accentuated by the lack of furniture in the 183 ft long building. All the same, there is much to see: the pinnacled cover that completely encloses the font; the chapel dedicated to the Blessed John Ball, priest and martyr, one of the leaders of the Peasants' Revolt in 1381; and the bright banners of six saints in the chancel. Memorials are relatively few for so large a church, but there is a charming though largely illegible one to Peter Platt, the early-19th-century builder who restored the tower.

'Where Peter lies, 'tis fit this tower should show,
But for his skill, itself had lain as low.'

A tower windmill shares the skyline with the church spire. The mill was built in 1804, and all its original machinery is intact. There is a small rural museum on the lower floors which opens on summer weekends.

CUTLERS' CASTLE *An early-15th-century Guildhall recalls the days when Thaxted was the cutlery capital of England. Part market house, part town hall and part craftsmen's meeting place, it proclaims the wealth of the cutlers who built it. So too does the large and austerely beautiful church, though part of its magnificence is also due to the great Essex family of Clare. Near the church is a fine double row of almshouses, which lead to a windmill that is preserved as a museum.*

THORNEY
CAMBRIDGESHIRE

7 miles north-east of Peterborough (page 432 Bd)

In the mid-19th century the Duke of Bedford decided to turn Thorney into a model village. He was concerned by the poor living conditions in the area, and put up a row of pale-yellow houses with leaded windows and gables for his agricultural workers. The bricks came from his brickyard at nearby Toneham, and he made sure that each house had piped water, gas lighting and a vegetable garden. The homes still line Wisbech Road, at the north end of the village.

In the 17th century, a previous Duke of Bedford gave asylum to French Protestants fleeing from the religious persecution of Louis XIV. They settled in the village – which was originally an island above the once waterlogged Fens – and until 1715 the abbey services were frequently held in French, and some of the surrounding gravestones bear French names and epitaphs. The Abbey Church is all that remains of a Saxon monastery which was refashioned by the Normans, whose sumptuous west front and towers survive.

Beside the church is a green surrounded by handsome houses dating from the 17th and 18th centuries. All are built on abbey foundations and most are constructed of masonry taken from the abbey buildings. To the west is the 16th-century Abbey House, which in 1979 was converted into two private homes, with the stables – for many years the village hall and cinema – turned into a 'character' residence.

Near the abbey is the former almshouse, which, until 1911, was used as the village post office and is now a general store. Not far away is Tank Yard, a group of Jacobean-style buildings with a water-tower erected in 1855. The block formerly housed the fire brigade and the Duke of Bedford's estate office and workshops. In 1979 a scheme was launched to turn the buildings into a new village hall.

A personal portrait of Westleton in Suffolk by

ROBERT DOUGALL

*It's a far curlew's cry from the lights and cameras of the BBC's television
studios to the reeded, wind-scoured estuaries and flat farmlands of the Suffolk coastline,
but the contrast sustained newsreader Robert Dougall over 30 years of a double
life . . . as the unflappable personality familiar to millions of viewers and listeners, and
the duffel-coated, binocular-hung, bird-watching country lover who has always
lurked behind the urbane image on the little screen. Now he's a countryman full-time,
'retired' to live and enjoy the life he loves best; to observe and describe the wild creatures of
his chosen habitat and relish the company of his Suffolk neighbours.*

❝ Thirty years ago my wife Nan and I began an affair with a stretch of Suffolk's coastline between Lowestoft and Aldeburgh. We came to it feeling battered by the war years, and have found there an abiding solace and sense of continuity – the ideal antidote to a febrile, media-ridden age.

This most easterly corner of England juts into the North Sea like a clenched jaw. The locals even talk with their mouths shut to keep out the east wind. There is nothing spectacular about the landscape – just low, crumbling cliffs, interspersed with marshes and solitary places where primeval man himself might still feel at home.

The very spirit of the land is island-like, unresponsive, elusive. There is no compromise: one either loves it or loathes it. Perhaps part of its charm lies in its ordinariness, and so I have chosen to write about one of the most unsung places of all – the little village of Westleton, which lies 2½ miles back from the lost port of Dunwich.

It had its beginnings when a Norseman named Vestlidhe stumbled across the site after the Romans left Britain. By the time the Normans arrived it had merged into the Saxon neighbourhood and so was entered in Domesday Book as Westlede's Tun, *tun* meaning 'a settlement'. Since then, English history has largely passed it by, and so has the worst of 20th-century development. The whole area is a network of nature reserves among estuaries and marshes, and a paradise for a moocher like me.

My introduction to Westleton was on a glorious Saturday afternoon in the first week of August 20 years ago, when I was honoured with an invitation to crown their Carnival Queen. The Queen's throne was placed on a wooden platform in the middle of the Green and the whole village – all 600 of them – were gathered round. A prettier sight you couldn't wish to see. The ducks on the pond took off, little dogs barked, two teenage girls reined in their ponies, and when I had placed the crown squarely on her head, no Miss World could have smiled more sweetly.

The Green has always seen all there is to see. For two centuries the parish butts were

here, in the days when archery practice was compulsory. Here, too, was the village pound where stray cattle were kept. Close by were the stocks – last used in the 1870s for chastening a poacher named Bob Randall. Near the pond was the ducking-stool where many a village scold had her tongue temporarily stilled.

Here, too, is the White Horse, once built of wattle and plaster with a thatched roof, but rebuilt at the turn of the century. Close to the Green, on a rise, is St Peter's Church, which has kept its thatched roof and has stood there since 1340. In past centuries smuggling and piracy were very much a part of life, especially on the east coast, and I was reminded of this by an entry in the Westleton Churchwarden's Account for 1731-2 which records the sum of one shilling and sixpence having been given to 'fifteen seamen in company, which had been taken by ye pyrates and very barbarously used'.

In all smuggling places ghost stories abound. Can it be that they were invented to keep law-abiding folk behind closed doors at night, when the deeds were being done? Westleton has more than its fair share of tales. The most persistent concerns a stone near the priest's door of the church over which grass never grows. Above it, in the wall, is an ancient iron grating. Place a piece of straw in the grating, run three times round the church, and on return there will be nothing there. Or you might even hear the Devil clanking his chains.

One of the many good things about Westleton is its strong sense of community. It is compact and independent, with the knack of inspiring loyalty, which explains why it has twice won the coveted title of 'Best-Kept Village in Suffolk'. For this, much of the credit must go to Jim Fisk, whose family have been in Westleton for 400 years. Jim is a nurseryman, specialising in clematis, and he has built up a business exporting 150 varieties to countries all over the world. One by-product is the Fisk Association of San Francisco, run by Howard Keith Fisk. He traces Fisks all over the world and, periodically, they foregather at the birthplace of their ancestors in Suffolk. That is one of the things I like about Westleton: it is an outgoing sort of place.

So, when I enquired what had happened to the little girl I had crowned Carnival Queen, I was not in the least surprised to hear that she had married an American from a nearby air base and was now living in Kermut, Texas, USA. 99

Robert Dougall

A sense of continuity—the ideal antidote
to a febrile, media-ridden age.

The very spirit of the land is island-like, unresponsive, elusive.
There is no compromise.

Jim Fiske exports 150 varieties of clematis to countries all over the world.

Near the priest's door there is a stone over which the grass never grows.

St Peter's Church has kept its thatched roof and has stood there since 1340.

THORNTON DALE
NORTH YORKSHIRE

2 miles east of Pickering (page 436 Cc)

Trout dart through the clear waters of Thornton Beck as it sparkles and chatters through the village on a great sweeping curve, like the flourish beneath a signature. In the upstream part of the village the lawns of graceful Georgian mansions slope down to the beck, and a footpath gives a close view of a beautiful thatched cottage with three dormer windows – the type that rise snugly into the thatch. The cottage is cruck-built, using the natural curve of timber to produce a bowed, A-shaped framework, and is believed to date from the early Tudor period. Set back from the main road near by is an eye-catching row of 12 dark-stone almshouses, built in 1656. They were endowed by the Lumley family, Barons of Scarborough. The largest building at one end, now used as a church hall, was originally the village's one-roomed grammar school, also endowed by the Lumleys.

Beside the road south to Malton, stone cottages with tiled roofs sit proudly among flower-filled gardens, reached by stone footbridges that span the beck.

TIGHNABRUAICH
STRATHCLYDE

24 miles south-west of Dunoon (page 441 Cd)

In the 1830s, Tighnabruaich was so remote and sparsely populated that a gunpowder factory was opened near by. The factory was closed in the 1920s because the village, with its mild climate and subtropical plants, was attracting many visitors.

Tighnabruaich – pronounced 'Tie-na-broo-ach' – is Gaelic for 'House on the Hill'. It is set on a narrow reach of the Kyles of Bute, and the houses and cottages – many of them Victorian – sweep up a wooded hillside overlooking the water. At one end of the village there is a little grey tea shop with a wooden pier running from it out into the bay. A Forest Trail and wild life hides lie 2 miles to the north-east. Blue hares, deer, wild geese, herons and duck can be discreetly observed from the hides.

TILFORD
SURREY

3 miles south-east of Farnham (page 422 Cb)

When William Cobbett, the author of *Rural Rides*, took his son to see the oak tree beside the green at Tilford in the early 19th century, he described it as 'by far the finest tree that I ever saw in my life'. The tree, known as King's Oak or Novel's Oak, has a girth of more than 26 ft and has been estimated to be about 900 years old.

Tilford still preserves by the green two medieval bridges, one with four stone arches, the other with six, spanning two different branches of the River Wey. Disastrous floods in 1233 caused much damage along the Wey, and the bridges may be two of the many rebuilt by the monks of Waverley Abbey, which stands 2 miles upstream.

The inn by the triangular green dates from 1700, and the Church of All Saints was built in 1867. The Tilford Institute by the green is an early work by Sir Edwin Lutyens, built in 1893.

TINTERN, Gwent (page 425 Eb)
(see St Briavels)

TISSINGTON
DERBYSHIRE

4 miles north of Ashbourne (page 430 Bd)

There are few more colourful customs in England than the Derbyshire tradition of well-dressing, and the place best known for this ancient ceremony is Tissington. On Ascension Day the village's five wells – Yewtree Well, Hall Well, Hands Well, Coffin Well and Town Well – are framed with biblical scenes made from thousands of flower petals pressed into moist clay. The ceremonies may date from pagan times, or from the 14th century when the purity of the water saved the village from the ravages of the Black Death. But, whatever its origin, well-dressing adds a splash of colour for a few days in the spring to what is already a village of great beauty.

Tissington lies on the southern edge of the Peak District National Park, and is an immaculate tribute to the FitzHerberts who have watched over its development since the reign of Queen Elizabeth I. It is a spacious place where buildings

Hall Well.

The green and vicarage.

Norman font.

of pale-grey limestone are sheltered by noble trees and overlook broad, grassy verges. Many of the houses and cottages bear dates showing that they were built between the 1830s and 1860s, when Sir Henry FitzHerbert and his sister Frances devoted their energies to improving the village.

The initials FF, together with the FitzHerbert coat of arms, appear over the door of the former village school which Frances built in 1837 to commemorate Queen Victoria's Coronation. The school, near the pond, is now a tea shop.

Beyond Town Well a footpath guarded by a stone stile leads to the tiny post office, reached by a garden path which passes Coffin Well. The vicarage, on the western side of the village and near the Yewtree Well, dates from 1730. It looks out towards St Mary's Church, which the Fitz-Herberts restored in Victorian times, but much of its Norman structure remains. The porch, approached between yew trees, shelters an early-Norman doorway whose pillars have marks said to have been made by local men sharpening arrows. Above the door are carved geometrical patterns flanked by two crudely drawn human figures. Even stranger figures decorate the circular font just inside the door: a weird beast swallowing a man; a bizarre creature swallowing its own tail; two human figures; a large bird; and the Lamb of God with a cross slung over its shoulder.

The church contains many monuments to the FitzHerbert family, the most splendid being the ornate, two-tiered memorial to Francis Fitz-Herbert, who died in 1619, his son John and their wives.

It was Francis FitzHerbert who, about 1609, built Tissington Hall. The house is not open to the public, but it can be admired from the broad, grass-flanked road which runs past the church towards Hands Well.

TOLLESBURY
ESSEX

7 miles east of Maldon (page 432 Cb)

Farmland ends and creeks and estuary marshes begin at Tollesbury, which lies close to the River Blackwater. A lane leads down to the marshes and a small boatyard on Woodrolfe Creek.

The village square is lined by plaster and brick houses, many with tiled roofs moss-covered and yellow with age. Behind a weathered brick wall the Church of St Mary is a colourful mixture of pebble, stone, brick and tiles. The 18th-century font bears the inscription: 'Good people all I pray take care, that in ye church you do not sware. As this man did.' The font was paid for by a drunken man who swore in church and was persuaded to make the donation to avoid prosecution.

The weather-vane of the church represents a fishing boat, a reminder that Tollesbury once had a fishing fleet. At the turn of the century more than 100 sailing smacks brought in their catches of sprats for pickling.

AN ECHO OF GRACIOUS LIVING

Shadows lengthen across a triangular village green; a late sun lights the pale grey stone of the vicarage, the restrained style of which endows it with a simple elegance. The effect is wholly felicitous – due largely to the efforts of the FitzHerbert family, who have nurtured the village of Tissington since the first Elizabeth sat the throne. Trees and grassy verges provide a park-like setting for the buildings that forms an ideal background for the ancient well-dressing ceremonies that draw visitors there every spring. There are five wells, Hall Well being the largest – the stream springing from it runs alongside the road. Inside St Mary's Church are many splendid monuments to the FitzHerbert family and a strangely carved, circular Norman font.

TOLPUDDLE
DORSET

7 miles east of Dorchester (page 421 Ca)

Wooden staves now prop up the old sycamore tree under which the six farmworkers known as the Tolpuddle Martyrs are said to have held some of their protest meetings in 1833–4. The tree stands on a steeply sloping triangle of grass not far from the centre of the village. The trade union martyrs were led by two brothers, George and James Loveless, and they were protesting against a reduction in their wages of 7 shillings a week to a starvation level of 6 shillings. They formed their own lodge of the Friendly Society of Agricultural Labourers to resist this third wage reduction in four years. For this, they were brought before a hostile judge and jury in Dorchester, in March 1834. They were found guilty of swearing unlawful oaths, and were sentenced to seven years' transportation to Australia. A public outcry later resulted in a pardon.

Memorials to the martyrs are found among the cob-walled cottages, 17th-century Manor House, and modern bungalows and houses which comprise the present-day village. Thomas Standfield's cottage, where the oaths were taken, still stands in the main street. Some of the martyrs were Wesleyan Methodists, and although the Methodist chapel has been rebuilt since their day it contains a document of 1829–30 which mentions the Loveless brothers as local preachers.

In 1934 the Trades Union Congress built a small museum and six cottages, which were named after the Loveless brothers and their four comrades.

The stone-and-flint Church of St John the Evangelist stands near by. It dates in part from the 13th century, and was much rebuilt in 1855. It contains a headstone to the martyrs by the 1930s sculptor and engraver Eric Gill. James Hammett, the only one of the martyrs to spend the rest of his life in Tolpuddle, is buried in the churchyard.

TOMINTOUL
GRAMPIAN

*10 miles south-east of Grantown-on-Spey
(page 443 Fc)*

Three generations of stonemasons were responsible for the limestone houses and slate cottages of Tomintoul, the highest village in the Highlands. It stands 1,160 ft up on the remote Banffshire moors and was the creation of the 4th Duke of Gordon. In 1776 he provided land for the village on either side of a military road built 22 years earlier. By 1794 37 families lived there, and the parish minister, the Reverend John Grant, wrote that the men, women and children lived to sell and drink whisky.

By the 1830s the population of Tomintoul, pronounced 'Tamintowel', had increased to 143 families, and there were four inns for travellers – as there still are today. In summer, visitors enjoy fishing and shooting in the nearby Avon Valley, and in winter they come for the skiing.

On a knoll 1 mile south-west of the village centre is the site of St Bryde's Church, which is believed to have existed since before the 12th century. Close by is the present, 18th-century Traquair Church.

TREGARON
DYFED

10 miles north-east of Lampeter (page 425 Cc)

In the remote heartland of Wales, where there are still far more sheep than people, Tregaron is a big place by local standards, with colour-washed buildings of grey stone spreading out from a riverside crossroads. The village square is overlooked by the Talbot Hotel, and has a bronze statue of Henry Richard. The son of a local minister, he was born in 1812 and became an MP. Richard's love of his homeland also earned him the nickname of 'The Member for Wales'.

Now a centre for pony-trekking, Tregaron was for many years a starting point for drovers who climbed eastwards over the wild mountains with cattle bound for the markets of England. The route they followed towards the Wye Valley climbs to almost 1,600 ft and is one of the most spectacular roads in Wales.

TREMADOG
GWYNEDD

1 mile north of Porthmadog (page 428 Bb)

St Mary's Church, set on a grassy hillock beside the main street, has a memorial to William Alexander Madocks, the man who founded Tremadog as a model town at the start of the 19th century. Madocks, the wealthy MP for Boston, Lincolnshire, intended Tremadog to be an important link on a road terminating at Porth Dinllaen, on the Lleyn Peninsula, where ferries would take passengers and mail on to Ireland. Unfortunately for him, a parliamentary committee voted in favour of Holyhead. Although Tremadog never developed into the bustling community envisaged by its creator, it has survived as a notable tribute to his vision.

The broad main street, flanked by neat buildings of local stone, runs into a square overlooked by what was originally the Market Hall. Behind the building, sheer cliffs crowned with trees run east and west to embrace the Coed Tremadog National Nature Reserve. The cliffs have tested the skill and courage of many climbers, but serious rockfalls in the 1970s have necessitated a major cliff-stabilisation project.

Madocks built his model town on land partly reclaimed from the sea, and was justifiably proud of the fact that it stood well below what was still the official high-water mark. Until then, the surrounding area was largely marshland. What is now the Christian Mountain Centre, at the southern end of the village, was the birthplace in 1888 of T. E. Lawrence, who was to become famous as Lawrence of Arabia.

WILL YE NO' COME BACK AGAIN? *It is said that the main gates of Traquair House were closed in the spring of 1746, after the Battle of Culloden, and will not open again until a Stuart ascends the throne. Equally poignant, but more prosaic, is the story that they were locked by the 7th Earl of Traquair after the death of his beautiful young wife in 1796.*

TRAQUAIR
BORDERS

1 mile south of Innerleithen (page 441 Fc)

One of Scotland's oldest inhabited mansions, the château-like Traquair House, has remained basically unchanged for the last 300 years. It was built in the 10th century, and has been visited by 27 Scottish and English monarchs. In 1566 Mary, Queen of Scots was at Traquair, and there are examples of her embroidery among its treasures. Also on view are an 18th-century library; a Priest's Room with secret staircase; and a Brew House, equipped as it was two centuries ago and licensed to sell its own beer, Traquair House Ale. The mansion is the home of the Stuarts of Traquair, and is open during the summer months.

The village – with its neat cottages and flower-filled gardens – lies in the valley of the River Tweed. In the past, when Highland cattle-drovers walked their herds to the English markets, Traquair was one of their overnight halts. The next day they started the tough climb over Minch Moor towards Selkirk. This is still a well-known Border right-of-way – although the hill grazings on the Traquair side are now covered by Forestry Commission plantations.

TROUTBECK

CUMBRIA

3 miles north of Windermere (page 435 Cd)

Like many Lake District villages, Troutbeck is spread along a hillside. For well over 1 mile, from Town End to Town Head, farms and cottages are scattered along a narrow lane.

Townend – a farm with whitewashed walls and stone-mullioned windows – was built in 1623 and still has much of the original oak furniture. It remained in the same family for nearly 300 years, but is now owned by the National Trust. The lovely old house has the tall, tapering chimneys that are a feature of Lake District architecture. Across the lane is one of several ranges of farm buildings that contribute much to Troutbeck's timeless character. Towards the far end of the village, farms and cottages cluster tightly round the Mortal Man, a 17th-century inn, and the delightful Clock Cottage.

Troutbeck's church and former school are down in the valley. The largely 18th-century church has an east window created in 1873 by William Morris, Edward Burne-Jones and Ford Madox Brown.

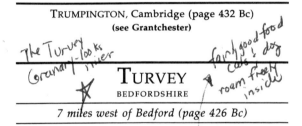

TRUMPINGTON, Cambridge (page 432 Bc)
(see Grantchester)

TURVEY

BEDFORDSHIRE

7 miles west of Bedford (page 426 Bc)

A stone bridge dating from the 13th century has 11 arches spanning the fast-flowing River Great Ouse at Turvey. Beside the bridge there is the 17th-century Ye Three Fyshes Inn.

Splayed around a central island of tree-shaded cottages are imposing, tall-gabled houses built in Victorian-Jacobean style by Charles Longuet-Higgins, who was lord of the manor in the mid-19th century. From the 13th century until 1783 the Turvey estate was held by the Mordaunts, but then it was bought by the Higgins family who built Turvey House in 1794.

Turvey House stands in parkland and is privately owned. Near its entrance in the main street is the Church of All Saints, which Higgins had restored by one of the most eminent architects of his day, Sir George Gilbert Scott, who designed the Albert Memorial in London. The church dates mostly from the 13th century, though the two small windows above the nave arches are Saxon. A beautiful 14th-century wall-painting of the Crucifixion was uncovered on the

(handwritten annotations:) The Turvey looks ordinary river / fairly good food cats & dog roam freely inside

south wall of the chapel during Scott's restoration.

The history of the Manor of Turvey unfolds in the church and in the churchyard, with the tombs of the Mordaunts dating from 1506 to 1601 followed by wall tablets to the Higgins family from 1840 to 1968.

On the river bank, near the bridge, stand two carved stone figures – one of which is known locally as Jonah. He stands 10 ft tall, has a dolphin at his feet, rather than a whale, but nevertheless this led to the statue's name. It came originally from Ashridge House in Hertfordshire and its age is unknown, but it was John Higgins who placed it on the river bank in 1844.

TURVILLE

BUCKINGHAMSHIRE

5 miles north of Henley-on-Thames (page 426 Ba)

A narrow lane flanked by high banks and hedgerows descends into Turville, and the black-and-white timbered Bull and Butcher Inn marks the beginning of a village that sits comfortably in the deep fold of the Turville Valley.

Beyond the inn the tiny, circular green makes an attractive frontage for a row of timber-framed cottages that leads to the churchyard gate. The Church of St Mary the Virgin was largely rebuilt towards the end of the 15th and early 16th centuries, although the tower may be 14th century. In the porch, a board listing Turville's vicars shows that the first incumbent was appointed in 1228. Like many of the nearby houses the church is built of flint, which was the principal building material in chalk country in the Middle Ages.

On the summit of a high ridge behind the village stands a black-capped windmill, the gaunt outlines of its sails silhouetted against the sky. It was featured in the film *Chitty Chitty Bang Bang.*

TUTBURY

STAFFORDSHIRE

4 miles north-west of Burton upon Trent (page 430 Bc)

Crumbling walls and jagged towers are all that remain of Tutbury Castle, standing 100 ft above the Dove Valley. The village below is large, sprawling down the hillside and yet retaining an air of dignity befitting its age. Its wide main street has sharp turns that almost divide it into three parts, each with a number of Georgian buildings. Ye Olde Dog and Partridge Hotel – 500 years old – is particularly attractive, with close-set uprights in its timber frame.

The castle dates from the 11th century when it belonged to Henry de Ferrers, one of William the Conqueror's barons who fought at the Battle of Hastings. Mary, Queen of Scots spent part of her long imprisonment there before being moved to Fotheringhay Castle shortly before her execution in 1587.

St Mary's Church, just below the castle, was founded as a Benedictine priory in 1080.

GOVERNED BY STATESMEN *Most of the older houses in Troutbeck were built by 'statesmen' – small yeomen farmers who made a subsistence living from the hillside fields. Of necessity, the buildings are strung out along a line of springs flowing from Wansfell; until recently, these were the only water supply. Wagoners used to water their horses there before the haul over Kirkstone Pass.*

UDNY GREEN
GRAMPIAN

5 miles east of Oldmeldrum (page 443 Gd)

Early in the 19th century, Udny Green church-yard was a favourite haunt of resurrectionists who dug up freshly interred corpses to sell to the medical school at Aberdeen. To prevent this, in 1832 the villagers built a mort-house where they kept the newly dead for a while before burial. The circular stone and slate building is still there, though the grisly trade has long ceased.

There has been a church by the village green since the Middle Ages. In 1604 the original church was replaced by Christ's Kirk of Udny, this was replaced in turn by the present towered building in 1821. The village is grouped around the green, with the village hall and Udny Arms Hotel on the south side. A group of old people's homes, called Academy Court, is on the site of a private school founded in 1786. Among famous pupils of the academy was Sir James Outram, hero of the Indian Mutiny.

The Udnys have been the leading family of Udny Green since the 14th century, and Udny Castle stands above the village. In the 17th century, ornamental turrets were added to this impressive, 100 ft high, five-storey tower-house, which has been modernised over the years.

After the lapse of an annual show, the Udny Castle Games were established in 1971. Eight neighbourhood villages compete in the Games, which include archery, croquet, field events, football and a display of Highland dancing. They are held on the last Saturday in June.

The village shop, Fleeman's, which stands on the green, is named after a local character, Jamie Fleeman, jester to an 18th-century laird of Udny. There are numerous stories about Fleeman, who first worked in the castle kitchen. Once, a noble guest asked him: 'Whose fool are you?' To which Jamie replied: 'The laird's – whose fool are you?'

UFFINGTON
OXFORDSHIRE

4 miles south of Faringdon (page 426 Aa)

The outline of a huge beast, as much like a horse as anything else, sprawls nearly 400 ft across the hillside below the Iron Age battlements of Uffington Castle. Who cut it, when or why, will never be known for certain, but the most reasonable theory seems to be that it is a cult-figure connected with Epona, Celtic goddess of horses.

The village is built almost entirely of chalk, except for some new houses built of creamy sandstone. A small, barn-like building of chalk blocks dating from the 17th century was once the school, and is now the village hall.

Uffington's church, St Mary's, is 13th century with an octagonal tower. Its spire blew down in 1740, and an extra storey was added to replace it. Inside, is a bronze of Thomas Hughes, who made the area the home of his hero in *Tom Brown's Schooldays*.

Dragon Hill, just below the White Horse, is said to be where St George slew the dragon. The naked patch on top is supposed to have been caused by the dragon's poisonous blood.

◆

ANCHORS AWEIGH *A fishing fleet fans out into the sheltered waters of Loch Broom. In its wake lies Ullapool, founded in 1788 as a fishing station. At first it prospered, but later fell on hard times when the herring trade slumped. Today, the village is once more a busy port whose boats work the fishing grounds of the Minch. It is also the mainland terminal for a car-ferry service to Stornoway and the Outer Hebrides.*

ULLAPOOL
HIGHLAND

On eastern shore of Loch Broom (page 443 De)

Although the name is of Norse origin, the present village of Ullapool was designed in 1788 by the British Fisheries Society as part of their plan to create employment based on the lucrative herring trade. But before the planned layout could be fully realised, the herring fishing slumped. Ullapool was bought by Sir James Matheson, a wealthy merchant, who completed the building of the village curving out on a promontory into Loch Broom. Whitewashed houses and shops look south-eastwards across a bay towards the towering peaks of the inland deer forests.

Behind the seafront, the village is neatly laid out, with street names signposted both in English and in Gaelic. Market Street is also *Sraid na Fèille*, and the fact that Ullapool used to be a port for coastal trading is recalled in *Sraid a' Schusduinn*, or Custom House Street.

The harbour is now a terminus of the Hebridean car-ferry service to Stornoway in Lewis, and the fishing grounds of the Minch attract many boats from east-coast ports. Sailing and sea-angling on Loch Broom, and further out among the Summer Isles, are among the attractions. There is a yachting centre half a mile away across the loch in a little bay surrounded by mountains.

UPPER ARLEY
HEREFORD AND WORCESTER

3 miles north of Bewdley (page 425 Ec)

The village of Arley clings to the steep eastern bank of the River Severn. It is sometimes known as Upper Arley, to distinguish it from the village of the same name in Warwickshire. Arley is right off the beaten track and its hilly main street, which dips down to the very edge of the river, is a cul-de-sac.

At one end of the village is the parish church of St Peter, a fine 14th-century building, with fragments of Norman ornament in the south wall of the nave, which indicate the existence of an earlier church. Its buttressed tower commands a fine view overlooking the river. Inside there are 19th-century memorials to the last Earl of Mountnorris and his son, Viscount Valentia, whose name is perpetuated by the Valentia Arms inn and restaurant near by.

Bordering the village street as it climbs away from the river is an attractive mixture of buildings: old red-brick and white-rendered cottages, a few modern bungalows, a large vicarage and the Georgian splendour of The Grange. The whole appearance is reminiscent of a small seaside fishing village, and attracts fishermen from a wide area.

Arley's ferry boat has been replaced by a single-span pedestrian bridge. This leads to the old Harbour Inn and the impeccably restored railway station, now part of the privately run steam-operated Severn Valley Railway.

The
SQUIRE
and the
Manor House

The squire and the manor house were as much a part of the English village as the parson and his church. Fiction has portrayed him as a moustache-twirling villain or a sport-mad drunk; but in real life he was often a progressive farmer and a pillar of society.

MOATED SPLENDOUR *One of the grand medieval manor houses to have survived to the present day is Ightham Mote in Kent. It is surrounded by a spring-filled moat and in turn surrounds a square central courtyard. The house dates in part from the mid-14th century. For nearly 300 years it was the home of the Selby family.*

Of all the traditional figures in the English country landscape, the squire is the best known. Kindly, bluff, quick to anger or to merriment, autocratic, hard-riding, hard-drinking, a fighter, a sportsman and a man's man from the top of his honest head to the tips of his spurred riding boots, he epitomises all the qualities the English secretly admire most.

He is Cromwell's 'honest, rus-set-coated captain'. He is John Peel, Squire Trelawney of *Treasure Island*, Squire Western of *Tom Jones* and Squire Brown of *Tom Brown's Schooldays*. He is the indomitable John Bull of the old *Punch* cartoons, waving a brawny, defiant fist from Dover's cliffs towards whichever nation was irritating us at the time. Sometimes nature mirrored art, and the real squire matched his countrymen's ideal. At least, he was a very English creation, for his like, in fact or fiction, occurs nowhere else on earth.

In his heyday – probably the 18th and 19th centuries – the squire occupied a very solid place in English society. Though his acreage was small compared to that of the great landowners – perhaps a parish or two and a few farms – he controlled every aspect of the lives of his tenantry, and his decisions for the most part went unquestioned.

He was the descendant of the feudal esquire, the lowest rank of the nobility, who held a manor of an overlord in exchange, when called upon, for military service – the provision of half-a-dozen or so armed men. He lived in the manor house, and the peasants on his land were allowed to work their portions of the village's open fields in exchange for a set number of days' labour on the esquire's domain.

It is generally reckoned that it was the Black Death of the mid-14th century that signalled the end of this system, though, in fact, the feudal structure had begun to crumble long before this. However, there is no doubt that the swathe cut by the plague through the agricultural labour force meant that the survivors became far more valuable than they had been a century before. For the first time they were able to demand cash wages.

This led to the growth of the

MASTER OF THE HOUNDS *George Osbaldeston was a daring 18th-century horseman – a man who typified the character of the sporting squire.*

Housemaid.   Coachman.   Head gardener.   Boot-boy.   Garden labourer.
           Housekeeper.   Kitchen maid.   Cook.

'TO KEEP A PERFECT GENTLEMAN GOING'   *The closing years of the Victorian era heralded the decline of many country squires, as their manor houses were converted into tenant farms and a new ruling class emerged. Nevertheless, the fortunate few managed to cling on to their old lifestyles until the turn of the century, maintaining a staff of servants sufficient – as Henry James, the expatriate American novelist observed – 'to keep a perfect gentleman going'.*

Milton Abbas – a planned model village built in the 18th century to replace an old market town.

TWO FACES OF THE SQUIREARCHY

Not all landowners were as indifferent to the welfare of their tenants as the squire depicted in the Punch *cartoon (right). Some made it their business to provide their retainers – both active and retired – with decent accommodation, such as the cottages built at Blaise Hamlet, in Bristol, and Selworthy in Somerset. Others, like the 1st Earl of Dorchester, were less philanthropic by intention but achieved similar ends. Between 1773 and 1779 he swept away the old market town of Abbey Milton – because he found it aesthetically displeasing – and created the village of Milton Abbas (above) on a new site, away from his home. The result was 40 thatched and whitewashed cottages flanking a broad main street with grass verges and chestnut trees. Even the church was rebuilt to match the model village.*

The iniquitous squire as observed by a Punch cartoonist.

yeoman class, small tenant farmers or owner-occupiers who stood socially and economically between the lord of the manor and the labourers that they both employed. Gradually, this pattern, too, was altered, chiefly through the enclosures that took place between Queen Elizabeth's day and the mid-19th century.

Most far-reaching in social and political effects were the enclosures of between 1750 and 1850, the era of the Agrarian Revolution, which gave rise to new techniques of crop rotation and animal husbandry demanding enclosed fields. The enclosing process was often little more than the legalised expropriation of the old field strips on which the villagers depended for a living. Small farmers, too, went to the wall, while many of the squirearchy grew rich.

Of these, William Cobbett,

author of *Rural Rides*, wrote in 1826: 'There is in the men calling themselves "English country gentlemen" something superlatively base. They are, I sincerely believe, the most cruel, the most unfeeling, the most brutally insolent ... they are the *most base* of all creatures that God ever suffered to disgrace the human shape.'

The gain in fertility and production that followed the enclosures was great, but the cost was a tragic decline in social variety. By the mid-19th century, the typical village was sharply divided between the landowning class and the landless, voteless and largely illiterate labourers. There were few other elements in the hierarchy. Apart from the parson, often the younger son of a landed family who had more in common with the squire than with his flock, the only interventions between the top and bottom of the village

pyramid were the odd innkeeper and the local craftsmen, all generally tenants of the squire themselves.

Despite Cobbett's bitter words, squires came in many different styles – harsh or benevolent, men of broad acres or few. Usually the village took what it got philosophically, since acceptance of the squire's leadership was bred deep in the bone. Neither did the landowner have many doubts.

A typical squire of the 1840s is described by William Howitt, a journalist of the period: 'He loves the constitution as he ought to do; for has it not done well for him and his forefathers? And has it not kept the mob in their places ... and given the family estate to him, the church to his brother Ned, and put Fred and George into the army and navy?'

To be fair, the class occasionally threw up remarkable men

– characters such as Jethro Tull of Berkshire, who, in addition to being a landowner, was a brilliant scholar and lawyer and an inventor of genius, whose treatise *Horse Hoeing Husbandry*, published in 1731, as well as his seed drill and other inventions, revolutionised British farming.

But by the middle of Victoria's reign, the image of the squirearchy was that displayed in the sporting prints of the time: hard-drinking, iron-faced men in hunting pink thrusting their horses at any obstacle, however difficult.

The archetype of the Victorian sporting squire was probably Sir Tatton Sykes of Yorkshire, who was a respected farmer and stockbreeder as well as a superb horseman. Among his feats is that of riding from Yorkshire to Aberdeen to compete in a race. He won the race and rode back to Doncaster in time for the St Leger, an event he never missed in all of his long life. The round journey of 740 miles was accomplished in slightly under five days.

Such legendary figures were scarcely the norm and, in fact, many landowners, the smaller ones especially, possessed a strong sense of duty. Often the squire had grown up with his tenants, whose families had known his family for generations. Continuity and stability were to everyone's interest, and the villagers expected, and frequently received, help from the manor house in times of trouble. Generally, too, the squire sat as the local Justice of the Peace, a task that involved not only passing judgments on petty crime, but the supervision of gaols, lunatic asylums, roads and bridges in the district, as well as the administration of the Poor Law and of fairs and licensed premises. Even when some of these powers passed to elected councils, the squire's influence remained, for politically he reigned supreme. Few tenant farmers would be rash enough to vote against his wishes, and few labourers had the vote at all before 1884. Sir John Thorold of Lincolnshire was perhaps exceptional in telling his tenants – in a two-member constituency – that he wanted only one of their two votes.

But, on the whole, the winds of change caused the late-19th-century squirearchy to button its coat more tightly. In the battle to establish the Agricultural Workers' Union in the 1870s, two Chipping Norton parson-magistrates awarded ten days' hard labour to women who had jeered at strike-breakers, while in Warwickshire Sir Charles Mordaunt issued notices to quit upon any of his tenants who joined the union. Lord Leigh, however, in the same county, readily agreed to advance his workers' pay

THE SQUARSON

The Reverend Charles Slingsby was one of the best-known (and best-loved) 19th-century squarsons – squires who were also parsons. Slingsby was lord of the manor at Scriven in North Yorkshire and patron of two livings, as well as being a magistrate and an accomplished sportsman.

He inherited the estate under the will of his uncle, Sir Charles Slingsby, who died while out hunting in 1869. Slingsby himself also died in the hunting field in 1912. But he at least had earned respect both as squire and parson, unlike many other squarsons who put their clerical duties in the hands of underpaid curates while they lived the lives of hard-riding, hard-drinking, sporting squires in the John Bull mould.

from 12 to 15 shillings a week.

In the end, it was not labour problems or legislation that caused the ancient fabric to crumble, but sheer economics. In the aftermath of the agricultural depression, which sullenly ran from the 1880s to the 1930s, old estates were broken up and the old manorial families replaced by newcomers.

Even so, the squire is by no means dead. But if he still rides to hounds, he also possesses a degree in agriculture, has let much of his shooting and probably a wing or two of the manor as well. His predecessors' monuments in church look on him without reproach, for in many ways he follows the style of living that they set and that the world has envied – that of the country gentleman.

SHOCK CURE *In order to stop a bout of hiccoughs, John Mytton, a 19th-century sporting squire – and a celebrated eccentric – set light to his nightshirt. Despite severe burns he recovered. He eventually died of* delerium tremens *in a debtors' prison – just 37 years old.*

VERYAN
CORNWALL

11 miles south-west of St Austell (page 418 Ba)

Narrow tree-lined lanes lead to Veryan, which lies in a beautiful wooded dell. It is a perfect setting for the village's whitewashed cottages, many of which are thatched. Veryan takes its name from St Symphoriana, who was martyred at Autun in central France in the 3rd century. The village church, with its granite nave and slate tower, is dedicated to the martyr.

Below the churchyard there is a water-garden sheltered by evergreen oak trees. Subtropical flowers and trees grow in profusion in Veryan, aided by its mild climate, in contrast to the bracken-covered slopes above Veryan Bay 2 miles to the east. Cornish folklore has it that the body of Gerennius, a 5th-century king of Cornwall, was rowed across nearby Gerrans Bay after his death and was buried beneath Carne Beacon. The boat that carried his body is said to have been made of gold, and the oars were made of silver.

There are two small fishing hamlets in Veryan Bay, Portloe and Portholland. Further east is the sandy Porthluney Cove, and above it the magnificent parkland of Caerhays Castle. The house was built in 1808 by John Nash, architect of London's Marble Arch, in Gothic style with turrets, towers and battlements. The house became 'Manderly' in the television production of Daphne du Maurier's *Rebecca*, and a cove in the area was 'Happy Valley'. Caerhays Castle is not open to the public, although its gardens are open twice a year, on Easter Sunday and on the first or second Sunday in May. The building can be seen from the road, which passes the lake.

◆

TO BEAT THE DEVIL *Cornwall is rich in myths and legends about the Devil, and at the beginning of the 19th century the villagers of Veryan feared that Satan might invade their homes. One man was so concerned for the community that he had five circular cottages built, each surmounted by a cross. The thatched and whitewashed buildings were said to be 'Devil-proof', as they contained no corners in which Satan could lie in wait for the inhabitants.*

WADENHOE

NORTHAMPTONSHIRE

4 miles south-west of Oundle (page 431 Db)

Instead of one of the lofty spires for which Northamptonshire is noted, Wadenhoe's parish church of St Michael and All Angels has a saddleback – or gable-roofed – tower. The church dates from Norman times, and stands on an escarpment above the village. From the church-yard gate there is a fine view of the willow-fringed banks of the River Nene as it flows towards a weir and mill-stream. The remains of a medieval ridge and furrowed field surround the church.

Wadenhoe's main street is lined with well-built old farmhouses and thatched stone cottages. A lane leads to the river and to the 17th-century King's Head Inn, whose garden sweeps down to the waterside. About 2 miles east of Wadenhoe is the basically 17th-century Lilford Hall, set in well-tended grounds. Although the hall itself is deserted, some of the outbuildings have been turned into a Rural Implements Museum and a crafts and antiques centre.

There are several notable buildings in Waden-hoe, including the gabled Wadenhoe House, once the home of George Ward-Hunt who served as Chancellor of the Exchequer under Benjamin Disraeli; a many-sided toll-house; and a circular dovecot with 500 nesting-boxes.

WADHURST

EAST SUSSEX

6 miles south-east of Tunbridge Wells (page 423 Eb)

Tile-hung cottages, shops and inns line the main street of Wadhurst, which stretches along a ridge in the heart of the High Weald, more than 450 ft above sea-level. Brick, made from local clay, is the principal building material. But it was another natural material – iron – that created Wadhurst's prosperity.

Snape Wood, to the south-west, was one of the last places in the South-East where iron ore was mined. Work went on intermittently as late as the mid-19th century.

Thirty iron tomb slabs are built into the floor of the Church of St Peter and St Paul, a unique collection that makes the floor ring as people walk over it. The slabs, some of which are inlaid with ornate heraldry and bear the names of local ironmasters, date from 1617 to 1772, roughly spanning the heyday of the local iron industry. The church also contains a 17 ft wrought-iron screen, built in 1957, depicting images of Sussex rural life interspersed by flowers and foliage.

It was a local ironmaster who built the Queen Anne vicarage in the High Street. Next door is the tile-hung Hill House, and close to the church-yard stands Churchgate House, timber-framed and tile-hung with an overhanging upper floor.

The village sign shows an anvil, recalling the iron industry, and also an oast-house, showing that this is also hop country. The estates around Wadhurst supplied timber for the hammer-beam roof of Westminster Hall in Richard II's reign, and also for repairs to the roof after it was damaged in the Second World War.

WANLOCKHEAD

DUMFRIES AND GALLOWAY

6 miles east of Sanquhar (page 441 Ec)

Gold from near Wanlockhead was used in the Crown of Scotland, remodelled for James V in 1540 and now kept in Edinburgh Castle as the most important item in the Royal Regalia, known as 'The Honours of Scotland'. Gold and silver have been mined in the area since Roman times, but lead mining was the village's main industry and the mines were worked until 1934. They went back into production briefly in 1957–8. Many of the mine-shafts, smelters and wagon-ways can be seen at the Silver-Lead Mine Visitor Walkway just north of the village. There are also a 19th-century beam-engine, a water-wheel pit and ruined miners' cottages on the site. The Mining Museum in Goldscaur Row is an exten-sion of the Miners' Subscription Library, founded in 1756. The present cottage-style library was opened in 1850.

Wanlockhead stands 1,380 ft above sea-level in the Lowther Hills, and is the highest village in Scotland. Most of the stone houses and cottages are scattered on high ground around the head of Wanlock Water. Many of them – in contrast to the surrounding heather-covered moors – are painted yellow, orange, blue and bright pink. They were built between 1755 and 1842, though the slate roofs date only from 1906, when a mining company bought the lead rights from the Duke of Buccleuch, and replaced the original thatch.

WARK

NORTHUMBERLAND

9 miles north-west of Hexham (page 438 Ac)

Until the 14th century, Wark-on-Tyne was in Scotland, and was the capital of Tynedale which thrusts northwards into the wild fell country of the Northumberland National Park. The village lies on a beautiful stretch of the North Tyne, where it is joined by the Warks Burn.

The road from the south passes a 16th-century farmhouse, now the Battlesteads Hotel, before reaching the village green with its quadrangle of greystone houses. A stone bridge spanning the stream gives fine views along the wooded banks.

Wark's history goes back to Saxon times, and it was here that Alfwald, King of Northumbria may have been murdered in 788. The Normans built a massive castle, and its remains can still be seen on the river bank. Across the river, 1½ miles south-east of Wark, is Chipchase Castle, a private residence dating from the 14th century.

SIMONBURN Lying 2 miles to the south, the stone and whitewashed village of Simonburn has associations with St Mungo, Glasgow's patron saint. He is said to have baptised converts at nearby St Mungo's Well in the 6th century, and the church, which bears his name, contains fragments of the same period.

WARMINGTON

WARWICKSHIRE

5 miles north-west of Banbury (page 430 Ba)

Buildings of rich, honey-coloured Hornton stone distinguish this enchanting village. It nestles beneath the steep, northern slopes of Edge Hill and looks out over an undulating patchwork of fields towards the valley of the River Cherwell. It was along this valley that Charles I's army marched in October 1642 to Edge Hill and the first major battle of the Civil War.

The army advanced westwards through Cropredy and Mollington before reaching Warmington and climbing the hill beyond St Michael's Church. People in the Manor House and many other buildings still surviving, watched the Royalist troops – 18,000 horse and foot – pass by on their way to the bloody, but indecisive, fray.

Much earlier, during the reign of Henry I, Benedictines from Preaux in Normandy were granted the manor of Warmington by the Earl of Warwick, and established a priory there. Like its counterparts in the neighbouring Cotswolds, the village thrived when the wool trade was at its peak during the Middle Ages. The oldest houses and cottages date from that period.

The village's centre is a spacious green surrounded by some of Warmington's most memorable buildings. It rises gently toward tree-clad slopes on which stands the ancient Church of St Michael. The foot of the green is dominated by the rectory with its early-18th-century facade.

At the top of the green, behind a pond attractive with ducks and water lilies, is the Manor House, built about 1600. Grove Farm House, in the south-east corner of the green, dates from the late 17th century.

The centuries-old houses of Court Close, below the church, at the opposite end of the village, blend remarkably well with their surroundings. They stand a short distance above the Plough, a cosy, early-17th-century inn. Near by, a short lane climbs steeply to the main road and is overlooked by the mullioned facade of Ivy Dene, an attractive old house flanked by a curved archway. Its neighbour, The Dene, has a quaint thatched porch.

Steps lead from Church Hill to the churchyard. A stone marks the last resting place of Alexander Gourden, a Scots 'captaine' who was buried two days after the Battle of Edge Hill together with Richard Sauner, one of Charles's officers, and seven other soldiers. The church itself, built of Hornton stone, dates in part from the end of the 13th century, and its nave has impressive Norman arcades.

CROPREDY Four miles to the east of Warmington, the River Cherwell flows into Cropredy under a bridge that in 1644 was the scene of another Civil War battle – with an equally indeterminate result. Most of the village, however, lies on the bank of the Oxford Canal, about whose lock is a group of tall poplars planted by the late Richard Crossman. A hump-backed bridge leads to Red Lion Street with its distinguished thatch and stone cottages. A cul-de-sac, the Cup and Saucer, derives its odd name from the hollowed remains of an old preaching cross.

The largely 13th-century sandstone church possesses a rare 15th-century lectern. During the battle it was hidden in the river for safety, and there it remained for many years, since, what with the excitement and confusion of the day, no one could remember where it had been sunk.

WELFORD-ON-AVON

WARWICKSHIRE

4 miles south-west of Stratford (page 430 Bb)

A loop in the meandering River Avon embraces Welford on all sides save the south. From the north a narrow stone bridge crosses the river to meet the long main street, off which lies the village green with its chestnut tree and tall, red, white and blue maypole.

Thatched, timber-framed houses and cottages abound in Welford. They stand in colourful gardens on both sides of the main street, down the lane leading to the church. The entrance to the churchyard is through a lych-gate, a replica of one that had stood there since the late 14th century until time and weather made it unsafe. Next to it, a plaque on the churchyard wall records the site of the village stocks and pound.

Welford has three inns – the Shakespeare and the Bell, near the village centre, and the Four Alls near the bridge.

For the greater part of its long history, the most discordant note at Warmington has been the conversation among the ducks on its pond. But in October 1642, tranquillity was shattered by blare of trumpet and beat of drum as King Charles and 18,000 men marched through the village to the Battle of Edge Hill. Most of the Royalist and Parliamentarian dead were buried on the battlefield, but a number lie in Warmington churchyard.

WELLOW
AVON

4 miles south of Bath (page 421 Cc)

Golden-stone cottages share Wellow's hillside main street with a handsome Manor House and ancient farm buildings. The oldest of them, Weavers Farm, has flanked the western side of the village square since the 14th century. Down Railway Lane, from the square, the signal box for the disused Somerset and Dorset line marks the start of a footpath to Wellow Brook. Pedestrians can cross the brook by a medieval packhorse bridge, its stone buttresses thick with moss. The watermill near by, converted into a dwelling house, is said to date from Saxon times, although it was altered and added to in 1827.

The Manor House, along High Street, was the home of the Hungerford family, who bought Wellow Manor in the 1330s and held it until 1711. The present house was built in 1634, but its dovecot, around the corner in Farm Lane, dates from about 1250. It has nesting places for about 600 pigeons.

St Julian's Church, further east, was rebuilt about 1372 by Sir Thomas Hungerford, the first recorded Speaker of the House of Commons. In Wellow's heyday, as the centre of a sheep-rearing area, the church drew its congregation from neighbouring settlements as well as from the village. Fine wall-paintings in the north chapel, representing Christ and the apostles, date from about 1500. A statue over the south porch shows St Julian blessing the parish – with an oar in hand, because he was adopted as the patron saint of ferrymen. Church Farmhouse, across the road, was built in 1620.

CLAVERTON A fine Bath stone house with splendid views is now the Claverton American Museum. Its rooms illustrate American domestic life from colonial days to the 19th century, and feature outstanding collections of quilts, textiles, pewter, glass and silver. There are special sections devoted to the American Indians, the Pennsylvania Dutch and the strict Puritan sect known as the Shakers. The museum, 5 miles from Wellow, is open on afternoons throughout the summer.

WELLOW
NOTTINGHAMSHIRE

9 miles east of Mansfield (page 430 Cd)

A maypole on the green at Wellow is one of only three permanent poles in Britain. At one time the pole was cut from Sherwood Forest, a few miles to the west, whenever a new one was needed. But the present one is made of steel and was erected in 1976. Around the green are 17th and 18th-century red-brick and pantiled houses and cottages, each one built in a different style. The Methodist chapel close by was built in 1847, but is in the late-Georgian style. Beside the main road is a white-painted cottage, Rock House, with an overhanging upper storey.

The small parish church of St Swithin dates from the 12th century and was built by the masons who had recently completed Rufford Abbey, 1½ miles to the south-west. Its sturdy tower rises above the cottages on the eastern side of the green, showing a clock face that was made by local craftsmen in 1953 to commemorate the Coronation of Elizabeth II.

A lane climbs up from the village to Wellow Park, the site of a circular hill-fortress, 250 ft in diameter, known as Jordan's Castle, which is surrounded by a broad moat.

◆

PART OF A KING'S REWARD *Thatched and tiled cottages line the slope leading to the village church in Wendens Ambo. Just around the corner, near the church, is Audley End Station, a name which recalls a 16th-century Lord Chancellor, Thomas Audley. His services to Henry VIII earned him 'a feast of abbey lands', including the estate on which his grandson built the magnificent 17th-century mansion of Audley End, which still stands in fine parkland 1½ miles north-east of the village.*

WENDENS AMBO
ESSEX

2 miles south-west of Saffron Walden (page 432 Cb)

Great and Little Wenden became one parish in 1662, hence the addition of *Ambo*, Latin for 'both'. The village lies in a shady vale by a winding stream, which gives rise to the first half of its name, from the Old English verb *windan*, 'to wind'. Thatched and tiled cottages line the lane to the church.

The Church of St Mary the Virgin has a Norman tower, topped by a short lead spire known as a Hertfordshire spike, because this type of spire is common in the neighbouring county. Inside the church are 15th-century wall-paintings depicting the life of St Margaret. The large thatched barn near the church is part of the farm buildings of the 15th-century Wendens Hall.

The railway station just south of the village bears the name of Audley End, the 17th-century mansion close by. The lands of Walden Abbey, on which the mansion stands, were given by Henry VIII to Thomas Audley as a reward for his help in the Dissolution of the Monasteries. It later passed to the Howard family, and the present house was begun in 1603 by Audley's grandson, Thomas Howard, Earl of Suffolk. Successive owners have altered it, but it still retains its Jacobean elegance.

Audley End is approached by a bridge over the River Cam built by Robert Adam, the 18th-century architect who also designed the circular Temple of Concord in the grounds which were laid out by Capability Brown.

Audley End is owned by the Department of the Environment, and is open to the public daily, except Mondays, from April to October.

WENSLEY
NORTH YORKSHIRE

9 miles south-west of Richmond (page 436 Bc)

One of Yorkshire's biggest and perhaps most beautiful dales takes its name not from a river, as most others do, but from this scattered little village of pale golden stone. Wensley was the market town of the dale for more than 200 years, until 1563. Then the plague struck. The parish register of crops notes grimly: 'This year nothing set down.' The townsfolk fled to higher ground at Leyburn, and few of those who escaped the disease chose to return. Leyburn became the market town, and the old market cross was laid in Wensley's churchyard where it was unearthed by schoolchildren in 1956. Holy Trinity Church, built in 1245 on Saxon foundations, has wall-paintings in the nave which are thought to date from about 1330 – perhaps the earliest in Yorkshire. There are old box pews, 16th-century choir stalls, and a notable memorial brass of 1375.

As you come down the hill from Leyburn, the road passes Bolton Hall and the Three Horse Shoes pub before crossing the River Ure.

WEOBLEY
HEREFORD AND WORCESTER

10 miles north-west of Hereford (page 425 Dc)

Timber-framed cottages and inns fan out from Weobley's wide central street. The island in the middle of the street, now a rose garden, was the site of a market in the heyday of this village, which until 1832 was a 'rotten' borough returning two members to Parliament. Benjamin Tomkins, a late-18th-century villager is said to have been responsible for originating the breed of red-and-white beef cattle, prized throughout the world, to which Hereford gave its name. Weobley's own name – pronounced 'Webley' – is derived from Wibba's ley, or meadow, and appears in the Domesday Book as Wibelai.

The road north from the Red Lion loops round the fine Church of St Peter and St Paul. Its commanding spire and traceried eight-sided font date from the 14th century, but other features remain from the Norman era. Among many interesting ornaments and monuments is a marble statue of Colonel John Birch, an officer in Cromwell's army who quarrelled with his leader and claimed after the Restoration that he had been imprisoned no fewer than 21 times.

WESTDEAN
EAST SUSSEX

6 miles west of Eastbourne (page 423 Eb)

There is a sense of seclusion in Westdean, a village of flint cottages and barns lying at the end of a narrow cul-de-sac. The beeches of Friston Forest shelter the village, and a small stream

MEDIEVAL SURVIVALS *The spire of Weobley's 14th-century church dominates a village having an abundance of timber-framed houses and inns, some dating from the early 1300s.*

leads to the River Cuckmere which flows into the sea less than 2 miles away.

Westdean is believed to be the town known as Dene, where Alfred the Great was met for the first time by his biographer, Bishop Asser. In Saxon times, when the Cuckmere formed a broader and deeper estuary, Alfred is thought to have kept a fleet at Dene. He may also have had a palace in Westdean, probably on the site in the centre of the village where the ruins of the medieval manor house and an adjoining dovecot are preserved as ancient monuments.

The flint-built village rectory dates from the 13th century. It still has the interior wooden shutters which were in use before glass was fitted in its windows. Near by is the part-Norman Church of All Saints. The memorials inside include a bronze head by Jacob Epstein, in memory of Lord Waverley who, as Sir John Anderson, was Home Secretary during the Second World War and introduced the air-raid shelter which bore his name.

Half a mile north of the village is Charleston Manor, part of which was built around 1200. It has Norman windows, and some Tudor and early-Georgian additions. A medieval dovecot stands near huge barns in the walled gardens, which are open to the public during the summer.

PRANCING FLAMINGOES *Weston Underwood's Flamingo Gardens claim to have one of the finest private collections of birds and mammals in the world. Among the birds are rare Andean and James flamingoes from the highlands of Peru and Bolivia, seen here prancing by the waterside. The mammals on show include bison, wallabies and llamas. The gardens are open during the summer.*

WEST HOATHLY

WEST SUSSEX

4 miles south-west of East Grinstead (page 423 Db)

Quiet lanes form a junction on a ridge of the High Weald, where West Hoathly stands in wooded country just west of Ashdown Forest. The Church of St Margaret, which is part Norman, stands on the junction opposite a 17th-century manor house. Tile-hung old cottages are clustered around the Cat Inn, said to have been a favourite spot for smugglers in the 18th century.

The village was a centre of the iron industry, and monuments of ironmasters who died early in the 17th century, when the industry was thriving, are set on the south wall of the church.

The manor house, originally built in 1627, is of local stone. Near by stands the 15th-century Priest House, timber-framed and roofed with Horsham slate, now owned by the Sussex Archaeological Society and open to the public. The house contains a small museum.

WESTMILL

HERTFORDSHIRE

8 miles east of Stevenage (page 426 Cb)

This is a quietly prosperous village set in an orderly landscape of well-spaced trees. Perhaps the village's charm lies in its spacing, in its wide grass verges and in its loved and cared-for look. The Sword in Hand, next door to the church, is a case in point – a fairly ordinary, pink-washed village pub, but given great dignity by the two magnificent trees that frame its entrance. The church, which is of Saxon origin, is approached through prim yews and immaculately carved flower beds. Sadly, its doors are generally locked.

A sense of neatness and order prevails throughout the village, from the triangular green with its tile-roofed pump and bow-fronted shop to the wide main street and its pollarded trees. The cottages are of respectable longevity, but in a wide mixture of styles – black and white, thatch, slate, tile, colour-washed and red brick.

The 18th-century Westmill Bury, with its great barn, gleams . with white paint, and is still a working farm. Up the road, in Cherry Green, is the tiny, thatched Button Snap cottage, the only property that the essayist Charles Lamb ever owned. He bought it in 1812 with 'the feeling of an English freeholder that all betwixt sky and centre was my own'. But he never lived in it, and sold it after three years for £50.

WESTLETON, Suffolk (page 433 Dc)

(see p. 378)

WESTON UNDER PENYARD

HEREFORD AND WORCESTER

2 miles east of Ross-on-Wye (page 425 Eb)

Houses of old red sandstone blend harmoniously with more recent buildings among a fine display of pretty gardens in the hillside village of Weston under Penyard. Men have lived on the site at least since Roman times. The Romans called it Ariconium. They founded it as a garrison town and later they used it as a smelting centre for iron ore from the nearby Forest of Dean.

Only a few fragments remain of the medieval Penyard Castle, 1 mile south-west of the village. But some of its original stone is thought to be incorporated in the Rectory and in Bollitree Castle, a 17th-century house just north of the village. Behind the house is a startling range of outbuildings with battlements and turrets – said to have been added by an 18th-century owner to please his bride, who wanted to live in a castle.

The Church of St Lawrence looks down from its position above the main village. It has a fine arcade of four Norman arches and a 14th-century bell tower which gives superb views across the countryside. In medieval times it was used as a watch tower – a function revived by the Home Guard in the last war.

WESTON UNDERWOOD
BUCKINGHAMSHIRE

4 miles north of Newport Pagnell (page 426 Bc)

Cottages and houses of honey-coloured stone line the single main street with its cobble-stoned pavement. The Lodge, in the centre of the village, was once the home of the poet William Cowper, and almost next door is the brick-and-stone Cowpers Oak Inn. A lane leads to Cowper's Alcove, a classically styled shelter with fine views across the countryside to the church spire at Olney, 2 miles distant. The alcove was erected by the Throckmorton family in 1753, and it is said that many of Cowper's works were written there. A plaque inside the alcove is inscribed with a verse of his poem *The Task*.

A high stone wall with an archway topped by stone eagles bounds Weston Underwood's Flamingo Gardens.

A stone gateway surmounted by stone pineapples forms an entrance to the village at its north-eastern end. Close by are Bolbec House and the Bolbec horse-breeding centre.

◆

WETHERAL *One of the loveliest stretches of the River Eden flows past the village, and is reached by lanes running down from the village green. A railway viaduct, completed in 1834 to carry the line between Carlisle and Newcastle upon Tyne, soars 100 ft above the river banks where boats wait for the anglers who fish the Eden's waters.*

WETHERAL
CUMBRIA

4 miles east of Carlisle (page 435 Ce)

Large houses grouped round a spacious, triangular green give Wetheral an air of quiet confidence and prosperity. Most are of local stone, but the green is dominated by the brick-built Eden Bank, an elaborate 19th-century 'chateau' with millstones set in its garden wall. Another contrast is provided by the Crown Hotel, a white building of simple elegance with Classical motifs above its columned porch.

Corby Castle, on the opposite side of the River Eden, towers above the trees. It has been owned by the Howard family since the 17th century, and incorporates an ancient pele tower built as a defence against the Scots.

Members of the Howard family of Corby Castle are buried in Wetheral's 16th-century Church of the Holy Trinity, which overlooks the river and has an octagonal tower. There are also effigies of Sir Richard Salkeld, who died in 1500, and his wife, Jane.

WHALTON
NORTHUMBERLAND

5 miles south-west of Morpeth (page 438 Bc)

Spacious green verges, dotted with trees, flank the broad main street through the village, which is lined with neat rows of brown stone cottages. Chains slung between white posts define the footpaths criss-crossing the greens, giving Whalton a trim and well-ordered air.

The manor house at the eastern end of the village was enlarged in 1908, when Sir Edwin Lutyens incorporated three cottages into the building. It is typical of his work of that period – a simplified Queen Anne style – and has a

striking roof of grey stone. The house is a private dwelling, but a glimpse of its attractive gardens may be caught through a picturesque archway.

St Mary's Church dates from the 13th century, though its narrow west tower is believed to be earlier. The former rectory incorporates part of a pele tower. These were small, fortified buildings erected during the medieval Border wars.

The traditional festival of Whalton Bale is held each year on July 4, when a bonfire is lit on the village green. There is folk-dancing to the music of fiddlers and Northumbrian pipers.

The festival probably dates from Saxon times, and 'Bale' comes from *bael*, meaning 'a great fire'.

Wherwell
HAMPSHIRE

3 miles south-east of Andover (page 422 Bb)

Anyone who feels that straw-thatching is a dying craft should visit Wherwell, which could well be the place where master thatchers take their apprentices to show them just how far the craft can go. There, crowning the mainly black-and-white timber-framed cottages in the centre of the village, it goes far indeed – almost to the ground in many instances, and in great curves and voluptuous billows above eaves and windows. Even the doors are sheltered by their own deep, luxurious mantles of thatch, and when the crafts-

men have exhausted the possibilities of roofs they thatch the tops of walls.

Among so much fine workmanship it is hard to pick out particular examples, but perhaps The Old Malt House, on which thatch flows over windows like a stilled sea over rocks, deserves pride of place. Close runners-up must be Gavel Acre, with its five tiny casements framed in clipped straw, and the plain white wall of Aldings, whose thatch almost brushes the road.

The place is full of small, pleasant surprises, from its Home Guard Club – there cannot be many of these left – to its Church of St Peter and Holy Cross, rebuilt in the 19th century with a tower clad in wooden tiles that looks just like a church in miniature perched on top. Within, there is a tomb believed to be that of a 14th-century abbess and some Saxon and medieval sculptures rescued from an earlier church on the same site.

Over the churchyard wall is The Priory, a splendid, 19th-century house with a pretty wooden cupola, defended by tall yews, immaculate lawns and an arm of the river acting as a moat. The house stands on the site of the Abbey of Wherwell, founded in 986 by Queen Elfrida, mother of Ethelred the Unready, to expiate the murder of her stepson, King Edward. A notice near the gate to the house relates how the abbey was destroyed by 'the zeal or avarice of King Henry' at the time of the Dissolution of the Monasteries. A few fragments of the original building still remain in the grounds of the house.

Bridge on the Test.

WHERWELL –
PEACE AND AN ANCIENT PENANCE

The tranquillity of the village is inherent in its deep-browed thatch, in the silent, swift-flowing stream where busy ducks balance themselves in the water over the heads of plump, two-pound trout, and in the fragmentary remains of its 10th-century abbey. This, it is said, was founded by Queen Elfrida in penance for murdering her stepson, King Edward the Martyr, to ensure that her own son, Ethelred ('the Unready'), would become king in his stead. The present village church was built in the 19th century, but fantastic heads from the original building are incorporated in a churchyard mausoleum.

Medieval heads.

Deep thatch at Wherwell.

WHITCHURCH CANONICORUM
DORSET

4 miles north-east of Lyme Regis (page 421 Ba)

A range of steep hills screens the village from the English Channel, 2 miles away. Whitchurch Canonicorum lies in a valley and is reached by narrow, winding lanes plunging between hedgerows. The parish extends to the coast and contains about 50 farms, some of which date from the 17th century. In the centre of the village are a number of thatched houses and cottages, standing in well-kept gardens.

The parish church of St Wite is the jewel of the village. It was built in Norman times, and extended several times in the succeeding centuries. Its interior is something of a treasure-house. There are massive Norman pillars on the south arcade of the nave. In the north arcade, the capitals feature splendid Early English carvings of flowers and plants. The oaken pulpit is Jacobean, and the choir stalls are finely panelled.

It is the only parish church in Britain to have what are thought to be the relics of the saint to whom it is dedicated. The bones of a woman, who may have been St Wite, are in a sealed casket contained in a shrine built into the wall of the north transept. The casket was last opened in 1900 – and, centuries before that, medieval pilgrims used to thrust their crippled limbs into cavities in the tomb in the hope of being healed.

WICKHAMBREAUX
KENT

5 miles east of Canterbury (page 423 Fc)

A triangular tree-lined green forms the centre of Wickhambreaux, a small village on the banks of the Lesser Stour near Canterbury. The 15th-century Old Stone House is the oldest house in the village and was once its shop.

Other old buildings include a tall, weatherboarded mill, its wheel still in working order; Wickham House, which is believed to have been built in 1713; and Bell House, from where the curfew was rung in Tudor times.

An avenue of lime trees leads from the north-west corner of the green to the Church of St Andrew, which dates from the 14th century with restoration work done in Victorian times. The church has a large stained-glass east window that was designed by Arild Rosenkrantz, and is a major piece of Art Nouveau, as well as a rare example of American craftsmanship in an English church. The window was donated by Count James Gallantin of New York. In contrast is a small fragment of 13th-century stained glass depicting the beheading of St John the Baptist.

Red-brick cottages of the 18th and 19th centuries flank the winding Gutter Street which leads to the far end of the village. Halfway down the street is timbered Dyke House, its name a reminder of the low-lying landscape.

WIDECOMBE IN THE MOOR
DEVON

5 miles north-west of Ashburton (page 419 Db)

The village stands on a knoll above water-meadows in the valley of the East Webburn River, and for 500 years has been dominated by the 120 ft tower of St Pancras Church. In 1638 one of the tower's pinnacles was struck by a thunderbolt and crashed through the roof, killing four people and injuring many more. This gave rise to the legend that the accident was due to a visit by the Devil, who tethered his horse to the pinnacle while he went inside to claim the souls of four men who were playing cards in the church. Beyond the church is the green, once known as Butte Park, where men practised archery in the days of the longbow.

The churchyard wall forms one side of the village square, the 15th-century Church House occupies another. This building is now owned by the National Trust and is used as a village hall and information centre.

On the moors around Widecombe there are many hut circles and burial mounds of prehistoric times. From the early Middle Ages, moormen depended on tin-mining for their livelihood. So successful was this occupation that the miners contributed to the cost of Widecombe's church tower – a monument to their gratitude.

MANATON Three and a half miles to the northeast of Widecombe, the stone village of Manaton rises from the ground like the outcrops of granite which surround it on the moorland. Prehistoric hut circles are found among the tors, or rocky hills, close to the village, where thatched and whitewashed cottages cluster around a tree-lined green. A mile to the south stands Hound Tor, where the wind, gusting through its crags and crevices, sets up a weird howling like a pack of hounds baying, perhaps giving rise to its name. Some local people believe that the tor gave Sir Arthur Conan Doyle the idea for his chilling story *The Hound of the Baskervilles*.

The granite-built Church of St Winifrede, by the green, dates from the 15th century.

DARTMOOR'S BEST-KNOWN VILLAGE

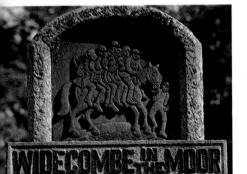

Widecombe in the Moor owes its fame to an annual fair that was established about 130 years ago – and the song which tells of the adventures of Tom Cobleigh, his friends, and the unfortunate grey mare who had to carry them on their celebrated journey (left). The words of Widecombe Fair *were written down and published by the vicar of another parish, who heard them sung by an old countryman. It was said that to be able to sing the chorus – wi' Bill Brewer, Jan Stewer, Peter Gurney, Peter Davey, Dan'l Whiddon, Harry Hawk, Old Uncle Tom Cobleigh and all, Old Uncle Tom Cobleigh and all – was proof of one's sobriety. If Tom Cobleigh and his friends existed, they probably came from Spreyton, 12 miles north of Widecombe. The parish church – the second largest in Devon and known as the 'cathedral of the moor' – has been at the heart of the community for more than 500 years. The west tower was partly paid for by local tin miners.*

Village sign.

'Cathedral of the moor'.

WILMINGTON
EAST SUSSEX

6 miles north-west of Eastbourne (page 423 Eb)

The village street is a long lane without pavements that runs from a large green by the main road, and climbs uphill towards a church and the substantial remains of a 13th-century priory. The cottages that line the street show flint and brickwork, and glimpses of thatch and medieval timbers. From the top of the hill, by the ancient church and priory, is an impressive view of the steep chalk escarpment in which is carved the mysterious figure known as the Long Man.

Wilmington is situated in farming country at the foot of the South Downs. The village school, store, stables, smithy, wheelwright's house, bakehouse and even some large flint barns have been converted into private houses. But the agricultural tradition is maintained by farm buildings which are still found among the dwellings. A few timbered cottages date from the 15th century. The small Chantry House, of flint and brick with a thatched roof, displays a grotesque face with bulging eyes on its outside wall.

An enormous yew tree, possibly as old as the church, stands in the churchyard; its trunk is 23

THE MYSTERY FIGURE ON THE HILLSIDE *Cut into the chalky soil of the Sussex Downs is the 226 ft high figure known as the Long Man of Wilmington. This featureless, enigmatic figure has intrigued generations of archaeologists, defying their attempts to unravel its secrets. When the figure was cut, why it was cut, and by whom – no one knows. Theories about its origins abound; some attribute it to the Romans; others claim it to represent a pagan god, or to be a Saxon cult figure. The mystery remains unsolved.*

◆

ft in girth and its heavy boughs are supported by poles. The church, part Norman and part Gothic, with wide stone ledges where the monks sat, was connected by a cloister to the Benedictine priory whose remains are close by. The surviving buildings of the priory, now owned by the Sussex Archaeological Trust, include a 13th-century hall, a gatehouse and an enclosed courtyard.

Wilmington's Long Man is carved into the slope of Windover Hill, overlooking the village. It is often in shadow. The simple outline of a human figure, 226 ft high, holds what appears to be a staff in each hand. The outline has been reinforced by concrete blocks in modern times, but its origin is a mystery. Some theories date it back to ancient times, pointing out that Roman coins found near by bear a figure with a similar stance. Others suggest that it may be of Saxon origin, or may even represent a medieval pilgrim.

WING
BUCKINGHAMSHIRE

3 miles south-west of Leighton Buzzard (page 426 Bb)

Tudor and Jacobean cottages, 16th-century alms-houses and modern buildings rub shoulders in this compact community. Standing slightly aloof from the village, on the brow of the hill over-looking the vale, is the Church of All Saints, one of the few Saxon churches in the country. It is believed to have been built by Aelfgifu, wife of the Saxon King Eadwig, in the 10th century. The apse, crypt and nave are original, and the Saxon chancel arch is one of the widest in England. The only additions to the building are the 14th-century south aisle and the 15th-century tower.

About half a mile to the east of Wing is Ascott House, a timber-framed building dating from 1606 but much enlarged in the same style in the 19th century. Its main attractions are the 30 acre gardens, laid out in both formal and natural styles, and the collection of works of art. The paintings include Italian and Dutch masters, and English artists are represented by Gainsborough, Reynolds, Turner, Romney and Stubbs. The collection of Oriental pottery is world famous.

WING, Leicestershire (page 431 Cc)
(see Edith Weston)

WINGHAM
KENT

6 miles east of Canterbury (page 423 Fc)

Approached from Canterbury, the green spire of St Mary's Church is the first indication of Wingham. Medieval houses and a grand 18th-century brick mansion are grouped around the church. The road then turns a sharp corner and opens northwards into a broad High Street, lined with Tudor and Georgian dwellings standing back behind trees and grass verges.

Near the church and the mansion, Delbridge House, is a row of timber-framed medieval build-ings, the Old Canonry, the Dog Inn and the Red Lion, two of them displaying the date 1286. This was when St Mary's became a college church, and six canons of Wingham College were housed in these buildings. Next to the Old Canonry is an 18th-century house which was once the site of a manor house for the Archbishop of Canterbury. Because of its position between the city and the medieval port of Sandwich, the manor house was often used as a stopping place for the highest in the land, including King John, Edward I, Edward III and the Black Prince.

When Elizabeth I stayed in Wingham on her royal progress through Kent in 1573, she com-mented on the poor state of the church. It is believed that some rebuilding work was already in hand by then, because in 1555 a Canterbury brewer embezzled the money raised for stone pillars. Wooden pillars were used in the nave instead, to no apparent disadvantage since they are still there more than 400 years later.

WINKBURN
NOTTINGHAMSHIRE

6 miles north-west of Newark-on-Trent (page 430 Cd)

A tiny stream, the Wink, flows through the village which lies in open countryside. Red-brick and pantiled cottages and farmhouses make up the tightly grouped settlement. The village and its church belonged to the Knights Hospitallers of the Order of St John of Jerusalem in the 12th century. The church is one of the few temple churches in Britain. It lies back from the road and consists simply of a nave, chancel and Norman tower. Inside are box pews, monuments to the Burnell family and a three-tiered Jacobean pulpit with a canopy.

The Burnell family were lords of the manor after the Dissolution of the Monasteries in 1536. Their home, Winkburn Hall, near the church, was built early in the 18th century.

WINSFORD
SOMERSET

8 miles south-west of Minehead (page 420 Ab)

All roads leading into Winsford are well worth travelling. None is more so than the lane that runs in from the south, from the Minehead to Tiverton road, through a wooded valley where massed rhododendrons bloom in June.

A CORNER OF EXMOOR *The River Winn joins the Exe at Winsford, a village of packhorse bridges – there are eight – set in a wooded valley on the eastern edge of the moor.*

A handsome thatched inn, the Royal Oak, stands opposite a cobblestoned packhorse bridge over the River Winn, and there are seven more bridges and a ford in the village. The road from the ford leads up to an impressive church with a 90 ft tower.

The Church of St Mary Magdalene is of Norman origin, but now has architectural features and memorials of every century from the 12th to the 20th. The big west tower is 15th century, and at some point around that time the church roof seems to have been in danger of collapsing – the pillars in the south arcade of the nave slope outwards to support it. The massive door has timbers that are later than its heavy 13th-century ironwork, which is the product of a master blacksmith – probably a monk from Barlynch Priory, the scant remains of which lie to the south, near Dulverton.

Opposite Winsford's Wesleyan chapel, a plaque on a house records that this was the birthplace in 1881 of Ernest Bevin, the trade-union leader and socialist MP who became Foreign Secretary in 1945. Bevin died in 1951, and his ashes are buried in Westminster Abbey.

Just off the road leading south-west from the village is the Caractacus Stone, believed to have been raised in memory of a descendant of the famous British chieftain Caractacus who unsuccessfully fought against the Roman invasion. The stone has a battered inscription – *Cargaci Nepus*, meaning 'descendant of Caractacus' – and has been dated from between the 5th and 7th centuries.

WISTOW
LEICESTERSHIRE
6 miles south-east of Leicester (page 430 Cb)

Two old villages, Wistow and Newton Harcourt, have been combined into a single parish as Wistow-cum-Newton Harcourt. They are linked by a short road, winding its way among spinneys, holly trees and streams.

Newton Harcourt has a tiny 13th-century church, dedicated to St Luke, and a 17th-century manor house with a handsome gate leading to its forecourt. Wistow's church is dedicated to St Wistan, and stands in a beautiful park. It is believed to occupy the very spot where Wistan, the Christian prince of the Saxon kingdom of Mercia, was murdered by his cousin in 849. The church has no electricity, and is open for services during the summer months only. Across the narrow, gated road running through the park towards Market Harborough stands Wistow Hall.

During the Civil War, Wistow Hall was the home of the staunch Royalist Sir Richard Halford, who was host to Charles I ten days before the Battle of Naseby in 1645. In the early 19th century it passed into the hands of Dr Henry Vaughan, head of the Royal College of Surgeons, who had changed his name to Sir Henry Halford. George III, the Duke of Wellington and William Pitt were among his distinguished patients. He also treated George IV, William IV and Queen Victoria.

WITHAM ON THE HILL
LINCOLNSHIRE
6 miles north of Stamford (page 432 Bd)

Approached from the east a steep incline leads to Witham's large village green, where the stocks survive as a relic of the village's ancient past. A tiled canopy protects the stocks, suggesting that in Witham justice was tempered with mercy. The Bywells Spring, which gushes out near the stocks, had never been known to stop flowing until the drought of 1976.

The parish is mentioned in the Domesday Book, the great land survey ordered by William the Conqueror in 1086; and Charles Kingsley in his book *Hereward the Wake* says that Hereward owned the estate. The spacious Church of St Andrew, largely 15th century, has several examples of Norman architecture – including the south aisle and the arch and doorway of the south porch. The church tower and spire were rebuilt in 1738 after the earlier ones had collapsed. Distinctive ornamental urns decorate the base of the spire.

On the opposite side of the green stands Witham Hall, an impressive mansion with bays dating from 1752. It is now a preparatory school for boys.

One of the wonders of Lincolnshire stands on farmland about 1 mile from the village but within the ecclesiastical parish. The Bowthorpe Oak, with a trunk about 40 ft in circumference, is thought to be at least 500 years old. The trunk had already been hollowed out in the 17th century, creating a room in which 39 people have stood together. On one occasion, it is said, 16 people sat down to afternoon tea inside the oak.

WITTON-LE-WEAR
DURHAM
3 miles south-west of Crook (page 438 Bb)

Tiers of stone houses give a fine elevation to Witton-le-Wear. The hillside village, which is noted for its fresh, invigorating air, has open views of moors and commons to the west. High above the village green – on the topmost tier – is a row of homes of different designs and periods with high-walled, tree-lined gardens. The buff-coloured Church of St Philip and St James – dating from Norman times and rebuilt in 1902 – stands among these houses. In the churchyard is the shaft of an ancient cross, upon which rests a sun-dial. The rest of the village slopes steeply south towards the River Wear and the grey battlements of Witton Castle, built in the 15th century but largely rebuilt 400 years later. Flanking the village green are several notable buildings, including the austere Methodist church; the picturesque Dun Cow Inn, with the date 1799 prominently displayed above the main door; and the remains of a medieval house, Witton Tower. The house is now privately owned, and contains a tall tower with perpendicular windows and a chapel with a Norman window.

The village
THEN AND NOW

For most of us, villages represent a way of life that conjures images of plodding ploughmen, winsome milkmaids and brawny blacksmiths. But mechanisation of work on the land and the attraction of town life destroyed those images, and most villages have had to adapt to new ways in order to survive.

From the car window most British villages look much as they always did. The old houses are still there – golden stone in the Cotswolds, grey stone in Yorkshire, cob and thatch in Devon, flint and brick in the Chilterns, brave white-wash in Cornwall and the Scottish Highlands, grey stone and slate in Wales.

But under the thatch and behind the rose-crowned doors the lives of the inhabitants have changed almost beyond recognition.

For the most part, villages grew up as centres for the time-less occupations of the country-side. They housed farm-workers, some of the outdoor servants of the big house, the vicar, the shopkeeper and agricultural craftsmen. Others were close-knit communities of coal-miners, fishermen, quarry-men or mill-workers.

Many of the old rural trades and industries have nearly vanished. Now fewer than three workers in 100 get their living from agriculture. In the quarter-century after the Second World War, farming lost half its work-force, the latest chapter in the long story of the drift from the land that began with the Industrial Revolution of the 18th century. Then, even the horrific

conditions of factory towns could offer many country people a better standard of living than was obtainable in their villages.

Late Victorian agricultural depression and the growth of mechanisation spurred the trend, while in this century, British farming has become the most highly mechanised in the world, resulting in the amalgamation of farms and an ever-steepening drop in the number of jobs available.

Similar factors have hit the other kinds of village. Coal-mining needs fewer men and the fishing ports once strung around the coast have dwindled to a mere handful.

But the village story is not entirely one of decay. Take the case of Ringmer, near Lewes in Sussex, for example.

Marriage patterns

Between 1857 and 1866, 75 marriages were celebrated in Ringmer's ancient parish church. In more than half these marriages, bride and groom both came from within the parish, and of the remainder, almost all were born within a radius of 20 miles. A century later – between 1961 and 1971 – there were 138 marriages in the same church. In only a

quarter of them were both partners from Ringmer. Then, too, in 1871, 53 per cent of the population was born in the parish and only 4 per cent came from outside Sussex. By contrast, in 1971, only 9 per cent were native to the village, though its population had more than trebled from 1,400 to 3,500. Most of that increase – a massive one in relation to Ringmer's original size – has taken place since 1945.

Slow pace of life

What happened to Ringmer was the direct result of a more mobile way of British life. In 1911, if the people of the Oxfordshire village of Berrick Salome wanted to go to Oxford, the only means of doing so was by a horse-drawn carrier's cart which made the journey each Wednesday and Saturday with eight or nine passengers. The 15 mile journey took three hours and the fare was two shillings return – about one-sixth of a farm labourer's weekly wages at that period.

Even as late as this, few villagers could afford a bicycle. But by the 1920s and 1930s bicycles were everywhere, and the better-off lads of the village even had motor-bikes. Bus companies, too, had extended a spider's web of routes even into the deepest countryside.

New freedom

This gave the villagers a new freedom, but when car owner-ship became commonplace in the 1950s and 1960s, many other people gained a new freedom too. For the city-dweller, the tie between home and workplace was finally broken. Increasingly, villages became suburbs in the fields, often giving rise to sad new divisions between 'them and us', the newcomers and the natives.

'Just lately,' said a villager from Walkington in Humberside, 'I have had a horrible feeling, which as a child I never thought could happen. I feel as though I am becoming a stranger in my own village . . .'

Walkington is one of the villages which the planning authorities have selected for expansion – one of the so-called

⇢ LOOKING BACK AT ASHWELL ⇠

THE VILLAGE FROM THE CHURCH TOWER *Something like 80 years separates these two pictures, which show how little the centre of Ashwell has changed over the years. The passage of time can be measured by the growth of trees, but there are more subtle differences which show how Ashwell has come to terms with the second half of the 20th century, such as the garages which have replaced outhouses and the new houses where thatched barns once stood.*

FACE-LIFT *At the turn of the century these old houses were already showing signs of decay, but extensive restoration has since given them a new lease of life. The pargeting on the centre house – a feature more often found in East Anglia – has been painstakingly restored, and the plaster fronts of the houses on either side have been removed to reveal the original timber framing in the upper storeys.*

TIMELESS HIGH STREET *Almost nothing has changed in the appearance of Ashwell's main street, though sadly two thatched cottages have gone. What changes there are show the trends in the modern way of life which have found their way into many villages. The village shop and post office is now a self-service store, and apparently no longer sells 'Thomson's Dye', while the house next door has been converted into an antiques shop.*

NATURE'S HAND *Cricket is still played on Ashwell's recreation ground, but the beautiful trees that must have cut short many a six-hit have gone, struck down by Dutch elm disease, and only their stumps remain beside the road. The Cricketer's Inn is now a private house; geranium-hung and minus its sign, but still clearly recognisable by its two chimneystacks and weather-boarded gable.*

'key villages'. In these, the idea is to bring in sufficient people to justify a concentration of such services as shops, buses and a primary school. Also, it is considerably cheaper to install power and mains drainage in an estate of, say, 40 houses than in one of half-a-dozen.

But village expansion has often been at the expense of the village community. Each new estate forms a separate community from the original village if, indeed, it forms a community at all. The newcomers commute to nearby towns where they work in jobs that have nothing to do with the traditional village pursuits. Generally, their incomes are considerably higher than those of the old village families.

This is particularly true in the village of Ashwell, Hertfordshire, but although the influx of outsiders may have disrupted community life, at least it has brought new prosperity to the village. Ashwell is one of the most attractive villages in Hertfordshire, but it is only in recent years that many of its old buildings have been restored and modernised.

The fight for schools

With some villages, the problem is precisely the opposite one. For them the refusal of planning permission to build new homes leads to stagnation. Young people cannot find homes in their own villages and are compelled to live elsewhere. Those who do stay find life difficult because there are not enough of them to sustain the bus service, the shop and the post office. Eventually, there are insufficient children to keep the school open – still another factor that drives young people out.

A Women's Institute member in Coldharbour, Surrey, gave a staccato summary of her village's experience in reply to a recent questionnaire by the Council for the Protection of Rural England: 'Static. No building permitted because in an area of outstanding natural beauty. No work in village. Young people move away when married because no houses they can afford. When houses become vacant, bought by middle-aged couples or weekenders.'

Some 800 village primary schools have been closed in England and Wales since the mid-1960s. Partly, this has been a matter of economy, since a larger number of pupils can be taught by fewer teachers if both are concentrated in a single school. But it has also been a matter of educational fashion. Small schools are thought to deprive children of the stimulus of their fellows, despite the fact that village schoolchildren do as well academically as others. Persuaded by this, local groups are now banding together in a national association to fight for small schools.

Turning tide

The case for the village school rests mainly on its value as a focal point for the community. Defending their school to the Education Authority, villagers at Purton Stoke, Wiltshire, claimed: 'Closure of the village school brings with it an attitude of mind that the village is dying. We submit that we are a small but independent and vigorous community with a strong local feeling, and we should be allowed to flourish.'

It seems that every possible pressure is against the village. If it is not being suffocated by new estates on a scale bigger than it can handle, it is being preserved instead in an aspic of picture-postcard prettiness. Its work base has been removed, its trains are long-vanished and the bus services are rapidly disappearing too. The shops have too often been beaten by the supermarkets of the nearby towns or by the complications of VAT.

But the tide is turning. In the mid-1970s the Development Commission – established originally by Lloyd George to fight rural decay – was given a new lease of life and money to spend. It built advance factories to attract new jobs to areas of rural depopulation, such as Northumberland and Lincolnshire. Similar agencies operated in Scotland and Wales.

The Council for Small Industries in Rural Areas, which is funded by the Development Commission, gave aid to small businessmen in village 'pockets of need', and district planners modified the rigidities of key village policies. Faced with the results of such policies, more counties now allow plans for small numbers of new homes, even in those villages where no long-term expansion is planned.

The National Trust, too, has come to the rescue and now owns more than 20 villages and hamlets. The Trust sets out to conserve the villages by banning all unsightly television aerials, overhead power lines and brash street lighting. Wherever possible it uses original materials in the repair of buildings. In letting cottages, priority is given to local people.

Self-sufficiency schemes

Most importantly, some villages are reverting to their oldest tradition – that of self-sufficiency. In Madingley, Cambridgeshire, for example, rather than see their school close, the villagers have bought it and staffed it themselves. In several schemes around the country, groups of villages are now running their own bus services. The pioneers in this venture were half-a-dozen villages near Holt, in Norfolk. There, the local bus company supplied a vehicle and enabled village volunteers to take Public Service Vehicle licences. The County Council guaranteed the scheme financially, and village committees worked out a timetable that suited everyone's needs – in contrast to many more conventional rural bus schedules.

Scores of villages, guided by a new breed of countryside officers in the county community councils, are making 'village appraisals' of their own needs and problems and presenting them forcibly to the planners.

British villages have undergone a revolution from which some will never recover. But the village is one of our oldest social institutions and it is hard to kill.

WOODGREEN
HAMPSHIRE

8 miles south of Salisbury (page 422 Bb)

In the early 1930s two young artists, R. W. Baker and E. R. Payne, came to Woodgreen to decorate the inside of the village hall with murals. They took as their theme the everyday activities of the village, and today their work is a valuable record of a now-vanished way of life. Many of the older villagers nostalgically identify themselves as children picking apples, helping with the harvest, carrying milk buckets, or singing at a Sunday School anniversary at the little chapel near by. Although the hall is usually locked, the key can be obtained from one of the cottages opposite.

Woodgreen lies between the River Avon and a hill on the edge of the central plateau of the New Forest. It is a typical Forest village, with brick and thatch cottages surrounded by thick hedges to keep out the cattle and Forest ponies which graze on the surrounding unfenced greens. Footpaths which were once cattle-tracks lead to the Forest table-land and to Woodgreen Common. Footpaths from the common lead down through the woods to the Drove, a broad, three-quarters-of-a-mile-long avenue of magnificent oaks. They are called the Napoleonic Oaks, and were planted nearly 200 years ago to provide the Royal Navy with timber for its men-of-war.

A few decades ago, the village was famed for its 'Merries' – sweet black cherries which have now all but gone. People from all over Britain came to eat the fruit and to enjoy themselves on Merry Sundays and in the Merry Garden.

WOODHOUSE EAVES
LEICESTERSHIRE

3 miles south of Loughborough (page 430 Cc)

The craggy Beacon Hill rises to 818 ft above sea-level behind Woodhouse Eaves, commanding fine views of Charnwood Forest. A small concrete obelisk marks the spot where beacons were lit during the reign of Elizabeth I to warn the country of the approach of the Spanish Armada. The hill, and the bluebell woods below, are a public open space.

Although much built up, the village has retained its charm with old cottages and almshouses of many-tinted Forest stone and topped with thatch or local Swithland slate.

Bronze Age tools found on Beacon Hill date from 800 BC, and a flat bronze axe from 2000 BC. For many generations part of the hill belonged to the Herrick family, one of whom was the 17th-century poet Robert Herrick. Beaumanor Hall, built by the Herricks in 1847, is now owned by the County Council.

NEWTOWN LINFORD Several old timber-framed houses with tall, curved beams stand in Newtown Linford's main street. The village is 3 miles south of Woodhouse Eaves, at the gateway to Bradgate

Park, 850 acres of natural splendour in the heart of Charnwood Forest. A spectacular ruin is all that remains of the 15th and 16th-century Bradgate House. Lady Jane Grey, the nine-day queen, was born there in 1537.

WOOLPIT
SUFFOLK

5 miles north-west of Stowmarket (page 432 Cc)

A village green, complete with a roofed-over village pump, lies near the centre of Woolpit, recorded in the Domesday Book as Wolfpeta – a pit in which wolves were trapped. The wolves have gone, but the centuries-old atmosphere lingers on amid the ancient dwellings, many of late medieval and Tudor design. The 400-year-old Swan Inn is still there, although its archway and yard no longer cater to the coaches that once used it as a staging post on the way to Bury St Edmunds. Modern traffic ignores the community since a by-pass was built, and leaves the village to go quietly about its business.

Tudor chimneys.

Guarding the pump.   Pump on the green.

Many of the village houses are built of white bricks, for which the local brickyard, now closed, was famous from the 17th century. Green is another colour that figures in local history, but for a different reason. There is a legend that in the 12th century, reapers saw two children climbing out of a pit. Their bodies were green, and after learning English they spoke of coming from a mysterious land called St Martin. The boy died young, but the girl grew up to marry. The story is said to have been the basis for Herbert Read's novel *The Green Child*, written in 1935.

St Mary's Church stands on the north side of the village, a building of flint and stone with a 140 ft high steeple that landmarks one of the most beautiful churches in Suffolk. It dates from the 11th century, but its later additions include a fine 15th-century porch and the tower and spire which were rebuilt in 1853. The nave is 14th century, and is crowned by a magnificent hammer-beam roof with spread-winged angels decorating the beam ends. Within the nave are carved pews, a lectern said to have been given by Elizabeth I, and a pulpit designed in 1883 by George Gilbert Scott junior, son of the Victorian church architect. The 15th-century screen still has traces of medieval decorations. But many of the church's contents were destroyed in the turbulent 1640s when a puritanical Parliament ordered the general demolition or removal of altars, pictures and candlesticks. St Mary's suffered at the hands of William Dowsing, a religious fanatic selected to carry out the destruction.

STATUES AND SUNFLOWERS IN A VILLAGE WHERE WOLVES ONCE ROAMED

It is said that the last wolf in Suffolk was killed at Woolpit, where only the occasional cat or dog now prowls the quiet lanes. The style of the village is mostly Tudor, from ornate chimneystacks down to the stuccoed windows of Tudor Rose cottage near the church. The present sunflower design is a replica of the original. Not replaced, however, are the statues from the niches in St Mary's south porch; they were probably smashed when the notorious William Dowsing, Suffolk's Parliamentary Church Visitor, had 80 of the church's pictures and statues destroyed in the 1640s. Statues also adorn the shelter over the village pump. The shelter was built in 1897 to commemorate Queen Victoria's Diamond Jubilee, and makes a charming focal point for this ancient village.

St Mary's Church.

Stuccoed windows.

WORSTEAD

NORFOLK

3 miles south-east of North Walsham (page 433 Dd)

When Flemish weavers settled in East Anglia during the Middle Ages they introduced a technique to the wool trade which produced a cloth of fine fibres and closely twisted yarn. Worstead became the centre for the manufacture of this new material, which came to be known as worsted – after the village.

The worsted industry thrived as a cottage craft until the 19th century, when production moved to the mills that came with the Industrial Revolution. Some brick-built weavers' houses – in which 12 ft high looms were used – remain in and around the village. The last hand-loom weaver, John Cubitt, died in 1882 aged 91. The old market place is now called Church Plain – 'plain' is the Norfolk word for 'square' – and it has several large 17th-century houses.

Worstead's church, St Mary's, is a splendid memorial to the prosperous weaving days. It was built from the wealth of the 14th-century clothmakers and has a 109 ft high tower. Inside there are copies of the designs made by Sir Joshua Reynolds for some of the windows of New College Chapel, Oxford, painted on panels in 1831.

WORTH MATRAVERS

DORSET

4 miles west of Swanage (page 421 Ca)

For centuries Worth Matravers was one of the main centres for the quarrying of Purbeck marble, and surface workings of the old quarries can be seen in the hills around the village. The dark grey marble supports the tower and spire of Salisbury Cathedral.

The Church of St Nicholas, which stands close to the centre of the stone-built village, is memorable for its Norman nave, chancel and windows. It was extensively restored in 1869 after it had become so dilapidated that services had to be held in the village school. In the churchyard is the grave of Benjamin Jesty, a Dorset yeoman reputed to be the first person to inoculate anyone with cowpox to ward off smallpox. Jesty is recorded as having carried out the experiments on his wife and two sons in 1774. It was not until 1798 that Dr Edward Jenner published his historic report concluding that cowpox inoculations serve as a protection against the fatal disease. The success of Jesty's experiment seems confirmed by the inscription on his wife's tombstone, which records that she died in 1824, aged 84.

The nearby seaside resort of Swanage was once merely a hamlet in the parish of Worth. A footpath over the downs, called the Priest's Way, links the two places. It was so called because it was the route used by the priest when he went to Swanage to hold services in the chapel there. To the south, another downland walk leads about 2 miles to a cave-riddled cape, known as St Alban's or St Aldhelm's Head, rising abruptly from the sea to a height of 354 ft.

Guillemots, razorbills and other seabirds make their nests on the precipices of the cape and carry on ceaseless traffic over the sea. On top of the headland is St Aldhelm's Chapel, a solid and perfectly square building erected around a central column supporting four Norman arches. The chapel was built in the latter part of the 12th century, possibly as a marker for vessels sailing along the channel coast.

WROXTON

OXFORDSHIRE

3 miles west of Banbury (page 426 Ab)

Most of the houses in Wroxton were built after a disastrous fire in 1666, giving the village an air of uniformity and dignity. The sloping Main Street is lined with grassy banks fronting thatched cottages built of red-brown ironstone. At the foot of the street is a large duck pond, and opposite are the gates of Wroxton Abbey.

Little remains of the 13th-century abbey, built as an Augustinian priory, and most of the house on the site dates from the 17th century. In the 18th century it was the home of Lord North, who was Prime Minister at the time of the American War of Independence. The house is now an American college.

The park has wide lawns sloping down to a lake and the remains of a cascade, and standing above the park is the early-14th-century Church of All Saints. The church contains an impressive monument to Sir William Pope and his wife; their marble effigies lie under an arched canopy supported by six black-marble columns. Near by is a simple stone in memory of Thomas Coutts, the 18th-century banker who died at Wroxton in 1822 worth nearly £1 million.

WYTHAM

OXFORDSHIRE

3 miles north-west of Oxford (page 426 Ab)

Wytham Great Wood almost engulfs this tiny village, set into the side of a Thames-side hill. It is approached by a narrow lane which follows the course of the willow-lined Seacourt Stream and emerges among greystone houses with thatched roofs, a church and the turreted Wytham Abbey.

The Earl of Abingdon rebuilt All Saints' Church in 1811, using material from Cumnor Place, his Berkshire house. Wytham Abbey, Lord Abingdon's home, was built in the 15th century, but had additions and improvements made over the succeeding centuries before being extensively remodelled in 1809–10.

To the north of Wytham is Godstow Nunnery, built in 1138 and destroyed by Cromwell in 1646. Across the river, the Trout Inn was built in 1138 as a hospice for the nunnery. It has riverside terraces patrolled by peacocks.

YATTENDON
BERKSHIRE

5 miles west of Pangbourne (page 426 Ba)

Royal jubilees are commemorated by trees of varying thickness in this proud, attractive village which was the home of Robert Bridges, the Poet Laureate, for 22 years. He was buried in the churchyard there in 1930. Houses patterned with black timbers set against white paintwork, and an elegant bow-fronted shop dominate one side of The Square. The opposite side, which includes the Royal Oak public house, is rose-red brick. Plaques at the village hall and on the Well House record the occasions that Yattendon has won Berkshire's Best-Kept-Village competition.

The Church of St Peter and St Paul is Victorian, apart from a few fragments and some monuments – including one to the 16th-century soldier Sir John Norris.

In centuries past, The Square resounded to the boisterous two-day activities known as the Yattendon 'Revels' when – in the 18th century – prizes were given to each man who broke a head with a cudgel.

OLD SOLDIER'S HOME *The sunlit Manor House at Yattendon was the last home of the Norris family, whose ties with the village go back to the Middle Ages. Among its most celebrated occupants was the great Elizabethan soldier, Sir John Norris, who sailed with Drake and died in Ireland in 1597. Due to his military travels, he spent little time at the house, which today is the home of Lord Iliffe.*

YETHOLM
BORDERS

7 miles south-east of Kelso (page 441 Gc)

The twin villages of Town Yetholm and Kirk Yetholm – pronounced 'Yettom' – lie in the foothills of the Cheviots close to the border between Scotland and England. Kirk Yetholm is the northern end of the Pennine Way, the 250 mile walking route from Edale in Derbyshire's Peak District.

Town Yetholm, the larger of the two, has solid stone houses overlooking a banked village green. But Kirk Yetholm across the valley of the Bowmont Water is by far the older place. The present kirk was built in 1836, on a site occupied by churches for many centuries. Scottish noblemen killed at the Battle of Flodden in 1513 are said to have been buried there.

For many years the villagers of Yetholm took advantage of the remote Cheviot valleys, where they could elude the revenue men in smuggling whisky across to England. The trade was stamped out in the 1830s, but in the best years the Yetholm men were said to have earned up to £20,000 from their illicit merchandise.

Kirk Yetholm was also known as Scotland's gipsy capital. Romanies are said to have come to Kirk Yetholm at the end of the 17th century. Will Faa, a self-styled 'King of the Gipsies', was buried at Kirk Yetholm in the 1780s. The small cottage which was his 'palace' is on the hill road to the south-east.

ZENNOR
CORNWALL

4 miles west of St Ives (page 418 Aa)

The road from St Ives winds and switchbacks across bleak moorland strewn with boulders, said to have been hurled by giants playing bowls. Then it dips into a hollow among granite cottages where the village shelters behind the bluff Zennor Head.

Zennor is a windswept place, surrounded by squat farm buildings of weathered granite looking like part of the natural landscape. It has one inn, the Tinners' Arms, and a cluster of grey-stone houses grouped around the sturdy Church of St Senara, from which the village takes its name.

The church dates from the 12th century, but has additions from every century until the 19th, when it was heavily restored. A 15th-century bench-end is carved with the figure of a mermaid who, according to legend, entered the church one day and lured the squire's son into following her back to the sea. He was never seen again.

By the side of a rushing stream is the Wayside Museum, housed in a disused mill. It displays domestic, agricultural and tin-mining exhibits.

Zennor Head is a granite cliff rising 200 ft above the sea. It can be reached by footpaths from the village, and more footpaths lead down to sandy coves. The view from Zennor Head is magnificent. To the north-east and south-west there are rugged headlands, where the Atlantic rollers burst over the jagged rocks. Facing inland, the view is across granite tors and heather-carpeted moorland climbing to more than 750 ft above sea-level.

On one of these tors, 1 mile east of the village, stands Zennor Quoit, a megalithic burial chamber. Five stones support the roof, a massive slab which has slipped from its original position and now has one end resting on the ground. Behind the chamber is the site where the Cornish Society meets each year on midsummer's eve and lights a ritual bonfire.

CORNISH KITCHEN *A huge fireplace dominates the kitchen of the old mill at Zennor, now the Wayside Museum. The simplicity of the countryman's life style in the 18th and 19th centuries is amply displayed, from the wooden settle with its patchwork seat to the flat-iron on the mantelpiece. A billhook by the fireplace, fishing floats hanging from the ceiling and a mining poster on the door are symbols of Cornwall's ancient industries – farming, fishing and tin-mining.*

LOCATING THE VILLAGES

How to use the maps

All the villages described in the book
are shown region by region on the maps on
the following pages. Each region's villages
are listed by counties alongside the map and have
grid references for speedy location.

WESTERN
ISLES

HIGHLAND | GRAMPIAN
13
TAYSIDE

FIFE

CENTRAL

LOTHIAN

STRATH
CLYDE | BORDERS
12
DUMFRIES
& GALLOWAY

NORTHLD

11

DURHAM

CUMBRIA

ISLE
OF MAN

9

N
YORKSHIRE
10
W
YORKS | HUMBER
SIDE

LANCS

GTR
MAN

MERSEYSIDE

DERBYS

CLWYD | CHES

GWYNEDD | NOTTS | LINCS

6

STAFFS

POWYS | SALOP | **7** | LEICS

W MIDS | NORFOLK

WARKS | **8**

POWYS | HEREFS
& WORCS | N'HANTS | CAMBS | SUFFOLK

DYFED | **4** | BEDS | ESSEX

W
MID | GWENT | BUCKS

GLAMORGAN | S | GLOS | OXON | **5** | HERTS

AVON | BERKS | GTR
LOND

WILTS | SURREY | KENT

SOMERSET | **2** | HANTS | W | **3** | E

1 | DEVON | DORSET | SUSSEX

CORNWALL | ISLE OF
WIGHT

SYMBOLS USED ON THE MAPS

■ Village   ———— Minor road
● Small town   ———— Major road
● Large town   —○— Motorway
– – – County boundary   - - - - Car ferry route
–·–·– National boundary   ⌒ River

1 SOUTH-WEST ENGLAND	5 WESTERN HOME COUNTIES	10 YORKSHIRE & THE HUMBER
2 WESSEX	6 NORTH WALES & THE BORDERS	11 NORTHUMBRIA
3 SOUTH-EAST ENGLAND	7 THE MIDLANDS	12 SCOTTISH LOWLANDS
4 SOUTH WALES & THE BORDERS	8 EAST ANGLIA & LINCOLNSHIRE	13 SCOTTISH HIGHLANDS
	9 LANCASHIRE & THE LAKES	

SOUTH WEST ENGLAND

Britain's mildest climate, a rugged Atlantic coastline of rocky headlands and sandy coves; a sheltered Channel coast where sub-tropical plants grow lushly, and vast tracts of wild moorland – all have helped to mould the character of South West England and the people who live there. Along the Atlantic coast, fishing villages cling precariously to every cleft in the rocks that provides a natural harbour. Inland, sturdy granite-built cottages cluster together in the folds of the windswept moors, and amid Devon's rich, red soil are farming villages built of timber, brick or cob.

The South-West is steeped in the romance of the smugglers, wreckers and pirates whose colourful exploits inspired writers like Robert Louis Stevenson and Daphne du Maurier. It is the land that bred the great seafaring adventurers Drake, Hawkins and Raleigh, and the steam pioneers Trevithick and Newcomen. The engine-houses of Cornwall's derelict tin mines still dot the landscape, and in the south the gleaming white hills formed by the china-clay quarries – the 'Cornish Alps' – rise like mountains of the moon.

NORTH COAST

Westerly gales, which lash the rugged north coast of Cornwall and Devon, stunt every exposed tree.

STARGAZY PIE

Mousehole is the home of stargazy pie. It is made of whole pilchards with their heads poking out of the crust.

1

BRISTOL CHANNEL

NEWPORT

CARDIFF

WESTON-SUPER-MARE

MINEHEAD

Barnstaple or Bideford Bay

Ilfracombe
Combe Martin
Lynton
Parracombe

Exmoor

S O M E R S E T

TAUNTON

Clovelly

BARNSTAPLE

Bideford

Sheepwash

HOLSWORTHY

D   E   V   O   N

Cheriton Fitzpaine

Broadhembury

HONITON

Sampford Courtenay

CREDITON

OKEHAMPTON

Drewsteignton

EXETER

Salcombe Regis

Axmouth

SEATON

Branscombe

SIDMOUTH

Lyme Bay

LAUNCESTON

Lydford

MORETONHAMPSTEAD

Dartmoor

North Bovey
Lustleigh

Manaton

Widecombe in the Moor

Buckland in the Moor

NEWTON ABBOT

TAVISTOCK

ASHBURTON

Meavy

TORQUAY

Berry Pomeroy

TOTNES

PLYMOUTH

Prawle Point

C H A N N E L

DARTMOOR PONIES

Ponies still run wild on Dartmoor, as they have done for centuries. They are a distinct breed, usually grey-brown, and 12.2 hands high.

SOUTH COAST

Sub-tropical plants flourish along the sheltered south coast of Cornwall and Devon. Palms are common in many fine gardens.

COB AND THATCH

Cob, a mixture of unbaked clay and straw, is built up layer by layer. Cob cottages, roofed with thatch are typical of South Devon.

SUNKEN LANES

Deep-cut narrow lanes often run along ancient ditches, dug as estate boundaries in medieval Devon and Cornwall.

WESSEX

The face of Wessex presents an enticing diversity – from the rolling chalk downs of Wiltshire to the high moors and hidden valleys of Somerset's Doone country; from the lush dairylands of Gloucestershire and the age-old tranquillity of Cotswold villages to the rugged rural fastnesses of Hardy's Dorset. The limestone cliffs of Portland Bill and the pebbled sweep of Chesil Beach on the southern shore contrast with the wide golden sands of the Bristol Channel. Dorset has its blue vinny cheese and Somerset its cheddar; and potent Somerset cider is a happy alternative to the sparkling real ales of a dozen and more local brews in the five counties. Everywhere there is mystery and legend – mystery in the stone circles of Avebury and Stonehenge, burial mounds, intricate hill-forts and giant figures cut by prehistoric hands on turf-clad chalk hills; legend that is almost tangible in places like Glastonbury, a cradle of Christianity and the fabled Avalon of King Arthur, whose Camelot is believed to be Cadbury Castle, near Sutton Montis.

DORSET THATCH

Thatching in Dorset is done with specially selected wheat straw – Dorset Reed –which gives a smoother finish than ordinary straw thatch.

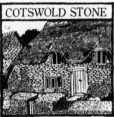

COTSWOLD STONE

Gloucestershire glows with the warm, honey-coloured stone quarried from the Cotswolds. It was used for churches and mansions – and humble village homes.

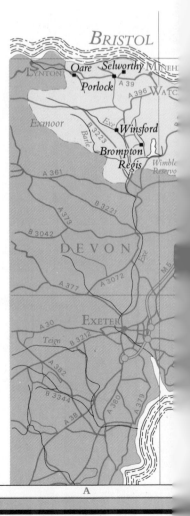

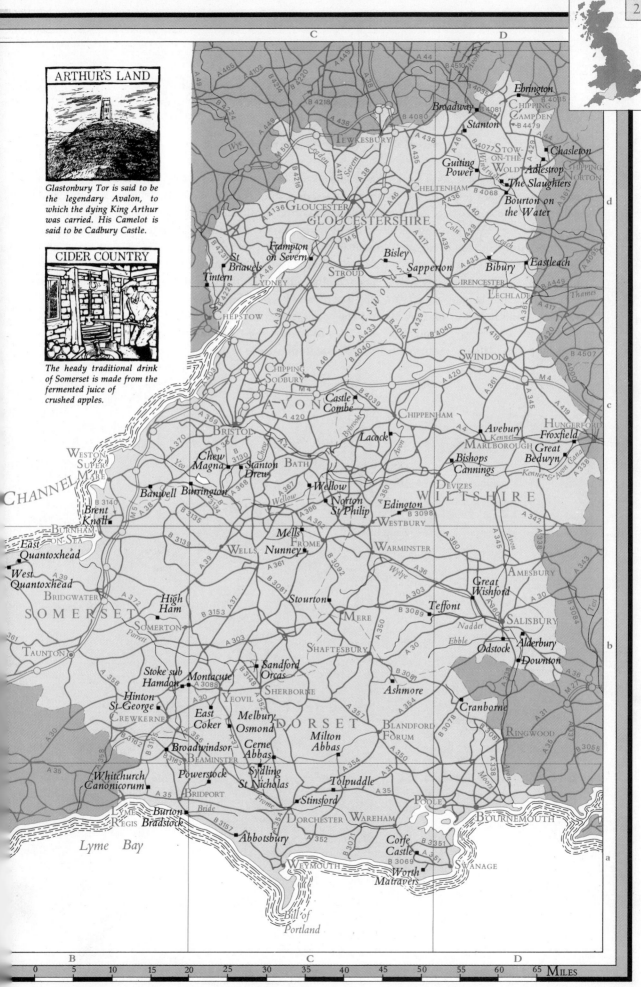

2

ARTHUR'S LAND

Glastonbury Tor is said to be the legendary Avalon, to which the dying King Arthur was carried. His Camelot is said to be Cadbury Castle.

CIDER COUNTRY

The heady traditional drink of Somerset is made from the fermented juice of crushed apples.

Ebrington
CHIPPING
CAMPDEN
Broadway
Stanton
Chasleton
STOW-ON-THE-
WOLD
Adlestrop
Guiting
Power
The Slaughters
CHELTENHAM
Bourton on
the Water
CHIPPING
NORTON
GLOUCESTER
GLOUCESTERSHIRE
Frampton
on Severn
Bisley
St
Briavels
Sapperton
Bibury
Eastleach
Tintern
STROUD
CIRENCESTER
LYDNEY
LECHLADE
Thames
CHEPSTOW
SWINDON
CHIPPING
SODBURY
Castle
Combe
Cotswolds
BRISTOL
CHIPPENHAM
Avebury
Froxfield
Hungerford
Lacock
MARLBOROUGH
Great
Bedwyn
Chew
Magna
Stanton
Drew
BATH
Bishops
Cannings
WESTON-
SUPER-
MARE
Wellow
DEVIZES
Banwell
Burrington
Norton
St Philip
WILTSHIRE
Edington
CHANNEL
Brent
Knoll
Mells
WESTBURY
BURNHAM-
ON-SEA
Nunney
FROME
WARMINSTER
East
Quantoxhead
WELLS
AMESBURY
West
Quantoxhead
Stourton
Great
Wishford
BRIDGWATER
High
Ham
Teffont
SALISBURY
SOMERSET
MERE
Odstock
Alderbury
SOMERTON
SHAFTESBURY
Downton
TAUNTON
Stoke sub
Hamdon
Montacute
Sandford
Orcas
Ashmore
Cranborne
Hinton
St George
YEOVIL
SHERBORNE
CREWKERNE
East
Coker
Melbury
Osmond
DORSET
BLANDFORD
FORUM
RINGWOOD
Broadwindsor
Cerne
Abbas
Milton
Abbas
Whitchurch
Canonicorum
Powerstock
BEAMINSTER
Sydling
St Nicholas
Tolpuddle
POOLE
BRIDPORT
Stinsford
BOURNEMOUTH
LYME
REGIS
Burton
Bradstock
DORCHESTER
WAREHAM
Abbotsbury
Corfe
Castle
SWANAGE
Lyme Bay
WEYMOUTH
Worth
Matravers
Bill of
Portland

0 5 10 15 20 25 30 35 40 45 50 55 60 65 **MILES**

SOUTH EAST ENGLAND

Time seems almost to stand still in the close-knit interlocking counties of the South-East, so powerful is the sense of affinity with the past that they induce. Even their most ancient and mysterious landscapes become somehow familiar and unintimidating – moulded, coaxed and nurtured though they were by a succession of invaders into a pattern unlike that found anywhere else in Britain. Kipling, living at Burwash in Sussex, captured the mood when he fused past and present in *Puck of Pook's Hill*. Romans, Saxons, Vikings and Normans landed all along the coast and on the banks of the Thames where it cuts deep inland. All left their marks on this land of marshes, wide beaches and high chalk cliffs which are backed by the fruit-laden Weald of Kent, the Surrey heathlands and high Sussex Downs, and the meadows and trout streams of Hampshire, with vast tracts of its New Forest looking almost as they did when the Conqueror hunted there. And across the Solent is the Isle of Wight, with little-frequented villages waiting to be discovered.

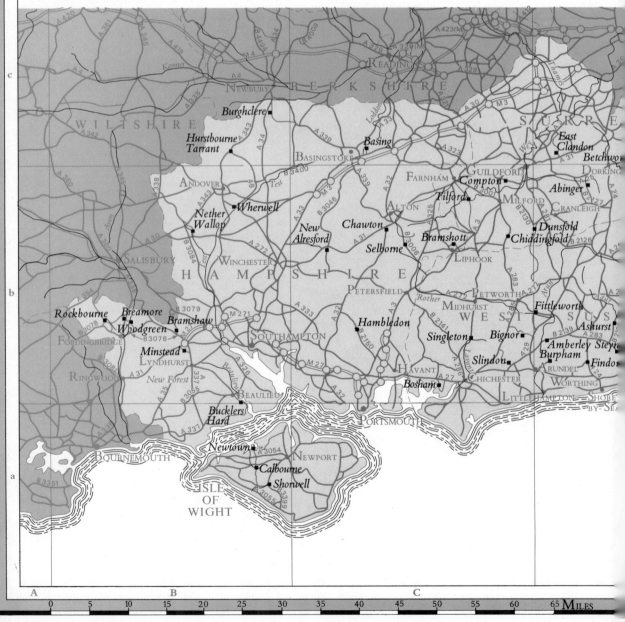

3

EAST SUSSEX

Alfriston 423 Eb
Brightling 423 Eb
Burwash 423 Eb
Mayfield 423 Eb
Northiam 423 Eb
Piddinghoe 423 Db
Sedlescombe 423 Eb
Telscombe 423 Db
Wadhurst 423 Eb
Westdean 423 Eb
Wilmington 423 Eb

HAMPSHIRE

Basing 422 Cc
Bramshaw 422 Bb
Bramshott 422 Cb
Breamore 422 Bb
Bucklers Hard 422 Bb
Burghclere 422 Bc
Chawton 422 Cb
Hambledon 422 Cb
Hurstbourne Tarrant
422 Bc
Minstead 422 Bb
Nether Wallop 422 Bb

New Alresford 422 Cb
Rockbourne 422 Bb
Selborne 422 Cb
Wherwell 422 Bb
Woodgreen 422 Bb

ISLE OF WIGHT

Calbourne 422 Ba
Newtown 422 Ba
Shorwell 422 Ba

KENT

Appledore 423 Eb
Biddenden 423 Eb
Brenchley 423 Eb
Brookland 423 Eb
Charing 423 Eb
Chiddingstone 423 Db
Chilham 423 Fc
Cobham 423 Ec
Elham 423 Fb
Eynsford 423 Ec
Fordwich 423 Fc
Goudhurst 423 Eb
Groombridge 423 Eb
Horsmonden 423 Eb
Ightham 423 Ec

Lenham 423 Ec
Offham 423 Ec
Patrixbourne 423 Fc
Penshurst 423 Eb
Pluckley 423 Eb
Smarden 423 Eb
Stone-in-Oxney 423 Eb
Wickhambreaux 423 Fc
Wingham 423 Fc

SURREY

Abinger 422 Db
Betchworth 422 Db
Bletchingley 423 Dc
Chiddingfold 422 Cb
Compton 422 Cb
Dunsfold 422 Db
East Clandon 422 Dc
Godstone 423 Dc
Limpsfield 423 Dc
Tilford 422 Cb

WEST SUSSEX

Amberley 422 Db
Ashurst 422 Db
Bignor 422 Cb
Bosham 422 Cb

Burpham 422 Db
Findon 422 Db
Fittleworth 422 Db
Horsted Keynes 423 Db
Lindfield 423 Db
Pyecombe 423 Db
Singleton 422 Cb
Slindon 422 Cb
Steyning 422 Db
West Hoathly 423 Db

TILE HANGING

Tiles hung on houses to protect them from the weather are typical of south-east England.

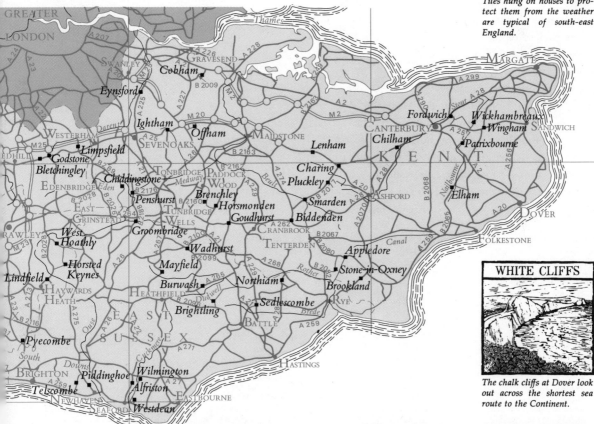

WHITE CLIFFS

The chalk cliffs at Dover look out across the shortest sea route to the Continent.

FIRST INNINGS

Modern cricket started at Hambledon in 1774 when the local team codified the rules.

SOUTH DOWNS

Chanctonbury Ring, a hilltop clump of beeches, commands views of Sussex.

HOP COUNTRY

Since the 16th century hops have flourished in the Kentish Weald.

SOUTH WALES & THE BORDERS

Echoes of stirring songs and the clangour of bygone battles haunt the mighty border castles and reverberate through the great, grey-green mountains of South Wales. Their very names sound an invitation to the time traveller ... Brecon Beacons, Black Mountains and Mynydd Prescelly, where the megaliths of Stonehenge were quarried. Even the new counties have old names: Carmarthen and Pembroke have gone back to being Dyfed, as they were in pre-Saxon times, Monmouthshire is Gwent again; Montgomery, Radnor and Brecon are Powys. Along the border the Welsh fought the Saxons, and the Normans fought both. But the battles are over – except perhaps on the rugby ground. The border strongholds now stand sentinel over languorous Hereford cattle in river-ribboned meadows, blossom-clouded Worcestershire orchards and sleepy hamlets.

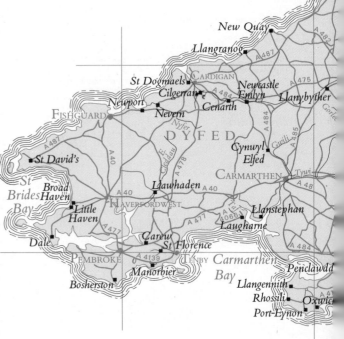

Cardigan Bay

New Quay
Llangranog
St Dogmaels
CARDIGAN
Cilgerran
Newport
Newcastle Emlyn
Nevern
Cenarth
Llanybyther
FISHGUARD
DYFED
St David's
Cynwyl Elfed
CARMARTHEN
Llawhaden
St Brides Bay
Broad Haven
HAVERFORDWEST
Llanstephan
Little Haven
Laugharne
Dale
Carew
St Florence
PEMBROKE
TENBY
Carmarthen Bay
Penclawdd
Manorbier
Llangennith
Bosherston
Rhossili
Oxwich
Port-Eynon

PEMBROKE COAST

Dramatic capes and headlands mark the rugged coast of Dyfed, which provides a safe haven for seabirds and a breeding ground for seals.

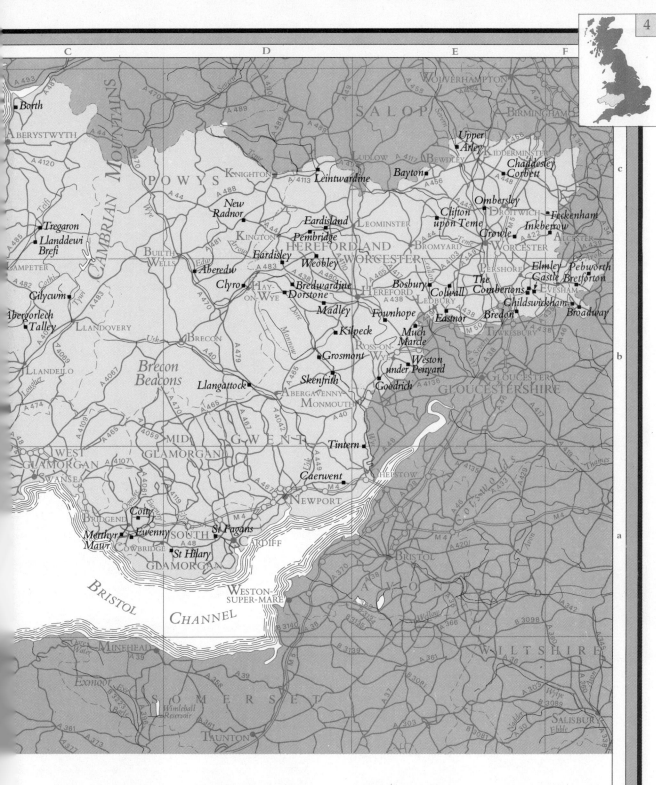

4

C   D   E   F

Map labels:

Borth, ABERYSTWYTH, CAMBRIAN MOUNTAINS, POWYS, Tregaron, Llanddewi Brefi, LAMPETER, Cilycwm, Abergorlech, Talley, LLANDOVERY, Llandeilo, Brecon Beacons, BRECON, Builth Wells, New Radnor, KINGTON, Aberedw, Clyro, HAY-ON-WYE, Eardisley, Pembridge, Weobley, Bredwardine, Dorstone, Madley, Kilpeck, Grosmont, Skenfrith, Langattock, ABERGAVENNY, MONMOUTH, Tintern, Caerwent, NEWPORT, WEST GLAMORGAN, SWANSEA, MID GLAMORGAN, BRIDGEND, Coity, Ewenny, Merthyr Mawr, COWBRIDGE, St Hilary, St Fagans, SOUTH GLAMORGAN, CARDIFF, WESTON-SUPER-MARE, BRISTOL CHANNEL, MINEHEAD, EXMOOR, SOMERSET, Wimbleball Reservoir, TAUNTON

KNIGHTON, Leintwardine, LUDLOW, BEWDLEY, Bayton, Upper Arley, KIDDERMINSTER, Chaddesley Corbett, SALOP, WOLVERHAMPTON, BIRMINGHAM, Eardisland, LEOMINSTER, Clifton upon Teme, Ombersley, DROITWICH, Feckenham, Inkberrow, ALCESTER, Crowle, WORCESTER, BROMYARD, HEREFORD AND WORCESTER, Bosbury, PERSHORE, Elmley Castle, Pebworth, Bretforton, The Combertons, EVESHAM, Colwall, LEDBURY, Childswickham, Broadway, HEREFORD, Fownhope, Eastnor, Bredon, Much Marcle, ROSS-ON-WYE, Weston under Penyard, Goodrich, GLOUCESTER, GLOUCESTERSHIRE, TEWKESBURY, CHEPSTOW, BRISTOL, AVON, COTSWOLD HILLS, WILTSHIRE, SALISBURY

0   5   10   15   20   25   30   35   40   45   50   55   60   65   70   75   80   85   MILES

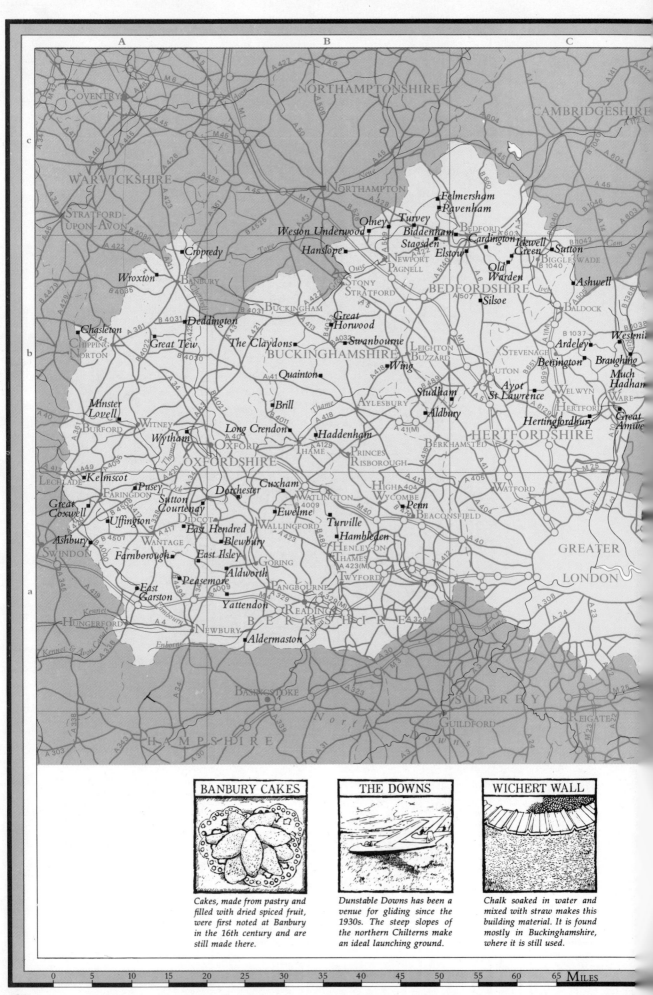

BANBURY CAKES

Cakes, made from pastry and filled with dried spiced fruit, were first noted at Banbury in the 16th century and are still made there.

THE DOWNS

Dunstable Downs has been a venue for gliding since the 1930s. The steep slopes of the northern Chilterns make an ideal launching ground.

WICHERT WALL

Chalk soaked in water and mixed with straw makes this building material. It is found mostly in Buckinghamshire, where it is still used.

0   5   10   15   20   25   30   35   40   45   50   55   60   65 MILES

5

WESTERN HOME COUNTIES

In the north-west corner of the five Home Counties the beautiful Cotswold Hills edge across the Oxfordshire border, and almost every village is built of grey or golden-tinted stone. Further south the green, chalk-flecked Chiltern Hills and Berkshire Downs are divided by the River Thames, flowing between slopes clad with dense beechwoods. There the villages are built mostly of durable flintstone, but in parts of Buckinghamshire the chalk is used to make a building material known as wichert.

Man has lived in this region for centuries. He left his mark more than 1,000 years ago in the shape of a white horse carved in the chalk above Uffington. The Romans built roads, military camps and towns, and from medieval times there is a rich legacy of grand houses and snug communities untouched by time.

CHURCH SPIKE

Although not confined to the county, this short, stubby spire caps many Hertfordshire churches. Many 'spikes' date from the 19th century.

CHALK LION

The chalk lion of Whipsnade, 483 ft from nose to tail, is one of many figures cut into the chalk of the North Downs and Chilterns.

THAMES VALLEY

The River Thames loops between the Berkshire Downs and Chiltern Hills. In autumn, riverside beechwoods blaze with colour.

FALLOW DEER

Wychwood Forest, in Oxfordshire, was once a royal hunting ground, favoured by Henry VIII. Today, the deer are protected.

NORTH WALES & THE BORDERS

Secret and unfrequented parts of Britain lie between the mountain-rimmed beaches of Cardigan Bay and the hump-backed hills of Wenlock Edge and the Long Mynd. Castles galore and villages like Clun, with its origins lost in prehistory, dot the Welsh Marches, once torn by border strife but mellow now with centuries of peace. Cattle and dairy farming support sandstone and timbered hamlets in the green, park-like Cheshire/Shropshire countryside. Lonely hill farms in Gwynedd, Clwyd and Powys produce tender Welsh lamb, and there are villages roofed with slate from the great quarries among the peaks of the Snowdonia National Park. These spectacular mountains, divided by dramatic passes, descend north to a coastline guarded by magnificent medieval castles like Conwy, Caernarfon and Harlech.

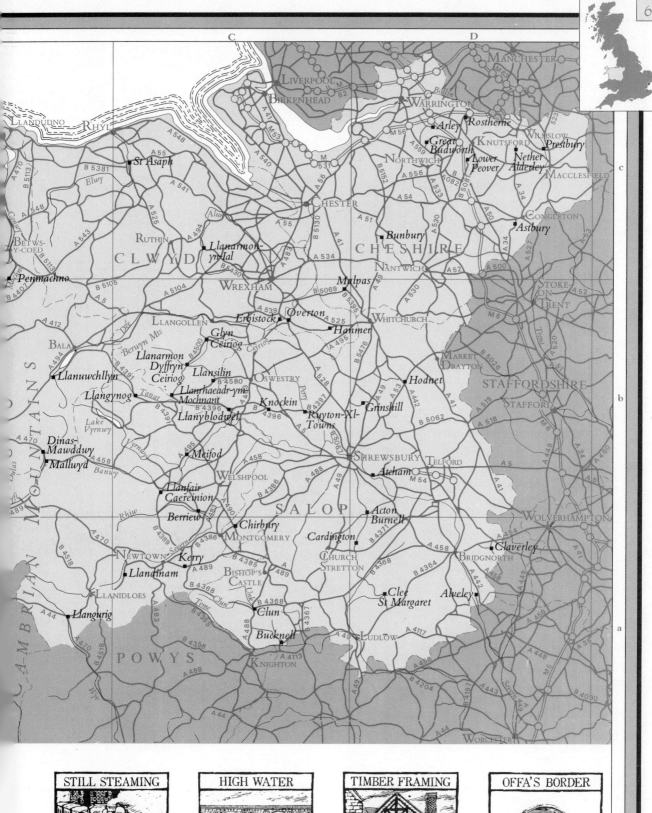

6

CLWYD

CHESHIRE

SALOP

POWYS

CAMBRIAN MOUNTAINS

STAFFORDSHIRE

LIVERPOOL
BIRKENHEAD
WARRINGTON
MANCHESTER
LLANDUDNO
RHYL
St Asaph
Penmachno
Betws-y-Coed
Ruthin
Llanarmon-yn-Ial
WREXHAM
Bala
Llanuwchllyn
Llangynog
Llanarmon Dyffryn Ceiriog
Llangollen
Erbistock
Overton
Glyn Ceiriog
Llansilin
Llanrhaeadr-ym-Mochnant
Llanyblodwel
OSWESTRY
Knockin
Ruyton-XI-Towns
Grinshill
Hodnet
MARKET DRAYTON
Hanmer
WHITCHURCH
Malpas
NANTWICH
Bunbury
Astbury
CONGLETON
Arley
Great Budworth
Rostherne
Knutsford
Lower Peover
Nether Alderley
Prestbury
WILMSLOW
MACCLESFIELD
STOKE-ON-TRENT
Dinas Mawddwy
Malluyd
Meifod
WELSHPOOL
Llanfair Caereinion
Berriew
Chirbury
MONTGOMERY
Cardington
SHREWSBURY
Atcham
TELFORD
Acton Burnell
CHURCH STRETTON
BRIDGNORTH
WOLVERHAMPTON
Claverley
Alveley
Newtown
Kerry
Llandinam
BISHOP'S CASTLE
Clun
Bucknell
KNIGHTON
Clee St Margaret
LUDLOW
Llangurig
Llanidloes
WORCESTER

Lake Vyrnwy

STILL STEAMING

The narrow-gauge railway built to carry slate from Blaenau Ffestiniog to Porthmadog in the 19th century now carries passengers.

HIGH WATER

The Shropshire Union Canal crosses the River Dee on Thomas Telford's 120 ft high Pontcysyllte Aqueduct, completed in 1805.

TIMBER FRAMING

Elaborate timber-framing is common in the 17th-century buildings of the wooded counties along the English-Welsh border.

OFFA'S BORDER

A coin of King Offa, who built a 168-mile dyke in 784 to define his boundary with Wales. Today, a footpath follows its full length.

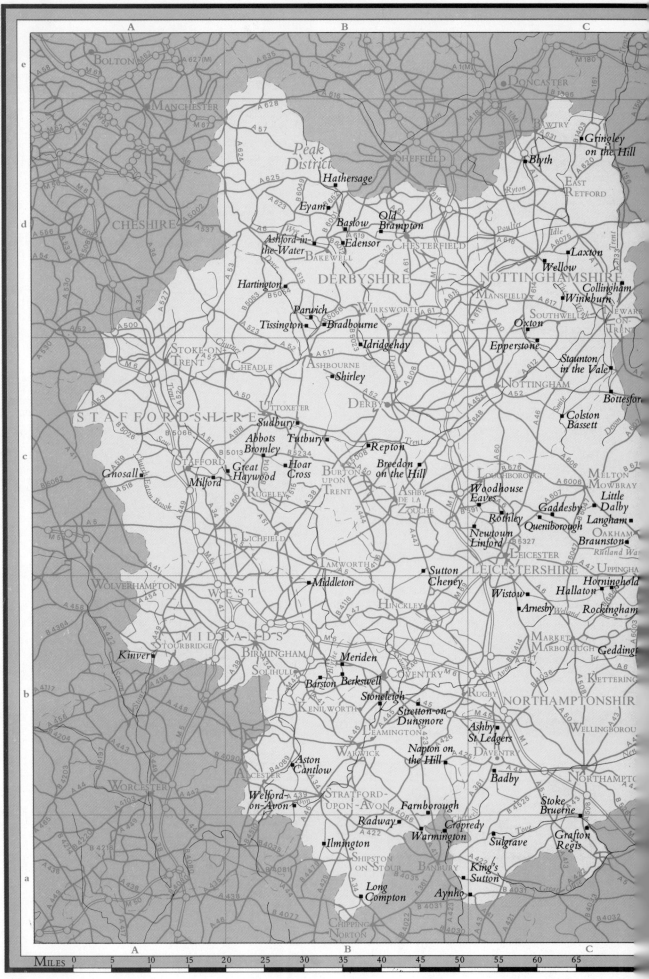

7

THE MIDLANDS

Here lies the heart of England. Not just the pounding heart of our vast Midlands industrial complex but the very core of our romantic and historic traditions. Here is Shakespeare's Forest of Arden, the Sherwood of Robin Hood, great castles like Warwick, and superb houses like Chatsworth; graceful crosses raised seven centuries ago by Edward I on the funeral route of his adored wife Eleanor of Castile; the crucial battlefields of Naseby and Bosworth. Here is the ancient hunting ground of Cannock Chase and the fox-hunting Vale of Belvoir, where yeomen of England fortified themselves – and still do – with the good ales of Burton and the succulent pies of Melton Mowbray; built their houses in a profusion of styles – timbered black and white, brick, and the creamy limestone of Northamptonshire. Here is the traditional centre of England, marked by a cross at Meriden, where it is said that Robin Hood himself drew his bow, and where archery contests continue to this day.

DERBYSHIRE
Ashford-in-the-Water **430 Bd**
Baslow **430 Bd**
Bradbourne **430 Bd**
Edensor **430 Bd**
Eyam **430 Bd**
Hartington **430 Bd**
Hathersage **430 Bd**
Idridgehay **430 Bc**
Old Brampton **430 Bd**
Parwich **430 Bd**
Repton **430 Bc**
Shirley **430 Bc**
Sudbury **430 Bc**
Tissington **430 Bd**

LEICESTERSHIRE
Arnesby **430 Cb**
Bottesford **430 Cc**
Braunston **430 Cc**
Breedon on the Hill **430 Bc**
Edith Weston **431 Cc**
Gaddesby **430 Cc**
Hallaton **430 Cb**
Horninghold **430 Cb**
Langham **430 Cc**
Little Dalby **430 Cb**
Newtown Linford **430 Cc**
Queniborough **430 Cc**
Rothley **430 Cc**

Sutton Cheney **430 Bc**
Wing **431 Cc**
Wistow **430 Cb**
Woodhouse Eaves **430 Cc**

NORTHAMPTONSHIRE
Ashby St Ledgers **430 Cb**
Aynho **430 Ca**
Badby **430 Cb**
Barnwell **431 Db**
Deene **431 Db**
Fotheringhay **431 Db**
Geddington **431 Cb**
Grafton Regis **430 Ca**
Grafton Underwood **431 Cb**
Grendon **430 Cb**
Gretton **431 Cb**
King's Sutton **430 Ba**
Rockingham **430 Cb**
Stoke Bruerne **430 Ca**
Sulgrave **430 Ca**
Wadenhoe **431 Db**

NOTTINGHAMSHIRE
Blyth **430 Cd**
Collingham **430 Cd**
Colston Bassett **430 Cc**
Epperstone **430 Cc**
Gringley on the Hill **430 Cd**
Laxton **430 Cd**

Oxton **430 Cd**
Staunton in the Vale **430 Cc**
Wellow **430 Cd**
Winkburn **430 Cd**

STAFFORDSHIRE
Abbots Bromley **430 Bc**
Gnosall **430 Ac**
Great Haywood **430 Bc**
Hoar Cross **430 Bc**
Kinver **430 Ab**
Milford **430 Ac**
Tutbury **430 Bc**

WARWICKSHIRE
Aston Cantlow **430 Bb**
Farnborough **430 Bb**
Ilmington **430 Ba**
Long Compton **430 Ba**
Napton on the Hill **430 Bb**
Radway **430 Ba**
Stoneleigh **430 Bb**
Stretton-on-Dunsmore **430 Bb**
Warmington **430 Ba**
Welford-on-Avon **430 Bb**

WEST MIDLANDS
Barston **430 Bb**
Berkswell **430 Bb**
Meriden **430 Bb**

TOBY JUG

One of Staffordshire's most popular products is the Toby Jug, named after Toby Philpot, a character in an 18th-century ballad.

WELL-DRESSING

Throughout the summer, village wells in many parts of Derbyshire are decorated with pictures made from flower petals.

PORK PIES

The pork-packed pies – and Stilton cheeses – of Melton Mowbray are savoured all over Britain and in many other countries.

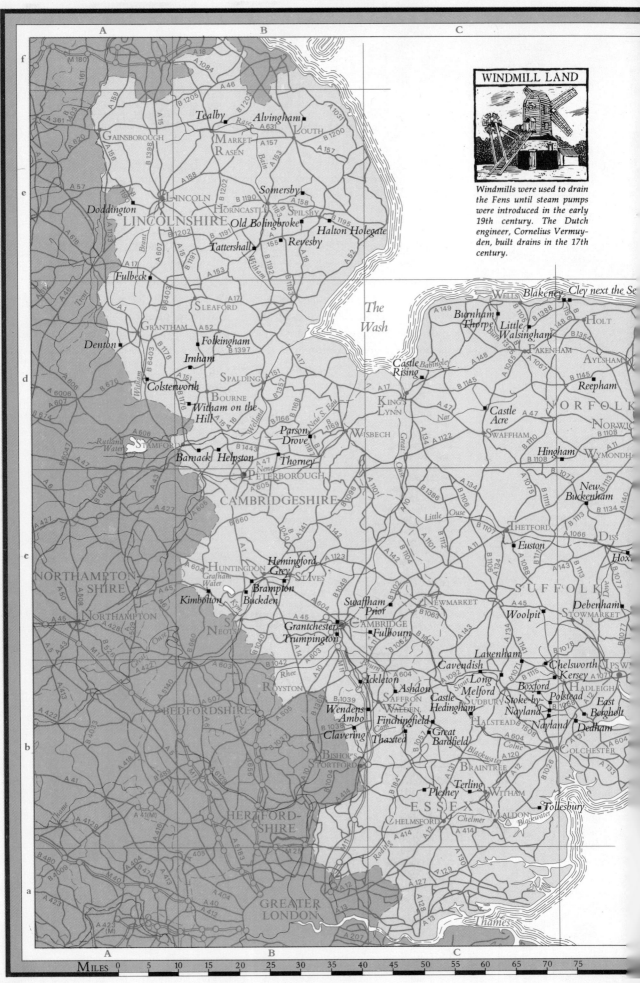

LINCOLNSHIRE & EAST ANGLIA

For thousands of years the bulging rump of England has been the settling place for invaders and immigrants from the Continent. The Angles came in the 5th century and gave their name to East Anglia, dividing it between the North Folk (Norfolk) and the South Folk (Suffolk). They found a sweeping coastline with no natural harbours, backed by marshland constantly washed by the sea. Beyond lay low hills and treacherous fens, forming a barrier to the land in the west.

Dutchmen in the 17th century found a land similar to their own, and used their skills to drain the fens and build ports which still show the Dutch influence in their gabled buildings. Windmills dot the landscape, bulb fields paint ribbons of colour in the spring, and in summer the Norfolk Broads swarm with yachts and motor cruisers.

This is a breezy corner of Britain, especially on the coast, but it is also the driest. The village of Great Wakering in Essex has the country's lowest average rainfall – 19.2 in. annually.

CAMBRIDGESHIRE
Barnack **432 Bd**
Brampton **432 Bc**
Buckden **432 Bc**
Fulbourn **432 Cc**
Grantchester **432 Bc**
Helpston **432 Bd**
Hemingford Grey **432 Bc**
Ickleton **432 Bb**
Kimbolton **432 Bc**
Parson Drove **432 Bd**
Swaffham Prior **432 Cc**
Thorney **432 Bd**
Trumpington **432 Bc**

ESSEX
Ashdon **432 Cb**
Castle Hedingham **432 Cb**
Clavering **432 Bb**
Dedham **432 Db**
Finchingfield **432 Cb**
Great Bardfield **432 Cb**
Pleshey **432 Cb**
Terling **432 Cb**
Thaxted **432 Cb**

Tollesbury **432 Cb**
Wendens Ambo **432 Cb**

LINCOLNSHIRE
Alvingham **432 Be**
Colsterworth **432 Ad**
Denton **432 Ad**
Doddington **432 Ae**
Folkingham **432 Bd**
Fulbeck **432 Ae**
Halton Holegate **432 Be**
Irnham **432 Bd**
Old Bolingbroke **432 Be**
Revesby **432 Be**
Somersby **432 Be**
Tattershall **432 Be**
Tealby **432 Be**
Witham on the Hill **432 Bd**

NORFOLK
Blakeney **432 Dd**
Burnham Thorpe **432 Cd**
Castle Acre **432 Cd**
Castle Rising **432 Cd**
Cley next the Sea **432 Dd**

Hingham **432 Dd**
Horning **433 Dd**
Little Walsingham **432 Cd**
New Buckenham **432 Dc**
Reepham **432 Dd**
Worstead **433 Dd**

SUFFOLK
Boxford **432 Cb**
Cavendish **432 Cb**
Chelsworth **432 Cb**
Debenham **432 Dc**
Dunwich **433 Dc**
East Bergholt **432 Db**
Euston **432 Cc**
Hoxne **432 Dc**
Kersey **432 Cb**
Lavenham **432 Cb**
Long Melford **432 Cb**
Nayland **432 Cb**
Orford **433 Dc**
Polstead **432 Cb**
Stoke-by-Nayland **432 Cb**
Westleton **433 Dc**
Woolpit **432 Cc**

THE BROADS

The Norfolk Broads provide more than 200 miles of navigable waterways. They were formed by medieval men digging for peat.

NORFOLK TURKEY

Norfolk is the home of the Christmas dinner. Britain's largest turkey farm, at Great Witchingham, produces 5 million birds a year.

MALTINGS

The Maltings concert hall at Snape, built on the site of a malt store, is the centre of the Aldeburgh music festival each June.

PARGETING

Fine, patterned plasterwork known as pargeting can be seen on buildings throughout East Anglia. It originated in Elizabethan times.

LANCASHIRE & THE LAKES

Lancashire, that great hotpot of a county, has ingredients and flavours enough to match the unique savour of its famous regional dish. The windswept slopes and moors of the western Pennines roll down to a rich and fertile coastal plain; stone and brick villages stand on the skyline of flat, black-soiled market-gardening country; sheltered farms and hamlets hide in wooded backwaters; magnificent houses and ruined castles are reminders of the winners and losers of the Wars of the Roses and other struggles. A flat, sand-duned coastline rolls north from Liverpool to the magnificent Lake District, 866 sq. miles of the largest National Park in the country that has changed little since Wordsworth lived and found inspiration there more than 150 years ago. Lancashire needs a different kind of author, someone like Walter (*Love on the Dole*) Greenwood, or an artist like L. S. Lowry, to capture the character of its homely and hospitable folk and their close-knit world, where the takeaways sell honeycomb tripe and cow-heels, pigs' trotters and delicious mushy peas. And the hotpot is like the people: simple, warm and satisfying.

HELVELLYN

The sharp ridge of Striding Edge sweeps by Red Tarn to the 3,118 ft summit of Helvellyn, the most popular climb in the Lake District.

HOME SPUN

Many old houses in Lancashire and Cumbria have first-floor spinning galleries, built when cloth-making was a cottage industry.

TIED ROOF

Low stone walls and a thatched roof held down by ropes tied to pegs in the walls, are typical of exposed cottages on the Isle of Man.

WORDSWORTH

The irresistible beauty of Lakeland drew William Wordsworth back to his native Cumbria to write some of his most heartfelt poetry.

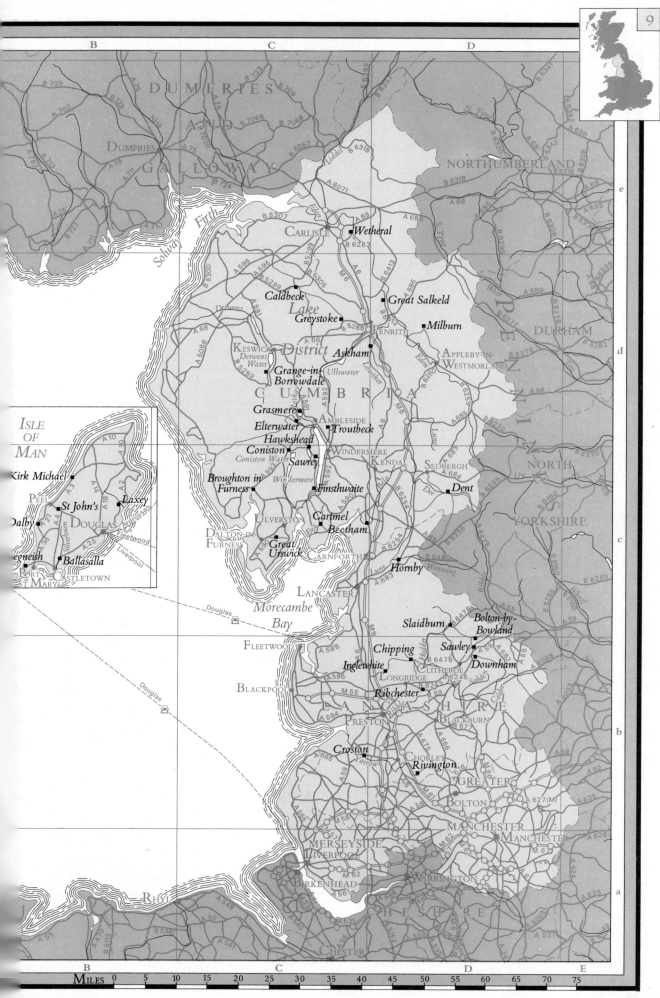

9

B   C   D

DUMFRIES
B 729
A 702
B 729
B 723
B 709
B 7068
B 7068
DUMFRIES
AND
A 75
A 78
GALLOWAY
B 724
A 75
B 727
A 710
NORTHUMBERLAND
N. Tyne
A 6071
B 6318
B 6318
B 6357
Solway   Firth
Liddel
B 6351
A 6
B 6318
B 6320
S. Tyne
B 6342
A 68
A 686
A 69
e

B 5307
CARLISLE ■ Wetheral
B 6263
A 69
A 689
A 695
B 6309
d

A 596
A 595
B 5299
B 5305
M 6
Calbeck ■
Lake
Greystoke ■
A 591
B 5288
PENRITH
A 686
Great Salkeld ■
Milburn ■
APPLEBY-IN-
WESTMORLAND
P E N N I N E S
DURHAM
B 6277
B 6276
B 6282
d

Derwent
Keswick
Derwent
Water
A 5086
B 5289
District
A 66
Askham ■
Ullswater
Lowther
Eden
B 6260
A 66
A 66
B 6270
B 6259
N O R T H
c

Grange-in-
Borrowdale ■
C U M B R I A
Grasmere ■
A 592
AMBLESIDE
Troutbeck ■
Elterwater
Hawkshead ■
Coniston ■
Coniston Water
Sawrey
Broughton in
Furness ■
Windermere
Finsthwaite ■
WINDERMERE
KENDAL
A 6
SEDBERGH
A 684
Dent ■
B 6255
Y O R K S H I R E
B 6160
c

ISLE
OF
MAN
Kirk Michael ■
A 10
A 10
PEEL
St John's ■
A 14
Laxey ■
Dalby ■
A 3
A 18
Douglas
A 25
A 27
eigneish ■
Ballasalla ■
ST MARY ■ CASTLETOWN
Ardrossan
Fleetwood
Liverpool
DALTON-IN-
FURNESS ■
ULVERSTON
Great
Urswick ■
CARNFORTH
Cartmel ■
Beetham ■
B 6254
Lune
Wenning
Hornby ■
B 6480
Ribble

Douglas
Morecambe
Bay
LANCASTER
M 6
Slaidburn ■
Bolton-by-
Bowland ■
Sawley ■
Downham ■
A 65
b

FLEETWOOD
A 588
Chipping ■
Inglewhite ■
LONGRIDGE
Hodder
B 6478
CLITHEROE
B 6246
A 59
A 56

Douglas
BLACKPOOL
A 584
M 55
Ribchester ■
L A N C A S H I R E
PRESTON
Ribble
Calder
BLACKBURN
B 677
b

Croston ■
A 565
A 59
Yarrow
CHORLEY
Rivington ■
A 6
G R E A T E R
BOLTON
A 627(M)

RHYL
A 585
M 58
M 62
MERSEYSIDE
Liverpool
BIRKENHEAD
A 561
M 62
MANCHESTER
MANCHESTER
M 62
WARRINGTON
C H E S H I R E
a

CHESTER

B   C   D   E

MILES 0   5   10   15   20   25   30   35   40   45   50   55   60   65   70   75

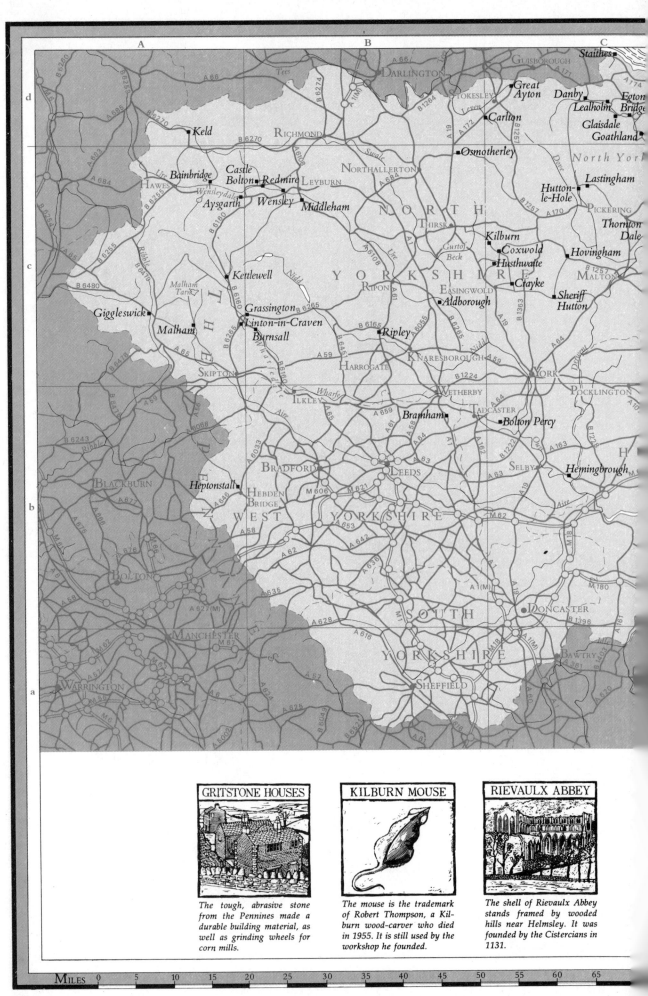

A B C
d
Staithes
B 6260
B 6270
Tees
A 66
B 6274
A 1(M)
GUISBOROUGH
A 171
DARLINGTON
A 19
B 1284
Great
Ayton
Danby
Egton
STOKESLEY
Leven
Lealholm
Bridge
A 172
A 19
Carlton
B 1257
Glaisdale
B 6270
RICHMOND
Swale
Osmotherley
Goathland
A 685
Keld
NORTHALLERTON
North York
B 6255
Bainbridge
Castle
Bolton
Redmire
Leyburn
A 684
Lastingham
Hutton-
le-Hole
B 1257
A 884
HAWES
Wensleydale
Wensley
Middleham
A 170
Aysgarth
NORTH
PICKERING
THIRSK
Kilburn
Thornton
Dale
B 6108
Coxwold
Hovingham
c
B 6255
B 6160
Gurtof
Beck
Husthwaite
B 1257
MALTON
B 6480
Kettlewell
YORKSHIRE
Nidd
Ure
Crayke
Sheriff
Hutton
Malham
Tarn
RIPON
A 61
B 1363
Giggleswick
Grassington
B 6265
EASINGWOLD
A 19
A 64
Linton-in-Craven
Aldborough
Malham
Burnsall
B 6165
Ripley
A 6055
Skipton
A 59
Knaresborough
A 59
York
Harrogate
Nidd
b
Ilkley
Wharfe
WETHERBY
A 64
POCKLINGTON
Aire
A 65
Bramham
TADCASTER
A 659
Bolton Percy
Bradford
A 61
Leeds
Selby
Heptonstall
A 646
Hebden
Bridge
WEST
YORKSHIRE
M 606
M 621
M 62
Hemingbrough
BLACKBURN
Aire
a
M 62
BOLTON
M 18
SOUTH
DONCASTER
M 1
YORKSHIRE
MANCHESTER
Bawtry
SHEFFIELD
MILES 0 5 10 15 20 25 30 35 40 45 50 55 60 65

GRITSTONE HOUSES

The tough, abrasive stone
from the Pennines made a
durable building material, as
well as grinding wheels for
corn mills.

KILBURN MOUSE

The mouse is the trademark
of Robert Thompson, a Kilburn wood-carver who died
in 1955. It is still used by the
workshop he founded.

RIEVAULX ABBEY

The shell of Rievaulx Abbey
stands framed by wooded
hills near Helmsley. It was
founded by the Cistercians in
1131.

10

D

YORKSHIRE & THE HUMBER

To a Yorkshireman, the cricket, the food, the ale, the scenery and the people of his broad-acred county are finer all round than those in any of the smaller counties that make up the rest of England. And to go there is to understand his pride. Hospitality rules in every snug stone village of the dales and vales. Every village seems to have at least one cricket field – and every inhabitant a profound insight into the game. This is a hard-working land of Pennine sheep farms, and rivers and waterfalls cascading down hillsides; of great abbeys and ruined castles in the fertile Vale of York and on the high moors; of superb beaches and rugged cliffs – and the crumbling coastline of Humberside. It is the land that bred talents like the Brontës, J. B. Priestley and David Hockney; men of action like Captain Cook; cricketers like Len Hutton, Fred Trueman and Geoffrey Boycott. It is a land that seems to demand achievement.

BRONTË COUNTRY

High Withins, on Haworth Moor, is thought to have been the original of the house described by Emily Brontë in **Wuthering Heights**.

FISHING COBLES

These flat-bottomed vessels are launched bow first from a beach. Grace Darling used a coble in her epic rescue of 1838.

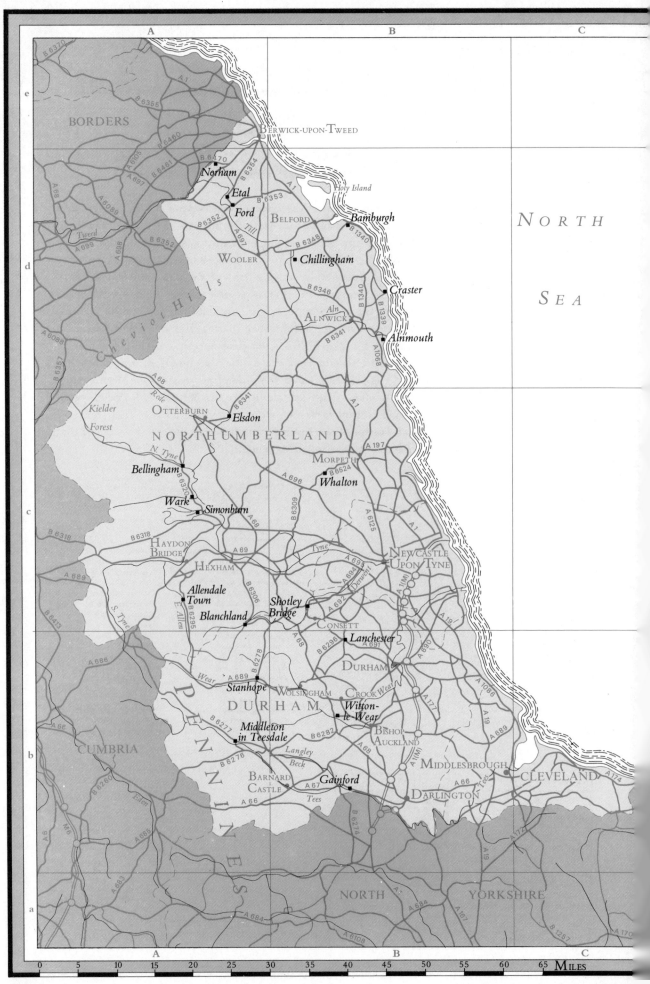

11

NORTHUMBRIA

Stand where the Roman legionaries stood on Hadrian's Wall, and the war cries of Pictish raiders can almost be heard on the wind. Cross the causeway to Holy Island – the Lindisfarne of old – and you are where St Aidan stood in the 7th century when he landed to bring Christianity to Northumbria. There is living history all over Northumbria, from its rugged fortress-dotted border country to the wooded valleys of County Durham. There is magnificent walking and touring country too, from the Cheviots and the high moors of Redesdale to the dales of Tyne, Wear and Tees with the Pennines rearing to the west. Houses stand close together in Northumbria's ancient villages, their stone walls thick and solid against the savagery of man and nature. Equally solid and sustaining is the local cooking. Tory Pan Haggerty – potato and onion cake sprinkled with cheese; or the Singin' Hinny of Tyneside – large fruit scones served hot, split and buttered.

FISHERMAN'S COAST

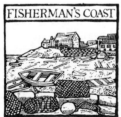

The north-east coastline is dotted with small fishing villages, where herring fleets set out from tiny harbours to wrest their harvest from the savage sea.

EMPEROR MOTH

On sunny days in April and May the male emperor moth can be seen zigzagging its way over the region's moorlands in search of the larger female.

BAMBURGH CASTLE

The massive walls and keep stand on a rocky clifftop high above Northumbria's rugged coast. The keep is Norman, but the walls date from the 19th century.

PELE TOWER

These towers were built in many border villages in the 14th century to serve as a refuge against marauders. This one is at Ancroft.

HADRIAN'S WALL

This is the Wall at Housesteads, near Hexham. It was built as a defence against northern tribes and was 73 miles long.

KIELDER FOREST

Kielder Forest, part of the Border Forest Park, grows spruce, larch and pine. Roe deer, badgers and otters are among its wildlife.

SCOTTISH LOWLANDS

A great surprise awaits a newcomer to the Lowlands: they are not low. They are in fact hillier than most parts of England, with ranges such as the Cheviots, the Lowthers and the Lammermuirs rising to 2,500 ft or more. The Lowlands offer scenes of beauty as compelling as anything in the Highlands. There are, too, the dreamy park-like landscapes of the river valleys around Melrose, where Sir Walter Scott wrote his romantic novels, and lush pastoral country across the Forth in Fife. The border country, castle-strewn from centuries of strife, is now the arena for less bloody conflicts – amid the traps and bunkers of hundreds of golf courses, and on salmon rivers, like the Tweed, where anglers pit their skills against splendid fighting fish.

Solid stone and whitewashed walls shield Lowland villagers when winters are harsh. Some of the houses are still thatch-roofed, like the gardener's cottage where Robert Burns was born in Alloway. Like Scott, he drew his inspiration mostly from Lowland landscapes. So, in modern times, did John Buchan, whose hero saw action around the remote peak of the Cairnsmore of Fleet in *The Thirty-Nine Steps*. This is also the Scotland of William Wallace, who thrashed the English at Stirling Bridge, and Robert Bruce, who routed them at Bannockburn.

NORTHERN PALMS

The sub-tropical gardens at Port Logan, on the west coast of Galloway, have flourished for a century in the mild Gulf Stream climate.

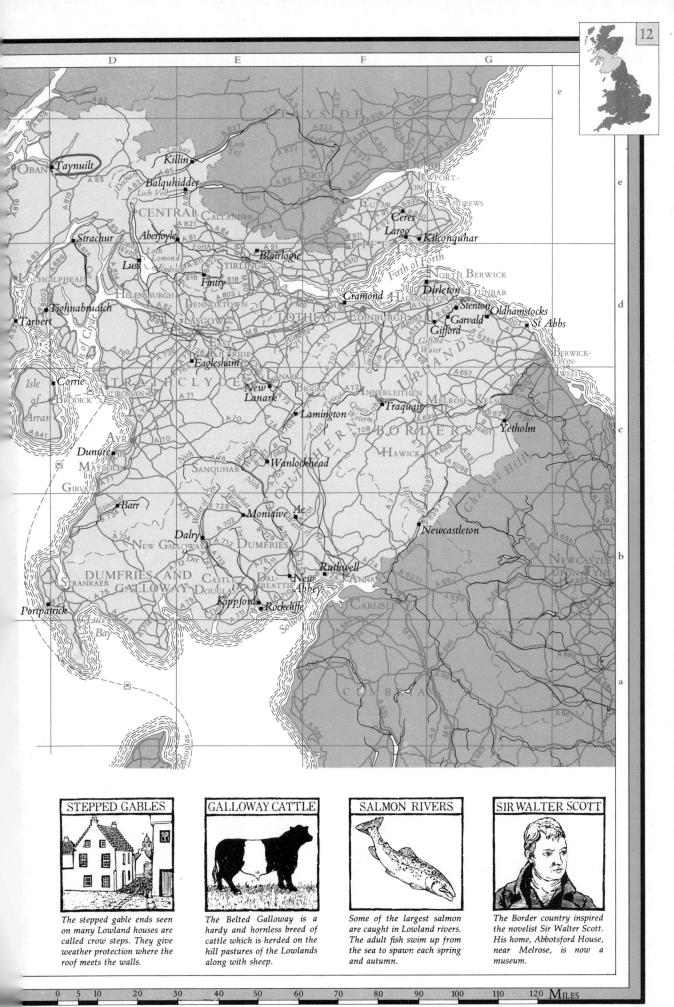

12

D   E   F   G

TAYSIDE

OBAN   Taynuilt

Killin

Balquhidder   Loch Tay   PERTH

CENTRAL   CALLANDER   DUNDEE   NEWPORT-ON-TAY   ST ANDREWS

Strachur   Aberfoyle   CUPAR   Ceres

Luss   Blairlogie   FIFE   Largo   Kilconquhar

Fintry   STIRLING

LOCHGILPHEAD   HELENSBURGH   LOTHIAN   Firth of Forth   NORTH BERWICK

Tighnabruaich   LENNOXTOWN   Cramond   HADDINGTON   Dirleton   DUNBAR

Tarbert   GLASGOW   EDINBURGH   Stenton   Oldhamstocks

EAST KILBRIDE   Garvald   St Abbs

Eaglesham   Gifford   BERWICK-UPON-TWEED

Corrie   STRATHCLYDE

BRODICK   ARDROSSAN   New Lanark   LANARK   Biggar   INNERLEITHEN   UPLANDS

Isle of Arran   Lamington   Traquair   MELROSE   KELSO

AYR   BORDERS   Yetholm

Dunure   Wanlockhead   HAWICK

MAYBOLE   Sanquhar   SOUTHERN   Cheviot Hills

GIRVAN

Barr   Moniaive   Ae   Newcastleton

Dalry   DUMFRIES

NEW GALLOWAY   NEWCASTLE UPON TYNE

STRANRAER   DUMFRIES AND GALLOWAY   CASTLE DOUGLAS   DALBEATTIE   Ruthwell   ANNAN

Kippford   New Abbey

Portpatrick   Rockcliffe   CARLISLE

Luce Bay   Solway Firth

CUMBRIA

STEPPED GABLES

The stepped gable ends seen on many Lowland houses are called crow steps. They give weather protection where the roof meets the walls.

GALLOWAY CATTLE

The Belted Galloway is a hardy and hornless breed of cattle which is herded on the hill pastures of the Lowlands along with sheep.

SALMON RIVERS

Some of the largest salmon are caught in Lowland rivers. The adult fish swim up from the sea to spawn each spring and autumn.

SIR WALTER SCOTT

The Border country inspired the novelist Sir Walter Scott. His home, Abbotsford House, near Melrose, is now a museum.

0   5   10   20   30   40   50   60   70   80   90   100   110   120 MILES

SCOTTISH HIGHLANDS

You can walk all day in the Highlands without seeing another soul; become an insignificant speck amid the majestic works of nature. There is more wild life than there are people: fierce wildcats and noble red deer; sometimes a soaring golden eagle or a ptarmigan, white-winged in winter. At the right time of year, salmon struggle up swift torrents; and lochs can be alive with the flash of trout. The few people who live in the Highlands would live nowhere else. Their stone villages and lonely crofts crouch low against the elements, heather roofs giving way grudgingly to tile and slate. Slashed across the region is the Great Glen, part-filled by Loch Ness, home of the monster, and with Ben Nevis rearing 4,406 ft at its western end. Then there are the islands – Skye, Lewis, Islay and a thousand others. 'My heart's in the Highlands,' wrote Rabbie Burns. And he was a Lowlander.

HEATHER THATCH

Cottages roofed with heather thatch can still be found on the Atlantic coast.

PTARMIGAN

This mountain bird is speckled grey in summer and white in winter.

STRONGHOLDS

Urquhart Castle, above Loch Ness, is a typical Highland stronghold.

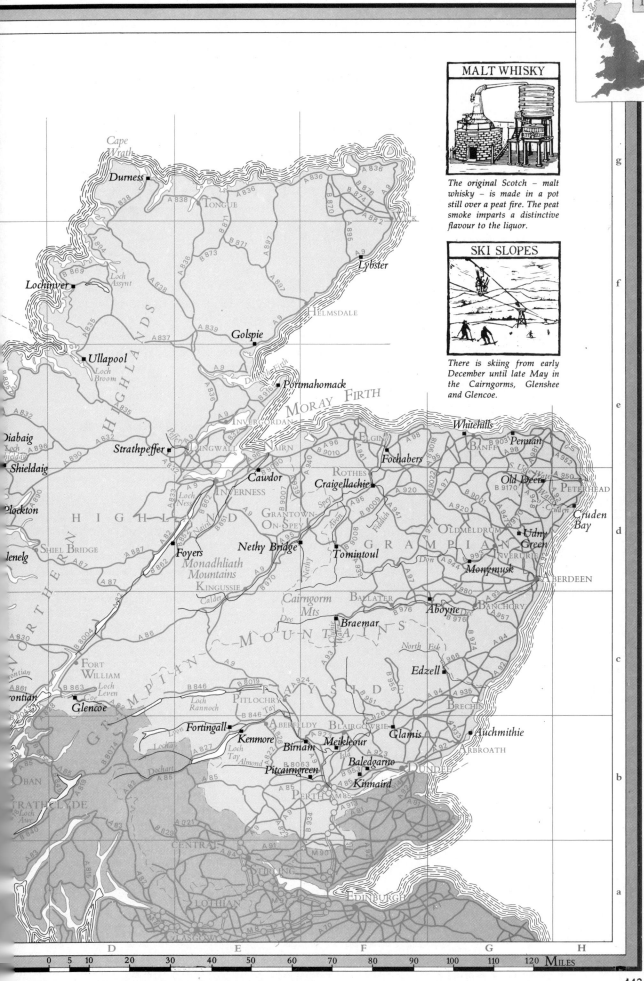

13

MALT WHISKY

The original Scotch – malt whisky – is made in a pot still over a peat fire. The peat smoke imparts a distinctive flavour to the liquor.

SKI SLOPES

There is skiing from early December until late May in the Cairngorms, Glenshee and Glencoe.

Cape Wrath

Durness

A 836

TONGUE

A 836

A 836

A 838

A 838

B 874

B 876

WICK

B 870

B 871

B 882

A 9

A 897

Lochinver

Loch Assynt

B 869

B 873

A 836

A 897

A 895

A 9

Lybster

A 894

A 838

A 838

A 9

HELMSDALE

HIGHLANDS

A 835

A 837

A 839

Golspie

A 832

A 836

Ullapool

Loch Broom

A 835

A 9

Portmahomack

MORAY FIRTH

INVERGORDON

Whitehills

Diabaig

A 896

Loch Maree Shieldaig

A 832

DINGWALL

NAIRN

Elgin

A 98

B 9018

BANFF

B 903

Pennan

A 952

Strathpeffer

A 832

A 9

A 96

A 941

Fochabers

A 98

B 9022

S. Ugie Water

A 950

Old Deer

Shieldaig

A 890

A 862

A 96

ROTHES

A 941

B 9170

PETERHEAD

Cawdor

Craigellachie

A 920

A 9001

A 947

Cruden Bay

Plockton

A 890

INVERNESS

B 9007

Spey

A 95

A 9009

A 920

OLDMELDRUM

Udny Green

HIGHLAND

A 862

A 9

GRANTOWN ON-SPEY

A 939

A 941

Fiddich

A 920

B 993

INVERURIE

Glenelg

A 887

A 862

Nairn

Foyers

Nethy Bridge

Nethy

Tomintoul

A 944

Monymusk

ABERDEEN

SHIEL BRIDGE

A 87

A 862

Monadhliath Mountains

GRAMPIAN

Don

A 944

A 980

A 87

KINGUSSIE

Calder

A 93

A 97

A 96

A 830

B 8004

A 86

Cairngorm Mts

BALLATER

Aboyne

BANCHORY

A 957

Dee

A 9

Dee

Braemar

B 976

B 976

A 93

FORT WILLIAM

B 863

Loch Leven

A 86

MOUNTAINS

Clunie

North Esk

A 974

Ardrontian

A 861

Loch Coe

B 8004

A 9

A 93

A 966

Edzell

A 94

A 935

Onich

Glencoe

GRAMPIAN

B 846

B 8019

A 951

B 966

BRECHIN

OBAN

B 8074

Loch Rannoch

PITLOCHRY

TAYSIDE

A 94

Tay

B 846

Tay

A 924

Fortingall

ABERFELDY

BLAIRGOWRIE

Glamis

Auchmithie

Lyon

Kenmore

Meikleour

A 928

ARBROATH

STRATHCLYDE

Loch Awe

A 85

Lochay

A 827

Loch Tay

Birnam

Isla

B 8063

Baledgarno

Almond

Pitcairngreen

B 953

DUNDEE

A 85

A 85

Dochart

Kinnaird

A 85

A 82

A 819

A 84

A 921

B 829

PERTH

A 912

A 91

CENTRAL

A 84

B 934

M 90

STIRLING

LOTHIAN

EDINBURGH

GLASGOW

M 8

A 70

| D | E | F | G | H |

| 0 | 5 | 10 | 20 | 30 | 40 | 50 | 60 | 70 | 80 | 90 | 100 | 110 | 120 | MILES |

g

f

e

d

c

b

a

Where to see Craftsmen at Work

'And all their desire is in the work of their craft.' Until the dawn of mechanisation, these biblical words fitted most villages as they were self-sufficient, with local craftsmen providing the needs of everyday living. Today, despite the mass production of most goods, the desire of some men and women is still in the work of their craft, and the following pages list the villages described in the book where traditional craft workshops can be visited and the skill of the potter, the smith, the woodworker and others can be seen. In most cases the workshops welcome visitors, but those marked (A) ask that an appointment be made for a visit.

ENGLAND

Federation of British Craft
Societies
43 Earlham Street
London WC2H 9LD
01-836 4722

AVON
Wellow
Wellow Crafts, Bath Hill.
Tel. Bath 833344. *Handicrafts.*

BEDFORDSHIRE
Pavenham
Mrs P. M. Morgan, Mill Lane.
Tel. Oakley 2393. **(A)** *Rushwork.*
Silsoe
Christine Boyce, BA, AMGP, 7
Vicarage Road.
Tel. Silsoe 60267. **(A)** *Stained glass.*

BERKSHIRE
Aldermaston
Aldermaston Pottery.
Tel. Woolhampton 3359.

BUCKINGHAMSHIRE
Haddenham
Ivor Newton & Son, Aston
Road. Tel. Haddenham 291461.
Woodwork.
Olney
The Olney Pottery, Holes Lane.
Tel. Bedford 712306. **(A)**

CAMBRIDGESHIRE
Fulbourn
Richard Sell,
1 Station Road.
Tel. Cambridge 880335. **(A)**
Lithographic illustration.
Pearl Soames, 7a Ludlow Lane.
Tel. Cambridge 880011. **(A)**
Ceramic tiled coffee tables.
Ickleton
Mrs Shirley Gant, 7 Church
Street.
Tel. Great Chesterford 639. **(A)**
Rush and cane work.
David Whitaker, 48 Frogge
Street.
Tel. Great Chesterford 304.
Furniture.

CORNWALL
Boscastle
Camelot Pottery, The Old
Bakery. Tel. Boscastle 291.
*Specialises in 'mochaware' – a
herbal form of decorated slipware.*
Polperro
Paula Humphris Pottery, Mill
Hill. Tel. Polperro 439.
St Agnes
John and Sue Sneddon,
Beaconsfield Place.
Tel. St Agnes 2842. **(A)** *Pottery.*
Veryan
C. E. Moore, Stella-Maris,
Pendower. Tel. Veryan 400. (1
mile south of village.)
Woodcarving.

CUMBRIA
Caldbeck
Greenrigg Pottery and Craft
Studio. Tel. Caldbeck 341.
(2½ miles out of village
towards Keswick.)
Coniston
Dunmail Studios, Waterhead.
Tel. Coniston 312. **(A)**
*Lakeland greenstone gifts and
fireplaces.*
Dent
Dent Glass Works,
Risehill Mill. Tel. Dent 323.
Engraved tableware.
Grasmere
Chris Reekie & Sons Ltd,
The Old Coach House,
Stock Lane. Tel. Grasmere 221.
Hand-woven fabrics.
White Bridge Forge.
Tel. Grasmere 414.
*Wrought ironwork and general
blacksmith.*
Great Salkeld
The Watermill,
Little Salkeld.
Tel. Langwathby 523. **(A)**
(1 mile south-east of Great
Salkeld.)
Stoneground flour.
Hawkshead
Ceramics and Glass,
Main Street.
Tel. Hawkshead 527.
Avis and Bernard Loshak,
Esthwaite Pottery.
Tel. Hawkshead 241.
(No craftsmen at work.)

DERBYSHIRE
Sudbury
Metwood Forge,
School Lane. Tel. Sudbury 232.
Wrought ironwork.

DEVON
Branscombe
Eric Golding,
Branscombe Pottery.
Tel. Branscombe 248.
(No craftsmen at work.)

DORSET
Abbotsbury
Roger Gilding,
Abbotsbury Pottery,
34 West Street.
Tel. Abbotsbury 506.
Cerne Abbas
Cerne Valley Forge. Tel. Cerne
Abbas 298.
Wrought ironwork.
Margaret Sayers,
6 Abbey Court. Tel. Cerne
Abbas 354. **(A)**
Period dolls.

ESSEX
Castle Hedingham
Humphries Weaving Co.,
Devere Mill,
Queen Street.
Tel. Hedingham 61193.
Handloomed silk for furnishings.
Open afternoons in summer –
other times by appointment.
Thaxted
Mrs Joy Parkin,
11 Mill End.
Tel. Thaxted 830696. **(A)**
Handicrafts – specialising in toys.
Glendale Forge,
Monk Street.
Tel. Thaxted 830466.
(1½ miles south of village.)
Wrought ironwork.
Jill Baines,
Coldhans Fee,
Bardfield Road.
Tel. Thaxted 830867.
Ceramics.

GLOUCESTERSHIRE
Bourton-on-the-Water
John and Judy Jelfs,
Clapton Row. Tel. Bourton-on-
the-Water 20173.
Pottery.
J. L. Kosmala,
Clapton Row. Tel. Bourton-on-
the-Water 15442. **(A)**
Jewellery.
W. George Martin,
12 Spring Vale. (No phone.)
Dry-stone walling.
K. A. Waterworth,
c/o Salon Phoenix,
Moore Road. Tel. Bourton-on-
the-Water 20133. **(A)**
*Hand-crafted furniture from
locally grown elm.*
Dymock
Mrs K. M. Pim,
Church Cottage.
Tel. Dymock 378. **(A)**

Costume dolls.
St Briavels
Gill McCubbin,
Forge Pottery.
Tel. St Briavels 297.
Domestic stoneware.
Betty Blandino,
Ivy Cottage,
Hudnalls Loop,
St Briavels Common.
Tel. St Briavels 510. **(A)**
(2 miles south-west of village.)
*Pottery – specialises in hand-built
large, thin pots.*

HAMPSHIRE
Burghclere
Grindon Pottery,
Penwood.
Tel. Newbury 253277. **(A)**
(About 2 miles north-west of
village.)
C. J. and S. A. James,
23a Breachfield.
Tel. Burghclere 455. **(A)**
Hand-painted canal-ware.
Chawton
Chawton Forge Pottery,
Winchester Road.
Tel. Alton 64105.
(No craftsmen at work.)
Hambledon
Hambledon Vineyards.
Tel. Hambledon 475.
Open Sunday afternoons in
summer.
Minstead
Will Selwood Art and Craft
Gallery,
Furzey Gardens.
Tel. Cadnam 2464.
(No craftsmen at work.)
Nether Wallop
Antony West,
The Smithy.
Tel. Salisbury 22333.
Selborne
Peter Ingram,
Limes End Yard,
High Street. Tel. Selborne 312.
*Building and restoring horse-
drawn vehicles – specialises in
gypsy caravans.*
Open weekends.

ISLE OF MAN
Ballasalla
Shebeg Gallery,
Ballamodha.
Tel. Castletown 3497.
(1½ miles north-west of
village.)
Pottery.
Kirk Michael
J. H. and E. Place,
Laurel Dene,
Rhencullen.
Tel. Kirk Michael 363.
*Gem stones, furniture, antique
restoring.*

Laxey
St George's Woollen Mills Ltd.
Tel. Laxey 1395.
Laxey Manx tweed.
St Johns
Tynwald Craft Centre.
Tel. St Johns 213.
*Mechanised weaving, glassblowing,
herbal cosmetics.*

ISLE OF WIGHT
Calbourne
Chessell Pottery.
Tel. Calbourne 248.
(2½ miles west of Calbourne.)
Stoneware and porcelain.

KENT
Appledore
R. A. R. Moseley,
The Forge. Tel. Appledore 358.
Wrought ironwork.
Biddenden
Winston and Sheila Moss,
The Potters Shop.
Tel. Biddenden 291339. **(A)**
Biddenden Vineyards,
Little Whatmans.
Tel. Biddenden 291237.
(1½ miles south-west of
village.)
Horsmonden
Jasper and Molly Kettlewell,
Capel Manor.
Tel. Brenchley 2769. **(A)**
Stained glass.

LINCOLNSHIRE
Alvingham
Alvingham Pottery and
Gallery,
Yarburgh Road.
Tel. South Cockerington 230.

NORFOLK
New Buckenham
Bakehouse Pottery and
Showroom,
King Street.
Tel. New Buckenham 512.
Reepham
Paul and Sue Taylor,
Church Hill. (No phone.)
Pottery.

NORTHAMPTONSHIRE
Grendon
John Timpany,
Shire Concertinas,
3 Chequers Lane.
Tel. Wellingborough 663008.
(A)
*Makes, tunes and repairs
concertinas.*
Gretton
Elizabeth Palmer,
Crown Cottage,
46 High Street.
Tel. Rockingham 770303. **(A)**
*Handweaving, handspinning and
corn dollies.*

NORTHUMBERLAND
Alnmouth
Aln Boatyard.
Tel. Alnmouth 294.
Boatbuilding.

NORTH YORKSHIRE
Coxwold
Mr P. Dick,
Coxwold Pottery.
Tel. Coxwold 344. **(A)**
Earthenware and stoneware.
Crayke
Woodcarvers of Crayke Ltd,
Stillington Road.
Tel. Easingwold 21512.
Furniture from English oak.
Danby
Camphill Village Trust Ltd,
Botton Village.
Tel. Castleton 424.
(3 miles south of village.)
*Candles, metal, dolls, glass
engraving, woodwork, furniture.*
Husthwaite
W. Hutchinson,
Squirrel Crafts.
Tel. Coxwold 352.
Traditional English oak furniture.
Hutton-le-Hole
Wold Pottery (Routh) Ltd.
Tel. Lastingham 527.
Kilburn
Robert Thompson's Craftsmen
Ltd,
Kilburn. Tel. Coxwold 218.
*Domestic and ecclesiastical oak
furniture.*

OXFORDSHIRE
Deddington
Michael and Heather Ackland,
Coniston House,
New Street.
Tel. Deddington 241. **(A)**
Jewellery.
Deddington Pottery,
Market Place.
Tel. Deddington 353.
Betty Francis,
3 Chapel Square.
Tel. Deddington 400.
Textiles.
Goldford Furnishings,
Hudson Street.
Tel. Deddington 165.
Furniture.

SOMERSET
Mells
Hive and Herb,
Laurel Cottage,
Little Green. Tel. Mells 812640.
(A)
*Hand-made herbal skin
preparations; ironware.*
Porlock
Waistel and Joan Cooper,
Studio Pottery,
Culbone Lodge.

Tel. Porlock 862539.
(Beside Culbone church.)
Porlock Pottery and Jewellery
Workshop,
High Street. (No phone.)

STAFFORDSHIRE
Tutbury
Webb Corbett Ltd,
Tutbury Glassworks.
Tel. Burton-on-Trent 813281.
(A)
*Glassblowing and decorative
tableware.*

SUFFOLK
Debenham
Aspall Cyder.
Tel. Debenham 860510.
(1½ miles north of village on
B1077.)
Modern equipment now used
but visitors can see 18th-
century equipment.
Deben Rush Weavers,
Bridge House.
Tel. Debenham 349.
Chairs, baskets, place mats.
A. Carter,
Kiln Cottage Pottery,
Low Road. Tel. Debenham 475.
Original modern ceramics.
Anthony Mowles,
6 Cross Green. (No phone.)
Leatherwork.
Kersey
Kersey Craft Workshops,
Kersey Uplands.
Tel. Hadleigh 3344.
(1 mile south-west of village.)
*Toys, woodwork, furniture –
specialists in rocking horses.*
Appointment needed for
Sunday.

EAST SUSSEX
Alfriston
Jonathan Chiswell Jones,
Drusillas. Tel. Alfriston 870234.
Appointment for vineyard
and furniture.
(1 mile north of village on
A27.)
*Vineyard, wood furniture,
leatherwork, pottery, bakery.*

WEST SUSSEX
Bosham
Bosham Walk,
Bosham Lane,
Old Bosham.
Tel. Bosham 572475.
*Spinning, weaving, clock restoring,
glass engraving, leather, silver and
gold work, miniature ships.*
Burpham
Aruncraft,
Riffards. Tel. Arundel 883143.
(A)
Period furniture restoration.

Horsted Keynes
The Blacksmiths Shop.
Tel. Sharpthorne 810292.
Wrought ironwork.
Steyning
Gordon Lawrie,
30 High Street.
Tel. Steyning 814056.
Gold and silver jewellery.
Geraldine St Aubyn Hubbard,
2 Charlton Court Cottages,
Mouse Lane.
Tel. Steyning 814204. **(A)**
*Silk, wool and cashmere
handwoven clothes, handblock
printed cushions and
handkerchiefs.*

WILTSHIRE
Lacock
Robert and Sheila Fournier,
The Tanyard. Tel. Lacock 266.
Pottery.
Graham and Jean Watling,
Lacock Gallery,
15 East Street. Tel. Lacock 422.
(A)
*Gold and silversmith – specialists
in silverware.*

SCOTLAND

DUMFRIES AND GALLOWAY
Moniaive
Mr Rolf Isler,
Dalya Crafts,
Kirkland. Tel. 372.
(2 miles east of Moniaive.)
Furniture, toys.
Mr H. Pouncey,
Stables Cottage,
Craigdarroch.
Tel. Moniaive 230. **(A)**
Spinning.
J. Mark Johnstone,
J. M. J. Designs,
Glencairn Workshops,
High Street. Tel. Moniaive 389.
Furniture and fitted interiors.
Sue and Tony Simpson,
Woodhead Cottage,
Craigdarroch.
Leatherwork in heavy cowhide.

FIFE
Largo
Anne Lightwood,
Largo Pottery,
Lower Largo.
Tel. Leven 320686.
Dust Jewellery,
7 Mill Wynd,
Lundin Links.
Tel. Lundin Links 320742.
(Just west of Largo.)
Silversmiths.

GRAMPIAN
Braemar
J. & I. Crichton.
Tel. Braemar 657.
*Woodcarving, kitchenware,
shortbread and butter moulds.*

HIGHLAND
Durness
D. Illingworth and Lotte Glob,
Far North Pottery,
Balnakeil. Tel. Durness 354.
(1 mile north-west of village.)
*Stoneware, earthenware, porcelain,
tiles, sculpture.*
Glenelg
Graham Noble and Janet
Gladstone,
Glenelg Studios,
The Old Ferry Inn.
Tel. Glenelg 253. **(A)**
(2 miles from village.)
Stoneware pottery.
R. Schipper & A. Marr,
Schimacraft,
Smithy Cottage.
Tel. Glenelg 278.
*Gold and silver, Skye marble
jewellery.*
Lochinver
Highland Stoneware Ltd,
Baddidaroch,
Inver Park. Tel. Lochinver 376.
*Hand-decorated gifts and
tableware.*
Sutherland Gemcutters,
114 Achmelvich.
Tel. Lochinver 312. **(A)**
Portree
Richard Townsend,
The Workshop,
9 Peinchorran,
The Braes. Tel. Sligachan 226.
(A)
(8 miles south-east of Portree.)
Hand-made furniture.
Andrew T. Prentice,
Marine Handweavers,
Quay Street,
Portree. Tel. Portree 2484. **(A)**
Handloom weaving.

STRATHCLYDE
Carradale
Stuart and Jo Leibbrandt,
Torrisdale Studios,
Torrisdale Square.
Tel. Carradale 623.
(2½ miles south of village.)
Hand-thrown stoneware pottery.
Mrs M. F. Arthur,
Grogport Rugs,
Grogport Old Manse.
Tel. Carradale 255.
(5 miles north of Carradale.)
Sheepskin rugs.

WESTERN ISLES
Tarbert
A. Campbell,
Croft Crafts,
4 Plochropool,
Drinishader.
Tel. Drinishader 217.
(5 miles south of village.)
Weaving Harris tweed.
Miss Joan MacLennan,
1A Drinishader. (No phone.)
(A)
(5 miles south of Tarbert.)
*Spinning Harris wool, hand-
weaving Harris tweed.*
Mrs Annie Morrison,
Post Office House,
Drinishader.
Tel. Drinishader 200.
*Spinning, dyeing and hand-
weaving Harris tweed.*
(Summer only.)

WALES
CLWYD
Hanmer
Stuart Bell,
Mere Pottery,
The Arrowry. Tel. Hanmer 352.
St Asaph
Dorothy Stopes,
Kentigern Studio Pottery,
The Old Shop,
Lower Street.
Tel. St Asaph 582412.
Glyn Ceiriog
Theo Davies,
Crefftau Ceiriog.
Tel. Glyn Ceiriog 218.
Furniture, antique restoring.

DYFED
Solva
Hugh and Betty
Loughborough,
The Craftsman,
Lower Solva. Tel. Solva 294.
Country-style furniture.
Tregaron
Tregaron Pottery Ltd,
Castell Flemish.
Tel. Bronant 639.
(3 miles north-west of village.)
Llawhaden
John and Ingrid Baum,
Ridgeway Pottery.
Tel. Llawhaden 268.
St Dogmaels
Dr Peter Saywood,
Cippyn Pottery,
Near Poppit Sands.
Tel. Cardigan 2875.
F. J. Paynter,
River View,
Penrhiw. Tel. Cardigan 2815.
Furniture.

Newcastle Emlyn
Cambrian Textile Mills
(Velindre) Ltd,
Drefach, Velindre.
Tel. Velindre 209.
(3½ miles east of village.)
Cenarth
James Davies (Abercuch) Ltd,
Newbridge Sawmills.
Tel. Llechryd 477 or 286.
(3 miles west of village.)
Wooden articles.
St David's
Maurice Riley,
Clegyr Isaf. Tel. St David's 701.
(1 mile east of St David's.)
Stone carving and masonry.
Newport
W. L. Rees,
Cemaes Pottery and Ceramics,
Brynhenllan,
Dinas. Tel. Dinas Cross 376. **(A)**
(3 miles west of Newport.)

GWYNEDD
Beddgelert
Snowdonia Pottery,
Caernarfon Road.
Tel. Beddgelert 304.
Hand-drawn wildlife.
Beddgelert Pottery,
Cae Ddafydd,
Penrhyndeudraeth.
Tel. Beddgelert 213.
(6 miles south of village.)
Dinas Mawddwy
Meirion Textile Mill,
Nr Machynleth.
Tel. Dinas Mawddwy 311.
Maentwrog
Trefor Glyn Owen and Gillian
Morgan,
Crochendy Twrog. (No phone.)
(1 mile from village.)
Pottery.
Penmachno
E. H. Boon,
Bod Afon. Tel. Penmachno 251.
Willow, cane, rushwork.
Penmachno Woollen Mill,
Nr Betws-y-coed.
Tel. Betws-y-coed 545.
(1½ miles from village.)
Textiles.

MID GLAMORGAN
Ewenny
Ewenny Pottery,
Nr. Bridgend.
Tel. Bridgend 3020.

POWYS
Clyro
Wye Pottery,
Hay-on-Wye. Tel. Hay-on-
Wye 820 510.
Earthenware and stoneware.

ACKNOWLEDGMENTS

The illustrations in this book were provided by the following artists, photographers and agencies.

Except where stated, credits read from left to right down the page. Work commissioned by the Reader's Digest is shown in italics.
1 Mary Evans Picture Library: **2 & 3** Royal Institution of Cornwall: **4 & 5** University of Reading, Institute of Agricultural History and Museum of English Rural Life: **6 & 7** Mary Evans Picture Library: **8** *Neil Holmes*: **11** *Colin Molyneux*: **12** artist Ivan Lapper: **13** *Lucinda Lambton*: **14 & 15** *Patrick Thurston*: **16** *Patrick Thurston*: **17** *Patrick Thurston*: **18** *Peter Keen*: **19** all *Malcolm Aird*: **20** artist Ivan Lapper: **21** *Lucinda Lambton*: **22** all *Patrick Thurston*: **25** *Patrick Thurston*: **26** both artist Peter Jones: **27** Dr V. Newall: artist Peter Jones: **28** top, Mary Evans Picture Library: others artist Peter Jones: **29** all artist Peter Jones: **30** *Lucinda Lambton*: **33** *Patrick Thurston*: **34** *Patrick Thurston*: **36** *Patrick Thurston*: **37** border, artist Gillian Coombes: top, Helen Allingham 'Happy England', Adam and Charles Black, London 1903: *David Gallant*: **38** box feature, Kenneth Scowen: artist Richard Jacobs: centre, J. Allan Cash: **39** Adam Woolfitt/Susan Griggs Agency: **41** *Patrick Thurston*: **42** both *Trevor Wood*: **43** *Trevor Wood*: **44** *Patrick Thurston*: **45** top left, Philip Llewellin: others, *Patrick Thurston*: **46** Photo Library International/ Marcus Brown: **48** *Ian Howes*: **50** *Trevor Wood*: **52** *Trevor Wood*: **53** artist Ivan Lapper: **55** *Patrick Thurston*: **56** Adam Woolfitt/Susan Griggs Agency: **58** all *Susan and Oliver Mathews*: **60** *Lucinda Lambton*: **61** *Colin Molyneux*: **62** both *Colin Molyneux*: **63** all *Colin Molyneux*: **64 & 65** *Trevor Wood*: **66** *Malcolm Aird*: **69** British Tourist Authority: **70** Nelly Peter/Bruce Coleman Ltd: **73** *Colin Molyneux*: **75** *Patrick Thurston*: **77** by permission of Lord Petre: Crown Copyright Reserved: **78** both Hertfordshire Office: **79** top left, Crown Copyright, Victoria and Albert Museum, London: others *Trevor Wood*: **82 & 83** *Trevor Wood*: **85** *Patrick Thurston*: **86** both *Trevor Wood*: **88** *Colin Molyneux*: **89** artist Ivan Lapper: **90** *Patrick Thurston*: **92** *Colin Molyneux*: **95** centre, *Michael St Maur Sheil*: others *Trevor Wood*: **98** *Patrick Thurston*: **99** *Ian Howes*: **100** *Ian Howes*: **101** *Colin Molyneux*: **103** *Ian Howes*: **104** both *Trevor Wood*: **106 & 107** *Patrick Thurston*: **109** John Vigurs: **111** *Colin Molyneux*: **112** artist Ivan Lapper: **113** G. F. Allen/Bruce Coleman Ltd: **114** all *Patrick Thurston*: **115** *Susan and Oliver Mathews*: **116 & 117** artist Ivan Lapper: **118** Heather Angel: Ann Ronan Picture Library: **119** *Trevor Wood*: Heather Angel: **120** *Colin Molyneux*: **122** in the ownership of the Earl of Shelburne: **123** *Patrick Thurston*: **125** all Neil Holmes: **126** *Colin Molyneux*: **128** all Crown Copyright, Victoria and Albert Museum, London: **132 & 133** *Ian Howes*: **134** *Patrick Thurston*: **138** *Patrick Thurston*: **139** Aerofilms: **141** *Colin Molyneux*: **142** *Trevor Wood*: **144** Patrick Eagar: **145** *Colin Molyneux*: **146** both *Colin Molyneux*: **147** all *Colin Molyneux*: **148** *Patrick Thurston*: **150** *Ian Howes*: **151** *Ian Howes*: **152** *Ian Howes*: **154** Sonia Halliday Photographs: **155** Sefton Samuels Photo Library: **156** artist Ivan Lapper: **157** by permission of the board of the British Library: **158** Pru Grice: **160** Richard Jemmett: **161** The Tate Gallery, London: **163** *Neil Holmes*: **164** Leo Aarons/Pictor International: **166** artist Lancelot Jones, based on National Trust model village of Acorn Magna, designed by T. Hopewell-Ash and created by Nick Pemberton: **167** artist Lancelot Jones: **168** Venner Artists: **169** Venner Artists: **170** artist Ivan Lapper: **172 & 173** *Patrick Thurston*: **175** both *Ian Howes*: **176** *Colin Molyneux*: **177** *Trevor Wood*: **179** all *John Wyand*: **181** *Patrick Thurston*: **182 & 183** *Ian Howes*: **184** Aerofilms: **186** Mansell Collection: **187** both Sonia Halliday Photographs: **190 & 191** *Lucinda Lambton*: **193** Richard Jemmett: **194** *Trevor Wood*: **197** *Ian Howes*: artist Ivan Lapper: **198** Aerofilms: **200** *Lucinda Lambton*: **201** Barnaby's Picture Library: **202** *Malcolm Aird*: **205** *Trevor Wood*: **206** both *Patrick Thurston*: **208** *Mike Burgess*: **211** *Colin Molyneux*: **212** *Patrick Thurston*: **213** *Chris Morris*: **215** *Chris Morris*: **216** *Lucinda Lambton*: **217** *Jane Lewis*: **218** both *Jane Lewis*: **219** all *Jane Lewis*: **221** *Trevor Wood*: **222** *Patrick Thurston*: **225** all *Trevor Wood*: **226** artist Ivan Lapper: **228 & 229** *Patrick Thurston*: **231** *Malcolm Aird*: **232** *Patrick Thurston*: **234** *Colin Molyneux*: **236** *George Wright*: **237** *Ian Howes*: **238** G. F. Allen/Bruce Coleman Ltd: **239** all *Patrick Thurston*: **241** *Trevor Wood*: **243** top left, *Patrick Thurston*: centre left, Philip Llewellin: bottom left, *Colin Molyneux*: bottom centre, G. Archbold/Robert Harding Picture Library: others *Trevor Wood*: **247** artist Ivan Lapper: **248** *Sefton Samuels*: **249** *Patrick Thurston*: **251** both *Colin Molyneux*: **252** *Sefton Samuels*: **255** *George Wright*: **257** Philip Llewellin: **258** artist Ivan Lapper: **261** both *Trevor Wood*: **262** *Patrick Thurston*: **263** artist Richard Jacobs: **264** *Patrick Thurston*: others artist Robert Micklewright: **265** artist Robert Micklewright: Suffolk Record Office, Ipswich: **266** bottom left, Janet and Colin Bord: others artist Richard Jacobs: **267** Devon County Library: **269** top two *Trevor Wood*: Barnaby's Picture Library: **271** *Patrick Thurston*: **273** *Trevor Wood*: **274** artist Ivan Lapper: **275** *Colin Molyneux*: **276** Sir Fitzroy Maclean: **277** Sir Fitzroy Maclean: **278** all Sir Fitzroy Maclean: **279** all Sir Fitzroy Maclean: **280** *Trevor Wood*: **281** *Patrick Thurston*: **283** *Colin Molyneux*: **285** *Trevor Wood*: **286** *Patrick Thurston*: **287** all *Patrick Thurston*: **288** artist Ivan Lapper: **289** *Patrick Thurston*: **290** *Neil Holmes*: **293** *Trevor Wood*: **294** artist Ivan Lapper: **296** *Malcolm Aird*: **298** J. E. Hancock: **299** Scottish Tourist Board, after Alan Sorrell (Royal Commission for Ancient Monuments of Scotland): **300** *Patrick Thurston*: Mitchell Library, Glasgow: **301** Rodney Legg: **303** both *Trevor Wood*: **305** all *Philip Dowell*: **306** both *Patrick Thurston*: **308** *Colin Molyneux*: **309** *Patrick Thurston*: **311** *Trevor Wood*: **312** artist Ivan Lapper: **314 & 315** both *Patrick Thurston*: **317** all *Timothy Beddow*: **318** both *Timothy Beddow*: **319** *Timothy Beddow*: **320** both *Patrick Thurston*: **321** *Patrick Thurston*: **322** artist Ivan Lapper: **324 & 325** *Colin Molyneux*: **327** all *Patrick Thurston*: **328** *Susan and Oliver Mathews*: **329** *Patrick Thurston*: **330** *Patrick Thurston*: **332** *Trevor Wood*: **333** *Neil Holmes*: **334** artist Ivan Lapper: **335** *Malcolm Aird*: **337** *Patrick Thurston*: **339** *Colin Molyneux*: **340** top left, John Tarlton: Venner Artists: bottom, Lancelot Jones: **341** top centre, *John Cook*: bottom centre, *Patrick Thurston*: others Venner Artists: **342** Welsh Folk Museum, St Fagans: artist Lancelot Jones: **343** top & bottom centre, Adam Woolfitt/Susan Griggs Agency: others Venner Artists: **344** top centre, J. E. Manners: bottom, Lancelot Jones: others Venner Artists: **345** all Venner Artists: **346** *Malcolm Aird*: **347** bottom right, *Martyn Chillmaid*: others *Patrick Thurston*: **348** *Patrick Thurston*: **349** *Colin Molyneux*: **351** 2 centre photographs, left, *Martyn Chillmaid*: others *Malcolm Aird*: **353** John Topham Picture Library: **355** both *Colin Molyneux*: **356** artist Ivan Lapper: **357** Leo Aarons/Pictor International: **359** artist Ivan Lapper: **360 & 361** *Neil Holmes*: **362** *Patrick Thurston*: **365** all *Neil Holmes*: **366** both *Neil Holmes*: **370** *Patrick Thurston*: **371** *Colin Molyneux*: **373** *Penny Tweedie*: **374** artist Ivan Lapper: **375** *Patrick Thurston*: **376** *Malcolm Aird*: **377** *Malcolm Aird*: **378** Mark Gerson: **379** *Neil Holmes*: **380** both *Neil Holmes*: **381** all *Neil Holmes*: **382** both *Colin Molyneux*: **383** *Colin Molyneux*: **384** *Trevor Wood*: **386** *Ian Howes*: **388** *John Bulmer*: **390** National Portrait Gallery, London: **391** *Patrick Thurston*: Mansell Collection: **392** Martin Gostelow: Radio Times Hulton Picture Library: **393** 'Sportsmen Parsons in Peace and War', Mrs Stuart Menzies: 'Life of John Mytton', C. J. Apperley: **394** *Patrick Thurston*: **397** Spectrum Colour Library: **398** *Patrick Thurston*: **399** artist Ivan Lapper: **400** *Patrick Thurston*: **401** Philip Llewellin: **402** both *Patrick Thurston*: **403** *Patrick Thurston*: **404** *Patrick Thurston*: Aerofilms: **405** *Malcolm Aird*: **406** artist Ivan Lapper: **409** Ashwell Village Museum: overlap, *Tim Stevens*: Ashwell Village Museum: overlap, *Tim Stevens*: **410** Ashwell Village Museum: overlap, *Tim Stevens*: Ashwell Village Museum: overlap: *Tim Stevens*: **412** both *Trevor Wood*: **413** all *Trevor Wood*: **415** *David Gallant*: **416** *Patrick Thurston*

The publishers also acknowledge their indebtedness to the following books, which were consulted for reference.

AA Stately Homes, Museums, Castles and Gardens in Britain (ABC Travel Guides Ltd); *ABC Rail Guide* (ABC Travel Guides Ltd); *Along the Chiltern Ways* G. R. Crosher (Cassell); *Along the Roman Roads of Britain* J. H. B. Peel (Cassell); *The Anatomy of the village* Thomas Sharpe (Penguin); *Ancient Monuments* (HMSO); *Antique maps and their cartographers* Raymond Lister (G. Bell and Sons Ltd); *Atlas of places to visit in England, Scotland, Wales and Northern Ireland* (National Trusts); *Bartholomew Gazetteer of Britain* Oliver Mason (John Bartholomew & Son Ltd); *Battles of the English Civil War* Austin Woolrych (Pan Books); *Berkshire* Ian Yarrow (Robert Hale); *Blue Guide: England* Stuart Rossiter (Ernest Benn Ltd); *Blue Guide: Wales* Stuart Rossiter (Ernest Benn Ltd); *Book of Common Prayer* (Collins); *The BP Book of Festivals and Events in Britain* Christopher Trent (Phoenix House); *Britain 1978: an official handbook* (HMSO); *The British Isles* L. Dudley Stamp and Stanley H. Beaver (Longmans); *Buckinghamshire* A. Uttley; *The Buildings of England* Nikolaus Pevsner (Penguin Books); *The Buildings of Scotland* Nikolaus Pevsner (Penguin Books); *The Buildings of Wales* Nikolaus Pevsner (Penguin Books); *Cambridge* Michael Grant (Weidenfeld & Nicolson); *Canals and rivers of Britain* Andrew Darwin (J. M. Dent and Sons Ltd); *Castles and Historic Places in Wales* (Wales Tourist Board); *The Castles of Scotland* Susan Ross (George Philip); *Catalogue of Rubbings of brasses and incised slabs* Muriel Clayton (HMSO); *The Central Highlands* Campbell R. Steven (The Scottish Mountaineering Trust); *Companion Guide to the Coast of North-East England* John Seymour (Collins); *Companion Guide to Kent and Sussex* Keith Spence (Collins); *Companion Guide to the West Highlands of Scotland* W. H. Murray (Collins); *A complete guide to heraldry* A. C. Fox-Davies (Nelson); *The Complete Welsh-English, English-Welsh Dictionary* H. Meurig Evans and W. O. Thomas (Christopher Davies); *A concise history of Scotland* Fitzroy Maclean (Thames and Hudson); *Craft workshops in the English countryside* (CoSIRA); *Crockford's Clerical Directory* (Oxford University Press); *Cumbria* John Parker (John Bartholomew & Son Ltd); *Daily Life in England in the reign of George III* Andre Parreaux (George Allen & Unwin Ltd); *Devon & Cornwall* Denys Kay-Robinson (John Bartholomew & Son Ltd); *A Dictionary of Architecture* John Fleming, Hugh Honour, Nikolaus Pevsner (Penguin Books); *Dictionary of Country Furniture* Marjorie Filbee (The Connoisseur); *Discovering Carts and Wagons* John Vince (Shire Publications); *Discovering Castles in England and Wales* John Kinross (Shire Publications); *Durham Villages* H. Thompson (Robert Hale); *English Cottage Gardens* Edward Hyams (Nelson); *English Cottages and Farms* O. Cooks; *The English Country Cottage* R. J. Brown (Robert Hale); *The English Country House* A. F. Kersting (Thames and Hudson); *English Folklore* Christina Hole (B. T. Batsford Ltd); *The English Home* Doreen Yarwood (B. T. Batsford Ltd); *English Parish Churches* John Betjeman (Collins); *English place-names* Kenneth Cameron (B. T. Batsford Ltd); *English River names* E. Ekwall (Oxford University Press); *English Villages* F. R. Banks; *An Englishman's Home* J. H. B. Peel (David & Charles); *Exmoor* S. H. Burton (Hodder and Stoughton); *The family house in England* Andrew Henderson (Phoenix House – London); *Field guide to archaeology* Eric S. Wood (Collins); *Folklore and customs of rural England* Margaret Baker (David & Charles); *Gaelic-English and English-Gaelic Dictionary* Neil Macalpine and John Mackenzie (Gairm Publications); *The gazetteer of England* Oliver Mason (David & Charles); *A guide to the prehistoric and Roman monuments in England and Wales* Jacquetta Hawkes (Sphere Books Ltd); *Guinness book of records* Norris McWhirter and Stan Greenberg (Guinness Superlatives Ltd); *Gypsies, wanderers of the world* Bart McDowell (National Geographic Society); *A Hampshire parish: Bramshott and Liphook* Roger Chatterton Newman (Frank Westwood); *Heart of England* Louise Wright and James Priddey (Robert Hale); *Highland Clearances* John Prebble (Secker & Warburg); *Historic Houses, Castles and Gardens* (ABC Historic Publications); *History of the English House* Nathaniel Lloyd (Architectural Press); *A History of Lancashire* J. J. Bagley (Darwen Finlayson Ltd); *A History of the Scottish People: 1560–1830* T. C. Smout (Collins/Fontana); *Horse racing 1979* Christopher Poole (Macdonald and Jane's); *How to study an old church* Arthur Needham (B. T. Batsford Ltd); *Illustrated glossary of architecture* Harris and Lever (Faber and Faber); *Illustrated guide to the ancient monuments* Department of the Environment (HMSO); *Illustrated handbook of vernacular architecture* R. W. Brunskill (Faber and Faber); *Inland Waterways of Great Britain* L. A. Edwards (Imray Laurie Norie and Wilson); *Inns and villages of England* Garry Hogg (Newnes); *The King's England* Arthur Mee (Hodder and Stoughton); *Lancashire Villages* Jessica Lofthouse (Robert Hale); *Landscapes of Britain* Roy Millward and Adrian Robinson (David & Charles); *Last of the Barons* Lord Lytton; *The Libraries, Museums and Art Galleries Year Book* Adrian Brink and Derry Watkins (James Clarke & Co. Ltd); *Lincolnshire & the Fens* M. W. Barley (E. P. Publishing Ltd); *Life below stairs* Frank E. Huggett (John Murray); *Life in Elizabethan England:* A. H. Doff, *Life in Georgian England:* E. N. Williams, *Life in Norman England:* O. G. Tomkeieff, *Life in Tudor England:* Penry Williams (B. T. Batsford Ltd); *Life in the English country house* Mark Girouard (Yale University Press); *Life and tradition in rural Wales* J. Geraint Jenkins (Dent); *Lives of the British Saints* Baring-Gould (Charles J. Clark); *Looking at place-names* Nicholas Gould (Kenneth Mason); *The Making of the English Landscape* W. G. Hoskins (Hodder and Stoughton); *Man at play* John Armitage (Frederick Warne); *Man the tool-maker* Kenneth P. Oakley (British Museum – Natural History); *Memorials of Old Lincolnshire* E. Mansel Sympson; *The Municipal Year Book* (The Municipal Journal Ltd); *Museums and Art Galleries* (ABC Historic Publications); *National Parks Illustrated Guides* (HMSO); *National Trust Guide* Robin Fedden and Rosemary Joekes (Jonathan Cape); *National Trust for Scotland Guide* Robin Prentice (Jonathan Cape); *New Forest, Forestry Commission Guide* H. L. Edlin (HMSO); *A New Oxfordshire* Frank Martin (Spurbooks Ltd); *New Shell guide to Scotland* Donald Lamond Macnie and Moray MacLaren (Ebury Press); *Nicholson's guide to the Thames* (Robert Nicholson Publications Ltd); *Nicholson's guide to the waterways* (Robert Nicholson Publications Ltd); *Not in front of the servants* Frank Dawes (Wayland); *Nottinghamshire* Roy Christian (B. T. Batsford Ltd); *Odd Aspects of England* Garry Hogg (David & Charles); *Old Engravings and Illustrations: Vol. II: Things* (The Dick Sutphen Studio); *Oxford Dictionary of English place-names* E. Ekwall (Oxford University Press); *Oxford Dictionary of Saints* David Hugh Farmer (Clarendon Press); *Oxford History of England* Sir George Clark (Oxford University Press); *The parish churches of England* Cox & Ford (B. T. Batsford Ltd); *Parish churches of England* Marvyn Blatch (Blandford Press); *The pattern of English building* Alec Clifton Taylor (B. T. Batsford Ltd); *The Peak District* K. C. Edwards (Collins/Fontana New Naturalist); *Pelican History of England: English Society in the early Middle Ages* Doris Mary Stenton, *Medieval and Tudor Britain* Valerie E. Chancellor, *Tudor England* S. T. Bindoff, *The Making of a Nation, 1603–1789* A. J. Patrick (Penguin Books); *A pictorial history of English architecture* John Betjeman (John Murray); *Portrait of Cambridgeshire* S. A. Manning (Robert Hale); *Portrait of County Durham* P. A. White; *Portrait of Dorset* Ralph Wightman (Robert Hale); *Portrait of Exmoor* J. H. B. Peel (Robert Hale); *Prehistoric Britain* Keith Branigan (Spurbooks Ltd); *Red guide: complete Scotland* Reginald J. W. Hammond (Ward, Lock Ltd); *Red guide: The Lake District* M. J. B. Baddeley (Ward, Lock Ltd); *Rural Rides* William Cobbett (Penguin); *Scotland's Castles* Hubert Fenwick (Robert Hale); *A selective guide to England* Jack Simmons (John Bartholomew & Son Ltd); *The Shell Book of Cottages* Richard Reid (Michael Joseph); *Shell Book of Country Crafts* James Arnold (John Baker); *Shell Book of exploring Britain* Garry Hogg (John Baker); *Shell County Guides* (Faber and Faber); *The Shell guide to Britain* Geoffrey Boumphrey (Ebury Press); *The Shell guide to Wales* Wynford Vaughan-Thomas and Alun Llewellyn (Michael Joseph in association with George Rainbird); *A short history of Lincolnshire* C. Brears; *South Wales* Ruth Thomas (John Bartholomew & Son Ltd); *The Squire and his relations* E. Wingfield-Stratford; *Staffordshire* Vivian Bird (B. T. Batsford Ltd); *Sussex* John Burke (B. T. Batsford Ltd); *The Thames Valley* F. R. Banks (Letts Motor Tour Guides); *This England* (National Geographic Society); *Traditional Country Craftsmen* J. Geraint Jenkins (David & Charles); *The Travellers Guides* Sean Jennett (Darton, Longman and Todd); *Trees and woodland in the British landscapes* Oliver Rackham (J. M. Dent and Sons Ltd); *Turner's picturesque views in England and Wales* Eric Shanes (Chatto & Windus); *Victoria County Histories*; *Victorian frames, borders and cuts from the 1882 type catalog of George Bruce's Son and Co.* (Dover Publications, Inc. New York); *The Victorian Home* Jenni Calder (Book Club Associates); *Villages: National Trust* (Heritage Books); *Villages in the landscape* Trevor Rowley (J. M. Dent and Sons Ltd); *Villages of vision* Gillian Darley (Architectural Press); *Wales* R. M. Lockley (B. T. Batsford Ltd); *Warwickshire* V. Bird (B. T. Batsford Ltd); *Warwickshire villages* L. F. Cave (Robert Hale); *The international book of Wood* (Mitchell Beazley); *Yorkshire: The West Riding* David Pill (B. T. Batsford Ltd); *Yorkshire Villages* G. Bernard Wood (Robert Hale); *Your House – the outside view* John Prizeman (Hutchinson)

Typesetting, separations, paper, printing and binding by:
Brown Knight and Truscott Ltd, Tonbridge; Gilchrist Brothers Ltd, Leeds; Jarrold and Sons Ltd, Norwich;
C. Townsend Hook Paper Co. Ltd, Snodland